Contents

Introduction

This is yet another inn book. But it's far more than that, too.

We enjoy reading all the others, but they rarely tell us what we *really* want to know, such as where to get a good meal and what there is to do. And the inns often are not grouped by location, so you don't get a feeling for what the area is like. We've found that out by talking with innkeepers, reading all the guidebooks and brochures, visiting tourist bureaus and Chambers of Commerce, and poring through the local newspapers.

That's what we now share with you. We start not with the inn but with the area (of course, the existence of inns or lack thereof helped determine the areas to be included). We sought out 32 extra-special areas, some of them New England's best-known and some not widely known at all.

Then we toured each area, visiting each inn, each restaurant and each attraction, as well as drawing on our experiences and memories of more than 30 years of vacationing in and 18 years of living in New England. We *worked* these areas as roving journalists, always seeking out the best and most interesing. We also *lived* them — staying in, eating in, and experiencing as many places as time and budget would allow.

The result is this book, a comprehensive yet selective compendium of what we found to be the best and most interesting places to stay, eat and enjoy in these 32 special areas.

The book reflects our tastes. We want creature comforts like private bathrooms and comfortable reading areas in our rooms; we like to meet other inn guests, but we also value our privacy. We seek interesing and creative food and settings for our meals. We enjoy unusual, enlightening things to do and places to see. We expect to receive value for money and time spent.

While touring the past year to research this second edition of "Inn Spots," we were surprised by how many innkeepers said we were among the few guidebook writers who ever visited their facility and did not simply expect them to fill out a form and forward it with a fee.

We also were struck — as we have been while preparing our other books — by how times and places change. Many of the inns and restaurants that were "in" a decade or so ago have faded, their places taken by any number of newcomers not yet widely known. Four new "inn" spots emerged, so we added chapters and substituted some for others that aren't quite so in these days. We're fortunate that our newspaper training and tight deadlines make this book as up-to-date as its 1989 publication date.

Yes, the schedule is hectic and we do keep busy on these, our working vacations that everyone thinks must be glamorous and nothing but fun. One of us says she never wants to inspect another inn bedroom (especially up on the third floor). The other doesn't care if he never eats another sun-dried tomato.

Nonetheless, it's rewarding to discover a little-known inn, to savor a great meal, to enjoy a choice musuem, to poke through an unusual store and to meet so many interesting people along the way.

That's what this book is all about. We hope that you will enjoy its findings as much as we did the finding.

Nancy Webster and Richard Woodworth
April 1989

About the Authors

Nancy Webster began her dining experiences in her native Montreal and as a waitress in summer resorts across Canada during her McGill University years. She worked in London and hitchhiked through Europe on $3 a day before her marriage to an American newspaper editor, whom she met while skiing at Mont Tremblant. She started writing her "Roaming the Restaurants" column for the West Hartford (Conn.) News in 1972. That led to half of the book, *Daytripping & Dining in Southern New England,* written in collaboration with Betsy Wittemann in 1978. She since has co-authored three editions of *Weekending in New England;* two more editions in the *Daytripping & Dining* series; two editions of *Getaways for Gourmets in the Northeast,* and *Water Escapes in the Northeast.* She and her husband have two grown sons and live in West Hartford.

Richard Woodworth has been an inveterate traveler since his youth in suburban Syracuse, N.Y., where his birthday outings often involved train trips with friends for the day to Utica or Rochester. After graduation from Middlebury College, he was a reporter for newspapers in Syracuse, Jamestown, Geneva and Rochester before moving to Connecticut to become editor of the West Hartford News and executive editor of Imprint Newspapers, for which he is now contributing editor. With wife Nancy Webster and their sons, he has traveled to the four corners of this country, Canada and portions of Europe, writing their findings for Imprint Newspapers and others. He co-authored both editions of *Getaways for Gourmets in the Northeast* with his wife. He also is Connecticut editor for the Original New England Guide. Between travels and duties as publisher of Wood Pond Press, he tries to find time to weed the garden in summer and ski in the winter.

Historical marker tells about Dorset outside Dovetail Inn.

Dorset, Vt.
The Town that Marble Built

There is marble almost everywhere in Dorset, a town that marble helped build and upon which it has long prospered.

You see it on the sidewalks all around the picturesque green, on the porch at the historic Dorset Inn and on the terrace at the newer Barrows House, on the side of the turreted United Church of Christ and on the pillars of the Marble West Inn. An entire mansion built of marble stuns passersby along Dorset West Road.

It seems as if all Dorset has been paved with marble — and with good intentions. Here is what residents and writers alike have called the perfect village. Merchant Jay Hathaway phrased it well in a Dorset Historical Society lecture: What could be better than running "a small country store nestled in the mountains of Vermont in a town that is as close to perfect as Dorset?"

A village of perhaps 1,200 (about half its population during the height of its marble-producing days a century ago), it's a mix of charm and culture in perfect proportion.

Dorset is unspoiled, from its rustic Barn Playhouse (the oldest summer playhouse in the state) to its handsomely restored inn (the oldest in the state) to its Dorset Field Club (the oldest nine-hole golf course in the state) to its lovely white, green-shuttered homes (many among the oldest in the state) to its two general stores, both curiously different relics of 19th-century life. Here is a peaceful place in which to cherish the past.

1

Yet barely six miles away is Manchester, one of the most sophisticated tourist meccas around. Many of its visitors don't know about nor are they particularly interested in Dorset, but people in Dorset can take advantage of all its urbane attractions as desired.

So the Dorset visitor has the best of both worlds — a tranquil respite amid a myriad of activities and attractions. What could be more copacetic?

Inn Spots

Dorset Inn, Route 30, Dorset 05251. (802) 867-5500.

Vermont's oldest continuously operated country inn, with a history dating back to 1796, was nicely renovated in 1984 and 1985 in what it bills as "the inspired revival of an historic site." That it is.

Under the aegis of new owners Sissy Hicks, the former chef at the Barrows House, and Gretchen Schmidt, the restored inn is a fine blend of history and contemporary comfort.

Overnight guests are greeted by a stunning collection of blue glass displayed in lighted cases at the top of the stairway on the second floor. All 35 rooms on the two upper floors have been redone with wall-to-wall carpeting, modern baths with wood washstands, lovely print wallpapers and antique furnishings. Two of the nicest are the third-floor front corner rooms, one with twin sleigh beds, two rockers, Audubon prints and floral wallpaper, and the other with a canopy bed, marble table and wallpaper of exotic animals and birds.

Downstairs, stuffed bears in little chairs welcome guests in the reception area. The main sitting room is appealing with comfortable furniture around the fireplace, a collection of blue and white china on the mantel, scrubbed wide-plank floors and a small television set. Beyond is a cheery breakfast room with Vermont-woven mats atop wood tables and green floral curtains against small-paned windows that extend to the floor. Out back are a pleasant tap room with a big oak bar and inexpensive pub menu, and an attractive, country-style dining room (see Dining Spots).

Doubles, $140, MAP.

Cornucopia of Dorset, Route 30, Dorset 05251. (802) 867-5751.

One of the more inviting and elegant B&Bs anywhere is offered by Bill and Linda Ley, who left Ipswich, Mass., to realize a goal of running a country inn. That they backed into Cornucopia of Dorset ultimately was as pleasing to them as it was to the guests who have been entertained there since. Their B&B lives up to its name, offering an abundance of warmth, comfort and personality.

Cornucopia has only four guest rooms and a cottage suite, but what accommodations they are! All with large, modern baths, they have poster or canopy beds ranging in size from king to twins, afluff with down comforters and pillows, and the front Scallop Room has a corner fireplace. Upholstered chairs flank three-way reading lamps. We found the Mother Myrick Room especially comfortable with a kingsize bed against a wall of shelves containing books and family photos, and a full bath with a double vanity. The rear cottage with a fireplaced living room and a loft bedroom is outfitted with a stereo and a private sun deck.

The common rooms are more than an adjunct; they are the focal point of Cornucopia. Off a small, cozy library is an inviting living room with overstuffed sofas; both have fireplaces. Beyond is an enormous dining room opening into a sun room, a contemporary area that's cool and shaded in the summer, warm and bright in winter. It is here that we like to gravitate to study the leather scrapbooks of restaurant menus and area attractions, browse through a cornucopia of magazines or pore through a hardbound

American flag and distinctive sign welcome guests to Cornucopia of Dorset.

book called "At the Movies," listing all the video tapes the Leys offer on their VCR. But there's little inclination to read or watch, given the innkeepers' hospitality and propensity for lively conversation.

Outside are a marble patio and a covered porch. Enough bird feeders are attached to the sun room windows to accommodate a flock.

Breakfast at the formal table in the airy dining room is a treat. Ours started with fresh orange juice and a colorful dish of honeydew melon, nicely pre-sliced into bite-size chunks and topped with fresh raspberries, strawberries, kiwi and banana slices, and creme fraiche. The baked raspberry pancake was so good that we asked Linda to share the recipe. Colombian coffee with a hint of cinnamon and Twining's English tea accompanied. Other specialties include baked croissant a l'orange, bread pudding with warm berry sauce, quiche lorraine, baked ham and egg cup with Vermont cheddar cheese and petite croissants, and baked cinnamon french toast with sausage patties.

The goodies don't end there. Tea is served in the afternoon, Bill may pour wine from a rack of many vintages, and brandy is in a decanter in the upstairs hall. A slice of buttercrunch from our favorite Mother Myrick's Confectionary store in Manchester is put out during nightly turndown service. And beside the bed are stationery and stamped envelopes and postcards upon which we'd spread the word, "great place — you ought to be here."

Doubles, $85 to $105; cottage, $145.

Birch Hill Inn, West Road, Box 346, Manchester 05254. (802) 362-2761.

Just across the Dorset town line and closely allied with it in spirit if not address, this imposing hilltop house was built in the late 1700s and has been in innkeeper Pat Lee's family since 1917. It housed her grandfather and her father; she and husband Jim live here and capitalize on the home-like atmosphere, serving breakfast and dinner and making their guests — many of them long-term and repeat — feel very much at home.

Guests dine family-style at two highly polished tables in the gracious dining room. They gather for games, reading or conversation in a cheery and comfortably furnished, 40-by-20-foot living room paneled in pine, or a new sun room lovely in wicker, pinks

3

and blues. Outside is a marble terrace where Jim may barbecue cornish game hens or beefalo steak (the beefalo, providing meat that is low-fat and low-cholesterol, are raised on the Lees' farm next door). Large windows frame the grounds, where stone fences and cross-country trails abound. In back is a kidney-shaped swimming pool.

All five large guest rooms on the second floor have private baths, and each is decorated in country style with family furnishings. Every room has a portable radio with a selection of interesting tapes. One has twin brass beds, another a queen bed with rose and green stenciling done by Pat, and one has a fireplace. Art by local painters (many by 85-year-old Luigi Lucioni, a friend of Pat's father) is everywhere. Also available is a small cottage with bedroom, sitting room, bath and refrigerator.

For breakfast, Pat serves fresh fruit, her popular homemade granola (in winter, hot cereal), and a choice of eggs or pancakes.

At night, meals are the kind she'd serve at a dinner party with a single entree (she was preparing a large salmon caught by a guest in British Columbia the night we first visited). Specialties are veal marsala, butterflied leg of lamb and chicken teriyaki. A soup (leek, tomato or zucchini-tarragon are some favorites) usually precedes. Green salad and vegetables from the large garden accompany, as do Pat's homemade chutneys, mustard sauce and herb jellies. Lemon souffle, rhubarb crunch, blueberry surprise or the Silver Palate's decadent chocolate cake might end the meal. The Lees have a beer and wine license, and serve hors d'oeuvres as guests gather for BYOB cocktails prior to dinner at 7:30. Cook's nights off are Wednesday, Thursday and Sunday, when guests are on their own.

Doubles, $96 to $106, B&B; $128 to $138, MAP.

Barrows House, Main Street, Dorset 05251. (802) 867-4455.

We don't know what is more appealing about the Barrows House: the comfortable rooms and cottages amid six acres of park-like grounds with swimming pool, tennis courts and an intricate gazebo, or the meals in the smashing new greenhouse addition that extends the dining room to the outdoors. You don't really have to choose. The choice is made for you with an MAP rate schedule that requires you to take your meals and encourages long stays, which is just fine with the numerous repeat guests who sometimes come for weeks at a time.

Black wicker rockers are at the ready behind the columns that front the 200-year-old main house, which has a fireplaced living room, the expansive dining room (see Dining Spots), ten upstairs guest rooms and, beside a canopied outdoor patio, a charming tavern notable for its trompe l'oeil walls of books.

The most popular rooms, however, are scattered in a number of outbuildings converted into sophisticated lodging. All but two of the 32 rooms in nine buildings have private baths. Most are carpeted, some have sofas and some in the cottages have fireplaces and sitting rooms. Many have coordinated wallpapers, draperies and quilts, and all are filled with nice touches like ruffled pillows and patchcraft hangings.

New innkeepers Tim and Sally Brown of New York and their children are putting their mark on the inn (son Thatcher has so enjoyed working in the kitchen that he transferred to Cornell's School of Hotel Administration). Guests also praise the new Brown's Bag Lunch ($7.50), good for midday on the patio or to take on a picnic.

Doubles, $150 to $180, MAP; B&B except on weekends in November.

Village Auberge, Main Street, Dorset 05251. (802) 867-5715.

The accommodations have been upgraded, the bar and waiting area expanded, and a comfy parlor and sun porch added since Helmut and Dorothy Stein of Boston took

Stone wall opens onto path to Little Lodge at Dorset.

over the Village Auberge in 1986. But the dining room, made famous by former chef-owner Alex Koks, remains familiar to guests who predate the Steins' arrival.

With their addition, the new innkeepers have created a new entry and reception area and a welcoming common area that was lacking earlier. No longer must arriving overnight guests share a small parlor with waiting dining patrons. Everyone can enjoy the expanded lounge, a large sitting room with a fireplace and two sofas, and an exceptionally nice enclosed porch full of white wicker sofas and chairs.

The four original guest rooms upstairs have been redecorated, and six more clean and tidy rooms with full baths have been added. All but one have queen beds, and are furnished with country antiques.

Breakfast is served to inn guests in the cheery, plant-filled bay-window end of the dining room. Eggs any style, pancakes, croissants and pain perdu with various fillings are among the offerings.

Doubles, $90, B&B; $150, MAP. Closed in April.

The Little Lodge at Dorset, Main Street, Box 673, Dorset 05251. (802) 867-4040.

"We have more places to sit per guest than any inn we've seen," says Allan Norris of the appealing, five-room B&B he and wife Nancy have run with T.L.C. since 1981.

Guests in those five rooms have access to a formal dining room with oriental rugs, shining silver and bone china for breakfast service, a living room with wood stove and large hooked rug, a large and luxurious den with barnwood walls, blue leather sofa, fireplace and shelves of books and games, an attached five-sided gazebo that has black garden furniture cushioned with yellow and green pads, a wet bar with refrigerator and a hallway with separate entrance for shedding and stashing skis and boots. Outside are a rope hammock and a garden sitting area overlooking a trout pond, the verdant fairways of the Dorset Field Club and the mountainside beyond.

Given all these inviting public areas, one might expect the Norrises, transplanted Baltimoreans, to have skimped on their upstairs guest rooms. Not so. All five have private baths, are furnished with twin beds usually made up as kings, have paintings by Nancy's great-uncle (one of the Boston School of Impressionists), quilts made by Nancy or bedspreads crocheted by Allan's sister, and exude an air of lived-in comfort.

Breakfast is continental-plus, Nancy supplementing juices and cereals with her homemade strawberry-pecan, orange-coriander and pear-walnut breads or muffins.

The grounds offer trails for cross-country skiing and hiking in the rear, the stocked trout pond (no fishing, but you can feed them) dug by the home's former owner who runs the Orvis sporting goods company in Manchester and a view of an oriental garden with colorful red bridges in front of the house next door. Enjoying all this with the guests is Columbine, an unusually friendly Doberman pinscher who nuzzles up to one and all. "More people write in our guest book about Columbine than anything else," Allan reports.

Dovetail Inn, Main Street, Dorset 05251. (802) 867-5747.

Nicely located in the heart of town just across from the Dorset Inn (in fact it was once an inn annex and housed chauffeurs and staff in the posh days) is the two-building Dovetail. Jim and Jean Kingston, he a marine engineer, moved up from Connecticut in 1984 and, as they say, picked a growing area.

They have redecorated the eleven rooms, all with private baths, in one structure; the other houses their quarters, a cheery "keeping room" for guests' use and a small gift shop in which are sold model wooden trucks that Jim makes. Rooms vary in size and have double, king or twin beds. Most have a couple of easy chairs (ours had a sofa) and pretty new wallpaper and curtains. There's a large new bedroom with a fireplace and wet bar. On the second floor landing is a nook with a window seat and many books for borrowing.

In the back yard is a 20-by-40-foot swimming pool, once the Dorset Inn's. The Kingstons have a beer and wine license and serve by the pool or in the keeping room. They also sometimes offer tea and cookies in the afternoon

Breakfast consists of juice, muffins (the orange ones were delicious) and coffee or tea. You may have it brought to your room in a basket, if you wish.

Why the name Dovetail? "I like quality building and furniture," says Jim, "and a cutesy name didn't fit Dorset."

Doubles, $57 to $125.

Marble West Inn, Dorset West Road, Box 22, Dorset 05251. (802) 867-4155.

The historic Holley-West house two miles southwest of Dorset, a Greek Revival built in the 1840s by the owner of a marble quarry, is graced with seven marble columns in front. A marble sign designates the inn since its extensive restoration and opening in 1985.

The renovation was done with taste, incorporating family treasures, by two young educators-turned-innkeepers, Hugh Miller and Edward Ferenc, the latter a Dorset native.

They salvaged the extraordinary stenciling (done by Honey West, one of the quarry owner's daughters) in the front entry and upstairs hall, and several other unusual decorative and architectural features, such as the low stairway banisters installed for a woman in the West family who was very short. A piano, sofas and rocking chairs around the fireplace beckon guests into the main parlor, open to the adjacent dining room used for breakfast. The library has a wood and copper Victorian bathtub (filled with gin at Honey West's wedding in the 1930s and now full of plants), a marble fireplace, small TV, stereo and a neat window seat with crocheted throws everywhere. The ornate

Marble sign designates Marble West Inn.

combination hat rack and walking-stick stand in the hall still bears several old Victorian hats.

Upstairs off two stairways are seven guest rooms with private baths, plus a small single. Each is amply furnished, most with colorful afghans and bedspreads crocheted by Edward's mother. We admired the rear-corner Dorset Room with an endearing collage of sheep over the bed, oriental rugs and blue crocheted spreads. A front suite has a pleasant sitting room with fireplace and a small bedroom. A new downstairs suite is striking in the "moderne" style: black and white tiled floor, black dots on white wallpaper, the bed against a white brick chimney wall, and a bathroom that is all black and white tiles.

A "lush continental" breakfast of fresh fruits (perhaps local melon with raspberry sauce), yogurt, homemade granola, orange blossom or poppyseed rolls and zucchini or cranberry breads is served. A pond out back provides skating in the winter.

The innkeepers also lead cross-country skiers on nearby trails. At our last visit, the inn was on the market, but it will likely continue as an inn.

Doubles, $70 to $90; suites, $120.

Dining Spots

Dorset Inn, Church and Main Streets, Dorset. (802) 867-5500.

Interesting, creative food has been emanating from the kitchen of this venerable inn since Sissy Hicks took over the chef's chores as co-innkeeper with Gretchen Schmidt.

The pleasant main dining room, which seats 85 at well-spaced tables, is predominantly blue, with frilly white curtains screening the windows from the street, oak chairs with upholstered seats, folk-art paintings on the walls, beige over blue linen and pewter service plates. Fresh flowers, classical music and candlelight enhance the mood.

A practitioner of the new American cuisine, Sissy Hicks changes her menu seasonally. Pre-dinner drinks are served with a basketful of french-fry-size cheese sticks. The crabmeat mousse with a cucumber-mustard dill sauce and a few slices of melba toast made a fine appetizer, enough for two to share. Smoked Norwegian salmon with dill creme fraiche, country duck and orange pate with pear chutney and warm Vermont goat cheese with radicchio and endive ($2.50 to $6.50) were other appetizers on the fall menu. Crusty French bread with sweet butter and green salads with excellent stilton or basil-vinaigrette dressings accompany.

Having been advised that the calves liver was the best anywhere, we had to try it. Served rare as requested with crisp bacon and slightly underdone slices of onion, it was superb. The fresh trout, deboned but served with its skin still on, was laden with sauteed leeks and mushrooms. These came with an assemblage of vegetables, including red-skin potatoes with a dollop of sour cream, and crisp cauliflower, broccoli and yellow squash. A Wente chardonnay for $14, golden and oaky, was a good choice from about 40 selections on the reasonably priced wine list.

Entrees range from $14 for breast of chicken stuffed with brie and coriander in pear and cider sauce to $19.50 for rack of lamb with fresh mint sauce. Veal medallions with a lime-ginger sauce, grilled duck breast with brown raspberry sauce, roast boneless quail, and broiled shrimp and scallops with aioli sauce are other possibilities.

Pies, wild rice pudding and chocolate terrine with raspberry sauce are on the dessert menu. One of the favorite fall desserts is Sissy's cider sorbet with spiced wine sauce.

The inn serves a hearty breakfast (sourdough or fruit pancakes, all kinds of eggs, bacon, ham and sausage), plus lunch in summer and fall. Many of the lunch items are available at night in the tap room, which is immensely popular with locals. Among the intriguing selections: warm chicken tenderloin salad, crisp garlic potato skins filled with avocado sauce, baked eggplant crepes and sauteed chicken livers on puff pastry with madeira tomato sauce, and a chilled goat cheese and walnut fettuccine that sounded great in summer. Most are in the $4.50 to $6.50 range.

Lunch daily in summer and fall, noon to 2; dinner nightly, 6 to 9; tap room menu, Sunday-Thursday 5:30 to 10.

Chantecleer, Route 7, East Dorset. (802) 362-1616.

As far as area residents are concerned, there's a surprising unanimity as to the best non-inn restaurant around: the Chantecleer in East Dorset, just north of the Manchester line. The food is consistent and the atmosphere rustically elegant.

Swiss chef Michel Baumann acquired the contemporary-style restaurant fashioned from an old dairy barn in 1981. His menu features Swiss and French provincial cuisine.

Appetizers run from $4.95 for bunderfleisch (Swiss air-dried beef) to $6.95 for smoked salmon and trout mousse, carpaccio, crab and shrimp with chilled pasta, and seafood sausage with saffron sauce. The Danish liver pate with lingonberries is highly rated.

Entrees are strong on veal dishes, the four running from wiener schnitzel to roulade madeira. Other entrees from $14.95 for braised pork and sweetbreads to $22 for rack of lamb provencale include frog's legs with garlic butter, filet mignon au poivre and duck with a lemon-whiskey sauce. You also might choose braised rabbit with apple-brandy sauce, roast duckling with apricot-walnut sauce, rack of lamb coated with herbs and garlic, beef fondue or any of the nightly seafood specials.

Favored desserts are chocolate fondue, coupe Matterhorn, bananas Foster and Swiss Tobler chocolate cake. A number of Swiss wines are included on the reasonably priced wine list, and Swiss yodeling music may be heard on tape as background music.

Dinner Wednesday-Sunday, 6 to 10.

Barrows House, Main Street, Dorset. (802) 867-4455.

The new greenhouse off to the left of the dining room is where we would choose to eat at the Barrows House, if we were lucky enough to snag one of its seven tables. Not that the larger main room with ruffled curtains, flowered china, and dark green flowered

Dorset Inn faces the village green.

and ferned wallpaper isn't inviting; it's simply a bit too brightly lit, while the greenhouse is dark and spectacular. The red tile floor and brick wall are graced with green plants and trees, and with the attractive grounds outside (flowers in summer, snow in winter), the setting is magical.

The menu, which changes nightly, is available a la carte or fixed price, $22.50 for four courses. The latter is the better deal. We started with smoked tuna with caper and red onion creme fraiche and a tartlette of smoked scallops and mussels with scallions and red peppers, both excellent. A small loaf of bread and a garden salad with a honey-mustard dressing came next.

The sirloin of beef with four-peppercorn sauce and calves liver with caramelized onions and smoked bacon were accompanied by a platter of vegetables served family style, on this night spaghetti squash Creole, lemon-scented broccoli, carrot puree with maple, and risotto with fennel and red peppers. Vegetables have always been a Barrows House strong point; one summer dinner brought carrots glazed with raisins and ginger, asparagus with hollandaise, squash and spinach with dill, and warm potato salad made by the innkeepers' son, Thatcher Brown.

A huckleberry tart and a wonderful cappuccino ice cream appealed from the dessert list, which included amaretto cheesecake, chocolate-cherry cake and maple-walnut pie. Innkeeper Tim Brown is proud of the wine list, which harbors our favorite Rutherford Hill cabernet for $22 as well as a Heitz Cellars Martha's Vineyard cabernet for $80. Matt's Choice, named in honor of the former chef who now owns and operates a deli-lunchroom in Bennington, is a special each night at a lower price — at our visit, grilled pork chop with lingonberries, salad, bread and beverage, just $10.95.

Dinner nightly, 6 to 9; weekends only in November. No smoking.

Village Auberge, Main Street, Dorset. (802) 867-5715.

Former chef-owner Alex Koks was a tough act to follow, but chef Richard Schafer is tailoring the inn's traditional French menu to his own style, and the clientele is responding. Striking built-in cabinets displaying china are a focal point in the attractive, restful dining room with a large bay window at the far end. Tables are covered with moss green linens and topped with stunning botanical service plates, and chairs are comfortable cane and bentwood.

A piping-hot cheese fritter is served to each diner with the menu. The new chef has

Bay window provides airy setting for dining at Village Auberge.

added more game dishes for main courses, but retained the ever-popular sauteed sweetbreads with morels and cream, which we remember fondly from years past, and roasted rack of lamb for two.

Among appetizers ($4.75 to $6.75), the rabbit terrine comes with hazelnuts, pinenuts and pistachios, the cold poached salmon with two mayonnaises, and the snails and mussels in puff pastry. Excellent sourdough bread and mixed green salad with zesty roquefort or vinaigrette dressings precede the main course.

Entrees ($15.50 to $21) range from roasted rabbit with endive and cream to roasted pork tenderloin with ginger. We savored the veal medallion with mushroom mornay sauce and the sweetbreads, both garnished with broccoli, tomatoes, spinach with nutmeg and duchess potatoes. Two or three seafood dishes vary nightly.

Desserts, if you can manage after all this, are $4. They include a fancy collection of sorbets and ice creams, a dense chocolate-orange almond torte made with ground almonds instead of flour, a fruit tart on a cheesecake base, and an apple spice cake. We enjoyed a colorful dish of three homemade sorbets — raspberry, mango and passion fruit — that was plenty for two.

With the opening of the expanded bar, Village Auberge offers a limited tavern menu. In the attractive room with dark green wainscoting and beams, the polished wooden tables are topped with English place mats. Such main courses as cold poached salmon, baked herbed chicken, fish mousse and sauteed tenderloin tips are about $6.50 to $8.25.

Dinner nightly except Monday, 6 to 8:30 or 9, Saturday only in winter; tavern serves nightly except Saturday in summer, Wednesday-Friday in winter.

The Garden Cafe, Southern Vermont Art Center, Manchester. (802) 362-4220.

This nifty cafe, halfway up a mountain, has been run for years by people associated with noted restaurateur Alex Koks — first his daughter Marianne, then Alex and lately an employee from his new Four Chimneys Inn and Restaurant in Old Bennington. A dining room and outdoor terrace at the back of the Art Center is the setting, with sculptures all around in the sloping gardens, and a view of distant mountains through the birch trees. On a nice day it could not be a more idyllic site for lunch or Sunday brunch.

Silk flowers in little baskets and Vermont woven mats decorate the tables; chairs are the ice-cream-parlor type with flowered seats. Everyone gets a small dish of celery and carrots with a savory dip. Fresh fruit daiquiris are a specialty, and the blanc de blanc for $5 a half carafe goes well with most lunches.

Soups, sandwiches and salads, with a few daily specials, are the fare, but everything has special touches. The tomato-orange soup, served in a glass bowl with a slice of orange and whipped cream on top, was wonderful, delicate yet tangy. Almost everyone we saw was ordering the chicken pot pie with croissant crust, but we tried a sandwich of chicken salad and snow peas (all sandwiches — $3.75 to $6.75 — are served open-face on a choice of farm, rye or sesame bread) and a pasta salad with parmesan cheese and mushrooms, both excellent. Crabmeat on a croissant and a burger with bearnaise sauce and avocado were other specials. A duck breast sandwich with olives and gherkins, a plate of English cold cuts, and sauteed sweetbreads with puff pastry (at $9.50, the most expensive item on the menu) are other interesting choices.

Homey desserts include apple crisp with vanilla ice cream, carrot cake, oatmeal square with coconut, pecan topping and whipped cream, and brownie a la mode.

Open Tuesday-Sunday, 11:30 to 3, June to mid-October. No credit cards.

Diversions

Dorset Playhouse. Tucked away in the trees just off Church Street, the rustic, all-wood barn with the red and white awning on the side was the first summer theater in Vermont. For fourteen years it has been home to the Dorset Theater Festival, a non-profit professional theater company committed to the revival of plays from the past and the development of new plays and playwrights. Its rediscovery of Cole Porter's 1938 musical "You Never Know" went on national tour; other new plays have gone on to New York and Washington, and in 1988 its production of "Taking Steps" was moving to off-Broadway. The season runs from mid-June through Labor Day.

Merck Forest & Farmland Center. These days it's rare to find so large and unspoiled an area so available for public use as this 2,700-acre preserve northwest of Dorset off Route 315 in Rupert. Twenty-six miles of roads and trails are available for hiking in the forests, meadows and mountains. Established by George Merck of chemical-company fame, it is a non-profit outdoor education center open to the public year-round. Scholars study the organic garden, the maple sugaring and forest management. Hikers, campers and cross-country skiers enjoy the trails to Birch and Beebe ponds and the vista of the Adirondacks from the Viewpoint. The forest is a New England treasure.

General stores. Peltier's General Store has been the center of Dorset life since the early 1800s, the more so since it was acquired in 1976 by Jay Hathaway and his wife Terri, who have augmented its everyday goods with exotica like Scotch smoked trout, cheddar cheese from Shelburne Farms, aromatic coffee beans and fine wines. Just back from New York with an array of new items, Jay said his store "is ever-changing because we don't want to be routine." History he has, but "we have a ton to offer in real life."

Equally historic but thoroughly unchanging is the **H.M. Williams Department Store,** two attached barns identified by a small sign at the south edge of town and an incredible jumble of merchandise placed helter-skelter (foodstuffs amidst the hardware, boxes of ladies' shoes identified with a cardboard sign: "With this quality and these prices, let the big boys compete"). Prices are marked by crayon and the cash register is a pouch worn around his waist by proprietor Dennis Bromlee. While we waited for 50 pounds of sunflower bird seed for a bargain $13.10, the woman ahead of us bought 50 pounds of rabbit pellets and was told where she could find a bale of hay.

A few other Dorset stores are of interest. Wildfowl carver Marilynn Morrissey offers decoys, pillows with wild life and stained-glass hangings at the **Wood Duck.** Lacy clothes and antiques are featured next door at **A Country Romantic.** South of town is the **J.K. Adams Co.** factory store, which has an exceptional assortment of woodware and housewares made from native hardwoods. Butcher blocks, knife racks, bowls, cutlery and homespun tablecloths are for sale at substantial savings.

More shopping. Since adjacent Manchester offers such fine shopping opportunities, here are a few favorites. Silk-screened greeting cards from the **Crockett Collection** are available at discount prices at the showroom on Route 7 north of Manchester; other cards and notes are stocked as well, and you can watch the cards being made. Fishermen gravitate to the **Orvis Retail Store** in Manchester Center, where fishing rods are made (and can be tried out at the adjacent trout pond). **Southwicks Ltd.** is a large, rather preppy store with gifts and conservative clothing for men and women (although it also sells Woody Jackson cow T-shirts). **The Jelly Mill,** a three-story barn, is crammed with gifts, cards, gourmet foods, kitchen ware and much more; the **Buttery Restaurant** on the second floor serves lunch and snacks. **Anne Klein, Ralph Lauren, Hathaway, Cole-Haan** and **Benetton** are among the growing number of fashionable outlet stores.

Southern Vermont Art Center. High up a mountainside off West Road in Manchester on the road to Dorset is this special place not to be missed. Inside are changing exhibits from early June through foliage season, plus the Garden Cafe for lunch. A summer film festival and concerts by such groups as the U.S. Military Academy Band, the New England Brass Consort and the Southern Vermont Chamber Orchestra are always well attended. The Manchester Garden Club restored and maintains the **Boswell Botany Trail,** a three-quarter-mile walk past hundreds of wildflowers and 67 varieties of Vermont ferns, all identified by club members. An hour's hike through the woods is another attraction, and the sculpture garden is bordered by amazing vistas.

Back roads. They're all around, but a few are special. Dorset West Road and adjacent West Road in Manchester take you past some interesting and impressive country homes. Dorset Hollow Road makes "an absolutely gorgeous circle that takes about ten minutes," in the words of innkeeper Bill Ley of Cornucopia. The Danby Mountain Road winds through secluded forests and, if you keep bearing right at every intersection, you eventually come to a dead-end with a spectacular wide-open view across the hillsides toward mountain peaks 50 miles away. The sight at fall foliage's height actually produced a few "wows" out of us and lived up to Dovetail innkeeper Jim Kingston's promise of one of the best foliage trips in Vermont.

Extra-Special

Mother Myrick's, Route 7A, Manchester Center. (802) 362-1560.

We can't seem to get through this area without stopping at Mother Myrick's, the ultimate ice-cream parlor and confectionary shop, but much, much more. One of the things that lures us is the fudge sauce — so good that a friend to whom we give it hides her jar in a cupboard and eats it with a spoon. Here you can buy the most extraordinary homemade chocolates, get a croissant and cappuccino in the morning, tea and a pastry in the afternoon, or a grand marnier truffle cake and espresso late at night. Ice-cream sodas, milkshakes, floats, sundaes and pastries are served in a fantastic art deco setting with etched-glass panels, bentwood cases, light columns and the like done by gifted Vermont craftsmen. Mother Myrick's also carries, appropriately, a line of greeting cards about diets. Open weekends from 8 a.m. to 11 p.m., weekdays 10 to 9.

Adirondack chairs are ready for lounging in front of placid waters of Lake Bomoseen.

Vermont Lakes Region
The Way It Used to Be

Vermont isn't known particularly for its lakes, other than, perhaps, Lake Champlain. But there was a time when a kosher resort on Lake St. Catherine was fondly likened to those in the Catskills and large hotels along Lake Bomoseen near the New York state line west of Rutland received guests by the trainload.

"Bomoseen used to be surrounded by old hotels, dance halls and casinos," recalls Cindy Soder, a transplanted Long Islander who now runs one of the inns proliferating across the area. "It was almost the Las Vegas of the East."

The hotels died with the trains after World War II, and the lakes and their surrounding towns languished in a time warp. Fair Haven, Poultney, Castleton and Middletown Springs harbor few of the embellishments of tourism that transformed nearby areas like Manchester, Woodstock and Killington.

Now the area's tourism cycle is starting over, and half a dozen inns and B&Bs have sprouted since 1985. Despite the Vermont Marble Exhibit's claim to being one of the state's premier tourist attractions since 1933, tourism is still in its infancy here. Other than inns, you'll find few restaurants, shops or points of interest (the first McDonald's opened in the area in the fall of 1988). "What we like is that this is rural Vermont the way it used to be," says Doyle Lane, who moved here with his wife to run a business and Priscilla's Victorian Inn.

Social life centers around the general stores, the Sunday evening band concert, the weekly farmers' markets. Green Mountain and Castleton State colleges provide cultural activity. There are historic sites in East Poultney and Castleton, mineral waters in Middletown Springs (much of the town is listed on the National Register), and a hilltop battlefield in Hubbardtown, where Ethan Allen and the Green Mountain Boys fought the only Revolutionary War battle in Vermont.

Lake Bomoseen, Vermont's largest, and Lake St. Catherine offer two state parks, good fishing and boating among water diversions. Ice fishing, ice sailing and cross-country skiing prevail in winter.

Except for the new Route 4 expressway that seems out of place as it cuts through the area, the roads are rural and undulating. You'll be struck by all the cows — and goats and sheep — grazing on the hillsides, and by all the domed hillocks and mountains that distinguish the area's landscape.

But there are stirrings in these rural hinterlands. "We came up here in 1986 to make this a destination area," Bea Taube of the Vermont Marble Inn says assuredly. "And we will."

Inn Spots

Vermont Marble Inn, 12 West Park Place, Fair Haven 05743. (802) 265-8383.

They were strictly novices when they bought the mansion in 1986, but they have thrown themselves into it with such abandon, you'd think they'd been innkeepers all their lives. Some guests even call Bea Taube and Shirley Stein "aunt" and Richard Taube "uncle" by the time they leave. "They come as guests and leave as friends," Bea says. "And they return as family."

Such is the spell cast by the ebullient innkeepers and their Italianate Victorian mansion, built in 1867 of Vermont golden marble. It has appealed to those seeking culinary treats and luxury since it was restored with great T.L.C. and money. Today, some people come simply to enjoy a bottle of Dom Perignon in the museum-like, formal drawing room with its incredible molding, crystal chandeliers, and soft rose walls (a slightly less formal library on the other side of the hall has a TV set, games and magazines). Others come for cocktails and dinner (see Dining Spots), while those in the know partake of it all — afternoon tea, dinner, overnight lodging, an elaborate breakfast and sumptuous surroundings.

Each of the innkeepers carries out his or her tasks with enthusiasm. Very visible as a team (at dinner they occupy a front table in the dining room, where they are part of the comings and goings), they welcome guests and oversee every detail. They serve afternoon tea with cookies, crudites or crackers and cheese at cocktail hour, and a full breakfast. We enjoyed fresh orange juice, currant and almond muffins, baked apple slices and feathery pancakes with premium maple syrup. You might find peaches and cream french toast or a croissant stuffed with scrambled eggs and smoked salmon.

The fourteen upstairs guest rooms (twelve with private baths) are as opulent as the common rooms. Named for favorite writers, they come in many shapes and sizes, but all are handsomely furnished with period pieces and items from the innkeepers' endless collections of antique beds, miniature shoes, candlesticks, paperweights and such. We stayed in the Shakespeare Room at the head of the long staircase (a third longer than usual), which was most spacious and had its own dressing room. The Elizabeth Barrett Browning room has a working fireplace, a four-poster bed and an antique lace bedcover; the Oscar Wilde, twin four-poster beds. Whimsical touches abound, and a tour is almost like visiting a fine house museum, a very personal one at that.

An art deco wing added in the '20s on the third floor must be seen to be believed. The bathroom in the George Bernard Shaw room is done up in black and chrome down to the all-black sink, toilet and tub. The pillow on the bed pictures a flapper with a fur boa, and the room's chairs are lacquered in black. Even the stair railings remind one of Radio City Music Hall.

Doubles, $62 to $92. Closed April and mid-November to mid-December.

Innkeepers Bea and Richard Taube and Shirley Stein in front of Vermont Marble Inn.

Middletown Springs Inn, On the Green, Middletown Springs 05757. (802) 235-2198.

The pink and white inn with gingerbread trim faces the tiny green in the center of what once was a mineral-springs resort that was Vermont's answer to Saratoga. Steve and Jane Sax, who previously ran a cottage colony in faraway Calais, Me., moved closer to the year-round action in 1986 when they took over this established inn, built in 1880. Victoriana is the theme of these hands-on innkeepers, and the inn exudes personality.

The inn has five common rooms with twelve-foot-high ceilings on the first floor and seven guest rooms upstairs, as well as three more in a rear carriage house. All have private baths and vary in size. Bright and cheerful, they are notable for elaborate Victorian furniture, lovely oriental rugs, interesting beds, books everywhere, and neat touches like a chest painted by talented Jane in an oriental mode and a carriage full of large dolls. She sells the wonderful wreaths that bedeck the house at all seasons.

Steve cooks the dinners served in the inn's two Victorian dining rooms (see Dining Spots) as well as breakfasts of egg puffs, German apple pancakes, Swiss eggs and such, plus the inn's trademark sticky buns.

The Saxes pack picnic lunches, give rides in their Austrian carriage, sell cottage crafts, offer package plans and generally keep things hopping year-round with their vivacious spirit.

Doubles, $110 to $140, MAP; two-night minimum on weekends.

Maplewood Inn, Route 22A South, R.R. 1, Box 4460, Fair Haven 05743. (802) 265-8039.

A mile south of town and denoted by a sign of colorful maple leaves, this restored Greek Revival is really three houses in one. Two were moved to the site to join the original 1850 structure, which accounts for its size and the number of public rooms.

Maplewood Inn is really three houses joined together as one

Cindy and Paul Soder, who used to run a wine and cheese cafe near St. James, Long Island, acquired the former dairy farmhouse in 1985 and renovated it into an appealing B&B with two suites and three bedrooms with private baths.

The rambling main floor has a fireplaced common room with TV, two breakfast rooms (one that doubles as a BYOB tavern), a formal dining room (with no fewer than seven doors), a large parlor, a country kitchen, a guest bedroom and the owners' quarters. Up various staircases are the rest of the bedrooms and suites, handsomely appointed with period furnishings, wing chairs, thick carpeting, wreaths, old costumes and abundant plants. We enjoyed the Hospitality Suite, with a pineapple motif, a comfy sitting room, a step-up four-poster queensize bed, and plenty of room to spread out — except in the cramped shower. A half-bottle of soave and a plate of crackers and cheese were presented upon arrival.

Breakfast is hearty, from cantaloupe and blueberry bread through scrambled eggs spiced with tomatoes, pepper and ham, and enough bacon to feed an army. Cindy, who champions the area, will send you on your way with ideas to keep you busy for many a day.

Doubles, $60 to $70; suites, $95.

Priscilla's Victorian Inn, South Street, Box 711, Middletown Springs 05757. (802) 235-2299.

A grand Victorian home with parlors on either side of the large front hall has been converted into a B&B by Priscilla and Doyle Lane, she an Englishwoman from Yorkshire and he a craftsman who restores player pianos, music boxes and such. Put their backgrounds together and the result is a small inn of great character.

Doyle's Chickering player grand piano, melodeons, wall clocks and other collector's items are shown to advantage in the parlors. More collections are evident in the dining room and in the library, where a full breakfast is served. Priscilla, who once owned a tea room in Hillsboroough, N.C., serves a different breakfast every day, catering to her whims and those of her guests. She serves afternoon tea at 4, complete with cream cakes and scones, and will prepare four-course dinners for guests at $13 per upon advance request. Roast beef with Yorkshire pudding is a favorite choice.

There are six large guest rooms with private baths, colorful furnishings, and pretty linens and towels.

Doubles, $56.

Tower Hall Bed & Breakfast, Bentley Avenue, Poultney 05764. (802) 287-4004.

A three-story turret graces this good-looking, mustard-colored Victorian charmer with a wicker porch facing the Green Mountain College campus. You'd hardly know it once served as a college dormitory and more recently as an office building for Ski Racing magazine. Parquet floors, stained glass, original woodwork and ornate mantels tell of a more elegant time.

Kathy and Ed Kann opened it in 1988 with three guest rooms, one with private bath and two sharing. Each is decorated with period furniture. Guests enjoy a lovely pink and blue Victorian parlor, and a second-floor sitting room with a fireplace is good for reading or watching TV.

Kathy makes and sells all the crafts that abound; the wooden items are particularly interesting. A continental breakfast of fruit and homemade breads and muffins is served in the large dining room.

Doubles, $45.

Eagle Tavern, On the Green, Box 587, East Poultney 05741. (802) 287-9498.

A new swimming pool surrounded by a deck and a wall of slate is a summer attraction at this historic hostelry, lately restored and reopened as a B&B by ex-New Jersey residents William and Gertrude Horridge.

Inside a building dating to 1785 is a gorgeous main floor, with a long entry hall, a grandly furnished living room and a formal dining room with Hitchcock chairs around a harvest table. Extravagant oriental rugs enhance the floors.

Upstairs are six bedrooms ranging in size from tiny to enormous. The two nicest are fashioned from the former ballroom, with striking arched ceilings, canopy beds, wing chairs and armoires. The largest, known as the Ballroom because it takes up two-thirds of its namesake, has six twelve-over-twelve windows. Moving from the sublime to the ridiculous, said Bill as he led a tour, the visitor sees next door a tiny single room that housed Horace Greeley, who was paid $40 a year while apprenticing to East Poultney's Northern Spectator before he went on to found the New York Herald Tribune.

"Goodie baskets" of fruit juices, crackers and candies are in each room upon guests' arrival. Afternoon tea or cider is served. Breakfast is described as in the European style, although we call it hearty — a sideboard laden with a buffet of cereal, juices, yogurts, muffins, croissants, a meat platter, Vermont cheeses, and possibly baked apples or pears.

Doubles, $50 to $65. Closed mid-October through December and mid-March through April.

Lake St. Catherine Inn, Cones Point Road, Box 129, Poultney 05764. (802) 287-9347.

A family-style inn like those you remember from the 1950s, this once was an exclusive kosher resort. Since taking over in 1984, Patricia and Raymond Endlich have made an informal, friendly inn out of the only commercial property along a dead-end road on a peninsula jutting into crystal-clear Lake St. Catherine.

Tucked between summer cottages are the two-story, weathered-wood main inn with sixteen simple, quaint guest rooms (all with private baths) and a motel-style annex with

Editor Horace Greeley stayed at historic Eagle Tavern when he worked in East Poultney.

nineteen deluxe units. Quilts and country items enhance these rooms and the main-floor living room and lounge, with cozy furniture and a feeling to match.

Hearty meals are served to house guests and the public by reservation in the large gold and brown dining room where windows look onto the lake. The five-course dinner is priced from $11.95 to $15.95, depending on the choice among three entrees. A typical Saturday night's offerings are prime rib, glazed roast duckling and rainbow trout amandine. Black Forest cake, fruit pies and bread pudding are favored desserts.

Guests like to take drinks onto the large free-standing deck beside the water. There are rafts for swimming and numerous canoes, paddleboats and rowboats are available.

Doubles, $110 to $134, MAP. Open mid-May through mid-October.

The Silver Fox, Route 133, Box 1222, West Rutland 05777. (802) 438-5555.

But for the restaurant canopy at the front entrance, the exterior of the structure reflects its heritage as a 1768 farmhouse, set amid 30 acres along the Clarendon River. The interior, however, has been renovated into a spiffy inn and restaurant (see Dining Spots).

Ex-New York restaurateur Frank Kranich is the front man for his retired parents who bought the place. He not only handles the cooking but did the decorating of the public spaces as well as the six guest rooms and two suites. All have new baths; some have two double beds, conveying a bit of a motel look. An inn feeling derives from the Queen Anne cherry or oak furnishings, four-poster beds, velvet chairs and gingham curtains.

Guests gather for cocktails and hors d'oeuvres in the elegant living room, which has a woodburning stove, an entertainment center with television, VCR and stereo, and a profusion of thriving green plants. One of the area's ubiquitous chess tables and backgammon are available in the library.

A full breakfast is served in one of the inn's two dining rooms. A fresh melon compote and honey bran muffins could precede the entree, perhaps an asparagus, mushroom and Swiss cheese omelet with bacon, french toast or strawberry waffles.

Doubles, $135 MAP.

Dining Spots

Vermont Marble Inn, 12 West Park Place, Fair Haven. (802) 265-8383.

The ubiquitous innkeepers here are heavily involved in their restaurant — Bea Taube does the baking and desserts, Shirley Stein makes the breakfasts, Rich Taube serves the wine and the breakfasts. But they leave the dinner menu and cooking up to Don Goodman, a 30-year-old chef from New Jersey, who calls his cuisine "gourmet American."

Candlelight dinners are served in two high-ceilinged, pink and white dining rooms seating about 60. We thought the mild country pate with leeks and grain mustard served warm ($4.50) and the assorted smoked fish plate ($5.50) were appealing appetizers.

Homemade rolls, a tossed salad and a small dish of sorbets — blueberry and seabreeze (grapefruit and vodka) — came next.

Among ten entrees ($10.95 to $15.50) were excellent braised duckling with port and raspberry sauce and a loin lamb chop grilled with garlic and served with onion-bell pepper salsa. Both were accompanied by snow peas and wild rice pilaf, with herbal and floral garnishes from the gardens out back. Scallops of veal with a sauce of basil and sun-dried tomatoes, breast of chicken with smoked ham and wild rice stuffing, and shrimp sauteed with endive, julienned vegetables and champagne were other choices.

A strawberry and cream roll with pecans and a very rich chocolate pate on a hazelnut creme anglaise were delicious endings. Gourmet magazine has published the recipe for Bea's berries and cream tart. She also

Dining room at Vermont Marble Inn.

does exotic sorbets like melon with Medori and pina colada, and garnishes them with pansies. Candies come with your bill, and if you are staying overnight, you will probably find chocolate-covered nuts and raisins in a chocolate cup on your pillow — this inn is definitely not for dieters without great will power.

A Davis-Bynum pinot noir ($15) was a hit from the well-chosen, extensive wine list, which goes up to $130 for a 1978 Chateau Lafite Pauillac.

Dinner nightly except Tuesday from 6. Closed April and mid-November to mid-December.

The Silver Fox, Route 133, West Rutland. (802) 438-5555.

Innkeeper Frank Kranich's fourteen-year background as a captain and chef in New York City (Le Madrigal, Smith & Wolensky) stood him in good stead for overseeing the dining room at his family's inn. He opened as a B&B, started serving dinner to house guests and, since 1988, has offered prix-fixe dinners to the public by reservation.

Up to three dozen patrons can be accommodated in two small, hushed dining rooms where decor is minimal and bare wood tables would be better off with cloth mats. Cocktails and hors d'oeuvres — in our case, crackers and cheese — are offered in the living room prior to the single seating at 7:30.

There's no choice among the dinner courses, priced at $16.95. Chilled raw vegetables and piping-hot French and dark breads are on the table as the server recites the menu. The appetizer the night we dined was a meal-size plateful of creamy fettuccine with mushrooms and shrimp. A warm spinach salad with bacon-mustard dressing came next.

By this time we barely had room for the entree, filet of sole sauteed with shrimp provencale. The slab of New York cheesecake that followed was simply too much. Although the waitress was touting the Montrachet ($45) or chardonnay ($23) with this meal, we settled on a perfectly nice Sterling sauvignon blanc for $16.75.

Entrees on other nights, Frank later informed us, could be cornish game hen stuffed with pecans, grilled salmon with dill sauce, prime rib and, on Sunday, roast leg of lamb, pork or turkey. Caesar is one of his favorite salads, and desserts could be Bavarian chocolate layer cake, sacher torte or homemade apple pie with Vermont cheddar cheese. All breads, pastas and desserts are homemade.

Dinner, one seating at 7:30.

Blossom's Corner, Routes 30 and 149, Wells. (802) 645-0058.

This rustic barn of a place is actually two restaurants, a casual pub in which bargains are the rule and a dining room featuring slightly more complex fare.

Chef-owner Bob Kapp makes little obvious use of his Culinary Institute of America training. Even the dining room menu follows the area's meat and potatoes tastes, from chopped sirloin to prime New York steak, $7.95 to $15.95. Oh, you can get vegetarian dishes (eggplant parmigiana or Italian manicotti), fried or broiled sole or scallops, veal cutlet parmigiana and — from the Delmarva Peninsula, according to the menu — duck a l'orange or teriyaki chicken with a spiced Vermont apple compote. Dinners come with relish dish, green salad, baked or fried potatoes or rice pilaf, vegetable and homemade bread. Chocolate mousse, cheesecake and apple pie are dessert favorites. Wine prices are in the low teens.

The pub menu offers some of the same appetizers served in the dining room plus sandwiches, burgers, pizzas and entrees from $4.95 for spaghetti and tomato sauce through clam strips and veal cutlet parmigiana to $11.95 for chargrilled sirloin.

Decorations brighten dining room at Silver Fox during holiday season.

White gingerbread trim over pink enhances Middletown Springs Inn.

The decor is barn-typical, with tiny white lights, hanging dried herbs and flowers dressing up the dining room. Seating is at benches, booths and captain's chairs in the high-ceilinged pub, where bar puzzles test the imbibers and a Lego set and coloring books amuse the kids.

Dinner, 5 to 10; closed Tuesday and Wednesday from November to Memorial Day.

Middletown Springs Inn, On the Green, Middletown Springs. (802) 235-2198.

By reservation, the public can join inn guests for dinner at communal tables in two high-ceilinged, Victorian dining rooms at this venerable inn. Innkeeper Steve Sax handles the cooking chores in a large country kitchen.

Hostess Jane Sax introduces guests at cocktail hour in the wicker sitting room next to the bar. When seated for dinner, they find a note with the dinner courses written in rhyme and everyone tries to solve the puzzle of each course before it is served. By the end of dessert, says Jane, strangers have become cohorts and friends.

The dinner tab is $20. The meal the day we visited started with cream of carrot soup and tossed salad with celery-seed and maple-syrup dressing. A blueberry sorbet primed the palate for the main course, chicken Kiev served country style with baked potato and broccoli with oregano. Homemade cheesecake with cherries was a worthy finale.

Other menu fixtures are corn chowder and cauliflower soup, baked herbed scrod and beef Victorian, and Jane Sax's rum torte and English trifle. Jane also provides munchies during cocktail hour.

Dinner nightly at 7 by reservation.

Ringquist's Dining Room, Route 30, Bomoseen. (802) 468-5172.

An attractive small white house with black shutters has been home since 1976 to Gordon Ringquist's pleasant little Colonial dining room, a tavern where lunch is served, and a side deck with tables facing Lake Bomoseen across the road.

The decor ranks among the fanciest in area restaurants. Eight tables are clad in white and brown, flanked by windsor chairs, and topped with gasoline lamps and blue and white china.

Dinner entrees start at $7.25 for roast turkey, roast loin of pork, beef liver and baked sole with mushroom and celery stuffing. Veal cordon bleu and filet mignon are the most expensive at $13.95. Start with Gordon's special clam chowder, barbecued chicken wings, marinated herring or escargots ($1.25 to $4.95). Wines and desserts are priced similarly.

Lunch, Monday-Friday noon to 2; dinner, Tuesday-Saturday 5 to 9, Sunday noon to 9. Open year-round, fewer days in winter.

Prospect House, Route 30, Bomoseen. (802) 468-5581.

This golfing resort with a motel and an annex includes a small lakefront restaurant, whose sunken dining room has windows on three sides facing the water. A fountain trickles outside the entry. Inside, tablecloths are rusty orange with white overlays.

The menu has French headings (les potages, les entrees) and vaguely French fare: mussels in saffron, onion soup gratinee, veal marsala, broiled scallops with lobster glace and baked haddock with shrimp. Sesame chicken, pork loin framboise, linguini with clam sauce, and broiled shrimp are other entrees, priced from $9.50 to $14.95. Salade maison comes with, and the dessert tray bears homemade specialties.

Dinner nightly except Monday, 6 to 9; open June to mid-October.

Fair Haven Inn, 5 Adams St., Fair Haven. (802) 265-4907.

Ex-Connecticut restaurateur John Lemnotis moved to Vermont to retire but ended up running a restaurant in an 1837 structure that had been known as the Cottage Inn. "If you have good food and good service the locals will find you," says John, who over nearly two decades has built such a clientele that in 1988 he added an enormous dining room geared for functions.

The stucco and barnwood walls of the long, narrow main room are enhanced by pictures of Greece. White and blue linens, windsor chairs and candlelight create a setting more attractive than one might expect from the exterior.

Chef John calls his cooking "American and continental with a Greek flair." Seafood is his specialty, and he has a wholesale business that supplies other restaurants. The lengthy menu offers shrimp a la Grecque, Grecian haddock, seafood kabobs and such rare-for-these-parts fish as red snapper and grouper under catch of the day. Prices range from $8.95 for Boston scrod to $15.95 for lamb chops. Veal francaise and lamb en brochette are among possibilities.

Spanakopita, stuffed grape leaves and calamari sauteed in pure olive oil are appetizer options, $1.95 to $5.95. Greek soup and salads and homemade pastas also are offered.

An enormous dessert cart, containing all the coffee cups as well, is laden with cakes and baklava. Seven Greek wines, $3 a glass and $12 a bottle, are among the wines.

The inn has a noisy bar, fortunately shut off from the dining room, and sixteen guest rooms on the second and third floors, some with private baths. Doubles are $40 to $60.

Dinner nightly, 5 to 9:30.

Diversions

The area offers few tourist trappings in the traditional sense. Instead, it has unspoiled scenery, rural hamlets and historic districts, and good fishing and boating. The attractions of Manchester, Rutland, Woodstock and Killington-Pico ski areas are nearby.

East Poultney. Although the college town of Poultney has a walking tour with a brochure detailing sixteen historic points of interest, the earlier settlement of East Poultney commands more attention. Editor Horace Greeley stayed at the town's Eagle

Lake Bomoseen is on view from front lawn at Prospect House.

Tavern while apprenticing in the 1820s at the National Spectator, where he was joined by George Jones, a founder of the New York Times. Here, time literally stands still. The hands on the clock of the United Baptist Church never move; they're painted on at 10 o'clock. The church in the center of the village green was organized in 1802 and reorganized in 1987, according to a sign. Across from the impressive green is St. John's Episcopal Church, left exactly as it was built in 1831, without heat and electricity. It's used one Sunday a year to retain its church status. The Baptist church, the 1895 schoolhouse where Horace Greeley gave his first talk, a melodeon factory and the 1791 Union Academy are opened by the Poultney Historical Society on Sunday afternoons from 1 to 5 June through August or by appointment. Band concerts are presented on the green at 7 p.m. Sundays in July. Just south of the green is a bridge over a beautiful gorge and waterfall.

Middletown Springs. The town center and 91 buildings are listed on the National Register of Historic Places as an example of an unchanged New England village. Blink your eyes and you almost could miss this remote hamlet, but tarry and you'll see remarkable architecture and get the flavor of old Vermont. "Take up the blacktop and you'd have the village as it was about the turn of the century," says innkeeper Steve Sax. The mineral springs that give the town its name (and inspired the construction of the large but shortlived Montvert Hotel in 1871) have been restored by the local historical society in a quaint park. Five springs are left, and each is supposed to be different, but the only one we could find tasted like ordinary spring water.

Castleton Historic District. The first college in Vermont was founded in 1787 in this lovely little town, whose Main Street lined with pillared Greek Revival houses and interesting churches makes up an historic district. A comprehensive state college since 1961, Castleton State has a pleasant campus. The Higley Homestead Museum, operated by the Castleton Historical Society, is open periodically, as are several historic homes.

North of Castleton — seemingly in the back of beyond — is the hilltop **Hubbardton Battlefield,** where Ethan Allen and Seth Warner planned the capture of Ticonderoga and staved off British invaders in the only battle fought in Vermont during the Revolution. The small visitor center is free, and the panoramic view of the surrounding mountains is priceless.

Lakes and Parks. Lake St. Catherine State Park south of Poultney has nature trails, a good sandy beach, picnic tables, fishing and boat rentals. **Bomoseen State Park,** a bit harder to get to on the west side of Lake Bomoseen, has the same facilities plus a wildlife refuge. Smaller but more accessible is **Crystal Beach,** a park operated by the town of Castleton on the east side of the state's largest lake.

Wilson Castle, West Proctor Road, Proctor, (802) 773-3284. This mysterious, red brick structure along a hillside doesn't look as much like a castle as one might expect, despite a facade of proscenium arches, turrets and parapets. Built in the mid-19th century and home for five generations of the Wilson family, it has 32 rooms furnished in Far Eastern and European antiques and museum pieces. The sight of the woodwork alone is said to be worth the admission price. Guided tours, daily 9 to 6, May-October. Adults, $2.75.

Shopping. Shopping is not this area's strong suit; indeed, the largest business in downtown Fair Haven appeared to be the Cleanarama. The best shopping is in Poultney, where the **Original Vermont Store** nearly corners the market. Nooks and crannies in its Thankful Mears House, an 1840 Greek Revival, offer up everything from specialty foods and maple syrup to books, bunnies, baskets, birdhouses and brass butterflies, including Original Vermont Design products made in Poultney. Across the street in an old train station is **Kay's Corner,** a mishmash of antiques and odds 'n ends; beyond in a second depot is the **Craft Seller,** with many quilted items. In a Victorian cottage at 27 College St., **Heartstrings** is stocked to the rafters with a potpourri of country gifts. A truck called the **Corn King** parks on Main street and sells vegetables, cider and the like. The **farmers' markets** staged on the Fair Haven Green on summer Fridays are good for local color.

Extra-Special

Vermont Marble Exhibit, 61 Main St., Proctor. (802) 459-3311.

The working-factory exterior belies the sophisticated wonders within. A truck loaded with raw marble arrived as we did, and from the second-floor overlook onto the vast production floor we could view all the steps of turning the slabs into walls, floors and works of art. A fifteen-minute film is a good introduction to one of only two marble-producing plants in the country. Then tour the Hall of Presidents, where the faces of 40 past presidents have been carved from pure white marble by a local sculptor. Another overlook allows a glimpse of the 120-foot waterfall that powers the factory, the town of Proctor, the Danby quarry and more. There are exhibits on the geology of marble, photos of quarries, and more examples of marble than one could imagine. You can watch a resident sculptor at work, and the sculptures in the entry lobby are worthy of a museum. The Boy and Girl on a Swing, circa 1900, was brought here in 1976 to be repaired; its owner never returned, so it's on display as "unquestionably the work of a master carver." An interesting gift shop purveys everything in marble, from picture frames to worry stones, lamps to vases, chess sets to earrings. Outside is a marble market for seconds, available at bargain prices — the trick is to be able to carry your purchase away. Open daily 9 to 5:30, mid-May to late October; winter, Monday-Saturday 9 to 4. Adults, $2.50.

Village of Stowe nestles in valley beneath Mount Mansfield.

Stowe, Vt.
A Resort for All Seasons

When Olympic skier Phil Mahre first saw Stowe clad in summer's green rather than winter's white, he was struck by its beauty. So were many in the Eastern Ski Writers audience he addressed that August day.

Most downhill skiers haven't been to Stowe in what for them is the off-season. But the undisputed Ski Capital of the East is a year-round destination resort, more than its newer, less endowed competitors can hope to be.

For one thing, Stowe is Stowe, a village unto itself about eight miles from Mount Mansfield, a ski area unto itself. The twain meets all along the Mountain Road, which links village and mountain. Such a marriage between town and ski area is unrivaled in New England and rich in history — a history unequaled by any other ski town in the country, according to Mount Mansfield Company officials.

The ski resort was led for years by Sepp Ruschp, who left Austria in 1936 to be ski instructor for the fledgling Mount Mansfield Ski Club. The alpine mystique of the area was enhanced by Baroness Maria Von Trapp and her family, whose story was immortalized by "The Sound of Music," when they founded the Trapp Family Lodge.

The rolling valley between broad Mount Mansfield on the west and the Worcester Mountains on the east creates an open feeling that is unusual for northern New England mountain regions. In Stowe's exhilarating air, recreation and cultural endeavors thrive.

Cross-country skiing complements downhill in winter. Other seasons bring golf, tennis, horseback riding, hiking, performing arts, art exhibits and enough sights to see and things to do to make credible the area's claim to being a world-class resort.

Foremost a ski center, Stowe is somewhat lacking in inns of the classic New England variety. Instead, it has resorts, motels, ski dorms, condominiums and more Alpine/Bavarian chalets than you'll find just about anywhere this side of the Atlantic.

Still, Stowe is Stowe, a storybook New England ski town dominated by Vermont's highest peak. It's a place to be treasured, by skier and non-skier alike.

Inn Spots

Edson Hill Manor, Edson Hill Road, Stowe 05672. (802) 253-7371.

A French Provincial-style manor with old English charm, built in 1940 as a gentleman's estate, became a country inn in 1954. It retains its original private-home flavor except in the four new carriage houses with modern accommodations.

A mile-long country lane leads from the white post gates to the manor, which innkeeper Anita Heath contends is "still the only true country inn in the Stowe area." Set high amidst 300 secluded acres, it has a spectacular terrace beside a spring-fed, kidney-shaped swimming pool, a pond stocked for trout fishing, a cross-country ski center and stables for horseback riding.

The manor was a prime location in 1980 for the filming of winter scenes for Alan Alda's movie, "The Four Seasons." The famous Mercedes scene took place on the pond.

Inside the manor are eleven guest rooms, a pine-paneled parlor with Delft tiles around the fireplace, orientals, and more books and magazines than anyone could possibly read, plus a beamed dining room where dinner is served to guests and the public by reservation (see Dining Spots). The beams in the large parlor are said to have come from Ethan Allen's barn. Some of the paintings were done by Effie Juraine Martin Heath, a grandmother in the Lawrence Heath family, innkeepers since 1954.

One family suite has a fireplace, sofa and armchair, and a large bathroom with tub. Next to it is a small room with shared bath and the best view of the mountains.

Each of the four new carriage houses, up a hill beyond the inn, has four spacious rooms done in the decor of the original manor with beamed ceilings, pine-paneled walls, brick fireplaces and private baths. Billed as the inn's luxury units, they accommodate two to four people.

All told, five rooms in the manor plus those in the carriage houses have working fireplaces — a great attraction for winter visitors. We'd happily settle any time for the manor's large Studio, which has queensize bed, fireplace, skylight (this was formerly an artist's studio) and an exceptionally nice sitting area with picture windows overlooking the pool, pond and gardens.

Doubles, $166 to $198, MAP; off-season, $50 to $60, EP.

Ten Acres Lodge, Luce Hill Road, Stowe 05672. (802) 253-7638 or (800) 327-7357.

Built as a farmhouse in 1826 with several later additions, this rambling and picturesque red frame house with white trim on a quiet hillside is better known for its restaurant (see below) than its accommodations, although the latter situation is changing under innkeepers Dave and Libby Helprin.

The dining rooms and the small tavern are altogether appealing, and the plush parlor and front library could not be more comfortable. The striking wing chairs and couches piled with pillows in the parlor are popular with houseguests. Large bay windows look out onto ever-changing vistas of valley and mountains.

On two floors, the lodge's ten guest rooms (eight with private baths) vary. Some are tiny and spare; others are quite a bit larger and more luxurious. One with kingsize bed even has two bathrooms, one containing the tub and the other the toilet and wash basin. Two newly redecorated rooms on the first floor are especially plush. Rooms are carpeted, walls are pine-paneled or wallpapered with pine trim, and good-looking quilts cover some of the beds.

26

Tree trunks support porte cochere at entrance of Stowehof Inn.

Two renovated cottages offer two or three bedrooms, kitchens, working fireplaces and terraces with great views in every direction.

Worth the extra tab are eight luxury fireplaced suites in the new Hill House. Each has a large sitting area, private deck, cable TV and phone. A hot tub open to the stars is at the ready.

A buffet breakfast includes fresh fruit, granola, yogurt, an egg dish, ham and Vermont cheese.

The grounds contain a small pool, tennis court, and flower and herb gardens that beckon white rabbits. Beyond, cows graze on neighboring farmlands. Who could ask for a more tranquil setting?

Doubles, $60 to $120; Hill House, $150.

Stowehof Inn, Edson Hill Road, Stowe 05672. (802) 253-9722 or (800) 422-9722.

"Slow — Deer Crossing," the sign warns as you drive up the steep road to the Stowehof, whose soaring Alpine exterior is a hilltop landmark hereabouts. "No parking — sleigh only," reads the sign at the door.

Such touches reflect the character of this unusual, thoroughly charming place that grew from a private ski house into one of Stowe's larger inns.

At the front entrance, the trunks of two maple trees support the enormous porte cochere above the small purple door. More tree trunks are inside the huge living room, nicely broken up into intimate nooks and crannies, the two-level dining room, the downstairs game room and the Tyrolean Tap Room. The bell tower, the sod roof laced with field flowers and the architecture are reminiscent of the Tyrolean Alps. The upstairs library and game room is a replica of the interior of an old Vermont covered bridge.

You'd never suspect that the owners are from Hawaii, but their decorating flair is apparent in most of the 46 guest rooms, some of them unusually large and sumptuous. All have balconies or patios with views in summer of lovely clumps of birches, a swimming pool, a trout pond, lawns and the mountains.

Breakfast and dinner are served in the well-appointed **Seasons** dining room with beamed ceiling, fireplaces and windows looking onto pool and mountains. Lunch is served in summer on the terrace. The regional American dinner menu changes weekly. When we visited, entrees ($16.95 to $21) included fricassee of shrimp with oyster ravioli, sauteed pork with maple-mustard sauce, medallions of lamb with fresh rosemary and mint, and grilled filet mignon with wild Vermont mushrooms. Smoked salmon crepes and an apple, walnut and watercress salad were among interesting starters. The wine list contains selections priced up to $420.

Locals advise going to Stowehof just to see it. We think it's an equally appealing place in which to stay.

Doubles, $170 to $190, MAP; off-season, $70 to $90, EP.

Ye Olde England Inn, Mountain Road, Stowe 05672. (802) 253-7558.

Stowe seems an unlikely spot for an English coaching inn, but this restored and expanded inn fashioned from the tired old Sans Souci is British all the way from the bright red phone booth out front to the menu in Mr. Pickwick's Pub.

All eighteen guest rooms have private baths and seven have jacuzzis. They are spacious, decorated in Laura Ashley style and, on the third floor, are notable for interesting shapes and views of the mountains. New in 1988 were three luxury two-bedroom English "cottages" in a building out back beside the swimming pool, each with fireplace, jacuzzi, cable TV, lounge-dining area and kitchen facilities.

Transplanted Englishmen Chris and Linda Francis, skiers both, are more in evidence at their inn than are many innkeepers in the area.

An English breakfast and four-course dinners are served in the beamed **Dickens Room** in season. A pub-type menu is available all day in **Mr. Pickwick's Pub** with a hearthstone fireplace or on the expanded quarterdeck, lined with umbrellas advertising British ale and presenting a scene straight from the English countryside.

The pub menu offers bubble and squeak, ploughman's lunch, bangers and mash, highland haggis and cornish pasties from $4.75 to $13.95, served from 11:30 to closing. A few non-British items like chicken fingers and chili are also listed. We enjoyed a lunch of spinach salad served in a tostada shell and a good steak and kidney pie served inexplicably with a side bowl of gravy (could it have been for dipping the french fries in?), all washed down with pints of Whitbread and Watneys ales, presented in proper pub glasses. The list of foreign beers is extraordinary, and one can even get ale by the yard. In the evening, live jazz and folk music are enjoyed by the laid-back crowd.

Doubles, $136 to $190, MAP in winter; $60 to $95, B&B in summer; cottages, $195.

Green Mountain Inn, Main Street, Box 220, Stowe 05672. (802) 253-7301 or (800) 445-6629.

Its deep red facade a landmark in the center of the village since 1833, the inn has been carefully restored and upgraded in the last few years.

The main-floor dining room is considered one of the area's best (see below) and the legendary Whip downstairs is still where the action is, in the appealing bar as well as in the cafeteria-style grill and on the outdoor deck by the pool. A couple of small parlors in front retain the New England inn charm.

Most of the 58 guest rooms are behind the inn in a motel-type configuration, albeit with an antique look. The modern baths, color TVs and phones are offset by twin or queensize canopy beds, custom-designed reproduction furniture manufactured specially for the inn, period wallpapers and stenciling. A health center offers a spa program.

An enclosed walkway connects the inn to the Old Depot shopping complex next door.

Doubles, $80 to $115, EP.

1860 House, School Street, Box 276, Stowe 05672. (802) 253-7351.

You enter right into the kitchen, so it comes as no surprise that guests — who must be non-smokers — have the run of the house in this spiffy B&B with five bedrooms, all with private baths, and uncommonly nice public rooms.

"Our guests share the house with us," says Rose Marie Matulionis, innkeeper with

her husband Richard Hubbard. "They can cook their dinners and we even provide the candlelight."

Fresh flowers abound in the rooms, especially the large living room with a comfy rust velvet sectional in front of the wood stove, a wall of bookshelves and a piano with 1950s sheet music.

Rose Marie and Rick serve fresh fruits, cereal, breads and muffins for breakfast in the charming dining room enhanced by hanging copper pots, a hooked rug and striking flower arrangements.

Cozy Vermont quilts top the extra-firm foam mattresses ("I think they're much more comfortable than inner springs," says Rose Marie) on the oversize beds in the spacious guest rooms. Baskets of Crabtree & Evelyn toiletries and splits of wine bearing the Trapp Family Lodge label are in the rooms.

In summer, guests enjoy the rear deck and a pretty back garden with yellow and white lawn furniture, the free use of bicycles and passes to the Village Athletic Club. In winter, they like the ski storage and waxing room, and at all times they like the laundry facilities and no-smoking policy.

Doubles, $75 to $95.

Foxfire Inn, Route 100, Box 2180, RD 2, Stowe 05672. (802) 253-4887.

An early 19th-century Vermont farmhouse now is the home of a locally acclaimed Italian restaurant (see Dining Spots) and five comfortable guest rooms with private baths.

Innkeepers for more than ten years, Art and Irene Segreto serve full breakfasts to inn guests on a sunny breakfast porch, which has white bentwood chairs, gold tablecloths and many plants in the windows on three sides.

The upstairs guest rooms are individually and handsomely decorated. One corner room has a bed with a crocheted, curtain-type affair swathing the headboard, centered by a lace-covered hanging lamp. Another with an oriental rug, sofabed and blue corduroy chair has a quilt and ruffled pillows on the bed, while a third has an ingenious corner shower. Tiny vases filled with flowers are on the dressers.

Watch your step in the upstairs corridor — there's a well-disguised two-inch rise that we tripped over coming and going, several times no less. The comfortable downstairs sitting room has a fireplace. Another parlor leads into the bar.

Out front is a lovely patio, lined with yellow lilies and redwood tubs ablaze with geraniums, under a huge maple tree.

Doubles, $60 to $65.

The Gables Inn, Mountain Road, Stowe 05672. (802) 253-7730.

What many consider to be the best breakfast in town is served at the Gables, either under yellow umbrellas on the front lawn (facing a spectacular view of Mount Mansfield), on the front porch or on picnic tables inside.

Twelve guest rooms in the main building and four in a small motel-type annex have charming country furniture, homemade wreaths and, an unusual touch, all rooms (and even a couple of bathrooms) are decorated with a few fine china plates from the extensive collection of owners Sol and Lynn Baumrind. All have private baths, most gleaming white and modern, some in what Sol laughingly calls a "toilet tower" he added just for the purpose. The newest master room has a queensize, lace-canopy four-poster bed, a sofa, TV and a modern bathroom with skylight.

A landscaped swimming pool, hot tub, a plant-filled solarium and a large, comfortably furnished den and living room with TV are other attractions in this homey place. In winter the downstairs den is used for apres-ski; the owners put out crockpots full of steaming hot soup, hot hors d'oeuvres, and cheese and crackers after 4 p.m. for hungry skiers, who BYOB.

As for that breakfast, it's open to the public, and some days the Baumrinds serve as many as 300. Says Sol with a smile, "service is leisurely — that's a code word for slow." Aside from all the old standbys, one can feast on kippers or chicken livers with onions and scrambled eggs, matzoh brei, and eggs Raymond, poached eggs in a puff pastry shell with smoked mussels topped with a chive and cream sauce. Stuffed french toast made with raisin bread, blueberry or banana pancakes and Belgian waffles are popular choices.

In ski season, family-style dinners are served in the dining rooms amid a wondrous collection of Royal Copenhagen plates. The picnic tables are covered with tablecloths, and candles glow.

Breakfast daily, 8 to noon, weekends to 12:30.

Doubles, $120, MAP in winter; $50 to $65, EP in summer.

Timberholm Inn, Cottage Club Road, RR1, Box 810, Stowe 05672. (802) 253-7603.

An inn with great potential. That's our impression of the Timberholm, shortly after its acquisition in 1988 by Susan and Wes Johnson of St. Louis. Taking over the old Coombs Inn, they gave it a new name and style and planned to upgrade the rooms.

The rustic, weathered cedar facade trimmed in Wedgwood blue hints that this 1949 house along a quiet road is more than just another ski lodge. Inside, the Great Room confirms it. This really is a great room — a huge, sunny space containing lots of sofas in two comfy sitting areas, a fieldstone fireplace, TV, shelves of books and, at the near end, an open dining area. Beyond are two walls of picture windows onto a wide, glorious deck — perfect for relaxing in summer — and a tree-framed view of the golf course and the Worcester Mountain range. We'd gladly curl up with a book in the Great Room or on the deck and spend the day.

The hitch comes at night. Under the existing room configuration in a lodge-style wing, the inn has six rooms and two suites. Four rooms are small and share baths. Two that are a bit larger are called deluxe and have full baths. The largest bedrooms are part of two-bedroom suites with living rooms that are superfluous given all the public space.

Susan serves lemonade and banana bread on summer afternoons, changing to tea, soup and cookies by the fire in winter. Breakfast is a serve-yourself buffet with yogurt, granola, fresh fruit, homemade breads and muffins, and a hot dish like french toast or eggs florentine.

Doubles, $56 to $70; suites, $86 for two.

Breakfast on the lawn is a tradition at the Gables Inn.

Butternut Inn, Mountain Road, RD 1, Box 950, Stowe 05672. (802) 253-4277.

The doorbell plays "The Eyes of Texas Are Upon You," and that's just the start at this recent transformation of the old Skimore Lodge. Texan owners Jim and Deborah Wimberly advertise theirs as "an award-winning, exclusive inn — a romantic couples' retreat — internationally famous for fine food and New England hospitality" and have a hallway wall of letters and thank-you notes to prove it.

The eighteen guest rooms, all with private baths and most air-conditioned, vary widely in size and remain true to their ski-lodge heritage, although each is furnished with antique dressers, country crafts, and black and white TVs. Ten have kingsize beds and one of the nicer on the third-floor corner has a balcony and an extra daybed, which jarred us, given the "romantic couples" motif.

There's a small living room on the main floor, but most of the action is on the lower floor: a parlor with a piano handmade from one large walnut tree, a billiard room with a 1905 pool table, a small sitting area and a large-screen TV (the room's walls are covered with photos Jim has taken of inn guests), and a large dining room. Christmas decor is on display all year, from the lights out front on the spruce tree to the sleigh filled with teddy bears.

Looking up toward Mount Mansfield, the eight-acre back yard is a showplace of flower and herb gardens, a terrace, a flagstone courtyard, a gazebo by the swimming pool, a fountain and a little park area for picnics by the river. There's plenty of room for eighteen romantic couples to be alone or together as they wish.

Breakfast is bountiful enough that most don't eat lunch, according to Jim. A favorite is eggs Butternut — poached eggs on pork chops with sauteed onions and Cajun peppers. The inn makes corned beef fresh daily for corned-beef hash. On summer afternoons, tea and homemade chocolate-chip cookies are served. In winter, there's an after-ski "soup bar" that also includes pheasant pate, and candlelight dinners are served.

Doubles, $70 to $120, B&B; winter, $130 to $160, MAP. No smoking.

Dining Spots

Ten Acres Lodge, Luce Hill Road, Stowe. (802) 253-7638.

The dining room is classically pretty — and the menus on the daring and innovative side — at Ten Acres, which usually is mentioned first when Stowe people are asked their favorite restaurants.

In summer, the airy porch with its small-paned bow windows and flowered wallpaper fills up first; the paneled interior dining room appeals more in winter. White-linened tables are set with Villeroy & Boch service plates in the Palermo pattern. The atmosphere is rather hushed, as Vivaldi music plays softly in the background, and young women in white blouses and long black skirts serve unobtrusively.

Chef Jack Pickett, who's been with Ten Acres for a decade, stresses regional foods and produce on his menus, which change weekly. One of the inn's waiters gathers the mushrooms, cepes and chanterelles, and a local man grows the melons, which are perfumed like flowers and so juicy you'd think they were from Persia, says the chef. Salads are special: one night, one of spinach, endive, radicchio, apple and walnuts with port wine and stilton dressing; the next, one of spinach, mushrooms, red onion, bacon and quail eggs.

We enjoyed generous drinks, crusty sourdough bread with sweet butter, an appetizer of lobster, shiitake mushrooms and creme fraiche in a cabbage leaf, and small house salads with excellent garlic-lemon and blue-cheese vinaigrette dressings. Both the butterflied leg of lamb with preserved black currants and cracked peppercorns and the chargrilled cornish game hen with tomato, basil and creme fraiche were superb, served with julienned zucchini and rice pilaf.

Other entrees are in the $16 to $21 range, except for a linguini with chanterelles, broccoli, peas and pattypan squash for $13.25. They could be a saute of monkfish and bay scallops with Italian parsley and scallions, chargrilled chicken breast with sun-dried tomatoes and basil, grilled veal chop with ragout of wild mushrooms, and tournedos of beef stuffed with roasted peppers, artichoke bottoms and smoked mozzarella.

For $4.75 to $6.50, you could start with a rabbit pate with coulis of three berries, shrimp with tomatillo and pineapple sauce, mushrooms stuffed with sausage and fennel, or buckwheat crepes with cured salmon, sour cream and dill.

Desserts like raspberry cheesecake, casaba melon sorbet, chocolate truffle cake and hazelnut lemon brioche go well with the good strong coffee.

The huge wine list includes a page of old and rare vintages, most over $100 and going up to $260. Ten Acres is a place to cherish for special occasions.

Dinner nightly, 6 to 9:30. No smoking.

Green Mountain Inn, Route 100, Stowe. (802) 253-4400.

The once-traditional Number One Main Street dining room is now country pretty with bare wood floors and nicely spaced tables set with white damask, candles, blue flowered plates and heavy polished silver. Lanterns and watercolors by the late Vermont artist Walton Blodgett adorn the walls.

The cooking is assertive, as in appetizers like chilled shrimp with avocado mousse and salsa, smoked trout with horseradish cream and stilton, lobster ravioli with ginger sauce, and mushrooms provencale with garlic sauce ("spicey!" warns the menu), priced from $4 to $6.50. Even the red bell-pepper soup is flavored with brie.

Entrees range from $13 for broiled turkey steak with Thai peanut sauce to $17 for a seafood sampler of three fish entrees or Vermont veal steak with watercress sauce and red peppers. Sea scallops with blackberry sauce, Cajun quail with crayfish-cornbread stuffing and filet mignon with fresh raspberry sauce are other summer offerings.

For dessert, how about frozen amaretto souffle or "sac de bon-bon," a chocolate shell filled with mousse and fresh fruit? Dinner nightly, 6 to 9:30.

Downstairs is **The Whip,** smartly redecorated and striking for the whips in the wall

Ten Acres Lodge is known in Stowe for fine dining.

divider separating bar from dining room and over the fireplace. Just outside is a most attractive deck, where the garden furniture is navy and white and tables are shaded by white umbrellas.

The day's fare is chalked on blackboards above cases where the food is displayed. Many of the dishes are calorie-counted for those who are there for the spa facilities. Country pate with cornichons on toast points, smoked salmon with capers, Mexican vegetable soup, salads with dressings devised by the Canyon Ranch in Arizona, crabmeat on a croissant with melted cheddar, open-face veggie melt (184 calories) — this is perfect "grazing" fare.

Main dishes like grilled blackened bluefish, poached salmon, grilled rib eye and sauteed veal with interesting presentations are chalked up at night. Prices are in the $8 to $12 range.

Frozen mocha cheesecake, oatmeal-maple pie, raspberry-rum sorbet and very berry bread pudding are some of the ever-changing desserts.

Open daily, 11:30 to 9:30.

Isle de France, Mountain Road, Stowe. (802) 253-7751.

Next door to the long-popular Shed but miles removed in terms of tone and atmosphere, this incredibly lavish (and almost out of place) restaurant was opened in 1979 by chef-owner Jean Lavina, a Frenchman from the Lyons area by way of the French Shack in New York City.

Formerly the Crystal Palace, the place shows its heritage, though some of it now seems a bit threadbare: cut-glass chandeliers, mirrors, gilt ornamental work around the ceilings, rose-bordered service plates with gold edges, heavy silver and a single red rose on each white-linened table. Three tables have sofas for two on one side. The cozy bar with apricot-colored sofas and a striking medieval chandelier features a menu of assorted specialties for under $10.

Dining in the two dining rooms with plush round-backed chairs is in the classical French style. For appetizers ($4 to $7), you might start with pork and veal country pate or oysters bourguignonne. The twenty entrees priced from $14 to $22 are supplemented by six to eight nightly specials like poached salmon in beurre blanc or fresh venison with a foie gras sauce. Eight beef presentations vary from entrecote bearnaise to

33

chateaubriand; one is slices of tenderloin with a creamy bourbon sauce. There are sweetbreads, frog's legs, Dover sole meuniere and many other French classics.

Desserts range from frozen meringues chantilly and creme caramel to bananas Foster, cherries jubilee and crepes Suzette for two. The large wine list is priced upward from the mid-teens.

Dinner nightly except Monday, 6:30 to 10:30.

Edson Hill Manor, Edson Hill Road, Stowe. (802) 253-7371.

The inviting dining room of this manor estate high up Edson Hill is open to the public for dinner by reservation.

The beamed room is rustic, with rusty orange curtains on the windows overlooking forests and mountains. Tables are set with woven mats for breakfast, white cloths and baskets of flowers for dinner. One particularly nice window table for two overlooks the pool and pond.

Veteran chef Jack St. Onge's dinner menu is a mix of New England and continental specialties at bargain prices. Among appetizers ($3.25 to $4.75) are escargots, pate forestiere, fettuccine alfredo and French onion soup gratinee. A selection of raw vegetables is served with an unusual maple-curry dip.

Entrees start at $12.50 for grilled mesquite chicken and top off at $15.50 for filet mignon bearnaise. In between are scampi provencale, sole florentine, veal du jour and broiled New England loin of lamb for an unbelievably low $12.95. The small but serviceable wine list is fairly priced as well.

Finish with pecan or Boston cream pie or bananas Foster. The value received is considerable.

When the inn's ski touring center is open, a fireside luncheon is available in the downstairs cocktail lounge from noon to 2:30.

Dinner nightly by reservation, 6 to 9.

Foxfire Inn and Restaurant, Route 100, Stowe. (802) 253-4887.

North of the village in an old farmhouse is this small inn and large restaurant serving some of the best Northern and Southern Italian cuisine in Vermont.

A few oriental rugs dot the wide-plank floors of the large blue main dining room at the rear. Windsor chairs are at bare polished wood tables, topped by different woven or quilted mats, fresh flowers in carafes and occasionally yellow cloths. On the other side of the bar is an enclosed, plant-filled porch.

Munch on homemade egg-glazed breadsticks as you await the hot antipasto (rolled eggplant, mushrooms and shrimp, $8.50) or garlicked red peppers with cured beef ($4.50), both popular appetizers. Pasta dishes, which include salad, run from $6.75 for spaghetti with meatballs or sausages to $11.25 for seafood linguini.

Six veal, five chicken, three steak and three seafood dishes make up the entrees, $11.25 to $14.50. There's also a nightly special — lobster fra diavolo when we visited.

A house salad with a dressing of olive oil and vinegar is served after the entree. "It helps to digest the meal and gets you ready for dessert," says chef-owner Art Segretto, who cooks "Italian like my mother made it."

You won't need much readiness for luscious desserts like Italian cheesecake, frozen lemon tortoni, a rum and coffee-flavored chocolate cake, cannoli and gelato. In cooler months, diners like to take their cappuccino with amaretto or Foxfire coffee (with frangelico and Italian brandy, the whipped cream topped with an Italian flag) into the parlor to sit in front of the fireplace. The mainly Italian wine list bears excellent values.

Dinner nightly, 6 to 10.

Dining room at Edson Hill Manor is open to the public as well as to its house guests.

Stubb's, Mountain Road at Edson Hill Road, Stowe. (802) 253-7110.

Vermont lamb and veal are featured entrees at this highly regarded dining spot, the reincarnation of a building that once housed the esteemed Steen's restaurant. Chef-owner Jim Dynan's fare, which changes with the seasons, is served in a candlelit setting of brass lamps, white linens and ladderback chairs. Entrees range from $9.75 for fettuccine with asparagus and asiago cheese to $16.75 for sauteed loin of veal with fresh chives. Grilled leg of lamb with sweet roasted-pepper salad, sauteed Vermont calves liver, crispy fish with Szechuan sauce and curried pasta with sea scallops and sun-dried tomatoes are other winners.

Standouts among appetizers ($4 to $6.75) include spicy grilled lamb sausage with endive and black bean salad, duck and scallion dumplings laced with ginger, and grilled shrimp with spiced pecans on watercress and Boston lettuce. Homemade pastries and ice creams are the dessert fare.

An appealing bar menu, including portions of the dining-room menu, is served in the lounge. We'd go there just for the lamb mixed grill — spicy sausage and grilled brochette, with garlic-roasted potatoes and pepper salad ($8.25).

Dinner nightly, 6 to 10.

Hapleton's, rear of the Carlson Building, Main Street, Stowe. (802) 253-4653.

Some people think Hapleton's serves the most interesting food for the price in town. It's a cozy downstairs restaurant with wooden booths and bar and much stained glass, all crafted by local artists. Hanging green lamps and a huge fireplace create a comfortable spot in which people love to hang out. A small side patio with Perrier umbrellas and black wrought-iron furniture off the main floor operates in warm months.

Appetizers, salads and light meals have always been served all day. Dinners ($13.50 to $15.50) were things like grilled lamb chops, sauteed liver and barbecued pork chops, augmented by blackboard specials. Popular at lunch was a "dog from Montreal," the Hebrew National brand, with pommes frites, and steamed shrimps en tabloid, served with complimentary newspaper.

When we last visited, the fare was in transition — the menu being eliminated in favor of "all kinds of food, from $3.95 to $14.95," according to our informant.

Open daily from 11:30.

The Shed, Mountain Road, Stowe. (802) 253-4364.

An institution among skiers for years, the Shed has grown from its original shed to include a greenhouse filled with Caribbean-style furnishings, trees and plants, and a menu offering something for everyone at all three meals. In the process, it may have lost some of its charm, but the variety and low prices keep it filled day and night.

Beige and green floral print cloths top the rattan-bamboo tables in the greenhouse and in the main dining room. Also popular is the rear deck brightened by planters full of petunias in summer and sporting a waffle buffet bar for brunch. The large lounge has a separate entrance.

The food is straightforward and with-it, from nachos to California salad to barbecued ribs to chicken in a basket. You can get seafood strudel, linguini verdi, shepherd's pie, lamb bourbon, prime rib and goodness knows what else at dinner prices ranging from $9.95 to $14.75. The omelet and Belgian waffle buffet that had people lined up outside for Sunday brunch on a holiday weekend is $8.50.

Breakfast, 7:30 to 11:30; lunch, noon to 4:30; dinner, 5 to 10; late-night menu from 10 p.m. on holidays and weekends.

Stowe-Away Lodge, Mountain Road, Stowe. (802) 253-7574.

The blenders atop the tiled bar at Stowe-Away, which doesn't sound like a Mexican restaurant but is, hum most of the time in summer, when up to thirteen gallons a night of chef-owner Michael Henzel's special homemade margarita mix get frothed up — $3.50 fetches a twelve-ounce portion.

Two small dining rooms with hand-painted tile tables flank the bar. The back dining room looks onto a small terrace used for summer dining, where a redwood hot tub is on a platform at the side. Relax in this with one of the margaritas and you may never make it to dinner.

Mike Henzel, who has cooked in Wyoming and California, designed the menu himself and it is used in several other Mexican restaurants across the country.

Soups, served with garlic toast, include a chile verde and a vegetarian chile. Guacamole salad is $3.75; super nachos, $3.50. Seven kinds of burrito ($4.95 to $6.25), tostadas and tacos, combination plates and huevos rancheros regular and deluxe are listed, as are crab enchiladas, quesadilla grande, enchiladas mole, arroz con pollo and piccadillo. Fajitas, shrimp kabob and chicken Ricky stuffed with cheese, black olives and jalapenos "for serious heat seekers" are in the $9.25 to $11.50 range. The homemade brownie is the only dessert in which the chef uses sugar; honey sweetens the sopaipillas, flan and homemade ice cream.

At Sunday brunch, egg dishes are $5.95 to $7.25, served with homefries, and six versions of Eggs Louie are variations of eggs Benedict. On the slow holiday weekend we were there, we were not thrilled with the excruciatingly laid-back service. We also were not thrilled with our huevos rancheros, missing the red salsa listed in the menu. When we pointed this out to the waiter, he checked with the chef, who responded that the menu was mistaken!

Dinner, 5:30 to 10; Sunday brunch, 11 to 2:30.

Restaurant Swisspot, Main Street, Stowe. (802) 253-4622.

Skiers have always been partial to fondues, and they're the specialty at this small and enduring place, brought to Stowe in 1968 after its incarnation as the restaurant in the Swiss Pavilion at Expo 67 in Montreal.

The classic Swiss cheese fondue with a dash of kirsch, $16.95 for two, made a fun meal for our skiing family. Also good is the beef fondue oriental ($13.95 for one), served with four sauces. There are six different quiches ($9.95) and a handful of entrees like bratwurst, chicken florentine and sirloin steak with a butter and herb sauce, $7.95 to $13.95.

Onion soup, eleven variations of burgers and many sandwiches ($3.50 to $7) are featured at lunch.

The dessert accent is on Swiss chocolate, including a chocolate fondue with marshmallows and fruits for dunking.

Open daily from noon to 10 p.m.; closed spring and late fall.

Austrian Tea Room, Trapp Family Lodge, Luce Hill Road, Stowe. 802) 253-8511.

In summer or foliage season, we know of no more appealing place for lunch or a snack than the rear deck of the Austrian Tea Room, with planters of geraniums and petunias enhancing the view across the countryside and horses grazing nearby. Surely you can feel the spirit of the late Maria von Trapp (who lived at the lodge until her death in 1987) and the Trapp Family Singers. It's a majestic setting where you feel on top of the world.

The fresh spinach salad looks great, as does the avocado stuffed with shrimp salad, and you can get broiled knockwurst or weisswurst served with sauerkraut and potato salad ($6.50). There are daily specials like chilled raspberry soup and shrimp and crab quiche as well as six open-face sandwiches, fancy drinks, cafe Viennoise and Austrian wines by the glass or liter.

Those Austrian desserts we all know and love, sachertorte, linzer torte, apfelstrudel and the like, as well as Bavarian chocolate pie, peach torte and jailhouse pie, are in the $3 range and — with a cup of cafe mocha — a delightful afternoon pick-me-up.

The trip up Luce Hill Road gives you a chance to see the rebuilt, exotic Trapp Family Lodge, which the locals consider the closest thing to Disneyland in Vermont. The tea room remains true to the lodge's heritage.

Open daily, 10:30 to 8:30.

Diversions

Mount Mansfield. Skiing is what made Stowe famous, legions of skiers having been attracted to New England's most storied mountain since the East's first chairlift was installed in 1940 (the Mount Mansfield Company is its official name, but everyone from near and far calls the ski area simply Stowe). Today, Mount Mansfield has six lifts and about one-third of its slopes are for expert skiers, including the awesome "Front Four" — the precipitous National, Goat, Starr and Liftline trails, so steep that on the Starr you cannot see the bottom from the ledge on top; they almost make the Nosedive seem tame. There's easier terrain, of course, and the related Spruce Peak ski area across the way has four more lifts, a sunny southeast exposure and a special section for new skiers. Combined with accommodations and nightlife, the total skiing experience ranks Stowe among the top ski resorts in the world. Adult lift tickets are $35.

Summer at Mount Mansfield. The four-passenger Stowe Gondola takes visitors 7,000 feet up to the Cliff House, just below Vermont's highest summit (adults $6, mid-June to mid-October). Cars can drive up the 4.5-mile **Stowe Auto Road,** known to skiers who ease down it in winter as the Toll Road (cars $6, daily late May to mid-October). The **Alpine Slide at Spruce Peak** appeals especially to children; you take a chairlift up and sled down (single rides, $4; open daily in summer, weekends in late spring and early fall).

Smugglers' Notch. Up the Mountain Road past the ski area you enter the Mount

Mansfield State Park, passing picnic areas and the Long Trail. A couple of hairpin turns take you into Smugglers' Notch, a narrow pass with 1,000-foot cliffs looming on either side. The closest thing we've seen in the East to Yosemite, it's a quiet, awe-inspiring place to pause and gawk at such rock formations as Elephant Head, King Rock and the Hunter and His Dog. Stop at Smugglers' Cave and, farther on, hike into Bingham Falls. The road is not for the faint-hearted (it's closed in winter, for good reason). We drove back from Jeffersonville after a thunderstorm and found waterfalls that had been trickles on the way over suddenly gushing down the rocks beside the lonely road.

The Arts. After a ten-year lapse, summer theater was revived in 1986 at the **Stowe Playhouse.** The **Stowe Performing Arts** Series offers three Sunday evening concerts in July, one usually featuring the Vermont Symphony Orchestra, in the concert meadow near the Trapp Family Lodge. The **Helen Day Art Center** has rotating exhibits in a restored 1863 Greek Revival structure that once was the high school on School Street.

The **Cold Hollow Cider Mill,** south of town on Route 100, is a large and intriguing red barn where you can watch cider being made (and drink the sweet and delicious free samples). For more than twenty years the Chittenden family also have sold tart cider jelly, cider donuts and other apple products as well as cookbooks, wooden toys, gourmet foods and about every kind of Vermont jam, jelly or preserve imaginable.

Shopping. Shops are concentrated in Stowe and scattered along Route 100 and the Mountain Road. In the village, **Shaw's General Store** considers itself 90 years young and carries most everything, especially sporting goods, sportswear, gifts and oddities. Nearby are the **Old Depot Shops,** an open, meandering mall of a place with **All Things Special** crafts, **Purcell's Country Foods** (where sensational fruit butters like strawberry daiquiri and peach bourbon are made every day), **Annie Van's** handpainted clothing, **Stuffed in Stowe** with thousands of stuffed animals and **Bear Pond Books.** Up the Mountain Road at 108 West is the **Stowe Kitchen Co.,** with practical cookware and gadgets; **Kookaburra,** with wild and woolly Australian sweaters, and **Pinnacle Antiques,** an exceptional antiques and handcrafts shop on three levels featuring furniture, jewelry, antique quilts, lacy pillows, mohair throws and such. Also on the Mountain Road is the **Christmas Place,** which speaks for itself; the excellent **Stowe Mountain Sports** is at Stowe Center. The **West Branch Shops** include **Betsy Snite Sports, Once Upon a Time** and **Samara,** an unusually good shop featuring works of Vermont craftsmen. At **Exclusively Vermont** you'll find jams, syrup, pickled fiddlehead ferns, beeswax candles, potpourri in large jars, boiled wool mittens and jewelry.

Extra-Special

Ben & Jerry's Ice Cream Factory, Route 100, Waterbury. (802) 244-5641.

Opened in 1985 just south of Stowe, this factory producing 130,000 pints daily of the ice cream that transplanted Vermont characters Ben Cohen and Jerry Greenfield made famous is one of Vermont's busiest tourist attractions. And with good reason. During half-hour guided tours ($1), you see a humorous slide show, watch the ice cream being made, learn some of the history of this intriguing outfit that donates one percent of its profits to peace and, of course, savor a tiny sample, obtained by lowering a bucket on a rope to the production area below. At busy times, the place is a madhouse — with live music outside, lineups of people waiting to buy cones, a gift shop filled with Vermont cow-related items, and every bit of publicity they ever got decorating the walls. If you can't get inside, at least buy a dish or cone of ice cream from the outdoor windows ($1.10 to $2.05). It's open daily year-round.

Skiers enjoy fresh powder conditions on a glorious sunny day at Sugarbush.

Waitsfield and Warren, Vt.
The Spirit of the Valley

Even more than most Vermont areas best known for skiing, the Mad River Valley is a year-round paradise for sportsmen.

The focus, of course, is on skiing — at the venerable and spartan Mad River Glen, a challenging area for hardy, serious skiers, and at the newer Sugarbush, the tony resort spawned by and for jet-setters. Both are very much "in" with skiers, for vastly differing reasons.

In the off-season, which extends from May into November, there are the conventional athletic pursuits associated with other destination ski resorts, such as golf and tennis. There also are the more unusual: mountaineering, polo, rugby and soaring.

Off-mountain, activity centers along Route 100, which links the two villages of Waitsfield and Warren. Ironically, Waitsfield (the home of Mad River Glen) is busier and more hip in the Sugarbush style. Warren (the address for Sugarbush) is in the Mad River Glen tradition, remote and seemingly bypassed by the times.

The spirit of the valley — considered unique by its adherents — emerges from its rugged terrain as well as from the contrasting mix attracted by its two skiing faces.

Unlike other ski resorts where one big mountain crowns a plateau, here mountains crowd the valley on all sides, forging several narrow valleys that leave some visitors feeling hemmed in. To understand, you have only to stay in a remote chalet at Mad River, the mountains rising in silence all around, or descend the back road from Roxbury Gap, one of Vermont's more heart-stopping drives, which rewards the persevering with awesome close-ups of some of the state's highest peaks.

The chic of Sugarbush joins with the rusticity of Mad River to present choices from racquetball to backpacking, from boutiques to country stores, from nightclubbing to roadhouses. For fine dining, the valley has no peer among Eastern ski resorts.

Although the valley is at its best and busiest in the winter, its spirit spans all seasons.

39

Inn Spots

The Inn at the Round Barn Farm, East Warren Road, RR Box 247, Waitsfield 05673. (802) 496-2276.

We had admired the Joslin Round Barn on previous travels, were surprised lately to find an ad touting it as an elegant B&B, and heard from an admiring area innkeeper that it oozes "countrified charm." But we were still unprepared for what we found.

The inn is not in the Round Barn as we had anticipated (that is being restored for conversion into a cultural center, artists' studios, a theater, a lap pool, and heaven knows what else). Rather, the inn occupies a gracious farmhouse next door, has six comfortable bedrooms, luxurious common rooms and a terraced, 85-acre back yard that rolls down a hill to a couple of ponds and meanders uphill past cows grazing in the distance. An idyllic setting, and an exciting B&B.

Innkeepers Jack and Doreen Simko, longtime skiers in the valley, retired from the family floral business in New Jersey to open the inn with daughter Annemarie in 1987. So expect to see flowers and greenery throughout the house, pots of flowering hibiscus on the terrace, and flowers sprouting from piles of rocks beneath a giant apple tree. Relaxing on the back terraces is a treat, what with animals grazing, a few barns scattered up the hill, whimsical things like a cow made out of iron and a pen with Jack's three pet pigs, Jessie, Bandit and Lobes — gifts for his 50th birthday.

Our visit coming at the end of one of the hottest summers ever, we passed up the two largest rooms with jacuzzi tubs in favor of the breezy Palmer Room at the rear corner. It had a highback Victorian queen bed sporting a crazy quilt made in 1915, lovely lace curtains and a framed fan on the wall. The draperies match the canopy on the kingsize bed in the Joslin Room, notable for cranberry walls and a heart and lace pillow. Besides stenciling and other interesting decorative touches, the inn has nightly turndown service with chocolates as well as toiletries like bath grains and moisturizers. At cocktail time, Jack, who Annemarie says is a creative cook with hors d'oeuvres, usually puts out something like guacamole or a hot shrimp dip.

The main floor offers a large, elegant library with walls of books, a fireplace and a fancy stereo system issuing forth Mozart or Vivaldi. A less formal game room downstairs has a pool table, TV and VCR. Breakfast is served in a large sun porch with skylights, wicker and chintz, and teal blue swags across the top of the windows. Here we feasted on raspberries and bananas in cream, followed by a fantastic omelet blending bacon, cottage cheese, onions, red peppers and basil from the garden.

About that round barn. It's a National Historic Landmark and one of the last remaining of its kind in Vermont. Restoration was under way for completion in 1989 and potential uses for its three floors of space remained open: artists' studios, cultural events, an aerobic studio, perhaps a lap pool, or a center for spa weekends.

The Simkos were planning to put in another two-acre pond with sandy beach for swimming and paddle boats. In the inn, they intended to add a solarium and three more guest rooms with kingsize beds, working fireplaces and jacuzzis by the rear windows. Based on requests of guests, they were starting to bottle the raspberry sauce they serve with their cottage-cheese pancakes. Said a California friend who was enjoying a reunion with the Simkos and joined us all at the breakfast table: "These are high-energy people with 85 irons in the fire. Staying with them is like being part of the family."

Doubles, $80 to $120.

Tucker Hill Lodge, Route 17, RD 1, Box 147, Waitsfield 05673. (802) 496-3983.

Since it was acquired by the Baron inn group early in 1987, this appealing inn of wide

Joslin Round Barn (left) is focal point of the Inn at the Round Barn Farm.

fame has had its ups and downs. When we visited in September 1988, former owner Zeke Church was back in active management, preparing the way for new innkeepers Meg and Chip Chapell and pronouncing the property and service once again up to snuff.

Innkeepers since 1976, Zeke and Emily Church were a tough act to follow. In 1985, Zeke won the Vermont Hospitality Association's "Restaurateur of the Year" award and the inn's dining room (see below) is highly regarded.

This is one of the more lavishly landscaped inns we have seen. In summer, the flower gardens are spectacular, with hanging clematis, flowering kale and (we had to ask Zeke what this strange-looking thing was) decorative mullen.

The twenty guest rooms vary in size and decor; fourteen have private baths. They are homey and rustic, with handmade quilts, bouquets of flowers and what the inn's brochure calls "a mountain cabin feeling." The nicest is the new Catamount Suite in the former cross-country building across the way. Also popular is the newly restored Eastman House, a three-bedroom farmhouse behind the pool, ideal for families or couples traveling together.

In the main inn, a nicely furnished, paneled living room has TV and a fieldstone fireplace. A barnwood lounge downstairs contains a rustic bar and a built-in sofa by another fireplace. Tennis courts, a swimming pool and a large outdoor deck ringed with cedar trees are attractions.

Breakfasts are hearty: seasonal fresh fruit, followed perhaps by cottage-cheese pancakes with fresh peaches, a broccoli, tomato and mushroom omelet, or Vermont toast, which is french toast with shredded cheddar cheese between the layers.

The innkeepers recommend hiking the local trails (the Long Trail is not far away). You'll need to after one of their breakfasts or dinners!

Doubles, $116 to $146, MAP; suite, $166.

The Sugartree, Sugarbush Access Road, Warren 05674. (802) 583-3211.

Thanks to Chicago corporate expatriates Howard and Janice Chapman, the Sugartree has undergone a facelift into an inviting inn from what essentially had been a ski chalet for 30 years.

Janice had never even seen skiing before they arrived in 1983. Summer's trees, incredible gardens and window boxes envelop the inn in its own delightful island of color and greenery but, she says, when the leaves are gone "we get the most gorgeous views of the mountains and can watch all the skiers" across the way. And the fall foliage, she adds with her infectious, hearty laugh, "takes your breath away."

An artist at heart, she has outfitted the inn with an extravagant potpourri of folk art, Vermont handicrafts and inanimate animals of all sizes and kinds, from stuffed teddy bears to duck napkin rings, wood hens to mouse dolls. They're at their showiest in the entry hall and large paneled living room, furnished like a home and with a fireplace, big windows and TV.

Colorful bedspreads, shams and dust ruffles perk up the ten guest rooms, all with private baths. Furnished in country style, they vary in size from a large main-floor room with stove and sink to a small third-floor room with hearts and birds on the wallpaper. Quilts, puffy country curtains, crocheted bed canopies and samplers brighten the rooms, and the bathrooms have glycerine soaps, herbal bath grains and built-in hair dryers.

Janice serves a full country breakfast in a dining room decorated to the hilt (from big ribbons tying pillows to the chairs to calico cats hanging from the shelves). French toast with homemade raspberry sauce, pineapple pancakes or scrambled eggs with oodles of cheese and pecan sticky buns could be the fare, presented at four tables amidst a painted cow, porcelain pigs, napkin-holders of all kinds of animals and such. She leaves the kitchen open for guests to get ice and to make sandwiches, and says "it's like a party in ski season" when Howard serves hearty soups, sweet and sour meatballs, homemade pizzas and desserts to returning skiers.

Doubles, $96 to $120.

The Lareau Farm Country Inn, Route 100, Box 563, Waitsfield 05673. (802) 496-4949.

This really is a farm with gardens, four dogs, two cats, three chickens and five horses. Only lately has the 1852 farmhouse been converted into an inn, with a barn, woodshed and appropriate country setting on flatlands that were farmed until a few years ago by the Lareau family. In the Mad River, just across the road, a ten-foot-deep swimming hole is flanked by rocks. You can dive into "water so clear you can see the brown trout," according to Susan Easley, innkeeper with her husband Dan.

The Easleys took over in 1984, Sue piecing together the squares for ten bed quilts in their first summer. Since then, they have added bathrooms and expanded to fourteen guest rooms. In the former woodshed, the dirt floors have given way to carpeting, but the four rooms retain some of the original posts and beams amid modern touches like private baths. Brass bedsteads and rockers are mixed with a profusion of hanging plants.

New in 1989 was an addition to the rear of the main house with four guest rooms, all with full baths and queensize beds, an enlarged dining room and a sitting room around the fireplace in the former kitchen. The other six rooms, which share baths, are in the oldest part of the house, built in the 1700s. The main structure was added to it, and has a parlor full of Victorian furniture and stuffed animals. Guests like to laze on the assortment of porches that wrap all the way around the house.

A cross-country center has been set up in the old slaughterhouse, where a wood stove provides warmth for fondue parties. An Arabian stallion and a pair of Canadian chunk horses give two-mile sleigh rides in the winter.

Dan Easley is the breakfast chef, whipping up homemade muffins or breads and perhaps an egg souffle casserole. The inn has a beer and wine license, and provides hors d'oeuvres and setups for guests in the winter.

Doubles, $80 to $90.

Tucker Hill Lodge is known for fine dining as well as overnight accommodations.

Beaver Pond Farm Inn, Golf Course Road, RD Box 306, Warren 05674. (802) 583-2861.

A farmhouse this may be, but an elegant one it is indeed. Located off a quiet country road overlooking several beaver ponds and the Sugarbush Golf Club fairways, the light green house with green roof has candles lighted in the windows even on a summer afternoon. Inside, golfers Betty and Bob Hansen share their home with guests, who enjoy a stylish living room, a rear deck with a barbecue, a small bar where setups and hors d'oeuvres are provided in the late afternoon, and a lovely formal dining room with a long table on an oriental rug.

Full country breakfasts are served there in the morning, hors d'oeuvres in the afternoon, and prix-fixe dinners are available three nights a week during winter.

Upstairs are five well furnished guest rooms, three with private baths and two sharing.

An advantage here is that guests are close to the clubhouse of the golf course, which in winter has a network of cross-country ski trails. A disadvantage for some is that standard booking periods are for two-day weekends and five-day weeks.

Doubles, $64 to $90.

The Waitsfield Inn, Route 100, Box 969, Waitsfield 05673. (802) 496-3979.

If you detect a California flair injected into this New England setting, that's because the former innkeepers emigrated from their corporate lifestyle in the Santa Cruz Mountains to take over the old Bagatelle Inn in 1983. They worked uncounted hours upgrading the original 1825 farmhouse from a ski lodge offering sleeping-bag space in a barn loft into attractive dining rooms (see below) and eight colorful, comfortable guest rooms. Their crowning achievement was the plush sitting room in the attached barn and woodshed plus six new contemporary-style guest rooms on its upper levels.

All fourteen rooms have private baths. The new barn guest rooms are particularly appealing, two with beamed lofts and skylights, and another very large with an oriental rug, skirted tables and tufted comforter.

Near the dining rooms is a rustic, fireside sitting room, but most overnight guests gravitate to the spacious Grand Room. It's a beauty, sensitively done with rag rugs and orientals on the floors, the original wood on walls and ceilings, no fewer than five sofas plus velvet wing chairs in separate conversation areas, a huge fireplace and a game table. A baby grand piano was added by new innkeepers Bill and Judy Knapp.

Full breakfasts are served daily to guests and the public.

Doubles, $110 to $150, MAP.

Dining Spots

Tucker Hill Lodge, Route 17, Waitsfield. (802) 496-3983.

The dining room is the big attraction at this inn, drawing people from all over the valley. The inner room is paneled and beamed; the outer addition is greenhouse-style, with skylights and brick floors. Quilts and watercolors decorate the walls, tables are white-linened and service is friendly.

New chef Gerry Nooney decides every morning what he will put on the dinner menu. He uses as many local products as he can, including veal and lamb, and the nearby Von Trapp Greenhouse (run by a grandson of Maria) supplies all kinds of lettuce and other vegetables for the inn. The assistant chef also furnishes produce from his organic garden and brings in eggs from his own free-range chickens with which to make the pasta.

There are usually two soups and three or four appetizers to start. In summer, soups include lentil with smoked ham, oyster and mussel chowder, and scallop with cilantro.

We began with "a warm summer night's seafood salad," a colorful plate of smoked Maine brook trout and Maine lobster, garnished with smoked Maine mussels, julienne of celery and baby carrots, local spinach, marigold petals and warm fresh dill-raspberry beurre blanc with local red raspberries — whew! The roast sirloin of western Black Angus beef was, according to the night's menu, "rubbed with shallots, garlic and kosher salt, with a madeira wine veal glace sauce with Italian porcini mushrooms, Vermont chanterelles and fresh savory." It was delicious, as were the medallions of pork loin with apples in a creme fraiche sauce with whole-grain mustard and honey.

Soups are $3.75, appetizers in the $5.75 to $6.50 range, and entrees start around $16.50 for panfried turbot with oysters and roasted red peppers or pheasant ravioli on a bed of braised red cabbage. Other summer tempters priced in the high teens were Vermont quail with a potato and leek nest filled with stewed mushrooms, broiled monkfish layered with smoked salmon and avocado, and wood-grilled rack of Vermont lamb in a cream sauce swirled with cotswold cheese. The vegetables that garnish each dish are wonderful and ever changing.

A summer innovation in 1988 in the downstairs lounge was the introduction of flatbreads cooked in an outdoor stone oven on Tuesday and Wednesday nights. Likened to gourmet pizzas, they included herbs from the garden and chanterelles, were $8.50 to $12.50 and big enough for two. They proved so popular that other innkeepers were stopping in regularly, and the chefs were trying to figure out how to continue in winter.

The wine list is fairly expensive, starting in the high teens.

Desserts ($3.75) change every day. Coffee sambucca cheesecake, frozen frangelico mousse, strawberries sabayon, chocolate-chip hazelnut ice cream and an orange genoise layered with apples, maple syrup and blueberry butter cream (deceptively called Vermont apple pie torte) are possibilities. We were content with passion-fruit sorbet and one of the lodge's special coffees with kahlua, brandy and creme de cacao ($4.50). This is truly special-occasion dining.

Dinner nightly, 6 to 9:30.

Greenery and mirrors grace dining rooms at the Phoenix.

The Phoenix, Sugarbush Village, Warren. (802) 583-2777.

The Phoenix could only be in Sugarbush and its desserts — well, they're nowhere else, either. Chef-owner Peter Sussman says his ratio of dinners to desserts is 106 percent desserts, because people often have more than one and some come only for dessert and coffee in the lounge.

Before dessert, however, comes the setting, the meal and a warning. "You can't have dessert until you eat your veggies," Peter admonished as we ogled the dessert cart he was wheeling by to another table.

The setting is multi-leveled with enormous windows filled with plants, twinkling lights even in summer, deep-blue linened tables bathed in candlelight, bentwood chairs, mirrors and greenery everywhere. An old brick fireplace and hand-hewn beams support an intimate, narrow dining balcony. The two-level lounge has velvet sofas, skylights and beautiful stained glass. The bar was transformed from an old altar rail, there's an enormous espresso machine and even an old barber pole is in a corner. Too chic for words!

The meals, though fine, are for some mere prelude to the desserts. Salads are extra, and appetizers like smoked Maine trout with watercress-horseradish sauce, marinated smoked rabbit or curried shrimp Mandarin ($4.95 to $6.25) might make you too sated for the finale. Anyway, the chewy rolls doled out with tongs helped tide us over and were good enough to call for seconds. (For big-eaters and bargain-seekers, the Phoenix offered a prix-fixe menu of four courses for $18.50 at our latest visit.)

Entrees ($13.95 to $17.95) include baked sole with lobster, broiled Norwegian salmon, medallions of beef, two veal dishes and roast loin of lamb. We had grilled chicken with pan-fried noodles (the noodles too crisp and the spicy sauce too salty and mostly soy) and a good roast confit of duckling with a homemade orange-pear-ginger sauce. The vegetables, a wild rice pilaf and a tasty mix of snap peas and strips of red and green pepper, were superb.

At the appropriate moment and with due fanfare, Peter wheeled up two carts containing six desserts each. They ranged from white chocolate mousse and napoleons to raspberry cheese souffle with raspberry puree and banana kiwi fruit tart filled with custard creme, all of which we sampled because each can order two half-portions — though they turned out to be what most would consider full portions.

Peter makes up to 40 desserts daily from his repertoire of 280 or more. "I eat six or seven of them a day myself," he says. "I have a pretty bad sweet tooth," although you'd never know it from his build. His tastes are eclectic and he only makes what he likes, he said as he showed off his sparkling kitchen and climate-controlled wine cellar the next morning.

He was about to prepare napoleons with amaretto and grand marnier and a mocha-macaroon pie with espresso cream topping among that evening's desserts. We groaned at the thought and toddled out into the noonday sun for a sandwich at a nearby deli.

Dinner, nightly 6 to 10 (closed Wednesday in non-ski season); desserts also available in the bar.

The Common Man, German Flats Road, Warren. (802) 583-2800.

Here is the ultimate incongruity: a soaring, century-old timbered barn with floral carpets on the walls to cut down the noise and keep out wintry drafts. Six crystal chandeliers hang from the beamed ceilings over bare wood tables set simply with red napkins and pewter candlesticks. The French-Swiss-Vermont fare is exceptional, yet a basket of herbed bread is served without benefit of a side plate.

Needless to say, the whole mix works, and thrivingly so since its establishment in 1972 in the site we first knew as Orsini's. Destroyed by fire in 1987, it has been replaced by a barn dismantled in Moretown and rebuilt here by English-born owner Mike Ware, who operates one of the more popular places in the valley with an air of elegance but without pretension.

At our visit, Vivaldi's "Four Seasons" played rather prominently in the background, the better to mask lively conversations and produce what Mike calls a soft baroque atmosphere. Winter's warming blaze in the massive fieldstone fireplace is replaced in summer by masses of fresh flowers.

Almost as you're seated, waitresses in long red printed skirts and white blouses serve smallish drinks with the aforementioned bread. The extensive wine list comes in two picture frames, hinged together to open like a book, and contains good values. "The saddest part of the fire was losing some of our finest wines," Mike recalls.

The escargots maison "served with our famous (and secret) garlic butter sauce" is the most popular of appetizers ($4.75 to $5.50), which include shrimp with feta cheese and duck salad with leeks and champagne mayonnaise. Main courses start at $10.25 for chicken supreme with tarragon and top off at $17.75 for rack of lamb provencale. With dishes like two quails in black currant sauce, sauteed Vermont veal with local mushrooms and salmon poached in champagne all under $15, this is uncommon fare — not to mention value — for common folk.

Entrees arrive after house salads of romaine, carrot slices and croutons with a zippy dressing hinting of garlic and curry. The fresh Vermont rabbit sauteed in olive oil, garlic and rosemary was distinctive, and the Vermont sweetbreads Normande with apples and apple brandy were some of the best we've tasted.

Desserts include kirschen strudel, mocha chocolate cake and meringue glace. The kirsch parfait sounded better than it turned out, the kirsch being difficult to detect. Six different ports, offered by the glass or bottle after dessert, make a mellow finale for an uncommon meal.

Dinner, weekdays 6:30 to 10, weekends 6 to 10:30; closed Mondays in off-season.

Sam Rupert's, Sugarbush Access Road, Warren. (802) 583-2421.

Skiers heading for Sugarbush once stopped at the Sugarbush Sugarhouse for pancakes and homemade syrup. Today, they stop at a vastly expanded dining establishment with a smashing greenhouse room for chef Lyndon Virkler's specialties, supplemented by a blackboard menu.

White linen with pink napkins sets the color scheme for the large dining room with the greenhouse full of massed flowers at one end, flowered lamps on tables spaced well apart, a wood stove and hanging plants all around. The windows in the greenhouse addition bring the outside in, and in summer the fabulous gardens and trees are illuminated at night.

Greenhouse dining at Sam Rupert's.

An unusual touch: the wine list is presented in a heavy album with color photos of the bottles against various backgrounds. One shows red roses in the snow amid branches covered with ice. The prices are reasonable and the choice extensive.

The dinner menu ($10.75 to $19.75) is a mixed repertoire of fresh seafood (grilled turbot bearnaise and monkfish with shrimps the night we visited), stuffed chicken Caribbean with spicy black beans, rack of lamb chambord, a Basque duckling dish and Vermont veal with chanterelles. On our summer visit, we liked the seafood on linguini and a fine roast pork tenderloin garnished with apples and flavored with apple brandy.

The terrine of smoked salmon and Chinese pancakes with shrimp, celery and ginger are popular starters. Finish with the house specialty, a frozen white and dark chocolate mousse pie, frozen peanut pie with hot chocolate sauce or peach melba deluxe with kiwi fruit and strawberries ($2.50 to $3.95). If you're as full as we were, settle for a cantaloupe sorbet.

Dinner nightly, 6 to 9:30; closed Tuesday and Wednesday in fall.

Chez Henri, Sugarbush Village, Warren. (802) 583-2600.

The longest-running of the valley's long runners, Chez Henri is in its third decade as a French bistro with an after-dinner disco in the rear. It's tiny, intimate and very French, as you might expect from a former food executive for Air France.

Henri Borel offers lunch, brunch, apres-ski, early dinner, dinner and dancing, inside in winter by a warming stone fireplace and a marble bar and outside in summer on a small terrace bordered by a babbling mountain brook.

The dinner menu, served from 6, starts with changing soups and pates "as made in a French country kitchen," a classic French onion soup or fish broth, and perhaps mussels mariniere, smoked trout with capers or steak tartare "knived to order" ($2.95 to $7.75).

Entrees range from $9.75 to $16.95. Served with good French bread and seasonal vegetables, they often include sauteed quails with vinegar and shallots, frog's legs provencale, tripe in casserole, rabbit with thyme and mushrooms, veal chop calvados and tournedos bearnaise.

Creme caramel, coupe marrons and chocolate mousse are among the dessert standbys. The wines are all French, and a carafe of the house Boulanger is $10.50.

Open from noon to 2 a.m. in winter; weekends in summer, hours vary.

Millbrook Lodge, Route 17, Waitsfield. (802) 496-2405. "Apple brown betty is the dumbest dessert we make, but we have to make it every night," says Thom Gorman, innkeeper with his wife Joan and chef at this small inn on the road to Mad River Glen. Such is the demand of regular patrons and houseguests in the popular dining room. Indeed, we were told everywhere we went that Millbrook was one of the better places to dine in the Valley.

MAP guests at the inn eat here, of course, in one of the two small dining rooms (one with a fireplace) at tables covered with paisley cloths. But the restaurant can seat 40, and people come in from all over. Annadama bread, a specialty, is made in house, as are pastas and desserts, from scratch. Start with mushrooms a la Millbrook, filled with a secret blend of ground veal and herbs. Entrees ($7.95 to $14.50) include a daily roast, veal roma (with Vermont veal), shrimp scampi, garden vegetarian lasagna, cheese cannelloni made with Vermont cheddar and fresh basil, and fettuccine Thom. There are also four dishes from the Bombay region, where Thom lived for two years. The badami rogan josh, local lamb simmered in all kinds of spices and yogurt and served with homemade tomato chutney, sounds wonderful.

The Gormans have a wine and beer license. As for those desserts, ice creams like chocolate chocolate chip and brickle candy are made here, as is a coffee-crunch pie filled with coffee mousse in a nut crust. In summer, open berry pies (maybe a raspberry and blackberry combination) are gobbled up.

Upstairs are seven bedrooms, four with private bath, decorated with stenciling and interesting quilts and comforters. A full breakfast, huge for skiers in winter, says Thom, is served. Doubles are $96 to $120, MAP.

Dinner nightly, 6 to 9; closed Wednesday in summer and month of May.

The Waitsfield Inn, Route 100, Waitsfield. (802) 496-3979.

A wide fieldstone path brightened by pink geraniums leads to the main entrance at the side of the Waitsfield Inn, where a stuffed bear greets patrons at the bar. The sprightly country look of the inn's five small dining rooms is embellished by Laura Ashley wallpapers, frilly curtains and woven mats atop patterned tablecloths. The main dining room opens onto a small outdoor patio, where breakfast and brunch are served at tables under bright yellow umbrellas.

Dinner entrees start at $12.95 for chicken with leeks, sweet onion and pinenut compote and go to $18.95 for tournedos of beef with artichoke bottoms. Fresh salmon with sun-dried tomatoes and cilantro butter in parchment and loin of lamb with wild forest mushrooms were specials the night we visited.

Among desserts are strawberries Romanoff, raspberry tarts and chocolate truffle cake.

Breakfast or brunch in the sunny dining room or outdoors on the patio is popular with the public as well as inn guests. Eggs Benedict and french toast are among the offerings.

Dinner nightly except Tuesday, 6 to 9; breakfast, 8 to 11; Sunday brunch to 2.

R.S.V.P., Bridge Street, Waitsfield. (802) 496-7787.

Located near the covered bridge, this intimate storefront restaurant has had a checkered career as the Bridge Street Cafe, Moonlight Cafe and now this establishment, whose initials stand for Richard's Special Vermont Pizza.

Using many local products, the pizza dough is made with unbleached white and stone-ground whole wheat flours, and toppings include double Vermont cheese, local sausage, fresh pesto, Moroccan anchovies and marinated peppers. A large pizza is $11; slices with one topping, $1.85. Wine and beer are served, as are Perrier and New York egg cream made with Vermont seltzer.

Patio dining is an attracion at the Waitsfield Inn.

For breakfast, try an egg-carton omelet with cob-smoked bacon or a breakfast burrito, two scrambled eggs in a warm flour tortilla ($1.75, with add-ons 50 cents each).

Open 7:30 to 10:30 a.m., and 11:30 to 9 or 11 p.m.; closed Wednesday.

Beggar's Banquet, Fiddler's Green, Route 100, Waitsfield. (802) 496-4485.

A canopied redwood deck with a view of the sheep at the Black Sheep Farm next door is a summer attraction at this casual spot billed as "the valley's finest dining alternative." Inside, all is rustic with booths, hanging plants, hanging lamps and a wide expanse of windows along the south wall.

The menu contains something for everyone: light fare from egg rolls and escargots to potato skins, zucchini sticks and baked brie, salads, burgers, sandwiches, pastas and entrees from $6.95 for lasagna to $10.95 for New York strip steak or saute of shrimp, chicken and snow peas. Honey-lemon pork chops, pecan chicken and Mexican items also are available, and Sunday is Mexican night.

Open daily, 11:30 a.m. to 11 p.m., Sunday 6 to 10.

The Odyssey, Sugarbush Village, Warren. (802) 583-2001.

Located underneath and run by the Phoenix, the Odyssey claims to be the least expensive place to eat in the valley. Italian dinners with fresh pasta run from $3.75 to $5.75 (for lasagna), but pizzas are the popular item here. Combination pizzas are $7.25 to $11 and vegetarian, $7 to $10.25. Spumoni and ice cream sundaes are the dessert fare. Beer, wine and liquor are served.

The decor is funky: blue or red checked tablecloths, blue bentwood chairs, bare floors, mirrors with infinity lights over the bar and a 20-foot metal sculpture welded to the wall.

Open daily, 5 to 11.

The Deli-Bakery at the Warren Store, Warren. (802) 496-3864.

At the rear of the old Warren Store is a delightful place for breakfast or lunch. You can get an egg McWarren for $1.50 and breakfast burritos (eggs in a flour tortilla) for

$1.50 to $2. A veggie pita pocket, salad nicoise, chef's salad and fruit salad plate are in the $3 to $5 range. Finish with a raspberry-almond square or a Haagen-Dazs milkshake. Take it all outside to tables on a deck under a green striped canopy beside the roaring falls of the Mad River, where our tomato-dill soup ($1.50) and a pesto-provolone sandwich ($3.25) tasted extra good on a summer day. The store also has a fine selection of rare wines. Open seven days a week.

Diversions

Downhill skiing reigns supreme and gives the valley its character.

Mad River Glen. Billed as a serious place for serious skiers, Mad River has been challenging hardy types since 1947. There are no frills here: little snowmaking, a few lifts including the original single chairlift (with blanket wraps provided to ward off the chill) to the summit, hair-raising trails like Paradise and the Fall Line, plenty of moguls and not much grooming, and a "Practice Slope" so steep it scares the daylights out of beginners. The Birdland area is fine for intermediates. There's a Mad River mystique (bluejeans and milk runs) that you sense immediately and attracts you back. Adult lift tickets: $22 on weekends, $20 weekdays.

Sugarbush. Founded in 1959 and among the first of Vermont's destination ski resorts, Sugarbush with its own "village" at its base appealed immediately to the jet set. From its original gondola lift to its expert Castle Rock area, from its clusters of condos and boutiques to its indoor Sports Center, Sugarbush appeals to those who appreciate their creature comforts — and good skiing as well (we think the Glades offer the best glade skiing in the East). Since Sugarbush acquired neighboring Glen Ellen (which has the valley's greatest vertical drop, 2,600 feet) and rechristened it first Sugarbush North and then Mount Ellen, it boasts a new diversity of skiing and mood. The two areas are not yet linked by trails, but a bus shuttles skiers back and forth. Adult lift tickets are $33.

Other sports. This is a four-season sports area with a difference. Yes, there is golf, at the Robert Trent Jones-designed **Sugarbush Golf Club** par-72 course with water hazards (pond or brook) affecting eight consecutive holes. Yes, the **Sugarbush Sports Center** has three indoor and ten outdoor tennis courts, racquetball and squash courts, indoor and outdoor pools, whirlpools and exercise facility.

But there's much more: this is something of an equestrian center with a number of stables offering trail rides. The **Sugarbush Polo Club,** started in 1962 by skiers using ski poles and a volleyball, now has three polo fields for games and tournaments, staged Saturday and Sunday afternoons June through September. Also for horse fanciers are the annual Valley Classic and Sugarbush horse shows in late July and early August.

Soaring via gliders and sailplanes is at its best from the Warren-Sugarbush Airport, where instruction and rentals are available. Biplane rides for one or two persons also go from the airport, which hosts an annual airshow early in late June.

For hiking and backpacking, the Long Trail is just overhead; innumerable mountain peaks and guided tours beckon. The Mad River and Blueberry Lake are ready for swimming, canoeing and fishing. The Mad River rugby team plays throughout the summer and fall at the Waitsfield Recreation Field. Finally, a round-robin English croquet tournament is staged in mid-summer.

Other pastimes. The list includes annual art shows, a crafts fair, house and garden tours, weekly bingo games, summer theater by the Valley Players, even poetry reading in a barn.

Scenic drives. The Lincoln Gap Road, the McCullogh Turnpike (Route 17) beyond Mad River Glen and the steep Roxbury Gap Road each have their rewards. For the most open vistas and overall feeling for the area, traverse Brook Road and Waitsfield Common Road out of Warren, past the landmark Joslin Round Barn and Blueberry Lake, Sugarloaf Airport and come the back way into Waitsfield.

Shopping. Waitsfield has three shopping complexes, each worthy of exploration: the Mad River Green and the Village Square along Route 100 and the new Bridge Street Marketplace beside Vermont's second oldest covered bridge. Among our favorites: the well-known **Green Mountain Coffee Roasters,** founded in Waitsfield with a retail store in Mad River Green, roasts 30 varieties of coffees and decafs, including founder Jamie Balne's special blend, and offers teas, coffee grinders and accessories, plus a cafe and espresso bar that's good for breakfast and lunch. At **The Store** in the 1834 Red Meeting House along Route 100 you'll find antiques, Vermont foods, books, Christmas things, and a lovely collection of handmade quilts and pillows. In Village Square, the **Blue Toad** gift shop specializes in particularly nice, inexpensive baskets from twenty countries and good greeting cards, as well as English tin boxes and jelly beans. **Tulip Tree Crafts** shows Vermont crafts and art, including lots of cows and many of the prints by Sabra Field, our favorite Vermont artist. South of town next to Fiddler's Green at the Black Sheep Farm is **Three Bags Full** with "ewe-nique" things, featuring wool, handmade sweaters, blankets, sheepskins and, of course, lots of grazing black sheep for the watching.

All Things Bright and Beautiful on Bridge Street, Waitsfield, is the ultimate collection of stuffed animals, mainly bears, outfitted in everything from a London bobby's uniform or a wedding dress to ski vests that proclaim "Save the Bear." The Victorian house has fifteen rooms and porches presided over by two sisters and Malcolm the cat perched atop the cash register. It's a bit overwhelming, but not to be missed. Just across the street is **Northeast Southwest,** a gift shop that has lovely things for babies, as well as a huge selection of wonderful candy. Here you can find gelato del conte, made in Burlington, in flavors like green apple, apricot and cappuccino.

In tiny Warren, the premier attraction is the **Warren Store,** an old-fashioned general store with provisions, fine wines and deli (see Dining Spots), plus upstairs, the **More Store,** with kitchenware, jewelry, apparel and cards. Lots of the things here are from India. Across the street, blue and white stoneware made on the premises is displayed on the lawn in front of the Warren Village Pottery.

The Von Trapp Greenhouse, run by a grandson of Maria off a dirt road east of Waitsfield Common, is worth a visit (limited hours). Beautiful flower and vegetable gardens surround the family's Alpine house. There's a retail shop in front of one of the two greenhouses, which furnish lavish floral displays and produce for the valley's inns and restaurants.

Extra-Special

Edison's Studio Movie Palace, Route 100, Waitsfield. (802) 496-2336.

This art deco cinema calls itself the most unique movie theater in the world. Two theaters seat 300 people, with half of the seating in "love seats" in the loges. Here there is bar and food service throughout the movie, which could be a first run, oldie or art film. You might sip a champagne cocktail or a courvoisier alexander, or munch on a slice of pizza or Ben & Jerry's ice cream. How about a frozen cocktail called Cecil B. DeMint? You may stop before or after the show in the small Magic Lantern Cafe for a snack or a drink as well. Shows nightly.

Wintertime scene along the green in Woodstock.

Woodstock-Quechee, Vt.
A Chic Blend of Old and New

Picture the perfect Vermont place and you're likely to picture Woodstock, the historic shire town portrayed by the media as the picture-perfect New England village.

Picture an old river town with handsome 19th-century houses, red brick mill, waterfall and covered bridge and you have Quechee, the emerging hamlet being restored to reflect Vermont as it used to be.

Join them with Rockefellers, Billingses, Pearces and other old names and new entrepreneurs, and you have an unusual combination for a chic, changing dynamic.

Carefully preserved and protected, Woodstock has such an impressive concentration of architecture from the late 17th and 18th centuries that National Geographic magazine termed it one of the most beautiful villages in America. That it is, thanks to its role as a prosperous county seat following its settlement in 1765 and to early popularity as both a summer and winter resort (Vermont's first golf course was established south of town around the turn of the century and the nation's first ski tow was installed on a cow pasture north of town in 1934).

That also was the year when Laurance S. Rockefeller married localite Mary Billings French, granddaughter of railroad magnate Frederick Billings. The Rockefeller interests now are Woodstock's largest landowner and employer. They buried the utility poles underground, provided a home and much of the stimulus for the Woodstock Historical Society, bought and rebuilt the Woodstock Inn, acquired and redesigned the golf course, bought and upgraded the Suicide Six ski area, opened the Billings Farm Museum, and built an indoor sports center in 1986.

Entrepreneur Simon Pearce, the Irish glass blower, is providing some of the same impetus for neighboring Quechee. He purchased an abandoned mill as a site for his glass-blowing enterprise, powered it with a 50-year-old turbine using water from the river outside, added more craftsmen and a restaurant, and sparked a crafts and business revival that is enlivening a sleepy hamlet heretofore known mainly for its scenic gorge.

In this inspirational setting of old and new, entrepreneurs are supported, and arts and crafts are appreciated.

Inn Spots

The Quechee Inn at Marshland Farm, Clubhouse Road, Quechee 05059. (802) 295-3133.

This venerable establishment — a beautifully restored 1793 farmstead built by Vermont's first lieutenant governor — is every Hollywood set designer's idea of what a New England country inn should look like: a pure white rambling Vermont farmhouse, red barns out back against a backdrop of green mountains, and across the quiet road the Ottauquechee River heading into Quechee Gorge.

The interior lives up to the expectation as well: a welcoming beamed and barnwood living room, lately expanded and so carefully integrated with the older section that many don't notice the change. The rustic, stenciled dining room (see below), in which some locally acclaimed fare is served. The new study, dressed in elegant draperies and valances, for reading or meetings. And 24 comfortable guest rooms, all with private baths, Queen Anne-style furnishings, brass and four-poster beds, wing chairs, braided and Chinese rugs on wide-plank floors and, a surprise for the purists, cable TV.

With fourteen rooms in the original farmhouse and ten more on the second floor of a new wing that houses the expanded common rooms and dining room, the inn is large enough to be a focal point for activity — a Christmas Eve open house for inn guests and townspeople, cocktails before a crackling fire in the lounge, summer get-togethers on the canopied patio, a cross-country learning center in the smallest barn (preparing skiers for touring through Quechee Gorge, in the upper meadow behind the inn or in what one describes as "a lovely tunnel through the pines"). The Vermont Fly Fishing School is based here, and guests have golf, tennis, swimming and skiing privileges at the private Quechee Club.

A full breakfast buffet — from fruits and yogurts to scrambled eggs and sausages — is served in the main dining room. Coffee, tea and fruit breads are offered in the afternoon.

Doubles, $128 to $158, MAP; suites, $168 to $188.

The Jackson House at Woodstock, Route 4 West, Woodstock 05091. (802) 457-2065.

If ever every room in a small country inn were worthy of coverage in an antiques or decorator magazine it would be these. All ten guest rooms are different and eclectically furnished with such things as antique brass lamps on either side of the bathroom mirror, a marble-topped bedside table, an 1860 sleigh bed, a prized Casablanca ceiling fan, Chinese carved rugs, old steam radiators painted gold, handmade afghans coordinated to each room's colors, bamboo and cane furniture, a blanket box made of tiger maple and so much more.

Suffice to say that the rooms vary from French Empire to British Oriental to old New England and bear such names as Gloria Swanson, who once stayed here when it was a guest house, and Mary Todd Lincoln, with furniture of the period. The floors in each

Two front porches beckon guests at the Jackson House at Woodstock.

room are of different woods because the house was built in 1890 by a sawmill owner. A lovely celadon collection is housed in a lighted stand at the top of the staircase with a highly polished banister of cherry wood. When we last chatted with innkeepers Jack Foster and Bruce McIlveen, they were excited about their latest acquisition, a 300-year-old grandfather clock made by Henry Merriman.

Each bathroom has a glassed-in shower, but that's about the only modern touch beyond the idea of luxury espoused by the innkeepers: elegant guest rooms, a parlor in which champagne and wine are poured and an elaborate buffet of hors d'oeuvres is set out at 6 p.m. (to the accompaniment on most Saturdays of a harpist or classical guitarist), an adjacent library where you can shut the door, turn on the 1937 Zenith radio and curl up with a classic, and a formal dining room in which elaborate breakfasts are served.

Bruce and Jack give you fuzzy brown slippers so your shoes won't mar the floors and take you to a bedroom that would do justice to a museum. When you return from dinner, you'll find a couple of those great Champlain Chocolate Company truffles on your pillows and perhaps two tiny bottles of liqueurs.

At breakfast, you gather around an 18th-century mahogany table from England for quite a feast. The first course is a plate of honeydew, cantaloupe and kiwi, bananas in cream or, in winter, baked apple with mincemeat in rum and wine. Juices, croissants and muffins are followed by such extravagances as mushroom and sausage omelet, poached egg harlequin with sherried chicken in a pastry shell, cheese blintzes, french toast Sante Fe with whipped cream, or a Creole dish of fried eggplant with poached egg in a hot sauce.

Doubles, $115 to $150. No smoking.

Woodstock Inn and Resort, 14 The Green, Woodstock 05091. (802) 457-1100 or (800) 448-7900.

The biggest institution in town, the Woodstock Inn sits majestically back from the green, its front facing a covered bridge and mountains, its back looking across the pool and putting green and down the valley toward its golf course and ski touring center. The resort's other leisure facilities include the Suicide Six ski area, ten tennis courts and two lighted paddle tennis courts, a new indoor racquet and sports center, and such attractions as sleigh rides, dogsledding, horseback riding and touring in the inn's Stanley Steamer.

The interior of the inn is impressive as well. Built by Rockresorts in 1969 after Laurance Rockefeller found the original Woodstock Inn beyond salvation, it contains a lobby warmed by a ten-foot-high stone fireplace around which people always seem to be gathered, a large dining room, coffee shop, Pine Room lounge and gift shop. All were being vastly expanded in 1989 as part of an $8 million improvement program that added a south wing with a new entrance and a veranda.

The inn has three stories in front and four in the rear, the lowest downstairs from the lobby. The 120 guest rooms are among the more luxurious in which we've stayed, with handmade quilts on the beds, upholstered chairs, three-way reading lights, television, telephones, and large bathrooms and closets. Walls are hung with paintings and photographs of local scenes.

The long main dining room, now doubled in size, has large windows onto a spacious outdoor terrace overlooking the pool and gardens. It offers a luncheon buffet Monday through Saturday and dinner nightly.

The Sunday brunch is popular, as is the Saturday night buffet, for which people start lining up before 6 o'clock for first crack at the 50-foot table laden with 200 items from stir-fried beef to halibut with a seafood sauce.

Otherwise, dinner entrees run from $16.50 for broiled chicken with Vermont apple wine sauce to $22 for broiled lamb chops with artichoke cream sauce. Sauteed duck breast is accompanied by pinenut spaetzle and morel sauce, and the roast rib eye of veal is done with spinach, prosciutto and a sun-dried tomato sauce. Daily specials might be sauteed veal with Vermont cheddar cheese and fresh morels gathered from the nearby woods or roast loin of pork glazed in maple syrup with apple-prune stuffing. Billings Farm ice creams and sherbets are among the desserts. Jackets are required for dinner.

The Woodstock Inn and Resort is a focal point for community activity.

Regional Alpine dishes, such as raclette and apple fritters Matterhorn, are served in the Coffee Shop, which is more attractive than most.

Doubles, $99 to $170, EP.

The Charleston House, 21 Pleasant St., Woodstock 05091. (802) 457-3843.

When we first saw the Charleston House, it was festooned for Christmas, inside and out, and looked like a spread for House Beautiful.

But the red brick 1835 Greek revival house is gorgeous at any time of year. Named for the hometown of Betsy Bradley, the former innkeeper, it remains the epitome of Southern charm and hospitality under new owners Barbara and Bill Hough from Maryland.

The house, listed on the National Register of Historic Places, is furnished with period antiques, eclectic art and oriental rugs. The Houghs aim not for a museum piece but rather for "the warmth and hospitality of a family homecoming." All seven comfortable bedrooms have private baths and most have queensize four-poster beds. The rear Gables room, which contains Barbara's childhood furniture, is the most popular, although honeymooners favor the Summer Kitchen room, downstairs in back with its own entrance.

Stunning floral arrangements and needlepoint pillows grace the dining room and comfortable living room, where a fire is usually going in the fireplace.

Breakfast is such a feast that Barbara has compiled her recipes in a small cookbook, "Breakfast at the Charleston House." Gingered or maple-sugar biscuits, shredded wheat

bread, chipped beef eggs, California omelet, egg and artichoke casserole, whole wheat almond pancakes, and macadamia nut waffles with papaya and strawberries are some of the inn favorites.

Coffee and tea with cookies or crackers and cheese are served in the afternoon.

Sander, the Houghs' golden retriever, wears a different bandana every day and sometimes meets guests with an inn brochure in his mouth.

The Charleston House.

Doubles, $92 to $115.

Quechee Bed & Breakfast, 753 Woodstock Road (Route 4), Quechee 05059. (802) 295-1776.

The waters of the Ottauquechee River can be seen from the back yard and rear upstairs guest rooms of this large 1795 house perched on a cliff not far from Quechee Gorge. It was converted into a luxury B&B in 1985 by Susan and Ken Kaduboski, transplanted Boston accountants, who have restored eight spacious, air-conditioned bedrooms with private baths.

Guests enter a large living-dining area with comfortable sofas gathered around a huge fireplace, a television set and breakfast tables topped with dusty rose cloths and paperwhites in pots. A large cactus stands in one corner, and an interesting art collection is on display.

A smaller parlor leads through heavy doors into the original house and the guest quarters, nicely secluded and private with a separate entry hall and staircase. Three rooms are on the first floor and five on the second, including two with beamed, half-cathedral ceilings. Each is suavely furnished with king or queensize beds (four of

Quechee Bed & Breakfast is cloaked in winter's snow.

them rice-carved four-posters) or, in one case, twin mahogany sleigh beds, antique dressers, two wing chairs, sprightly wallpapers and decorative touches like swags and stenciled lamp shades, and large bathrooms with colorful towels. Sheets and pillow cases are white and lavishly trimmed with lace. One new bathroom is all in pink and pretty as can be.

The Kaduboskis serve a full breakfast of juices, baked apple or broiled grapefruit, homemade Swedish breads with different jams, and such main dishes as herbed scrambled eggs, apple pancakes or french toast stuffed with cream cheese and walnuts.

Doubles, $80 to $115.

Parker House, 16 Main St., Quechee 05059. (802) 295-6077.

This elegant red brick and white frame Victorian mansion with steep black mansard roof crowned by an ornamental wrought-iron railing is a registered National Historic Site. A Vermont state senator and mill owner, Joseph C. Parker, built the mansion in 1857 next to his mill on the Ottauquechee River. It was acquired in 1986 by Roger Nicholas of the Home Hill Country Inn & French Restaurant in nearby Plainfield, N.H., who brought in chef Barry Snyder and his wife Claire as innkeepers.

Long known for fine dining (see Dining Spots), the inn has four large, high-ceilinged guest rooms with private baths upstairs. Emily's room in front, named for the original Mrs. Parker, has twin white enamel and brass poster bedsteads joined by a kingsize mattress, oriental rug, a small sofa, dressing room with desk and an enormous modern bathroom. Even larger is another room running the width of the back of the house with a fine view of the river. Joseph's Room, actually a sitting room plus a bedroom, has a double bed in an alcove with towering windows on three sides (no doubt so the owner could keep his eye on the mill outside; today, the view toward the falls and covered bridge is reason enough).

A continental breakfast with fresh pastries is served in one of the dining rooms.

Doubles, $95 to $120. Closed two weeks in November and April.

The Abel Barron House, 37 Main St., Box 532, Quechee 05059. (802) 295-1337.

Mark Olivere, who was in sales at the Quechee Inn at Marshland Farm, bought this house that was an established gift shop in 1988 and quickly opened four guest rooms with private baths as a B&B. The rooms are spacious in the Victorian manner and notable for spectacular Pamela Hill quilts and Indian hand-knotted wool rugs. When we visited, the rooms had been open only a short time and lacked finishing touches, including places to sit. Downstairs is a small common room with a television set.

The focus of the place, besides the shop-gallery with interesting art and handicrafts, is a greenhouse full of orchids. That's where Mark serves a breakfast of apple turnovers, omelets or french toast.

Doubles, 95.

Three Church Street, 3 Church St., Woodstock 05091. (802) 457-1925.

Classical music is heard throughout the several common rooms of this 1830s brick and white-pillared Georgian mansion listed on the National Register of Historic Places. Fires are ablaze in a small front sitting room with a sofa and parquet floors, way out back in a more casual room with a modern black wood stove, and sometimes in others of the nine fireplaces, some made of marble with hand-carved mantels.

Most of the downstairs — including a large formal parlor and music room with plush sofas and oriental rugs, a spacious dining room and rear gallery overlooking the lawn leading to the Ottauquechee River — is available for guests. So are the tennis court and swimming pool with changing room and cabana out back.

The Spanish-style foyer has a spindled staircase leading upstairs, where six of the eleven guest rooms have private baths and beds are about equally split between doubles and twins. Rooms are spacious, nicely decorated and enhanced by striking art works.

Eleanor Paine, who raised eight children in her home, sold her inn as this edition was going to press to an unidentified buyer who she said planned to continue it as a B&B.

Doubles, $62 to $90; one three-room suite, $250.

The Applebutter Inn, Happy Valley Road, Box 24, Woodstock 05091. (802) 457-4158.

On a hillside behind the Taftsville Country Store in rural Taftsville is this B&B in a restored Federal house, opened in 1987 by Beverlee Cook, manager of Woodstock's Cuddledown store. That association explains all the gorgeous down comforters and fine linens in the four guest rooms, which share two baths.

The rooms, properly Vermonty and historic, are named for apples. One has a half-canopy bed, old pine floors and its own porch. The Granny Smith room is enormous, with a barnwood wall, skylights and three beds.

The living room is large and appealing, there's a fireplaced TV room with a VCR, and a harvest table is a feature in the dining room. Beverlee serves a continental breakfast of all natural foods, including her own granola. She's been known to do omelets or puff pancakes upon request.

Doubles, $55 to $70

Dining Spots

Simon Pearce Restaurant, The Mill, Quechee. (802) 295-1470.

The restaurant that opened in 1985 has as much integrity as the rest of Irish glass blower Simon Pearce's mill complex. The chefs all train at Ballymaloe in Ireland, and they import flour from Ireland to make Irish soda and Ballymaloe brown bread.

You sit on sturdy ash chairs at bare wood tables (dressed with white linens at night).

The brown and white tableware and heavy glassware are all made by Simon Pearce and his family. Irish or classical music plays in the background. Through large windows you have a view of the river, hills rising beyond. A new dining addition looks out onto the falls and, in summer, a canopied outdoor deck is almost over the falls. The setting is spare, but plants and antique quilts soften the brick walls and bare floors.

Several wines are available by the glass. At lunches we've tried both the house white and red ($3.50 a glass) as well as spicy bloody marys with a real kick, while nibbling the sensational bread (seconds were offered and accepted).

The menu changes frequently but there are always specialties like beef and Guinness stew (which is delicious — for $8.50 a generous serving of fork-tender beef and vegetables, plus a small side salad of julienned vegetables). Soups at our latest visit were hearty split pea with ham and creamy broccoli with cheese ($3). Entrees ($6 to $10.50) included curried lamb and rice, brie with fresh fruit, spinach and cheddar cheese

in puff pastry, and shepherd's pie. The pasta salad ($7.25), a huge heap of spirals, featured many vegetables and a splendid dressing of oil, vinegar, basil and parmesan cheese. Hickory-smoked coho salmon with potato salad and a skewer of grilled chicken with a spicy peanut sauce and a green salad with vinaigrette also were extra-good.

The walnut meringue cake with strawberry sauce, a menu fixture, is crisp and crunchy and melts in the mouth. Cappuccino cheesecake also is super, as are bittersweet chocolate tart with an espresso sauce, chocolate almond torte and homemade sorbets. Chocolate rum cake, Irish apple cake and pecan pie are other possibilities, but when we go back, which we seem to do often, nothing but the walnut meringue will do.

At night, a candlelight dinner might start with some of the luncheon entrees as ap-

Table for two at Simon Pearce Restaurant.

petizers ($4.25 to $6.50), like that grilled chicken with spicy peanut sauce, country pate with onion jam, scallops with beurre blanc or fettuccine tossed with roasted red pepper, scallions, cream and cheese. Entrees ($11.50 to $19.50) could be chicken sauteed with spinach and cheddar cheese, poached salmon with saffron sauce, roast duck with mango chutney sauce, veal with a two-mustard sauce, medallions of beef with port and bearnaise sauces, and roast rack of lamb with a spinach duxelle, rosemary, pinenuts and madeira sauce. Desserts are more of the delectable luncheon choices ($4), and the coffee tastes like espresso.

The wine list ranges widely, with plenty of good vintages, priced from $12 to $110. Naturally, you can get beers and ales from the British Isles.

Here's a restaurant that's so unpretentious but so appealing that we're not surprised that several of the friends we've directed there for lunch liked it so much they have returned the next day.

Lunch daily, 11.30 to 2:30; dinner nightly, 6 to 9.

Parker House, 16 Main St., Quechee. (802) 295-6077.
Texas-trained chef Barry Snyder talks a good game ("with all due modesty," says he,

"this is the best restaurant in Vermont"). He backs it up with some innovative menus and outstanding cooking that put his claim within the realm of plausibility.

The atmosphere is elegant in the three small dining rooms of this Victorian inn. Graceful chairs are at well-spaced tables topped by white over burgundy linens and fresh flowers. Hand-screened French wallpaper lends a touch of owner Roger Nicholas's native Brittany to the rear Fleur de Lis Room, which opens onto a balcony overlooking the Ottauquechee River (used for dining in summer).

The chef's Texas background is evident in his cooking, which Roger (himself no slouch in the kitchen) says is more adventurous and more nouvelle than his. The meal is prix-fixe for $30, and the menu is in French with English translations.

Begin perhaps with a choice of crepe stuffed with seafood mousse, a warm salad with homemade sausage and mushrooms, or a seasonal soup. Priming the palate for the main course is a sorbet, perhaps lemon tarragon or prickly pear from Texas.

The entree could be rack of lamb roasted with rosemary, baby pheasant braised with marsala and cabbage, tenderloin of beef with stilton and bordelaise sauce, roast veal stuffed with a duxelle of mushrooms or a selection of fish "fresh from the Boston market." A salad of hydroponic greens, endive and vinaigrette follows.

Favorite desserts are a Queen of Sheba torte with passion fruit sauce and white chocolate mousse in a box of Belgian bitter chocolate over raspberry coulis.

The wine list contains a page each of red bordeaux and burgundies and is priced from $15 up.

Dinner nightly except Wednesday from 6; Sunday brunch.

The Prince and the Pauper, 34 Elm St., Woodstock. (802) 457-1818.
A new cocktail lounge with a wine bar and the shiniest wood bar you ever saw has freed up space for more tables in what many consider to be Woodstock's best restaurant.

Tables in the expanded yet intimate L-shaped dining room (some surrounded by dark wood booths) are covered with brown linens, oil lamps and flowers in small carafes. The lamps cast flickering shadows on dark beamed ceilings, and old prints adorn the white walls, one of which has a shelf of old books.

Chef-owner Chris J. Balcer refers to his cuisine as "creative continental." His soup of the day could be billi-bi, the pasta perhaps fettuccine primavera with pinenuts, and his pate a mixture of duck, pork and chicken livers flavored with grand marnier and served with cumberland sauce.

Meals are prix-fixe for $25, not including dessert. There's a choice of six entrees, perhaps the signature dish of boneless rack of lamb in puff pastry, veal forestiere, roast duckling with green peppercorns, fresh grilled wahoo, baked swordfish with leeks and fresh basil-tomato coulis, and tournedos Rossini.

Homemade bread, house salad and seasonal vegetables accompany. The interesting wine list is heavy on Californias.

Desserts include strawberry sabayon with triple sec, pears Helene, profiteroles or fresh fruit, topped off with espresso, cappuccino or an international coffee.

Dinner nightly, 6 to 9 or 9:30.

Quechee Inn at Marshland Farm, Clubhouse Road, Quechee. (802) 295-3133.
Most people enjoy a drink by the fire in the expanded living room-lounge before adjourning for dinner in the antiques-filled dining room. Beamed ceilings, wide-plank floors and lovely stenciled borders on the walls provide the setting for some inspired cuisine.

The pink and blue stenciling is repeated on the covers of the menu, wine list and the

Quechee Inn Dessert Cookbook, a wonderful collection of the recipes of the inn's baker and dessert chef, Erma J. Hastings, including her renowned French silk pie (the recipe for which also appeared in Gourmet magazine).

Chef Kevin Lane's dinner menu changes seasonally. The summer offerings start with petite California snails in puff pastry, fresh fruit compote, grilled shrimp and bacon with pernod, scallops ceviche and a house pate.

The eight entrees run from $14.25 for "trailfire trout" tossed in cornmeal to $18.50 for black angus sirloin. Others include broiled halibut with pistachio lime butter, Isle au Haut seafood pie, roast duckling with shiitake mushrooms and strawberries, and baby back pork ribs accompanied by fresh maple apple puree.

Innkeeper Michael Madeira's hobby is wine, as evidenced by the wine cellar and racks he built as well as the 100-plus offerings on the reasonably priced wine list notable for its narrative descriptions. The California house wines bear the inn's own label.

Dinner nightly, 6 to 9. Reservations required.

Bentleys Restaurant, 3 Elm St., Woodstock. (802) 457-3232.

Entrepreneurs David Creech and Bill Deckelbaum Jr. started with a greenhouse and plant store in 1974, installed a soda fountain, expanded with a restaurant catering to every taste at every hour, added a specialty-foods shop, opened another Bentleys in 1983 in Hanover, N.H., and lately developed the colorful Waterman Place with retail stores and a Mexican restaurant called Rosalita's in a 100-year-old house along Route 4 in Quechee.

The flagship of it all is the original Bentleys, a casual and eclectic spot at the prime corner in Woodstock. On several levels, close-together tables are set with small cane mats, Perrier bottles filled with flowers, and small lamps or tall candles in holders. Old floor lamps sport fringed shades, windows are framed by lace curtains, the plants are large potted palms, and walls are covered with English prints and an enormous bas-relief.

The menu is eclectic as well. For lunch, we enjoyed a house specialty, torta rustica ($6.95), a hot Italian puff pastry filled with prosciutto, salami, provolone and marinated vegetables, and a fluffy quiche ($5.95) with turkey, mushrooms and snow peas, both accompanied by side salads. From the dessert tray came a delicate chocolate mousse cake with layers of meringue, like a torte, served with the good Green Mountain coffee.

Appetizers, salads, sandwiches and light entrees such as the torta rustica, chicken chimichanga and cold sliced marinated flank steak make up half the dinner menu. The other side offers such entrees as three-mustard chicken, duckling with cranberry-bourbon glaze, veal Romanoff, Jack Daniels steak, Shanghai stir-fry and four Cajun-Creole specialties ($13.95 to $17.50).

With choices like these, it's little wonder that Bentleys is always crowded and bustling.

Lunch, daily 11:30 to 2:30; dinner, 5:30 to 9:30; Sunday brunch, noon to 3.

The Corners Inn & Restaurant, Route 4, Bridgewater. (802) 672-9968.

The exterior is unassuming and the interior is plain ("our inn is old New England," the owners concede). But the food is exciting at this restaurant favored by the locals about seven miles west of Woodstock. We've heard great things about the garlic bread (a house specialty, $2), and the caesar salad is proclaimed the best ever by Barbara Hough of the Charleston House, a self-styled "caesar salad freak" who frequently sends her guests here. The restaurant has a gold medal in the Taste of Vermont competition to show for its efforts.

Start perhaps with the cold antipasti plate ($7.95) or fettuccine alfredo with prosciutto ($5.95). Entrees run from $6.95 for pasta with sausage to $15.95 for Sicilian steak. Other possibilities are chicken lemone, veal with artichoke hearts, roast duckling, and shrimp and scallop scampi.

The Corners won a prize for its red cabbage salad, and the wine list is considered one of the best around. The inn has six bedrooms with two shared baths ($50 double), but the food is what it's known for.

Dinner, Wednesday-Sunday 6 to 10.

Spooner's Restaurant, Sunset Farm, Route 4, Woodstock. (802) 457-4022.

The lower floor of the old Spooner Barn built in 1850 at the east end of town was converted into a handsome restaurant in 1983. It's all bare woods, dark greens and beiges, with bentwood chairs and inlaid tables in a modern greenhouse section, and velvet-covered benches from the old Woodstock Inn as well as booths made of old church pews in other sections. Colorful Sabra Field prints hang on the walls, and a classy bar centers the whole affair.

Mesquite broiling is featured, everything from marinated chicken ($8.95) to chicken, shrimp and sirloin ($15.95). Other entrees ($7.95 to $14.95) include steak kabob, teriyaki sirloin, filet mignon bearnaise and prime rib, plus a variety of surf 'n turf combinations. Eggplant parmesan and pasta of the day are available for those who prefer. Seven items are listed on a children's menu.

The few desserts are pies, mud pie, ice cream and the wonderful cheesecake made by the nuns of New Skete in upstate New York.

The limited wine list is exceptionally priced from $9.95 to $20.95.

Dinner nightly, 5 to 10 or 11.

Lincoln Covered Bridge Inn, Route 4, West Woodstock. (802) 457-3312.

Continental cuisine is served in this inn's pretty Victorian dining room with soft green cloths, windsor chairs, crystal globes and huge vases filled with plants. A few tables are set up for overflow in the small adjacent bar.

Entrees range from $13.95 for chicken calvados to $18.95 for sirloin steak with hunter sauce and loin of lamb dijon. Veal saltimbocca or marsala, sole amandine, shrimp provencale and roast duckling with strawberry sauce are other possibilities.

Start with stuffed mushrooms or marinated artichoke hearts with roasted red peppers. Finish with an unusually light, mile-high cheesecake.

A well-balanced wine selection lists some of our favorite Californias at bargain prices.

Upstairs, innkeeper Marilyn Dolan offers seven small but pleasant guest rooms with private baths for $75 to $100, including continental breakfast.

Dinner, Tuesday-Saturday 6 to 9; Sunday brunch, 11 to 3.

Rumble Seat Rathskeller, Woodstock East, Route 4, Woodstock. (802) 457-3609.

The cellar of the 1834 Stone House houses this casual-elegant little establishment with intimate niches and crannies in three small dining rooms, one with four tables — "a cozy little room for cozy little couples," according to the hostess. It's well away from the large lounge beyond.

The original stone and brick walls have been lacquered, gray linens are accented by cranberry napkins, and it's all more attractive than one might expect from the name.

Dinner entrees run from $9.95 for orange roasted chicken and crumb-baked scrod to $15.50 for veal and shrimp dijon. There's a choice of five dressings for the house salad. Baked stuffed artichokes and potato skins with different fillings are popular appetizers.

Open daily, 11:30 to 10 or 11.

The Mill at Quechee houses Simon Pearce enterprises.

Extra-Special

Simon Pearce, The Mill at Quechee. (802) 295-2711.

Every time we're in the area, we stop at Simon Pearce's magnificent mill, partly because it's all so fascinating and partly because there's always something new.

Simon Pearce is the 43-year-old Irish glass blower who left Ireland in 1981 to set up business in the abandoned flannel mill beside the Ottauquechee.

The site is inspiring: thundering waterfalls, covered bridge, beautifully restored mill and classic white Vermont houses all around. The interior has a fine restaurant (see above) and a wondrous shop offering glass, pottery and Irish woolens, all beautifully displayed.

Downstairs is a glass-blowing area where you can watch Simon Pearce and eight associates turn out 120 pieces a day, the pottery where Miranda Thomas is at work, the hydro station with enormous pipes from the river and a steam turbine that provides enough power to light the town of Quechee as well as serve the mill's energy needs (melting sand into glass, firing clay into porcelain and stoneware).

"The whole idea was to become self-sufficient and provide an economic model for small business in Vermont," says Simon. The mill is zoned utility in the sub-basement, manufacturing in the basement, retail in the restaurant and shop, office on the second floor and residential on the third, where Simon lived with his family until he moved out in 1985.

The enterprise is growing all the time, expanding to other locations (Cambridge, Greenwich Village and Keene, N.H.) and adding ventures (furniture, wooden bowls, brother Stephen Pearce's Irish pottery and Shanagarry by their father, Phillip). We defy anyone not to enjoy, learn — and probably buy! Beautiful clear glass balls, $8 each, are marvelous ornaments for a Christmas tree.

Open daily, 9 a.m. to 9 p.m.; glass-blowers work Monday-Friday except for lunch from 1 to 2.

Diversions

The sportsman and the sightseer have plenty to do in the Woodstock-Quechee area. You can ski at Suicide Six, not far from Gilbert's farm where Woodstockers installed the nation's first rope tow in 1934, or you can ski at nearby Killington, the East's largest ski area. You can golf at the historic Woodstock Country Club, site of Vermont's first golf course and home also of the fine Woodstock Ski Touring Center, or at a newer golf course in Quechee. You can hike through the Quechee Gorge area or the hundreds of acres of forests maintained by the Woodstock Inn. You can walk around the village green and center, marveling in the architectural variety and browsing through the Woodstock Historical Society. But it is arts, crafts and shopping that make Woodstock so appealing for many.

Shopping. The Vermont Workshop, 73 Central St., is said to be the oldest gallery in Woodstock, having evolved from a summer workshop established in 1949. Everything from woven mats and interesting lamp shades to wall hangings and cookware is for sale in room after room of great appeal. Nearby on this artsy section of Central Street is one of the two locations of **Gallery 2;** the gallery at 43 Central has paintings, sculpture and art glass pieces. The print room around the corner at 6 Elm St. holds lots of Woody Jackson cows and woodcuts of Sabra Johnson Field, whose studio in nearby East Pomfret, Tontine Press, is worth a visit (by appointment).

The Pomfret Shop offers unusual garden ornaments, plant containers, fine arts and handcrafts, and a Christmas Treasures shop upstairs. Check out the Colorways china at **Aubergine,** a kitchenware shop, where you might find a thermos full of chocolate raspberry coffee to sample. **Log Cabin Quilts** has everything for the quilter plus the finished products, including a marvelous selection of pillows. Next door is the **Unicorn,** a gift shop with jewelry and woodcrafts by New England artisans.

F.H. Gillingham & Co. at 16 Elm St. is the most fun store of all. Run by the Billings family for 100 years, it's a general store, but a highly sophisticated one — from specialty foods and wines to hardware — and so popular that it does a land-office mail-order business. Owner Jireh Swift Billings's newborn son represents the ninth generation of the Swift family, dating to the 1600s. Next door is the **Village Butcher** where you can get a good sandwich, or maybe a bowl of lobster bisque or chili. There's a table full of maple sugar and maple syrup products.

In Quechee, the **Shop on Main Street** features art and handmade crafts. Shops seem to come and go on the three levels of **Waterman Place,** a 100-year-old restored house with a new glass atrium and elevator above Quechee village off Route 4.

The Marketplace at Bridgewater Mill, west of Woodstock on Route 4 in Bridgewater, is a restored 1820 woolen mill with small shops, crafts outlets (wooden clocks are made in one), outlet stores and open markets.

Billings Farm & Museum, Route 12 north of Woodstock. This is an artfully presented display of life-like exhibits portraying the Vermont farm year of 1890. Housed in four interconnected 19th-century buildings on the working Billings Farm, it shows how crops were planted and harvested. Farm life also meant making butter and cider, cutting ice and firewood, sugaring and darning socks, as well as going to school and the general store and participating in community life; such activities are imaginatively shown. Down a path the modern farm is evident: visitors can see the Jersey herd, calves, sheep, oxen and two teams of Belgian horses, and the milking barn is open. Special events include a 19th-century crafts day and a cow-milking contest. Open daily 10 to 5, early May to late October; adults, $4.

Newfane/West River Valley
The Essence of Vermont

There's not much to do in Newfane and Vermont's surrounding West River Valley. And that's the way the inhabitants like it.

The interstates, the ski areas, the tony four-season destination resorts are some distance away. This is the essence of old Vermont, unspoiled by tourism and contemporary commercial trappings.

The meandering West River creates a narrow valley between the mountains as it descends toward Brattleboro. Along the way are covered bridges (one is the longest in Vermont), country stores, flea markets and a couple of picture-book villages.

The heart of the valley is Newfane, the shire town of Windham County, without so much as a brochure to publicize it. In 1824, Newfane "moved" to the valley from its original site two miles up Newfane hill and now has fewer residents than it had then. The Newfane green is said to be Vermont's most-photographed. Clustered around the green are the white-columned courthouse, the matching Congregational church, the town hall, two famed inns, two country stores and, nearby, some houses — and that's about it.

Upriver is Townshend ("Historic Townshend," one of the area's few tourist brochures calls it), with a larger green and more business activity, though that's relative. Beyond is Jamaica, an up-and-coming hamlet with some good new crafts and gift shops.

There are back roads and country stores to explore, but for many visitors this quiet area's major blessing is its collection of fine inns and restaurants amidst a setting of Vermont as it used to be.

Inn Spots

The Four Columns Inn, 250 West St., Newfane 05345. (802) 365-7713.

Ever since French chef Rene Chardain left the Old Newfane Inn to open the Four Columns, this spot has been widely known for outstanding cuisine (see Dining Spots). Under the auspices of subsequent innkeeper Jacques Allembert, it has become known for comfortable overnight accommodations as well.

Six guest rooms and three suites, all with private baths and most with king or queensize beds, are located in the main columned inn, built in 1830 by General Pardon Kimball for his Southern-born wife as a replica of her girlhood home. Another five rooms and a suite are in the main restaurant building, while the rear Farm Cottage has two suites, one in rustic, masculine style and another cheerier with cathedral ceiling, decoys and a coffee table made from an old sleigh.

All rooms are colorfully decorated with antiques, hooked rugs, handmade afghans and quilts. An 84-year-old craftsman made the canopied four-poster bed in one.

We're especially fond of the third-floor hideaway suite in the front building. Centered by an exposed chimney that divides the room into unusual spaces, it has a canopied bed set into an alcove, a sitting room with a private front porch overlooking the Newfane green, thick beige carpeting and Laura Ashley fabrics.

Several common rooms are good for relaxing or watching television, and the tavern to the rear of the dining room is a popular gathering spot. Continental breakfast is served to houseguests, who can order a full breakfast for an extra charge.

The spacious and attractive grounds include a landscaped swimming pool, a trout pond beloved by ducks, rock gardens and Jacques Allembert's large herb garden behind

Guest rooms are in front and restaurant at rear of Four Columns Inn.

a vine arbor. Beyond are a trout stream and hiking trails up the inn's own little mountain. Doubles, $75 to $95; suites and cottages, $95 to $115.

The Inn at South Newfane, Dover Road, South Newfane 05351. (802) 348-7191.

What better way to approach a country inn than through a covered bridge? The one we have in mind is in Williamsville, the town next to South Newfane, where the handsome Inn at South Newfane, with its olive green trim and masses of pink impatiens surrounding the porte cochere, opened in 1984.

A private turn-of-the century estate on 100 acres, it was purchased by Connie and Herb Borst of Westchester County. They had traveled extensively in Europe, always enjoying small inns more than hotels, so decided to open one of their own. Their daughter Lisa is the exceptional chef (see Dining Spots).

Herb Borst does the baking for breakfast, when dishes like Alsatian kugelhofs, fruit pancakes and french toast made from three slices of different homemade breads are served in a sunny morning room. His tiny Scandinavian pancakes with whipped honey butter and Vermont maple syrup were about the best we've had.

An expansive, well-furnished living room with fireplace and the "Great Room" that is just inside the front door, in shades of gold and with shelves of books, are available for guests' use.

The porch in back is set with garden furniture and beyond are extensive grounds, embracing grand gardens and a fair-size pond for swimming in summer and skating in winter. Hiking and cross-country trails abound, some on the mountain behind the inn.

The six bedrooms, of different sizes, have queen or twin beds and all have been totally redone by the Borsts, who added private baths. Quilts made by "the ladies in the church across the street," floral wallpapers, frilly curtains, and stuffed animals or quilted cat pillows on the beds add to the charm. One room has a reproduction of an old Colonial bed, so high you must use a stool to climb up, and another has twin cannonball beds. The windowed back room has a bathtub in which, says Connie, you can soak and look out at the birds and trees. Flowers and small bowls of fruit are in the rooms.

In the big hall upstairs is a large and attractive reading and writing alcove, where a chest holds all kinds of good books and magazines, and old glass bottles of many colors are displayed to good advantage in front of the window.

Quiet and tranquil, the Inn at South Newfane is the perfect place to relax and read that book you haven't had time for.

Doubles, $160 to $196, MAP; $130 to $166, B&B. Closed November and April. No credit cards.

Windham Hill Inn, West Townshend 05359. (802) 874-4080.

Up a steep hill so far off the main road that we had to stop to ask if we were on the right track is this gem of an inn, a speckled brick and white wood structure built in 1825 and distinguished by a suave oval sign and a commanding view of the West River Valley. Ken and Linda Busteed took over the inn in 1982 and, with skilled decorating touches and hospitable nuances like small decanters of Harvey's Bristol Cream in each room, have turned it into a destination unto itself. "There's not much to do but relax, admire our 150 acres of trees and hills, and enjoy two good meals a day," says Ken.

Linda's touch as an interior designer is evident throughout the inn's common rooms and guest rooms, which rated a six-page photo spread in Country Decorating magazine. The fifteen spacious guest rooms, all with private baths, are furnished with oriental rugs, old photographs and paintings, old quilts and such delights as handmade wreaths, high-button shoes, a christening dress on a wall and a hat over a bed.

One rear room Linda calls the tree house because "when you wake up in the morning you feel you're in the trees;" it has a sofa, a corner window seat and a private balcony. An upstairs corner room has dainty wallpaper, a quilt on a stand in front of the fireplace, candlesticks atop the mantel, and old farm furniture painted, Ken tells guests, with milk and manure. Among the most coveted rooms are the five new ones fashioned from nooks and alcoves in the White Barn annex, particularly the two sharing a large deck overlooking the mountains.

Guests are served full breakasts, Ken offering bananas in sour cream with brown sugar and eggs mornay on Canadian bacon amidst a background of taped chamber music, antique silver and crystal when we stayed.

Linda cooks five-course dinners, which are served at large mahogany and maple tables in the main dining room or at four tables in the Frog Pond Room overlooking the pond and lawns. Dinner is at 7 and the public may be served by reservation ($20) if the inn is not full. Linda's aim is to "make basic things interesting." When we were there, a spinach custard with tomato vinaigrette preceded a mushroom bisque. A salad of leaf lettuce with dijon vinaigrette laced with garlic and dill, homemade poppyseed rolls and a pineapple sorbet preceded the main course, a wonderful scallops provencale. Dessert was a linzer torte. A Silverado sauvignon blanc for $14 was a good choice from Ken's well-selected wine list.

Other rooms at guests' disposal are a cozy parlor with blue velvet sofa, a sunny back room filled with wicker furniture, wood stove, television set and game table (guests usually congregate here for cocktails and munchies before dinner), and in the barn annex, an acoustically fine space in which Musica Vermont of the Brattleboro Music Center presents the occasional chamber music or jazz concert.

In winter, ex-banker Jonathan Tobey runs Windham Hill's new cross-country learning center, offering guided tours and instruction on the inn's groomed trails.

Doubles, $140 to $150, MAP.

Three Mountain Inn, Route 30, Jamaica 05343. (802) 874-4140.

The aromas of dinner emanating from the kitchen and a wood-paneled living room with a fireplace welcome guests to this charming inn, now encompassing five buildings and offering sixteen guest rooms, a small conference center and good meals (see Dining Spots).

Charles and Elaine Murray took over the old Jamaica Inn with eight rooms in 1978, and have been adding rooms and private baths ever since. Accommodations in the main house vary from a corner room with private balcony and kingsize four-poster bed done up in greens and rose shades in the new "Wing Up" above a stable to a couple of simple rooms sharing a bath on the first floor. Architect Rodney Williams of the nearby Inn at Sawmill Farm designed the new wing with his trademark barnwood and beamed-ceiling touches, as well as a new rear house with a queensize bed and a fireplace, perfect for honeymooners.

Next door in the Robinson House are six more guest rooms, one notable for a square bathtub and another that Elaine decorated around a lovely patterned rug. The house also has a small parlor with a wood stove and a room in which Elaine planned to open a shop featuring Vermont products. Across the street is the Sage House, a once-primitive place that the Murrays were upgrading with a redecorated living room, two bedrooms, a new kitchen and a jacuzzi tub.

An appealing swimming pool is a favorite back-yard gathering spot in the summer.

Pecan waffles, french toast, local sausage and eggs, homemade biscuits and blueberry muffins are typical fare at breakfast, served in one of the two pretty fireplaced dining rooms.

Doubles, $130 to $170, MAP. Closed November and March.

The Country Inn at Williamsville, Grimes Hill Road, Box 166, Williamsville 05362. (802) 348-7148.

Situated on 115 country acres, this elegant white clapboard house with green shutters has been home for six years to Bill and Sandra Cassill, who opened it as an inn in 1986. Guests hike the trails in summer and cross-country ski in winter, relax or fish at a trout pond out front, or walk through the fields to a perfect swimming hole in the Rock River, which borders the property.

The Cassills lived for many years in France and England, and have furnished their inn with antiques they collected abroad. Their son Jon, an artist in New York, painted the murals and his fine paintings are in most of the rooms. Sandra, who studied French cooking in Paris and London, and worked in a two-star restaurant for the experience, prepares five-course dinners for guests on Friday and Saturday nights.

Six bedrooms, all with private baths (some off the hall) and one with a fireplace, have a variety of beds from king to twins. One even has a little bunk room beside it (children over 8 are welcome here). All are nicely furnished and have lovely comforters from Carriage House Comforters, a shop nearby. A rear terrace, an appealing living room and a library with a TV, stereo, tapes, books and games (the only room in which smoking is allowed) are also available.

A full breakfast is served at the refectory table in one of the two small dining rooms. It might include blueberry-buttermilk pancakes or pecan waffles with Vermont maple syrup, and always delicious homemade granola.

Following a cocktail hour in the living room, a typical weekend dinner at 7 o'clock would start with a delicate watercress soup, go on to a spinach roulade with a sauce of tomatoes and red pepper, and the main course could be tenderloin of beef with a mustard sauce or chicken breast with wild mushroom sauce. Herbed Vermont lamb chops are sometimes offered. A green salad follows, and for dessert Sandra may make a grand marnier souffle, a cheesecake with raspberries and elderberries, or profiteroles with chocolate sauce. The convivial, leisurely experience takes at least two hours, and you may order wine to accompany, as the Cassills have a beer and wine license.

Doubles, $92 to $112, B&B; $136 to $156, MAP (weekends only).

The Old Newfane Inn, Route 30, Newfane 05345. (802) 365-4427.

Built in 1787, this classic New England inn along the green proclaims itself "virtually unchanged for nearly 200 years" and proud of it. Even the spectacular banks of vivid phlox outside the entrance have stood the test of time.

German chef Eric Weindl and his wife Gundy run the place in the continental style, with an emphasis on their dining facility (see below). Theirs is one of the few area inns we've heard of requiring a two-night minimum stay anytime.

The ten old-fashioned (the Gundys call them quaint) guest rooms upstairs are meticulously clean, most furnished with twin beds, pretty floral wallpapers, samplers and wall hangings, wing chairs and rockers. Eight have private baths and one is a suite. Several rooms, which once were part of the ballroom, have gently curved ceilings and access to a side balcony looking onto the green.

Guests enter via a front porch with a lineup of rocking chairs into a lobby whose walls are hung with framed but faded magazine articles touting the inn. Off the entry on one side is a dark, beamed parlor with fireplace, upholstered chairs and sofa. On the other side is a narrow and dark beamed dining room.

Doubles, $88 to $95, including continental breakfast. Closed November to mid-December and most of May.

Dining Spots

The Inn at South Newfane, South Newfane. (802) 348-7191.

Lisa Borst, who loves to cook, reigns over the big kitchen at her parents' inn. "I enjoy what I do so much," says she, "that it rubs off in the presentation of the food." Always looking for that extra oomph, she gets drenched picking blackberries early in the morning from her extensive vegetable, herb and fruit garden out back, and she makes preserves, purees and sauces (even watermelon pickles) from her produce to carry over to winter.

The summer menu featured shanks of spring lamb with tomatoes, onion and lots of garlic, California duckling served with a ginger oriental sauce, Pacific coho salmon with bearnaise sauce and a loin veal chop with sorrel sauce, among entrees from $16.95 to $19.95. We began with a country pate of game, veal and pork and a dish of escargots,

leeks and mushrooms in a garlic cream with Cajun tasso. The roast breast of pheasant with lavender-garlic sauce and the oven-roasted poussin on a coulis of red pepper were unforgettable. A light grand marnier cheesecake and ginger-peach ice cream were refreshing desserts. On our latest visit, an apple-walnut salad with a mint-strawberry vinaigrette and a fig and cinnamon sorbet were two of Lisa's recent creations. "Every night there's something new coming out of the kitchen," her proud father says.

In winter, you might find a prime rib of buffalo ($19.50) or Lisa's "killer" rack of lamb for one with a sauce of red wine vinegar and rosemary.

The large, almost exclusively American wine list is interesting as well, with many bottles from Idaho.

Dining room at the Inn at South Newfane.

From the French bread at the meal's beginning to the chocolate truffle at the end, everything is homemade and served in a serene dining room with comfortable bow or Queen Anne wingback chairs, beige linens, candles in brass holders, crystal water glasses and large wine glasses. The Mikasa china is rose colored, and the wallpaper features big tulips in beiges and mauves, with matching valances and draperies.

Dinner nightly except Monday, 5:30 to 9 or 9:30. No credit cards. Reservations required by 4 p.m.

The Four Columns Inn, 250 West St., Newfane. (802) 365-7713.

Beamed timbers from the original barn, a huge fireplace, antiques on shelves and walls, and tiny white lights aflickering make the dining area at the rear of the inn a charming setting. Add the magnifcent old French pewter bar decorated with country things like calico hens and an inventive menu that changes seasonally and you have one of the premier dining experiences in southern Vermont.

The culinary tradition launched by Rene Chardain, who left to open a restaurant bearing his name in South Salem, N.Y., is continued by Jacques Allembert and his head chef, Gregory Parks, who was sous chef under Rene.

The hand-written dinner menu is limited but supplemented with blackboard specials so that chef Parks can take advantage of local seasonal products. Appetizers ($7 to $9) seem to get more interesting with every visit: the last time, they included wild boar pate, mushroom mousse with goat cheese, escargots and artichoke with garlic served over fried polenta, and gorgonzola-filled cappelletti with shrimp and roasted pinenuts.

For entrees ($19 to $24.50), it would be hard to choose among such dishes as broiled salmon with ancho chili pepper sauce, braised rabbit with armagnac and creamy polenta, grilled pheasant with a chardonnay-mustard sauce, and loin of venison with cranberries. Even the lowly chicken is stuffed with basmati rice, mozzarella, hazelnuts and sun-dried tomatoes.

Desserts change nightly (perhaps raspberry cream tart or chocolate and vanilla mousse tart with seasonal berries), and you can stop in the lounge to pick one from the cart, even if you haven't dined at the inn.

Dinner nightly except Tuesday, 6 to 9.

Three Mountain Inn, Route 30, Jamaica. (802) 874-4140.

Overnight guests — and the public, by reservation — partake of innkeeper Elaine Murray's straightforward cooking in the two fireplaced dining rooms dressed with pink and white linens and ladderback or bow chairs.

The handwritten menu changes nightly. Favorites among the five appetizers ($3 to $5.50) are tomato dill soup, a hot carrot vichyssoise and scallops maison, served in cream wine sauce with mushrooms and Swiss cheese.

Folks rave about the seafood kabob, trout amandine, chicken paprikash and veal parmesan among the five changing entrees, priced from $12.50 for baked ham to $16 for filet mignon.

Kahlua mocha fudge pie, butter-pecan ice-cream pie, apple crisp with Vermont apple ice cream and a French gateau made without flour are in Elaine's dessert repertoire. A small but good wine list contains such bargains as Firestone cabernet and Beringer fume blanc for $12.

Dinner, 6 or 6:30 to 8:30 or 9.

Townshend Country Inn, Route 30, Box 3100, Townshend. (802) 365-4141.

Down-home country cooking and good values are enjoyed by patrons of this farmhouse-turned-restaurant with three upstairs guest rooms and more in the works.

Table is set for fine dining at the Inn at Windham Hill.

Joseph Peters, formerly manager of the Yankee Pedlar Inn in Holyoke, Mass., picked up his culinary skills while observing the kitchen there. Assisted by wife Donna and three of their four children, he presents an extensive menu at both lunch and dinner, an old-fashioned Vermont Sunday buffet brunch with more than twenty items for $8.75, and some enticing gourmet wine-tasting dinners monthly for $30 a head.

Donna's festive seasonal decorations enhance the main dining room, with bare pine floors, white-linened tables, windsor chairs and a fireplace mantel topped with striking German chocolate pots. A smaller dining room has tables with white woven mats, and there's a lounge at the entrance.

The dinner menu offers something for everyone, from vegetarian platter ($7.95) and pasta to eleven house specialties topping off at $15.95 for filet mignon with bordelaise sauce. Baked scrod, Nantucket seafood casserole, baby coho salmon stuffed with crabmeat, pork gruyere, veal piccata and roast Long Island duck are a few of the offerings.

Joseph is proud of his homemade sherbets, pies and Indian pudding. Most of the 70 wines are bargain-priced at $15 or less, but a page of private-cellar vintages goes up to $50.

Yankee pot roast, chicken pot pie, sauteed calves liver, fish and chips, seafood canneloni and sandwiches are among the lunchtime offerings. The Friday night all-you-can-eat prime rib dinner for $9.95 packs in the locals.

Upstairs are three guest rooms with shared baths, $45 to $55 double. The Peterses have plans to expand a barn and add ten rooms with private baths.

Lunch, 11:30 to 2:30; dinner, 5 to 9; Sunday, brunch 11 to 2:30, dinner 5 to 9.

The Old Newfane Inn, Route 30, Newfane 05345. (802) 365-4427.

Chef-owner Eric Weindl, who trained in a Swiss hotel, cooks in what he calls the Swiss-Continental style at this classic New England inn dating to 1787. The food is as predictable as when we first went out of our way to dine here nearly two decades ago during a ski trip to Mount Snow — that is to say good, but not exciting.

A few daily specials spark up the enormous printed menu, which remains virtually unchanged over the years and lists most of the standards, starting with a slice of melon for $2.75 through marinated herring and escargots bourguignonne to Nova Scotia salmon for $7.75. Capon florentine, duckling a l'orange or with peppercorns, veal marsala, brochette of beef bordelaise, frog's legs provencale, shrimp scampi and pepper steak flamed in brandy are a few of the entrees, priced from $14.50 to $20.95 and accompanied by seasonal vegetables and salad. Chateaubriand "served the proper way" and rack of lamb bouquetiere are $46 and $48 for two. Featured desserts include peach melba, Bavarian chocolate cream pie, cherries jubilee and pear Helene.

The decor matches the vision of what people think a New England inn dining room should look like. Narrow and beamed with a wall of windows onto the green, it has white lace curtains, pink and white linens, lamps on the window tables, shiny dark wood floors, floral wallpaper and a massive fireplace.

Dinner nightly 6 to 9, Sunday 5 to 8 or 8:30. Closed November to mid-December and most of May.

West Townshend Village Cafe, Route 30, West Townshend 05359. (802) 874-4152.

The outdoor deck high up in the trees over a creek and a casual, semi-contemporary interior are draws in this attractive blue wood building down a steep hill. Richard and Debbie Carusona opened in 1982 and renovated in 1984 to produce a dining room with knotty pine paneling and a large bar and lounge with a pool table. It's a mix of gold cloths and white paper mats and napkins, old wood beams and fireplace, herbal wreaths and hanging plants, and is favored by the pickup-truck crowd at night.

The all-day menu lists sandwiches, salads, light dinners and full dinners (the last from $8.95 for rib-eye steak to $16.95 for surf and turf). For dessert, besides ice cream, two or three kinds of pies are baked every day — maple pecan and apple, on our visit. The soup and salad bar (all you can eat for $4.50) would be fine for lunch under the colorful Bolla umbrellas on the deck above Tannery Brook.

Lunch daily, 11 to 4; dinner, 4 to 9:30

Diversions

There aren't many diversions — at least of the traditional tourist variety. For those, head for Brattleboro, Wilmington, Weston or Manchester, all within less than an hour's drive. In the West River Valley, you simply relax, hike or drive scenic back roads, and browse through flea markets, crafts shops and country stores.

Shopping usually begins and ends at the **Newfane Country Store.** Mary and Peter Loring claim the best selection of custom-made quilts in all New England in their store chock full of "country things for country folks." Some of the quilts, which the Lorings say represent a local cottage industry, hang outside and beckon passersby in for herbs, jams and jellies, penny candy, maple syrup, sweaters, Christmas ornaments and such.

Other general stores are the **Newfane General Store,** a family-operated grocery store and deli across from the Newfane green, the **South Newfane General Store** ("experience nostalgia in a working general store and post office"), and the **West Townshend Country Store,** a fixture since 1848 with foods, gifts, cookware, old pickle and cracker barrels (would you believe pickled limes?), spruce gum and two-cent penny candy; there's an entire wall of beer steins with family crests for $9.50.

Along Route 30 in Townshend, **Lawrence's Smoke Shop** has maple products and corn-cob smoked bacon, ham and other meat products as well as jellies, honey and fudge, and they'll make up sandwiches. The factory outlet for **Mary Meyer** stuffed

Vermont's longest covered bridge crosses West River near Townshend.

toys on Route 30 in Townshend is where doting grandmothers and the objects of their affections can go wild. The **Townshend Furniture Co.** factory has an outlet store with Colonial, country and contemporary pine furniture, plus English country antiques and used furniture in the **Back Store.** In Harmonyville, **Alia** is a crafts store and studio purveying wonderful earrings, pins, bracelets and such featuring shell mosaic inlays of semi-precious stones. You can pick up remarkable handcrafted coverings for the bed and body (from pillows to nightshirts) at **Carriage House Comforters,** manufacturing shop in Williamsville and retail shop on Route 30 west of Brattleboro.

Jamaica is abloom with nifty little shops of late. **American Country Designs** is where Jennifer and Thomas Connor offer contemporary accessories and gifts; we acquired a piece of striking sponge pottery. **Butter Up** is a homey kitchen gift store, and the **Bavaria House** sells homemade fudge as well as nutcrackers, cuckoo clocks and other German imports. We coveted absolutely everything at the **Gallery at Jamaica,** from found-metal sculptures for a cool $2,000 to pottery, paintings and wondrous glass marbles called "inhabited planets."

Flea markets seem to pop up all along Route 30. The original Newfane flea market, Vermont's largest now in its 24th year, operates every Saturday and Sunday from May through October one mile north of the Newfane common. The Old Newfane Barn advertises an auction every Saturday at 6:30. The Townshend flea market, beginning at the ungodly hour of 6 a.m. every Sunday, is considered a bit schlocky.

Swimming is extra-special in the Rock River, just off Route 30 up the road to South Newfane. Cars and pickup trucks in a parking area identify the path, a long descent to a series of swimming holes called locally "Indian Love Call," with sections for skinny-dippers, the half-clothed and the clothed. More conventional swimming is available in the West River reservoir behind the Townshend Dam off Route 30 .

Extra-Special

Grafton. For some, this postcard-perfect hamlet just north of Windham Hill and the West River Valley is a destination in itself, and it's worth a day trip from this area. Off the beaten path, it was put on the map by the Windham Foundation, which was launched in 1963 after the town had gone downhill. More than twenty buildings in town have been restored.

The foundation-owned Old Tavern at Grafton has beautifully appointed guest rooms and serves lunch and dinner. Also worth a look are the Grafton Village Cheese Co., nature trails and a museum showing area crafts and tools.

West Dover, Vt.
Fun Place in the Snow

If it weren't for the late ski pioneer Walter Schoenknecht and his vision for a showy ski resort called Mount Snow, West Dover might still be little more than a stagecoach stop on the back road from Wilmington to who-knows-where. It could have followed the path of Somerset, the sprawling township beyond Mount Snow's North Face, which has one of Vermont's largest lakes and nary a human resident — just the remnants of a ghost town vanished in the wilderness.

Flushed with success from his Mohawk Mountain ski area in northwest Connecticut, Walt Schoenknecht developed something of a skiing Disneyland on a 3,556-foot peak slumbering above West Dover. It had a glitzy gondola, enclosed bubble chairlifts, easy wide slopes and a heated outdoor swimming pool in which people frolicked all winter. Here was the the closest major ski and fun resort to Eastern metropolitan areas, and the snow bunnies turned out from the city in droves.

Other ski areas, inns and lodges, restaurants and condos followed, and the boom was on along the river that gives the Deerfield Valley its name. Mount Snow pioneered as a four-season resort with its own Snow Lake Lodge and an eighteen-hole golf course. Two pioneering inns, catering to an affluent clientele, set a standard for elegance and dining among New England inns.

Still, winter fun reigns around West Dover, and cross-country skiing is growing faster than the downhill variety. High season is winter. Lodging rates generally are lower in summer, and vary widely depending on weekday or weekend, length of stay and holiday periods.

While Mount Snow has evolved since its acquisition by the owners of Killington, so has the Deerfield Valley. Inns and restaurants are proliferating as West Dover takes ever more advantage of its place in the sun and snow.

Inn Spots

The Inn at Sawmill Farm, Route 100, Box 367, West Dover 05356. (802) 464-8131.

To hear Ione and Rod Williams tell it, they never planned to live in Vermont, much less run an inn. He was an architect and she an interior designer in New Jersey. On a ski trip to Mount Snow, a blizzardy day forced them off the slopes and into a real-estate office. The agent took them directly to the old Winston Farm they had been admiring for years. "We've never been sure who was more surprised that day when we bought the farm — we or the realtor," the Williamses recall.

That was in February 1968. Their creative minds went to work and the idea for an inn evolved. They spent the next few years turning the 1799 columned farmhouse, a dilapidated barn, a wagon shed and other outbuildings on the site of an 18th-century sawmill into an inn that is a model of sophistication and distinction.

Not the usual country inn, this — even though it's in the country and is one of the world's most perfect hideaways, as Travel & Leisure magazine once described it. Rod Williams kept elements of the barn (hand-hewn beams. weathered posts, boards and doors) so guests would know they're not in the city. Dining rooms, the small bar, living room, loft room, entry, lobby and corridors to guest rooms all meld together fashionably and with unfolding fascination.

Public and private rooms are a decorator's dream. The twenty guest rooms in the inn, sawmill studios and fireplace cottages are large and unusually comfortable. Our

74

Skiers watch evening torchlight parade on slope at Mount Snow.

mid-price master bedroom typified the place. Extra-spacious, it had a kingsize bed, a desk-like table and chair, three upholstered chairs in a sitting area around a wood table with a good porcelain reading lamp, two sinks in a dressing area outside the bathroom, a dresser and a large plant in a wooden stand. Wallpaper, upholstery, bedspread and even the shower curtain were in the same country floral print, and the lush green towels matched the thick carpeting. Beyond was a small balcony overlooking the pool.

And then there are the extras: little packages of Godiva chocolates in your room, afternoon tea with nut bread and ginger cookies in front of the large brick fireplace in the living room, superb dinners (see Dining Spots), hearty breakfasts, a sparkling swimming pool, a spring-fed trout pond, a tennis court and the historic part of West Dover just below.

The hearth of the cathedral-ceilinged living room, festooned with copper pots and utensils, is the focal point for guests who luxuriate on comfortable sofas or wing chairs covered in chintz and read the magazines displayed on a beautiful copper table. Other groupings are near the huge windows that give a perfect view of Mount Snow. The loft room upstairs has more sofas, an entire wall of books and the inn's only television set, which is rarely in use.

Breakfasts are a delight in the sunny greenhouse dining room facing the pool in summer and a flock of chickadees at the bird feeders in winter. You get a choice of all kinds of fruits, oatmeal and fancy egg dishes. We especially liked the baked eggs Portuguese and the eggs Buckingham, the latter an intriguing mix of eggs, sauteed red and green peppers, onion and bacon seasoned with dijon mustard and worcestershire sauce, served atop an English muffin, covered with Vermont cheddar cheese and then baked. What a way to start the day!

Doubles, $220 to $260, MAP. Closed Thanksgiving to mid-December. No credit cards.

The Hermitage, Coldbrook Road, Box 457, Wilmington 05363. (802) 464-3511.

Nestled into a hill overlooking the Haystack Mountain ski area stands an 18th-century farmhouse that once was the home of the editor of the Social Register, the blue book for blue-blood society. Today it's the nucleus of an unusual inn, restaurant (see Dining Spots) and enough other enterprises to stagger the imagination.

"Please do not ask if you may bring your pets," the room confirmation card warns. Any doubts as to why are dispelled as you near the inn at the end of a dirt road. You hear the quacking of ducks and the squawking of geese. Off to the side is the liveliest group of gamebirds you ever saw. You can ogle the inn's peacocks and English setters, try your hand at fishing in the trout pond, cross-country ski at a large touring center, see the results of a vast maple-syrup operation, view the innkeeper's collections of decoys and paintings, and examine some of the bottles that comprise the largest wine list of any New England restaurant in the inn's wine and gift shop. Now a large dining addition that also triples the size of the wine cellar provides space to show off a huge collection of wooden decoys and 200 lithographs from three artists, among them the largest hanging group of French artist Michel Delacroix.

The Hermitage is the expanding restaurant-turned-inn-turned-showcase of owner Jim McGovern, a man of many talents and interests. He pursues most of them 18 hours a day through the changing seasons on his 24-acre property. Part of the Hermitage experience is to wander the grounds, viewing the maple-sugar shed in which the innkeeper also produces more than 10,000 jars of preserves and the outdoor pens with as many as 60 different species of gamebirds, which are for sale and which also turn up on the lunch and dinner menus.

If the scene is busy and the lodging almost seems an adjunct to all the other goings-on, no matter. The fifteen guest rooms in the main inn, the converted carriage house and the new Wine House have private baths, and eleven have working fireplaces. Rooms are generally large and modern, individually decorated and furnished with antiques. In the Wine House, where pictures of ducks grace the small parlor, one room has a heavy carved bed with chenille spread, fringed curtains and a tiny sofa; another has old wood and leather rockers in front of the fireplace. The carriage house with four guest rooms has its own living room and sauna.

Brookbound Inn, the Hermitage's latest adjunct a mile down the road, conveys a ski-lodge atmosphere through and through. Ten of its fourteen paneled rooms have private baths and are pleasantly if spartanly furnished in a cross between country-inn and ski-lodge style. The attractive grounds astride a hill off Coldbrook Road contain a swimming pool and a clay tennis court. Guests here travel to the Hermitage for dinner, and for breakfast in slow periods.

A choice of eggs, omelets, pancakes and the like is offered at breakfast. All the maple syrup and preserves, of course, come from the Hermitage enterprises.

Jim McGovern considers the Hermitage an extension of his home and an expression of his hobbies. His eight-page inn brochure asks rhetorically: "Where else would one also find under one roof the breeding and training of English setter dogs...all with names like Cognac, Burgundy and Yquem. They're assistant innkeepers and will be here to join in welcoming you and making you feel at home."

No cuddly inn cats or feminine frills here. It's an eclectic, sporty, fun and, yes, offbeat place.

Doubles, $180 to $200, MAP; Brookbound, $130 to $200, MAP.

Deerhill Inn, Valley View Road, Box 397, West Dover 05356. (802) 464-3100.

High on a hill overlooking the valley and the Green Mountains, this inn is quiet and comfortable. The sixteen rooms and a suite, some in the main inn and some in a wing

Birch tree flanks entrance to Deerhill Inn.

by the swimming pool, have private baths. They and the public rooms were originally decorated by Ione Williams of the Inn at Sawmill Farm, a former innkeeper's aunt, which helps explain their flair.

The large first-floor living room, with comfy sofas, wing chairs, copper table and massive fireplace, pewter candlesticks and tankards on the mantel, is most welcoming. So is the second-floor living room with another large brick fireplace, conversation groupings and enormous pillows to sit on. A reading alcove with shelves of books and a TV set is at the head of the stairs.

Bedrooms are furnished with queen and kingsize beds, some with canopies, and modern bathrooms with thick colorful towels. We like the room that looks over the swimming pool, with a print canopy over the bed, and a newly redone room with a striking oriental ironwood four-poster bed that innkeepers Robert and Joan Ritchie acquired from Hong Kong.

Besides the 20-by-40-foot pool (a great setting for cocktails on the deck while watching the sunset over the mountains), there is a tennis court.

A full breakfast menu — eggs, french toast or pancakes — is served in the handsome dining room, the site for highly acclaimed dinners (see Dining Spots).

Doubles, $160 to $180, MAP.

Doveberry Inn, Route 100, West Dover 05356. (802) 464-5652.

The former Tollhouse bed-and-breakfast establishment was upgraded in 1984 into the Doveberry Inn, with a pleasant restaurant, a great outdoor dining deck with colorful Schweppes umbrellas and eight fine guest rooms, all with private baths.

The renovated inn has a contemporary air, some rooms having skylights and one luxury suite having a private deck and sitting area with color TV. The deluxe Blue Room has two double beds, a duck cushion resting on one and a butterfly cushion on the other, and a basket of apples at our fall visit. A typical smaller double has two cat pillows on the chairs, flowered curtains matching the wallpaper (which also covers the ceiling) and a bathroom with copper in the sink and shower.

Wood stoves and an open brick fireplace warm the common rooms, where there are some lovely oriental antiques, from the travels of new innkeeper Pat Rossi and her associate, Richard Wright. Overstuffed dark blue sofas are grouped around the hearth. Classical music plays on tapes, and books and games are available. Hot cider or mulled wine is served in ski season, this being the closest inn to Mount Snow.

Pat, a recent New England Culinary Institute grad, whips up a dynamite breakfast: perhaps raisin french toast stuffed with cream cheese one day, blueberry pancakes the next. Her sister, Kathleen Snyder, is the dinner chef (see Dining Spots).

Doubles, $90 to $110. Closed April-May.

Snow Den Inn, Route 100, Box 625, West Dover 05356. (802) 464-9355.

Since Andrew and Marjorie Trautwein took over the Snow Den Inn, they have been receiving high marks from fellow innkeepers. And with good reason: the 100-year-old farmhouse that became the first ski lodge in the Mount Snow area in 1952 has been vastly upgraded, retaining few vestiges of its past. Andy says he frankly patterned the changes after the Inn at Sawmill Farm across the street, where he'd been a frequent guest over the years; Sawmill Farm reciprocates by sending his inn its overflow.

Four different staircases lead to the upstairs and a Hammond organ is in one of the halls of this long, rambling house. It has eight guest rooms, five with fireplaces and all with private baths and cable TV. Electric candles are lit all year in the front windows, and rooms are handsome with canopy or brass beds, good-looking quilts and wing chairs. Although rooms with fireplaces have comfy sitting areas, guests also gather in the attractive living room, done up in rusts and greens with country accessories and ducks in various guises.

Mary Trautwein serves a full breakfast in a pretty pink dining room with Hitchcock chairs at one large and four small tables. Coffee and fruit are available in the hall all day, and wine and beer and snacks are offered in the afternoon.

Doubles, $80 to $120. Closed early November and May.

The Inn at Quail Run, Smith Road, Box 28, Wilmington 05363. (802) 464-3362.

Young innkeepers Jerry and Jackie Bonney, he a former FBI agent and she once a bank vice president, took over the quiet and secluded On the Rocks Lodge in 1987 and rechristened it with this neat name. The place is neat, too — a large house that gives way to room after room of surprises, to say nothing of the outdoor swimming pool, the tennis court and the patio framing a great view of Mount Snow.

The Bonneys are upgrading twelve lodge-style guest rooms with private baths, iron or brass beds, and nice touches like baskets of bath amenities, assorted chocolates and splits of sparkling wine for guests on arrival. Hors d'oeuvres are put out at 4, and dessert and coffee at 8. A separate house has three suites with working fireplaces.

The common rooms are remarkable here: an enormous living room furnished in Victorian pieces with windows onto the mountains, a flagstone and glass-walled breakfast room, a BYOB lounge with complimentary wine and, downstairs, an exercise room, a nice television room/library with overstuffed chairs, a game room with pingpong table and bumper pool, and an eight-person sauna. All this for 30 or so guests amid a surprisingly homey atmosphere.

A full breakfast of the guest's choice is served in the morning.

Doubles, $100.

Trail's End, Smith Road, Wilmington 05363. (802) 464-2727.

Tucked beneath towering trees off a country road, Trail's End is an architecturally interesting blend of ski lodge and inn with eighteen guest rooms and private baths.

Bedrooms vary from small with one double bed to family suites with fireplaces. "They're not fancy-fancy but clean and nice," as innkeeper Bill Kilburn described them. Most have bleached pine or oak furniture, and the oldest and smallest in back appeal to bargain-seekers.

The centerpiece is the striking living room/dining room area, with soaring windows and cathedral ceiling, a gigantic fireplace, two stories of stone walls and an unusual wall of cistern wheels that must be seen to be believed. Against the windows is a lineup of built-in beige sofas, capable, no doubt, of seating half the house. Above is a ramp crossing to a corner loft television area overlooking the whole scene.

The low-ceilinged dining room has three large round tables, where guests dine family style. Mary Kilburn, who has shared her recipes in a cookbook, serves dinner to house guests at 6:30 for $14. The fare consists of soup, homemade bread, garden salad, an entree such as veal marsala or stuffed flounder, three vegetables and a dessert like apple pie or berry clafouti. Bill says his summer steak fry by the pool is a hit every Thursday. Dinner is available nightly in summer, weekends the rest of the year, if at least fifteen people sign up.

Featuring homemade granola and omelets, a full breakfast of the guest's choice is available in the morning.

A large, rustic fieldstone-floored room has games, books and bumper pool, and there's a BYOB bar. The ten acres of grounds are very becoming with a stocked trout pond, pool, tennis court and beautiful English gardens.

Doubles, $60 to $120, B&B; $84 to $144, MAP. Closed most of November and April.

Dining Spots

The Inn at Sawmill Farm, Route 100, West Dover. (802) 464-8131.

The food served up by engineer-turned-chef Brill Williams, son of innkeepers Rodney and Ione Williams, is worthy of the magnificent setting they created.

The three candlelit dining rooms are as attractive as the rest of the inn and display the owners' collection of folk art. The most formal has wrought-iron chandeliers, chintz draperies and Queen Anne-style chairs contrasting with a cathedral ceiling and barnwood walls. The main dining room has white beams, theorem and oil paintings, rose and ivory wallpaper (even on the ceiling), a lovely china cabinet and tables set with white linens, heavy silver and pretty flowered china. We like best the Greenhouse Room, a colorful plant-filled oasis. And, for the ultimate in decor coordination, the waitresses wear long peasant-style dresses made of the same print as the wallpaper.

The menu is rather larger and more ambitious than one might expect, comprising more than a dozen appetizers and twenty entrees, many of the favorites remaining on the list year after year. For starters ($6 to $10), how about salmon mousse with black American caviar, backfin crabmeat cocktail, sauteed quail or shrimp in beer batter? We liked the thinly sliced raw prime sirloin with a shallot and mustard sauce, and dug into the delicate green salads and a basket of good hot rolls and crisp, homemade melba toast.

Entrees run from $19.50 for Indonesian curried chicken breasts to $28 for steak au poivre flambee. Duck is prepared two ways and frog's legs come with sliced truffles. A roasted free-range chicken stuffed with shallots and mushrooms is available for two. Pork is sauced with cognac, cream and walnuts, and veal loin steak with morels and calvados sauce. We found outstanding both the rabbit stew and the sweetbreads chasseur garnished with french-fried parsley.

Desserts are grand. Fresh coconut cake, apple tart with hard sauce, chocolate whiskey cake with grand marnier sauce and bananas Romanoff were among the choices when

Greenhouse Room is plant-filled oasis for dining at the Inn at Sawmill Farm.

we visited. The espresso is strong, and better-than-usual decaffeinated coffee is served in a silver pot.

Brill Williams's wine cellar, which he says he has developed "more as a hobby than a business," has been ranked one of the top 100 in America by Wine Spectator. Prices start in the mid-teens and rise sharply, but you can find some rare treats for a splurge.

Dinner nightly by reservation, 6 to 9. Jackets required; no credit cards.

The Hermitage, Coldbrook Road, Wilmington. (802) 464-3511.

The dinner menu at the Hermitage rarely changes. It doesn't have to. Innkeeper Jim McGovern, one of whose talents is cooking, specializes in gamebirds that he raises on the inn's property. He also is a connoisseur of wines. Combine the three interests and he has a going concern indeed.

In season, lunch and brunch are served outside on a marble patio, inside on an intimate sun porch or in one of the two small, elegant dining rooms. The large new rear dining room is simply gorgeous, with upholstered and wing chairs around widely spaced tables set with white linens and blue overcloths, fresh flowers, white china and heavy silver. Walls are covered with the "naif" prints of Michel Delacroix. Pretty patterned carpeting, huge windows looking onto the grounds, a grand piano, and hand-carved decoys everywhere complete the picture. A wreath made of corks graces one wall in the lounge.

The relatively small dinner menu lists ten entrees from $13 for filet of sole or chicken amandine to $19 for frog's legs provencale. You can get boneless trout, shrimp scampi, veal marsala or wiener schnitzel. But who wouldn't opt for the nightly game specials — perhaps pheasant, quail, duck, goose or, the last time we visited, partridge?

As you dine, Jim McGovern may table-hop, chatting about his gamebirds or the wine cellar, now containing 40,000 bottles, remarkable for their quality and variety. The black-bound, typeset wine lists more than 500 choices (86 California chardonnays and 50 montrachets, for instance), priced from the low teens to $1,000.

For a weekend brunch (the same menu is offered weekdays for lunch), we sampled the mushroom soup with a rich game pate on toast triangles plus a house specialty, four mushroom caps stuffed with caviar and garnished with a pimento slice and chopped raw onion on a bed of ruby lettuce. Chicken salad for $6.95 was a winner: an ample plateful colorfully surrounded by sliced oranges, apples, green melon, strawberries, grapes and tomatoes on a bed of bibb lettuce. The portions were large enough that we could not be tempted by such desserts as a hot Indian pudding, a maple parfait made with Hermitage syrup or fresh strawberries on homemade shortcake.

Lunch weekdays in season, noon to 2; brunch weekends and holidays, 11 to 3; dinner nightly, 5 to 11.

Two Tannery Road, 2 Tannery Road, West Dover. (802) 464-2707.

Since this restaurant opened in 1982, it has been a favorite of summer and winter visitors as well as locals. Now the historic house has been renovated to perfection. A new entrance hall is decorated with quilts and a deacon's bench. The focus of a large and inviting lounge is the dark oak and mahogany bar, from the original Waldorf-Astoria Hotel and purchased at auction in upstate New York in 1983. A jukebox in the corner plays oldies like Glenn Miller.

Large windows on three sides of our favorite rear Garden Room look onto the spotlit lawns and trees. Copper pans and pots glow on the brick fireplace; the lushest poinsettias we've seen hang in profusion from the beamed ceiling, and folk art is everywhere. The Fireplace Room and two more small dining rooms are beamed and stenciled; oriental patterned rugs dot the wide-plank floors.

Chef Brian Reynolds stayed on with new owners who took over in 1987. His summer menu includes such appetizers ($4.50 to $7.50) as smoked seafood medley, baked artichoke hearts and Acadian pepper shrimp. Soup of the day could be tomato basil or salmon bisque; the cold cucumber with dill is particularly good.

Entrees run from $14 for three versions of chicken (including one stuffed with four cheeses and a leek cream sauce) to $22 for filet mignon or grilled lamb chops with mint jelly. Stuffed shrimp, veal Kiev, roast Long Island duck, grilled medallions of veal with homemade garlic mayonnaise and steak au poivre are other choices. We can vouch for a couple of the specialty veal dishes from past visits.

For dessert ($3.50), apple crisp with oats, chocolate mousse cake and homemade peanut-butter chocolate-chip ice cream are favorites. The wine list is richly varied, at reasonable prices.

The house, moved to its present location in the 1940s, is the oldest frame building in Dover. In the early part of the century it belonged to President Theodore Roosevelt's son and daughter-in-law; the President is reported to have used it as a retreat. .

Dinner, Tuesday-Sunday 6 to 10, open Monday of holiday weeks. Closed mid-April to Memorial Day and first three weeks of November.

Le Petit Chef, Route 100, Wilmington. (802) 464-8437.

The outside of this low white 1850 farmhouse smack up against the road to Mount Snow looks deceptively small. The inside houses three intimate dining rooms, a spacious lobby abloom with spring flowers in midwinter, and an inviting lounge. Tables are set with white cloths, blue napkins, handsome white china and oil lamps. Cabinets full of antique china and glass. Oriental rugs and grapevine wreaths are accents.

Chef-owner Betty Hillman, whose mother Libby is the cookbook author, studied in France and her formerly classic menu has become more contemporary of late. Appetizers ($5 to $8.50) include marinated goat cheese en croute, home smoked beef with maple mustard sauce, orange-scented sea scallop salad, lemon linguini with smoked salmon and black caviar, and crabmeat imperial in pasta shells.

Entrees run from $13 for oriental stir-fried vegetables to $21 for noisettes of venison with red currant sauce and chutney. Among others are fish of the day poached Mediterranean style, duckling with juniper-honey sauce and cranberry chutney, two versions of veal (cream or herbs), and filet of beef with a five-pepper sauce.

Fresh fruit tarts, chocolate torte, and special ice creams and sorbets are among the homemade desserts.

Dinner nightly except Tuesday, 6 to 9 or 10.

Deerhill Inn, Valley View Road, West Dover. (802) 464-3100.

Chef Pamela Grey-Storey and her husband Tom Storey, maitre-d' and wine steward, have continued a tradition of fine dining at this inn since they took over Deerhill's restaurant operation.

The two dining rooms are light and airy, their expansive windows looking over the valley to the mountains beyond. One has a tartan rug and a fireplace, and the other a lovely moss-green carpet with round oriental-style inserts. Pink and white linens, huge wine glasses and candles with flowered bobeches create an elegant backdrop.

Typical appetizers ($4.50 to $6.75) are raclette fondue, shrimp toasts, salmon crepe and French onion tart with gruyere cheese. Entrees range from $15.50 for pasta of the day to $25 for roast rack of lamb. Poached salmon with pasta and julienned vegetables, gulf shrimp with braised leeks, filet mignon with roquefort and bacon in pastry and medallions of veal with artichokes and sun-dried tomatoes are other choices.

Finish with the ever-changing desserts, maybe pumpkin caramel brulee, chocolate decadence cake with raspberry sauce, apple strudel or linzer torte.

Dinner nightly except Monday, 6 to 9. Closed mid-April to mid-May.

Elsa's European Deli & Cafe, Route 100, West Dover. (802) 464-8425.

Since Elsa's is one of the few places where you can have lunch in the area, we're happy to report that it is worth the stop. It's small, but in summer you can eat on decks in front by the road or in back by a stream. Inside, a few chairs face a right-angle counter; green mats and flowers in mustard jars top the small tables. The open kitchen where copper pots hang is bordered by a canvas awning in many colors, and skylights make the place bright and cheery, especially in the small, brick-floored front room. Posters, lots of tile, a wood stove, and shelves with pastas, pickles and such for sale add to the cafe feeling.

A blackboard lists many specials to supplement the menu, which is comprised mostly of sandwiches, burgers, omelets and salads. Bratwurst with potato salad, barbecued ribs, chili and cream of mushroom soup were specials at our winter stop. We enjoyed a cup of wild rice florentine soup, a plate of duck-liver pate (all the pates come from Trois Cochons in New York) with a delicious cumberland sauce, served with crusty warm French bread ($5.25), and an unusually bountiful salad nicoise ($6.25). Sandwich prices are in the $1.50 to $4.75 range; the latter includes the Hans C. Andersen, a warm croissant with pate, bacon and horseradish sauce.

Wines and beers are available; seven wines are served for $2.25 to $2.50 a generous glass. For dessert, tollhouse-cookie pie and chocolate-chip cheesecake are in the $2.75 range.

Elsa's also puts up box lunches for two, and is a good place for a late breakfast of bagel and cream cheese ($1.50) or Vermont cheddar and ham omelet ($4.25). Chef Mark Longo's blackboard dinner specials the day we last visited were fried flounder, veal marsala and beef brochettes, $6.95 to $10.95.

Open daily except Tuesday, 11:30 to 9. No credit cards.

Outdoor dining on the deck is popular at Doveberry Inn.

Doveberry Inn, Route 100, West Dover. (802) 464-5652.

The sign outside the inn says "Home cooking and old-fashioned charm," but when did you last make duck confit on mixed greens or salmon tartare, fresh and smoked salmon with capers, onion and egg? Chef Kathleen Snyder, the new innkeeper's sister, is a graduate of the New England Culinary Institute, and her repertoire is ever changing. Soups might be cream of carrot, avocado, bean with bacon or gazpacho; appetizers, rumaki, baked brie with seasonal fresh fruit, or fettuccine alfredo.

Dinner entrees ($14.50 to $16) include New York strip steak with a choice of sauces, pork tenderloin with apples and calvados, stuffed boneless chicken breast en croute, scampi in a pungent pesto sauce and scallops florentine wrapped in Vermont ham. The house salad of many greens, including radicchio and spinach, is served with a red wine vinaigrette and blue cheese dressing.

With a cup of the good Green Mountain coffee, try a chocolate terrine on raspberry coulis or mud pie made with heath-bar crunch.

The two beamed country-style dining rooms in this renovated inn have ladderback chairs and bare wood tables topped with woven mats and cutlery tucked inside brown napkins for breakfast and lunch; linens cover the tables at night. A collection of pink depression glass is on the shelves and a tartan rug covers the floors.

Lunch is served on the spacious front deck if the weather warrants. The new owners planned to expand the wine list.

Lunch in season; dinner Wednesday-Sunday, 6 to 9:30 or 10.

The Bakery, Route 100, West Dover. (802) 464-5914.

Stop at this little bakery in a small shopping center with its five tables for coffee or hot chocolate with raspberry turnovers, banana muffins and frangipane tarts. The peanut-butter swirl bars are delicious and the sticky buns the stickiest ever.

On weekends, owner Wendy Cote makes turkey or ham and cheese croissants, so it's a good bet for a quick lunch.

Diversions

Skiing. Mount Snow virtually put West Dover on the map and remains the stellar attraction today. Long known as a great beginners' area and a lively place for apres-ski (with the stress on apres more than ski), it nonetheless always has appealed to us for its wide-open, almost effortless intermediate skiing. Since founder-showman Walter Schoenknecht sold to the business types from Killington, Mount Snow has been upgraded in terms of snowmaking and lift capacity. Gone is the heated swimming pool; more emphasis is on the North Face, a challenging area for advanced skiers, blessedly away from the crowds. Newly accessible from Mount Snow is the former **Carinthia** ski area, a low-key place the larger area acquired for beginners, intermediates and families. Now any skier can find his place — and space — at Mount Snow. Adult lift rates, $32.

More Skiing. Haystack, a smaller mountain (1,400-foot vertical, compared with Mount Snow's 1,900), has had its ups and downs, but the 'Stack is back, as its advertising proclaims, with a new base lodge, four new chairlifts, base-to-summit snowmaking and uncrowded, family-type skiing (its $15 weekday lift tickets are the cheapest in Vermont). The Haystack vicinity is aboom with condominium villages, a golf course and an indoor sports center under construction.

Cross-Country Skiing. Where skiers gather, cross-country is usually available, too. So it is with the Deerfield Valley, which has three major touring centers. The best is the **Hermitage Touring Center,** run by the Hermitage inn, which has 55 kilometers of groomed trails next to Haystack. It is part of the rugged new Ridge Trail, a five-mile-long mountaintop touring trail that winds up and down four peaks between Haystack and Mount Snow. The **Sitzmark Ski Touring Center** offers 25 kilometers of trails on its golf course and adjacent wooded hills off East Dover Road in Wilmington. The **White House Ski Touring Center,** run by the White House Inn in Wilmington, has fourteen miles of trails through woods and hills east of Wilmington.

Other Seasons. Two of southern Vermont's largest lakes are close at hand for boating, fishing and swimming, Somerset Reservoir in the wilderness north of Mount Snow and Lake Whitingham southeast of Wilmington. Golf is available at the eighteen-hole Mount Snow Country Club, the par-three Sitzmark golf course and the new eighteen-hole Haystack championship course. Special events are scheduled throughout the summer and fall.

Shopping. West Dover is little more than a hamlet with some landmark structures that make up what one innkeeper says is an emerging "Historic Mile." Most of the shopping opportunities are down the valley in Wilmington, where there are fascinating shops. The usual ski clothing boutiques abound, of course, and more trendy little shopping clusters open along Route 100 every year. Try **Swe Den Nor Ltd.** for Scandinavian gifts and **Marge's Touch of Country** in the North Country Stores for handcrafted items. **Silver Chalice Ltd.** at the North Commercial Center has crafts and jewelry.

Extra-Special

The Marlboro Music Festival, Marlboro.

Popular with West Dover visitors is the summer tradition at Marlboro College in nearby Marlboro, where three chamber-music concerts are presented each weekend from early July to mid-August. Since 1952, pianist Rudolf Serkin has directed the 70 festival players whose concerts are incidental to their studies. Tickets usually are sold out by spring, but seats may be available on the screened porch outside the 650-seat concert hall. For advance tickets, contact Marlboro Music Festival, 135 South 18th St., Philadelphia, Pa. 19103; after June 6, Marlboro Music Festival, Marlboro 05344, (802) 254-8163 or 254-2394.

Lake Sunapee is quiet in early morning in this view from Three Mile Loop.

Lake Sunapee Region, N.H.
Clubby Air and Sports Galore

The fortuitous combination of lakes, mountains and meadows makes the Sunapee Region a choice year-round attraction, especially for the sportsman.

Lake Sunapee, New Hampshire's third largest, and its neighbors, Little Sunapee and Pleasant Lake, provide all kinds of water pleasures within view of Mount Kearsarge, central New Hampshire's highest peak, and Mount Sunapee, a state park and ski area. In between on the rolling flatlands are four golf courses and two tennis clubs.

So it comes as no surprise that historic New London, the largest village in the region (year-round population, 2,900, but swelled by second-home residents, tourists and students at Colby-Sawyer College), is a mecca for the affluent. Its hilltop setting with posh contemporary homes, trendy shops and country clubs casts an unmistakable aura of prosperity. Legend has it that the song made famous by Kate Smith, "When the Moon Comes Over the Mountain," was written by a Colby student as she watched it rise above Mount Kearsarge.

Little Sunapee and Pleasant lakes, hidden from the tourists' path, are happily unspoiled. Some of the Lake Sunapee shoreline is surprisingly undeveloped as well, and old Sunapee Harbor — the heart of the lake resort region — looks not unlike a cove transplanted from the coast of upper Maine.

The area's inns, most of which have been around a while and bill themselves as self-contained resorts, reflect the solitude and variety of the region. Some have a detached and clubby air, but a new breed of innkeepers is giving most a breath of fresh air.

Inn Spots

Seven Hearths, Old Route 11, Sunapee 03782. (603) 763-5657.

While this inn may look like an old farmhouse from the outside, take one step inside and you know that sophistication reigns. A small table in the middle of the reception area holds a large, clear round bowl with a beautiful arrangement of flowers, brilliantly spotlit from above; beyond it is another table with a display of wine bottles. To the right, through glass doors, is a stunning living room dominated by a huge fieldstone fireplace and two plush, mushroom-colored velvet sofas.

The farmhouse dates from 1801 and its last incarnation was as an antiques store. Vacant for a period, it was acquired in 1983 by a Harvard design graduate and his wife, who restored it with taste and tender loving care, opened it as an inn in the summer of 1984, and then decided they didn't like the inn business. They sold a few months later to Mary Ann Callahan and Miguel Ramirez, corporate types from Boston, who brought their extensive art collection to the inn, but who didn't have to do much else.

There really are seven hearths, five of them in the bedrooms (there are ten guest rooms, all with private baths). We certainly enjoyed the fire in ours in a large front corner room on a chilly September night.

Rooms vary in size from very large to quite small; some have twin beds, but most have queensize. All are elegant, with touches like needlepoint luggage racks, sofas or velvet wing chairs in sitting areas, good artworks, interesting area rugs and antique furnishings. The back corner room has a round window through which you can see white birch trees; a picture of birches hangs on the opposite wall. Bowls of fruit are placed in each room.

Spacious grounds contain flower gardens, a large vegetable garden well-used by the chef and, in back, a swimming pool up a slope landscaped with rocks and flowers.

Before dinner (see Dining Spots), guests gather in the Hearth Room for cocktails and hors d'oeuvres. Breakfast at Seven Hearths is an event, from the fresh orange juice ("I get up every morning at 6:30 to squeeze it," says Mary Ann) served as a first course with homemade breads or muffins, to the dish of fresh fruit with creme fraiche (nectarines and blueberries at our visit), accompanied when we were there by a slice of spicy gingerbread and a piece of brie. Hearty eaters may then order eggs any style, pancakes or waffles. One of us thought the preceding was more than enough. Accompanied by good coffee and music from "The Magic Flute," it was a breakfast fit for a king.

Doubles, $108 to $138. Closed in April.

Wonderwell, Philbrick Hill, Springfield 03284. (603) 763-5065.

This imposing shingled mansion on a hill seemingly in the middle of nowhere has been the summer home of innkeeper Samuel Alexander's family since 1934. Built in 1911 by the Stoddard family of Washington, D.C., it is unique to the area, says Sam, because of its formal center hall and its two-story living room (the Great Room) with a Caesar's balcony all around, two huge stone fireplaces and rustic beams. Sam and his wife Susan, who have traveled across the world, opened Wonderwell as an inn in 1988 with the help of Wolf Heinberg, former owner of the renowned Hide-Away Lodge in New London, as consultant.

Not yet 100 percent finished, they have plans for screening in the west porch, enclosing the south porch and outfitting it with a pingpong table and bumper pool, adding a tennis court for 1989 and eventually building a swimming pool.

In the meantime, there are eight elegant bedrooms on the second and third floors, two of which can be used as a suite. They are named for flowers and herbs. Hollyhock has a four-poster queen bed and a fireplace; Dandelion, twin beds and a jacuzzi. All have private baths, vary in size, and are stylishly decorated with lots of teals and pinks in rugs, comforters and the like.

Guests are given a card in the evening to fill out for their breakfast the next morning. Along with the usual fare (fresh orange juice, cereals, eggs any style), a special is offered

Imposing shingled mansion built in 1911 is now Wonderwell.

each day. It could be a poppyseed flan with apricot relish, Scottish kippers and cottage fried potatoes, scrambled eggs and smoked salmon with fresh dill in pastry shells or walnut waffles with strawberry cream.

The innkeepers love music, and offer musical evenings in the Great Room (which has excellent acoustics) with perhaps musicians from the Portland Symphony. One of the first, titled "Absolutely Amadeus," included a four-course dinner with wines for $75.

Guests may order dinner in advance any night for $28.50 a head. Sam will prepare something like Gaspe salmon with a dill-hollandaise sauce, a watercress-avocado salad with lime dressing, and chocolate truffle cake. Lunch is also available on request, and the Alexanders will put up special picnic lunches and box lunches for skiers. "Our philosophy," says Sam, "is to give guests more service, hospitality and better food than they expect for what they're paying."

Add tea in the afternoon, and hors d'oeuvres and wine at night, and you can appreciate the value.

Doubles, $100; suite $180. Closed in April and from Thanksgiving to Christmas.

New London Inn, Main Street, Box 8, New London 03257. (603) 526-2791.

This village inn next to the Colby-Sawyer College campus has been around since 1792, but never more spiffily than since it was taken over and grandly refurbished in 1986 by Maureen and John Follansbee, whose grandfather started the Follansbee Inn. A focal point in the community, it is now a full-service inn worthy of its landmark status, and its dining room is receiving acclaim for inspired regional cuisine (see Dining Spots).

With T.L.C., the Follansbees have remodeled and redecorated 30 guest rooms on three floors, replacing many a carpet, 28 beds and 101 windows ("we found windows that hadn't been washed in 195 years," recalls Maureen). Mini-print and sprigged wallpapers, brass and spool beds, decoys, tin wall sconces and sitting areas enhance many of the rooms, which come in various sizes and configurations. All have private baths. Choicest are the larger corner rooms (one of which accommodated Ronald Reagan years ago when he campaigned in the New Hampshire primary), furnished in blue and white with two double beds, a sofa and two wicker chairs. From a long front porch off the second floor, guests can view the passing scene and get a bird's-eye view of some of the award-winning gardens below.

Returning Colby-Sawyer and Dartmouth types are surprised by the refurbished main floor, with a new entrance lobby, graceful parlors and a relocated tavern. John tells how they redid the kitchen to allow for a bigger dining area near the fireplace, only to open up the fireplace and discover it was fake. Undaunted, they constructed one with 200-year-old bricks from the foundation.

Breakfast from a full menu is included in the room rates. Red flannel hash with poached eggs and eggs baked in cream with wild mushrooms (both $4.50) are specialties that attract the public as well.

Doubles, $65 to $85. Two-night minimum stay in summer and fall.

Follansbee Inn, Route 114, Box 92, North Sutton 03260. (603) 927-4221.

"Welcome to the Follansbee Inn — a great place to relax and enjoy a slower pace of living," greeted the sign at the porch entry to this rambling old inn fronting on Kezar Lake. And on a blackboard underneath: "Today's saying: Swallowing your pride occasionally will never give you indigestion."

Such are the distinctive touches that imbue the Follansbee with plenty of personality. A big place with a hotel-style main floor and 23 guest rooms, it seems smaller and is much more friendly, thanks to new innkeepers Sandy and Dick Reilein. Thus it is not unrealistic for Sandy to say that theirs is "like the country home you've always wanted to have — with none of the work." They do it, seemingly effortlessly, for you.

Outgoing hosts who are apt to join arriving guests for a late-afternoon swim, they share the work with eleven-year-old son Matthew. The youngest of six children, he greets guests, helps with luggage, tends to the waterfront and entertains with magic tricks if prompted. Between dinner preparations and making small talk during cocktails in the living room, the Reileins can be counted on to bring out a tray of munchies to those seeking solitude on the porch or chatting in the common rooms.

Off a second-floor hall full of antiques are eleven guest rooms with private baths, all spruced up with Eisenhart Vintage wallpapers, new mattresses, carpeting, large towels and bayberry soap made specially for the inn. Our corner room overlooking the lake had good cross-ventilation, a must on a sultry night. The third floor has twelve more bedrooms with shared baths.

Where the Follansbee once thrived on numbers, the Reileins stress intimacy and conviviality. They downsized the operation, closed the restaurant to the public and made the inn totally non-smoking. That last brave move has increased business, says Dick, a former IBM executive. "In our own small way, we feel we are helping people to live a healthier life style."

The homey main floor has a cozy sitting room paneled in barnwood and furnished with patchwork cushions, baskets and all kinds of games, and a large front parlor, a bit more formal but most comfortable. It opens onto a dining room, where breakfast is served partly buffet-style, starting with fresh fruit and Sandy's homemade granola and featuring an entree such as french toast, puffed apple pancake, egg souffle or a choice of omelets. Guests are encouraged to sit at tables of six or eight to get acquainted.

At night, Sandy cooks an optional, all-you-can eat dinner for house guests. Peaches and cream soup, salad, homemade bread and baked Alaska pie surrounded the main course, stuffed shrimp, the night we were there. The price depends on the single entree, ranging from $7.50 for lasagna to $20 for rack of lamb. Dick, who helps serve, oversees an interesting stock of beer and wine.

Besides partaking of the Reileins' hospitality, guests enjoy peaceful Kezar Lake, where Matthew's armada now includes a sailboard, rowboat, canoe and paddle boat, and 500 wooded acres for hiking and cross-country skiing.

Doubles, $65 to $80. No smoking. Closed part of April and November.

The English House, Route 4 & 11, Box 162, Andover 03216. (603) 735-5987.

Gillian Smith, a talented craftswoman, and her husband Ken moved from Surrey, England, in 1986 to open a B&B with an English name and tradition next to the Proctor Academy campus. "The house looked derelict from the outside, like a brown tooth in a jaw," recalls Ken. "I first saw it two months after Gillian bought it and was horrified."

Hard work, arty touches and good taste have transformed seven bedrooms on three floors into accommodations of distinction. There's afternoon tea, of course, served with cakes or biscuits. An attractive dining room with windsor chairs is the setting for a full breakfast: fruit salad, a choice of five juices, granola with twelve ingredients, and scrambled eggs with bacon or pancakes. Sometimes there's kedgeree made with haddock or smoked cod from Canada.

All seven guest rooms have private baths. Decorated in bright colors, most are spacious and accented by wicker, plants, dhurrie rugs, quilts and landscape paintings done by a relative who is a watercolorist of some repute, Ken says. We were intrigued by one room with a niche above the bed containing a painting framed by plants.

Guests use an attractive living room with TV and fireplace, and may get a peek at Gillian's studio, where she teaches classes in needlecrafts.

Doubles, $60.

Dexter's Inn and Tennis Club, 150 Stagecoach Road, Sunapee 03782. (603) 763-5571 or (800) 232-5571.

Its facilities and location a mile or so up a country lane, high above Lake Sunapee, make this self-contained small resort a retreat for sports enthusiasts.

The main house, painted a pale yellow, was built in 1801, extensively remodeled in 1930 and converted into an inn in 1948. Longtime innkeeper Frank Simpson turned over the reins in 1988 to his son-in-law and daughter, Mike and Holly Simpson Durfor, but still lives next door and retains the title of innkeeper emeritus. It was he who added "Tennis Club" to the name in 1973. Tennis buffs have use of three all-weather courts, with a tennis pro and tennis shop at hand, "and we've never heard of anyone who didn't get enough court time," Frank says proudly.

Tennis players — and others, for this is by no means exclusively a tennis resort — can cool off in the attractive swimming pool. The twenty-acre property offers shuffleboard, croquet and a horseshoe pit.

The sports theme continues inside the large barn recreation room, with bumper pool and pingpong tables.

The main inn has a long narrow entry with red velvet Victorian chairs, a living room full of chintz and walls of books, a pine-paneled lounge with games, fireplace and an alcove for TV, and a small gift shop. Particularly appealing is the screened porch with more chintz and wicker, a ceiling painted with red and white stripes, and tables covered in red and white oilcloth.

All ten guest rooms in the main inn and seven in the annex have private baths. Each is decorated in vivid colors coordinated with the striking wallpapers. The front rooms offer glimpses of the distant lake. Rooms in the annex and barn have high ceilings; one has twin canopy beds, another has sliding doors leading to a patio, and all are bright and cheery.

Coffee and juice are served in the bedrooms (and you could have your whole meal there), but most guests gather for breakfast near the bay window in the dining room for a view of the lake. In summer, salads and sandwiches are served for lunch on an outdoor terrace.

Dinners are table d'hote, the fixed menu augmented by a nightly special. A soup like chilled melon and a salad of tossed greens or kidney beans lead off the meal. The four

Lake Sunapee is on view in distance from the Inn at Sunapee.

entrees might be honey-sesame chicken, scallops baked with cheddar cheese and sauterne, lamb chops or filet mignon. Desserts could be homemade cheesecake, lemon meringue pie and chocolate crepes with strawberries.

Doubles, $110 to $150, MAP. Bed and breakfast available May, June and September, $85 to $125 double. Open May-October.

The Inn at Sunapee, Burkehaven Hill Road, Box 336, Sunapee 03782. (603) 763-4444.

Kate Crawford, who formerly managed the Highland House in Vermont and before that was a Washington lobbyist, found a home for herself and her possessions at the Inn at Sunapee, which she acquired in 1985. Although the previous owners had done basic renovations, the inn was in need of some cosmetics and deplasticizing, which Kate has accomplished with great success.

Perched high on a hill, with a distant view of Lake Sunapee and the surrounding mountains, the inn has spacious grounds with a swimming pool and tennis courts, and there's a decidedly "out-in-the-country" feel to it. Beyond the pool are four motel-like units and an old milk house that was being turned into a honeymoon cottage.

The rest of the sixteen rooms are on two floors of the main inn. All have private baths and there are family suites, one with two bedrooms and one with three. All have been freshly painted and have new wallpaper, painted floors and scatter rugs. A local seamstress made pillow covers from Kate's grandmother's linens. Armoires and dressers from her family are in some. Kate has mimeographed a personal guide called "Pretty and Interesting Places" that's helpful for first-time visitors.

Guests gather on overstuffed chairs or at the bar in a cheery fireplaced lounge, where the walls are decorated with Grandmother's gilt paintings on glass and an old ship's masthead.

Breakfast, which on summer days can be taken on the back deck, includes fresh fruit, a choice of eggs, pancakes or french toast, and sausage or bacon. On terribly creative mornings, says Kate, "we might do omelets or eggs ranchero." Skiers could find hot cider and cookies in the lounge when they come back, tired and hungry. Dinner in the inn's pleasant dining room (see below) is a treat.

As this edition went to press, the inn was for sale, but Kate was sure that a new owner would continue it as an inn.

Doubles, $79; family suites, $110 to $140.

Mountain Lake Inn, Route 114, Box 443, Bradford 03221. (603) 938-2136.

Carol and Phil Fullerton of suburban Montreal spent six years looking for a country inn of their own and found it the night they stayed here. They bought it the next day.

That was early in 1987, and Carol — who ran a catering business at home — has gained a reputation for her country cooking. She and her husband have upgraded the nine homey guest rooms, all now with private baths. Stenciling, attractive quilts, wallpapers, eyelet curtains, paintings, the inn's own soaps and Phil's grandfather's clock, an 1820 Scottish gem, grace the rooms. Contemporary furnishings blend unobtrusively with American and English antiques in an atmosphere that lives up to the Fullertons' description as "small, relaxed, cozy and comfortable."

The front parlor, wallpapered with Currier and Ives prints, has a large fireplace. A screened porch looks down across the highway to Lake Massasecum, where the Fullertons have seven acres of frontage and a private sandy beach.

Breakfast with five kinds of fruit, four kinds of muffins, cereal, scrambled eggs and sausage or perhaps eggs Benedict are served in the spacious Pine Room, aptly named and with a rooster atop the wood stove and big windows onto the front lawn.

Optional dinners are served Wednesday-Sunday for $15 at polished wood tables covered with woven mats and surrounded by mismatched chairs. Dinner is at 6:30, following a half hour of hors d'oeuvres and cocktails. A typical meal would be cold cucumber soup, garden salad, gingered chicken breasts with lime, whole-grain rice and honey-tarragon carrots, and kahlua or blueberry pie.

Doubles, $70 to $80.

Pleasant Lake Inn, Pleasant Street, Box 1030, New London 03257. (603) 526-6271.

Down a long hill north out of New London at the end of Pleasant Lake is the area's oldest operating inn.

"The view from our front window is the most spectacular in the area," claim innkeepers Grant and Margaret Rich, and they could be right. The exceptional setting with a beach across the road and Mount Kearsarge at the far end of the lake has attracted visitors for more than 100 years.

All twelve guest rooms on the second and third floors have private baths. "We've been adding baths left and right since we took over with one private bath in 1983," says Marilyn. She's particularly proud of the second-floor rooms that have been completely refurbished in what she calls country antiques style. Her favorite is No.7 with a brass bed, an armoire with an old marble sink, and blue floral Laura Ashley wallpaper that she hung herself.

For years, the handsome dining room was the main attraction, although that has changed with the upgrading of rooms and the downscaling of the restaurant (now open to the public only by reservation made before 2 p.m.). The wraparound flagstone patio room that originally served as the restaurant is now a wicker sun porch and a family room with TV, upright piano and games.

Dinner is served at heavy barnwood tables in a small front room with bare wood floor, oriental carpet and a view of Pleasant Lake. The tariff varies with the changing, no-choice menu. One night it was $13 for fresh fruit, spinach salad, lasagna with marinated mushrooms and garlic bread, spumoni and cookies. The next it was $17.50

for vichyssoise, caesar salad, duck with cointreau sauce, rice and green beans, topped off by chocolate icebox cake. The house Georges Duboeuf wine is dispensed from a small service bar.

For breakfast, guests have the choice of eggs, pancakes, french toast and "Whatchamacallit" — scrambled egg on English muffin with cheese and sausage. Doubles, $75 to $80.

Dining Spots

New London Inn, Main Street, New London. (603) 526-2791.

This inn's serene dining room, with its wondrous windows yielding full-length views of the colorful gardens outside, offered up one of the best meals of our travels lately.

Chef Mary Richter, who trained at the Culinary Institute of America, changes portions of her menu nightly. Among appetizers ($4 to $6.95), perhaps warm asparagus strudel or oysters poached in champagne on artichoke bottoms, we shared — for obvious reasons — one priced at the low end: roasted garlic puree served with crostini and tiny nicoise olives. Really zippy! Italian, zucchini and corn breads were accompanied by swirls of butter. Next came a perfect green salad dressed with a mellow raspberry and walnut vinaigrette and pretty as a picture with two raspberries and edible nasturtiums on a white plate.

The main courses ($16 to $18.50) were triumphs. One was grilled lamb medallions with a smoked tomato coulis sauce and roasted eggplant and the other was grilled Maine rabbit with a spicy mole sauce and corn flower pasta. Vegetables came family-style: green beans with bacon and potatoes with balsamic vinegar, served at room temperature.

Desserts included a marvelous peach clafouti with vanilla-bean ice cream, bittersweet chocolate torte with brandied raspberries and creme fraiche, and homemade plum ice cream.

The flawless service included a complete change of silver with each course and provision of real wine globes for our $13.50 bottle of Tyrell's Long Flat Red, a zesty Australian from the well-stocked cellar. Wines are remarkably priced from $7.50 to $27.50 (for a 1982 Margaux).

The airy room is a match for the meal: pale green wallpaper depicting white peacocks and well-spaced tables flanked by windsor chairs and set with dark green cloths, white china, hurricane lamps and vases of alstroemeria.

Dinner nightly, 6 to 8:30; closed Sunday and Monday in winter and spring.

Seven Hearths, Old Route 11, Sunapee. (603) 763-5657.

The suave, handwritten menu changes nightly in the restaurant at this elegant inn. Candles, lanterns and recessed lighting illuminate the dark main dining room, pretty as a picture with pink and plum linens accented by vases of fresh flowers, wide pine floors, bay window and a hearth with beehive oven. Another room has three tables with a view onto the spectacular gardens and pool area. A smaller room behind the dining room is good for private parties, of which Seven Hearths seems to have many.

Meals are preceded by cocktails in the inn's large living room. Inn guests are urged to be there 45 minutes before their dinner reservations for drinks and complimentary hors d'oeuvres (brie with crackers and hot cheese quiche strips, very good and very filling, the night we stayed). Co-innkeeper Miguel Ramirez, clad in white trousers, is a genial host and mixes hefty drinks. How the cocktail get-together works depends entirely on the crowd. The two of us shared the room with an outside party of five retired couples chatting about their golf games and, later, a group of eleven women educators; we felt a bit like intruders at a party.

New London Inn is known for some of the region's finest dining.

Chef Michael Rhodes's menu is $28, prix-fixe, including the hors d'oeuvres in the living room. Dinner begins with the night's soup, possibly chilled Georgia peach with sour cream or Mediterranean seafood bisque, or an appetizer like fresh asparagus flan over a tomato-basil coulis.

Five entrees are offered, perhaps roast duckling with apricot-ginger glaze, roast loin of Vermont lamb with a basil-garlic demi glace, broiled filet mignon with a green peppercorn sauce, and chicken breasts with mushrooms, scallions and artichoke hearts dijonnaise. We thought the last was excellent, as was a spicy shrimp dish with such bite as to leave the mouth burning. Duchess potatoes, broccoli fleurettes and vichy carrots were accompaniments, and the plate was decorated with nasturtiums.

A green salad with aioli-herb vinaigrette followed the main course.

Two desserts are offered daily: perhaps chocolate chocolate ganache torte and fresh raspberry tart with creme anglaise. The wine list is interesting but limited, starting in the high teens.

Dinner, Wednesday-Sunday 6 to 8:30, Thursday-Saturday in winter. Reservations required.

The Inn at Sunapee, Burkehaven Hill Road, Sunapee. (603) 763-4444.

The dining room at the Inn at Sunapee is cheery, granting wondrous views of the lake and mountains through bay windows. Paper narcissuses in the windows and flowers on the white-linened tables add to the color, and a gorgeous accent is the breakfront that belonged to innkeeper Kate Crawford's grandfather, who was involved in the China Trade era, filled with her grandmother's Royal Worcester plates.

The chef has devised a menu that keeps diners coming back for more. Appetizers ($3.75 to $7.75) include baked brie, gravlax and shrimp and avocado in a spicy smoked pepper sauce. For entrees ($10.50 to $16), choose among grilled Norwegian salmon, cornish game hen in lemon tarragon marinade, shrimp in garlic cream over pasta, grilled sirloin or steak au poivre. Kate's aim is for "sophisticated country dining" and she feels strongly about using local produce, going so far as to find someone to raise corn-fed chickens for her.

Desserts by the former pastry chef from Boston's Museum of Fine Arts are knockouts. Raspberry chocolate torte, old-fashioned peach cobbler, chocolate cherry cake and Austrian nut roll are specialties. The limited wine list is reasonably priced.

Dinner nightly except Monday, 6 to 8:30.

Woodbine Cottage, River Road, Sunapee Harbor. (603) 763-2222.

Eleanor Hill, a very peppy 83, is still much involved in the restaurant she and her late husband Bob began 62 years ago in their home. They had a small screened porch that they built around and, says she, it just grew from there. Now a thriving enterprise, the vine-covered cottage incorporates two pine-paneled inner dining rooms and a garden porch beyond, as well as a large gift shop, for which Mrs. Hill is the buyer. Next door is the Holly Shop, chock full of everything for Christmas.

Lunch, tea and dinner are served. In fact, the atmosphere is rather endearingly tea roomish, with lacy paper mats on the tables. An arrangement of mums and berries is over the mantel of the fireplace (which is lit on cool days), and gorgeous flower gardens, spotlit at night, are outside. Each table sports a different colored candle and flowers to coordinate.

"Full-course luncheons" (meaning with soup or juice, muffin, relish tray, salad wagon, vegetable, potato, dessert and beverage) are priced from $9.95 for turkey pie or grilled sandwich to $14.25 for lobster salad or newburg. Ordered a la carte, sandwiches and salads are in the $2 to $5 range. At teatime you may have, for $4.50, tea sandwiches and cake or a fruit salad, with tea in a proper pot.

Full dinners are $14.95 for chicken and mushroom casserole to $18.95 for steak, lobster salad or newburg. This is good solid New England fare — broiled halibut, salmon or Cape scallops, roasts and chops.

Desserts get the most raves at Woodbine. Among the goodies are strawberry shortcake, pecan, date macaroon and chiffon pies, tortes, cheesecake, homemade

Woodbine Cottage started as a porch and grew from there.

sherbets and ice creams, served with a choice of six sauces including French apricot and ginger, and frozen cake balls (choose your own flavor of ice cream and sauce). Fresh fruit in season, meringue glace and Dixie crunch ice-cream ball are more.

A little cookbook of "Our Favorite Recipes" is for sale in the gift shops, as are jars of the house caesar salad dressing.

Lunch, tea and dinner daily daily except Monday; Sunday brunch, 10 to 3. Open May to mid-October.

Millstone Restaurant, Newport Road, New London. (603) 526-4201.

A lofty cathedral ceiling with skylights lends an airy feel to this casually elegant place that is popular with the Colby-Sawyer College crowd. Owned by Tom Mills, who has another Millstone in Concord, it has a pleasant, canopied brick terrace for dining in the summer. Inside are well-spaced tables, covered with beige linen and blue napkins.

Entrees ($10.50 to $17.95) on the large and varied dinner menu run the gamut from pasta dishes (scampi on angel hair is one), Swiss-style veal and Bavarian schnitzel to pork tenderloin oriental (served with the house sweet and sour apricot-plum sauce), sweetbreads mimosa (glazed in an orange-champagne sauce) and charbroiled New Zealand venison with chambord sauce.

Among appetizers ($3.95 to $5.95) are stuffed artichoke hearts, grilled Carolina quail on Texas toast, and hummus served with Syrian bread points. Desserts include profiteroles aux chocolat, pecan flan, Belgian chocolate mousse pie and maple-syrup cream custard.

The same desserts are on the lunch menu, as are some of the interesting entrees, plus an array of salads, sandwiches and omelets. Eggs Benedict and florentine as well as entree specialties are available at Sunday brunch.

Lunch daily, 11:30 to 2:30; dinner from 5:30; Sunday brunch, 11 to 2:30.

Peter Christian's, Main Street, New London. (603) 526-4042.

A spinoff of its Hanover namesake, Peter Christian's occupies intimate, dark quarters with low beamed ceilings and booths in the mid-section of the former Edgewater Inn.

The fare and prices on the all-day menu are geared to the college crowd. A handful of dinner entrees runs from $6.25 for beef stew, served with salad and bread, to $10.50 for hot crab and cheese bake or chicken breast stuffed with shrimp and mushrooms. There are Chinese chicken stir-fry, quiche du jour (summer squash when we visited) and, for starters, spinach and ham balls to be dipped in mustard, boursin cheese and crackers, parmesan artichoke dip and, natch, nachos. Three cheese and meat boards are priced from $4.50 to $5.95. Desserts include rum fudge mousse, fudge swirl cheesecake, hot fudge sundae and, if you're not into fudge, strawberry cream puff. The few wines are appealingly priced, by the glass or bottle.

Open daily, 11:30 to midnight.

Waterlilies, The Gallery, New London. (603) 526-2442.

A good place for a snack or lunch is this new cafe-deli-bakery in a shopping center on the Newport Road. You place your order at the counter, find a table and then hope the two meet (we say hope advisedly, for we had to ask twice whether our order had been overlooked — finally, the owner overheard and found to her chagrin that it had).

At any rate, when they finally arrived we enjoyed a curried carrot soup with a quiche St. Tropez and a grilled Canadian bacon and cheddar cheese sandwich. Sandwiches are priced from $2.75 to $3.95; the quiche with a salad, $2.95. Bagels, muffins, pastries, cheesecake and the like are offered from the bakery.

Open daily until 8 p.m.

Boats in busy Sunapee Harbor provide entertainment for outdoor patrons at Harbor View.

Gourmet Garden, Main Street, New London. (603) 526-6656.
Primarily known as a specialty-foods shop par excellence ("send something tasteful with a local flavor"), this establishment run by Sarah and Michael Cave also puts up great salads and sandwiches to go. Curried chicken with water chestnuts and tortellini with artichoke hearts and turkey are two of the salads. Smoked turkey or ham, summer sausage and pate sandwiches are $3.95. Locally baked German nut corners, Ishler tortes, madeleines and florentiniers are available, as are natural juices, wine and beer. Gift boxes contain all kinds of New Hampshire goodies.

Harbor View, Sunapee Harbor. (603) 763-4777.
There's nothing special about this long, narrow room with white-and-blue oilclothed tables and a rear deck with open-air bar, tables and umbrellas. Nothing special, that is, except for the view of the water and the harbor goings-on. You can't get much closer to the water without being on or in it.
The old Dock and Boathouse Tavern was upgraded in 1988 by a restaurateur from Hanover, although its status was uncertain pending harbor redevelopment in 1989. Soups, salads and sandwiches were the all-day fare ($5 to $7), plus a few more substantial items up to $9.25, like pasta of the day, chicken dijonnaise and shrimp kabob. Out front, and open to the Harbor View, is a Haagen-Dazs ice-cream stand.
Lunch, 11:30 to 3; dinner, 5:30 to 9; seasonal.

Diversions

Cultural offerings. For 55 years, the **New London Barn Players,** New Hampshire's longest operating summer theater, have presented matinee and nightly performances of musicals and comedies from mid-June to Labor Day. Seven Thursday evening concerts are staged in a pops atmosphere during the **Summer Music Associates** series at King Ridge ski area. Sunday afternoon concerts feature guest performers throughout the summer at **Saint Gaudens National Historic Site** at Cornish. Despite its generally low-key flavor, the area bustles during the League of New Hampshire Craftsmen's annual crafts fair, the nation's oldest, which attracts 1,500 craftsmen and 50,000 visitors for a week in early August to Mount Sunapee State Park.

Mount Sunapee State Park. A 700-foot-long beach is great for swimming in the crystal-clear waters of Lake Sunapee. Across the road is the 2,700-foot high Mount Sunapee, criss-crossed with hiking and ski trails and its summit lodge accessible in summer and winter by a 6,800-foot-long gondola lift. The park is also the site of such special events as a gem and mineral festival, the Great American Milk Bicycle Race and the New England championship Lake Sunapee Bike Race.

Sports. All the usual are available, plus some in abundance. Golfers have their choice of four semi-public country clubs and smaller courses: the venerable Lake Sunapee Country Club and Inn, the hilly and challenging Eastman Golf Links in Grantham, picturesque Twin Lakes Villa beside Little Sunapee, and the Country Club of New Hampshire, rated one of the nation's top 75 public courses by Golf Digest. Downhill skiers get their fill at Mount Sunapee or King Ridge ski areas, and cross-country skiers take over the fairways at the area's golf clubs in winter.

Lake excursions. From Sunapee Harbor, the 150-passenger M.V. Mt. Sunapee II gives 90-minute narrated tours the length of Lake Sunapee at 10 a.m. and 2:30 p.m. daily from mid-June to Labor Day, and 2:30 weekends in spring and fall. The steamer M.V. Kearsarge offers buffet-supper cruises at 5:30 and 7:45 nightly in summer. Another way to view the lake is to drive the Scenic Three-Mile Loop around Sunapee Harbor; you'll find striking new houses interspersed with old traditional cottages.

Shopping. For a town its size, New London has more than its share of good shopping — spread out along much of the length of Main Street and clustered in shopping centers and a new mall along Route 11 on the southwest edge of town. **Campion's** for clothing and **Kearsarge Bookshelf** are highlights of the attractive new Gallery Mall. Along Main Street are shops like **Pennyweights,** a jewelry store under the New London Inn, good crafts stores like **Artisans Workshop** and the **Crafty Goose,** and the kind of clothing stores one finds in college towns like the **College Sport Shop. C.B. Coburn** has "unique gifts for home and palate." In Guild, to the southwest of Sunapee, is the **Dorr Mill Store,** a large and attractive shop specializing in woolens. Despite its location at the mill, this is no mill outlet and the prices are what you'd expect to pay back home.

Extra-Special

The Saint-Gaudens National Historic Site, Route 12-A, Cornish. (603) 675-2175..

If the Sunapee region's lakes and mountains are a place for reflection as well as activity, the house and property of noted turn-of-the-century sculptor Augustus Saint-Gaudens is its epitome. It is here that he did some of his best work, set up his own bowling green and nine-hole golf course, and gathered literary and artistic luminaries who formed the Cornish Colony (artist Maxfield Parrish's home is just up the road). Like the sculptures for which he is known, the artist molded his 149-acre estate to suit his creative vision. Besides the white-columned "little studio" he fashioned from a barn, there are sunken gardens, high hedges and reflecting pools, a tree-lined walk, a bowling green and, tucked into appropriate niches, copies or casts of his best-known works. Three main-floor rooms of his 200-year-old house are open for tours by the National Park Service. The important things are elsewhere on the property. Visitors are given a map to wander on their own through the gallery, the ravine studio, the temple and the rest to get a feeling for the man, his work and his special world. Open daily 8:30 to 4:30, late May-October; adults, $1.

Franconia-Sugar Hill, N.H.
The Road Less Traveled

The lines are from Robert Frost: "Two roads diverged in a wood, and I — I took the one less traveled by, and that has made all the difference."

They were written when the poet lived in Franconia beneath Cannon Mountain, and the road less traveled has made a difference historically in maintaining the Franconia area as an island of serenity just beyond the crowds.

Even the 1988 opening of the beautiful Franconia Notch Parkway connecting completed portions of Interstate 93 on either side of the notch failed to stimulate the hordes. "Many people don't know about our history and beauty," said former innkeeper Richard Bromberg. "They think that beyond the Old Man of the Mountains, there's just woods and Canada."

Indeed, Franconia and its upcountry neighbor, Sugar Hill, are remote and almost untouched by the usual trappings of tourism. They retain much of the look and the flavor of the late 19th century when they were noted mountain resort areas. In the 1930s, Austrian Sig Buchmayer established the country's first ski school at Peckett's-on-Sugar Hill (now designated by a primitive historic marker) and Cannon Mountain dedicated skiing's first aerial tramway.

But for the mystique of the name, one might not be aware of the area's storied past. Gone are the large hotels and, as ski areas go, Cannon keeps a low profile. Today, the crowds and the condos stop at Franconia Notch to the south, leaving Cannon Mountain, Franconia, Sugar Hill and even the "city" of Littleton for those who appreciate them as vestiges of the past.

For those who want action, the magnificent Franconia Notch State Park stretching eight miles through the notch offers some of the Northeast's most spectacular sights and activities.

But the road less traveled takes one beyond. There are few better places for fall foliage viewing than from Sunset Hill or the ridge leading up to Sugar Hill above Franconia. The heights afford sweeping vistas of the towering White Mountains on three sides and toward Vermont's Green Mountains on the fourth.

In winter, downhill skiers can revel in the challenges of Cannon Mountain, the venerable World Cup area so full of skiing history that the New England Ski Museum is located at its base.

In spring and summer, the quiet pleasures of an area rich in history and character suffice. The Frost Place, the Sugar Hill Historical Museum and the Sugar Hill Sampler are classics of their genre.

Don't expect trendy inns, fancy restaurants or tony shops. Immerse yourself instead in the beauty and the serenity of New England as it used to be.

It's little wonder that long after he left, poet Frost wrote, "I am sitting here thinking of the view from our house in Franconia." It's unforgettable.

Inn Spots

Rabbit Hill Inn, off Route 18, Lower Waterford, Vt. 05848. (802) 748-5168.

If you have an iota of romance in your soul, you'll love this white-columned inn in a tiny hillside hamlet just across the Connecticut River from New Hampshire. Where else would you find, upon retiring to your room after a candlelight dinner, the beds turned down, the radio playing soft music, the lights turned off, a candle flickering in

Robert Frost worked at this desk in Franconia with a view of Cannon Mountain.

a hurricane lamp, and a small stuffed and decorated heart on the bed to use as a "do not disturb" sign and yours to take home?

That's just a sample of the care and concern that Maureen and John Magee, who bought this venerable inn in April 1987, show for their guests. "We set the stage," says Maureen, who has an air for the theatrical, "and our guests are the players." Upon arrival, John is apt to greet you with a "welcome to our home" and in your room is a personal note of welcome from Maureen. You'll find iced tea, flavored with red clover, and delicious chocolate-chip cookies in the afternoon in the cozy parlor. Next to it is a pub, the Snooty Fox, with comfortable sofas as well as game tables. Across the road is a pond for swimming and fishing with a small gazebo nearby.

The eighteen guest rooms, all with private baths, are in the main inn, a carriage wing and a building next door. The last has a gift shop, the **Crafty Rabbit,** and a newly decorated common room where wintertime guests often find chili or stew on the stove, mulled cider, and even maple syrup on snow accompanied by pickles.

The Magees have decorated with loving care. Each room has a theme and some have working fireplaces with, of course, andirons in the shape of rabbits. In Caroline's Chamber, the bed is draped with blue curtains. The Samuel Colby suite (named after the original owner in the late 18th century) has a king bed covered with lacy pillows and a Georgian fireplace. Even in the carriage wing, where the rooms are in a motel-like configuration, they are done in a most unmotel-like way. Our room, Clara's Chamber, was named for Maureen's grandmother and contained many mementos of her life as well as the standard room diary in which guests describe their feelings and rave about the innkeepers.

Two front porches, one on the second floor, are where guests like to sit and watch the distant mountains. There's a reading nook upstairs, and downstairs in the parlor Maureen keeps adding to a collection of books written by guests. Everywhere are rabbit items, many of them gifts sent by people who have stayed here.

Breakfast is an event at Rabbit Hill; it is served in the dining room from 8:15 but you can find coffee in the pub earlier. To the accompaniment of "The Sound of Music," we enjoyed fresh orange juice, a cup of melon pieces and tiny blueberries, and a poached egg on a croissant with cheese sauce, homefries and bacon. The music and the entree change daily, but you might hit the day they're serving the breakfast banana split with yogurt. And the granola is so good that guests buy packages to take home.

The inn's restaurant is considered among the best in the area (see Dining Spots).

Doubles, $110 to $160, MAP; deluxe fireplaced suites, $180.

Sugar Hill Inn, Route 117, Franconia 03580. (603) 823-5621.

Nestled into the side of Sugar Hill, this old white inn, built as a farmhouse in 1789, its wraparound porch sporting colorfully padded white wicker furniture and a telescope for viewing Cannon Mountain, welcomes guests all year except for spring mud season.

When Barbara and Jim Quinn of Rhode Island took over as innkeepers in 1986, they knew they'd see deer but were quite unprepared for the bear that "pitched his camp at our dumpster for the summer," Barbara recalls. The bear since has departed, but the deer remain.

The ten inn rooms, all with private baths, exude country charm, with hand-stenciling, rocking chairs, quilts, eyelet curtains, and even a teeny pillow shaped like a duck on most beds. All rooms are different, with choice of twin, double, queen and king beds.

The six cottage units in back (not open in winter, because the water lines freeze) are nicely done, some with stenciling, and with new front porches, plush carpeting and television sets.

Two living rooms in the inn are available for guests. One next to the dining room is rather formal with a white brick fireplace and a piano, and the other has a small TV set.

Breakfast is an occasion, with enough food for a lumberjack, as our waitress said. First course is choice of juice and a homemade muffin (ours was zucchini-walnut and outstanding), followed by a dish of fresh fruit in season (blueberries and peaches at our September visit) and then a choice of several hot dishes. We can only say that the eggs Benedict were splendid and as for the country souffle, we requested the recipe to add to our repertoire.

Dinner is served nightly from 6:30 to 7:30 in fall and winter and on summer weekends to house guests.

The dining room is country-pretty, with dark green and rose calico quilted mats on the polished tables, draperies to match, Hitchcock chairs, and spotlit theorem paintings on velvet. A white candle in a hurricane lamp and a small carafe of flowers (fall asters, on our visit) are on each table.

Jim Quinn does the cooking, a talent harkening back to his days in the grocery business in Westerly, R.I. He offers a choice of two entrees a night from a repertoire of beef Wellington, veal Oscar, baked stuffed shrimp and chicken Washington, a breast stuffed with crabmeat and topped with hollandaise. Guests trade recipes to obtain the one for mushroom dill soup, and many are partial to the salad of broccoli, raisins and almonds with a sweet and sour dressing. A choice of homemade pies with ice cream is the usual dessert. The inn has a full liquor license.

As we were warned upon making our reservations, there is no smoking anywhere in this inn (we did spot an ashtray on the porch), a rule we heartily endorse.

Doubles, spring and summer, $90, B&B. Rest of year, $140 to $150, MAP.

Carriage is trademark of Sugar Hill Inn.

Franconia Inn, Easton Road, Franconia 03580. (603) 823-5542.

Classically situated by a meadow with Cannon Mountain as a backdrop, this rambling white structure looks the way you think a country inn should look and is the area's largest and busiest. "We have a reputation for lots of activities," says Alec Morris, innkeeper with his brother Richard for their parents who run a resort in the Ozarks.

Thirty-four rooms on two floors have been gradually upgraded since the Morrises took over the vacant inn in 1980 after it had lapsed into bankruptcy. Most of the changes were cosmetic, but every guest room now claims a private bath and carpeting.

Rooms vary in size and beds; some connect to become family suites. The Morrises are gradually upgrading the room decor, adding matching window cornices and bedspreads. We liked pine-paneled Room 27 with a pencil-post, canopied queensize bed, a duck bedspread, matching curtains and a lamp base in the shape of a duck. The corner rooms are best in terms of size and view.

The main floor has an attractive dining room (see below), living room and oak-paneled library with fireplaces, a pool room, a game room with pinball machines, and a screened porch with wicker furniture overlooking a large swimming pool. Downstairs is the spacious **Rathskeller Lounge,** with entertainment at night, and beyond, a hot tub in a large redwood room.

Outside there is swimming in the pool or in a secluded swimming hole in the Ham Branch River. Four clay tennis courts and a glider/bi-plane facility are across the street ("soaring lets you see the mountains from the ultimate vantage point — the sky," says Alec Morris). The stables next door house five horses for trail rides in what the inn touts as a western adventure. In the winter, the barn turns into a cross-country ski center; sleigh rides and snowshoeing are other activities. Movies are shown every night.

Doubles, $65 to $85; family suites with connecting bath, $110 to $120. For MAP, add $27.50 per adult. Closed most of April and May, and from mid-October to mid-December.

Lovett's Inn By Lafayette Brook, Profile Road, Franconia 03580. (603) 823-7761 or (800) 356-3802.

Although this inn, a fixture for two generations, added a swimming pool a few years ago for its summer clientele, it's at its best in the winter — and we'll always remember it that way. We were lucky enough to stumble into one of its fireplaced cottages during a snowstorm nearly twenty years ago and liked it so well we stayed for two nights.

Many of the patrons have been coming here for years, such was the spell that longtime innkeeper Charles H. Lovett Jr. and family cast on his inn and dining room. Jim Peters, a ten-year employee who became innkeeper for the new owners in 1987, was maintaining the reputation and upgrading the decor.

The main house, dating from 1784, has seven guest rooms (three with private baths) upstairs, an acclaimed dining room, a basement rec room, a living room with TV and an adjoining sun porch full of video games — great for the kids while parents linger over dinner. The porch is used as a cross-country ski center in winter. The rooms here are simple but adequate and bear a few interesting decorative touches.

Summer or winter, we'd choose one of the sixteen cottages in duplex chalets scattered beside the pool and around the lawns. Each has a small patio with chairs for gazing upon Cannon Mountain in summer. The nine with fireplaces are positively idyllic on chilly nights. All have sitting areas and small television sets. The elongated narrow bathrooms at the rear are ingenious as well as serviceable.

A full breakfast, including shirred eggs with mushrooms or herbed tomatoes, and several renditions of pancakes (including chocolate or parsnip!), is served, as is dinner (see below).

Doubles, $82 to $132, MAP; off-season, $35 to $55, EP.

Beal House Inn, 247 West Main St., Littleton 03561. (603) 444-2661.

A large, cheery breakfast room chock full of antiques, where guests eat on blue and white willow china at a long table covered by a red cloth, is the central feature of the B&B and antiques shop run by Ann and Jim Carver and their sons in the heart of Littleton. A collection of 93 antique cookie jars — "the largest in the north country," says Ann — is prominently displayed on shelves at the end of the breakfast room.

All the antiques here — as well as in the cluttered, cozy parlor, the glassed-in front porch furnished in wicker, up the various staircases and in the fourteen guest rooms — are a logical extension of the Carvers' antiques shop in the barn, connected to the inn by a carriage house.

Besides the public rooms, guests have use of an outdoor deck up a hill in back of the house, illuminated at night.

Rooms are furnished with four-poster, canopied, brass and spool beds, colorful quilts, hooked and braided rugs, wing chairs and rockers. The front-corner Garden Room on the main floor is attractive with wicker chairs and a queensize four-poster bed. The canopy bed in the back Lavender Room, named for the hillside of lilacs and wildflowers outside its windows, has a lovely decorator coverlet; the towels and shower curtain in the bathroom are a striking lavender.

Twelve of the fourteen rooms on the main floor, upstairs and in the annex have private baths. Rooms at the rear of the house, away from the street, are quieter.

Hot popovers are the Carvers' specialty at breakfast, which also includes seven kinds of juices, scrambled eggs, waffles, bacon and sausage. A fire blazes in the brick fireplace, and the conversations are spirited — "where else can you talk with people from six other areas of the country at once?" asks Ann. Coffee and 50 varieties of herbal tea are offered at breakfast, as well as all day long.

Doubles, $40 to $90.

The Horse and Hound Inn, Wells Road, Franconia 03580. (603) 823-5501.

A secluded farmhouse converted into an inn in the 1940s, the Horse and Hound has twelve guest rooms, six with private bath.

Rooms vary in size and decor — the tiny Honeymoon Room is so named because "it's all bed," according to a former innkeeper. The Meditation Room, with a view onto the rear yard and hillside, is done in shades of blue, with blue velvet chairs and a blue tiled bathroom.

The rear lounge is called the library because of its large collection of books and magazines, plus games and stereo. A pleasant patio overlooks the rear gardens. Three fireplaces in the lobby and dining rooms warm things up in winter.

Breakfast and dinner are served in two rustic, beamed dining rooms made attractive by tall white candles, white linen, brown carpeting and beige napkins intricately folded on white and green floral china.

Appetizers are standard, from baked French onion soup to shrimp cocktail ($2.50 to $5.95). Entrees ($12.50 to $20.95) are more ambitious, with three versions of roast Long Island duckling (l'orange, Normandy and Bombay), scampi a la francaise and steak au poivre.

Homemade Thomas Jefferson ice cream, Swiss pastry and "fancy pie" — a cross between pudding and cake with a dollop of blueberry sauce — are favorite desserts. Two dozen wines are priced from $7.50 to $37.

Dinner nightly, 5:30 to 9:30, June-October and winter holiday weeks; Thursday-Sunday in winter.

Doubles, $55 to $80. Closed April and November.

The Inn at Forest Hills, Route 142, Franconia 03580. (603) 823-5525.

Once the private reception house for the old Forest Hills Hotel and later the residence of the president of the short-lived Franconia College, this 1894 English Tudor-style mansion has been a B&B since 1987.

Seven guest rooms on three floors are nicely appointed with oriental rugs, colorful fabrics and plump quilts. Some are unusually spacious with intriguing alcoves and window seats, upholstered sofas and wicker chairs. Three have private baths.

Guests gather in a large, fireplaced living room or on the front veranda. Innkeeper Bernice Keeney, who leases the structure from the developer of the adjacent Forest Hills four-season recreation community, serves a full country breakfast.

Doubles, $50 to $80.

Dining Spots

Tim-Bir Alley, 28 Main St., Littleton. (603) 444-6142.

Tim and Biruta Carr, who both worked for the Sheraton Corporation and were transferred all over, met when they landed in Oklahoma City at the same time. When they decided to open a restaurant of their own in 1984, they settled in, of all places, Littleton, N.H.

Their teeny establishment is really down an alley and hard to find, but their menu is outstanding, the most sophisticated and inventive in the area.

With seven tables, seating 22 lucky people (plus a small counter with a few stools), their place is simple but pleasant. Glass covers the antique lace tablecloths, and a votive candle in a crystal bowl and a cactus plant are on each table. The cafe curtains are trimmed with eyelet embroidery, walls are hung with posters and macrame, and classical music plays at night.

The dinner menu changes weekly, with usually one soup, two appetizers and a pasta dish, and five entrees. Shrimp and corn chowder and cream of mushroom, leek and brie are a couple of the soups. Among other starters ($4.75 to $5) are grilled shrimp with zucchini cakes and basil hollandaise, terrine of three smoked seafoods, chilled fresh asparagus with smoked salmon mayonnaise or, our choice, an absolutely outstanding scallop mousse with fresh dill and dijon vinaigrette, more than enough for two to share. The house salad was an interesting mix of greens, mushrooms, red peppers and Swiss cheese, served on glass plates with piquant vinaigrette or blue cheese dressings.

Rabbit Hill Inn is nestled in trees on hillside that is Lower Waterford.

At $15.95, the mixed grill was the most expensive entree — an unusual mix of lamb chop with rosemary and feta, veal scaloppine with banana, rum and cream (rather sweet for our tastes) and tournedo of beef with choron sauce. It was beautifully presented around asparagus spears, red caviar on sour cream over roast potatoes, and bits of asparagus and zucchini in the middle. A smoky flavor pervaded the linguini with duck, scallions, tomato and smoked Swiss cheese ($10.25), an unusual and memorable combination.

Other entrees could be fresh swordfish with papaya salsa or pork scaloppine with plums, brie and brandy cream.

Desserts are limited, a pound cake with peach-blueberry sauce, a double chocolate pate with strawberry coulis and two ice creams when we visited. A carafe of the house Pierre Dourthe wine was a reasonable $8.

The lunches are just as good, we found on our latest visit. An excellent mixed salad with blue cheese dressing preceded an equally good linguini with tomatoes, artichoke hearts and goat cheese. The seafood citrus salad, also $6.95, was a bountiful plateful of shrimp, scallops, grapefruit and orange slices with a fruity dressing. The appetizer of shrimp mousse with two caviars at the next table looked so wonderful that we vowed to return another day to try it.

Lunch, Wednesday-Saturday 11:30 to 2; dinner, Thursday-Saturday 6 to 9; Sunday brunch, 9 to 1.

Rabbit Hill Inn, Lower Waterford, Vt. (802) 748-5168.

Innkeeper Maureen Magee keeps the doors to her dining room closed until dinner begins at 6, so that if it's your first visit, you will appreciate the drama of a room lit mostly by candles, silver gleaming on burgundy mats on polished wood tables, and napkins folded into pewter rings shaped like rabbits. Even the chandeliers have candles in them. Fresh flowers and porcelain bunnies on each table add to the charm, and a spinning wheel stands in the middle of the room.

Chef Bob Reney (aided by the Magees' son Jeremy as sous chef) offers some of the most interesting food in the area, with a choice of appetizer or soup, three entrees (four or five on weekends), salad and dessert. The cost to the public is a bargain $22 prix-fixe.

We feasted on cream of celery soup with pimento and chives and a small dish of tiny scallops in a dijon sauce on linguini, delicate salads with a creamy dressing, and a small loaf of piping-hot whole wheat bread served with the butter pat shaped like a bunny, with a sprig of parsley for its curly tail. Sorbet drenched in champagne cleared our palates for very spicy red snapper and a tender breast of chicken with a havarti cheese and dill sauce with sun-dried tomatoes. Sauteed potatoes shaped like mushrooms were a novel touch. A Beringer fume blanc ($16) went nicely with all this. With desserts of bourbon pecan pie and chocolate crepes with grand marnier sauce came brewed decaf coffee with chocolate shells filled with whipped cream to dunk in — a great idea!

Other nights might bring smoked salmon with cucumber-dill sauce, veal francais, rack of lamb with a plum-cranberry sauce, duck in a honey-pear sauce or a specialty of the house, trout with fresh fruit in a liqueur sauce.

Maureen, a classical flutist, often plays during dinner, but in the adjacent parlor, so as not, she says, to upstage the diners. The Magees' college-student son, Matthew, might join in on classical guitar in the summer. This is a quiet dining room, where no detail has been overlooked and solicitous service is well-paced. Plan on at least two hours for a fulfilling meal and evening.

Dinner nightly by reservation, 6 to 9.

Edencroft Manor, Route 135, Littleton. (603) 444-6776.

Although this inn has guest rooms and conference facilities, it is best known for its restaurant. New innkeepers Phil and Maryann Frasca, earlier of Marblehead, Mass., inherited chef Andrew Fink, who they found was so revered by the clientele that people visit the kitchen to shake his hand and one woman said she wanted to marry him.

Dining is in two formal, candlelit rooms with classical music as a backdrop. Entrees run from $9.50 for chicken citron to $17.95 for tournedos Rossini. Five presentations of veal (including one with shiitake mushrooms) and three of shrimp, filet of sole with peanuts, lamb chops with chutney and two fettuccines are among the choices.

Shrimp cocktail and oysters Rockefeller are the most expensive appetizers at $4.95. The dessert cart is laden with Maryann Frasca's pastry creations, among them praline and double chocolate cheesecakes, key lime pie, a variety of mousses and Aunt Agnes's snow pudding with fresh lemon dacquoise.

Upstairs are six large guest rooms, four with private baths, named for the colors that set the decorating theme. The rambling floor configuration is such that the entry to the green room with its two double beds covered with pink and green quilts is through the bathroom. A full breakfast for $3.50 is served guests in the sunny rear lounge. Doubles are $65 to $80.

Dinner, Tuesday-Saturday 5:30 to 9, Sunday 5:30 to 8.

Lovett's by Lafayette Brook, Profile Road, Franconia. (603) 823-7761.

The offerings of longtime chef Peter Tavino continue to please a coterie of regulars as well as visitors to the area. Before dinner, guests usually gather in the inn's small bar (where the marble bar is from a Newport mansion) for socializing. Then they're seated in one of the three beamed-ceilinged dining rooms for three-course table d'hote dinners priced at $20.

A plate of pates and cocktail spreads with crackers makes a good appetizer, as do things like fresh salmon mousse, tabouleh or cold poached striped bass with green yogurt sauce. Unusual soups include such summer offerings as cold bisque of fresh watercress with chervil, cold black bean soup with Demarara rum, wild White Mountain blueberry soup or strong mutton broth with fresh vegetables and barley.

Among the dozen entrees might be curried turkey or lamb with Lovett's grape chutney, sauteed Colorado trout, poached Norwegian salmon, veal marengo, chicken in apples and calvados, and such standbys as chicken livers, ham steak with gravy and broiled scrod.

The wine list, limited but serviceable, is pleasantly priced in the teens except for two red imports at $20 and $21.50.

Desserts are extravagant, from hot Indian pudding with ice cream to meringue glace with strawberries, macaroon crumble pie and butterscotch ice-cream puff. We remember with gusto the chocolatey Aspen crud from eighteen years ago and, yes, last we knew it was still on the menu. Some things, like Lovett's, don't change much over the years. And that's rather reassuring.

Dinner nightly, 6:30 to 7:45. Reservations required; jackets suggested.

Franconia Inn, Easton Road, Franconia. (603) 823-5542.

The large dining room with well-spaced tables and small-paned windows looking out toward the mountains rather resembles a ballroom. It's quite handsome with pink and white linens matching a new floral red carpet, peach walls and chairs with curved cane backs. The limited menu changes frequently and is considered locally a bit pricey.

A typical dinner might begin with escargots in puff pastry, broiled artichoke hearts or herring with sour cream and capers ($4.25 to $6.95). Entrees ($14.95 to $21.95) might be seafood pernod, veal Oscar, lamb chops dijon, spicy ginger shish kabob, filet mignon with pink peppercorn sauce and, for the vegetarian, fresh vegetables sauteed and served in a pastry shell.

"We're not all that elaborate with our desserts," says innkeeper Richard Morris. Cakes, pies and fruit melbas make up most of them. The many fancy after-dinner drinks and coffees are an alternative.

Dinner nightly, 6 to 9.

Sunset Hill House, Sunset Road off Route 117, Sugar Hill 03585. (603) 823-5522.

There could be no more spectacular setting for a restaurant/inn than the Sunset Hill ridge commanding nearly 180-degree vistas both east and west. The four adjoining dining rooms at Sunset Hill House take full advantage of the view to the east.

The rooms are formal: fireplaces, red draperies framing the views of Cannon Mountain, red coverings over the backs of the chairs, blue water glasses and fancy china.

The printed menu changes nightly. Table d'hote dinners including fruit cup, soup or juice, choice of dessert and beverages range from $14.95 to $16.90, according to entree. Billed as country French but surely Yankee American, typical offerings might be baked stuffed shrimp, broiled swordfish, roast leg of lamb with mint jelly, grilled ham steak and filet mignon. Some of the desserts are Indian pudding, pies, Harvey Wallbanger cake and creme de menthe parfait.

The inn, housed in what was once the annex of the original Sunset Hill House, has 35 rooms, most with private baths, available at $52.50 to $66 per person, MAP. In summer, the outdoor patio overlooking mountains and the free-form swimming pool and jacuzzi is a pleasant spot in which to relax.

Dinner nightly, 6:30 to 9.

Polly's Pancake Parlor, Hildex Maple Sugar Farm, Route 117, Sugar Hill. (603) 823-5575.

Polly and Wilfred "Sugar Hill" Dexter opened their pancake parlor in 1938, when they charged 50 cents for all you could eat, mainly to have a way to use up their maple syrup. Their daughter, Nancy Dexter Aldrich, and her husband Roger operate the farm

Lovett's By Lafayette Brook in winter.

and restaurant now. They charge considerably more than 50 cents, but it's still a bargain and a fun place to go for breakfast, lunch or early dinner and a slice of local life.

Bare tables sport red mats shaped like maple leaves, topped with wooden plates handpainted with maple leaves by Nancy Aldrich, who, in her red skirt and red bow, greets and seats diners. Red kitchen chairs and sheet music pasted to the ceiling add color to this 1820 building, once a carriage shed. Its most appealing feature is big louvred windows with a view of the gorgeous Mount Lafayette range beyond.

You can watch the pancakes being made in the open kitchen. The batter is poured from a contraption that ensures they measure exactly three inches.

Pancakes are served with maple syrup, granulated maple sugar and maple spread; an order of six costs $3.80 for plain pancakes made with white flour, buckwheat, whole wheat or cornmeal. All are available with blueberries, walnuts or coconut for $4.80. The Aldriches grind their own organically grown grains, and make their own breads, sausage and baked beans (with maple syrup, of course). Waffles, seven inches wide, are available in all the pancake versions, except for blueberry.

If, like us, you don't really crave pancakes in the middle of the day, try the homemade soups (lentil is especially good), quiche of the day (our ham and cheddar melted in the mouth) or a super good BLT made with cob-smoked bacon ($3.60). Cereals, eggs, muffins made with pancake batter, salads and sandwiches like grilled cheese and cob-smoked ham, croque monsieur, and even peanut butter with a maple spread are available.

The homemade pies, $2.75 (add $1 for a la mode), are outstanding. Hurricane sauce, made from apples, butter and maple syrup, is served over ice cream. The back of the menu lists, for extra-hearty eaters, all-you-can-eat prices.

No liquor is served, but the coffee, made with spring water, is great and, as a matter of fact, a glass of the spring water really hits the spot. In the shop you pass through to get to the dining room, you may purchase pancake packs, maple syrup and sugar, jams and jellies and even the maple-leaf painted plates. Polly's also does a large mail-order business.

Open Friday-Sunday from 7 a.m. to 7 p.m., Monday-Thursday 7 to 3, late April to late October.

Village House Restaurant, Route 18, Franconia. (603) 823-5912.

Pine-paneled walls covered with old signs and artifacts mark this family restaurant of the old school. It consists of a main dining room with a bar in the middle, a dining porch and the Tack Room lounge in back.

Three meals a day are served, including such breakfast items as Cajun eggs, breakfast burritos, apricot toast, raspberry crepes, and a bagelwich — "a little unorthodox, a grilled bagel topped with ham, bacon, tomato slices and cheese sauce" (the most expensive item at $4.25).

Dinner entrees ($8.50 to $14.95) run the gamut from Bombay or coconut chicken to scalloped oysters, Cajun scrod and New York strip steak. Five items combine sea and grill, and there are curried chicken casserole, California salad and burgers for lighter appetites.

Breakfast, 7:30 to 11; lunch, 11:30 to 2; dinner, 5:30 to 9.

Diversions

Franconia Notch State Park, south of Franconia. The wonders of one of the nation's most spectacular parks are well known. Thousands visit the Flume, a 700-foot-long gorge with cascades and pools (adults $4), and the Basin and gaze at the rock outcroppings, most notably the Old Man of the Mountains. Echo Lake at the foot of Cannon Mountain is fine for swimming. Cannon Mountain has retired its original 1938 aerial tramway but a modern replacement carries tourists to the summit for the views that skiers cherish — and gets them back down without the challenges that hardy skiers take for granted. In the large new visitor center at the southern entrance to the park, a good fifteen-minute movie chronicles years of change in the area and advises, "when you see Franconia Notch today, remember it will never be quite the same again."

Cannon Mountain. In an era of plasticized, free-wheeling skiing, the serious ski areas with character are few and far between. One of the last and best is Cannon, which considers itself the first major ski mountain in the Northeast (1937). Operated as a state park, it remains virginal and free of commercialism. The setting is reminiscent of the Alps, when you view the sheer cliffs and avalanche country across Franconia Notch on Lafayette Mountain and the majestic peaks of the Presidential Range beyond. From the summit, much of the skiing varies from tough to frightening, as befits the site of America's first racing trail and the first World Cup competition. But there is plenty of intermediate and novice skiing as well. Lift prices are downright bargains: $26 on weekends, $21 on weekdays, with a $4 surcharge for weekend use of the tram.

New England Ski Museum, next to the tram station at Cannon Mountain, Franconia. Skiers particularly will enjoy this small museum that opened in 1982 with themed displays that change annually. The maroon parka belonging to the founder of the National Ski Patrol is shown, as is a photo of him taken at Pecketts-on-Sugar-Hill. One of the more fascinating exhibits traces the evolution of ski equipment. "Ski Tracks" is an informative and impressive thirteen-minute audio-visual show with 450 slides tracing the history of New England skiing. Open daily 11-5, Memorial Day-Columbus Day; daily 11-4, Dec. 15-March 31. Adults $1.

Sugar Hill Historical Museum, Sugar Hill. Sugar Hill people say not to miss this choice small place, and they're right. Established as a Bicentennial project by proud descendants of Sugar Hill founders, it displays an excellent collection in a modern, uncluttered setting and gives a feel for the uncommon history of this small hilltop town, named for the sugar maples that still produce maple syrup ("everyone who can, taps the trees," reports museum director Mitchell Vincent). The life of the community is thoroughly chronicled in photographs and artifacts. The Cobleigh Room recreates a stagecoach tavern kitchen from nearby Lisbon, and the Carriage Barn contains mountain wagons and horse-drawn sleighs, including one from the Butternut estate that used to belong to Bette Davis. Open July-October, Thursdays and Saturdays 1 to 4, Sundays 2 to 5. Adults $1.

Sugar Hill Sampler, Route 117, Sugar Hill. A horse was grazing out front on our last visit to this place behind the Homestead Inn, where commercialism gives way to personality and history. The large dairy barn, with nooks and crannies full of New England items for souvenir shoppers, is literally a working museum of Sugar Hill history. Owner Barbara Serafini Parker is the sixth-generation descendant of one of Sugar Hill's founders and takes great pride in sharing her thoughts and possessions, even giving hand-written descriptions on the beams. In one rear section full of family memorabilia, she displays her grandmother's wedding gown, which she wore in a pageant written by her father and presented for President Eisenhower on the occasion of the Old Man of the Mountain's birthday in 1955. Amid all the memorabilia is an interesting selection of quaint and unusual merchandise, including maple syrup made by the Stewart family on Sugar Hill, and a special spiced tea mixture called Heavenly Tea. Many New Hampshire foods are featured, and you can taste samples of several of them. Toys and Christmas decorations are displayed in nooks off the main barn.

Shopping. In Sugar Hill, **Harman's Cheese and Country Store,** a tiny place with a large mail-order business, proclaims "the world's greatest cheddar cheese." Many of its food and local items are one-of-a-kind, according to owner Maxine Aldrich, who is carrying on the late Harman family tradition. In Franconia, the **Garnet Hill** catalog store shows fine bedclothes (English flannel sheets, comforters and the like), as well as pricey children's clothing, all in natural fibers, although you cannot buy anything here. Its main retail outlet is on Newbury Street in Boston — enough said. At the **Grateful Bread,** you can pick up a cinnamon-raisin bagel for 40 cents or a loaf of soy-sesame bread for $1.75. Twenty-five varieties of breads and rolls are made; "we mill our own flour and our sourdough starter came from Germany 40 years ago," says the owner. The **Gale River Outlet** is an outlet for pretty cotton clothes (and has some of the things offered in the Garnet Hill catalog), while **Valar Sports** is the ski and sportswear shop of tradition. A collection of frogs is featured amid the country gifts at the **Green Frog.** A casual place for breakfast or lunch is the bakery (with a few tables) called **Not Just Desserts** at 24 Main St., Littleton. Its Touch of New Hampshire sandwich includes ham, turkey and cheese on oatmeal-honey bread with a maple-honey dressing. Have a German chocolate square for dessert.

Extra-Special

The Frost Place, Ridge Road off Route 116, Franconia. (603) 823-8038.

The farmhouse in which the poet lived from 1915 to 1920 and in which he summered through 1938 is a low-key attraction not to be missed. It was here he wrote most of his best-known works, executive director Donald Sheehan said of the property opened by the town of Franconia as a Bicentennial project in 1976. The house remains essentially unchanged from the 1920s. Each summer a different visiting poet occupies most of it, but the front room and a rear barn are open with displays of Frost memorabilia, including his handwritten "Stopping by Woods on a Snowy Evening" and a rare, large photo of Frost at age 40 working at his desk in the room. Out back, a half-mile nature trail has plaques with Frost's poems appropriate to the site; in two cases, the poems are on the locations where he wrote them. As if the poetry and setting weren't awesome enough, the stand of woods happens to contain every variety of wildflower indigenous to Northern New England. Open July and August, daily except Tuesday 1 to 5; weekends 1 to 5 Memorial Day-June and Labor Day-Columbus Day. Adults, $2.

Squam Lakes, N.H.
Midas Touches Golden Pond

The movie "On Golden Pond" cast the largest private lake in the country quietly into the public eye.

"Before the movie, not that many people knew the lake was here," said Pierre Havre, who with his wife Jan restored a rundown resort into the Manor in 1983. They started something of a boom in year-round innkeeping in an area that long has been a low-key haven for homeowner-members of the influential Squam Lakes Association, whose membership reads like a Yankee who's who.

Now, the Holderness area between Squam and Little Squam lakes has three relatively new inns and the surrounding area has two bed-and-breakfast establishments. Just east of the Squam Lakes at the closest sections of better-known Lake Winnipesaukee, Meredith and Center Harbor are the sites of large new inns.

"All of a sudden," notes Bill Webb of the Inn on Golden Pond, "the Squams have 50 beds and, with skiing close by, we're making this a destination area year-round."

Passersby see the striking sign in front of his inn and "stop just to ask if this is the place where the movie was filmed," Bill Webb says. It isn't, but like most of the Squams' new entrepreneurs, he takes full advantage of the association.

Pierre Havre boards inn guests and the public on his 28-foot pontoon craft for twice-daily cruises along the 50-mile shoreline of Squam Lake. Its water is so pure that the 1,000 or so homeowners drink straight from the lake and its setting is so quiet that it's a nesting place for loons, which are the lake's trademark. Other than by private boat, Havre's Lady of the Manor is the only way visitors can see the sights that Katharine Hepburn and Henry Fonda made famous (the Thayer house, Purgatory Cove) and sample the changing moods of a very special lake.

Besides the lakes, the nearby historic town of Center Sandwich — a picturesque crafts colony that is everybody's idea of what an old New England village should be — and the upscale pleasures of Meredith beckon visitors.

Now, thanks to the emergence of some good inns, they have a home base from which to enjoy the charms of Golden Pond.

Inn Spots

The Manor, Route 3, Box T, Holderness 03245. (603) 968-3348.

Sometimes called the Manor on Golden Pond, this is the largest and most luxurious of Squam Lake inns. It is also the only one with lake frontage and access, which is a major plus.

Built from 1903-1907 by an Englishman who had made a fortune as a Florida land developer, the mansion with its leaded windows, gigantic fireplaces and oak and mahogany paneling is a gem. High on Shepard Hill, commanding a panoramic view of mountains and glimpses of the lake, the honey-colored stucco structure has a porte cochere guarded by a statue of a German shepherd. Other bits of sculpture are dotted around the grounds. A large swimming pool off to one side, a clay tennis court in the pines and a lawn set up for croquet complete the picture. Down at the beach, a raft, canoes, a sailboat and paddleboats are available, and you can gaze at innkeeper Pierre Havre's new powerboat, nicknamed Thayer 5 from movie fame but officially called Loon Magic.

An elegant living room done in shades of blue and apricot, a cozy library with a small

Squam Lake is visible through porte cochere at the Manor.

TV and many games plus a deck off one side, a lounge and a piano bar are available for guests. Innkeepers Pierre and Jan Havre, he a retired American Airlines pilot, have done a splendid job of restoring the formerly run-down Squam Lakes Resort. Jan, an artist, did the decorating with a California flair.

All seventeen guest rooms (with English names) in the manor house and newer Mountain View wing are different, though they share plush, wall-to-wall taupe carpeting. Most of the bathrooms are small but modern; a few have old-fashioned pedestal sinks. Some bedrooms have working fireplaces, and some have good views of the lake. Most are spacious and all are pretty. We especially liked the Buckingham — a huge corner room with marble fireplace and kingsize bed. There are fifteen more bedrooms in the Carriage House and four cottages as well. The Dover Cottage, which has two bedrooms and a kitchen-living room with fireplace, is smack beside the lake and available in season for $850 a week.

A full breakfast is available in the lounge, and light lunches (hot dogs, croissant sandwiches) are offered at the boathouse. The inn's elegant restaurant (see below) is known for fine dining.

Doubles, $65 to $138.

Red Hill Inn, Route 25B, Box 99M, Center Harbor 03226. (603) 279-7001.

The red brick summer estate that served as the administration building for the short-lived Belknap College was restored in 1985 after eleven years of dormancy into a full-fledged inn and restaurant atop a rural hillside with a view of Squam Lake.

"From your room you can see where they filmed 'On Golden Pond,'" the inn's brochure proclaims. All ten guest rooms on the second and third floors of the mansion have private baths. They vary from double rooms with twin beds to five suites with sitting rooms and working fireplaces, two with private balconies and a pleasant view. A separate stone cottage contains another suite, and a second cottage has two guest rooms with Franklin fireplaces and jacuzzis. Co-owner Rick Miller, a Meredith native who returned to the area after ten years of innkeeping in the Bahamas, was readying ten more guest rooms in outlying farm buildings when we last visited.

Room rates include a full country breakfast, with a choice of cereal, eggs, toast, muffins and such, served buffet style in a front dining room.

Dinner is served nightly in two other dining rooms (see below), one an airy sun porch with large windows capitalizing on glimpses of Squam Lake and another with a fireplace for cool nights. Another large fireplace is in the comfortable living room, also with picture windows.

In the spacious Runabout Lounge in the rear woodshed, an old mahogany runabout was cut in half lengthwise to become a bar and the walls are lined with innkeeper Don Leavitt's old auto license plates.

Guests relax in the many lawn chairs and stroll through the labeled herb garden in which hardy varieties are grown for the kitchen. In winter, the paths through the inn's 50 acres of fields and forests are used for cross-country skiing.

Double rooms and suites, $65 to $115.

The Inn on Golden Pond, Route 3, Box 126, Holderness 03245. (603) 968-7269.

Franconia native Bonnie Webb and her Massachusetts-born husband Bill returned from three years in California to open this bed-and-breakfast inn in a 110-year-old residence with a rear section dating back 200 years.

No, the inn is not on Golden Pond (it's across the road from Little Squam, which is hidden by trees in summer) "and other than the fact that Jane Fonda once used the upstairs bathroom, we have no connection with the movie," the inn's fact sheet tells guests.

The Webbs have spruced up the place considerably, each of the nine guest rooms (seven with private bath) handsomely appointed with queen or twin beds, pretty curtains with matching cushions, hooked rugs and needlepoint handwork done by Bonnie. Each room, named for an animal (Bear's Den, Raccoon's Retreat), has its needlepointed sign with the appropriate animal thereon. Bonnie also makes the mints that are put on the pillows when the beds are turned down at night.

The spacious, comfortably furnished living room, with a fireplace and numerous books and magazines, is particularly inviting for reading and quiet conversations. The large rear window looks onto a treed lawn with garden chairs and a hillside of 55 acres for cross-country skiing. A smaller room offers cable TV and a fascinating map with colored pins locating "our guests' other homes." A 60-foot-long front porch is a relaxing spot in summer.

A full breakfast is served at individual tables in the attractive pine dining room. Bacon and eggs as well as another hot dish are among the daily choices.

Doubles, $65 to $75.

The Inn at Mill Falls, Mill Falls Marketplace, Route 3, Meredith 03253. (603) 279-7006.

This 54-room luxury hotel opened in 1985 after being erected in five months by a crew of 150 in what manager Kathy Cummings called "a minor miracle."

With two Bostonians as partners, a 38-year-old local real estate broker, Edward "Rusty" McLear, developed the $2.5 million inn as the last phase of an ambitious shopping and restaurant complex fashioned from an old mill site at the western end of Lake Winnipesaukee, about eight miles southeast of Holderness. "We couldn't understand why a beautiful resort area like this had nothing more than a couple of cottages in which to stay," explained his wife, Linda McLear, proprietor of the Cupola bookstore in the marketplace.

A white frame structure on five levels, the inn has rooms of varying size and color schemes, decorated in contemporary French country style with matching draperies and

Winter scene at the Inn on Golden Pond.

bedspreads, plush chairs, television sets and spacious baths, each with a basket of amenities. Old samplers on the walls, framed pictures of 19th-century Meredith, plants in an old sleigh and antique headboards lend a bit of history.

The inn has a small indoor swimming pool, jacuzzi and sauna, but no grounds to speak of. A bridge over the waterfall that gives the project its name connects it to the busy marketplace, in which inn guests and the public can dine at the Millworks restaurant or the Provisions delicatessen.

In 1988, the partnership began construction of a second, similar inn and marketplace facing the lake at Center Harbor.

Doubles, $78 to $120. Four luxury rooms with balconies, $145.

The Nutmeg Inn, Pease Road, Meredith 03253. (603) 279-8811.

An early stagecoach inn on a quiet rural road, this 225-year-old structure was grandly redone in 1988 by new innkeepers Daryl and Cheri Lawrence. Taking over what had been primarily a restaurant, they scaled down the food operation and upscaled the guest rooms.

Eight bedrooms, six with private baths and two with fireplaces, are handsomely outfitted with country furnishings, hooked rugs, homemade quilts and dolls. Downstairs are a gracious parlor with two blue sofas and a breakfast room with oak floorboards, brick fireplace and wide wallboards indicating the place was granted by the King of England. A swimming pool and seven acres beckon outside.

Cheri Lawrence cooks a full breakfast for guests, offering a choice of eggs, blueberry or apple pancakes, raisin toast and the like. The Lawrences were considering doing private dinners for groups in the immense rear dining room.

Doubles, $60.

Country Options, 27 North Main St., Ashland 03217. (603) 968-7958.

For a time the most creative restaurant in the area, this is now a B&B with breakfast open to the public and a bakery specializing in desserts.

The onetime rooming house was renovated in 1983 by Sandy Ray, formerly of the nearby Common Man restaurant, and partner Nancy Puglisi. They've given it a charming country look, with wreaths and baskets everywhere, and a special teddy bears' table in the dining room.

Upstairs are five freshly decorated guest rooms (all sharing two adjoining bathrooms marked for men or women). Downstairs are **Divine Desserts,** a small bakery living up to its name, and a dining room with a pretty enclosed porch where breakfast is served. The breakfast mat lists the menu, its items named after quilt patterns.

Complete breakfasts, including orange juice and coffee, are priced from $2.95 to $5.95.

Doubles, $35 to $45. Breakfast for public, Saturday and Sunday 8 to noon.

Dining Spots

The Corner House Inn, Center Sandwich. (603) 284-6219.

In eight years, innkeeper Jane Kroeger and chef Don Brown have created one of the area's more popular restaurants in this delightful Victorian house in the center of town. They also teamed up with fellow restaurateur Alex Ray of the Common Man to open Glove Hollow, the area's fanciest restaurant, and found time to get married.

Dinner is by candlelight in a rustic, beamed dining room with blue and white tablecloths and red napkins, or in three smaller rooms off the other side of the entry. The striking handicrafts on the walls and shelves are for sale by Anne Made; the same for the art works from Surroundings gallery.

Lunches are bountiful and bargains; we saw some patrons sending half of theirs back for doggy bags. We, however, enjoyed every bite of the Downeaster ($5.95), two halves of an English muffin laden with fresh lobster salad (more than you'd ever get in a Maine lobster roll costing nearly twice as much), sprouts and melted Swiss cheese. We also tried a refreshing cold fruit soup (peach, melon and yogurt, sparked with citrus rinds) and an interesting crepe filled with ground beef and veggies ($3.95). Sesame chicken, baked ham with brandied peach sauce and broiled scallops were the entrees for $6.95. Most people seemed sated with soup and half a sandwich, and possibly a dessert of cappuccino cheesecake, frozen chocolate kahlua pie or pina colada sherbet.

For dinner, you might start with lobster salad in an avocado half ($5.95), mussels casino or sesame chicken with honey dip (both $3.95). Entrees run from $9.95 for vegetable primavera to $16.95 for tournedos Normandy. One diner said the double two-inch-thick broiled lamb chops were the best she'd ever had. The limited wine list starts at $12 for Entre deux Mer and the house wine is a William Wycliff from California. "Sandwich was a dry town when we came here and they finally granted us a beer and wine license," Jane Brown said, "so they must think we're all right."

Upstairs, she is gradually redecorating four guest rooms — one up a separate steep staircase with a private bath, the other three sharing one bath. A handstitched teddybear sits atop each bed, surrounded by plants, antiques and handmade quilts. Doubles are $60 to $70 and include a full breakfast.

Lunch, daily 11:30 to 2:30, dinner 5:30 to 9:30 in summer; shortened hours and closed Monday and Tuesday in winter.

Glove Hollow, Route 3, Plymouth. (603) 536-4536.

Upscale American cuisine is served in a fancy Victorian setting in this new restaurant, opened in 1988 by Jane and Don Brown of the Corner House in partnership with Alex Ray and Diane Downing of the Common Man. Their aim was to provide the finest dining in the area, which once was the site of a glove factory.

Three small dining rooms hung with interesting paintings are in the main 1849

Windowed alcove has view from small dining room at Corner House Inn.

structure. The owners were eyeing a barn for more dining space, and planned eventually to open a B&B with three or four guest rooms in a cottage beside the river on the 44-acre property.

Appetizers range from $3.95 for escargots provencale to $5.95 for lobster bisque, which, the menu states, originated at the Roosevelts' summer home in Campobello. Entrees like veal tenderloin wrapped around a dumpling and topped with bordelaise sauce, rack of lamb, medallions of pork tenderloin, chargrilled chicken and scallops on fresh linguini are in the $12.95 to $19.95 range.

Eggs sardou, lobster Benedict and grilled homemade crab cakes are offered at Sunday brunch ($5.95 to $8.95), as is a brunch buffet. Sunday afternoon dinner, also including the brunch buffet, brings roast prime rib with a horseradish-stuffed popover, poached salmon and fettuccine alfredo in the $8.95 to $11.95 range.

Dinner nightly except Monday; Sunday brunch and afternoon dinner.

The Common Man, Ashland Common, Ashland. (603) 968-7030.

Founded in 1971 by Alex Ray and hailed for food that is the most consistent in the area, the Common Man attracts enormous crowds — we faced a half-hour wait at 8:30 on a Wednesday evening — and has spawned many other restaurateurs, Jane and Don Brown of the Corner House among them.

A jigsaw puzzle is at the ready on a table near the entrance. Inside, old records, sheet music and Saturday Evening Post covers are for sale. Upstairs is a vast lounge with buckets and lobster traps hanging from the ceiling, a long pine counter set for Chinese checkers and chess, plush sofas in intimate groupings and an outside porch overlooking the shops of Ashland Common. The rustic, beamed main dining room, separated into sections by a divider topped with books, is crowded with tables sporting a variety of linens and mats, chairs and banquettes.

The dinner menu is plain but priced right, from $8.95 for London broil or fresh vegetable kabob to $12.95 for prime rib or veal Oscar. A "grate steak" serving "from one ridiculously hungry person to three very hungry people," complemented with a medley of fresh vegetables, is $26.95. The chef says he gets creative with specials, perhaps scrod with oyster sauce, duckling with kiwi fruit or bouillabaisse in winter.

Desserts vary from hot Indian pudding to a creamy cheesecake and white chocolate mousse. The house wines are Craftsbury Creek, Californias bottled specially for the Common Man.

Lunch, Monday-Saturday 11:30 to 2:30; dinner, 5:30 to 9, Sunday 5 to 9.

The Sweetwater Inn, Route 25, Moultonboro. (603) 476-5079.

Veteran restaurateur Mike Love, who had a Northern Italian eatery in Red Bank, N.J., and his wife Donna took over the old Stone Hearth here in 1986, rechristened it the Sweetwater Inn (for no particular reason other than they moved from saltwater to sweetwater) and have been impressing local diners ever since.

Patrons enter through a spacious cocktail lounge. Beyond is a large and comfortable dining room, which would be quite at home in New Jersey, its two levels done up in beiges and browns amid beams and plants.

Mike and his head chef, who accompanied the Loves from Red Bank, make their own pastas, naturally, for such dishes as lobster ravioli and fettuccine jambalaya ($9.95 to $14.95). Entrees on the wide-ranging menu run from $9.95 for baked haddock with lemon butter to $16.95 for a medley of shellfish. Two kinds of paella, four versions of veal and four of steak also are available.

Donna Love is responsible for the desserts, among them "a mean peach pie," raspberry cheesecake with hazelnut-almond meringue and a white chocolate mousse with fresh raspberries. The wine list, voted the state's best by New Hampshire Profiles magazine, offers a number of Californias in the low teens.

Dinner nightly.

The Manor, Route 3, Holderness. (603) 968-3348.

The area's most luxurious inn also contains its most sumptuous dining room, a picture of elegance from its leaded windows and tiled fireplaces to the crystal chandelier hanging from the beamed ceiling covered with rich floral wallpaper. Exotic lilies and beige napkins fanned in crystal wine glasses accent the tables dressed in white over burgundy linen. The brochure advertises romantic candlelight dining and, believe us, it is so dark it's hard to read the menu — the waiter had to bring us a flashlight. A second dining room off the lounge is less formal.

Hot popovers and a house salad of greens laced with peanuts and mandarin oranges preceded our entrees, nicely herbed lamb chops dijonnaise and heavily sauced steak Diane. Dinner entrees are priced from $10.95 for chicken in mustard sauce to $18.95 for two presentations of veal. Salmon in saffron cream sauce is topped with black and red caviar for $16.95, and shrimp madagascar is sauteed with pernod and pink peppercorns on a bed of spinach and saffron rice. A Martini merlot for $16 was the best bet from a wine list that offered a few inexpensive vintages and then rose in price dramatically. Mocha ice-cream pie and Irish coffee made worthy endings, and you might find lemon cloud pie with fresh blueberries or chocolate grand marnier torte.

Dinner nightly, 5:30 to 9:30; Sunday brunch, 11 to 2:30.

Red Hill Inn, Route 25B, Center Harbor. (603) 279-7001.

Colorful china with a pattern of morning glories, garden flowers and candles in hurricane lamps complement the pink-linened tables in the two dining rooms and airy sun porch of the Red Hill. The front dining room and the end of the porch offer a view of Squam Lake. A warming fireplace compensates for the lack of view in the inner room.

The kitchen is the special preserve of Elmer Davis, a chef of the old school who worked in long-gone American Plan hotels and never takes a day off. "From scratch" cooking is his motto, and he even makes all twelve dressings that grace the house salads. The ambitious menu ranges from old-fashioned (marinated herring) to contemporary (curried shrimp on angel-hair pasta) for appetizers, roast Long Island duckling to chicken with lemon and pepper for entrees. Prices range from $7.95 for breast of chicken natural ("for the purist") to $19.95 for surf and turf or steamed Alaskan king crab. There is a good selection of dishes for the vegetarian. A rich chocolate silk pie, amaretto cheesecake and berry pies are among the popular desserts.

The wine list is limited but reasonably priced (eight reds from $12 to $18).

Lunch in summer and fall, noon to 2; dinner nightly, 5 to 10; Sunday brunch, 11 to 2.

The Pasquaney Inn, Route 3-A, Bridgewater 03222. (603) 744-9111.

Dining is the main claim to fame at this venerable summer inn, which has been offering respite and a gorgeous view of crystal-clear Newfound Lake to visitors since 1840, but never more smartly than since new innkeepers took over in 1987.

A long porch with handsome wooden furniture fronts the main floor, which has a cozy bar, an intimate dining room with pretty green and peach wallpaper and matching curtains, and a much larger dining room used on busy nights. French/Belgian cuisine is prepared by chef-owner Bud Edrick, who trained at the French Culinary Institute and formerly was at Flamand Restaurant in New York City.

Duck with braised cabbage and raspberry sauce, quails with grapes and port wine sauce, monkfish with leek sauce, veal sweetbreads madeira and tenderloin of beef with truffle sauce are among the seasonal entrees ($12.75 to $22). Start with dandelion salad with sauteed bacon or smoked Norwegian salmon with endives and finish with creme brulee or gateau marjolaine. Belgian touches are evident in such desserts as dame blanch (vanilla ice cream with melted Belgian chocolate) and croustillant aux pommes (sauteed caramelized apples in phyllo on creme anglaise). The well-chosen wine list offers a mix of French, California and Australian vintages.

Upstairs on the second and third floors are eighteen guest rooms with private, private continental, and shared continental baths. Eight summer rooms in the adjacent Lilac House are among the nicest. Doubles, $86 to $96, B&B; $116 to $136, MAP.

Dinner nightly except Monday, 6 to 9; Sunday brunch, 11 to 2.

Christopher's, Route 25, Moultonboro. (603) 476-2300.

A rambling blue house that has been home to a number of restaurants over the years took on its latest reincarnation in 1987. Chef-owner David McDonald, who named it for his brother Christopher, said it was so successful he was converting the upstairs guest rooms into another dining area.

Tables are spaced well apart in the main, dark-beamed white and blue dining room (with a view of Berry Pond) and two smaller rooms in front. Mesquite grilling and wok frying are featured.

Appetizers could be lobster and corn chowder, wild mushroom strudel or baked salmon and crab cakes ($2.50 to $6). Six salads from grilled chicken to classic caesar are $2.50 to $5. Entrees run from $9 for two chicken dishes to $16 for pan-roasted filet mignon medallions with buttom mushrooms and a sauce of roasted sweet red peppers and brandy glasage. Mesquite-grilled pork loin, veal boursin and sauteed salmon on a bed of beefsteak tomatoes with lobster bordelaise are other possibilities.

What are billed as "flourishes of seasonal vegetables" turned out to be an assortment of six — snow peas, corn, baby carrots, Chinese green beans, brandied beets and cauliflower with cheese on our visit.

Desserts vary from a chocolate ganache to peach and strawberry cobbler. The limited wine list is priced from $9.95 to $36.95.

Dinner nightly from 5.

Mame's, Plymouth Street, Meredith. (603) 279-4631.

Owner John Cook takes pride in the fine restoration of the brick house and barn once owned by a 19th-century physician. A meandering series of small dining rooms on the main floor is topped by a large lounge on the second.

The menu is standard steak and seafood with a continental flair, from seafood Diane and lobster divan to steak Medici and veal Pierre. The prices are gentle (generally $10.95 to $14.95), and the atmosphere intimate and romantic.

New England mud pie, chocolate silk pie, orange decadence and liqueur parfaits are favored desserts.

Lunch daily, 11:30 to 3; dinner, 5 to 9 or 9:30; Sunday brunch, 11:30 to 2.

The Millworks, Mill Falls Marketplace, Meredith. (603) 279-4116.

The outdoor patio and an upstairs greenhouse overlook the town docks and lake at this popular, multi-leveled restaurant in a central location in the Mill Falls Marketplace. There are intimate fieldstone alcoves, booths, tables with placemats or linen, an abundance of hanging greenery, exposed pipes on the ceilings, mill artifacts and local paintings on the arched brick walls.

Also owned by John Cook, this restaurant offers something for everyone, from nachos to frog's legs, and the cuisine suffered somewhat when we were there. For dinner, we sampled baked stuffed shrimp and veal marsala ($12.95 and $11.95). Salads with poppyseed or buttermilk dill dressings came on clear glass plates; a bread board with two big Pepperidge Farms-style rolls was accompanied by pads of butter in aluminum wrap.

The Millfalls Magic dessert ($3.25) of vanilla ice cream, Bailey's Irish mist, chocolate cookie crust, hot fudge sauce and whipped cream is really good, our earnest waitress said. We passed in favor of black raspberry ice cream in a homemade waffle cone (merely sensational) at Nuage Ice Cream Gallery just outside.

Open daily for breakfast, lunch and dinner, 7:30 a.m. to 10 p.m.

Up Country Cafe, Mill Falls Marketplace, Meredith. (603) 279-7229.

Part of the fine Up Country Provisions shop on the third floor of the marketplace, this is a good bet for a light breakfast or an interesting lunch, and *the* place to pick up a picnic.

A dilly dally deli platter, chicken fingers with honey-dijon sauce, sandwiches (most $3.50) and entrees like open-face vegetarian sandwich, Parisian lobster salad on a croissant, turkey divan, spinach mushroom salad and gourmet grilled cheese (made with three kinds of cheese, ham, turkey and bacon) are some of the offerings, priced up to $6.95.

Open daily from 7 a.m. to 9 p.m.

The Good Egg, Route 3, Holderness.

The locals gather for gossip and breakfast at this lunch counter and decor-less dining room in the center of Holderness. Portions are ample and the prices from olden days. We ate breakfast here when it was the Chef's Hat and the service was fast; on our last visit it was so slow as to be catatonic and we had to go through incredible gyrations just to get some coffee.

The "baker's secret" hash with poached eggs and Swiss cheese ($2.95) set us up to skip lunch. The "good eggcellence" (the house version of an egg McMuffin) was a meal in itself for $1.35.

At lunch, burgers are from $2.75 for basic to $3.95 for deluxe, and you can get an onion-pepper steak sandwich for $5.75.

Open for breakfast and lunch.

"On Golden Pond" sights are seen from Lady of the Manor pontoon boat.

Diversions

Squam Lake. The lake made famous in the movie "On Golden Pond" is so screened from public view that passersby get to see it only from a distance or up close at precious few points. But you can — and should — experience it via Pierre Havre's **Lady of the Manor,** a 28-foot covered pontoon boat with a 90-horsepower motor. Former airline pilot Pierre is a knowledgeable and talkative guide as he conducts two-hour tours of the lake twice a day from late May through October.

He tells the history, relates vignettes, stops to watch resting loons and visits the places made famous in the movie. "That's the Thayer cottage," he says from a distant vantage point before discreetly passing the house loaned for the summer's filming and so remote that many locals have yet to find it. Purgatory Cove with Norman's famous rock was as foreboding the stormy day we visited as it was during the climactic scene in the film. "On a sunny day," he relates, "you'll see no more than a dozen boats on the second biggest lake in New Hampshire."

Chocorua Island, also called Church Island, is a favorite stop. The site of the first boys' camp in America, it now has an inspiring outdoor chapel in which summer worship services, complete with crank organ, have been conducted continuously by area churches since 1903. At 10 a.m. Sunday, the dock area is said to resemble the approach of the Spanish armada as upwards of 250 churchgoers arrive in a variety of boats.

Boat tours leave from The Manor at 10 a.m. and 4 p.m. Monday-Friday and 11 and 4 on Sunday. Adults $8, children 12 and under $3.50.

Center Sandwich, an historic district, still looks much as it did two generations ago when Mary Hill Coolidge and the Sandwich Historical Society organized a display of hooked and braided rugs that led to the opening of a crafts shop. Known as **Sandwich Industries,** the shop became the first home for the League of New Hampshire Craftsmen. It is open daily from Memorial Day through mid-October with myriad craft and gift items. Free crafts demonstrations are given several days a week in summer, and an outdoor art exhibit is staged during Sandwich Old Home Week in mid-August.

119

The **Sandwich Fair,** one of New England's outstanding country fairs scheduled in mid-October, celebrates its 80th anniversary in 1990. Summer residents might go home after Labor Day, but they often return for the Sandwich Fair.

The main roads and byways of this picturesque village lead to any number of interesting crafts and antiques shops. **Surroundings,** a gallery in the center of town, is known for fine art. We were intrigued by the handweaving (vests, pillows, jumpers and much more) done by Roberta and Robert Ayotte, on display and for sale at **Ayotte's Designery,** their fascinating shop and studio in the former high school, open Thursday-Saturday 10 to 5. We also admired the wonderful pillows, especially those with cat portraits, done by Anne Perkins of **Anne Made** at **Hill Country Antiques.** Her wall hangings, quilts and pillows decorate the walls of the nearby Corner House Inn and are snapped up by purchasers as fast as she puts them up.

Shopping. It seems that shopping is not where it's at in Squam Lakes. We were disappointed that Brick Village Square, a mini-mall in the center of Holderness with ten small, open shops and the office of the Squam Lakes Association, had disappeared on our latest visit. Nor could we raise anyone at mid-morning at the **Loon's Nest,** a gift shop with loon items on the edge of town.

Other than the arts and crafts shops of Center Sandwich (see above), the best place for shopping is the **Mill Falls Marketplace** in Meredith, with twenty enterprises from **Irish Tweeds** to the expansive **Leighton Tracy Gallery. Provisions Ltd.** is a large gourmet food shop par excellence. Absent are the souvenir shops indigenous to much of the Lakes Region. At Linda McLear's **Cupola,** one customer asked if she had any T-shirts with "Meredith" printed on the front. No, was the reply — you have to go to Weirs Beach to find that kind of thing. Lamented the customer: "But then it won't say 'Meredith.'" Similarly, the loon items in Holderness signify, but do not say, Squam Lakes.

Extra-Special

Ice Creams, Old and New.

A trek to the ice-cream stand is an after-supper tradition at many a family resort area like Squam Lake. "The world's best ice creams" (as described by one restaurant that serves them) have been dispensed for years at **Squam Lakeside Farm** on Route 3, across from Little Squam Lake. Mocha walnut fudge, heath bar crunch (we tried it and although good, it didn't hold a candle to Ben & Jerry's), pumpkin, amaretto nut, rum raisin and banana strawberry are among the flavors of cones priced from $1 to $2 (for a colosso cone). Greatly expanded lately, the place offers breakfast, snacky items, lobster rolls, onion rings, nachos, tacos, burritos and the like plus beer and wine at picnic tables overlooking Little Squam Lake. Fried haddock with sauteed zucchini and potato salad was $6.95 at our last visit.

Ice cream becomes a work of art in a high-tech setting at **Nuage Ice Cream Gallery** in the Mill Falls Marketplace, Meredith. Although no longer made on the premises (it's produced in Manchester by the original owner who has expanded), it's upscale as ever. Hazelnut chocolate, amaretto, white chocolate chip, raisin marsala, blueberry and many more are served in homemade waffle cones ($1.75 and $2.25), sundaes or what have you. "We try not to mask the flavors but to enhance them," the manager informed us. They do that very well.

Cross-country skiing is great on trails throughout Jackson.

Jackson, N.H.
A Rugged Mountain World

Drive through the old red covered bridge into Jackson and you enter another world.

It's a world isolated from the hubbub of the lower Mount Washington Valley and enveloped by mountains of the Presidential Range, tiptoeing toward the East's highest peak (6,288 feet). It's a highland valley of pristine air, scenic beauty, and peace and quiet. It's a European-style mountainside village of 600 residents and often a greater number of visitors.

Jackson is one of the nation's earliest year-round destination resorts, dating to pre-Civil War days (and not all that changed since its heyday around the turn of the century). It's a village of spirited tradition and pride, from the local book based on recipes used in Jackson's early lodges to the Jackson Resort Association's claim that "nowhere else in the world will you find a more concentrated area of diverse recreational opportunities."

Today, skiing is the big deal in Jackson and its sister hamlets of Glen and Intervale. There are two downhill ski areas, Wildcat and Black Mountain; a world-class cross-country center in the Jackson Ski Touring Foundation, and fabled Tuckerman Ravine, where the diehards climb to the headwall of Mount Washington for one last run in June.

The two worlds of skiing — alpine and nordic — co-exist in friendly tension. Explained Betty Whitney, who was staffing the village information center when we stopped: "Thom wanted to advertise 'Ski Tour Jackson' and I wanted to stress alpine, so we ended up simply 'Ski Jackson.'" Betty Whitney and her husband came to Jackson in 1936 to establish Black Mountain and Whitneys' Inn; Thom Perkins is the energetic executive director of the prestigious Jackson Ski Touring Foundation.

There are modern-day amenities, two golf courses among them. But this is a rugged area, better epitomized by the Appalachian Mountain Club hiking camp at Pinkham

121

Notch than the Mount Washington Auto Road (its bumper stickers boasting "This Car Climbed Mount Washington"), better experienced from a secluded mountain inn than from one of the chock-a-block motels down the valley in North Conway.

Inn Spots

Christmas Farm Inn, Route 16B, Box 176, Jackson 03846. (603) 383-4313.

A basket of bright red buttons proclaiming "We Make Memories" is beside an arrangement of garden flowers inside the entrance to this ever-expanding property where Christmas is reflected, if not celebrated, all year long. The buttons are part of Sydna and Bill Zeliff's promotion effort for their lively inn (he was in marketing with duPont and handles this venture accordingly). The flowers are from the pretty grounds, which won the valley's annual garden competition in 1985.

Few inns have such a fragmented history: part jail, part church, part inn, part farmhouse, part sugarhouse. The property was given by a Philadelphian as a Christmas present in the 1940s to his daughter, who tried and failed at farming on the rocky hillside before the place was revived as an inn. Hence the name, and whence all nicely detailed on the back of the dinner menu (see Dining Spots).

"We'd never stayed in an inn before we bought this one in 1976," says Bill Zeliff, and they're obviously making up for lost time. Located off by itself above Jackson Village, the entire place has a palpable inn air that starts with the guest list beside the reception desk naming and welcoming the day's arrivals. The Zeliffs aim to bring people together for an inn-family experience, putting on everything from lobster bakes in summer to cross-country trail lunches in winter. They publish the North Pole Ledger, a fancy newsletter for guests, and keep a scrapbook for every year in the cozy Mistletoe Lounge "so that the guest experience becomes part of the memory," says Bill. Patrons reciprocate; many of the wreaths, samplers and such on the walls are gifts from guests.

A new brick fireplace is the focal point of the 200-year-old inn's living room, which is done appropriately in red and green with plaid loveseats, a big red velvet duck and holly on the pillows. Bingo, games and movies on the VCR are nightly features of the adjacent TV-game room. The rear barn has a huge game room with pingpong, bumper pool, large-screen TV, an enormous fireplace and a sauna. Across the road are a swimming pool with a cabana where lunch is available, a putting green, shuffleboard and volleyball court. Everywhere you look are paths, brick walls and gardens with flowers identified by labels.

Oh yes, about the guest rooms, of which there are 38, all but two with private baths. Ten in the main inn have Christmasy names like Three Wise Men and those of Santa's reindeer, and have lately been redecorated in sprightly Laura Ashley style; the spacious Blitzen and Vixen have jacuzzis as well. The red and green 1777 saltbox out back has nine deluxe rooms, and most luxurious of all are the four suites in the barn, each with a living area with sofa and velvet chair, television, high sloped ceilings, large baths and loft bedrooms. Three cottages, each with two bedrooms and private baths, large sun decks, TV and fireplace, are first to be rented in the winter. Other accommodations are in the Log Cabin, the Sugar House and a bunk room for four.

Doubles, $136 to $164, MAP; many package plans.

The Inn at Thorn Hill, Thorn Hill Road, Jackson 03846. (603) 383-4242.

Quite possibly Jackson's best view of the Presidential Range is from the front porch of this neat yellow inn, built as a private residence in 1895 and converted into an inn in 1955. All the mountains are labeled for identification purposes on the 48-year-old painting at the end (it's a bit weatherbeaten, and we heard a new one was being painted).

Lush flowers greet summer guests of Christmas Farm Inn.

An even broader view, wide enough to encompass the weather station atop Mount Washington, opens through the picture windows in the long, lovely living room. Dressed in antiques, velvet upholstered furniture and fine oriental rugs, the room is Victorian to the hilt and overseen by mannequins in Victorian dresses. Between the living room and the entry hall is a more casual parlor with television and VCR.

The valley's best meals are served in an attractive dining room at the rear (see below). Next to it is a cozy pub with a fireplace.

New innkeepers Peter and Linda LaRose are dropouts from the corporate world in Washington, D.C., where he was vice president for finance for MCI. "We'd never been to an inn before," said Linda, who described its acquisition as a friend's fantasy. "This popped up as a lark, so I guess fate brought us here."

With their young family, they moved here in 1987 to broaden the inn's traditional clientele of what they call WOOFS — well-off older folks. They continued the room renovations of their predecessors, added fine antiques and orientals, upgraded the dining and enhanced the Victorian feeling, which is comfortable and not at all overpowering.

The most choice rooms are the ten on the second and third floors of the main inn. They are richly furnished with Victorian antiques, colorful floral wallpapers and oriental rugs. Sachet pillows are scattered about the large antique beds, and there are many special touches. The Ramsey Suite is stunning with a queensize canopy bed, ruffled curtains and a gorgeous patterned rug over wall-to-wall carpeting.

A new deck has been added to the carriage house, which is losing some of its ski-chalet appearance. It has seven large carpeted bedrooms with modern baths off a pine-paneled living room with plump sofas near the raised fireplace. Linda redid the East Room in an all-lamb motif: lambs on the quilt, rugs, lampstand, wallpaper and pictures, and there's even a big stuffed lamb.

On a wickedly hot night, we enjoyed our quarters in the nicely furnished, two-room Notchview cottage, where the front porch caught what little breeze there was. Two other

123

cottages are close by, and a very pleasant swimming pool is screened from view by a hedge.

"I changed the rooms I wanted to change," says Linda. "But there's a lot more to do — we want to expand, and turn the third-floor rooms into suites."

Breakfast, served formally on white china, lives up to the inn's culinary reputation. You help yourself to a buffet spread with four kinds of juice, yogurt, granola, fresh fruits, baked goods and cheeses. Then you order a main course, perhaps a potato and cheese omelet or grand marnier french toast with peach conserve, both excellent.

Doubles, $136 to $156, MAP.

Dana Place Inn, Pinkham Notch, Route 16, Jackson 03846. (603) 383-6822 or (800) 423-2766.

Undergoing rapid expansion, the historic Dana Place is an inn in transition. It's at once a rural country inn with quaint rooms sharing baths, juxtaposed against luxury suites in two new additions. Its rustic, high-ceilinged Lodge Room with a fireplace is traditional, and an airy new addition with an indoor swimming pool and a jacuzzi is anything but. When we visited, the lobby and entry were being expanded, with a glassed-in wraparound porch around the front and side, and an addition was nearly doubling the size of the dining room.

Whew! No wonder that innkeeper Roger Bintliff was breathless from the construction pace, and that the new owner was staying out of the way in New York. By the summer of 1989, all the activity caused by four additions and a nearly doubling in size in two years was to have slowed down.

The out-of-the-way location of this inn, which still carries the name of the original owners of the Colonial farmhouse/inn from which all these additions have sprung, is special. It's up in the mountains some 2,000 feet above North Conway, just before you reach Pinkham Notch in the midst of the White Mountain National Forest, and right beside the Ellis River.

The Ellis River cross-country ski trail, one of the most skied trails in the country, ends at the inn, and skiers often come inside for lunches of hearty soups and chili in the lounge. In summer, inn guests cool off in a scenic swimming hole in the rushing river and, in all seasons, picture taking is in order, with Mount Washington rising behind the birch trees.

A small patio outside the common Lodge Room faces the lawn leading to the river, and a hammock strung between the trees is a great place for relaxing. Crabapple trees on the property burst into color in the spring and the inn gardens outside the dining rooms are spotlit at night.

The 29 guest rooms, all but four with private bath, vary in size and decor from rustic to contemporary. All had been redone with pretty floral wallpaper and white spreads when we stayed. Our large room with sitting area in the original inn had a view over the gardens toward Mount Washington, a kingsize platform bed and a large modern bathroom with tub and shower. Most of the twelve new rooms are spacious and have kingsize beds; those on the rear have private decks facing the river and mountains.

A country breakfast is served (and available to the public for $5.95). Eggs any style, buttermilk pancakes, french toast and omelets are the choices.

Doubles, $55 to $85, suites, $75 to $95, B&B; $95 to $125, MAP.

Riverside, Route 16A, Intervale 03845. (603) 356-9060.

Located beside the east branch of the Saco River on the Intervale loop between North Conway and Glen, this is a homey country inn with a gourmet restaurant that serves dinners on weekends (see Dining Spots).

124

Restored Wentworth retains style of its turn-of-the-century beginnings.

Geoff and Anne Carter, who had several restaurants in her career, moved in 1983 from Portsmouth to the turn-of-the-century summer house built by his grandfather, an industrialist from Lynn, Mass. It's a summery place, steeped in family history.

Three of the seven guest rooms have private baths and two used as suites share adjoining baths. Our favorite is Esther's Room (all are named for members of the family, down to the chauffeur and governess). Formerly the master bedroom, it has a brass bed, a pink chaise longue and a great bathroom. A painting by Anne's mother adorns Lolly's Room, pretty in chintz and the deep-green carpeting that runs through all the bedrooms, with matching shower curtain and bed covers. Rooms are as comfortable as they were when this was a lived-in home. "People feel as if they're coming to Grandma's house," says Anne.

Common areas include a fireplaced parlor with a jigsaw puzzle in progress, a front porch, the dining room and "Auntie's Bar," the enclosed side porch where Geoff presides over cocktails and liqueurs.

The sumptuous breakfasts were featured in a recent edition of New Hampshire Profiles magazine. There's a choice of three fruits, followed by perhaps English toast (as opposed to french toast, it's English muffins in an egg batter), scrambled eggs with croutons and cheddar, or corned-beef hash. "We always have a sweet dish and an omelet," says Anne, who has a repertoire of twenty items. Eggs from local chickens and blueberries grown by the local county extension agent are used.

Doubles, $55 to $95.

The Wentworth Resort Hotel, Route 16A, Jackson Village 03846. (603) 383-9700 or (800) 637-0013.

The Wentworth was the grand hotel of Jackson at the turn of the century when Jackson had 24 lodging establishments. Abandoned for a time, it was restored in 1983 into a luxury resort with modern conveniences but retaining much of the style and charm from its golden era.

The eighteen-hole golf course behind the hotel is part of the Jackson Ski Touring

125

Center layout in the winter. Other facilities include clay tennis courts, swimming pool, cocktail lounge and an elegant restaurant (see below).

The turreted, yellow and green Victorian structure plus annexes and outbuildings (some with great views of the golf course) contain a total of 60 guest rooms.

Plushly carpeted halls lead to twenty spacious guest rooms on the second and third floors of the main inn. All are beautifully restored in different shapes and sizes, with private baths (most have refinished, old-fashioned Victorian claw tubs with showers), French Provincial furnishings, an upholstered chair under a reading lamp, and color television. Beige patterned draperies and bedspreads are coordinated with restful cream walls and rust carpeting.

The large, formal lobby is richly furnished in French Provincial as well. Sofas and arm chairs are scattered across the green carpeting, and a wood stove is at the ready in the brick fireplace.

A buffet breakfast is available for $5.95.

Doubles, $75 to $125, EP.

Wildcat Inn and Tavern, Route 16A, Box T, Jackson Village 03846. (603) 383-4245.

If the Wentworth is the deluxe renovation, the Wildcat exemplifies Jackson's timeless past. Looking like something out of yesteryear, it exudes a sense of history in fifteen upstairs guest rooms, nine with private baths, as well as in a two-bedroom cottage (we were told there were plans to upgrade the lodging). Rooms vary but are furnished with antiques and hooked rugs. We liked the corner room in peach and green with a quilted bedspread. One homey twin-bedded room has a sitting room as well.

With two fireplaces and a large-screen TV, the huge Tavern is a popular gathering place for apres-skiers and others. Folksingers perform on weekends.

A full breakfast featuring pastries baked on the premises is served guests. Innkeepers Pam and Marty Sweeney are proud of their birchemusli, a European dish of chilled oatmeal mixed with fruit and nuts and topped with fresh whipped cream, and sometimes spike their hot chocolate with schnapps.

Doubles, $66 to $74, B&B; $106, MAP.

The Bernerhof, Route 302, Box 240, Glen 03838. (603) 383-4414 or (800) 548-8007.

Long known for its European food, the Bernerhof is becoming a great place to stay. "Food has provided 85 percent of our revenues, but I want to get lodging up to 50-50," says Ted Wroblewski, owner with his wife Sharon.

To do that, they expanded in 1988 with a three-room addition featuring private baths, kingsize brass beds and, the crowning touches, jacuzzi tubs in window alcoves, where you can gaze at the stars as you soak. Eight of the eleven rooms now have private baths, and one room has a fireplace and a spa tub under a skylight. Two other rooms share a sauna.

Guests have use of a second-floor sitting room with cable TV and VCR, and can walk to a secluded swimming pool in summer.

The main floor is devoted to things culinary, including the restaurant, the European-style lounge called the Zumstein Room (after the original owners), and the Taste of the Mountains Cooking School. A full breakfast (perhaps eggs Laurent, with onions and wine over poached eggs) is included in the rates, and a complimentary champagne breakfast is served in bed on the third morning of one's stay.

Doubles, $64 to $100, B&B; $120 to $133, MAP.

Whitneys' Inn, Route 16B, Jackson 03846. (603) 383-6886 or (800) 252-5622.

A somewhat Bavarian feeling pervades this self-contained resort owned by Judy and

Terry Tannehill at the foot of Black Mountain, a rambling complex of inn, outbuilding, barn and cottages totaling 35 guest rooms.

Although primarily a winter place (with the family-oriented Black Mountain ski area out back, a lighted skating rink, sledding and tobogganing), summer fun is not overlooked. Tucked away in the trees across the street, the skating rink turns out to be a lovely spring-fed pond for swimming and lazing. The inn has a tennis court and volleyball, croquet and other lawn games. Once you're here, you're away from everything but nature. No wonder it's popular for an old-fashioned country vacation.

Fifteen guest rooms in the inn have private baths and four on the third floor share. Rooms are carpeted, nicely furnished in country style, and have good-looking quilts. Some at the rear have two upholstered chairs by a table with a floor lamp for reading and a great view onto the ski slopes. Some have desks and bureaus. Two two-bedroom cottages have fireplaces. Eight family suites with bedroom and living room are in an outbuilding, and two deluxe and two standard units are in the Brookside cottage.

The inn has a front parlor with jigsaw puzzles in various stages of completion, a formal parlor with piano, the Greenery lounge with a flagstone floor and sliding glass doors opening onto a patio, and downstairs, a recreation room with pingpong table, games and TV. In winter, there's the rustic Shovel Handle Pub in the barn for lunch and apres-ski.

Breakfast and dinner are served in a country dining room, which has stenciled wallpaper above pine paneling, beige linen cloths, rose napkins and green carpeting. Dinner entrees run from $11.95 for chicken Marguerita to $15.95 for broiled sirloin. Smoked seafood and vegetables over pasta made a good summer appetizer ($4.95).

Doubles, $134 to $154, MAP.

Eagle Mountain House, Carter Notch Road, Jackson 03846. (603) 383-9111 or (800) 527-5022.

A picturesque row of high-backed rockers is lined up on the 380-foot-long veranda that's longer than a football field in front of this grand old hotel dating to 1879. The interior was restored in 1986 into a 94-room hotel and condominium center.

Although the establishment has a bit of an institutional-condo feeling, there's no denying the location — up in the mountains, facing a beautiful golf course and a colorful little pool and tennis court. Many of the rooms have sitting areas with sturdy mountain furniture, TVs hidden in the armoires and queensize beds.

Off a rambling front lobby are the Eagle Landing Tavern (where lunch is served in busy seasons), a huge white-linened dining room and a health club. The signature dish at dinner is sauteed shrimp in Spanish saffron sauce, finished with brandy and pistachios and served in a cornbread ring. Prices range from $9.50 for New England pot pie to $18 for filet mignon bearnaise.

Doubles, $95 to $110, EP; suites, $130 to $145.

Veranda at Eagle Mountain House

127

The Village House, Route 16A, Box 359, Jackson 03846. (603) 383-6666.

A greenhouse-style porch for breakfast, a tennis court and a small swimming pool out front are attractions at this cheery yellow and white B&B on seven peaceful acres in the valley at the edge of Jackson Village. A small gazebo atop a hill and a wicker-filled front porch provide fine views of the mountains.

A cozy parlor has rustic furniture and a wood stove. In summer, innkeepers Robin Crocker and Lori Allen serve a continental plus breakfast of fruit salad, cereal, homemade granola, muffins and fruit breads. A full breakfast is offered in winter.

Eight of the ten guest rooms on three floors have private baths. Each is named for a New England resort village the innkeepers like, and books from the particular area are displayed in each room. The Sturbridge is done up in peaches and greens, while Kennebunkport is all violet and white. Mints are placed on the pillows at night, and snacks are served in the afternoon.

Doubles, $60 to $80.

Ellis River House, Route 16, Box 656, Jackson 03846. (603) 383-9339.

At this working farm, guests can help gather eggs from the hens in the morning. Barry and Barbara Lubao keep pigs, geese, rabbits, ducks and a pony as well. They have won prizes for their vegetable gardens, and have begun a vineyard and plan to make burgundy-type wine.

The five bedrooms are traditional and share baths, except for a two-floor suite with its own bathroom and color cable TV. On the second floor is a game room with TV and VCR; the innkeepers also planned to put balconies on the bedrooms that face the Ellis River. On the main floor are a parlor with grand piano (where there are occasional concerts) and in back, a garden room with a large jacuzzi.

Guests are served a full breakfast (eggs any style, french toast, cinnamon raisin oatmeal bread) in the pretty dining room. Barry, who was chief engineer for the Sheraton hotels but always wanted to be a chef, cooks dinner for guests by reservation at 6:30 p.m. Broiled trout, cornish hen or steak might be the fare. His beer bread is renowned, and dessert could be blueberry pan dowdy.

Doubles, $60 to $100.

Jackson House, Route 16, Box 378, Jackson 03846. (603) 383-4226.

Eleven country-decorated rooms, three in a new wing with private baths, are offered at the 1868 Jackson House, where two golden retrievers welcome you in. Ex-stock broker Laraine Hill makes the patchwork ducks, quilts and pillows. Her husband Peter, a former race-car driver, tends to the couple's horses, among other chores.

Laraine serves a full breakfast at a long table for twelve in the dining room: fresh fruit platters, blueberry pancakes with berries picked on the property, and maybe banana bread. There's usually a choice of three entrees.

Public spaces include a handsome sitting room with fireplace, and a solarium with a six-person jacuzzi, perfect for relaxing after hiking and skiing.

Doubles, $65 to $90.

Dining Spots

The Inn at Thorn Hill, Thorn Hill Road, Jackson. (603) 383-4242.

The pretty dining room here is long and narrow with pressed-oak, high-back chairs at well-spaced tables set with white linens, white china, antique oil lamps and baskets of flowers from the gardens. Dark green floral wallpaper, white wainscoting, stained glass and a multitude of baskets complete the setting.

Dining room at the Inn at Thorn Hill is known for fine cuisine.

Head chef Hoke Wilson and three assistants, including his wife, are responsible for what the inn amusingly calls "Hoke Cuisine." That translates to exciting menus that change fortnightly and meals that are summed up in our notes with the exclamation, "stupendous!"

Consider our dinner: a cucumber soup with red bell peppers, diced tomato and mint; grilled shrimp on a bed of julienned cucumber and tomatoes with coriander; a basket of herbed sourdough bread, and salads bursting with croutons, scallions, carrots, tomatoes, sprouts, mushrooms and impeccable greens, served with mini-carafes of the house dressings — creamy radish, creamy curry with scallions, creamy mint with feta, and vinaigrette, so good that we sampled them all. Main courses were twin filets of beef Sisone topped with swirls of pistachio-garlic cream on a plate of tomato puree and grilled quail on a bed of peanut and scallion couscous, served with a peach, basil and black pepper relish.

Assertive fare this, and there was no letdown at dessert: a perfect grand marnier parfait with blackberries, homemade plum sorbet, a chocolate velvet mousse and a chocolate pecan pie. From start to finish, the presentation of each dish was pretty as a picture, perhaps due to the chef's training as a graphic artist before he went into cooking at New York's Hotel Carlyle.   - - -

A good wine list is supplemented by house wines that change with the menu. We found the Vicomte de Padirac bordeaux a bargain at $10.

Entrees are priced from $12.75 to $19.50 for such creations as roulade of veal stuffed with lobster and spinach, Indian chicken with coriander, cumin and chii sauce accompanied by Indian flat bread, and breast of duck on a lime and garlic sauce. If this be Hoke cuisine, let us have more of it!

Dinner nightly, 6 to 9. No smoking.

The Bernerhof, Route 302, Glen. (603) 383-4414.

A turreted Victorian inn with sloping greenhouse addition is home for notable Swiss cuisine in an old-world setting, plus the noted cooking school, A Taste of the Mountains.

Here is where Steven Raichlen, the Boston food and restaurant writer, teaches five-day and weekend courses in spring and fall, assisted by owner Ted Wroblewski and executive chef Richard Spencer.

"Our kitchen and cooking school set us apart," says Ted, creating a culinary dynamic that pervades the establishment.

We can vouch for lunch, when we enjoyed the pate platter ($4.95) and the day's raw plate of gravlax and vegetable salad ($3.75), both appetizers but plenty for a meal after a hearty breakfast. The three pates of duck, trout and seafood-vegetable were memorable, and the smoked salmon was a generous serving around a salad in the middle, much enhanced by the melba toast that, upon request, the chef prepared from good French bread.

At dinner, the specialty is fresh Delft blue provimi veal, deboned by the chef and used in wiener schnitzel, emince de veau au vin blanc, piccata a la Suisse and schnitzel cordon bleu. Other entrees ($10.95 to $19.95) are veal steak persillade and veal chops with pears, filet of salmon with shrimp, and scallops provencale. Delices de gruyere and shrimp remoulade are favored among appetizers ($4 to $7.95). A delectable array of desserts includes a concoction of vanilla ice cream and kirsch in a meringue topped with bing cherries and whipped cream, profiteroles aux chocolat, chocolate silk pie made with Myers's dark rum, and chocolate fondue for two. (Cheese and beef fondues are available in the bar and dining room as well.)

Meals are served in three dining rooms amidst pine paneling, beamed ceilings, crisp white linens, a piano and a Swiss stove. The Zumstein Room cocktail lounge has an oak-paneled bar and a limited taproom menu.

The wine list, large by New Hampshire standards, includes a few Austrian, German and Swiss vintages along with the predominantly French, priced from $14 to $120.

Lunch, noon to 3; dinner nightly, 6 to 9:30; Sunday brunch, 10:30 to 2:30.

Dana Place Inn, Route 16, Jackson. (603) 383-6822.

The four dining rooms here are country elegant with an accent of Danish contemporary. There's a cozy center room with Scandinavian teak chairs. The skylit and airy lower level has large windows for viewing the spotlit gardens, crabapple trees and bird feeders outside, and a new addition offers round tables at bay windows with views of the river. Pink linen, burgundy napkins and pink candles provide a romantic atmosphere.

The menu ranges widely, the fifteen entrees ($14.95 to $18.95) including wiener schnitzel, grilled swordfish, roast duckling and tournedos with a watercress-ginger sauce. The chef prepares chicken four ways — saltimbocca, braised apple, spicy with tequila and seasoned with peaches, coconut and raspberries.

Manager Roger Bintliff, who used to operate delis in New York and was a captain at Le Bibliotheque, serves up a knockout caesar salad with caviar and capers, $11.90 for two. Desserts include fresh strawberries to dip in a zabaglione flavored with grand marnier, chocolate bourbon mousse, fresh fruit crepes and coconut flan with fresh raspberry coulis.

The wine list is one of the valley's finest, with more than 100 California boutique labels, priced from $14 to $50.

Breakfast, 8 to 10; lunch in winter, 11 to 3; dinner nightly, 6 to 9 or 10.

Christmas Farm Inn, Route 16B, Jackson. (603) 383-4313.

With everything else going for it, the Christmas Farm Inn also aims to be "an MAP experience," says innkeeper Sydna Zeliff. "We've tried to make the food the focal point," and its quality was enhanced following the arrival in 1988 of chef Joseph Kubik from the Four Seasons in Boston.

Old wagon is filled with autumn bounty at entrance to Dana Place Inn.

The large candlelit country dining room is pure Christmas, of course, what with the red, white and green color scheme, plates with red bows, wreaths over the fireplace and the hutch filled with Christmas plates.

The menu has become more adventuresome lately, with appetizers like warm salad of grilled scallops with fresh pasta and sun-dried tomatoes, ravioli of crab with saffron and chives, and a terrine of wild mushrooms with a salad of pea pods, croutons and roasted shallots. Among entrees ($13.75 to $18) are brochette of shrimp over Chinese cabbage, roast pork tenderloin with cream of garlic and thyme, grilled marinated lamb, and breast of duck over pasta with watercress and scallions.

Bill Zeliff sings the praises of the pastry chef, who is known for decorated tortes and gorgeous cakes, among them a strawberry cream cake.

The huge wine list is heavily into Californias, at prices from $9.50 for valpolicella to $39 for a 1981 Chateau Montelena cabernet.

Dinner nightly, 6 to 9. No smoking.

Wildcat Inn and Tavern, Route 16A, Jackson Village. (603) 383-4245.

Food is what the Wildcat Inn is known for. The old front porch had to be converted into dining space to handle the overflow from the original two dining rooms, as ancient, cozy and homey as can be.

Sitting beneath a portrait of Abraham Lincoln, we enjoyed an autumn lunch in a small, dark inner room with bare floors, mismatched chairs and green linens. An exceptional cream of vegetable soup was chock full of fresh vegetables; that and half a reuben sandwich made a hearty meal for $5.25. We also liked the delicate spinach and onion quiche, served with a garden salad dressed with creamy dill.

Dinner entrees run from $9.95 for lasagna to $17.95 for filet of beef Oscar. Wildcat chicken is served like cordon bleu but wrapped in puff pastry and topped with mustard sauce; bulgogi is a dish of thinly sliced beef with Korean sauce over a bed of rice. You also can get mondo chicken with Italian sausage and apricot brandy, shrimp and scallop

131

scampi and "the extravaganza" — shrimp, lobster and scallops sauteed with vegetables and rice.

The wine list is limited; the desserts slathered with whipped cream are memorable. Chocolate silk pie, mocha ice cream pie, blueberry cheesecake, frozen lemon pie and the Mount Washington brownie topped with vanilla ice cream, hot fudge sauce, whipped cream and creme de menthe are tempters.

In summer, you can dine out back at white, umbrella-covered tables in the attractive tavern gardens, which won the local garden club award for 1984. In winter, the historic tavern is a popular watering hole for skiers.

Breakfast daily, 7:30 to 9:30; lunch, 11:30 to 3; dinner, 6 to 9 or 10.

Riverside, Route 16A, Intervale. (603) 356-9060.

Although dinner is served only on weekends, it's worth mentioning for the ambiance (a turn-of-the-century country summer home) and the food (innkeeper Anne Cotter, a former restaurateur, does the cooking). "Creative country cooking — hearty, neighborly and abundant" is what it's all about, according to the tiny menu.

An inventive cook who decides her menu by whim ("I cook by the seat of my pants," she says), Anne is likely to offer a handful of entrees, perhaps shrimp Rajah with candied ginger, chicken diablo with sweet mustard butter, and filet mignon with a mushroom and sour cream sauce. Scallops on angel-hair pasta or pork tenderloin might be the nightly creation. Entrees are priced from $11.50 to $17.50 and include a crisp garden salad, fresh vegetables, potatoes and rolls. Chilled scallop bisque or smoked sausage are possible starters; desserts could be homemade ice creams, rum brickle, lemon meringue puff or nutty fudge brownie.

Pink cloths and pale green napkins dress the dining area, which runs the width of the house behind a front parlor and adjacent to the pleasant side porch bar, a great place for cocktails or cordials.

Dinner, Friday and Saturday 5:30 to 9.

The Plum Room, Wentworth Resort Hotel, Jackson Village. (603) 383-9700.

A huge calico wreath in plum shades sets the stage for dining in the Plum Room, aptly named and pretty as a picture with dark rose carpeting, upholstered French Provincial chairs with plum backs and seats, and tables set with pink napkins on white cloths over plum undercloths reaching to the floor. The flowers are apt to be pink carnations, the wine glasses have pink stems and the white china is bordered in plum.

Scottish chef Billy Haggarty features an international menu. Among entrees ($17 to $19) are pasta primavera, seafood pot-au-feu, wiener schnitzel, medallions of lamb with a hazelnut and frangelico sauce, roast duckling a l'orange and filet mignon rossini. Entrees come with marinated mushrooms, choice of potato or wild rice, and homemade bread; vegetables and salads are extra.

Oysters pesto, escargots en croute, marinated herring and smoked Scotch salmon are appetizers ($5 to $7). Lemon mousse pie, strawberry tarts and chocolate banana cake are favored desserts.

Dinner nightly, 6 to 10.

Thompson House Eatery (T.H.E.), Route 16A at 16, Jackson Village. (603) 383-9341.

An old red farmhouse dating from the early 1800s holds a rustic restaurant renowned for salads and sandwiches and an old-fashioned soda fountain.

In the decade-plus since he opened, chef-owner Larry Baima has created so many unusual dishes that, legend has it, he had no room on the menu for hamburgers or french fries. Instead, sandwiches have flair: turkey with asparagus spears, red onions, melted Swiss and Russian dressing; knockwurst marinated in beer and grilled with tomatoes, bacon, cheese and mustard. Salads are creations: pasta spirals tossed with marinated artichoke hearts and mushrooms atop a bed of greens, garnished with salami, cheese, eggs, tomatoes and more; shrimp on a bed of greens with tomatoes and vegetables; curried chicken, almonds and raisins atop greens and garnishes. At both lunch and dinner, such items are $5 to $7.

Dinner entrees ($9.50 to $13.50) include "Baked Popeye," a notable spinach casserole with fresh mushrooms, bacon and cheese, with an option of scallops. Other artful combinations are chicken and sausage parmigiana, filet of sole crowned with crabmeat and artichoke hearts, seafood on linguini, broiled sirloin and several stir-fries. Beer and wine are available. The Swiss chocolate truffle, Dutch mocha ice creams and wild berry crumble make great desserts.

Patrons eat in several small, rustic rooms and alcoves at tables covered with pastel floral cloths, or outside on canopied. flower-bedecked patios flanked by huge pots of tomatoes and basil.

Lunch daily, 11:30 to 4; dinner, 5:30 to 10. Closed November to Memorial Day.

Red Parka Pub, Route 302, Glen. (603) 383-4344.

This is the perfect place for apres-ski, from the "wild and crazy bar" with a wall of license plates from across the country (the more outrageous the better) to the "Skiboose," a 1914 flanger car that pushed snow off the railroad tracks and now is a cozy dining area for private parties. Somehow the rest of this vast place remains dark and intimate, done up in red and blue colors, red candles and ice-cream-parlor chairs.

The menu, which comes inside the Red Parka Pub Table Times, features hearty steaks, barbecued ribs, teriyakis and combinations thereof ($9.95 to $15.95), a salad bar with 30 items and breads, and homemade desserts like mud pie and Indian pudding.

Next door is the new **Red Parka Company Store,** doling out such provisions as meats, cheeses and salads along with gifts and local crafts.

Dinner nightly, 5 to 10.

Yesterday's, Route 16B, Jackson. (603) 383-4457.

Yellow striped awnings and pretty flower boxes identify the exterior of this unassuming little restaurant in Jackson Village, billed as the "home of the all-day breakfast."

The countryman's special of two eggs, pancakes or french toast, homefries and coffee goes for $4.25, and everything else is considerably less.

For lunch, burgers, sandwiches and salads start at $1.25 for a hot dog. Chef's salad and turkey club at $4.95 are the most expensive items. No wonder we couldn't even get in for a weekday lunch without a long wait. The proprietors, who also own the Christmas Farm Inn, are onto a good thing.

Breakfast daily, 6:30 to 3; lunch, 11:30 to 3.

As You Like It, Jackson Falls Marketplace, Route 16B, Jackson. (603) 383-6425.

This bakery-deli is a good stop for picking up a picnic to eat in the mountains, or to have a snack at one of the three tables. How about a corned-beef sandwich on oatmeal molasses bread, a mushroom-bacon quiche or some curried wild rice salad? You could have a blueberry crumb coffee cake or a banana-apple muffin for breakfast, a cup of zesty gazpacho for lunch, or pick up lasagna for dinner. Fine cheeses, meats and wines are also sold here, as are interesting mustards, salsas, cheese spreads and so forth. A piece of toll house pie or chocolate-praline cheesecake hits the spot, too.

Open Tuesday-Sunday, 9 to 4, 5 or 6.

Diversions

Downhill Skiing. Wildcat, looming across Pinkham Notch from Mount Washington, is a big mountain with plenty of challenge, a 2,100-foot vertical drop from its 4,100-foot summit, top-to-bottom snowmaking, four chairlifts and a gondola (adult lift tickets, $31 weekends, $25 weekdays). **Black Mountain** is half its height and far smaller in scope, but its sunny southerly exposure and low-key, self-contained nature make it particularly good for families. Nearby are **Attitash** in Bartlett and **Mount Cranmore** in North Conway, a revered place that celebrated its 50th anniversary in 1989. **Tuckerman Ravine** on Mount Washington is where the hardy ski when the snows elsewhere have long since melted, if they're up to the climb (a 1,500-foot vertical rise for a half-mile run down).

Hikes and Drives. The Jackson Resort Association publishes a handy guide to nine walks and hikes, from the "Village Mile" stroll to Thorn Mountain trails. A good overview is offered by the Five-Mile Circuit Drive up Route 16B into the mountains east of Jackson, a loop worth driving both directions for different perspectives. Look for spectacular glimpses of Mount Washington, and stop for a picnic, a swim or a stroll through the cascades called Jackson Falls, part of the Wildcat River just above the village. The Appalachian Mountain Club has a guide for tougher hikes in the White Mountains.

Shopping. It's no surprise that the biggest store is the **Jack Frost Shop,** a distinctive landmark that's a serious ski shop as well as a fine apparel store with a few gift items plus a Nordic rental shop and ski school. Other than a couple of small galleries and antiques shops, "downtown" Jackson consists of a post office, town hall, the Jackson Community Church and the tiny red 1901 Jackson Library, open Tuesdays from 10 to 4 and Thursdays from 10 to 4 and 7 to 9. For a more rigorous shopping foray, head down valley to the boutiques of North Conway and its ever-expanding factory outlet centers and shopping complexes like the new, upscale Settlers' Green.

Other Attractions. Heritage-New Hampshire and **Storyland** are side-by-side destinations, suitable particularly for families. The former lets visitors walk through stage sets in which dioramas, costumed guides and talking figures depict 30 events in state history. Storyland is a fairytale village with buildings, fourteen themed rides and performances for children. Nearby is the **Grand Manor,** a museum of antique automobiles. Children and non-skiers also enjoy riding the Wildcat gondola, a 25-minute round trip to the summit looking across to Mount Washington. You can look down on Wildcat and the rest of New England from the top of the Mount Washington Auto Road, a 90-minute round-trip drive.

Extra-Special

Cross-Country Skiing. Jackson was rated by Esquire magazine as one of the four best places in the world for ski touring. That's due in large part to the efforts of the non-profit Jackson Ski Touring Foundation, founded in 1972 and now with 91 miles of well-groomed and marked trails starting in the village of Jackson and heading across public and private lands into the White Mountain National Forest. They interlace the village and link restaurants and inns, as well as connecting with 40 miles of Appalachian Mountain Club trails in Pinkham Notch. It's possible for cross-country skiers to take the gondola to the summit of Wildcat and tour downhill via a twelve-mile trail to the village of Jackson 3,200 feet below.

Sherburne House (circa 1695) is one of oldest structures at Strawbery Banke.

Portsmouth, N.H.
A Lively Past and Present

Settled in 1623, the Portsmouth area ranks as the third oldest in the country after Jamestown and Plymouth. In many ways it looks it, the early Colonial houses hugging the narrow streets and the busy riverfront conceding little to modernity.

This is no Jamestown or Plymouth, nor is it Newport, a similarly sized and situated community with which it occasionally is compared. The city has only one large hotel, its downtown blessedly few chain stores or trendy boutiques, its residents little sense of elitism. What it does have is a patina of living and working history, a pride in its past and present, a noticeable joie de vivre.

The sense of history is everywhere, from the famed restoration called Strawbery Banke to the ancient structures dating back to the 17th century tucked here and there across town. Named for the profusion of wild berries found on the shores by the English settlers, Strawbery Banke after more than 25 years of restoration efforts is a living museum of 37 historic buildings at the edge of downtown.

Portsmouth's pride in past and present evidences itself in the six museum homes of the Historic Portsmouth Trail, the creative reuse of old buildings around Market Square and on the Hill, and the pending renovation by the Henley Group of the magnificent old Wentworth-by-the-Sea resort hotel out in Newcastle.

You can sense Portsmouth's joie de vivre in its flourishing restaurants (good new ones pop up every year), the number and scope of which are far beyond the resources of most cities of 26,000. You can see it in its lively Theatre by the Sea and its Music Hall. You can feel it in its Prescott Park Arts Festival, the Ceres Street Crafts Fair, the Seacoast Jazz Festival. The people on the streets and in the shops exude friendliness.

Happily, Portsmouth retains its historic sense of scale. It is an enclave of antiquity

Martin Hill Inn is decked out for Christmas.

along the Piscataqua River, four miles inland from the Atlantic. The Portsmouth Navy Yard is across the river in Kittery, Me. The Pease Air Force Base is west toward Dover. The shopping centers and fast-food strips are out in Newington. The beach action is down in Rye and Hampton. Most tourists stay at motels at the Portsmouth Circle.

While travelers pass by on the New Hampshire Turnpike, Air Force jets stream overhead, and tugboats and ocean vessels ply the river to and from the sea, Portsmouth goes its merry, historic way.

Inn Spots

Martin Hill Inn, 404 Islington St., Portsmouth 03801. (603) 436-2287.

The first B&B in Portsmouth (1978), the Martin Hill was acquired in 1983 by Jane and Paul Harnden, who with another couple were visiting their favorite town from Nashua, where they lived. "We had hardly heard of bed and breakfast," says Jane, "but during breakfast at the inn the owners said they would like to sell in about three years and, I thought, this is me."

It turned out that medical problems forced the owners to sell that summer, and now the Harndens are the friendly innkeepers who dispense gobs of information about the many restaurants in town, historic attractions and whatnot, as well as cooking delicious breakfasts.

The handsome yellow house, built in 1820, is within a long walk of downtown. Although it is on a commercial street, it's quiet because of air-conditioning and one can retreat in summer to a nicely landscaped back yard where 400 plants thrive and where tea is served about 4 p.m.

Although the inn lacks a common room, guests have plenty of room to spread out in the three spacious guest rooms in the main inn and four suites in the Guest House. The downstairs front room, called the Library, is in shades of rose and has a twin and a

136

double pineapple poster bed. Upstairs, the Master Bedroom, in white and Wedgwood blue, has a queensize canopy bed and oriental rugs on the wide-board floors. The Greenhouse Suite in the spiffy side annex contains a small solarium of wicker looking onto a lovely courtyard, rattan furniture in an inside sitting room and a queensize bedroom with full bath. Balloon curtains frame the windows in the Green Room, which has a small sitting room, an antique tub with a hand-held shower apparatus, and a queensize iron and brass bed that's so frilly it reminds Jane of a big crib. All rooms have modern baths, loveseats or comfortable chairs, good reading lamps, writing desks, armoires, and nice touches like potpourri in china teacups.

Breakfast is served on a long, gleaming mahogany table in the antiques-filled dining room. Orange juice might be followed by Jane's scrumptious baked apple, the core filled with brown sugar. Paul makes dynamite french toast with Italian sourdough bread, slathered with almonds and accompanied by Canadian bacon and homemade cranberry relish. Our scrambled eggs with cheese and chervil were served with a pork chop and sliced cranberry bread, and the coffee pot was bottomless. It's a great time to compare notes on the restaurants of the night before and to plan the day, with the help of Paul, who can even plot you out a trip up to Canada and back. Clearly the Harndens love their role as innkeepers and go out of their way to be helpful.

Doubles, $70 to $85.

Sise Inn, 40 Court St., Portsmouth 03801. (603) 433-1200 or (800) 232-4667.

The first United States branch of a five-inn Canadian chain called Someplace(s) Different Ltd., this is a magnificent operation. The company took the original Queen Anne home built in 1881 for the John E. Sise family, remodeled it in 1986 with exquisite taste and put on a large rear addition that blends in very well. Walk in the front door past the stained-glass windows on either side, gaze at the rich and abundant butternut and oak throughout, marvel at the graceful staircase and three-story-high foyer, peek into the sumptuous living room and you're apt to say, as marketing director Cyndee Wild did upon first seeing it, "this is the real Portsmouth."

The 34 rooms and suites on three floors vary in bed configuration, size and decor. All are elegantly furnished in antiques and period reproductions with striking window treatments and vivid wallpapers. Geared to the business traveler, they have vanities outside the bathroom, writing desks, chairs or sitting areas, clock radios, room phones, and remote-control television and VCRs often hidden in armoires. Businessmen must like to watch TV in bed, for in many of the rooms we saw it wasn't visible from the chairs or, as is too often the case, the single chair. Windows that open, English herbal toiletries and mints on the pillow may compensate for the occasional lack of places to sit.

Or you can sit in the stylish main-floor living room, very much like an English library with several conversation areas and fresh flowers all around. Carl Jensen, innkeeper with his wife Gisele, is the usually visible host.

A help-yourself breakfast of fruits, juices,

Graceful staircase at the Sise Inn.

yogurt, cheese, cereals, granola, croissants, bagels and all kinds of preserves and honey is available amidst much ornate wood in the dining room.

The lower floor, notable for an antique English phone booth in the hallway, has three function rooms. A modern elevator shuttles guests between floors of this deluxe inn, which really feels more like an inn than a small hotel.

Doubles, $78 to $99; suites, $109 to $150.

The Inn at Strawberry Banke, 314 Court St., Portsmouth 03801. (603) 436-7242.

You can't stay much closer to Strawbery Banke than here, although you may wonder why innkeepers Tom and Martha Laurie add the extra "r" to the attraction upon which they capitalize. They inherited the name from their predecessors, and perhaps it reflects the updating both couples have done to the 1800 ship captain's house situated right up against the street, as so many in Portsmouth are.

The Lauries took over in 1988 and added baths, so that now all seven rooms have private baths, although two are in the hall (and one in the attic suite is open to the room). Two rooms on the main floor share a common room. Strawberry stenciling, strawberry comforters and strawberry candies on the pillows accent the prevailing green and white color scheme here. More rooms go off an upstairs common room, where decanters of sherry await. One, done up in blues, has inside shutters, two rattan chairs and pineapple stenciling. The aforementioned attic suite, with the open toilet and shower added in the corner, is for young, short people, said Tom as he led us up the steep stairs and ducked to avoid the roof as we entered the sleeping alcove.

A continental breakfast of juice, cereal and breads from the great Ceres Bakery is set out on an old Duchess Atlantic cookstove in a cheery, skylit sun room. The room looks onto the trellised rose garden of the historic Governor Langdon House just behind.

Doubles, $89 to $98.

Leighton Inn, 69 Richards Ave., Portsmouth 03801. (603) 433-2188.

A stark white clapboard house that once was in the Sise family (see above) was transformed about the same time as the Sise Inn into a stately B&B by Catherine Stone, a stickler for authenticity, who was looking for a home for her collection of Empire furniture. She took the name of another occupant of the 1809 home built by a local cabinetmaker. There's a piano in each of the formal parlors on either side of the staircase, an architectural delight that climbs majestically to the third floor.

Three of the five large guest rooms have private baths, the two on the third floor sharing one down a far-away hall. One second-floor front room with a chintz-draped canopy four-poster has a dramatic red, white and black bathroom and an old brocade sofa. The clothing hooks from the 19th century in the closet of a second room are worthy of their builder; this queensize room in blues and peaches has a hall bath with colorful tiles around the tub. Catherine calls one of her third-floor rooms the bridal suite because its pencil-post canopy bed is dressed in white eyelet. The room across the hall has an enormous, free-standing Empire cheval mirror that dwarfs the twin converted rope beds, bentwood rocker and Sheraton tiger maple table.

A full breakfast is served in the kitchen or on the small rear porch. Fresh fruits, homemade muffins with berries grown in her garden, an egg dish, homefries and breakfast meats are the fare.

Doubles, $65 to $75.

The Inn at Christian Shore, 335 Maplewood Ave., Portsmouth 03801. (603) 431-6770.

An abundance of antiques, an inviting dining room with a fireplace, and quite lavishly

Dining room at Strawbery Court is elegant and subdued.

decorated, air-conditioned guest rooms with television are attractions in this 1800 Federal house, located in the historic Christian Shore area.

Across from the Jackson House, Portsmouth's oldest, the structure was renovated and redecorated in 1979 by three antiques dealers, Charles Litchfield, Louis Sochia and Tom Towey. "It was a neighborhood eyesore," Tom says, but you'd never know it today.

In the main entry hall is a desk with baskets of candies and nuts, a grandfather clock and an etched-glass light. The richly furnished sitting room crammed with antiques is used as a sixth guest room in summer.

Upstairs are five guest rooms, several with canopy or four-poster beds and one a tiny single. Three rooms have private baths (including one with peach towels resting on a leather couch), another with a double and twin bed has a half bath, and two share. All have handsome furnishings like crocheted afghans.

A long harvest table dominates the beamed breakfast room, with its large brick fireplace and an organ in the corner. Three smaller dining tables with upholstered wing chairs are around the sides. The innkeepers' collection of rabbits covers every shelf in the room — some ceramic, some cement, some in a 1900 lacquered Japanese cabinet, some on the floor.

A full breakfast including ham or perhaps steak is cooked by any of the three innkeepers, with the other two waiting on tables. The partners were tiring of the pace, however, and had the inn up for sale as this edition went to press.

Doubles, $60; single $30.

Dining Spots

Strawbery Court, 20 Atkinson St., Portsmouth. (603) 431-7722.

In this city of restaurants, most discriminating diners consider Strawbery Court the leader in consistently fine dining.

It certainly is the most elegant, restful and refined: eleven well-spaced tables in the large dining room of a brick 1815 Federal House that is home to talented young chef Douglas Johnson and his dentist-partner, Dr. Frank Manchester. The platinum-colored walls and carpet seem to turn a restful dark gray at night. A few spotlit oil paintings and

139

a large bouquet of gladioli on the service table provide accents. A perfect long-stemmed pink rose is in a vase on each white-linened table. A tall white candle is lit on each; the rest of the lighting comes from candles on a sideboard, a crystal chandelier and discreet ceiling track lights. Even the restrooms are lit by candles, as are two small upstairs dining rooms with warming fireplaces for overflow and private parties.

Service is solicitous and formal, the menu being explained knowledgeably if a bit by rote, and the silver and china place settings being changed with each course.

Dinner can be ordered prix-fixe for $37 or a la carte. Among appetizers (escargots, souffle of coquilles St. Jacques and marinated chicken terrine with port, sausage and pistachios, all $6.95), we sampled the Norwegian smoked salmon, thinly sliced pieces garnished with capers, onion and caviar. Good, crunchy and hot French whole wheat bread slices were served from an enormous basket. Lemon slices flavor the ice water. The colorful house salad ($4.95) was composed like a painting: Boston lettuce and radicchio topped with a fan of enoki mushrooms, shredded radish, purple kale, beets, carrots and snow peas.

Entrees ($20.95 to $22.95) include such seasonal specialties as pheasant Normande and loin of venison, along with traditional items like tournedos with brandy and peppercorns and breast of chicken stuffed with foie gras. We liked the sweetbreads sauteed with orange zest and cointreau and the thick and rosy medallions of lamb, served with pimento (red) and pesto (green) sauces. Between them was a ribbon of whipped potatoes; on the side, a bundle of crisp white asparagus tied with red pepper.

The desserts ($6) are triumphs. The popular gateau au fromage is a delicate cheesecake laced with armagnac and grand marnier on a layer of genoise. A real wow of a dessert was a pear poached in red wine, cored and stuffed with frangelico and hazelnut ice cream, the top dipped in a caramel glaze, the bottom in a fresh red raspberry glaze, and served on a bed of semi-sweet chocolate sauce. Chef Doug also offered samples of his chocolate chestnut terrine on raspberry coulis and a chocolate tart with fresh mint and raspberries that were too good to pass up.

The house Lucien Simone rouge and blanc de blanc wines are $11.25, the best bargains on a rather expensive wine list.

Doug Johnson, a native Rhode Islander and Culinary Institute of America grad, cooks in the classical French style with a nouvelle presentation. He does it all himself, assisted occasionally by some of the staff of five who accompanied him to Strawbery Court in 1983 from his acclaimed restaurant, L'Armagnac, in Columbus, Ohio.

Dinner, Tuesday-Saturday 6 to 9.

Seventy Two Restaurant, 45 Pearl St., Portsmouth. (603) 436-5666.

The name comes from young chef James J. Miceli's original success, 72 Islington, a small and highly rated restaurant he opened in 1982 on Islington Street. In 1984, he moved around the corner into what was formerly a Baptist church, a smashing site to be converted into a restaurant. So it's not surprising that Jim, now a justice of the peace, performs weddings in his restaurant.

From the front entrance you ascend stairways on either side to what was once the airy sanctuary. It's an incredible space, with high rusty red ceiling, tall arched windows and well-spaced tables for 75. At the far end over the kitchen is a balcony that must have been the choir loft. It's now a cocktail lounge with an ornate metal banister, tables, piano and a sofa seating a family of stuffed bears from Jim's collection.

Tiny lamps are on each table, crisply set with white linen, pink napkins folded in porcelain rings and white china. The setting could not be more regal, if a bit intimidating, especially when the dining room is not filled.

Locals fault the service while applauding the dinner fare. "French food with a New

England flair" is how self-taught chef Miceli describes it. The ambitious menu might list octopus, chilled lobster remoulade and veal sausage with shallot cream sauce among appetizers ($6.25). Soups could be French brie with sherry or oyster stew.

Entrees range from $14.95 for haddock amandine to lobster-stuffed lobster tails for $21.95 and chateaubriand, $45 for two. Changing preparations of lamb and tenderloin, veal Oscar, roast duck Montmorency, shrimp scampi and saute of quail in chambord and raspberry vinegar are typical. Salad is extra, but plates come with three or four vegetables, artfully presented.

The dessert cart might contain hazelnut torte, poppyseed and frangelico cheesecakes, a midnight layer cake and a linzer torte. The rather pricey wine list comes in a little wine-colored book.

Dinner nightly, 6 to 10; Sunday brunch, noon to 3.

L'Auberge, 96 Bridge St., Portsmouth. (603) 436-2377.

A one-room, very personal restaurant in the French provincial style is run rather casually by Francois Rolland and his wife Kathy — he in the kitchen and she out front, and neither crosses the line. It's of the old school and open at the chef's whim; "when I make enough money I close the doors and take off to France," he says.

A sign inside the canopied entrance to the out-of-the-way house warns "this is not a diner," intending to convey that the meal will take some time. The decor is unpretentious: hurricane candles and brown linens, pretty beveled windows and stained glass.

All the French classics are offered, from $12 for frog's legs provencale or linguini with white clam sauce to $18 for beef Wellington or Dover sole meuniere. Tournedos rossini or bearnaise are $15, sweetbreads $14 and roast duck $13.50. Dinners include crusty French bread, potato or rice pilaf, vegetable and caesar salad. The French wines are a bargain, and the crepes Suzette and cherries jubilee outstanding.

Lunch is locally popular. How could it not be with entrees priced from $5.50 to $8.50 for some of the dinner items, plus shrimp Creole and Hungarian goulash?

Lunch, 11:30 to 3; dinner, 5 to 10; closed Sunday and Monday, plus June and part of July.

Guido's Upstairs Trattoria, 67 Bow St, Portsmouth. (603) 431-2989.

"Guido is just back from Italy with the new fall menu," said the sign directing us upstairs over the natural-foods store. There in the kitchen was Peter ("call me Guido") Yosua, young, dark and handsome and in the kitchen alone in the early afternoon, preparing for the evening's dinner.

We'd heard raves from other restaurateurs as well as criticisms (for inconsistency), but there's no denying Guido's purity — he's into healthy cooking with natural foods, bans smoking and tries to make "everything as authentic as possible." There's no denying, either, the pristine quality of the dozen white-clothed tables set amid beamed ceiling and brick walls, flanked by windows onto the harbor.

Guido, who claims to be self-taught, travels to Italy two or three times a year to bone up on Tuscan cuisine. Among appetizers ($3.50 to $6), the most expensive appealed — seafood antipasto, with clams, shrimp, calamari and mussels delicately steamed in wine, garlic and olive oil.

Seven pastas ($9.50 to $12) are available in half portions if ordered as appetizers. We liked the sound of penne with porcini mushrooms, prosciutto and peas, and gorgonzola-stuffed tortellini in a cheese and pinenut sauce.

All ten entrees are a bargain $13 or $14 for the likes of veal stewed in a white wine and sage broth, jumbo shrimp dredged in garlic and olive oil, tenderloin of beef braised in chianti, and roasted pork with veal sausage and beef tenderloin.

Lion statues greet diners outside the Library restaurant.

Desserts include tirami su, casatta, fresh fruit and Italian cheeses. The all-Italian wine list is priced from $12 to $50.

Dinner, Tuesday-Saturday 6 to 10.

Anthony's Al Dente, 59 Penhallow St., Portsmouth. (603) 436-2527.

Popular locally, usually jammed and considered rather expensive is this institution in the Custom House Cellar, dark and grotto-like with stone and brick walls and slate floors, accented with paintings and oriental rugs.

The six-page menu combines both northern and southern Italian specialties, and while it appears expensive, patrons are expected to share. The small antipasto ($7.75, as opposed to large, $13.50) is enough for four. It's such a work of art that one hates to disturb it. Twelve pastas, made on the premises, are listed as "first main courses" ($9 to $16) and make a meal in themselves. Ten "second main courses" of veal, chicken and scampi (from $12 to $17, calamari of the day to scampi diavolo) are supplemented by daily Italian specialties featuring beef, lamb or game.

Everything costs extra (remember, you're supposed to share), from garlic bread ($2.50) to mixed salad ($3.50) to minestrone ($4).

Most desserts are $4.25, things like almond cake with amaretto whipped cream, zuppa Inglese, ricotta cheesecake, cannoli and spumoni.

The wine list stresses Italian vintages, with some good buys for $9 and most priced in the teens.

Dinner, Tuesday-Saturday 5:30 to 10, Sunday 5 to 9.

The Library at the Rockingham House, 401 State St., Portsmouth. (603) 431-5202.

The old Rockingham Hotel has been converted to apartments, but Michael Hallinan restored part of the ground floor into an extravagant restaurant in 1975. Its ornate carved-wood ceiling, mahogany paneling, fireplaces, huge mirrors and bright blue napkins set the stage for books, books and more books on shelves in three rooms. Some bookshelves enclose booths for intimate dining.

The appealing menu is reasonably priced and the specials interesting (sweet and sour chicken, veal amandine, tournedos Oscar and cream of eggplant soup the last time we were there). For lunch, we tried a fennel and gruyere quiche ($5.25) that was as tasty

142

as it was generous, accompanied by a super-good spinach salad with a mustard dressing and homemade croutons. The mussels mariniere ($6.25) arrived in a large glass bowl abrim with garlicky broth in which to dip chunks of the homemade rolls. The strawberry cheesecake for dessert was at least three inches high.

For dinner, Thailandese beef salad, Middle Eastern eggplant dip and broiled pork with peanut curry sauce are among provocative appetizers ($2.75 to $5.25). Entrees run the gamut from the aforementioned mussels mariniere ($7.50) through oriental chicken, roast Long Island duck and sole florentine to $18.50 for rack of New Zealand lamb with mint-apricot sauce. Three steak and two shrimp dishes are in the $15 range.

Lunch, 11:30 to 3; dinner, 5 to 11 or midnight; Sunday brunch, 11:30 to 4.

The Toucan, 174 Fleet St., Portsmouth. (603) 431-5443.

How could you not like a restaurant where the focal point is a toucan named Piwi in her own glassed-in cage, and the restrooms are labeled "He Can" and "She Can?" The food is fine, and the atmosphere upbeat, at this cafe brought to us by the folks who operate the more sedate and established Library at the Rockingham.

Up a flight of stairs beside a waterfall flowing over a stone wall, you can see, up high, an enormous mechanical toucan on a perch, its head bobbing from side to side. Toucan is divided by curved glass brick walls into an oft-crowded lounge with a green marble bar, above which is written, in neon, "grab a beakful," and a bistro-like restaurant with green and white tile floor, tables covered with shelf paper (crayons are provided for doodling), bentwood chairs, colored theatrical lights on a track and framed posters on the walls. Gracefully curved windows provide glimpses of downtown Portsmouth. Cactus plants in clay pots are here and there; toucans in stained glass and other guises are colorful accessories.

Served all day, Toucan's menu is basically Mexican, with a smattering of American, South American and, after 5 and for lunch specials, Cajun dishes like blackened snapper. Crisp homemade tortilla chips and a snappy salsa are served as soon as you sit down. The tortilla soup ($2.75) is a meal in itself, loaded with cheese and spicy enough to bring out the Kleenex. Calamari salad ($5.95) is served with artichoke hearts and pimentos in a terrific marinade.

The oyster shot ($2.25) is one of the favorite appetizers. It's a blue-point oyster in a shot glass with a bit of champagne, spicy sauce and chopped cilantro.

Mexican pizza, nachos various ways, big red chili burger, taco salad, and barbecued ribs or chicken are other treats. With the barbecued dishes you get whirley bird fries, cole slaw and jalapeno corn bread. N'awlins seafood linguini, Cajun blackened sirloin, jumbo shrimp gumbo and grilled mustard shrimp are some "down by the bayou" entrees. For dessert, try an apple burrito or deep-fried ice cream.

Sangria is about $10 a liter; the wines are inexpensive (but beer is better with many of these dishes). You can get Cajun steak and eggs, french toast bayou or huevos rancheros at Aunt Chilada's brunch on Sunday.

Open daily, 11:30 to 11.

The Metro, 20 High St., Portsmouth. (603) 436-0521.

Very popular locally is this art nouveau bar and cafe, pleasantly decked out with brass rails, stained glass, old gas lights, mirrors and dark wood, leather banquettes, bentwood chairs and nifty Vanity Fair posters.

The Metro's award-winning clam chowder (which once won first prize in the New England competition at Newport) is a popular starter among the standard continental appetizers. Salads, sandwiches, fettuccine alfredo, baked spanakopita and several entrees are offered at lunch.

Dinner in owner Sam Jarvis's convivial establishment is a mix of American and continental (lamb chops and haddock casino, steak Diane and veal Oscar), $10.95 to $14.95. Desserts, attractively displayed on a fancy old baker's rack, include baklava, walnut pie and caramel custard.

Lunch daily, 11:30 to 3; dinner, 5:30 to 9:30 or 10; closed Sunday.

The Oar House, 55 Ceres St., Portsmouth. (603) 436-4025.

Located in an old grain warehouse dating from the early 1800s, this casual restaurant has quadrupled in size since its opening in 1975. But the ancient aura remains: rough brick and stone walls hung with nautical photos, dark beams, bare floors, a jolly bar and two dining rooms — one upstairs, with a glimpse of the waterfront. One table in the downstairs dining room is enclosed in a brass bedstead.

Tiny oil candles flickered as we lunched in a booth in the tavern after sipping a very good bloody mary made with clamato juice. Thick clam chowder studded with clams, potatoes and corn was fine; the accompanying turkey and avocado sandwich a bit dry. Shrimp marinara crepe and a green salad loaded with carrot strips, bean sprouts, sunflower seeds and a creamy dill dressing made a great lunch combination.

Dinner is a mixed but interesting bag, with seafood the specialty and plenty of other choices. Priced from $11.50 to $16.96, entrees include teriyaki beef kabob, medallions of tenderloin bearnaise, chicken en papillote, veal barbara and bouillabaisse.

Lunch and dinner daily, Sunday brunch.

Karen's, 105 Daniel St., Portsmouth. (603) 431-1948.

Some of the most interesting dinners (to say nothing of breakfasts and lunches) in town are served by Karen Weiss and staff in this unassuming little place with bare floors, stenciled walls and ten or twelve tables flanked by windsor chairs.

The weekend dinners are exciting. How about this November menu that included spicy jalapeno quesadillas with blackeyed-pea salsa or Indonesian chicken sate with cucumber relish and spicy peanut sauce for appetizers ($3.50 and $3.95), and main courses like fresh tuna with putanesca sauce, sauteed tenderloin with Hungarian spiced cognac sour-cream sauce and veal medallions sauteed with pancetta, oyster mushrooms, shrimp and cilantro lemon demi-glace ($11.95 to $17.95)?

If you can't get in for dinner, settle for lunch, perhaps a hot eggplant sandwich, Mexican chicken club, grilled swordfish kabob, chicken faijita or pesto quiche and salad. Prices are in the $5 to $6 range.

Breakfasts are memorable: five versions of scrambled eggs, whole wheat pancakes, french toast with Karen's cinnamon-raisin bread and hot seven-grain cereal. Splurge for eggs Benedict ($4.25) or steak and eggs ($5.95).

Breakfast and lunch, Monday-Saturday; dinner, Friday and Saturday 6 to 10; Sunday brunch, 8 to 2. BYOB. No credit cards.

The Dolphin Striker, 15 Bow St., Portsmouth. (603) 431-5222.

Fresh seafood and a few entrees with a creative flair are the hallmarks of the Dolphin Striker, a plain but historic restaurant upstairs with a cozy stone-walled tavern beneath. Natives rave about the seafood, from the simple broiled haddock served with lemon butter ($11.50) to seafood provencale ($16.75). Lobster is an accent to the sole Andrea and Hannah Mariner's pie, filled with seafood in a rich sherry and sour cream sauce ($14.25). Noisettes of veal madeira, rack of lamb dijon and steaks also are available. French silk and key lime pies, fruit sorbets, black magic chocolate cake and a "strawberry bazaar" are among the scrumptious desserts.

Lunch, 11:30 to 2; dinner, 5:30 to 9:30.

Sakura, 40 Pleasant St., Portsmouth. (603) 431-2721.

Portsmouth's first and only Japanese restaurant is in the old Post Office building, with a long sushi bar, blond wood tables, stucco walls, hanging lamps and screens. The two sushi chefs work magic and we enjoyed, for a gentle $7.95, a plate of beautifully decorated sushi, miso soup and tea. Another lunch special, breaded and fried codfish with rice, salad and shrimp dumplings, was only $4.95.

Other choices at lunch are shrimp tempura ($6.75), teriyaki dishes for $6.75 to $8.25, and seven noodle dishes, $4.75 to $6.75 (for noodles with tempura, fish cake, vegetables and egg).

At night, sushi comes in several dishes. "Heaven" is comprised of twelve pieces and two rolls of sushi and ten pieces of sashimi. Baked halibut with soybean sauce, breaded cutlets, sukiyaki, teriyakis and tempuras are $7.25 to $15. Enjoy a Sapporo beer with your meal, and finish up with ginger or green-tea ice cream.

Lunch, Monday-Friday 11:30 to 2:30; dinner nightly, 5 to 10 or 11.

BG's Boat House Restaurant, Wentworth Road, Portsmouth. (603) 431-1074.

If you're hankering for lobster and down-home surroundings, head for this popular little restaurant with outdoor decks and a marina out past the old Wentworth resort in Newcastle. Windows look onto what longtime owners Bruce and Joanne Graves say is Sagamore Creek; to us it looks more like an ocean inlet.

The walls are pine paneled, the floors bare and tables have captain's chairs and paper mats, the better for gorging oneself on a lobster dinner ($9.95), a lobster roll with french fries ($7.25), fried oysters in a basket ($5.95) or a seafood platter ($12.95). The lobsters are delivered to the back door by boat by BG's own lobstermen. The Graveses accommodate other tastes with BLT sandwiches, hamburgers, potato skins and mozzarella sticks, but most people go here for lobster and seafood, plain and simple.

Lunch, Monday-Friday 11 to 4; dinner nightly, 5 to 9. Closed December-February.

The Blue Strawbery, 29 Ceres St., Portsmouth. (603) 431-6420.

Portsmouth's restaurant renaissance was inspired by chef James Haller and the Blue Strawbery, which opened in a narrow 1797 restored ship's chandlery across from the waterfront in 1970. It's known far and wide, better regarded nationally than locally, especially since a spate of letters in the daily newspaper revealed a consensus that the restaurant was resting on its laurels.

Buddy Haller has since left; the author of "The Blue Strawbery Cookbook" now is into holistic cooking and prepares candlelight dinners at the Shaker Village in Canterbury, N.H. Longtime chef Phillip McGuire, who cooked during Haller's frequent absences, was still on board, but Gene Brown, the last of the original partners, had the restaurant up for sale. Although some say the food is as good as ever, we know increasing numbers of people who have been disappointed,

Prix-fixe dinners of six courses ($36) are served at two seatings nightly. The choice of entree includes one each from land, sea or air. Waiters serve the meals family style from huge platters, sometimes telling people they can have "seconds" of their order but not a sample of something else.

145

Dinner by reservation only, Monday-Saturday 6 and 9 p.m., Sunday 3 and 6 p.m.; single seating at 7:30 Tuesday-Thursday from Columbus Day to Memorial Day. No credit cards.

Cafe Brioche, 14 Market Square, Portsmouth. (603) 430-9225.

Portsmouth's only sidewalk cafe (in summer) is a good place to stop anytime for a light breakfast like a pastry with cappuccino. It's also popular for lunch, with several kinds of quiche (ham and tomato, spinach and mushroom) at $2 a slice and great soups (lentil-vegetable and creamy carrot and ginger for $1.50 or $2 at our last visit). Sandwiches are $2.50 to $3.50 and you could have one of hummus or country pate. A broccoli feta croissant is $1.50 and garden salad $2. Take out, or enjoy on one of the seven glass-covered tables. A strawberry-banana-kiwi tart would make a good dessert, or maybe just a bourbon truffle?

Open daily 8 to 5 or 6, Friday to 9.

A few other good places for a snack: **Ceres Bakery** at 51 Penhallow St. offers wonderful breads and pastries. On a recent visit we saw a spinach, tomato and cheddar quiche ($2), split pea soup with coriander, and an almond mocha tart for $1.25. **Moe's Sandwich Shop** at 22 Daniel St. is famous for grinders; a regular half is $1.50, a super half $2, and "x-tras" 20 cents to 40 cents. For handmade ice cream, stop at **Annabelle's** on Ceres Street; a small cone of cashew caramel turtle or raspberry chocolate chip is $1.75. Soups and sandwiches are offered as well. **A Movable Feast** at 41 Congress St. is an outstanding deli-gourmet store with soups, salads, sandwiches and pizza. The Greek pasta salad and curried chicken puffs looked great.

Diversions

Portsmouth offers much for anyone with an interest in history. The Greater Porstmouth Chamber of Commerce publishes an excellent "Walking Tour of Downtown Portsmouth's Waterfront," which also can be driven (although directions get confusing because of one-way streets). The 2.3-mile tour takes in most of the city's attractions, including some we had passed for years unknowingly — such is the charm of an area crammed with discoveries at every turn.

Strawbery Banke. Billed as "an American original," this walk-through museum is the careful restoration of one of the nation's oldest neighborhoods, its 37 structures dating from 1695 to 1945 and depicting four centuries of cultural and architectural change. Some have simply been preserved; some are used by working artisans (independent of the museum, they are earning their living rather than merely re-enacting history); others are used for educational exhibits including archaeology, architectural styles and construction techniques and, on the outside, historic gardens. Strawbery Banke's collection of local arts and furniture is shown in six historic houses. Significantly, these are not all homes of the rich or famous, but rather of ordinary people. As the museum's 25th anniversary program noted, "This is the real story of history — the dreams and aspirations, the disappointments and frustrations of common people." That is the glory of Strawbery Banke, and of much of Portsmouth. Open daily 10 to 5, May-October; adults $6.

The Portsmouth Trail. Six of Portsmouth's finest house museums are open individually and linked by a walking tour and common ticket ($6). Considered the one not to miss is the 1763 **Moffatt-Ladd House,** a replica of an English manor house located just above Ceres Street restaurants and shops. The yellow 1758 **John Paul Jones House** and the imposing **Governor John Langdon House** (1784) are others.

Historic structures are visitor attractions at Strawbery Banke.

Shopping. Most of the traditional tourist shopping attractions have passed Portsmouth by, heading for the upscale outlet strip along Route 1 north of Kittery or the shopping malls of Newington. In town, the most interesting shops are around Market Square. **Salamandra Glass** has colorful, exquisite hanging glass pieces and vases with fluted edges among items made in the adjacent studio. We liked the birch-bark planters at **Habitat,** a very modern store with everything from toys to closet systems. The backpacks for kids were extra colorful. **Gallery 33** at Ceres and Bow streets has some of the wildest jewelry we've seen. **Little Dickens** is good for toys. **The Square Rigger** is a large gift shop with many nautical things; the same owner has the **Bow Street Candle and Mug,** which name is self-explanatory. **Wholly Macro** offers good educational toys; **Macro Polo** has some trendy clothes. **Tulips** for crafts and woodwork, **Worldly Goods** for interesting baskets and adorable cat pins, and **Prelude** for Crabtree & Evelyn goods are more. We liked almost everything at **Les Cadeaux,** a fine gift store, and did some Christmas shopping at the **N.W. Barrett Gallery,** which has a good selection of Sabra Field woodcuts and some fantastic jewelry. **Kingsbury House** at 93 State St. is the gift shop run by the Guild of Strawbery Banke. **Strawbery Banke** has working crafts shops offering the wares of potters, a cabinetmaker, a weaver, and dories made in the boat shed.

An unusually good outlet mall on the south side of town is **Artisan Outlet Village,** where in the anchor store the man of the family stocked up on shirts, sweaters and ties and hoped to return when he was feeling more flush for a Burberry raincoat.

Extra-Special

Newcastle. Drive or bicycle out Newcastle Avenue (Route 1B) through the quaint islands of Newcastle, the original settlement in 1623, dotted with prosperous historic (and new) homes. The meandering roads and treed residential properties, many with water views, mix contemporary-style houses with those of days gone by. You can view Fort Constitution and visit the new seacoast park at **Great Island Common** (parking $2 a person), where there are a playground, waterfront picnic tables and views of the Isles of Shoals. Take a gander at the restoration of Wentworth-by-the-Sea, a majestic resort hotel if ever there was one. The Henley Group planned to invest more than $100 million in the 275-acre property, including a large marina, an underground parking garage for 800 cars, an expanded and rebuilt resort hotel and a year-round conference center to open in 1991.

The Yorks
Great Gateway to Maine

The visitor quickly agrees with what the Chamber of Commerce directory proudly proclaims: "The Yorks are a perfect introduction to Maine. They have everything for which the Great State is famous: rocky coast, sandy beaches, a lighthouse, a mountain, rivers,...lobsters, folks who really do say 'ayuh.'"

The focal point of the Yorks is, of course, the water — specifically, the harbor where the river confronts the sea. From fashionable York Harbor, whose waters are as protected as its seaside homes, it's barely a mile inland along the York River to historic York Village, the oldest surviving English settlement in Maine. From the harbor, it's also barely a mile along the shore to York Beach. Abruptly, the rocky coast yields to sand; the trailer parks symbolize the transition from tree-shaded affluence to honky-tonk strand. Beyond are Nubble Light, one of America's most photographed lighthouses, and Cape Neddick Harbor, a quieter and quainter fishing site. Sand gives way again to rocks as Bald Head Cliff rises off the forested Shore Road near the Ogunquit town line.

Yes, the Yorks provide a good introduction to Maine, from the Cape Neddick fishermen to the amusement areas at crowded York Beach.

But much of the appeal of the Yorks is elsewhere. It's in York Village, where a national historic district embraces both private structures and eight house museums. It's in York Harbor, a verdant enclave of Colonial homesteads and gracious estates whose occupants in 1892 formed the York Harbor Reading Room men's club, an offshoot of which was the York Harbor Village Corporation. It established the first zoning laws in Maine and prevented the hordes and development of York Beach from spilling into York Harbor.

Growing numbers of inns are concentrated in York Village and York Harbor, allowing visitors to partake of private places in which past melds into present.

Inn Spots

Stage Neck Inn, Off Route 1A, Box 97, York Harbor 03911. (207) 363-3850 or (800) 222-3238.

Once an island and now a promontory where the York River becomes a harbor, Stage Neck was the site of the Marshall House, the first of the area's resort hotels. It was razed and rebuilt in 1973 as the Stage Neck Inn, a low-profile contemporary resort whose understated luxury fits the setting.

Disproportionate numbers of Cadillacs are in the parking lot, hinting of the clientele for whom Stage Neck is designed. There are tennis courts, a swimming pool and private beach, golf privileges, posh public rooms with water views, and a gorgeous dining room in which jackets are required for dinner.

There also are water views from the private patios or balconies of 60 guest rooms on three floors, the sprawling building having been designed into the landscape and opening on three sides to ocean, river and beach. Guest rooms are comfortably furnished in restful deep rose and moss green, with twins, two doubles or kingsize beds, two comfortable chairs and a table, color TV and phone. Rates vary with the view. The most choice are corner rooms with wraparound porches and views of the water in two directions.

Three meals a day are served in the grill or the main dining room (see Dining Spots). The inn is now open year-round, and offers good package prices in the winter.

Doubles, $120 to $160, EP.

The ocean is just beyond guest rooms at Stage Neck Inn.

York Harbor Inn, Route 1A, Box 573, York Harbor 03911. (207) 363-5119.

A history dating back to 1637 and a family's labor of love. That's the story of this busy turn-of-the-century inn restored and reopened in 1981 by twin brothers Joe and George Dominguez, their younger brother Garry and Joe's wife Jean.

Listed in the National Register of Historic Places and built around a 1637 post-and-beam sail loft that was moved to the site and now serves as a common room, the inn once served as headquarters for the York Harbor Reading Club, which continues to this day. The Dominguez brothers, all graduates of Colgate University, spent a year and a half restoring the inn, and are still adding to it (in 1988 they opened an addition housing a gift shop, banquet hall and twelve guest rooms upstairs).

Except for the new rooms, this is an old-fashioned, full-service inn with a character you sense immediately when you enter the main Cabin Lounge, its pitched ceiling (the former sail loft) now covered with tiny white Christmas bulbs lit all year. The dark, English-style Wine Cellar pub with a long solid cherry bar and lots of sofas clustered around the corner fireplace has weekend entertainment, and the dining rooms serve three meals a day (see below).

All but five of the oldest rooms in the main inn have private baths. Eaves and dormers contribute to interesting shapes, nooks and crannies in many rooms. They are nicely furnished with touches like white wicker headboards and rocking chairs, pink puffy quilts, good-looking prints and perhaps a writing desk. One room has a four-poster bed, white frilly curtains, oriental rug and towels stashed in an antique crib. Seven have fireplaces, and some have spa tubs. Decanters of sherry are set out in the upstairs hallways each evening.

In the newer Yorkshire House, a large front room has an oak bed, a working fireplace and a case full of books. From most rooms you can hear the ocean rolling up against the inn's beach across the street beneath the Marginal Way.

Guests are served a continental breakfast of fresh fruit, juice, and homemade blueberry or cranberry muffins. A full breakfast is available for a charge in the summer.

Doubles, $60 to $120.

Elegant furnishings enhance guest bedroom and parlor at Wooden Goose Inn.

Wooden Goose Inn, Route 1, Cape Neddick 03902. (207) 363-5673.

Wonderful aromas and spirited classical music greet visitors to the Wooden Goose Inn. The aromas come from the kitchen, where innkeepers Jerry Rippletoe and Tony Sienicki may be taking turns baking their specialties, perhaps a flourless chocolate torte for afternoon tea or date bread for breakfast. The music comes from myriad speakers, which send Mozart and Vivaldi across the wonderful house.

This is one decorated inn, from its Terrace Room breakfast area and two comfy parlors to the seven guest rooms. All would do any decorator magazine proud. Jerry was a decorator in New York and New Jersey before he and Tony acquired the derelict house in 1984; he still commutes to the metropolitan area for consulting jobs. As befits the inn's name, geese and ducks are everywhere — even on the gorgeous, white-lit Christmas tree on our latest visit. Most are gifts from guests.

The rooms have been sumptuously outfitted with Victorian country furnishings in a masculine style and the walls hung with paintings. Each has a private bath and a sitting area. Blinds are down and curtains drawn to screen out the view and the noise from the road outside; there are bedside lights for reading, and the setting epitomizes escape and romance. Since we like an airy feeling and open windows, the rooms are a bit dark for our taste.

"The room is the important part of the stay," contends Jerry, who also keeps his charges well fed. Afternoon tea is taken in the Terrace Room or outside in lush gardens around a trickling pond bordered by rocks. Eleven varieties are offered, and come with pates on toast rounds and a choice of desserts, perhaps a tart of Granny Smith apples and lemons, a butter pecan cheesecake or other fancy desserts prepared by Tony.

Breakfasts are sumptuous as well. Fresh juice and homemade baked goods precede such fruit courses as strawberries Romanoff or peach and cherry soup. Then comes the piece de resistance: eggs Oscar, or hard-boiled eggs with shrimp and creamy dill sauce, or baked egg in puff pastry on smoked Canadian bacon with hollandaise sauce,

150

garnished with pimento and black olives. After that, the bedroom looks good, no doubt, for a snooze.

Doubles, $95. Closed in January.

Dockside Guest Quarters, Harris Island, Box 205, York 03909. (207) 363-2868.

Just across the river from Stage Neck on an island unto itself is the Dockside, which 33 years ago began taking in boaters in the handsome late 19th-cenury white homestead. Owners David and Harriette Lusty enjoyed innkeeping so much they added the Crow's Nest with an apartment and two studios on the water, then built the Quarterdeck cottages, and finally added the contemporary Lookout on the hill. They retain the name "guest quarters" (which is something of a misnomer), such is the tradition of this place.

The lovely grounds, very homelike, lead to water's edge and are spotted with lawn chairs, flower gardens and picket fences.

The day's tides are posted on the blackboard in the Maine House, where the dining room and parlor are furnished with antiques, marine paintings and models of ships, and the rambling wraparound porch opens to sea views. There's a TV set in the parlor, and a table holds tea bags and apples for afternoon snacks.

The house has five guest rooms, ranging from a twin room without private bath ($43.50 a night) to a studio sleeping two to four. The front corner room is the choice of many, with its full-length porch from which to view the buoys bobbing in the harbor.

The three multi-unit cottage buildings scattered around the property have twin or double bedrooms, studios, an efficiency and apartment suites for two to four. Each has use of a porch or deck with a view out the harbor entrance to the ocean. You can't get much closer to the water than the balconies in the Crow's Nest, but some prefer the wider decks of the Lookout, higher up on the lawn. All told, there are 21 units.

A continental breakfast buffet featuring fresh fruit and just-baked muffins is offered in the dining room for $3. Lunch and dinner are available next door at the Dockside Dining Room (see below).

Doubles, $65 to $69.50; studios, $66 to $74.50; apartment suites, $104.50. Two-night minimum in season. Closed mid-October to Memorial Day.

Scotland Bridge Inn, One Scotland Bridge Road, York 03909. (207) 363-4432.

The rural 19th-century farmhouse in which she and her late husband raised five children has been turned into a B&B full of personality by Sylvia S. Batchelder, a gregarious woman originally from Prince Edward Island.

The living room is most inviting with a rear expanse of windows enhanced by a window seat, a striking stained-glass hanging that Sylvia made and plants all around. Fine oriental rugs grace this room as well as the dining room, where she serves a fancy breakfast amid Wedgwood china, fine linens and crystal at a long table flanked by Hitchcock chairs. French toast made with French bread, blueberry pancakes or eggs Benedict (a weekly Sunday treat) could be the fare.

Afternoon tea is poured from her silver service in the living room, accompanied by whatever Sylvia has handy in the kitchen — little sandwiches, cookies, gingerbread or banana bread. Guests also enjoy the back yard with an umbrella table, chairs and a lovely English garden.

Upstairs are three guest rooms sharing a large bath, plus a suite with private bath. Rooms are named for their prevailing colors — grape, lemon, peach and pear — and are cozily decorated with Sylvia's handcrafted country touches "to make this a home away from home." A special one it is at that.

Doubles, $60; suite, $75.

Hutchins House, 173 Organug Road, York 03909. (207) 363-3058.

Another family house, this one a lovely manse in a quiet area of substantial homes beside the York River, was converted into a B&B in 1987 by Melinda Hutchins, whose six children had left the hearth.

The common rooms are a delight. There's a long, airy sun porch full of wicker with wonderful views of the river at the rear of the house. It's decorated in blues and whites with a collection of willowware, a TV and VCR, and books and games. A sundeck goes off it. A lovely formal living room with a restored baby grand player piano resounds upon occasion with classical scores.

Upstairs are three guest rooms with private or semi-private baths. One huge room has windows on three sides, while another contains a queensize four-poster bed with mounds of down pillows and is decorated in Laura Ashley pinks and whites.

Melinda, an outgoing woman who loves to cook, serves a full breakfast in the rear sun porch: perhaps eggs Benedict, quiche, omelets or blueberry pancakes. She has skippered and cooked on a 50-foot charter sailboat, so knows the ropes. Incidentally, she has a power boat for sunset cruises up the river to York Harbor, as well as a canoe for rent. The large back yard is a great place for lounging and watching the placid tidal river.

Melinda is proud that hers is the only B&B in the historic district. "We're small enough to be family," she says, "but the house is so large there's a lot of peace and quiet." It's refined and formal, and the only one we've encountered where a sign advises: "Please ring doorbell and await your host. No unannounced entries, please."

Doubles, $68 to $85. Closed November-April.

Canterbury House, Route 1-A, Box 881, York Harbor 03911. (207) 363-3505.

A compact, unassuming white house in the heart of York Harbor holds seven guest rooms sharing two baths. It's owned by James Pappas and Jim Hagar, who also own the York Harbor Chowder House and an adjacent market across the street.

The common rooms are beautifully decorated, the living room with bleached maple floors and chintz sofas in shades of pinks and blues, and a rear dining room with lacy cafe curtains, a crystal chandelier and five small tables set with Royal Albert china, silver and linen napkins. Here is where a complimentary continental breakfast is served; for an extra $14 a couple, you have a choice of things like eggs Canterbury (eggs Benedict with the addition of spinach or asparagus), scrambled eggs with homefries and biscuits, or Belgian waffles. Afternoon tea, with scones, clotted cream and black currant jelly or maybe quiche or cucumber sandwiches with nasturtium blossoms, is taken in the living room or on the front porch. Dinners are served as part of special packages on holiday weekends.

Up a stairwell of pecan wood are guest rooms on two floors in a variety of bed configurations. The Iris Room, with a double and single, is light and airy with irises on the comforters and linens. All the rooms have striking colors and abundant plants.

Doubles, $55 with continental breakfast, $69 with full breakfast.

Edwards' Harborside Inn, Stage Neck Road, Box 866, York Harbor 03911. (207) 363-3037.

An inn for five years with a grand location at the entrance to Stage Neck, "where harbor and ocean meet," this three-story, turn-of-the-century residence was renovated in 1985 by new innkeeper Jay Edwards. A Portsmouth auto dealer and third-generation innkeeper, he says he jumped at the chance of acquiring what he thinks is "the prettiest place in the world."

Edwards' Harborside Inn has own wharf where harbor meets ocean.

The property faces water on three sides, has its own long wharf (from which Jay sometimes takes guests on his boat for whale-watching or moonlight cruises) and a small beach beyond the lawn.

Each of the ten rooms has one or two double beds, television, air-conditioning and a view of river or harbor — or both. Friends who stayed in the second-floor York Suite ($150) with water views on three sides felt as if they were on a yacht. The suite is a beauty: a sofa against one picture window, two velvet upholstered rockers, a queen bed and a sofa bed, green carpet, colorful floral wallpaper and an enormous blue bathroom with a tub, shower, double sink and what Jay says is "the only potted bidet on the East Coast" (a plant sprouts from inside). A tiled jacuzzi in the entry overlooks the harbor.

Other rooms are of different sizes and shapes, individually decorated, and four have private baths.

In the off-season, the Bay View queensize bedroom becomes a welcoming parlor. It's richly furnished with a plush white sofa, chairs and red patterned rugs, and sherry is available for guests on the sideboard. A small lobby area has books and games. Coffee and danish pastries are served for breakfast in the sun porch.

Doubles, $60 to $90.

The Willows Inn, Long Beach Avenue, York Beach 03910. (207) 363-8800.

Rooms are named after trees in this turn-of-the-century Victorian on a hill with a view of York Beach from a wraparound veranda full of wicker chairs and rockers. Long a private house, it was restored at great expense and converted into what innkeeper Lisa M. Arone bills as "a romantic B&B" in 1988.

The original woodwork was retained, but six of the eight bedrooms on two floors have modern baths and an airy if somewhat unfinished feeling, as if the budget did not stretch quite far enough to complete the furnishings. Queensize antique beds are the focal points, and several rooms have window seats.

The parlor and dining room on the main floor are furnished in high Victorian style. Pressed oak chairs and round oak tables set with woven mats and pink napkins enhance the breakfast room, where Belgian waffles, blueberry pancakes or thick french toast are served in the morning. Lemonade, cheese and crackers are the fare in the afternoon.

Doubles, $95 to $150. Closed December-April.

Dining Spots

Cape Neddick Inn, Route 1 at Route 1A, Cape Neddick. (207) 363-2899.

This interesting combination of restaurant and art gallery burned to the ground in May 1985. Undaunted, owners Robbie Wells, Pamela Wallis and Glenn Gobeille had the place rebuilt to the original plans, with a twenty percent expansion in size, and celebrated a grand reopening at Thanksgiving the same year.

That's fortunate, for this is one of the more artistic settings and one of the more creative menus for dining along the southern Maine coast. On two levels, the dining room has windsor chairs at nicely spaced tables covered with beige cloths, mismatched china and candle holders, rose napkins and cobalt blue water glasses. Potted palms, flowers in vases, fancy screens, paintings and sculptures emphasize the feeling of dining in a gallery.

A huge fieldstone fireplace, a collection of baskets, art books to read and a cherry bar enhance the inviting, tomato-colored cocktail lounge.

The limited menu changes every six weeks. Nightly specials revolve around duck, fish, chicken, veal and tournedos — the varying preparations not decided until that afternoon.

Soups ($2.50) might be lamb broth with roasted vegetables, roasted garlic, cauliflower-fennel or potato, leek and cream. Appetizers ($5 to $7) when we visited were goose liver, duckling and pistachio pate with cointreau, scallops ceviche, falafel with toasted pita bread, and beef curry wontons with ginger-honey sweet and sour sauce.

Entrees are priced from $16 for roast Long Island duckling or chicken marengo to $22 for chateaubriand on a crouton with goose liver pate and green peppercorn mustard sauce. We passed up one of the night's specials of swordfish grilled with ginger and gin for a fantastic special of fettuccine with chicken breast and a Korean-style lamb kabob on rice with sesame sauce and a spicy vegetable relish. Served on large oval plates, the entrees came with glazed parsnips, broccoli and yellow beans. A complimentary plate of raw vegetables with dip accompanied drinks, followed by salads swathed in warm creamy bacon or cucumber-dill dressings.

"Don't forget our desserts," the menu correctly urges. They range widely from tortes and tarts to chocolate confections from a repertoire of more than 500 developed over the years. But we had to refrain from a choclate grand marnier torte and amaretto cheesecake and requested a doggy bag for our left-over pasta, which provided a delicious supper the next day.

The wine list is small but select; a $15 Franciscan merlot was perfect with our meal.

Dinner nightly in summer, 6 to 9, Wednesday-Sunday in winter; Sunday brunch, noon to 3, mid-October to May.

Pipers Grill & Oyster Bar, Route 1, York Corner. (207) 363-8196.

A small, one-story house has a jaunty outdoor deck with a raw bar, a busy cocktail lounge and a spare dining room of bare wood tables on pedestals, a few baskets on the rafters, Laura Ashley print wallpaper and curtains, a large picture of an artichoke on one wall and not much else. The emphasis is not on decor but rather on eclectic food at reasonable prices.

The dinner menu is ever-changing as the owners try to find their niche, but two things are certain: the cooking is interesting and the values enticing. The fare includes mesquite-grilled burgers and all kinds of pizzas (one of them topped with shrimp, sun-dried tomatoes and pesto), chicken nachos and barbecued ribs as well as some attractive entrees priced from $11 for grilled game hen with roasted garlic butter and potato pancakes to $13 for lobster ragout with lemon pasta or sizzling shrimp and

Rebuilt Cape Neddick Inn offers dining in an art gallery setting.

scallops with Chinese mustard and black-bean sauces and fried red-pepper noodles. Grilled skirt steak with roquefort and garlic sauce and paillard of veal with smoked tomato and grilled red onion vinaigrette also appealed on our latest visit, as did the night's seafood specials of grilled tuna with tomato-cumin and chili pepper sauce and grilled swordfish with lemon mayonnaise.

The tenderloin of pork might be done with Granny Smith apples and black currant sauce, the daily pasta with scallops and prosciutto, and the grilled tuna marinated with artichokes and bell peppers. Seasonal vegetables could be sauteed green beans, shredded beets and yams.

Steamed mussels in tomato and garlic and a grilled flank steak with spicy Szechuan peanut sauce are among appealing appetizers ($4.95 to $5.50). The wine list is limited but chosen with an eye to price, a number of fine Californias going for $3 to $4 a glass.

Lunch, Monday-Saturday 11:30 to 2:30; dinner, 5 to 10, to midnight Friday-Sunday; Sunday brunch, noon to 3.

York Harbor Inn, Route 1A, York Harbor. (207) 363-5119.

From their hilltop perch, three of the four charming dining rooms here look onto (and catch the salty breeze from) the ocean across the street. One room, the main Cabin Loft lobby with fireplace, is used in winter; another is an enclosed porch, and a third beamed room looks like a pub.

Mismatched chairs, small paned windows, blue and white plates displayed below the beamed ceiling, overcloths of varying colors and prints over white with pink napkins, small oil lamps and sloping floors convey an old-fashioned feeling.

Chef Gerry Bonsey's dinner menu features Yankee seafood with contemporary accents. Among appetizers ($4.50 to $6.75) are mussels provencale, smoked salmon, broiled oysters covered with crabmeat and bearnaise sauce, and a dish called Tatnic Bay Treasure — scallops, shrimp and crabmeat in a creamy veloute sauce. Brie cheese soup, a concoction of mushrooms, cream, julienned vegetables and white wine, is a popular starter.

Entrees run from $12.95 for vegetable strudel to $17.95 for filet mignon. The recipe for veal Swiss was requested by Gourmet magazine; pasta with shrimp and scallops, and chicken stuffed with lobster and boursin cheese are other specialties. The innkeeper's clambake is priced daily.

155

Original section of expanded York Harbor Inn houses dining rooms.

Special desserts are the Toblerone Swiss chocolate walnut confection and chocolate sundae, plus a chilled lemon and caramel souffle. The well-chosen wine list is fairly priced.

Six salads and croissant creations are offered on an extensive luncheon menu.

Lunch, Monday-Friday 11:30 to 2:30; dinner nightly, 5:30 to 9:30 or 10:30; Sunday brunch, 10:30 to 2:30.

Stage Neck Inn, Off Route 1A, York Harbor. (207) 363-3580.

Meals in the elegant, chandeliered dining room with floor-to-ceiling water views from windows on three sides are what natives consider special-occasion deals. In shades of beige and peach, the spacious room is restful with velvet round-back chairs and swagged balloon draperies.

The large dinner menu embraces American and continental fare. Appetizers start at $3.50 for melon with prosciutto and rise rapidly to the $7 range for oysters and zucchini sauteed in sweet champagne sauce and served over peppercorn pasta or poached salmon fillet served with cumin sauce and deep-fried celery leaves. The lobster bisque for $7.95 is a house specialty. The twenty entrees ($13 to $18.95) run the gamut from boiled lobster to filet mignon bearnaise. Szechuan shrimp, medallions of pork with apple brandy, paillards of veal rolled with spinach, prosciutto and cheese, and roast duckling with raspberry sauce are among the more interesting choices.

Dinner also is available in the grill, bright and cheery in raspberry colors, with upholstered chairs at well-spaced tables and views of the water. Grilled salmon, broiled or blackened swordfish and open-face steak sandwiches are among the choices, $12.95 to $19.50 (for baked stuffed lobster).

Sandwiches, salads, pizzas and entrees like pan-fried filet of sole or scallop and crabmeat scampi ($5.25 to $11.25) are offered at lunch in the grill, which also serves as the dining room in winter. Sunday brunch is served in the main dining room.

Lunch and Sunday brunch, noon to 2; dinner, 6 to 9 or 10. Jackets required.

Dockside Dining Room, Harris Island, York. (207) 363-4800.

Overlooking the harbor next to the Dockside Guest Quarters, this gray-shingled structure houses an airy dining room on two levels, several round tables on the porch screened from floor to ceiling, and a small gift shop.

The decor is slightly more "au courant" than that of the inn next door, with white

156

bentwood ice-cream parlor chairs, flowers in beer or Perrier bottles, green mats with paper napkins on Formica tables, green carpet and blue walls, and everywhere a water view.

It's an especially fine setting for a nautical lunch. For $5.50 to $9.75, you can get broiled scrod, fried or baked scallops, lobster salad in a croissant, roast duckling and a few other items. Most are accompanied by cheese and crackers, cheese bread and the "salad deck" — items from a salad bar set in half of an old boat.

The same appetizers are offered at lunch and dinner: seafood tostada, baked onion soup, herring and sour cream, seafood chowder and shrimp cocktail ($4.95). Dinner entrees run from $9.50 for broiled scrod to $14.25 for lobster-stuffed sole. Favorites are the roast stuffed duckling (from Hickory Stick Farm in Laconia, N.H.), baked scallops, carpetbagger steak and boiled lobster.

For nineteen years Steve and Sue Roeder have been managing the restaurant. Their formula obviously works too well to change much.

Lunch, noon to 2; dinner, 5:30 to 9, Sunday noon to 2 and 5 to 8:30. Closed Mondays, also mid-October to Memorial Day.

Chef Mimmo's Restaurant, Route 1A, York Beach. (207) 363-3807.

This restaurant is recommended highly by several area innkeepers, who say the decor is somewhat tacky but the food is wonderful. The location at the Windbreaker in the thick of the York Beach action is uninspiring. But Chef Mimmo is apparently an Italian of the old school, a big man who flings the pots around and when he leaves the kitchen for the dining room, the fun begins.

The food is Tuscan; we hear great things about the pasta with shrimp, calamari and scallops. Prices range from $9.95 to $15.95 for pastas, seven veal dishes, six chicken dishes and four seafood items. All are served with garden salad and garlic bread.

Appetizers, all for two, are $7.50 and include a cold antipasto platter, artichokes and pimento, calamari salad, stuffed mushrooms and mussels marinara or fra diavolo.

Dinner only; open year-round.

Rick's All Seasons Restaurant, 240R York St., York Village. (207) 363-5584.

Nothing could be more down home than this restaurant that looks as if it's been there forever. Two downstairs rooms have brick walls, pseudo-beamed ceilings, hanging plants, a lunch counter and tables topped with red oilcloth.

The locals pack the place for burgers, subs, sandwiches, vegetarian specials and lunch entrees like grilled ham steak, salisbury steak, homemade beans and franks, and a beer-batter haddock dinner (prices start at $1.25 for a hot dog and top off at $6.99 for fried clam or scallop dinners).

Breakfast, served from 4 a.m., brings an array of dishes like three-egg omelets, egg and cheese quiche, blueberry pancakes, french toast and RcMuffins. Almost everything is in the $2 to $3 range, except for steak and eggs, $5.25.

Dinner, for some reason, is served only on Wednesday and Thursday nights til 8. Blackboard specials when we visited were baked stuffed chicken for $7 and open-face sirloin sandwich for $5.95, both with potatoes and vegetables.

Open 4 a.m. to 2:30 p.m. Monday, Tuesday and Friday, to 2 p.m. Saturday, to 1:30 p.m. Sunday, to 8 p.m. Wednesday and Thursday.

Cafe Shelton, Ocean Avenue, York Beach. (203) 363-3810.

A white-pillared dining room with white cafe tables and chairs, high ceilings and a mix of hanging plants, chandeliers and spotlit posters characterizes this spacious place with an outdoor patio in the heart of downtown York Beach. It's the answer to a tour-bus

157

operator's dream, and the tour buses were there in force when we stopped for lunch one September day.

The mix-and-match menu offers no fewer than ten salads and uncounted sandwiches, a few crepes and quiches, and "everyday specials" of twin lobsters and seafood newburg (market price). At night, the menu is supplemented by entrees like shrimp scampi, seafood Wellington, salisbury steak and grilled kielbasa ($7.50 to $12.50).

Parfaits, crepes, Belgian waffles and pie a la mode are listed for dessert. Lobster Benedict highlights the breakfast menu ($7.25), and a pianist entertains on weekends.

Breakfast, lunch and dinner from 7:30 a.m. to 11 p.m. daily in summer; fewer hours in off-season. Closed Columbus Day to Memorial Day.

York Harbor Chowder House, Varrell Lane at Route 1A, York Harbor. (207) 363-4130.

Just up from the harbor, in the restored gray Lancaster Building, is this plain and tiny restaurant owned by Jim Hagar and James Pappas of the Canterbury House B&B.

The limited menu is supplemented by daily specials. For lunch, try a lobster roll ($8.95), tomatoes stuffed with crabmeat, shrimp or chef's salad or quiche du jour.

At night, the name changes to the Whale's Tail for "fine dining" and the fare is a bit more ambitious. Sole mornay, chicken dijon, baked jumbo shrimp, steak au poivre and steak Diane are priced from $8.95 (for pasta primavera) to $15.95. Lobster is baked, stuffed or sauteed. The vegetable du jour is an extra $1.25. Three chowders are $3.25 a cup and $3.95 a bowl. Other starters include frog's legs, artichoke hearts baked with garlic and cheese, shrimp cocktail and caesar salad for two.

Wines are priced from $10 to $20. Desserts might include fruit salad, chocolate truffles or brownies a la mode.

Lunch, 11:30 to 2:30; dinner, 5:30 to 9:30. Closed Monday.

Scuttlebutt, Route 1A, York Harbor. (207) 363-3121.

You probably wouldn't write home about the food or the decor of this new restaurant right across from the beach. What is worth noting is the open upstairs deck with a stunning view of Long Sands Beach and the Nubble Light, though on the sunny day we were there for lunch most of the people stayed under an enclosed red-canvas canopy strung with white lights.

There are bars upstairs and down, glass-covered tables and a flamingo standing in a ficus tree. No matter. This is grazing food, from nachos and fried veggies to peel-'n-eat shrimp, burgers and Boston cream pie. The young crowd eats it up; you don't really come here for much more than the view, the action and a very basic steak and seafood menu ($8.95 to $12.95) at night.

Open daily except Monday, 11:30 to 10.

Cape Neddick Lobster Pound, Route 1A, Cape Neddick. (207) 728-6777.

A gray shingled building practically over the water, the Cape Neddick cries out for an outdoor deck. However, there are glorious views (especially at sunset) from every window inside the two-level bar and dining area, which has shiny wooden tables, deck chairs and paper mats decorated with lobsters. Loud music plays in the background — live on weekends — and it's all very picturesque and casual.

Offering more than just lobster, the menu lists things like bouillabaisse ($14.50) and teriyaki steak. Boiled lobster and the Cape Neddick Down East shore dinner are priced daily; lobster stew is $5.95. Broiled haddock or scallops and shrimp scampi are $11.95 to $13.25. The chef satisfies his creative urges with specials like curry stir-fried shrimp, grilled swordfish with shrimp hollandaise sauce or fettuccine with scallops, smoked

Boats are moored outside Dockside Guest Quarters and Dining Room.

tuna, plum tomatoes and romano cream. The "Fisherman's Luck" special could be charbroiled tuna. Fried clams, lobster salad, fish and chips, and lobster roll and fries complete the selection.

Open from 5 p.m., summer only.

Diversions

Beaches. Inn guests probably will be grateful for the peace and quiet of the inn grounds and sheltered beaches. Or you may be as lucky as we were and find a parking spot and place at Harbor Beach, next to a private club. But if you want surf, join the throngs on Long Sands Beach, one of Maine's sandiest and deservedly crowded. It was a refreshing oasis on one unforgettable 100-degree day when we and everyone else placed our sand chairs in the ocean and lounged in the water trying to keep cool. If there's not enough action on the beach, surely there is in the amusement area of downtown York Beach. On past Short Sands Beach at Cape Neddick Harbor is a sheltered beach good for children.

Nubble Light. Don't miss the landmark Cape Neddick Lighthouse on the nubble separating Long Sands and Short Sands beaches. From the bluffs you can see up and down the coast and out to Boon Island and the Isles of Shoals off Portsmouth. Along Nubble Road you'll pass tiny cottages and institutions like Fox's Lobster House (serving noon to 9) and Brown's Old Fashion Ice Cream ("We make our own"). Another spectacular view is from Bald Head Cliff off Shore Road. Not far inland is 673-foot-high Mount Agamenticus, a landmark for sailors and the highest spot on the southern Maine coast.

Marginal Way. A three-mile walk along the ocean between shore and homes begins at Harbor Beach and extends to Nubble Light. It's more rugged than Ogunquit's better known Marginal Way, but well worth the effort for the views and the natural landscaping (wild roses, bayberry, blueberries and ground juniper).

Cape Neddick Park. Off River Road are 100 acres of woods preserved by Brenda Kuhn as a memorial to her parents. The park contains the **Walt Kuhn Gallery,** which

159

has the late artist's Maine landscapes and circus drawings as well as works of other local artists, the **Vera Spier Kuhn Sculpture Garden** of contemporary sculpture (including a colorful one that looks like a jigsaw puzzle atop a chariot and another that's all pink dots on posts), and a performing arts amphitheater for summer entertainment. Picnic tables are scattered about.

The York Historic District. The history of the first chartered English city in North America (a refuge for early Puritan settlers from Massachusetts) is on display in York Village. The Chamber of Commerce has an excellent brochure detailing walking and driving tours. The **Old Gaol Museum,** once the King's Prison, is the oldest surviving public building of the British Colonies in this country; on view are the dungeon, cells, jailer's quarters and household effects. The **Emerson-Wilcox House** (1740), the enormous **Elizabeth Perkins House** (1730) beside the river and the rambling **Sayward-Wheeler Mansion** (1720) are open, as are **Jefferds Tavern** (1750), the 1745 **Old School House,** the **George Marshall Store** and the **John Hancock Wharf,** with old tools and antique ship models in a warehouse owned by a signer of the Declaration of Independence. Most are concentrated along Lindsay Road, which leads to **Sewall's Bridge,** a replica of the first pile drawbridge in America. Nearby, Route 103 passes an intriguing looking mini-suspension bridge for pedestrians (called the "wiggly bridge," for good reason), which leads to a neat pathway along the river from York Harbor to Sewall's Bridge. Out Route 91 is a small stone memorial next to the trickling **Maud Muller Spring,** which inspired John Greenleaf Whittier's poem.

Shopping. The Goldenrod, which has been operated every summer since 1896 by the same family in York Beach, is where everyone stops for taffy kisses — choosing from dozens of flavors. It's also a restaurant with a nice old-fashioned menu, listing sandwiches like fried egg and bacon or cream cheese and olives, cinnamon toast, club sandwiches and lots of soda-fountain items. Also in York Beach is **Shelton's Gift Shop,** which offers attractive clothing, cards and jewelry. At the **York Harbor Inn** there's a large gift shop with a good choice of country things, made-in-Maine items and souvenirs. The **York Village Emporium** is a large store with many stalls that are rented out to craftspeople; there's plenty of flea-market stuff as well. Popcorn in many flavors is available here. Also in the village are **Classic Clothiers,** with tailored clothing, and the **Williams Country Store,** which is a real general store with sewing notions beside the classy gifts and penny candy. "There aren't many of us left," says owner Don Williams; "they've all gone to chrome and glass."

Extra-Special

Factory Outlet Shopping. Anyone who rejoiced when **Dansk** opened its first large factory outlet at Kittery is probably ecstatic about the several miles of outlets along Route 1 from Kittery to York. Although some are the same kinds of clothing outlets that you find in Freeport, the specialty here seems to be china, glass and kitchenware. We have found tremendous bargains at **Villeroy & Boch** (place settings and oversized dinner plates at up to 75 percent off), **Mikasa, Royal Doulton** and **Waterford-Aynsley.** You can admire the river view from benches outside the **Corning Designs** store at the Maine Gate Outlets, and pick up an assortment of bargains at **Reading China & Glass.** There are **Lenox** and **Oneida, Scandinavian Design** and **Georges Briard, Van Heusen** and **Samuel Roberts** (ultrasuede at 50 percent off) in various malls and small plazas on both sides of the highway. New ones pop up all the time, and it takes policemen to untangle the bumper-to-bumper shopper traffic on summer weekends.

Harbor at Cape Porpoise is on view through rose trellis at the Inn at Harbor Head.

The Kennebunks, Me.
The Most and Best of Everything

For many, the small coastal area known as the Kennebunk Region has the most or best of everything in Maine: the best beaches, the most inns, the best shops, the most eating places, the best scenery, the most tourist attractions, the best galleries, the most diversity.

And now it has a new role as the summer home of President Bush.

All have combined to produce what oldtimers like gift shop owners Henry and Priscilla Pasco see as overkill. Concerned over a gradual deterioration in the century-old traditions of one of Maine's earliest summer havens for the wealthy, they were instrumental in Kennebunkport's hosting of a conference on "Preserving Town Character," sponsored by Maine Citizens for Historic Preservation and Kennebunkport's business and historical associations, among others.

The Kennebunks offer a case study in town character. Actually, there are at least three Kennebunks. One is the town of Kennebunk and its inland commercial center, historic Kennebunk. The second is Kennebunkport, the changing coastal resort community that draws the tourists. A third represents Cape Arundel, Cape Porpoise and Goose Rocks Beach, their rugged coastal aspects largely unchanged by development in recent years.

Even before George Bush's election as President, Kennebunkport and its Dock Square and Lower Village shopping areas had become so congested that a bus started shuttling visitors from vast parking areas on the edge of town. The streets teem on summer evenings with strollers who have spent the day at the beach.

And yet you can escape: walk along Parson's Way; drive out Ocean Avenue past Spouting Rock and the Bush estate and around Cape Arundel to Cape Porpoise, a working fishing village; bicycle out Beach Avenue to Lord's Point or Strawberry Island; visit the Rachel Carson Wildlife Preserve; savor times gone by among the historic homes of Summer Street in Kennebunk or along the beach at Goose Rocks.

One of the charms of the Kennebunks is that the crowded restaurants and galleries co-exist with the annual Unitarian Church blueberry festival, the Rotary chicken barbecue and the solitude of Parson's Way.

Watercolorist Edgar Whitney proclaimed the Kennebunks "the best ten square miles of painting areas in the nation." Explore a bit and you'll see why.

Inn Spots

The Captain Lord Mansion, Pleasant Street, Box 527, Kennebunkport 04046. (207) 967-3141.

For starters, consider the architectural features of this beautifully restored 1812 mansion: an octagonal cupola, a suspended elliptical staircase, blown-glass windows, trompe l'oeil hand-painted doors, an eighteen-foot bay window, a hand-pulled working elevator.

The inn is so full of historic interest that public tours are given in summer for a nominal fee. You'd never guess that it was converted from a boarding house for senior citizens as recently as 1978.

Guests can savor all the heritage that makes this a National Historic Register listing by staying overnight in any of the sixteen sumptuous guest rooms and enjoying hot or iced tea in the parlor or games beside the fire in the Gathering Room. Each of the guest rooms on three floors has been carefully decorated by Bev Davis and her husband Rick Litchfield, whose innkeeping energy and flair are considered models by their peers. Eleven rooms have working fireplaces, much in demand in the winter; all have private baths (though some created from closets are rather small), and the corner rooms are especially spacious. Nice touches like sewing kits, Poland Spring water, and trays with wine glasses and corkscrew abound.

Bev makes pin cushions and needlecraft "Do Not Disturb" signs for the rooms and oversees the gift shop on the main floor. Breakfast is served family-style at large tables in the kitchen. It includes Rick's soft-boiled eggs plus fresh muffins and breads — Bev's zucchini bread is renowned, as are some of the hors d'oeuvres she prepares for wine gatherings for guests at Halloween and New Year's.

Always on the move, the Captain Lord recently opened two annexes that add eight ultra-deluxe rooms and suites. The first was the Captain's Hideaway, which has two honeymoon quarters three doors away in a house that Rick calls "our gourmet B&B" and bills as even more romantic than the mansion. The second-floor suite has to be seen to be believed: you enter through an enormous bathroom complete with fireplace, two-person whirlpool tub, an oversize shower and the commode hidden around the corner; beyond is a room with queensize canopy bed and another fireplace. Chocolates come with turndown service at night, and Hideaway guests enjoy breakfast by candlelight.

Phoebe's Fantasy is the latest addition with six rooms in a house behind the inn. When we visited, Rick and Bev were flat out restoring and decorating a breakfast room with a seven-foot harvest table and the guest rooms, including a large corner bedroom with

The Captain Lord Mansion is full of historic interest.

windows on three sides, Indian shutters, a pineapple-carved king bed, a Franklin stove and a jacuzzi.

Doubles, $89 to $199; two-night minimum on weekends.

Old Fort Inn, Old Fort Avenue, Kennebunkport 04046. (207) 967-5353.

The main lodge in a converted barn is the heart of the Old Fort Inn. You enter through the reception area and Sheila Aldrich's antiques shop. Inside is a large rustic room with enormous beams, weathered pine walls and a massive brick fireplace, the perfect setting for some of Sheila's antiques.

That's where she and husband David, transplanted Californians, set out a buffet breakfast each morning — guests pick up wicker trays with calico linings, help themselves to bowls of gorgeous fresh fruits and platters of pastries, and sit around the lodge or outside on the sun-dappled deck beside the large swimming pool. Sheila bakes the sweet breads (blueberry, zucchini, banana, oatmeal and pumpkin are some); the croissants are David's forte and there are sticky buns on Sundays.

The stone and brick carriage house out back has twelve large and luxurious guest rooms off a central corridor on the second floor. All are decorated in different colors, all have private bathrooms, plush carpeting and color television, plus such nice touches as velvet wing chairs, stenciling on the walls and handmade wreaths over the beds. "My wife agonizes over every intricate detail," says David. "I call her Miss Mix and Match." Her decorating flair shows; even the towels are color-coordinated.

The elegant suite on the lower floor of the carriage house has two bedrooms and two baths with a connecting living room. A handsome chest of drawers hides the TV, the kingsize beds are topped with fishnet canopies, and the baths are outfitted with jacuzzis and Neutrogena amenities. The newly furnished sitting room in the carriage house has two settees and a pine hutch; a small adjoining room has wicker furniture.

The inn is a quiet retreat away from the tourist hubbub but within walking distance of the ocean; at night, David says, the silence is deafening. The inn offers a tennis court as well as the pool. Most guests are repeat, long-term customers, and it's easy to see why.

Doubles, $90 to $195; three-night minimum in summer. Closed mid-December to mid-April.

The Captain Jefferds Inn, Pearl Street, Box 691, Kennebunkport 04046. (207) 967-2311.

If you like antiques and pets, you'll love the Captain Jefferds, which has an abundance of both. Tessie Fitzharris, the Maine coon cat, was snoozing on the porch chair when we came through the ornate white iron fence and up the brick walk.

Innkeeper Warren Fitzsimmons, an antiques dealer from Long Island, bought the inn in 1980 and moved his collection in. A decorator and antiquarian, he has made the 1804 sea captain's mansion into a stunningly colorful and comfortable spot, one that was pictured on the cover of House Beautiful.

Warren cooks breakfast in the small but efficient kitchen; it's served formally in the handsome dining room, or outside on the delightful front porch or the new flagstone terrace. Guests may eat at 8 or 9 o'clock seatings. Eggs Benedict, blueberry crepes, quiche, frittata with seasonal vegetables and flannel (hash with poached egg) are in Warren's repertoire and he never repeats a breakfast in a week.

A living room with an amazing collection of majolica, a sunlit solarium, a rear brick terrace, the front terrace and an expansive lawn with comfortable loungers are places where guests can relax with a book or whatever. Tea and hors d'oeuvres for cocktails are served in the late afternoon.

All twelve guest rooms have private tiled baths. All are luxurious and perfectly decorated, with chaise longues, Laura Ashley linens, firm mattresses, woolen blankets and four pillows on each bed. Warren collects antique white cotton spreads and quilts; he has such an extensive collection that he changes them around from time to time.

Most of the rooms have Victorian wicker pieces. "I hate plastic," says the innkeeper — we defy anyone to find a bit of it in this enchanting place.

Doubles, $75 to $95. Two-night minimum, July-October.

White Barn Inn, Beach Street, R.R. 3, Box 387, Kennebunkport 04046. (207) 967-2321.

Long known as one of the area's premier restaurants (see Dining Spots), the White Barn is moving to become a top-rate inn under new Australian owner Laurie Bongiorno and his partner-manager, Carol Hackett. When we visited, renovation and redecoration were in progress and rooms were to be available year-round. Carol assured that by 1989 the reality would be "an elegant inn with a fine dining room."

What was in store was evident in the inn's refurbished main floor, with a reception area, three sitting rooms with comfortable furniture and an inviting sun porch with a TV set. Flowers, mints, decanters of sherry, newspapers and magazines were all around, and oriental rugs were scattered over the polished wood floors.

The thirteen rooms upstairs in the inn have private baths (some with old-fashioned tubs), four-poster and brass beds, and pampering amenities including turndown service with a homemade sweet and a note from the innkeeper at night.

The six suites in May's Annex were being renovated to the height of luxury with library-style living rooms, dressing rooms, spacious baths with jacuzzis, Queen Anne four-poster beds and secretary desks, and chintz-covered furniture. Six large rooms in the Gatehouse and the Cottage already had been renovated with cathedral ceilings, sitting areas with wing chairs, ceiling fans and queensize beds, chintz spreads and fine art on the walls.

After the rooms were upgraded, Carol planned to train her sights on the grounds, already lush with prolific flowers. Herbal gardens, a pond and a gazebo were a glint in her eye.

Guests enjoy a substantial continental buffet breakfast in the quietly elegant Colonial dining room. Bowls of fresh fruit, juices, assorted cereals, yogurts, many kinds of

164

White fence surrounds spacious grounds at Captain Jefferds Inn.

muffins and pastries, bagels and cream cheese, and, at our visit, steaming baked apples are set out.

Doubles, $95 to $170.

The Kennebunkport Inn, Dock Square, Box 111, Kennebunkport 04046. (207) 967-2621.

In a nicely landscaped setting just off busy Dock Square, with a view of the river, is the graceful 19th-century mansion housing the Kennebunkport Inn, plus a 1930 motel-style annex in the rear. A small octagonal swimming pool with a large wooden deck fits snugly in between.

Excellent meals can be sampled in the inn's lovely dining rooms (see below). Drinks are served in a recently renovated piano bar or by the pool.

Innkeepers Rick and Martha Griffin have decorated the twenty guest rooms in the annex with period pieces, Laura Ashley wallpapers and different stenciling everywhere. One of the larger rooms has a four-poster bed, sofa and velvet chair. All rooms have private baths and color TV.

Five more bedrooms are upstairs in the main inn. Nine deluxe rooms with four-poster beds were added in 1987 in a wing behind the restaurant that also provided the handsome piano bar and lounge.

Breakfast is extra, but includes such interesting dishes as custard french toast with pear-honey sauce and potato skins stuffed with scrambled eggs and mushrooms in a mornay sauce.

Doubles, $82 to $139, EP.

Sundial Inn, 46 Beach Ave., Kennebunk Beach 04043. (207) 967-3850.

When Pat and Larry Kenny first inspected the old Sundial Inn built in 1891, "we wouldn't buy it, it was such a dump," Larry says. "But we came back a month later and did." They gutted the place and, after a total transformation, reopened in 1987 with a sparkling renovation — 34 rooms with private baths on three floors, nine with great views of the ocean across the street.

On the main floor is a large, beamed living room, all in chintzes and wicker with the fieldstone fireplace ablaze and numerous conversation areas. A continental breakfast with homemade muffins is served in the cheery breakfast room overlooking the ocean. Hot chocolate or cider are available in the afternoons.

An elevator leads to the upstairs bedrooms, which meander off sprawling corridors.

Rooms are tastefully decorated with matching bedspreads and curtains in colorful fabrics and wicker furniture upholstered in chintz. Many of the beds are white wrought iron. All have modern baths, TV, old-fashioned hand-painted phones and enough individual touches like Tiffany-style lamps or chandeliers to compensate for a somewhat motelish feeling. A couple of top-floor rooms facing the ocean are larger with cushioned window seats, skylights and jacuzzis.

Doubles, $85 to $160.

The Ocean View, 72 Beach Ave., Kennebunk Beach 04043. (207) 967-2750.

With a prime beachfront location, it's little wonder that Carole and Bob Arena have given their small B&B a summery, beachy feeling. "We're deliberately trying not to be antique-y," says Carole. That's not to say theirs doesn't have its own special features, however.

The sunny breakfast room, for instance, is colorful indeed. Three tiny white tables flanked by white chairs are set with striking California china, each piece in two bright colors; there's a collection of masks on the wall, and the whole scene is a stage set for photographers. Here is where Carole serves a hearty breakfast — the day we visited, cantaloupe, yogurt and wheat germ, ham and cheese croissants, and scrambled eggs with brioche.

The fireplaced, pine-paneled living room is full of books, and there's a TV room with two sofas. At the end of the living room is a small boutique for guests, who can acquire some of the colorful dishes as well as unusual ornaments, jewelry and the like.

On two upstairs floors are five oceanfront rooms, three with private baths, cheerily furnished with good reading lamps over the beds, colorful sheets, skirted round tables and such. For the summer of 1989 Carole planned to convert two rear apartments into four deluxe rooms with private baths, canopy pencil-post beds and splashy fabrics.

Doubles, $73 to $95. Closed November-March.

The Inn at Harbor Head, Cape Porpoise, RD 2, Box 1180, Kennebunkport 04046. (207) 967-5564 or 967-4873.

The location of the rambling shingled home of David and Joan Sutter on a rocky knoll right above the picturesque Cape Porpoise harbor is a special attraction at this small B&B. Out front are exquisite gardens with a sundial; a private rear terrace and lawns lead down to the shore for swimming from the floats or just relaxing in a garden chair, watching the lobster boats go by.

Breakfast is another special attraction. From Joan's country kitchen come dishes like pineapple boats decorated with edible flowers, pears poached with lemon and vanilla and topped with a cointreau-laced custard sauce, and broiled grapefruit with nutmeg. The "Maine" course could be puff pastry with eggs, spinach and feta cheese or mushroom omelet topped with salsa — no one ever leaves a bite of the roast beef hash made from scratch with red and green peppers and a touch of garlic. Pecan sticky buns and fruit croissants might accompany this feast. The meal is served at 9 in the dining room at a long table where there is lots of camaraderie; coffee is put out in the sitting room at 7.

The four bedrooms, two up and two down, have private baths and are decorated to the nth degree by Joan, who is a sculptor and artist. Her murals are exquisite. The Harbor Suite's murals are of Cape Porpoise on the walls, with clouds and sky on the ceiling. The entrance to the Garden Room is paved with stones; with a fishnet canopy bed and exotic plants, it has an oriental feel. The Greenery has a kingsize bed covered in white with tons of lacy pillows. Joan painted the dresser here with butterflies and flowers.

The innkeepers, who say they like to do things in the "poshest way possible," put out

Wall of masks and colorful china enhance breakfast room at the Ocean View.

a decanter of wine with cheese and crackers in late afternoon and, after guests leave for dinner, turn down their beds, light soft lights and leave silver dishes of Godiva chocolates on the pillows. It's little wonder that some guests stay for up to two weeks, and many are honeymooners.

Doubles, $85 to $130; two-night minimum. No smoking.

Bufflehead Cove, off Route 35, Box 499, Kennebunkport 04046. (207) 967-3879 or 967-5151.

Down a long dirt road and past a lily pond is this little-known treasure: a gray shingled, Dutch Colonial manse right beside a scenic bend of the Kennebunk River, the kind of summer home you've always dreamed of. Owner Harriet Gott doesn't advertise and doesn't need to. Her five-room B&B is filled by word of mouth.

The public rooms and the setting are special here. A long porch faces the river, one of the lovelier spots around; there are porches along the side and in back, too. A large and comfy living room has window seats with views of the water, and the dining room, which is shaped like the back of a ship, has a dark beamed ceiling, paneling, stenciling and a carpet painted on the floor. There are a dock with boats and five acres of tranquility with which to surround oneself.

All bedrooms are bright and cheerful, but the Balcony Room is perhaps the most appealing. It has a fabulous, wicker-filled balcony overlooking the river, a queensize brass bed and an antique armoire. In the Teal Room, the bathroom is stenciled like the bedroom with ribbons and bouquets of flowers. The walls and ceilings are hand-painted with unusual designs in the Suite, two rooms that share a bath. The Garden Studio in back has its own entrance and patio, a sitting area, queensize brass bed and a kitchen.

Harriet serves a full breakfast on the porch or in the dining room. A typical repast might be a baked apple with sour cream and quiche with a croissant. Eggs Benedict, souffles, homemade waffles and popovers are other specialties. Sherry or white wine and cheese are served in the afternoon.

Harriet's husband Jim is a lobster fisherman. Guests may not see much of him unless they get up to join his fishing expedition at 4:30 a.m., but they know he's around by the lobster in the quiche and omelets.

Doubles, $65 to $85.

Cape Arundel Inn, Ocean Avenue, Kennebunkport 04046. (207) 967-2125.

A choice location facing the open ocean and an excellent dining room commend this Maine-style inn containing seven oceanview rooms with private baths and seven motel units at the side.

Innkeeper Ann Fales has upgraded the rooms upstairs in the inn, which are spacious and pleasantly traditional. Master Bedrooms 2 and 3 are most coveted, the former with twin beds, a loveseat and chair by the picture window, and a private balcony. We liked ours on the far-front corner, where white organdy curtains fluttered in the breeze and a white chenille spread covered the kingsize bed. The walls were wood and the carpeting attractive, but the view was all: two chairs in the corner from which to take in the bird's-eye panorama of the George Bush compound and the ocean.

Also coveted are the motel rooms, each with a double and a twin bed, full bath and TV, and a little balcony with striped chairs and a front-on view of the ocean beyond the wild roses.

The spacious front porch of the inn is a super place to curl up with a good book, enjoy a cocktail or a nightcap, or the morning newspaper before breakfast. Breakfasts are extra but well worth it; we know people who drive miles for the Downeast sampler (sausages, blueberry pancake, scrambled egg and grilled tomato, $4.75) and the view. We can vouch for the fried codfish cakes served with baked beans and grilled tomato and the omelet of the day (sour cream, avocado, tomato and chives), accompanied by unlimited refills of coffee.

Doubles, $85 to $105. Open mid-May through October.

Dock Square Inn, Temple Street, Box 1123, Kennebunkport 04046. (207) 967-5773.

"I make people feel at home," says Bernice Shoby, who with her husband Frank operates this six-bedroom B&B that is the epitome of Victoriana, "and most of them come back."

They have run the inn for twenty years, for many years just in summer when Frank was on vacation from his industrial-arts teaching job. In 1982 they moved from Connecticut and now open from March through November.

The common rooms and bedrooms are filled with the Shobys' collections of antiques. They were planning to open a small shop to house the overflow.

The house originally belonged to David Clark, Kennebunkport's most prolific shipbuilder, and the bedrooms are named after his ships. Most have private baths, some ingeniously built into small spaces, and color cable TV. Some are air-conditioned.

We stayed in the spacious upstairs front corner room with carved walnut bed, a chaise longue and Laura Ashley wallpaper. Though the inn is near Dock Square, the street noise didn't bother us after we closed the street-side window and turned on the fan.

The Shobys provide a bicycle built for two, free beach passes, and bowls of fruit and candy to nibble on. A ring on the old school bell summons guests to the kitchen at 9 to feast on fresh fruit cups (which could include mango and papaya), choice of cereals with a big bowl of blueberries, and maybe a cheese omelet with sausages, rolled ham stuffed with cheese and eggs, or blueberry pancakes with Bernice's own blueberry syrup (she bakes all her own breads, puts up her own preserves, and politely declines requests for her recipe for the best blueberry muffins ever).

Doubles, $80 to $85. Closed December-February.

Harbor Inn, Ocean Avenue, Box 538A, Kennebunkport 04046. (207) 967-2074.

The large, wraparound front porch with river view is appropriate at the Harbor Inn. Texans Charlotte and Bill Massmann find themselves right at home on the wicker rocking chairs on the Southern-style veranda of the 1903 Victorian summer house they converted into a B&B in 1985. A decanter of sherry awaits guests in the large front parlor. At one side is a small antiques shop stocking Waterford glass and old quilts, among other things.

To the rear is a lace-curtained dining room with wallpaper patterned with pretty iris, where Charlotte serves a full breakfast of seasonal fruits, cereals, bagels with cream cheese, blueberry pancakes or crepes with ham and egg souffle, all prepared in a Texas-size kitchen created from four downstairs rooms.

Two of the eight guest rooms on the second and third floors are suites and all have private baths. They are handsomely furnished with canopy or four-poster beds, comfortable chairs, antique coverlets and

Veranda awaits guests at Harbor Inn.

fresh flowers. An efficiency cottage in the rear has one bedroom and sliding glass doors onto a patio.

Doubles, $80 to $110; two-night minimum in summer. Closed November-May.

Arundel Meadows Inn, Route 1, Box 1129, Kennebunk 04043. (207) 985-3770.

Colorful flowers and a lovely brick terrace greet visitors at this B&B in a bright yellow, 165-year-old farmhouse.

The six rooms, all with private baths, have antique beds and armoires and three have working fireplaces. The stairway wall is a allery, displaying the works of co-owner Murray Yaeger, an accomplished artist. We enjoyed the quiet first-floor suite with a queensize bed, decorated in an oriental motif. A new suite over the kitchen with two rooms and a bath was in the works for 1989.

A highlight here is the extra-special breakfast prepared by innkeeper Mark Batchelder, a professional chef, and served by Murray in the art-filled dining room. From Mark's large kitchen came some of the best croissants we've tasted, plus a plate heaped with a codfish cake, a dropped egg with bearnaise sauce, a zucchini fritter and cherry tomatoes. Belgian waffles and Monte Cristo (ham and cheese french toast) are other favorites.

Teatime brings such treats as fresh raspberry tarts, lemon squares, small cream puffs and applesauce cake.

Doubles, $60 to $80.

The Kennebunk Inn, 45 Main St., Kennebunk 04043. (207) 985-3351.

Dating back to 1799, this was little more than a flophouse when Arthur and Angela LeBlanc acquired it in 1978. "We took a street walker and turned her into a lady," Angela is fond of saying. A decade later, this convivial inn and restaurant full of personality is an example of what a couple with talent, energy and help from their five children can do.

Over the years the LeBlancs have modernized and upgraded the downtown hotel facility, to the point where it now has 34 rooms, 29 with private baths. Rooms vary in size and decor (there are ten kingsize and three queensize beds); some have working fireplaces and cathedral ceilings. Prevailing colors are pink, rose and raspberry, and the rooms we saw were very attractive. All have amenity packages, hair dryers and a rubber duck (one of Angela's whimsical touches) in the bathrooms.

Public areas include a parlor with a wood stove, an outdoor courtyard and the Fly Fishing Lounge, with a fishing wall containing a mounted salmon that Art caught and an old auto license plate, "Dry Fly." Angela presides over a large and eclectic gift shop, which sells the pottery and table settings for which she is known. The indefatigable Angela, who sings with the Choral Art Society, was starring in a musical and about to write a cookbook featuring Maine inns when we visited.

Lunch and dinner are served daily in the pleasant, pink-linened Victorian dining room (see below). The back of the menu tells the family's story in charming detail, and their enthusiasm is infectious.

Doubles, $35 to $80.

Dining Spots

Seascapes, On the Pier, Cape Porpoise, Kennebunkport. (207) 967-8500.

On our last visit to the Kennebunks, we were thrilled to find Seascapes, an elegant restaurant owned and operated by Angela and Arthur LeBlanc of the Kennebunk Inn, in the waterside space that formerly was Spicer's Gallery. The large square room is decorated simply (you wouldn't want to compete with the view of lobster boats through the picture windows), but the table settings are anything but simple. The plates are of handpainted Italian pottery in heavenly colors; candle holders are of the same pottery and napkins are ringed with fishes. The wine glasses are fluted and the linens (green overcloths that match the color of the rim of the pottery dishes, over white cloths topped with white straw mats at noon) are the finishing touch. And, glory be, the chairs are upholstered and comfortable, and classical music is the background.

Chef Jim Thomson, who was chef at the late Whistling Oyster in Ogunquit, has put together one of the area's more interesting menus. For dinner you might start with steamed mussels in coconut cream with fresh mint, or cornbread fried oysters with red pepper salsa ($4.95 or $6.95). The Maine bouillabaisse is the most expensive entree at $16.95, except for lobster braised in drambuie cream, which is priced daily. Christina's shrimp a la turkolimani is sauteed with fresh tomatoes and feta cheese, and scallops with arugula and lime pesto. The fresh haddock filet ($12.95) has a corn and bacon sauce, and the broiled breast of chicken with fresh rosemary and walnuts is sauced with apple vinegar. For the house salad ($2.50) you might order a tomato-roquefort dressing. A small dish of sorbet (perhaps grapefruit and pineapple) is served before the main course. Desserts could be fresh raspberries and chantilly cream or a pecan pineapple torte. The wine list is well chosen, with some comparative bargains, and the house Trefethen and Riverside labels are a treat.

At lunchtime, we loved the pasta of the day, with red and yellow peppers, feta cheese and many sprigs of coriander, and thought the Maine crab cakes with crispy outsides and a tomato-rosemary sauce even better than the ones we've had in Maryland. They were served with crisp potato bits and beets cooked in red wine vinegar. Mussels steamed in saffron cream, lobster ragout with vanilla, bourbon and fresh thyme, and baked pollack filet with tomato-onion compote were also available, about $4.95 to

Dining tables with colorful place settings overlook wharf at Seascapes.

$10.95 (for the Maine bouillabaisse). At brunch you might have parsnip and potato rounds with smoked salmon, sour cream and caviar ($4.95), marinated chicken livers with pecans, raisins and bourbon, or scallop mousseline wrapped in Napa cabbage, with orange-basil beurre blanc ($11.95). New American cuisine has arrived in the Kennebunk area with a flourish!

Lunch daily, 11:30 to 2; dinner, 5:30 to 9:30 or 10; after Labor Day, closed Tuesday and at 9 p.m. Closed January and February.

Cape Arundel Inn, Ocean Avenue, Kennebunkport. (207) 967-2125.

What could be more romantic than dining at a window table at the Cape Arundel, watching wispy clouds turn to mauve and violet as the sun sets, followed by a full golden moon rising over the darkened ocean? That the food is so good is a bonus.

The ocean and sky outside provide more than enough backdrop for a plain but attractive dining room with lots of windows and plants, dark wood and white linens. An excellent warm pheasant salad on radicchio with Thai dressing ($7.95) preceded our main courses, sweetbreads with a tart grapefruit sauce and roast loin of lamb, accompanied by rice pilaf, crisp ratatouille, and julienned carrots and turnips. Other entrees ($14.25 to $19.95) included duck with apricots and ginger, poached salmon with creamed leeks and sorrel, shrimp and scallops tossed with pesto, swordfish with pistachio butter and tournedos madagascar. The wine list offered a liter of River Oak red for $12.50.

The dessert tray harbored some interesting indulgences, a fruit shortcake among them. Dinner, Monday-Saturday, 5:30 to 8:30 or 9. Open mid-May through October.

White Barn Inn, Beach Street, Kennebunkport. (203) 967-2321.

Soaring up to three stories with all kinds of farming artifacts hanging from beams and pulleys, the White Barn is almost too atmospheric for words. It's also long been way up on everyone's list of favorite restaurants hereabouts.

Diners sit at tables that are blessedly well spaced in the main barn and in an addition.

The convivial gather at the gorgeous solid brass bar, and the truly jovial perch around the baby grand and sing along with the pianist. The tables are set with silver and pewter, linen and oil lamps, and the colorful impatiens on the deck beyond the large rear windows are spotlit at night.

The appealing menu lists five appetizers ($6 to $9.95) and fourteen entrees ($14.95 to $23.95). A fine house salad on chilled glass plates and some heavenly whole wheat rolls come with. For starters, the escargots in puff pastry, heady with garlic, and the summer salad of warm duck breast with an orange honey vinaigrette are excellent. Among main courses, we enjoyed grilled breast of chicken with a tomato-mint salsa ($14.95) and poached salmon ($19.95). Others in our party liked the blackened tuna with

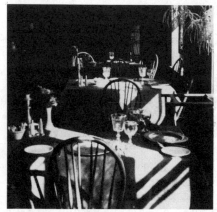

peaches, brandied cream and Cajun spices and the two whole stuffed quails with a grand marnier orange butter. Snow peas, new potatoes and other fresh vegetables accompanied this September dinner.

Cheesecake with raspberries, a pear tart, sweet potato pie and banana mousse were good choices from the dessert tray. The well-chosen wine list, evenly divided between French and California choices, has some good vintages at fair prices.

With candlelight flickering and classical music playing, the setting for such a repast could not be nicer.

Dinner nightly, 6 to 9:30; Sunday brunch, 11:30 to 1:30. Closed Mondays off-season.

Dining area at White Barn Inn.

Kennebunkport Inn, Dock Square, Kennebunkport. (207) 967-2621.

The pristine dining rooms on either side of the inn's entry are extra pretty, with fringed valances, lace curtains, Laura Ashley wallpaper and stenciling, hurricane lamps, jars of fresh flowers on the fireplace mantels and well-spaced tables done up in white over beige.

Innkeepers Martha and Rick Griffin have garnered quite a culinary reputation and go to France frequently to learn new dishes with which to dazzle their frequent repeat customers. Blackened carpaccio, terrine of pork and veal with truffles, and steamed mussels in a cognac and saffron cream sauce are among appetizers, $5.25 to $7.95.

The fourteen entrees ($14.95 to $21.95) on the changing menu might be breast of chicken stuffed with fruits and herbs and served with a pinenut and sherry cream sauce, grilled veal chop with a fricassee of wild mushrooms, seafood ravioli and bouillabaisse with a side of spicy red pepper sauce. We remember an artfully presented grilled duck breast with raspberry sauce and an extraordinary mustard-ginger rack of lamb.

An ethereal key lime pie and a white chocolate mousse with strawberries in kirsch were good choices from the dessert cart ($4.50).

Dinner nightly, 6 to 9; closed November-March.

The Tides Inn By-the-Sea, Goose Rocks Beach, Kennebunkport. (207) 967-3757.

Some of the area's more intriguing fare comes from a seaside inn of the old school. Chairs line the front porch facing the ocean, a pot-belly stove is in the pub, the cluttered dining room is partitioned by a screen from the entrance to the kitchen, and there's a rustic dining porch.

Marie Henricksen, who runs what she calls "a casual, crazy place with a true Maine

Kennebunkport Inn has built a reputation for fine cuisine over the years.

air," has upgraded the inn gradually over the last seventeen years, and chef Tim Mavrakos's menu reflects an eclectic regional cuisine.

The decor is fairly nondescript with bentwood chairs, tables covered with paisley cloths and blue napkins, and fake flowers. Classical music plays in the background. The food is assertive: Szechuan grilled eggplant, warm lobster taco with yellow tomato salsa and Tex-Mex tortilla soup among appetizers, grilled catfish with a Cajun tartar sauce and sauteed veal tenderloin with chili hollandaise among entrees, and, for dessert, fruit tuilles and a chocolate bombe that one addict called unreal. The price is right: appetizers, $2.95 to $7.95; entrees, $11.95 to $16.75, and many wines in the low teens.

We ordered the grilled lamb and vegetables, a large plate bearing chunks of nicely seared lamb, tender new potatoes, zucchini and red peppers, plus a side portion of salsa laced with coriander as well as the regular minted pear chutney. Also good was the grilled shrimp and fettuccine with green onions, sun-dried tomatoes, basil and garlic cream. Dessert was an extraordinary almond cake with a fresh peach sauce.

Twenty-two guest rooms upstairs and in a new annex range in age and decor from extra-plain and old-fashioned to modern, and are $60 to $125 a night. Marie has been gradually redecorating the rooms and adding more private baths. The annex rooms, with kingsize beds and modern baths, are the more expensive.

Dinner nightly, 6 to 9; closed November-April.

The Olde Grist Mill, Mill Lane, Kennebunkport. (207) 967-4781.

Owner David Lombard says his father was the miller in the 1930s in this, the last remaining tidal mill in the country, built in 1749 and in his family ever since. His mother opened it as a tea room in 1940 and it evolved into a full-scale restaurant that underwent a major renovation and expansion in 1985. The mill's old features were preserved and many of the original accoutrements remain, but the immense new bar and lounge is posh as can be with wing chairs, sofas and a piano gracing the wide-board floors. The rear dining room is all in pink, with bentwood chairs, old farm implements on the walls and lots of windows opening onto the tidal river.

173

Long a favorite luncheon spot for tour buses and the blue-rinse crowd, the restaurant has become more serious (and pricey) lately and is decidedly popular with the locals. Lunch no longer is served, and dinners start at $13.75 (for filet of haddock) and rise rapidly through the high teens to $27.75 for baked stuffed lobster. Among the choices are salmon en papillote, baked stuffed shrimp with macadamia nuts, sea scallops with an Amontillado sherry sauce, veal cordon bleu, roast duckling chambord and steak au poivre. A full shore dinner with clam chowder, steamed clams or scallops or shrimp cocktail, lobster and all the trimmings is $32.50.

Mocha raspberry torte, strawberry cream torte, chocolate mousse and lemon rum cheesecake are favorite desserts.

The property, listed on the National Register, includes a good country store and gift shop across the lawn.

Dinner nightly from 5:30; closed Monday in spring and fall. Open April-December.

Windows on the Water, Chase Hill, Kennebunkport. (207) 967-3313.

The windows are architecturally interesting at this sleek restaurant of recent vintage on a hilltop above the water; they also offer one of Kennebunkport's better water views. So the name was a natural, as is the attractive two-level outdoor deck, which may be the best place in town for a summer lunch.

Lunch is the perfect opportunity to try the restaurant's highly touted lobster-stuffed potato, which has been featured in national magazines. Fresh lobster meat, jarlsberg cheese and cream top a hot baked potato, and the $8.50 tab is probably more justifiable as a luncheon main course than as an appetizer at dinner. Salads, sandwiches and entrees are in the $5.50 to $8.50 range. We were a bit disappointed in the small size of the chef's salad ($7.50), mostly turkey and ham; for some reason the shrimp-based salad with cheese was much more ample. The poppyseed vinaigrette dressing was excellent, and the Whitbread's ale so cooling on a hot summer day that we had two.

The main dining room has a cathedral ceiling, track lighting, and a green color scheme accented by vases of black-eyed susans. A smaller room beyond is even nicer with a bowed front window. Upstairs is a lounge with a cathedral ceiling and a Palladian window overlooking the river.

The dinner menu has given up its original Chart House touches (the owner was formerly with that chain) for more continental fare: scallops en croute, shrimp scampi, veal Oscar, beef Wellington and the local staple, prime rib, $13.25 to $18.95.

Lunch daily, 11:45 to 2:30; dinner from 5:30; Sunday brunch, 11 to 3.

Cafe Topher, Western Avenue, Kennebunkport. (207) 987-5009.

The smart-looking cafe opened by Christopher Riley in 1983 was such a success that he and his wife Hylah added Topher's Tavern underneath and, in 1988, expanded into a former shop in front with a large new dining room. Gone is the old, intimate cafe, now a formal reception area and a larger kitchen. And gone is the cafe feeling, but at least the tables are better spaced for privacy.

The menu is a mixed bag from the nachos, potato skins and chicken wings for "munchins" to marinated beef kabob or prawns Venice. Topher's chicken stuffed with green beans, wrapped in bacon and served with a bearnaise sauce appeals, and baked haddock with garlic butter is a perennial favorite.

Dinners are priced from $8.84 for fettuccine alfredo to $17.26 for lobster newburg.

At lunch, salads, shrimp or lobster rolls, burgers and sandwiches are available. A fine setting is the nicely landscaped outdoor patio, decked out with linens and white molded chairs.

Lunch daily, ll:30 to 2:30; dinner, 5:30 to 10; Sunday brunch.

174

Alisson's, 5 Dock Square, Kennebunkport. (207) 967-4841.

Ensconced in a large downtown storefront, Alisson's is a local tradition, possibly because of its motto: "where the nicest people meet the nicest people." (Another motto reads "Eat, drink and grow port-ly.") Everyone seems to know everyone else, and the place is full for three meals a day seven days a week.

The atmosphere is casual, both downstairs in the bar and in a dining room with bare wood tables and ladderback chairs and upstairs in a larger room with skylights, small glass-over-pink tables and large windows onto Dock Square. Here people can dig into the fried seafood and dishes like honey shrimp, baked stuffed sole and steak teriyaki at prices that won't break the bank (dinner entrees, $9.95 to $13.95). Nachos, potato skins and shrimp cocktail are among the "preliminaries" ($2.95 to $4.95); "afterthoughts" include carrot cake, Maine raspberry chocolate cake and chocolate peanut-butter pie.

Heaping sandwiches at earthy prices are the rule at lunch. Breakfast is a downright bargain, from a complete mini-breakfast for $2.50 to amaretto french toast for $2.95. Eggs Benedict is $3.95.

Open daily from 6 a.m. to 11 p.m.

Kennebunk Inn, 45 Main St., Kennebunk. (207) 985-3351.

This cheerful-looking 1799 inn has an esteemed hotel-style dining room with high upholstered chairs, pink and white linen, candles in hurricane lamps and Tiffany-style stained-glass windows.

The food is consistent — considered a compelling virtue in the area — and reasonably priced. Dinners range from $10.95 for haddock chablis to $14.95 for filet mignon or lazy man's lobster.

This is very much a family-run place. Owners Art and Angela LeBlanc and their children are evident on the menu and in the dining room (even the chef, James Thompson, was engaged to their "adopted daughter" Sarah, one of their extended family.

The featured dishes (two veals, seafood fettuccine, shrimp, chicken, surf and turf, and duck) are named for family members, all of whose names begin with "A." Angela's mother lends her name to Ma Mere's scallops and a dessert of trifle, and her first granddaughter Christina was about to be honored with a "C" dish.

Hidden from the front, a patio off to the side of the inn is attractive for lunching. Haddock veronique, chicken Oscar, Maine seafood cakes and honeyed scallops are among the offerings, most in the $4 to $8 range.

Lunch daily, 11:30 to 2:30; dinner, 5:30 to 9 or 10.

Extra-Special

Tilly's Shanty, Cape Porpoise.

If you prefer your Maine lobster in an informal outdoor setting by the water, shun the better known Nunan's Lobster Hut nearby, which is deservedly popular in its own right. Head right onto the pier at Cape Porpoise. Behind Seascapes is a shanty where you place your order and then sit at a battered picnic table beside the harbor (or inside at a few tables and a counter facing the water). When we were last there, lobster dinners ranged from $8.95 to $11.95, depending on size. Twin lobster tails and "frys" were $9.95, a lobster roll, $6.75, and lobster stew, $4.75 a cup and $6.25 a bowl. Homemade muffins and omelets are featured at breakfast; fishermen start gathering at 5:30 a.m. Hours vary, but Tilly's is generally open weekdays for breakfast from 5:30 to 10, lunch and dinner daily until 8 p.m.

Diversions

Beaches. Gooch's and **Kennebunk** are two sandy strands with surf west of town (parking by permit, often provided by innkeepers). The fine silvery sand at **Goose Rocks Beach** looks almost tropical and the waters are protected. The beaches are at their uncrowded best at non-peak periods and early or late in the day.

Parson's Way. A marker opposite the landmark Colony Hotel notes the land given to the people of Kennebunkport so that "everyone may enjoy its natural beauty." Sit on the benches, spread a blanket on a rock beside the ocean, or walk out to the serene little chapel of St. Ann's Episcopal Church by the sea.

Ocean Avenue. Continue past Parson's Way to Spouting Rock, where the incoming tide creates a spurting fountain as waves crash between two ragged cliffs, and Blowing Cave, another roaring phenomenon within view of Walker Point and the impressive George Bush summer compound. Go on to Cape Porpoise, the closest thing to a fishing village hereabouts, with a working lobster pier and a picturesque harbor full of islands.

History. The Kennebunkport Historical Society has its attractions: the 1853 Greek Revival Nott House called **White Columns** and the 1899 **Town House School** with exhibits of local and maritime heritage. But inland Kennebunk is more obviously historic: The 1825 **Brick Store Museum** has an excellent collection of decorative and fine arts, Federal period furniture, artifacts and textiles. It mounts a couple of major exhibits each year (photos of the great fire of 1947 were on when we last visited) and offers walking tours of Kennebunk's historic district. Summer Street (Route 35) running south of downtown toward Kennebunkport is considered one of the architecturally outstanding residential streets in the nation; the 1803 **Taylor-Barry House** is open for tours, and the aptly named yellow-with-white-frosting "Wedding Cake House" (1826) is a sight to behold (though not open to the public).

Arts and Crafts. Its scenery has turned Kennebunkport into a mecca for artisans. The Art Guild of the Kennebunks numbers more than 50 resident professionals as members and claims the Kennebunks are the largest collective community of fine art on the East Coast. Art and galleries are everywhere, but are concentrated around Kennebunkport's Dock Square and the wharves to the southeast. Fine crafts are shown at **The Pascos,** the shop and home of civic boosters Henry and Priscilla Pasco, a brother-sister team whose 48-year tenure makes theirs "by far the oldest shop around." Nearby in the new Wharf Lane Shops are the **Priscilla Hartley Gallery,** in its 28th season and the oldest in Maine, the **Van Sinderen Furniture** and woodworking shop, and out over the water, Lou and Bob Lipkin's distinctive **Goose Rocks Pottery.** For a change of pace, visit the grounds of the **Franciscan Monastery** (where, as some savvy travelers know, spare and inexpensive bedrooms are available) and St. Anthony's Shrine. The shrines and sculpture include the towering piece that adorned the facade of the Vatican pavilion at the 1964 New York World's Fair.

Shopping. Dock Square and, increasingly, the Lower Village across the river are full of interesting stores, everything from the **Tipsy Mouse** with gourmet foods and wines to the **Port Canvas Co.,** with all kinds of handsome canvas products. **Zamboanga** has a fine array of gifts, home furnishings, tiles and kites. **Alano Ltd.** has super clothes, and Charlene Romanos makes unusual jewelry, flower arrangements and more at her **Back Porch Boutique.** The **Dannah Collection** at the Schooner Shops is an exquisite gift shop and flower store. The splendid **Kennebunk Book Port, Paper Plus,** the **Haberdashery** and the **Zoo Apparel** (clothing), **Amicus** and **Plum Dandy** (crafts), **Once a Knight** (games), **Port Folio** ("paper with panache"), the **Whimsy Shop** and the shops at the new **Union Square** and **Village Marketplace** are some favorites.

Fine Camden Harbor view is offered from porch at Smiling Cow gift shop.

Camden, Me.
Where Mountains Meet Sea

From where she stood in 1910, all that native poet Edna St. Vincent Millay could see were "three long mountains and a wood" in one direction and "three islands in a bay" the other way. Her poem, written at age 18 and first recited publicly at Camden's Whitehall Inn, captures the physical beauty of this coastal area known as the place where the mountains meet the sea.

Today, the late poet might not recognize her beloved Camden, so changed is the town that now teems with tourists in summer. The scenery remains as gorgeous as ever, and perhaps no street in Maine is more majestic than High Street, its forested properties lined with the sparkling white homes one associates with the Maine coast of a generation ago. Back then, when you finally reached Camden after the slow, tortuous drive up Route 1, you had unofficially arrived Down East.

Those were the days, and visitors in ever-increasing numbers still try to recapture them in a town undergoing a bed-and-breakfast inn boom and a proliferation of smart, distinctive shops. A sign in the window of Mariner's Restaurant, proclaiming itself "the last local luncheonette," caught our eye: "Down Home, Down East; no ferns, no quiche."

A small-scale cultural life attracts some; others like the outdoors activities of Camden Hills State Park. But the focus for most is Camden Harbor, with its famed fleet of windjammers setting forth under full sail each Monday morning and returning to port each Saturday morning.

Camden has an almost mystical appeal that draws people back time and again. Sometimes, amid all those people, you just wish that appeal weren't quite so universal.

Inn Spots

Norumbega, 61 High St., Camden 04843. (207) 236-4646.

Imagine having the run of a grand Victorian castle overlooking Penobscot Bay — a "castle to call home," in the words of businessman-turned-innkeeper Murray Keatinge.

It's possible, thanks to Murray and his wife Elisabeth, Californians who summer in Camden and acquired Norumbega in 1987. "There's only one way to run a business and that's to run it myself," he's finding as he commutes back and forth from Pasadena. "We're trying to build the best inn in the U.S.A., and we're close to it."

One of the great late-19th-century villas along the Maine coast, the 1886 cobblestone and slate-roofed mansion was built for Joseph B. Stearns, inventor of the duplex system of telegraphy, and for a few years was the summer home of journalist Hodding Carter. It has seven sumptuous guest rooms on the second and third floors, two more plus a pub in the walk-out basement, and a main floor with public rooms like those in the finest estates.

Indeed, this is a mini-Newport-style mansion, from its graceful entry with oriental carpets and ornate staircase (complete with a cozy retreat for two beside a fireplace on the landing) to the smallest of guest rooms on the third floor. Even it has two Victorian rocking chairs around a skirted table, a queensize bed, an oak dresser with pieces of Blue Hill's Rackcliffe Pottery on top, a bathroom with an old clawfoot tub and separate shower stall, and costs a cool $160 a night.

The other rooms, all high-ceilinged and airy, are decorated in a fresh California style with lots of pastels and plush rugs. The Sandringham has a kingsize bed, a fireplace in the corner and a sofa and two chairs beneath balloon curtains in the curved window. The Carnerveron, full of wicker, has its own little rear porch with deck chairs. Even the new basement rooms, with windows onto the garden, are cheery.

The parlors, the library, the conservatory, the second-floor reading room, the downstairs pub with pool table and TV, the flower-laden rear porches on all three floors and the expansive lawns are available for guests.

The Keatinges' resident manager, who greets guests, pours tea or wine in the afternoon. In the morning, guests gather at the large damask-covered table in the formal dining room or outside on the deck for a breakfast feast for the eyes as well as the palate: platters of fresh fruits, homemade muffins and breads, breakfast meats and, the piece de resistance, the main course — perhaps crabmeat omelet, Belgian waffles or, in our case, french toast topped with a dollop of pink sherbet and sliced peaches, which all eight at our table agreed was the best we'd ever had. Being thrown together with strangers somehow works here — there's enough room for togetherness and also for escape, if you like.

The price is steep, but the value is received. All nine rooms have private baths and four have fireplaces. The best (and quietest) are those away from the road in the rear with spectacular views of the harbor.

Doubles, $160 to $180.

Edgecombe-Coles House, 64 High St., Camden 04843. (207) 236-2336.

Another substantial summer home, on a hilltop almost across the street from Norumbega, opened for bed and breakfast in 1984.

Innkeepers Terry and Louise Price named it for their fathers and furnished it rather spectacularly with antiques, oriental rugs, original art, stenciling that Louise did herself (she also loves to wallpaper), and interesting touches like draperies around the showers and English soaps and herb shampoos for guests.

Each of the six guest rooms with private baths is different, but most have quilts and bedspreads made by Louise's mother. The most elegant is the huge front room with kingsize bed, fireplace and picture window framing a grand ocean view.

In the luxurious living room are a leather sofa, piano and many books.

A full breakfast is served in the rear dining room or outside in the garden. Strawberry waffles, blueberry pancakes and giant sweet popovers are among the specialties. Or the innkeepers will bring continental breakfast to your bedroom, if you wish.

Doubles, $75 to $120.

178

Norumbega is a grand Victorian mansion overlooking Penobscot Bay.

Windward House, 6 High St., Camden 04843. (207) 236-9656.

Guests enter this handsome B&B through the dining room, which is appropriate, for its gourmet breakfasts are well-known. A gleaming silver service, lace curtains, blue patterned rug and lots of plants immediately catch the eye. Innkeepers Mary and Jon Davis may greet you here and lead you to the nicely furnished parlor, or a pine-paneled TV room with all the current magazines, for orientation purposes before showing you to your room.

Upstairs on the second and third floors are five guest rooms, each with private bath. We're partial to the Rose Room with queen canopy bed and lots of antiques, but were charmed also by the Wicker Room in pink and blue and the Camden Room with an eyelet cover and a doll on the bed. Special touches in each room include mints and Crabtree & Evelyn toiletries, and a decanter of sherry awaits in the parlor.

About those breakfasts. Mary Davis, who was a caterer in Bernardsville, N.J., prepares things like apple-puff pancakes, waffles with blueberry-lemon nut sauce, crepes, quiches, ham and cheese souffles, and grand marnier strawberry puffs. Fresh fruit comes first, followed by homemade muffins and rolls, then the entree, accompanied by breakfast meats. After that, you may be temporarily immobilized; take your coffee to a back room full of wicker furniture, or out onto the deck overlooking a pleasant back yard.

Doubles, $60 to $85.

The Whitehall Inn, 52 High St., Box 558, Camden 04843. (207) 236-3391.

This rambling inn (built in 1834, an inn since 1901) is a fixture on the Camden scene, generations of families returning annually for vacations to partake of the hospitality offered by the Dewing family and their offspring. The front porch is supplied with the obligatory rocking chairs, and youngsters play lawn games alongside the inn.

Edna St. Vincent Millay of nearby Rockland gave the first recitation of her lyric poem, "Renascence," in 1912 in the inn. Her sister was on the dining room staff and one of the guests, recognizing the poet's talent, arranged for her acceptance at Vassar College. Her pictures and high-school diploma hang over the piano.

Forty guest rooms, all but two with private baths, are entered from meandering corridors on the second and third floors of the main inn. Each is furnished simply with a double or twin beds and contains an old-fashioned, in-house telephone. Ten additional rooms are in two houses across the street.

Breakfast and dinner are served in the large, old-fashioned and pleasant dining room with paned windows overlooking the side lawns. The changing dinner menu in the $15 to $17 range might list sauteed chicken breast, broiled haddock and veal St. Millay with shallots, wine and cream. House specialties include boiled lobster, poached salmon and crabmeat florentine. Local blueberries show up in everything from pancakes to bread puddings.

Doubles, $115 to $130, MAP; two- and three-day minimum stays required at peak times. Closed mid-October to Memorial Day.

Lord Camden Inn, 24 Main St., Camden 04843. (207) 236-4325.

If the Whitehall is Camden's grand dowager, the Lord Camden is the new kid on the block — and feels it. An 1893 brick storefront and the Masonic Temple in the heart of downtown Camden were restored in 1984 into a modern, rather impersonal 28-room inn with elevator, private baths and in-room television.

Most rooms on the second, third and fourth floors are ersatz Colonial with original brick walls and brass or mahogany four-poster beds. Coveted rooms with balconies overlook the harbor beyond the stores across the street (the higher the floor, the higher the price).

Continental breakfast is delivered to rooms. Chocolates are put out when the covers are turned down at night.

Doubles, $98 to $138.

The Belmont, 6 Belmont Ave., Camden 04843. (207) 236-8053.

Billed as Camden's oldest inn, this cottage-style Victorian on a residential side street has sheltered guests first as the Green Gables and then, until 1988, as Aubergine. That's when David and Kerlin Grant, widely known for their French cuisine, sold to Gerald Clare and John Mancarella.

The new owners changed the main-floor layout, added a side porch and switched the cuisine from French nouvelle to regional American (see Dining Spots). They kept the upstairs guest rooms the same, although they were planning some remodeling for 1989. All are nicely decorated with antique furnishings, floral wallpapers and a light, sunny quality in keeping with the exterior. The two third-floor rooms we once occupied with our sons have been converted into one extra-large room. Four of the six rooms have private baths.

The old-fashioned swing on the side porch and the bar with tiny marble tables in a separate room off the parlor invite dalliance for a pre-dinner drink. The parlor, done up in rose and celadon with an oriental rug over the bleached wood floor, has a nifty window seat made from mattress ticking and small built-in seats beside the fireplace.

A full breakfast, perhaps with shirred eggs, is served in the country-pretty dining room, on the enclosed porch sparkling with white summer furniture, or in the bedrooms.

Doubles, $72 to $90; two-night minimum on weekends. Closed November-April.

Hartstone Inn, 41 Elm St., Camden 04843. (207) 236-4259.

Built in 1835 by a local merchant, this house on Camden's main street near the business district was renovated into an inviting inn in 1986 by Peter and Elaine Simmons.

They offer seven bedrooms, all with private baths and two with fireplaces, on three floors — from one on the third floor, you can glimpse the harbor. One bathroom has a marble sink, another an old wood-encased tub, and several beds have carved-oak headboards.

A restored carriage house in the rear offers two housekeeping suites. Done in contemporary barn style, they have dark beams tempered with light walls and skylights, complete kitchens and futon beds.

A quiet parlor has a fireplace, and a common room is full of books, games and a TV. A pleasant dining room is where a complete breakfast including egg dishes, french toast or waffles is served.

A four-course dinner featuring perhaps stuffed breast of chicken is available for house guests for $15 to $20, depending on Elaine's choice of entree.

Doubles, $75 to $85.

Blackberry Inn, 82 Elm St., Camden 04843. (207) 236-6060.

Gray with berry-colored trim, this 1860 Italianate structure exudes Victoriana, from the incredible tin ceiling colored in pastels in innkeeper Edward Doudera's law office to the colorful moldings and gilt where the walls meet the ceilings throughout. Ed and wife Vicki offer seven guest rooms, two with new private baths and five with half-baths (sinks and toilets), plus a studio apartment in a rear carriage house.

The ornamental plasterwork crafted by an Italian artisan, original brass fixtures, shiny parquet floors and ornate mantels provide a backdrop for period furnishings and oriental rugs. The main floor includes two living rooms (one a morning parlor furnished in antique Bar Harbor wicker and the other all in Victoriana), a dining room and the Library guest room, which has a white iron bed and a fireplace. Spacious rooms on the second floor — one named for Bette Davis, who stayed there — have queensize brass beds.

The Douderas serve breakfast buffet style at the extra-long table in the dining room. Cheese-sausage strata, blueberry pancakes or blackberry blintzes might be the fare. The makings for the last come from the inn's back yard, which is crammed with blackberry bushes.

Doubles, $55 to $75.

The Owl and the Turtle, 8 Bay View St., Camden 04843. (207) 236-9014.

Most visitors know this as a good bookstore and, until recently, as an appealing tea room with a balcony overlooking the harbor. But it also has three comfortable motel-style guest rooms with television, air-conditioning and wall-to-wall carpeting even in the bathrooms. Each has an outdoor balcony overlooking the harbor. Continental breakfast is served in the room.

Doubles, $65 to $70. No smoking.

Dining Spots

The Belmont, 6 Belmont Ave., Camden. (207) 236-8053.

The first fine restaurant in the Camden area (indeed, a pioneer in nouvelle cuisine on the Maine coast), Aubergine gave way in 1988 to the Belmont and new chef-owner Gerry Clare, who had a restaurant in Fort Lauderdale and a guest house in Nantucket. He changed the emphasis from French to American cuisine, but otherwise repeat guests would be hard-pressed to tell the difference.

The serene dining room still looks lovely with its white linens and aubergine carpet; the adjacent sun porch still has its pristine white tables and chairs. Floral china and field flowers in tiny clear-glass vases provide color.

The menu changes every three days. You might start with a Nantucket fish chowder

181

Breakfast is served to house guests in summery dining room at the Belmont.

or appetizers ($6 to $7.50) like a plate of exotic pates, seafood salad, codfish cakes with Maine crab and red pepper mayonnaise, or pasta "du moment" (sauteed vegetables and pesto on angel hair the night we were there).

The five entrees are priced from $13.50 for chicken en croute to $19 for filet mignon au poivre. Roast duckling with ginger-peach sauce, medallions of veal with a wild mushroom strudel and salmon with a champagne-grapefruit beurre blanc were other offerings when we visited. Vegetable accompaniments were a puree of broccoli with sour cream and horseradish, carrots braised in grand marnier and garlic cheese grits. Sourdough bread and salad come with.

Desserts could be bete noir (a deep chocolate cake filled with beach plum preserves and chocolate ganache), fresh raspberries with champagne sabayon, lemon curd tarts or amaretto cheesecake.

The wine list is extensive and fairly priced, from $10 to $190.

Dinner nightly except Monday. Closed November-April.

Cassoulet, 31 Elm St., Camden. (207) 236-6304.

Tiny, cute and very colorful is Cassoulet (the former Secret Garden). Pinks, greens, purples and floral prints are the colors; the china is plain white for a nice contrast.

Featuring "classic country cooking," the menu lists such appetizers as clams casino and oysters Giannini ($4.95 to $6.95). The cassoulet, made with lamb, pork and sausage, is $13.95. Entrees go up to $17.95 for bouillabaisse and include shrimp a la Grecque, filet mignon with a cognac sauce and cannelloni verde. The catch of the day could be salmon with a lemon-caper butter or halibut broiled with pesto; the pasta of the day, seafood alfredo, with lobster, scallops and shrimp on fettuccine.

Desserts change nightly; a popular one is a flourless chocolate-raspberry torte. Profiteroles with homemade fudge sauce, creme de menthe cheesecake and walnut-apricot tart are others. Eight house wines are available by the glass.

Dinner, Monday-Saturday 6 to 9:30.

Mama & Leenie's, 27 Elm St., Camden. (207) 236-6300.

Stop in at this little cafe and bakery for a cup of that good Green Mountain coffee and a breakfast of waffles, french toast or a blintz with fruit and sour cream ($3.50 to $3.75).

At lunch you might order Mama's special peasant soup with beef, kielbasa and vegetables, or a caesar salad with Leenie's homemade croutons. Melted cheese and tomato on a bagel might hit the spot, or how about Chinese chop suey with rice?

Mama does a lot of the cooking. Daughter Leenie is a master baker as evidenced by the apricot strudel with coconut and walnuts, the double chocolate fudge brownies with orange zest, and the pure butter shortbread (85 cents a wedge). The fresh berry pies with real whipped cream are masterpieces.

The decor is simple, with ladderback chairs, and wild flowers in little jars. There's also a nice little patio on one side.

You may bring your own wine for dinner, when you might find Indonesian marinated chicken on a skewer or a bowl of chili with homemade bread. The local Miss Plum's ice cream is offered, and nothing costs over $6.

Open 8 a.m. to 9:30 p.m., Sunday 8 to 4, fewer hours in off-season.

Cappy's Chowder House, 1 Main St., Camden. (207) 236-2254.

"The Maine you hope to meet" is one of the catchy slogans surrounding Cappy's, and local color is said to be its strong point. The scene is barroom nautical: lobster traps hang above the bar, and green billiard-room lamps light the bare wood tables. The something-for-everyone menu is Down East cutesy: Maine pig skins, burgers on the bounty, Camden Hills frittata, mussel beach pasta and desserted islands.

The place packs in the crowds for one of the best clam chowders anywhere ($3.95 a bowl; by the pint or quart to go), fried scallops with remoulade, a lobster croissant, fish cakes topped with salsa on a bed of spinach, seafood stir-fry, Cajun lamb tenderloin and the like. Main courses, accompanied by French bread from Cappy's Bakery below, rice pilaf and salad with a good house dressing, are $8.95 to $11.95. Burgers, salads and lighter fare are in the $4.75 to $8.95 range.

The locals gather here for breakfast. The placemat is the menu, offering things like "pure eggstasy" and blueberry pancakes in the $1 to $4 range. For a snack, try the morning special at Cappy's Bakery: an apple croissant and coffee, $1.10.

Shrimp by the bucket is served from the raw bar during happy hour in the Crow's Nest.

Open daily, 7:30 a.m. to midnight.

The Waterfront Restaurant, Harborside Square off Bay View Street, Camden. (207) 236-3747.

There's no better waterside setting in Camden than this appropriately named establishment with a large outdoor deck shaded by a striking white canopy that resembles a boat's sails.

You can watch the busy harbor as you lunch on fried clams (the most expensive entree and including a good gazpacho and french fries), a California salad or lobster roll. Other interesting selections include lemon chicken salad, smoked salmon with toasted bagel, seafood on a toasted roll with remoulade sauce, crabmeat rarebit, mussels mariniere and enchiladas.

Many of the luncheon salads also are available as dinner entrees, and the homemade sweet and sour bacon, lemon-parmesan and blue cheese dressings are outstanding.

The accent is on seafood among main courses at dinner ($10.95 to $16.95). Mediterranean seafood stew, sole boursin, New England crab cakes and poached haddock with

Outdoor dining is popular at the Waterfront Restaurant.

artichokes and hollandaise are popular choices. Apricot chicken and New York sirloin are available for those who prefer.

For appetizers, the smoked fish sampler with the local Duck Trap River Trout Farm smoked salmon, mussels and trout appeals, and all kinds of shellfish are available at the raw bar.

Lunch daily, 11:30 to 2:30; dinner, 5 to 10.

Peter Ott's Tavern and Steakhouse, Bay View Street, Camden. (207) 236-4032.

We can't imagine why people would want to eat at a steakhouse on the coast, but those who tire of seafood apparently do and Peter Ott's is usually jammed. Antique and contemporary local photographs brighten the dark decor.

Grilled swordfish, chicken Creole and sirloin dijonnaise are featured on the menu, which runs from $9.95 for pork chops to $17.95 for sirloin and sauteed lobster. The salad bar is billed as Camden's original, and its offerings (including pastas) are said to be quite good.

Dinner nightly, 5:30 to 10.

O'Neil's, 21 Bay View St., Camden. (207) 236-3272.

Pass the main-floor bar and head upstairs to a pleasant dining room with glimpses through the windows of the harbor and a small rear deck that's best described as cozy. This is casual dining with some Mexican touches.

Start with Buffalo chicken wings, nachos, quesadilla or Mexican pizza, or try the French country (chicken) or smoked turkey salad. Heavier eaters can try chargrilled swordfish or salmon, seafood stir-fry, pasta vera cruz, fish and chips, baby back ribs or New York sirloin, $7.95 to $14.95. The menu's specials include four Mexican dishes and a "cheeseburger in paradise,"

Open daily from 11:30 a.m. to 11:30 p.m.

Gilbert's Publick House, 12 Bay View St., Camden. (207) 236-4320.

In 1988, this was the newest restaurant in a town in which restaurants seem to come and go with the tides. The top of the bar was fashioned from the backs of pews from an old Catholic church in Rockland, and some of the seats are church pews. All kinds of chairs from pressed oak to wrought iron surround tables in various sections of the spacious room, and Tiffany lamps hang from the ceiling. The dance floor (live music Wednesday through Saturday) is very much in evidence.

The all-day menu features international pub food, which translates to "entrees from pubs all over." Among them are antipasto, Aegean shrimp salad, fried native seafood, pasta santini, burritos, sesame stir-fry, German wurst platter and Long Branch barbecue ribs, gently priced from $5.95 to $7.95. "International starters" include nachos, baked brie and fried egg rolls. Sandwiches are all-American.

Open daily, 11:30 to 11.

Francesca's, Public Landing, Camden. (207) 236-9660.

Our favorite Blueberry Puffin food shop was gone in 1988, its place taken by Francesca T. Brown and the deli and catering shop bearing her name.

Interesting sandwiches range from $3.95 for Sicilian to $6.75 for lobster with lemon mayonnaise, lettuce and tomato, advertised as "a weight-watcher's nightmare." All kinds of side salads are available, 95 cents a serving, and quiches (broccoli-scallion, artichoke-red pepper or sausage-cheese) with a salad are $4.95. No fewer than three versions of chicken salad are offered. For those who can't choose, there's a salad bar. Desserts are featured in the evening.

Open Tuesday-Saturday 8 a.m. to 10 p.m., Sunday 8 to 8.

Round Top and Galley Takeout, Bay View Street, Camden.

Twenty-six flavors of ice cream are available at this old-fashioned ice cream counter and take-out restaurant, which has a few tables on the wharf.

A lobster roll is $5.95 (in a box with french fries, $6.85) and a hot dog, $1.25. But the ice cream is the main attraction: everything from bubblegum, ginger and cappuccino to rum raisin, watermelon sherbet and Brand X (vanilla with M&Ms) available in cones (95 cents to $1.55), frappes and sherbet freezes.

Open from 11:30 a.m. in season.

Diversions

Water pursuits. Any number of boat cruises on Penobscot Bay leave from the Camden landing, where there are benches for viewing the passing boat parade. For a longer cruise or ferry rides to the islands, go to Rockland or Lincolnville Beach (a favorite excursion is the ferry trip to Islesboro for lunch at the Islesboro Inn). The Lincolnville Beach is popular for swimming. A more secluded, picturesque setting is the little-known Laite Memorial Beach with treed lawns sloping down to the water, a small beach, picnic tables and old-fashioned fireplaces off Bay View Street.

Inland pursuits. Some of the East Coast's most scenic hiking is available on trails in Camden Hills State Park. Mount Megunticook is the highest of the three mountains that make up the park and the second highest point on the Eastern Seaboard. If you're not up to hiking, be sure to drive the toll road up Mount Battie, an easy one-mile ride. The view is worth the $1-per-person toll. A scenic drive is out Route 52 to Megunticook Lake, an island-studded lake that emerged eerily from the clouds the first foggy afternoon we saw it. A walking tour of Camden and a bicycle or car tour of Camden and adjacent Rockport are available through the Camden-Rockport Historical Society.

Cultural pursuits. Founded in 1978, the **Camden Shakespeare Company** gives four plays in repertory in summer in the natural, stone-tiered Bok Amphitheater behind the Camden Public Library. The sylvan setting adds much to matinee or evening performances of the likes of "Macbeth," "Much Ado About Nothing" and "A Midsummer Night's Dream." Each play takes place on a different "stage" on each side of the 200 seats set up and taken down for each performance. The **Farnsworth Museum** in the center of Rockland ranks among the finer regional art museums in the nation. The collection focuses on American art from the 18th century to the present, with prized works by the Wyeth family. The **Farnsworth Homestead** next door, open for $2, is considered one of the most beautiful Victorian houses in the country. Nearby in Rockland is the **Shore Village Museum,** locally called the lighthouse museum because of its intriguing collection of lighthouse and Coast Guard memorabilia.

Shopping pursuits. Camden is a mecca for sophisticated shopping, and all kinds of interesting specialty stores and boutiques pop up every year. Among our favorites: **The Smiling Cow,** a large and venerable gift shop with a myriad of Maine items, has a great view from its rear porch over the Megunticook River, which ripples down the rocks toward the harbor; you can take in the picturesque scene while sipping complimentary coffee or tea between shopping forays. **Unique 1** specializes in natural fiber sweaters, but also has pottery, baskets, gifts and even a wind socket with a moose on it. **Heather Harland** offers interesting kitchen items, tableware, cookbooks and cards — we especially liked the selection of wrapping paper. A large carved gull wearing a windjammer tie drew us into the **Ducktrap Bay Trading Co.,** a gallery of wildlife from decoys to paintings. **The Admiral's Buttons** has preppy clothing and sailing attire. We bought a handcrafted Maine wooden bucket for use as a planter from **Once a Tree,** which also has great clocks, toys, bracelets and everything else made from wood. At **Pen Bay Glassware,** we liked the wild hats by Susan Sherman — some with bells and sequins, perfect for a magician. **The Winemporium,** with excellent Maine food products including local goat cheese, Ducktrap River Trout Farm smoked fish and fine wines, is a must stop for provisions; you could put together a great picnic here. **The Grasshopper Shop** is good for gifts; pottery, cards, and Crabtree & Evelyn things are among its wares. Traditional favorites are **Haskell & Corthell** and the **House of Logan,** both apparel stores, and **Margo Moore,** for distinctive clothing and gifts.

Extra-Special

Camden Windjammers. Long known as the windjammer capital of the world, Camden Harbor is quite a sight when the windjammers are in. On Sunday evenings from June through September, people sit at the wharf to watch as passengers board the old-time sailing vessels for their week's cruise through Penobscot Bay. After breakfast on Monday, the seven windjammers set sail for who knows where; their routes depend on whim, wind and tides. Mates sleep and eat on board, helping the crew if they like but most relaxing and savoring a sail from yesteryear. Many beds are bunks, but at least one of the newer windjammers has double beds, and some have running water for showers. Generally, the captain handles the seagoing chores while his wife does the cooking — everything from chowders to roasts — on a wood stove. The evening lobster bake on a deserted island is usually the week's highlight. On Saturday afternoon, the watching resumes in earnest as the windjammers return to Camden. Passengers pay $400 to $500 each for the experience; landlubbers can watch the comings and goings for free.

Rowantrees Pottery put Blue Hill on the map.

Blue Hill, Me.
Treasure of Tranquility

Between the chic of Camden and the bustle of Bar Harbor lies an unspoiled area jutting into East Penobscot Bay. Its focus is the tranquil treasure known as Blue Hill.

So small that the unknowing tourist almost could miss it, the village lies between the 940-foot-high hill from which it takes its name and an inlet of Blue Hill Bay. A few roads and streets converge from different directions and, suddenly, here it is: Blue Hill, Maine, population 1,644.

This is the center of an area long known for fine handicrafts, especially pottery. Indeed, Rowantrees Pottery owner Sheila Varnum says it is the pottery that "put Blue Hill on the map." Founded more than 50 years ago, the pottery has inspired a number of smaller ventures by craftspeople who cherish the simplicity of the area.

Not for water or resort pursuits do visitors come to Blue Hill. It's the kind of place where the sign at the outdoor phone booth warns, "This phone doesn't work the way you're used to. Dial your number, wait for the loud tone and after your party answers, deposit twenty cents." We managed to get through the second time around.

There are no town beaches nor marinas, no shopping emporiums to speak of, and only one motel. What there are, instead, are world-famous potteries and crafts cooperatives, a handful of exceptional inns and restaurants, rural byways that remain much the way they were a generation ago and invite aimless exploration, and a sense of serenity that draws the knowing few back time after time for the utter peace and quiet of it all.

Go, but don't tell too many other people about your find.

Inn Spots

John Peters House, Peters Point, Box 916, Blue Hill 04614. (207) 374-2116.

Looking somewhat like a Southern plantation, this white pillared and red brick structure commands a hilltop location just outside Blue Hill with water on two sides.

Barbara and Rick Seeger, who acquired the former Altenhofen House in 1986, rebuilt the kitchen, added a dining porch and moved all the guest rooms upstairs. The eight comfortable bedrooms have private baths and five have fireplaces. Everybody's favorite is the Blue Hill Room, which has a kingsize bed, lovely carpets, wet bar with refrigerator and a large private deck looking up at Blue Hill.

Nice touches are fresh fruit and flowers in the rooms, the morning newspaper, a living room with a grand piano (many musicians stay here), and cozy sofas and chairs for reading or socializing, an old-fashioned swimming pool, and a canoe and a couple of sailboats.

The Seegers put out quite a spread for breakfast, served on the side porch amid fine china, silver and classical music. Our three-course repast began with cantaloupe with ice cream or fresh berries with champagne (extra champagne is poured in glasses for those who wish it; one couple finished off a bottle and retired to their room for an early nap, Barbara reported). Then came fresh orange juice with sliced and grilled blueberry and corn muffins. The main event was a choice of eggs Benedict, peach waffles, cheese and eggs or, the piece de resistance, a lobster and artichoke omelet — so colorful that it cried out for a picture. Garnished with lobster claws, it was accompanied by bacon or ham and hash browns and was so good that one of us ordered it two mornings in a row.

Doubles, $70 to $120.

Blue Hill Inn, Union Street, Box 403, Blue Hill 04614. (207) 374-2844.

Its flag flying out front, this trim white Colonial inn with Wedgwood blue shutters — a landmark in the heart of Blue Hill for nearly 150 years — has been considerably spiffed up since Mary and Don Hartley assumed ownership in 1988. Plush carpeting, modernized bathrooms and new wallpaper eliminate the slightly rundown atmosphere we experienced when we stayed here a few years ago.

All ten guest rooms have private baths and four have fireplaces. Some have sitting areas that once were small bedrooms. They are furnished with comfortable, traditional pieces reflecting "a homey Down East style." Homemade chocolates are put out when the beds are turned down at night.

A small parlor, where old Life magazines are displayed, is furnished in antiques. The

John Peters House has the look of a Southern plantation.

188

Arcady Down East is imposing brown-shingled Victorian mansion.

larger main parlor is where the Hartleys serve hors d'oeuvres (perhaps smoked bluefish or local goat cheese) during a nightly innkeepers' reception at 6. Wines and liquors are available from the bar.

"Dining is an integral part of our inn," says Mary, who cooks a six-course dinner for guests (and for the public by reservation for $20 if there's room). Starting at 7, a leisurely meal is served in an intimate dining room lit by ten-inch candles (they go through a set every other night) in a striking Persian chandelier.

A typical meal might begin with gazpacho, a salad of broiled montrachet and walnuts on a bed of watercress, and smoked salmon with dill sauce. A kiwi or raspberry sorbet prepares the palate for the main course, perhaps leg of lamb with asparagus and sweet red peppers (steamed lobster is usually a choice in summer). Chocolate mousse torte, cheesecake with rhubarb sauce, sacher torte with custard and raspberries, or nutmeg shortcake in grand marnier could be the desserts.

"We concentrate on dinner and let breakfast be traditional," says Mary. Eggs any style, omelets and blueberry pancakes are served in the sunny breakfast and game room behind the dining room.

Outside, guests enjoy the Hartleys' new garden with lawn furniture, a gazebo and a profusion of huge yellow lilies. The innkeepers occasionally charter a schooner to take guests out on East Penobscot Bay and offer sleigh rides in winter.

Doubles, $140, MAP. No smoking.

Arcady Down East, South Street, Blue Hill 04614. (207) 374-5576.

A large, brown-shingled Victorian mansion on a hilltop south of town has been converted into an elegant B&B by Floridians Tommie and Andy Duncan, who dole out Southern hospitality in an atmosphere of turn-of-the-century splendor. A century old and listed on the National Register, the structure offers on its main floor an enormous entry foyer, a library, a game room, a dining room and porches looking onto the distant bay. A knight in armor guards the entry to the dining room.

A lovely staircase from the foyer splits in two directions to the second-floor guest rooms. Of the eight rooms, five have private baths and three share.

The Duncans have furnished the rooms with items collected from their travels. The Juan Carlos master suite has an ornate kingsize bed, fireplace, lamps and rugs from Mexico and Spain. The Victoria and Albert rooms have twin beds, antique furniture and pretty quilts. Three rooms at the rear share a vast skylit bathroom containing what's said to be the oldest tub in Blue Hill.

Tommie Duncan offers a fresh fruit bowl, a dish like upside-down apple cake over sherried fruit and a main course — perhaps what she calls a farmer's breakfast of eggs, potatoes, cheese, bacon, onions and green pepper. It's served buffet style and taken at a long table in the formal, dark-paneled dining room with needlepoint chairs and a fireplace or outside on the porch at tables fashioned from the bases of old sewing machines.

Doubles, $50 to $90. Open Memorial Day to mid-October.

Blue Hill Farm, Route 15, Box 437, Blue Hill 04614. (207) 374-5126.

Located out in the country east of Blue Hill, this B&B really has a farm feeling — from the barn exterior of a new addition to the garden, stone wall and trout pond out back.

The barn, full of fanciful touches and furnishings, has a spacious and lofty main floor where meals are served and where there are all kinds of sitting areas. Upstairs are seven modern, smallish guest rooms with private baths. Seven more guest rooms that share baths are in the original farmhouse to which the barn is attached. It has a cozy, old-fashioned parlor for those who prefer more seclusion.

From an ample kitchen, innkeepers Marcia and Jim Schatz serve what they call a Maine continental breakfast: fresh orange juice, a plate of fresh fruit and cheese, homemade granola, yogurt, cereals and, every third or fourth day, a treat of lox and bagels.

The table settings are lovely: woven cloths and napkins, blue and white china with ducks depicted thereon, and dried flowers in baskets. Dinners are served by advance request. A typical meal might be seafood Wellington or peasant bouillabaisse plus salad and a dessert of homemade ice cream for $15.50 to $17.50, BYOB.

Blue Hill Farm gives off good vibes. It's the kind of simple, homey place that many inn-goers look for.

Doubles, $53 to $63.

The Pilgrim's Inn, Deer Isle 04627. (207) 348-6615.

A welcoming, tasteful Colonial inn run by Dud and Jean Hendrick beckons visitors south from Blue Hill to Deer Isle. The striking, dark red 1793 house is on a spit of land with harbor in front and mill pond in back.

Listed on the National Register of Historic Places, the inn exudes an aura of history, from its pumpkin pine wide-paneled floors to its Victorian parlor hung with changing works of local artists.

Jean Hendrick has decorated the rooms in sprightly Laura Ashley style, mixing and matching art and plants. Oriental rugs and quilts lend elegance to the prevailing simplicity. Each of the thirteen guest rooms has a wood stove and eight have private baths. Duvets and down pillows were new when we last visited. Nestled amid Deer Hill's stores down the street is a deluxe seaside cottage; it has a living room with cathedral ceiling, a kitchen-dining area, an upstairs bedroom and a rear deck overlooking the water.

Dud Hendrick, a former Dartmouth College lacrosse coach, tends to an extensive herb and vegetable garden on the grounds behind the inn during the day. At night he tends bar in the paneled tap room, serving drinks to guests (he even made a fresh raspberry daiquiri for one when we were there) who gather at 6 o'clock in the comfortable downstairs common room with its eight-foot-wide fireplace and beehive oven for abundant and delicious hors d'oeuvres.

A single-entree dinner is served at 7 in the charming dining room (a former goat barn), simply decorated with farm utensils and quilts on the walls, mismatched chairs, tables with fresh flowers and green cloths, and ten outside doors that open to let in the breeze.

If there is room, the public is welcome by reservation except on Thursday, lobster night for guests. Dinner is $20 and worth every penny. We'll never forget a Sunday night dinner: Jean Hendrick's salad with goat cheese, homemade peasant bread, her heavenly paella topped with nasturtiums (such a pretty dish it should have been photographed for Gourmet magazine) and her sensational raspberry chocolate pie on a shortbread crust. The week's menu includes grilled butterflied or roasted lamb on Monday, pork loin on Tuesday and fresh fish on Friday, and many are the repeat guests who return for a week of interesting meals. The Hendricks are currently into grilling on their large outdoor barbecue, which occupies a prominent spot on a new rear deck. A mixed grill marrying lamb sausage, marinated scallops, cornish hen and tenderloin was a highlight of 1988. Arugula and raddichio from the garden turn up in the salads.

Homemade granola, scones, fresh melon and omelets are featured at breakfast.

The inn has several bicycles for guests' use; the lawns sloping down to the mill pond in back are great for lounging. The Hendricks do not allow smoking in bedrooms or the dining room.

Doubles, $130 to $150, MAP. Three-night minimum in August. Closed mid-October to mid-May. No credit cards.

Dining Spots

Firepond, Main Street, Blue Hill. (207) 374-2135.

It's hard to imagine a more enchanting setting than the dining porch beside the stream at Firepond. The screened porch, which wraps around the small bar and interior dining room, is the place to be on a summer evening, its garden-type glass tables lit by candles and topped by woven mats, fresh flowers and Blue Hill pottery, the sounds of water rippling below and spotlights illuminating the gleaming rocks. It's almost magical, and usually must be booked well in advance.

The food is often magical as well. We like to start with the selection of pates ($8.50) — country pork, salmon mousse and vegetable on one visit — with croutons, cornichons, and interesting mustards and chutneys. Other recent choices included a souffle made with local sea urchins, baked brie en croute, mushroom ravioli, and hot or cold soups (cream of red bell pepper and gazpacho on one visit).

Four kinds of homemade breads are served: whole wheat, a light French, pumpkin and a dill roll. The chef makes his own cerano chili vinegar and grows his own herbs and nasturtiums for garnishes.

Entrees range from $11 for a sensational chicken with creme fraiche and mustard to $18.75 for medallions of lamb with wild mushrooms. On our latest visit, we enjoyed the latter, served with brown rice pilaf, carrots and snow peas, as well as a fabulous dish of veal sweetbreads with oysters in a lime butter sauce. New owner Peter Berley, a natural-foods cooking instructor from New York, is teaming with longtime chef Peter Johnson to lighten the menu, grilling several seafood and vegetable dishes with herbs and wine. A composed salad of marinated vegetales, roasted peppers, eggplant chutney and smoked fish with herbed aioli intrigued when we were there, as did fettuccine with crabmeat, cilantro and tomato concasse. The roast duckling with mangoes and ginger and the tournedos with roquefort and lingonberries remain fixtures on the menu.

Porch dining beside the brook at Fire Pond.

Desserts are few but select, among them a silken praline cheesecake, grand marnier chocolate mousse, fresh fruit tarts, and mango or ginger ice cream.

Peter, who greets patrons at the bar, has put together a sensational wine list with informative descriptions. About ten of the seventy offerings are organic, reflecting a predilection of his. Prices are so reasonable you think they're a mistake.

Dinner nightly, 5 to 9:30, Memorial Day through December.

Jonathan's, Main Street, Blue Hill. (207) 374-5226.

How can one small town support two such good restaurants? Who knows, but Blue Hill does, and they both get better and better. A rear addition in 1985 doubled the size of this cheery, informal spot where some creative fare is turned out by Jonathan Chase. In contrast with the front's somewhat close and intimate quarters, the new back section with rough wood walls, bar, bow windows and pitched ceiling is airy and open, a welcoming and comforting place for an assertive summer meal.

Interesting specials supplement the printed menu. Our latest visit produced an appetizer of roasted elephant garlic with local chevre, served with ripe tomatoes and grilled French bread, and a remarkable smoked mussel salad with goat cheese and pinenuts. Other choices for starters ($4 to $8.50) included smoked halibut with anjou pears, spanakopita and a spicy Indian turkey salad.

Among dinner entrees ($12.50 to $16.75), we enjoyed a special of scallops nicely sauteed with mint and tomatoes, and Jonathan's signature dish, shrimp flamed in ouzo and served with feta on linguini. A tasty Greek lemon soup and a fish provencale soup with cumin, included in the price of the entree and served in clear glass bowls, preceded. A chocolate cointreau mousse, frangelico cheesecake and raspberry sorbet topped with fresh berries are among the worthy endings. The exceptional and extensive wine list is reasonably priced.

Lunch, Monday-Friday 11 to 2:30; dinner nightly, 5 to 9:30.

Left Bank Bakery & Cafe, Route 172 north, Blue Hill. (207) 374-2201.

This rustic place with wooden tables, brick floor, shelves of books and a porch at the side opened in 1988 for breakfast, lunch, light dinners and late-night suppers. It's run by Arnold Greenberg, who closed his Left Bank cafe along the Delaware River in Frenchtown, N.J., for a new life with his family in Maine. "What we wanted was to live in the community where we work, with our children alongside us," explained Arnold, in a "place that would welcome us when we came downstairs each morning."

Though without a river, the Left Bank retains its New Jersey motto, "a home away from home." It's obviously low-key and casual, with jazz and folk music on weekends, and the menu features "unique fun foods" to eat in or take out.

Breakfast brings things like bagels and lox, a spicy Left Bank omelet with jalapeno cheese and salsa, french toast made with homemade challah, homemade oatmeal and granola, at mix-and-match prices from 50 cents for a sticky bun to $5.50 for a Nova platter of lox, bagel with cream cheese, tomato, red onion and cucumber.

Salads, spinach pie, quiche and hefty sandwiches served on bagels, croissants or French bread are in the $2 to $5 range. At dinner there are stir-fries and deep-dish pizzas, as well as all the other goodies.

Baked goods are made with flour imported from France and Germany, and no preservatives are used.

Patrons can bring their own wine, read a book or whatever, says Arnold, who was planning to add an outside cafe for 1989. The Greenbergs will be there, and happy to oblige.

Open daily, 7 a.m. to 10 p.m.

Sarah's Shoppe, Main Street, Blue Hill. (207) 374-5181.

Named for its owner's granddaughter who was born just before he opened it in 1980, this ice cream parlor and cafe with a screened porch is popular with locals for breakfast, lunch and dinner.

Blueberry pancakes, a ham and cheese omelet with generous amounts of sliced ham, and egg McSarah are among breakfast choices in the $3 to $4 range. Country-style dinners are priced from $6.95 for southern fried chicken to $12.95 for a sixteen-ounce sirloin with potato and salad. A lobster dinner with choice of salad and potato is $12.95, and sauteed lobster with sherry and mushrooms $13.95. Or you can get a hot dog and french fries for $1.95. Among the homemade ice creams are Swiss almond, orange-pineapple, M&M and grapenut. Draft beer and wine are $1.25 a glass.

Open daily, 7 a.m. to 10 p.m., mid-May to October.

S.L. Phillips Gallery & Cafe, Main Street, Blue Hill. (207) 374-2711.

Breakfast pastries, lunch and afternoon tea at four tiny tables inside the gallery or outside on a spacious outdoor deck with a view of Blue Hill Bay are served by Smedley Manion in this establishment she opened in 1987.

A creamy clam chowder, oversize sandwiches, broccoli quiche, tuna salad and a fresh fruit and cheese plate are the main offerings ($3.95 to $5.95). They're supplemented by muffins, apple crunch coffee cake, rich pies and cakes, and treats like a chocolate boat filled with ice cream and topped with a confectionary sail.

Smedley does the hand-screened cards ($1.50) and offers paintings, prints, hand-crafted jewelry, brass and salvaged nautical items.

Open daily, 9:30 to 4:30.

Pie in the Sky Pizza, Mill Street, Blue Hill. (207) 374-5570.

This rustic, shingled building is on an out-of-the-way street, which is probably why we'd missed it on previous visits. But it's just about every local denizen's favorite spot for pizza and more.

It's high style for a pizza parlor, a melange of booths and tables with paper balloon lamps, ladderback chairs and fans hanging from the high ceilings.

A mug of Budweiser is 95 cents, a bottle $1.50. A blackboard lists soups — sweet and sour cabbage, cream of celery and chilled potato-dill at our visit — as well as desserts like chocolate silk pie, lemon cheesecake and raspberries in triple sec cream.

Pizzas are served on homemade white or whole wheat dough by the slice or in assorted sizes (the Hawaiian with ham, pineapple and mozzarella was a new one on us) and there's a choice of sixteen toppings. Calzones, subs and sandwiches (grilled tempeh and hot falafel with salad are two for vegetarians), nachos and stuffed potatoes round out the menu, priced in the $2 to $4 range.

Open daily, 11 to 9.

Blue Hill Gourmet Shop, Main Street, Blue Hill. (207) 374-2276.

Local food products (like Nervous Nellie's Jams and Jellies), outstanding salads and gourmet sandwiches are the fare at this neat establishment on the ground level of the building occupied by Firepond restaurant. Tarragon chicken and tabbouleh with carrots are among the salads. Sandwiches, made with Schaller & Weber meats and freshly baked bread, include roast beeef, smoked turkey, Black Forest ham, pate, and hummus and sprouts, $3.25 to $4.25. Lemon squares are 65 cents each. Closed Sunday.

Diversions

Crafts. Pottery and handicrafts abound in Blue Hill and, indeed, all across the East Penobscot Bay peninsula and onto Deer Isle and Stonington. The **Brooklin Crafts Cooperative** in Brooklin, the **Eastern Bay Cooperative Gallery** beside the water in Stonington and **North Country Textiles** in South Penobscot are within driving distance.

The world-famous **Haystack Mountain School of Crafts** at Sunshine on Deer Isle, which sometimes has shows, is worth the drive simply for the breathtaking view from its unsurpassed setting on a steep, forested slope with stairs down to East Penobscot Bay. Visitors are welcome from Thursday to Sunday, 10 to 4.

Rowantrees Pottery, the institution inspired in 1934 by Adelaide Pearson through her friend Mahatma Gandhi, is still going strong in a rambling house and barn reached by a pretty brick path through gardens at the edge of Blue Hill. Inside, you may be able to see potters at work; veteran employees like Grace Lymburner in the upstairs shop might recall for you the days when as children they joined the story hours and pottery classes run by Miss Pearson and her protege, Laura Paddock. Sheila Varnum, who was associated with the founders since she was 3, has owned the pottery since 1976 and has continued its tradition. Named for the mountain ash trees above its green gate along Union Street and one of the few production potteries in the country, Rowantrees is especially known for its jam jar with a flat white lid covered with blueberries, as well as for unique glazes. Items are attractively displayed for sale. Summer hours: weekdays 7 to 5, Saturday 8:30 to 5, Sunday noon to 5.

Rackliffe Pottery at the other end of town is an offshoot of Rowantrees, Phil Rackliffe having worked there for twenty years. He and his family make all kinds of handsome and useful kitchenware in a work area next to their small shop on Route 172. The soup tureens with blueberry, strawberry or cranberry covers are especially nice.

Kneisel Hall Chamber Music Series. Concerts by well-known faculty members are given Wednesday evenings and Sunday afternoons from late June to early August in a

Stairs lead to ocean from Haystack Mountain School of Crafts.

rustic concert hall off upper Pleasant Street. The series is part of the summer session of the Kneisel Hall School of Music, founded by Dr. Franz Kneisel. Innkeepers say a summer tradition for many of their guests is to arrive on Wednesday and stay through Sunday, taking in two concerts, visiting the potteries and dining at Jonathan's and Firepond.

Blue Hill Farmer's Market, Route 172 at the Blue Hill Fairgrounds. Each Saturday in July and August from 9 to 11:30 a.m., local farmers and artisans gather here for a real downhome event. Horse-drawn wagons give the youngsters hayrides, while residents and visitors enjoy a small but interesting display of everything from local produce to goat cheese, jellies, handmade gifts, lamb's wool and patterned ski sweaters.

Shopping. We like the art-quality quilts displayed in a gallery-like setting at **Cole House Quilts,** 10 Union St. **Saltwater Seasons** is an old brick house, a garage-turned-art gallery and a barn full of country furnishings, kitchen paraphernalia, garden accessories, stuffed animals, linens and distinctive cards. Even non-smokers are enticed by the aromas at **Blue Hill Tea & Tobacco Shop,** something of an anachronism modernized by a selection of fine wines. The open-air **Handworks Gallery** offers handknit clothing, jewelry and toys

Extra-Special

Palmer Day III Excursions, Stonington, (207) 367-2207. Capt. Reginald Greenlaw conducts daily cruises on his 45-passenger boat in the waters off Stonington. He is as entertaining as is his excursion, a sixteen-mile trip that goes near Isle au Haut, offering closeup views of untold varieties of birds, deer and a small island covered with seals, one of which jumps up beside the boat for the raw fish the captain brings along. It's the most interesting nature cruise we've taken. Daily, July 4 to Sept. 1, 2 p.m.; adults $7, children under 10, $4; reservations advised.

Mount Desert Island, Me.
The Other Harbors

Mount Desert Island has long held a special appeal, first as a summer resort for society and later as the site of a national park beloved by campers and naturalists.

Its focus for us, as well as for increasing numbers of others, has always been Bar Harbor and the eastern part of Acadia National Park. Since our first vacation there more than 25 years ago, we've witnessed the changes — for better and worse — as tourism impacted relentlessly, and still Bar Harbor remains dear to our hearts.

Be advised, however, that there are other harbors and another side to Mount Desert Island. The other side is the quieter side, one that its devotees call "the right side" of this fabulously varied island.

Even the right side is wonderfully diverse. Northeast Harbor and Southwest Harbor are barely two miles across Somes Sound from each other, but far apart in spirit and character.

Northeast Harbor is the yachting harbor, a haven for Rockefellers and some of the world's great boats, a moneyed place where yachting is the seasonal preoccupation. Southwest Harbor is the working harbor, where fishing and boat-building are the year-round occupation. Here and in Bass Harbor, the native flavor of coastal Maine remains.

Some of the choice parts of Acadia National Park are close at hand: Seawall, Wonderland, Beech Mountain, Echo Lake and Eagle Cliff. Thuya and Asticou gardens are special treats, and we know of few better views than those up and down Somes Sound, the only natural fjord in North America.

For a different perspective than most visitors get of Mount Desert, try the other harbors on the "right side."

Inn Spots

Asticou Inn, Route 3, Northeast Harbor 04662. (207) 276-3344.

Majestically situated at the head of Northeast Harbor on a hillside where the mountains slope to the sea, the Asticou has been a bastion of elegance since 1883.

The fireplace in the lobby is always ablaze — "to take the chill off foggy mornings or late afternoons," our friendly guide informed. The lobby with its huge oriental rug and wing chairs gives way to a parlor decorated in blues, beiges and a cheery rust. Beyond is a bright and breezy cocktail lounge with sliding doors onto the outdoor deck; amid white furniture, yellow umbrellas and petunias in planters, it's a great place from which to view the goings-on in the harbor. The enclosd east porch is used for games and television viewing. The spacious dining room (see below) serves three meals a day and a Thursday evening buffet that draws people from all over the island.

A carpeted staircase and an 88-year-old elevator lead to 50 guest rooms on the second and third floors. Rooms vary from those with twin beds, rose carpeting and frilly white curtains framing views onto the harbor to a suite with a sofa, two peach chintz chairs and a desk in a sitting room plus two twins in the bedroom. Four have private balconies viewing the water. Seventeen more rooms are available in the Cranberry Lodge, Bird Bank and Blue Spruce guest houses and the Topsider cottages. Most striking are the contemporary, circular Topsiders with decks, full-length windows, attractive parlors and kitchenettes.

The perfectly landscaped grounds offer a swimming pool, tennis, gardens and, all the

Rear deck and grounds of Asticou Inn overlook Northeast Harbor.

while, changing vistas of the harbor. Guests have privileges at the Northeast Harbor Golf Club.

Rates are MAP in season (mid-June to mid-September), EP with continental breakfast served in Cranberry Lodge in the off-season when only the guest houses and cottages are open.

Doubles, $158 to $186, MAP; off-season, $62 to $85, EP. Two-night minimum in season. Open April-December.

The Claremont, Clark Point Road, Southwest Harbor 04679. (207) 244-5036.

The other grand dowager of Mount Desert, the Claremont marked its 100th anniversary in 1984, a year later than the Asticou. It's the island's oldest continuously operating inn, with only three owners in its first century.

Entered in the National Register of HIstoric Places in 1978 as a reminder of the "prosperous, relaxed and seasonal way of life" of Maine's early summer-resort era, the original light yellow structure has been considerably spiffed up of late and the name has been shortened from the Claremont Hotel and Cottages. But the inn's wraparound veranda and the heavy white wood slant-back chairs lined up side by side on the rear lawn still provide a relaxing view of Somes Sound, and croquet is the sport of choice. The annual Claremont Croquet Classic is known as the home of nine-wicket croquet.

The main inn building contains a lobby and living rooms full of wicker and sofas, a handsome dining room (see below) and 21 guest rooms (singles, doubles and suites) on the second and third floors, all with private baths. Also available for longer stays are eight cottages (with living rooms, fireplaces and decks) and two guest houses (the Phillips with a massive fieldstone fireplace in the parlor is particularly inviting).

Besides croquet, boating and tennis are offered, and the hardy can swim from the dock in chilly Somes Sound. The Boathouse is a fine spot for a light lunch or cocktails.

Doubles, $120 to $127, MAP. Cottages and Clark House Suite available EP or MAP. Inn open mid-June to mid-September, cottages and guest house mid-May to mid-October.

The Harbourside Inn, Harbourside Road (Route 198), Northeast Harbor 04662. (207) 276-3272.

Built in 1888 in the style of the Seal Harbor Club, this shingled hilltop mansion is run very much their way by the Sweet family (take it or leave it, and most people take it). "We're old-fashioned and intend to keep it that way," Geraldine Sweet explains. She and her husband, who formerly managed the Jordan Pond House, acquired the mansion in 1977 from a woman who would sell only to Maine residents who would maintain the heritage.

The heritage indeed remains, from the nasturtiums nurtured from the original seeds still brightening the entry circle to the original carpets from China, somewhat worn but too prized to be discarded. Guests gather in a pleasant parlor with wing chairs in shades of blue or on the front sun porch, all done up with bright cushions and curtains in appropriate Northeast Harbor colors, preppy pink and green.

Nine guest rooms on the first and second floors have working fireplaces, and three have their own porches. All fourteen units ("I hate the word, but that's what we have," says Geraldine — "we get children and nannies") have private baths and are furnished in 19th-century style. "We had great fun with the wallpapers," she said; one bathroom's paper has small red bears with big hearts on the borders, and a bedroom is papered with irises. Room 1 with a wallpapered ceiling has a Wallace Nutting bed, a collector's item. The honeymoon suite has a kingsize bed and an enclosed porch with cathedral ceiling, wicker rockers and a lounger. A first-floor suite offers a sitting room with comfortable chairs grouped in front of the fireplace and a kitchenette in an alcove, a room with a kingsize bed and an old-fashioned tub in the bathroom.

A complimentary breakfast of homemade blueberry muffins is served on the sun porch.

Lest the inn's name mislead, the Sweets stress that the once-sweeping view of the harbor from their hilltop is now obstructed by a century's growth of trees.

Doubles, $85; suites to $210. Open June-September.

Grey Rock Inn, Harbourside Road, Northeast Harbor 04662. (207) 276-9360 or 276-5526.

Remarkable gardens and a prolific hanging begonia at the door greet visitors to this little-publicized inn, said to have been a gathering place for socialite Northeast Harbor families after it was built in the 1890s as a private residence.

Inside the inviting large fieldstone and shingled mansion with yellow trim is a veritable showcase for British innkeeper Janet Millet's decorating tastes: an array of wicker like you've never seen, fans and paintings from the Orient, fringed lamps, masses of exotic flowers — rather overwhelming, we found, particularly since Janet shunned publicity, saying she had all the business she wanted.

People who stay at Grey Rock must like eclectic elegance, for that's what they get. The two fireplaces in the living room and parlor are kept aglow, even in mid-summer, because the innkeeper finds her guests want it that way. Wicker serves as furniture and art, from table lamps to loveseats, from desk to plant stand.

The nine guest rooms are equally exotic. The huge main-floor corner room with canopied four-poster bed, oriental screen and private balcony could not be more romantic. The upstairs rooms are lacy, frilly and flowery, with much pale pink and green, all kinds of embroidered towels, and porches all around. Some have fireplaces, and all have views of the trees or gardens atop this wooded hilltop high above and back from the road.

The aptly named Tree House cottage has two bedrooms, two baths and a full kitchen.

Janet serves an exemplary continental breakfast, including a fruit compote with eight

Lush plantings and hanging begonia grace entrance to Grey Rock Inn.

to ten kinds of fresh fruit, assorted baked goods and bacon, occasionally eggs, and what she states is "a good cup of coffee for a British lady."

Doubles, $110 to $145; cottage, $160 for two, $200 for four. Open spring through October.

The Moorings, Shore Road, Southwest Harbor 04679. (207) 244-5523 or 244-3210.

Genial Leslie and Betty King have run this delightfully informal, old-fashioned place for 25 years in a location they call the "Little Norway of America," and one we find the most appealing on the island, smack on the shore at the start of Somes Sound in Manset.

The rambling white house with dark shutters in the Maine style contains eight guest rooms, all with private baths. There also are five motel units (one with two exposures billed as having "probably the finest view on the coast") and seven units in three trim white cottages with wicker porches and a garden apartment. New for 1989 was a three-story structure with three apartments. The Kings have upgraded their rooms with cheery new wallpapers and furnishings, and the five on the inn's second floor now sport delightful decks and balconies to take advantage of the view. Peruvian lilies from Holland grace each room.

We dubbed our corner bedroom the Agatha Christie Room because several of her paperbacks were on the bureau (Betty makes the rounds of all the lawn sales to pick up the books, her son volunteered). It's the only one without a water view but, as with the other rooms, the towels were large and fluffy, the beds had colorfully patterned sheets, and a candle was in a ceramic holder beside the bed.

The fireplace glows on cool mornings in the living room, which has a television set in a windowed alcove and enough books and magazines to start a library. The coffee pot is kept filled all day in the adjacent office, where complimentary orange juice and donuts are served every morning.

Outside, two rowboats filled with geraniums brighten the path to the front door. In back are canoes, bicycles and a stony shoreline for swimming, beachcombing, clam-

Wraparound veranda creates pleasant entrance for guests at Kingsleigh Inn.

ming and musseling. The Kings provide charcoal for the grills beside the shore, a memorable spot to barbecue a steak for dinner as you watch the sunset.

Doubles, $50 to $70 (two small singles, $40); motel units, $60; cottages, $70 to $80.

The Kingsleigh Inn, 100 Main St., Southwest Harbor 04679. (207) 244-5302.

A wraparound veranda full of wicker, colorful pillows and flowers distinguishes this B&B with an unusual pebbledash stucco-stone exterior.

Inside are inviting common rooms and seven guest rooms, five with private baths, each notable for Waverly wall coverings and fabrics, lace window treatments, plush carpeting and gleaming hardwood floors, and many with four-poster beds and wingback chairs. The new Turret Suite has a great view from a telescope placed between two cozy bentwood rockers. Sewing kits and candy kisses are in each room, and the scent of potpourri is everywhere.

Pink and green china and deep-green tablecloths enhance the breakfast room. For breakfast, innkeepers Jim and Kathy King serve cereals, homemade blueberry breads and jams, and entrees like oatmeal pancakes with fresh fruit, eggs with home fries and cinnamon french toast. The country kitchen is for guests' use; cookies and wines are served there.

Doubles, $55 to $75; suite $95.

The Maison Suisse Inn, Main Street, Box 1090, Northeast Harbor 04622. (207) 276-5223.

Pick a couple of blueberries along the entry path as you arrive at this new inn, surrounded by gardens designed by a previous owner who trained as a landscape architect in Switzerland. Beth and David White took over in 1987, did a total renovation and ended up with seven bedrooms and three suites, all with private baths.

Canopy and spool beds, silkscreened wallpaper, feather pillows, down comforters, dust ruffles, antiques and Bar Harbor wicker comprise the decor. We like the upstairs suite, which has a small balcony with a wicker loveseat, and the Garden Room with a separate entrance and a charming little garden ringed by cedars to make it private.

200

The common rooms downstairs are nicely furnished. Beach stones form an unusual inset in the mantel of the brick fireplace in the main hall.

Room rates include a full breakfast with the inn's compliments at Colonel's Restaurant across the street.

Doubles, $85 to $125; suites, $135 and $155. Open June to mid-October. No smoking.

The Inn at Southwest, Main Street, Box 593, Southwest Harbor 04679. (207) 244-3835.

New owners Ted and Kathy Combs from Connecticut have "chintzed and softened up" this old rooming house that has been taking in guests since 1884. A mannequin in the hall, a baby grand piano, balloon curtains, stenciling and a living room with a big sofa, TV and stereo, a game table and an ornate fireplace mantel are features.

Seven of the nine guest rooms have private baths, and all are furnished with down comforters, wicker or rattan tables and desks, potpourri, plants and the like.

Full breakfast is served at three tables in a pink-walled dining room or on a porch lined with geraniums. Blackberry-cinnamon or five-grain pancakes, basil stratas, omelets and french toast are among the specialties.

Doubles, $50 to $85.

Lindenwood Inn, Clark Point Road, Box 1328, Southwest Harbor 04679. (207) 244-5335.

Towering linden trees shade this turn-of-the-century sea captain's home, now run as a homey B&B by Gardiner and Marilyn Brower. The front porches on both the first and second floors contain nice old rocking chairs and the entry parlor and living room have their share of nautical books and Gardiner's color photographs on the walls. A harpsichord is available for those who play.

Upstairs are seven guest rooms, three with private baths and four sharing two more. The Browers have opened a new room in the rear with a queensize four-poster bed, eyelet curtains, plush carpeting, a clawfoot bathtub and its own deck with a view of the harbor.

Behind the house is a cottage with a deck, a super water view through the picture windows of the living room, a small kitchen and two bedrooms. It goes for $95 a night (three-night minimum in season).

A full breakfast is served in the cheery dining room warmed by a fireplace on cool mornings. Among specialties are cinnamon-blueberry pancakes, cheese stratas and cinnamon french toast.

Doubles, $45 to $75

Bass Harbor Inn, Shore Road, Bass Harbor 04653. (207) 244-5157 or 244-7432.

This striking structure with high peaked roofs would seem more at home in Mendocino than in what the manager says is the area's oldest fishing village, "the place where the fishing action is." It looks and smells new, but actually only the interior of an 1832 house was gutted and restored in 1985 into a sleek B&B by Kim Strauss and Carl Taplin.

Nine modern rooms with white walls and private or half baths are nicely decorated with hooked and throw rugs, vases of wildflowers, and paintings collected in his world travels by the grandfather of one of the owners. Three ground-floor rooms have private baths and open onto a large deck that wraps around two sides of the building. A third-floor suite with the original beamed cathedral ceiling includes a full kitchen and a balcony with a super view of the harbor. A new cottage offers a kitchen and fireplace.

A continental breakfast, perhaps with fresh blueberry muffins or poppyseed cakes, is served in the fireplaced common room that doubles as an office.

Doubles, $45 to $60; suite and cottage, $90. Closed December-March.

Dining Spots

The Claremont, Clark Point Road, Southwest Harbor. (207) 244-5036.

The comparatively new dining-room addition with views on three sides, excellent service and consistently good food make this popular with residents on the quiet side of the island.

They like to have drinks at the **Boathouse** (which also serves sandwiches and salads for lunch) and then head into the high-ceilinged dining room, a picture of elegance with fancy china on white over pink linens, pink napkins, a moss green carpet and pink and green wallpaper. It's as pretty as the view across the lawns onto Somes Sound.

The appetizer du jour is often the best choice on the limited menu; otherwise go for the iced Maine crabmeat cocktail ($4.50). Native crabmeat also turns up among dinner entrees, baked in a ramekin with artichoke hearts, sherry sauce and gruyere cheese. Other entrees ($13 to $15) include baked shrimp stuffed with scallops or crabmeat, coquilles St. Jacques duglere, shrimp and sole baked in parchment, veal rib chop, herb-roasted chicken with three-peppercorn butter and rack of lamb.

The produce comes from the inn's gardens and the baked goods from its bakery. The chef's homemade desserts include cheesecake, a daily special and either ice cream or lemon ice with Claremont cookies.

Lunch at the Boathouse, noon to 2, mid-July through August; dinner, 6 to 9, late June through Labor Day, jackets required. Cocktails at the Boathouse, 5 to 9.

Asticou Inn, Northeast Harbor. (207) 276-3344.

The $33 buffet every Thursday night draws up to 300 people in peak season to the posh dining room of the Asticou Inn. Thursday happens to be maid's night off hereabouts, so summer residents join inn guests for the extravagant spread followed by live music and an evening of socializing.

The pillared dining room is decorated with handpainted murals of trees and flowers on the deep yellow walls, a brass chandelier, oriental rugs, lovely flowered china and tiny plants in clay pots. Most coveted seating is in the adjacent enclosed porch, with great views through picture windows onto the harbor beyond.

Dinners are $25 prix-fixe, the mimeographed menu changing daily. Typically there are three entrees from broiled scallops, baked stuffed shrimp and boiled lobster to prime rib and broiled lamb chops. Meals begin with assorted relishes, breads and perhaps fish chowder, shrimp cocktail or lobster and shrimp in phyllo, include a salad, and finish with desserts like frozen chocolate mousse, key lime pie, or a fruit and cheese tray.

Lunch, 12:30 to 2; dinner, 7 to 8:30, mid-June to mid-September. Jackets required at dinner.

Clark Point Cafe, Clark Point Road, Southwest Harbor. (207) 244-5816.

Right up against the street in "downtown" Southwest Harbor, this storefront cafe opened in 1985 and was just what the area needed: something between the formality of the aforementioned inns and the rustic seafood houses all around.

Proprietors Carole and Vance O'Donnell have a simple restaurant divided into two sections with pine paneling, a small bar and tables sporting beige cloths and red napkins.

The menu ranges widely: entrees like pasta of the day, seafood stew, poached Norwegian salmon, Granny Smith chicken, veal francaise and lobster thermidor, priced from $10.95 to $15.95. Shrimp or duck pate, scallops ceviche and baked brie are favorite appetizers, and a section of the menu called lighter fare includes baked haddock and shrimp and lobster salad.

Dinner nightly, 5:30 to 10.

Seafood Ketch, On the Harbor, Bass Harbor. (207) 244-7463.

"For gosh sakes, come in quick before we both starve to death," demands the sign on this shanty beside the harbor. Here is the real thing, a delightful, down-home place run by Ed and Eileen Branch with lots of fresh seafood and everything homemade, to the last loaf of crusty French bread served on a board with pads of butter at dinner.

Arriving twenty minutes late for an 8 o'clock reservation, we found we had lost our table. "That's okay, the same thing happens to Casper Weinberger," explained Ed, referring to a regular customer. Dining is by candlelight with white linens at tables in the rear room beside the water, each decorated with a bottle of wine. The jaunty outdoor deck is usually too buggy for dining outside at night.

Speedy service produced garden salads with homemade blue cheese or creamy Italian dressings and entrees like baked halibut with lobster sauce and the night's special, stir-fried halibut on rice. A Roos Leap fume blanc ($12.25) from a good wine list accompanied, and a fresh raspberry pie with ice cream was a superb dessert. Entrees are $8.95 to $12.95 (for a twenty-ounce porterhouse steak), and starters run from $2.25 for seafood bisque to $5.95 for a plate of fried clams, scallops and shrimp.

The menu also includes light or luncheon fare, $2.95 for a toasted BLT to $7.95 for a lobster roll. Among regular desserts are Ed's secret mocha pie and, according to the menu, "the world's best carrot cake — Ed says so," and he does all the baking.

These folks do have fun with their meals, as attested by their motto, "What foods these morsels be." The fun continues non-stop from 7 a.m. to 9:30 p.m. daily, May to November.

Drydock Cafe, 108 Main St., Southwest Harbor. (207) 244-3886. Seating 50 at booths and tables with sprigged cloths, the Drydock has upgraded its decor and prices since we first visited. At lunch try one of the burgers (most $3.95) served on English muffins — the Maniac comes with cheddar and bacon. Specialty sandwiches include a crabmeat croissant, $7.95, and a tuna caesar salad is $4.50. The fajitas here are delicious; choose between grilled steak or chicken served with all manner of toppings, $6.25.

For dinner you might start with scallops wrapped in bacon ($5.95) or mushrooms stuffed with crabmeat ($4.95). Twenty-six entrees are priced from $7.95 for fettuccine alfredo to $15.95 for a six-ounce filet with broiled scallops or scampi. Seafood imperial, stuffed haddock, chicken moutard and blackened scallops are among the choices.

There's a full bar, a fairly good wine list (Fetzer chardonnay is $10.95) and a large selection of beers. The dessert tray might bear Kentucky Derby pie, cheesecakes, mousses and truffles.

Drydock also offers five lodging units with kitchenettes and private baths upstairs.

Lunch, 11:30 to 3:30; dinner, 5 to 10. Sunday breakfast from 8. Open May to October.

Tea on the lawn is a tradition at the Jordan Pond House.

Jordan Pond House, Park Loop Road, Acadia National Park. (207) 276-3316.

Rebuilt following a disastrous fire in 1979, the new Jordan Pond House is a large, strikingly contemporary complex with cathedral ceilings, two levels, outdoor porches and decks, huge windows and one of the good Acadia Gift Shops. The majestic setting remains the same, with lawns sloping down to Jordan Pond and mountains rising beyond.

Lobster stew ($9.50 a bowl) or soup and a Jordan Pond popover served with strawberry preserves and butter ($6) are popular luncheon items. On our last visit we enjoyed a fine seafood pasta and a curried chicken salad, garnished with red grapes and orange slices, and shared one of the famous popovers — good but a bit pricey at $2, considering it was hollow!

Dinners get more formal, featuring steaks and lobster (boiled, stuffed, saute, stew and salad) as well as baked chicken and broiled halibut, priced from $9.50 to $19.50. The fresh fruit ice creams are made on the premises from original recipes dating back to the late 19th century.

Even if you don't eat here, do stop for tea on the lawn, an island tradition. You sit on old-fashioned chairs and sip tea with popovers ($4.75).

Lunch, 11:30 to 2:30; tea on the lawn, 2:30 to 5:30; dinner, 5:30 to 9. Open mid-June to mid-October.

Janet's, Route 102, Southwest Harbor. (207) 244-5131.

Creative home cooking is featured three meals a day at this new restaurant named for a waitress who took over the old Happy Crab. There's a two-tiered deck outside between the highway and the woods, where you sit at rustic, custom-built square wood tables a bit too high for the chairs. Inside are a bar and a couple of simple but pleasant dining rooms.

The prices are from yesteryear — for breakfast, a western sandwich for $1.65 or two eggs, toast and coffee for $1.75; for lunch, soup and salad for $2.95. At dinner, try crab Victoria in a mild cheddar sauce over fettuccine ($8.95), scallops au gratin or a lobster saute, the most expensive item at $11.95. Janet makes her own bread pudding and maple walnut pies, and obtains homemade fruit pies from a woman in the next town.

Open daily from 5:30 a.m. to 10 p.m.

204

A sampling of other, more casual eating spots, particularly good for seafood or sea atmosphere:

Beal's Lobster Pier, Clark Point Road, Southwest Harbor. Beside the Coast Guard Station, Beal's offers lobsters to go as well as to eat at picnic tables on the working dock. The last time we visited, they were priced at $6.29 a pound boiled (boiling ends between 6:30 and 7:30). A lobster roll (all lobster meat with a dab of mayonnaise in a toasted hot dog bun, $6.95) makes a fine lunch, supplemented by great french fries, lemonade and ice cream from the **Captain's Galley** next door (open 9 a.m. to sunset).

Kay & John's Lobster Pier, Clark Point Road, Southwest Harbor. Across the wharf from Beal's is this new place with more picnic tables, purveying Philly cheese steaks, steamers, pizza burgers and lobster dinners ($6.25 a pound) with cole slaw, french fries and a roll. Open from 11 a.m. to dusk.

Head of the Harbor, Route 102, Southwest Harbor. A lobster dinner was $11.95 when we last stopped at this rustic indoor-outdoor restaurant on a hill above Somes Sound. You see the lobsters steaming and place your order at a window, then eat on an expansive outdoor deck or on a screened porch overlooking the water. A fried clam platter with cole slaw and potato salad or french fries ($5.95) and chowder with a clam roll ($4.95) made a good lunch, washed down with a wine cooler and a Bud Lite. Open daily 11 to 10, Memorial Day to Labor Day.

The Docksider, Sea Street, Northeast Harbor. Strangely, the outdoor deck is on the wrong side of the building (away from the harbor view), so many prefer to eat inside at booths with paper mats and paper plates. The fare runs the gamut from fried haddock sandwich and fried clam roll to seafood crepes and lobster newburg, priced from $1.50 for a hot dog to $16.95 for a shore dinner. Wine and beer; breakfast, lunch and dinner served.

Maine-ly Delights, Ferry Road, Bass Harbor. Over the years, Karen Holmes has expanded her place from a van that dispensed hot dogs and crabmeat rolls to a room with open kitchen and an outdoor deck. A hot dog still costs $1 and a lobster roll $6.25; you can get a complete lobster dinner with french fries and cole slaw for $6.95. Fish chowder, mussels scampi, shrimp basket, carrot cake and bread pudding are among the fare. At breakfast, a muffin with egg and sausage is $1.50. Open daily from 8 a.m. to 8 p.m.

Diversions

Acadia National Park. The most famous sites are along Ocean Drive and the Park Loop Road out of Bar Harbor, but don't miss the park's other attractions on this side of the island. The Beech Mountain area offers Echo Lake with a fine beach, changing rooms and fresh water far warmer than the ocean. Hike up Beech Cliff for a great view of the lake below (yes, you may hear your echo). Past Southwest Harbor and Manset are Seawall, created naturally by the sea, and the Wonderland and Ship's Harbor nature trails, both well worth taking.

Somes Sound and Somesville. Follow Sargent Drive out of Northeast Harbor along the fjord-like Somes Sound for some of the island's most spectacular views (it's the closest thing we know of to the more remote areas around Lake Tahoe). At the head of the sound is Somesville, a classic New England village and a joy to behold: the whites of the houses brightened patriotically by geraniums, petunias and morning glories in flowerboxes that line the street. Check out the old library with the new-fangled, wired-for-sound lounge chairs, and maybe an arts and crafts show outside. The entire town is listed on the National Register of Historic Places, and the **Mount Desert Historical Society** buildings chronicle the history of the island's earliest settlement.

The Masonic Hall in Somesville is home of the **Acadia Repertory Theater,** which stages a full summer season.

Boat cruises. Untold numbers of cruises — public, private and park-sponsored — leave from Northeast Harbor and Bass Harbor. You can take a naturalist tour to Baker Island, a lobster boat or a ferry ride to Swans Island or the Cranberry Islands, and the park's cruises are particularly informative. If you'd rather observe than ride, poke around one of the ten or more boat-building yards in Southwest Harbor.

Museums. Southwest Harbor is widely known for its variety of birds (many consider it the warbler capital of the country), so fittingly this is the home of the **Wendell Gilley**

Museum, a monument to the memory of one of the nation's outstanding bird carvers. Opened in 1981 in a solar-heated building, it shows birds and decoys, special exhibitions, and daily films and programs on woodcarving and natural history (admission, $2.50).

Also in Southwest Harbor is the **Mount Desert Oceanarium,** a building full of sea life and lobster lore, with a touch tank, whale exhibit, fishing boats and more (adults, $3.50).

Shopping. The area's best shopping is in Northeast Harbor. **The Kimball Shop** is one of the snazziest gift shops we've seen, a pageant of bright colors and room after room of zippy clothes, pretty china, furniture, kitchenware, and almost anything else that's in. Try **Animal Crackers** for adorable clothes for children, **Sherman's** for books, and **Impressions** for gifts. **Town & Country Tweeds** sells the kind of clothes one would wear to the yacht club, and **Provisions** has the suavest groceries. The **Holmes Store** has more preppy clothes, and there are several fine art galleries to browse in, including **Form & Function Gallery,** with wonderful pottery. Slip into **Mount Desert Apothecary** for a Harbor Bar, 95 cents. In Southwest Harbor, the **Alternative Market** is where the gourmet foods and good cheeses are. A good selection of children's books is at **Oz Books,** there's some smashing jewelry at **Aylen & Son,** and at **The Gallery,** we discovered some lovely Christmas ornaments and crafts. More gifts, pottery, crafts and books may be found at the **Live Yankee.**

Extra-Special

Asticou Terrace and Thuya Gardens, Route 33, Northeast Harbor.

You can drive up, but we recommend the ten-minute hike nearly straight up a scenic, well-maintained switchback path and stairs to the prized gardens above Northeast Harbor. A plaque relates that landscape architect Joseph H. Curtis left this "for the quiet recreation of the people of this town and their summer guests." Who would not enjoy the showy hilltop spread combining English flower beds with informal natural Japanese effects, some common and uncommon annuals plus hardy rhododendron and laurel that appear as a surprise so far north. As you might find on a private estate, which this once was, there are a gazebo, a free-form freshwater pond, and a shelter with pillowed seats and deck chairs for relaxing in the shade. Open daily. Free.

Victorian architecture prevails in Kingfield, as shown at Inn on Winter's Hill.

Kingfield-Sugarloaf, Me.
Sophistication, Wilderness Style

You can't get much farther north and east in the United States and still be in the vicinity of civilization. That's one of the advantages of the Victorian town of Kingfield and its large northern neighbor, Sugarloaf USA.

This is rugged, backwoods, outdoors country, a place where moose-watching is a common pastime and where lumberjacks and logging trucks share trails and roads with cross-country skiers and jeeps topped with rafts and canoes. Maine's second highest mountain, Sugarloaf, is surrounded by 900 square miles of wilderness and lakes, a few settlements with names like West Carry Camp and Portage, the whitewater rapids of the Kennebec and Penobscot rivers, and beyond, Mount Katahdin, the Allagash and French Quebec.

Against this backdrop are two clusters of civilization — a sort of sophistication, wilderness style.

Kingfield (population 1,000) is a 19th-century mill town that gave birth to the inventive Stanley family of Stanley Steamer fame. Three mills still produce rolling pins, pepper mills and drum sticks. It also has three inns with restaurants of note.

Sixteen miles northwest is Sugarloaf USA, a rapidly emerging four-season resort area with snowfield skiing, a tough new wooded golf course designed by Robert Trent Jones Jr., a summer performing arts program and all the amenities of a self-contained resort village, including a seven-story hotel. Sugarloaf's recent expansion from a well-known but isolated ski area into what it calls "a mountain of things to do all year long" represents the largest investment ever in a resort in Maine.

A worthy counterpoint for the tasteful chic of the new Sugarloaf is Kingfield, which retains its Victorian look. A small band of restorationists have recreated period inns in which history resides and have saved the 1903 schoolhouse from the wrecker's ball to become the Stanley Museum.

Inn Spots

The Inn on Winter's Hill, Box 44, Kingfield 04947. (207) 265-5421.

A wealthy merchant named A.G. Winter, whose son Amos began the Sugarloaf development, and his inventor friends, the Stanley twins, built this Georgian Colonial Revival country mansion on a hilltop at the edge of Kingfield for his bride from New York in 1898. The deep mustard-gold structure with white trim and curved facade is listed on the National Register of Historic Places and open for tours, such is the mark of Michael Thom, architect turned innkeeper.

But rather than tour you'd have more fun staying in one of the eleven elegantly furnished guest rooms, dining on excellent French fare in Le Papillon restaurant (see Dining Spots) and savoring the treasures of some extraordinary public rooms.

A velvet sofa in front of a huge grand piano is a focus of the Grand Hall, with a small lounge and bar off to one side and two dining rooms off the other. The main focus is the flowing Georgian oak staircase that ascends past a Palladian window at the midway landing to a comfortable sitting area with sofa, wood stove and chess set for the use of guests in the luxurious rooms on the second floor. Another sitting area serves the third floor.

A Canadian from Toronto, ebullient Michael Thom had admired the house for years on his way to Sugarloaf from Boston, where he worked as an architect. He stopped on impulse one day, soon acquired the structure, and set to work restoring it into an inn. When he uncovered the original Stanley blueprints, he realized the magnitude of his treasure. He and his cat, Balthazar Jr. (succeeding his namesake, who died in 1988 at age 20), share it with overnight guests and lend it for some of Kingfield's more gala parties.

Michael's skill as an architect, designer and collector is evident throughout, from the gladioli in oriental vases and the stuffed armadillo over the fireplace in the Grand Hall to the small bedrooms fashioned from attic-type crannies on the third floor. The five second-floor bedrooms, each smashingly decorated in vivid colors and Victorian furnishings, are sumptuous. One has an old curved iron bedstead; another is all in blues and purples with velvet chairs and a sofa beside the window, a kingsize bed, a lamp with a base sculpted like a jade tree, and a sunny yellow bathroom. The four guest rooms on the third floor include a single and a suite converted from the bunkroom in which our skiing family once stayed. The upstairs rooms share two baths.

The exterior facilities are as luxurious as the interior. There's a tennis court, and Sunday brunch is served in season on the deck around the large swimming pool in the rear yard, looking up toward Sugarloaf. From the pool area, the sunset over the mountains on our latest summer visit was as spectacular as any we've seen. Michael agreed; "I tried to get a sunrise over there for you, too," he quipped as we arose the next morning, "but it didn't work out." Breakfast by the pool was enjoyable as well, with a tray full of fresh fruit, granola, and choice of croissants, muffins and raisin toast.

Doubles, $68 to $88, B&B; $110 to $140, MAP. Closed Easter to Memorial Day and most of November.

The Herbert, Main Street, Box 67, Kingfield 04947. (207) 265-2000.

The handsome exterior of this three-story hotel, described in its history as located at "Main Street on the Corner," is nicely lit by spotlights at dusk — an inviting oasis in the wilderness on a dark evening. Built in 1918 by a Maine legislator and judge, it had been abandoned for several years and was "a mess" when Sugarloaf skier Bud Dick first saw it. He carefully restored it and reopened it in 1982 as an inn bearing the first name of its original owner, Herbert Wing.

Novel historic touches abound: the exposed sink on the dining room wall, just inside the entrance, where diners arriving by stagecoach could wash up before eating; the old Western Electric phones in each room, by which guests can call the front desk (when they work); the brass fixtures, light switches and outlet covers from the first electrified building in Kingfield.

A moose head stands guard over the marble fireplace in the oak-paneled lobby, which has much Victorian furniture and two plush sofas of deep plum velvet. Downstairs is the Woodworks, a vast brick bar and lounge full of video games and a pool table. A steam room with sauna and hot tub is popular with skiers.

The 33 guest rooms, including three suites but mostly small doubles, are pleasantly furnished with double or twin beds, white bedspreads and fresh wallpaper. Each has a private bath with steambath and sauna or jacuzzi. The original glass windows above the doors in each room open to the hallway, letting light and noise in or out.

Doubles, $46 to $50, EP.

Three Stanley Avenue, 3 Stanley Ave., Kingfield 04947. (207) 265-5541.

One of two Stanley homes still standing on Stanley Avenue, this Queen Anne-style, late-Victorian house is run as a B&B by Dan Davis, owner of the acclaimed One Stanley Avenue restaurant next door (see Dining Spots).

Located on a residential street across the Carrabassett River from the center of Kingfield, it's simple and quiet, almost eerily so. At least it was the time we were the only guests there and slept right through the 7:30 to 9 breakfast service next door. No matter; Dan Davis gets up at 5:30 every day to get the kids off to school and start dinner preparations, "so I'm here anyway," he said as he served up juice, blueberry pancakes and superior coffee at the indecent weekday breakfast hour of 10.

The six guest rooms, three each on the first and second floors, are simply furnished and decorated with a number of Victorian pieces. The three upstairs share two baths; one has two beds and a sofa. Our room, the downstairs front opening onto a large porch, was the largest and had a spacious and modern bathroom. Arriving after dark, however, we were on our own since Dan was cooking at the restaurant and we missed not having a common room or a place to sit and read before dinner. Most guests enjoy sitting in the parlor with its small bar at One Stanley Avenue.

Doubles, $50 to $60.

Sugarloaf Inn Resort, Carabassett Valley 04947. (207) 237-2000 or (800) 451-0002.

This pleasantly alpine-contemporary inn off to one side of the foot of Sugarloaf ski area is a cut above many of its genre, thanks to the touch of local skier-entrepreneur Peter Webber, board chairman of Sugarloaf.

One of Stanley family homes is now a B&B, Three Stanley Avenue.

A full-service inn with the Sugartree indoor sports complex nearby, it offers 36 deluxe rooms on the upper three floors, plus many more in 225 surrounding condominiums, ranging from studios to five bedrooms. The inn's large parlor with velvet sofas arranged in groupings before a fireplace and television set is especially comfortable. The inn advertises "ski-to-the-door convenience," and a chairlift takes skiers up to the main lifts in the base village.

Three meals a day are served at the inn or the Sugartree Club. The **Seasons** restaurant is an attractive, angular room with plant-filled dividers, subdued wallpaper and sconces plus a couple of old sleds on the walls. The greenhouse addition, with tile floor and windows looking onto a clump of birch trees, is airy and inviting.

The fairly standard dinner menu offers beef and seafood, from $7.95 for a burger or pasta of the day to $14.95 for shrimp scampi. A Downeast smoked seafood sampler is one of the appetizers.

Doubles, $80 to $150, EP.

Sugarloaf Mountain Hotel, On the Mountain, Carrabasset Valley 04947. (207) 237-2222 or (800) 527-9879.

What's a seven-story hotel doing at the foot of a wilderness ski area? Adding sophisticated hotel accommodations to the lodging options already available, that's what.

Built in 1986 as a condominium hotel (which explains the kitchen counters and wet bars in most of the rooms and the lack of a real lobby), the resort changed management and added a suave main-floor restaurant and lounge in 1988.

The 119 rooms are in a variety of configurations, from double-double to executive king to one-bedroom and loft suites and a plush three-story penthouse (renting for $345 a night at peak periods, which is to say, winter). Off angled corridors, the rooms are spacious, with blond wood furniture, blue and white quilts, and comfortable wing chairs. All have cable TV and phones.

The hotel is centrally located near the ski lifts, base lodge and alpine village.

Doubles, $88 to $132, EP.

Dining Spots

One Stanley Avenue, 1 Stanley Ave., Kingfield. (207) 265-5541.

Native Mainer Dan Davis was looking for a home and a restaurant site in 1971 when he spotted a for-sale sign on a tree outside an unimposing house at the head of Stanley Avenue, a residential street named for Kingfield's best-known family. A skier who had been cooking at Vail, he painted the exterior an attractive white, restored the interior and scrounged enough furnishings to open a restaurant in 1972.

The Queen Anne-style Victorian was listed on the National Register of Historic Places in 1982 and is a trove of elegant Victoriana. Be sure to check out the old oak reach-in refrigerator that keeps the wine collection at the right temperature in the front hall and the Chickering square piano in the small parlor with a bar.

It is the food, however, for which One Stanley Avenue is famous, and justly so. Dan is basically self-taught, though in 1976 he studied with Louis Szathmary at the Bakery in Chicago. It was he who advised Dan to start cooking with the foods of Maine, applying classic techniques to indigenous products. His continuing interest in food and techniques took him in 1987 to six countries of Europe, a working tour that increased his awareness of regional styles and cuisines. That accounts for the interesting local specialties that outnumber the continental entrees on the menu, which changes seasonally. Amazingly, Dan does all of the cooking, with assistance from 16-year-old daughter

Elegant Victorian setting is match for food at One Stanley Avenue.

Sarah, serving an ambitious menu to up to 65 people in two small dining rooms and an enclosed porch on a busy night.

On the autumn night we dined, entrees included a maple cider chicken, dilled lobster on zucchini, roast duck with rhubarb glaze, and pork loin with juniper berry and port wine sauce. We delighted in the alluvial chicken, served with fiddlehead ferns and two-rice pilaf, plus side dishes of glazed carrots and sweet and sour cabbage. Even more memorable was the succulent mound of sweetbreads with applejack and chive cream sauce. A loaf of good whole wheat bread with sweet butter, green salads, coffee and orange sherbet came with the price of the entree ($11.50 to $19). With a $12 bottle of Rodney Strong cabernet, two of us feasted for less than $45. Another occasion brought veal and fiddlehead pie and saged rabbit, sliced in medallions with raspberry sauce.

For appetizers, Dan serves things like smoked Maine salmon and mussels, rumakis, and cream soups (lovage, chard, beets or beet greens). He obtained the recipe for his chocolate Maine guide cake from a man in his 80s, who got it from a man in his 80s who cooked it over a fire with a reflector oven. His mignonettes Mercurio, named for his next-door neighbor, are two noisettes of beef tenderloin, sauteed with mushrooms and garlic, and served with a burgundy and cream sauce. Such are some of the endearing and enduring Maine touches of an outstanding restaurant.

Dinner nightly except Monday, 5 to 9; closed Oct. 20-Dec. 22 and Easter to July 4.

Arabella's, Sugarloaf Mountain Hotel, Carrabasset Valley. (207) 237-2222.

Executive chef Steve Skaling put together this fancy restaurant in the new hotel at the base of Sugarloaf in the winter of 1988 and headed a team of three chefs whose food was highly regarded in its first year.

Against a backdrop of green linens, polished wood and rattan chairs, they served an ambitious menu priced from $10 for filet of sole with grapes and champagne sauce to $14.75 for seafood fettuccine enlivened with cilantro and a jalapeno cream sauce. Blackened chicken with salsa, lobster ravioli, roast duckling and steak Diane are other favorites.

The pastry chef changes the dessert selection daily. The wine list is quite expensive by Maine standards. Complete breakfasts (one is huevos rancheros) are $6 or $7. Dinner nightly, 6 to 9 or 10.

Hug's, Route 27, Carrabasset Valley. (207) 237-2392.
Here's a place with character. The character is provided as much by chef-owner Jack Flannagan as by his rustic, tiny restaurant transformed in 1986 from a sauna.

Starting with a tiny kitchen, half a dozen glass-covered tables, hearty northern Italian cuisine and more than a dollop of fun, Jack and his wife of French-Canadian descent, Hug (for Hugette), packed in a coterie of devotees year-round. By the fall of 1988, they'd doubled their size with a second room in which twenty "private" seats at $300 each were sold out in a week.

Jack, who said he has had seventeen restaurants and is at the age when some think of retiring, jokes with diners between stints in the kitchen where he whips up a dynamite pesto-pizza flat bread, some ethereal pasta dishes we heard about from a chef in lower Maine (a dozen choices, $5.95 to $12.95), plus shrimp scampi, chicken limone, and veal scaloppine or francaise. A full salad comes with, so you'll likely not need either of the appetizers, fontina fritter or antipasto ($7.95 for two). Jack offers a chocolate truffle mousse, but says "if they have room for dessert, I'm really upset."

The cafe atmosphere with a couple of wooden booths, calico cloths, candles in hurricane lamps and painted captain's chairs is extremely cozy. If there's a wait, have a drink in the Hard Core ante room and gawk at the walls autographed by patrons (some of them quite famous) and bearing the list of Hug's board of directors, which includes Pepper Oni and Prima Vera. Now that's fun.

Dinner nightly from 5.

Le Papillon at the Inn on Winter's Hill, Kingfield. (207) 265-5421.
The two dining rooms are as elaborate as the rest of the house, except for the comfortable brown canvas directors' chairs to sit on. Gold over white tablecloths, draperies over lace curtains, ferns in the windows, oil paintings on fancy wallpaper, fireplaces, mirrors and candlelight make for romantic dining. From every window are views of the rugged countryside, a contrast to the poshness within.

Innkeeper Michael Thom scaled down his dining hours and his menu in 1988. Serving in winter only, he offered "le grand menu" on Saturdays and "le petit menu" three nights a week. The Saturday dinners included such continental entrees as steak au poivre, beef Wellington, roast duckling, chicken, and veal and seafood du jour. Escargots, brie en croute and pate were favored appetizers; desserts tended toward chocolate mousse and creme caramel. The petite menu was comprised of appetizers, stew or a sandwich and dessert.

Sunday brunch is served by the pool in summer. It includes a choice of eggs Benedict or florentine ($5.25), french toast, blueberry pancakes and pepperoni scrambled eggs as well as fruits and desserts.

Dinner in winter, full menu, Saturdays and holidays, 6 to 6:30 and 8 to 8:30; light menu, Thursday-Sunday 5 to 10.

The Herbert, Main Street, Kingfield. (207) 265-2000.
White lace tablecloths, gray fabric-upholstered chairs, gray walls, lace curtains, candles and pillared columns are featured in this airy, high-ceilinged dining room of the old hotel school. The open sink along the wall inside the dining room entrance — in which stagecoach passengers washed up for dinner — adds an historic if not especially esthetic note.

The menu is categorized by chicken and game choices (chicken, duck and rabbit), salad and vegetable items, and seafood and farmyard selections. They run the gamut from pistouille, a vegetarian dish containing eggplant, tomatoes and peppers ($8.95), to filet bearnaise ($15.25), and include a homemade cheese spread with crackers and a house salad. Chicken Cherryfield is topped with a blueberry sour cream sauce ($11.50).

The menu suggests wines to go with each entree, right down to the spinach and cheese crepes (house white zinfandel). They come from a list of 100 nicely chosen selections at wallet-pleasing prices. For dessert, you can get bananas Foster ($3.95 for two), baked Alaska and pies, cheesecake and ice cream of the day.

Dinner nightly, 5:30 to 9; Sunday, brunch 11:30 to 2, dinner 5 to 8.

The Truffle Hound, Village West at Sugarloaf. (207) 237-2355.

Established a year before One Stanley Avenue and Le Papillon enticed skiing gourmets off the mountain down to Kingfield, this is considered the fanciest of older restaurants in the Sugarloaf village.

The continental menu ranges from $11.50 for chicken dijon or marinated pork kabob to $14.50 for petit filet au poivre. Veal piccata, roast duckling with orange, honey-lime or raspberry sauce, and shrimp and scallop saute are other choices. The wine list is extensive, and the dessert menu lists such goodies as English trifle, baked Alaska, chocolate hazelnut cake and triple chocolate terrine grand marnier.

Lunchtime brings eggs Benedict, chicken divan and fettuccine carbonara in addition to soups, salads and sandwiches. After a long morning on the ski slopes, we had a great curried carrot soup, a hearty cheeseburger topped with Swiss cheese, and a not-so-successful open-face fresh haddock sandwich with a supposed hollandaise sauce on a toasted hot dog bun.

The restaurant, with three rooms done up in beige and blue and lit by tiny candles at night, is a peaceful respite from the crowds at the nearby base lodge.

Winter hours, lunch 11:30 to 3, dinner 5:30 to 9:30; summer, dinner Thursday-Sunday 6 to 10.

Longfellow's, Main Street, Kingfield. (207) 265-4394.

Established in 1980, Longfellow's restaurant and Riverside Lounge is a rustic, casual affair with polished wood tables, beamed ceiling, homespun curtains, old glass lamps and plenty of local color coming and going at the bar. It also has a dining room upstairs with an outdoor deck overlooking the Carrabassett River.

We thought it a find for an inexpensive lunch, as we enjoyed a cup of soup du jour (hearty vegetable) with a tabbouleh salad and a vegetable quiche with garden salad for a bargain $6.50 for two, plus tip.

At night, the extensive menu is divided into Italian, garden, seafood and "some of our favorites" sections, priced from $4.50 for spaghetti with meatballs to $10.75 for seafood scampi. Stir-fry vegetables, Cajun chicken, and shrimp and steak teriyaki are among the choices. Quite a list of desserts and liquered coffees concludes both lunch and dinner menus.

Open daily, lunch 11 to 5, dinner 5 to 9 or 9:30.

Gepetto's, Village West at Sugarloaf. (207) 237-2192.

Casual and always crowded, and considered to be the place where the action is, Gepetto's serves up lunch, dinner, and apres-ski and evening entertainment in a greenhouse with butcherblock tables or a tavern with a loud bar and large-screen television.

This is not for tete-a-tete dining. The fare tends to be basic chicken, pork, steaks and

Sugarloaf ski trails are backdrop for new Sugarloaf Mountain Hotel and base villlage.

broiled or fried fish, from $8.95 for broccoli-stuffed chicken or fried clams to $13.95 for surf and turf. One wintry night we tried the oversize porterhouse steak with onion rings, which was quite adequate. The others in our party had an interesting chicken dish with mushrooms, artichoke hearts and cheese ($9.50) and a ham pizza ($5.50), washed down with a carafe of the house Sebastiani red.

Besides sandwiches and a raw bar, the menu urges: "Don't forget to ask about our daily specials — the help sometimes thinks it's a secret." Lunch sandwiches include "Play it again, ham" and the "Veggie Jackson," grilled cheese and garden greens.

Open daily in winter, lunch 11 to 3, dinner from 5:30. Limited menu served daily in summer from 11 to 8.

Diversions

Skiing. Starting in the 1950s, **Sugarloaf USA** is what put Kingfield on the map. Its isolated site made it a destination resort, its distance from population centers made it uncrowded and a relative bargain, and its wilderness location gave it a character all its own. The above-the-treeline snowfields are known for open European-style spring skiing — a Down East version of Mount Washington's Tuckerman Ravine with lifts. The 2,637-foot vertical drop, one of the greatest in the East, is steep at the top, intermediate in the middle and easy at the bottom, and the extensive lift system follows suit so that skiers can ski the level that suits them. The rapidly growing alpine village at the base has several clusters with numerous restaurants and pubs, boutiques, condominiums and a hotel conference center, complete with auditorium and stage for performing arts festivals. After averting bankruptcy in 1987, Sugarloaf stopped developing real estate and went back to the skiing basics, adding snowmaking and a new area with two quadruple chairlifts for 1989. Adult lift tickets, $31.

Sugarloaf Gondola. Non-skiers can enjoy the exhilarating view from the summit of Sugarloaf by riding the gondola in the off-season. The gondola operates June 15 to Labor Day, Wednesday-Friday 1 to 5 and weekends 10 to 5, and daily 10 to 5 from Labor Day to Oct. 10. Adults $5, children $3.

Ski touring. The **Carrabassett Valley Ski Touring Center,** just south of Route 27 near the Sugarloaf access road, is considered Maine's premier cross-country facility. More than 50 miles of marked trails, most former logging roads, slice through the semi-wilderness with varying degrees of difficulty and with nary a building, power line or road crossing in sight. In the winter of 1988-89, the center was the site for an international race, the highest-caliber cross-country ski meet ever staged in Maine.

White-water rafting. Since a group of bear hunters first rafted down the Kennebec River in 1976, rafting has been a boom sport in these parts from May into October. The

Kennebec, the Penobscot, the Dead and the Carrabassett rivers each has its own fans. Outfitters like Downeast Rafting, Eastern River Expeditions, Northern Outdoors and Rolling Thunder River Co. guide trips and package tours through swift rapids and calm pools, usually stopping for a steak cookout at lunch and often ending up in a hot tub or bar.

Golfing. Since 1985, golfers have enjoyed the new eighteen-hole Sugarloaf golf course designed by Robert Trent Jones Jr. at the foot of the mountain. From what was once impenetrable woodland, he created a course that's scenic, bold and, in his words, "really in the wilderness and that's unusual." It's a heavily wooded course, which gives golfers a sense of isolation, like walking through a forest. The designer calls the course one of his best ever, and it's a Golf Digest award-winner.

Summer arts. Sugarloaf has become something of a center for performing arts. In 1988, the innovative **Feld Ballet Company** of New York succeeded the Hartford Ballet in residence for two weeks in early August; free outdoor rehearsals daily in the Richard H. Bell Chapel on the mountain and a farewell review were among the public attractions. The **Berklee School of Music** in Boston presents a series of jazz concerts on weekends from mid-July through mid-August. The biggest draw of all is the annual art show, featuring two dozen painters and sculptors during Homecoming Weekend each October.

Shopping. Sugarloaf has boutiques that one normally associates with ski resorts. Kingfield's tiny Main Street has three places of interest: **Patricia Buck's Emporium of the Western Mountains** is full of custom-knit sweaters, hats, legwarmers and such that she designs, plus items by Maine craftsmen, quilt squares, books, potpourri, coffees, spices and Maine mustards. Upstairs she has opened an art gallery featuring works of Maine artists as well as antiques. The **1850 House** has an excellent collection of antiques and art, gift items, baked goods, specialty foods and fine wines; we liked the blue and white Shard pottery, the Maine wood block cards, the rabbit pot pie and Bob's No Problem Bloody Mary Mixer. The biggest store in town is **Keenan Auction Co.,** a factory outlet with good bargains on clothing, ski apparel, shoes, Woolrich knits and the like.

Extra-Special

The Stanley Museum, School Street, Kingfield. (207) 265-2729.

Founded in 1981 in the former Stanley School that was slated to be razed, this fledgling museum has an ambitious $1 million plan to preserve and show the Stanley tradition of painting, photography, music and steam transportation. Sue Davis, the museum's executive director, calls herself the museum's "guiding force" — she's "the engine that makes it run," according to a Boston Globe report. The inventive Stanley twins — Francis Edgar and Freelan Oscar — and their American Renaissance family are inextricably woven into the fabric of old Kingfield; their legacy is gradually being collected and exhibited at the museum. A 1905 four-passenger Stanley Steamer car greets visitors inside the entrance and a five-passenger Model 70 from 1910 was totally restored in 1988. Air-brush portraits by F.E. Stanley, photographs by Chansonetta Stanley Emmons (sister of the twins), the violins they made, family scrapbooks and other memorabilia are fascinating. Still in the developmental stage, the museum is open free from 1 to 4 p.m. daily except Monday, summer through foliage, and by appointment at other times.

Oxford Hills and Lakes, Me.
Not Where It's At — Yet

The famous — some locals call it infamous — milepost sign out in the middle of nowhere giving distances to nearby places like Norway, Denmark, Mexico, Poland, Paris and Naples would deceive no one.

This is anything but the center of the universe. It's more like the name on the school bus we passed, "State of Maine, Unorganized Territory."

The Oxford Hills region is an unspoiled land of sparkling lakes, hills that back up to the mighty White Mountains and tiny hamlets with English-sounding names like Center Lovell and Lower Waterford. It's an area of great beauty — we hear that the National Geographic called Kezar Lake one of the nation's ten most beautiful (its other claim to fame is that Bridgton native Stephen King has a summer home along its forested shore). There's a fortuitous concentration of small country inns that epitomize the genre.

Unusual as a time capsule from the past, the area offers little in the way of formal activity or tourist trappings. "You are on your own," the Westways inn brochure advises.

More and more people seek the serenity of western Maine, area innkeepers report. "We're really out in the country," concedes Barbara Vanderzanden of the Waterford Inne. "But we have a central location not far from North Conway or the Maine coast."

The charms of this rural retreat have yet to be discovered by the crowds. But that may be only a matter of time. Says restaurateur Suzanne Uhl-Myers of the Lake House: "Western Maine is where it's going to be at."

Happily, it's not there yet. That remains its special joy.

Inn Spots

Westways on Kezar Lake, Route 5, Center Lovell 04016. (207) 928-2663.

Each of the inns in this area has its distinctive appeal. At Westways, it's the great location right on the east shore of upper Kezar Lake, plus its heritage as a small, private luxury lodge from the past.

Built in the 1920s by the owner of the Diamond Match Company as a corporate retreat, it was opened to the public in 1975 with its original furnishings, from the books in the guest rooms to the 1925 billiards table and vintage bowling alley in the recreation hall. "We're unique as a time capsule," says Nancy C. Tripp, manager for the four owners from Boston. "It has been left as it was in the '20s."

The main floor contains a large kitchen and an immense living room, with many Italian antiques, a huge stone fireplace and, at either end, hand-carved oak tables that each seat twelve for meals. Beyond is a long dining porch running the width of the lodge with windows right above the water, and a grand old boathouse where cocktails and nibbles are served on the screened porch as the sun sets over the White Mountains (see Dining Spots). A small interior dining room, with many Japanese prints on the wall, is used for winter dining. The downstairs also has a restroom with an ornate wraparound needle shower that invigorates the entire body and compensates for the lack of showers upstairs.

Three of the seven guest rooms have private baths, while the rest share four baths in the hallways. Nicest is the Master Room with two double beds, hand-carved furniture and windows on two sides. Many think the Horses Room, named for the series of Fox Hunt prints on the walls, has the best view in the house. Only one of the three smaller rooms in the former servants' quarters lacks a water view.

Dock and boathouse at Westways on Kezar Lake.

Westways also rents out a former stableman's cottage by the day and six houses on the grounds (two brand new), accommodating up to fourteen at weekly rates of $600 to $1,200.

Lodge guests are served full breakfasts, with choice of pancakes, french toast, eggs any style or omelets. They also have the run of the forested, 100-acre property, which includes a dock at the boathouse with a swimming area in the crystal-clear waters of the quiet, almost private lake and a sand beach a quarter-mile down the shore. If you're into handball, try the "fives" court in an outbuilding (tournaments are sometimes held here).

Across the lake, you can see the former estate of Rudy Vallee, who built a treehouse for one of his pianos and sometimes rowed over to Westways, playing his ukelele and serenading guests during barbecues.

Doubles, $80 to $120, B&B; $110 to $150, MAP. Closed April and November.

The Waterford Inne, Chadbourne Road, Box 49, East Waterford 04233. (207) 583-4037.

This handsome inn and antiques shop really is out in the country — half a mile up a rural lane, its pale yellow and mustard exterior commanding a hilltop view and containing ten well-furnished guest rooms, a comfortable and charming living room full of folk art, a more formal parlor, and a semi-public dining room of note.

Former New Jersey school teachers Rosalie and Barbara Vanderzanden, a mother and daughter team, carefully restored and furnished the 1825 farmhouse in 1978, eventually augmenting the original five bedrooms with five more in the old woodshed leading to the red barn out back.

The common rooms and porch are unusually nice and ever so tasteful. Special touches abound in each bedroom, seven of which have private baths. Duck pillows, duck wallpaper and a duck lamp grace the deluxe Chesapeake Room, which has a kingsize bed, a working fireplace and a super second-story porch overlooking the farm pond and mountains. A quilted whale hangs behind the bed in the Nantucket Room, complete with a map of the island and a bathroom almost as large as the bedroom itself. The

217

Waterford Inne and antiques shop occupy hilltop setting way out in the country.

Strawberry Room in the woodshed has strawberries on the lamp, rug, quilts, pillow and sheets, and even strawberry-scented potpourri in a strawberry-shaped dish.

Fresh flowers decorate each room in summer. Electric blankets are provided in winter. And "you should see this place at Christmas," says Barbara. "Every nook and cranny is decorated and red bows are put on even the smallest folk-art lambs." In summer, the principal activity is watching the bullfrogs and birds, including a great blue heron, around the farm pond.

Full breakfasts for $6 ("we'll cook whatever you want," says Rosalie) are served in the beamed dining room or in good weather on the porch.

Dinners for $25 are served to guests and, by reservation, to the public in the dining room filled with the women's pewter collection. Up to twenty can be served when the front parlor and porch are used as well. Although there is no choice, Rosalie will work around special diets and asks large parties for their preference.

A typical dinner might start with cream of broccoli soup, go on to dilled scallops over angel-hair pasta with vegetables and salad not long out of the garden, and end with a fresh berry pie. Chilled cucumber soup and veal marsala might make up another dinner. Leg of lamb often appears, as do shrimp with pernod, game hens, duckling, sole, and pork or beef tenderloin. Grand marnier souffle and pumpkin ice cream cake are frequent desserts, and guests may bring their own wine.

Doubles, $55 to $80, EP. No credit cards.

Olde Rowley Inn, Route 35, North Waterford 04267. (207) 583-4143.

History fairly oozes from every nook and cranny of this rambling red building with the sagging roof smack up against the road atop the hill that is North Waterford. Built in 1790 and opened as a stagecoach inn in 1825, it had been abandoned when two young sisters and their husbands found it in 1980 and restored it with care as to its history. With the departure of one couple, Pamela and Peter Leja now share the innkeeping duties.

Dried herbs hang over the massive open hearth in the keeping room, where inn guests gather under a low-beamed ceiling. A rocking chair and a high-backed bench surround the fireplace, and atop the mantel is a needlepoint picture of a Colonial lady done by Pamela's mother. There are pumpkin pine floors and wainscoting made of fourteen-foot-long boards that had been hidden under fifteen coats of paint.

A "tightwinder" staircase ascends to the second floor and the five guest rooms, two with private baths. Authentic pierced-tin lanterns cast light on the uneven floors of the hallways. The cozy beamed bedrooms, named after local dignitaries, are furnished with period wallpaper and furniture, white bedspreads, colorful towels, hooked rugs, and perhaps a half bath or washstand.

A full country breakfast is included in the rates. In winter, Irish oatmeal is popular with skiers. Guests also have a choice of eggs, sometimes there are blueberry pancakes, and the homemade oatmeal bread tastes terrific as toast.

A 1779 stage ticket found by an elderly lady in her attic across the street is in the frame of a picture of the old inn in the bar. Pamela Leja has a great reputation as dinner chef (see Dining Spots).

Doubles, $45 to $55.

The Noble House, Highland Road, Box 180, Bridgton 04009. (207) 647-3733.

Once a senator's home in a residential section overlooking Highland Lake, the Noble House is now a comfortable B&B with eight bedrooms and two suites, run with much warmth and personality by Jane and Dick Starets and their three teen-agers. Although they share a Victorian-antique theme, six of the newer rooms in the rear carriage house seem more modern — some jacuzzi baths, large windows, a window seat and perhaps

the Noble House

a private porch. They're decorated primarily in white, furnished in wicker and have wall-to-wall carpeting, period antiques, floral quilts with matching draperies, and frilly touches like eyelet curtains and pillows, one in the shape of a heart.

Guests gather in the the fireplaced parlor, which has lots of books and a grand piano outfitted with sheet music, or in the pine-paneled family room in back, with its huge mushroom-colored sectional and a grand fireplace.

Breakfast is served at a table for six in a Victorian dining room clad totally in pale greens, except for the rug. Tropical fruit salad, whole-grain cereal, raisin bran muffins and vegetable frittata were served the morning we were there.

Guests can swim or canoe from the inn's lakefront property across the road, where a hammock, barbecue grill and picnic table are available. Jane Starets has printed up a handy guide to restaurants and attractions in the area.

Doubles, $62 to $90; suites, $90 to $110. No smoking.

Kedarburn Inn, Route 35, Box 61, Waterford 04088. (207) 583-6182.

Built in 1858, this handsome white Colonial house with dark green shutters and broad lawns brightened with flower beds was in transition when we visited. It had just been acquired in the summer of 1988 by Margaret and Derek Gibson, who had run a B&B in their native Bournemouth, England.

They added three guest rooms for a total of nine and were putting in four more private baths for a total of six. Rooms come in a variety of configurations from kingsize to one with three twin beds and another a double-deck affair with stairs up to a single bed (the rear barn portion was Maine's first boys' camp, Margaret advised).

Country decor enhances the bedrooms, and Margaret sewed the curtains bearing ducks. Mints, thick colorful towels and stuffed Paddington bears are special touches.

219

The spacious country dining room and the airy breakfast room are attractive, as is the front guest parlor with a television set, comfortable sofas and books. An outdoor patio is within earshot of Kedar Brook.

What the Gibsons call a full camper's breakfast is complimentary for inn guests and available to the public for $5.25, with choice of eggs, omelets, pancakes or french toast.

Doubles, $55 to $65.

Center Lovell Inn, Route 5, Center Lovell 04016. (207) 925-1575.

The screened porch that wraps around this 1805 homestead appeals to guests as much as it did to Susie and Bill Mosca from Connecticut, who first saw the abandoned farmhouse in 1974. "We sat on the front porch and admired the view and that was it," Susie recalls. The view, with a glimpse of Kezar Lake down a long hillside and the White Mountains etched against the western sky, is indeed special.

The Moscas have renovated room by room the three-story structure, which has something of a Mississippi steamboat appearance thanks to the Floridian who added a mansard roof topped by a cupola in the 1860s. The 1835 Norton House, a former barber shop, was moved to the site from Lovell and now adds five more guest rooms at the side.

The annex has large rooms with country furnishings and the rear room with double bed and a settee has a modern bathroom. Some of the guest rooms in the homestead have neat old chests for storing extra blankets. A large painting of pansies in an ornate frame graces one room, and all have country curtains. There are private baths in seven of the eleven rooms.

The common living room with a hooked rug has a wood stove and small organ. Glowing fireplaces, lit even on fairly warm days, cheer the dining rooms, where Bill Mosca's cooking is highly regarded (see below). The standard MAP plan includes a single-item set menu that changes nightly; a deluxe MAP plan with the pick of the full menu is extra.

Doubles, $96 to $115, MAP; $116 to $145, deluxe MAP; $52 to $79 EP when dining room is closed. Closed late October to Christmas and mid-March to May 1.

Tolman House Inn, Tolman Road, Box 551, Harrison 04040. (207) 583-4445.

A landscaper is one of the partners in this new inn, and his work is evident in the formal gardens with statues and a croquet court on view from a pleasant deck with wrought-iron furniture. The 100-acre property near the Bear River, situated not far from two lakes, is supremely quiet and rural.

Nine guest rooms with private baths are available in the restored carriage house, a substantial adjunct to the stately main house built in 1870 by a prosperous businessman and now occupied by the innkeepers, Alex and Mary Soutter and Joyce and Paul Cotton.

Stenciled walls and frilly curtains grace the rather spare rooms, which are furnished with antique and brass beds. There's a small parlor with a TV, and the old ice house has been converted into a game room.

The innkeepers take turns preparing breakfast, perhaps eggs with homefries, blueberry pancakes or french toast. It's served in a rear dining room with Hitchcock chairs overlooking the gardens.

Doubles, $70. Closed in April.

Lake House, Routes 35 & 37, Waterford 04088. (207) 583-4182.

A landmark structure that had been Waterford's first inn (operating until the 1940s) was reopened in 1984 as the Lake House, with a well-regarded restaurant on the main floor and four guest rooms upstairs.

Oxford House Inn is known for good dining and accommodations.

The restaurant (see below) and a small parlor take top billing on the main floor, and owners Suzanne and Michael Uhl-Myers live with their young daughter on the third floor. Two rooms and two suites with private baths are available on the second floor.

The Waterford Flat Suite had more than enough space in which to spread out during a record hot spell, in spacious sleeping quarters with a ruffly double bed and an adjoining reading room with a sofa, shelves lined with books and a prominently displayed coffee-maker. Two other rooms are smaller, but like ours had a homey, lived-in feeling. Not at all home-like is the grand ballroom suite, which lives up to its name with a huge curved ceiling, a canopied double bed, seven windows, a sitting area and an open, carpeted platform for a bathroom.

A split of riesling is put out in each guest room, and a bowl of peanuts in the parlor staves off hunger. Breakfast, taken in the rear dining room or on the front porch, could be scrambled eggs, pancakes or waffles, accompanied by juice and a fresh fruit salad — bananas and blueberries with cream, in our case.

Doubles, $59; suites, $79.

The Oxford House Inn, 105 Main St., Fryeburg 04037. (207) 935-3442.

Known primarily for its food (see Dining Spots), this inn run by John and Phyllis Morris has five guest rooms as well. They're located upstairs in an attractive, pale yellow and green country house fronted with a wraparound piazza.

Three rooms have private baths, including one front corner room with a bow window and two double beds. Velvet is draped behind the queensize bed in another room, and all the rooms are furnished with period furniture and antiques.

Guests share a front parlor with waiting dinner patrons, but can retire as well to a large downstairs pub with four small tables and a sitting area with a wood stove and a large TV favored by the innkeepers' young sons. The wicker-filled wraparound porch is great for relaxing, and the back yard opens onto a super view of the Presidential Range.

The Morrises serve a complete breakfast. Eggs Benedict, grand marnier french toast, berry pancakes and french toast with cream cheese and marmalade or raspberry jam are among the possibilities.

Doubles, $60 to $75.

Dining Spots

Lake House, Routes 35 & 37, Waterford. (207) 583-4182.

Almost since it reopened in 1984, the restaurant at Waterford's first inn has been making culinary waves in western Maine. A changing menu of creative regional cuisine, flaming desserts and a remarkable wine list are offered by proprietors Suzanne and Michael Uhl-Myers.

Each dining room is pretty as a picture. The small front room has burgundy wallpaper above pale green woodwork, green carpeting, shelves of glass and china, a corkscrew collection and a picture of puffins over the fireplace. The larger rear, pine-paneled dining room has burgundy and pink linens, tables set with two large wine glasses at each setting and oriental rugs on the floor. Patrons can enjoy the antics of birds at feeders behind a couple of one-way mirrors.

The owners consider their award-winning wine list "the best in Maine." Notable more for depth than breadth, it reflects Suzanne's former career as a wine consultant. Prices are extremely reasonable (seven bottlings of beaujolais, $12 to $18) and each is accompanied by an intelligent description.

We chose to dine on the narrow front porch, which was rather too brightly illuminated for our tastes. The Rhode Island squid sauteed with spinach ravioli and a garlic sauce ($5.95) was an excellent starter. Other choices included duck and goose liver pate seasoned with grand marnier, and three phyllo pastries filled with various cheeses. The changing soups might be a creamy red onion with a shot of sherry on the side, curried carrot or smoked salmon.

A dollop of kiwi sorbet preceded the entrees, a generous portion of sliced lamb sauced with curry and vodka and a roast duckling in a sweet sauce of blackberries and raspberries. Sliced potatoes, cucumbers, tomatoes and pickled corn accompanied. Peppered veal, shrimp New Orleans, fettuccine with smoked salmon, chicken stuffed with ricotta cheese and filet mignon were other choices, priced from $12.95 to $18.95.

Served after the entree, the salad of fresh fruit on a bed of lettuce was so refreshing we didn't need dessert, although one of us succumbed to a parfait pie. Apples Normandy, bananas Foster and crepes Suzette are flamed tableside for two, a duty that keeps Michael hopping on busy nights. Some people come just for the desserts, which are available separately with coffee and cordials after 8 p.m.

Dinner nightly, 5 to 10; closed Tuesday and Wednesday in off-season.

The Oxford House Inn, 105 Main St., Fryeburg. (207) 935-3442.

Opened in 1985, this 1913 country house is run very personally by John and Phyllis Morris, formerly of North Conway. Their creative cuisine has quickly gained a wide reputation.

Seventy-five people can be seated on white chairs (their tops hand-stenciled by Phyllis) on the rear porch with a stunning view of Mount Kearsarge North, in the former living room called the Parlor, and along the screened front piazza. The back rooms are done up in rust linens, the napkins tied like a necktie. Green floral wallpaper, Phyllis's handmade curtains and draperies, and lovely paneling enhance the parlor.

Tables are set with delicate pink crystal, heavy silver and Sango Mystique peach china, with candles in clay pots and fresh daisies at our visit.

Lake House offers fine dining in Waterford.

The menu, which changes seasonally, comes inside sheet music from the 1920s. Dinner begins with complimentary homemade crackers and a cream-cheese spread, a salad of fresh greens and fruits (berries and melon), perhaps with a tomato-tarragon dressing or a cranberry vinaigrette, and fresh nut and corn breads. Appetizers ($4.50 to $6.95) are Maine crab chowder, a house pate, hot smoked Atlantic salmon, baked camembert in puff pastry with fruit and a smoked seafood plate. Crayfish bisque, cream of asparagus and chilled strawberry wcrc among summer soups when we visited.

The ten entrees ($16 to $19) include such creations as turkey Waldorf splashed with applejack, poached salmon pommery, pork with pears and port, scallops in puff pastry and veal madeira. John does most of the cooking, but the desserts are Phyllis's: fruit trifles, walnut torte with orange cream filling, amaretto chocolate cheesecake, fruit flans and tarts, and an acclaimed bread pudding with peaches and blueberries.

The wine list bears its share of bargains, the house offerings going for $2.25 a glass. Dinner nightly, 6 to 9; Sunday brunch, 11 to 2.

Olde Rowley Inn, Route 35, North Waterford. (207) 583-4143.

Three candlelit dining rooms in a 1790 roadside stagecoach inn couldn't be more historic or romantic. That the food is so good is a bonus.

Stenciled reproduction wallpaper and a handful of tables with assorted overcloths are in one small dining room. Beyond and down a few stairs is the 1825 carriage house connecting inn to barn. In one dining room here, the exposed-beam ceiling is hung with old baskets and dried herbs; frilly white curtains surround the small windows. Copper wall lanterns illuminate the hand-stenciled wallpaper in the third room.

Chef Pamela Leja's traditional menu starts with deep-fried Monterey Jack cheese with dill sauce, stuffed mushrooms, a scallop tart or wonderful cream soups — the carrot bisque and mushroom laced with cognac being standouts.

Fresh homemade breads and a mixed salad of greens, vegetables and fruits with house dressings come with the meal. Entrees ($10.50 to $15.75) include hunter's chicken, veal piccata, haddock provencale, shrimp amandine, lobster pie, roast pork Normandy and filet mignon with choice of three sauces. Wild rice pilaf and seasonal vegetables accompany.

Desserts are to groan over: trifles with raspberries and peaches or chocolate, strawberries and bananas, walnut bourbon pie, bread pudding with butter bourbon sauce,

French silk pie and a four-layer French chocolate cake filled with rum mousse. The wine list has some good bargains in the $10 to $14 range.

Dinner nightly, 5 to 10; sometimes closed one or two nights a week in winter.

Center Lovell Inn, Route 5, Center Lovell. (207) 925-1575.

The heritage of five generations of Italian cooks, whose recipes chef-owner Bill Mosca grew up with along the Connecticut shore, is the dining attraction at this farmhouse-turned-inn overlooking Kezar Lake. The tables in two small, plain dining rooms have peach cloths and red napkins; in summer, there's outdoor dining on the wraparound porch as the sun sets over the Presidential Range.

Dining is taken seriously here, Bill Mosca going so far as to prepare special feasts of six or seven courses for holidays and other occasions. Roast suckling pig and baby leg of lamb stuffed with prosciutto are featured main courses; a Mediterranean fish course of pastry shells filled with lobster, oysters, scallops and eggplant in a cream sauce is a treat.

Regular dinners begin with a choice of six appetizers ($2.50 to $4.95). Favorites are fresh fruit chilled in champagne, artichoke hearts and steamed mussels. Among entrees ($11.95 to $17.95), the milk-fed veal marsala and veal Margarita are outstanding. Shrimp is baked and stuffed with crabmeat or sauteed in olive oil with spices and wine. Baked filet of Maine hake is stuffed with shrimp and flavored with sherry. Entrees are served with Italian bread, salad with an Italian dressing (an acclaimed homemade blue cheese dressing is $3 extra), and vegetable. Six pasta dishes are listed after the entrees for $10.25 to $12.95, and a house specialty — lobster fra diavalo — can be ordered with two days' notice.

Susie Mosca makes the desserts: a rich Italian cheesecake, spumoni and parfait de menthe, ice cream Nero and occasionally a trifle, $2.75 to $3. A demitasse of espresso is served for two, or you may order French roast coffee with anisette. The wine list is reasonably priced, with the emphasis on Italian and French vintages.

Dinner, nightly from 5. Reservations required.

Westways on Kezar Lake, Route 5, Center Lovell. (207) 928-2663.

As the sun sets over Kezar Lake, the porch and the adjacent living room are a memorable setting for dinner at Westways. Meals begin with cocktails in the lounge above the boathouse, where raw vegetables with a curry dip and a plate of cheese, grapes and crackers might be served.

The menu starts with shrimp by the piece, country pate and baked camembert with almonds ($6.95). Soup choices could be a chilled cantaloupe, hot cream of parsnip or mushroom consomme with Japanese noodles. The chef is especially fond of his maple-pecan salad dressing, atop salads he makes colorful with seasonal lettuce and vegetables. His basket of homemade breads always includes one made with cheese, and sometimes rum-pumpkin bread, served with rosettes of butter.

The six entrees ($14.95 to $17.95) include scallops tossed with vegetables and pasta in a pesto cream sauce, gingered duck breast with raspberry-peach glaze, Cajun-blackened chicken, baked salmon and a changing veal preparation, plus such specials as leg of lamb or chicken marsala. Herbs and vegetables, from basil to string beans, come from one of the waitress's garden. A baker in town is responsible for the desserts ($3.25), among them Sicilian rum cake, white chocolate raspberry mousse, peanut-butter/chocolate-chip cheesecake and Hungarian torte.

The wine list is reasonably priced.

Tables are set with white linens, dark rose napkins and interesting floral arrangements on the porch, where dinner is served with a water view on summer nights, inside the

Handsome Colonial structure houses Kedarburn Inn.

main room at hand-carved oak tables warmed by a fieldstone fireplace, or in the small winter dining room.

Dinner, nightly 6 to 9; reservations required by 4 p.m.

Kedarburn Inn, Route 35, Waterford. (207) 583-6182.

A pianist plays for singalongs on Friday and Saturday evenings in the blue and beige dining room of the Kedarburn. New innkeepers Margaret and Derek Gibson refurbished the kitchen and hired a chef.

Dinner entrees ($8.95 to $14.95) include things like chicken cordon bleu, veal piccata, seafood newburg, crab-stuffed shrimp in puff pastry and individual beef Wellington. Marinated steaks are barbecued on the inn's charcoal grill for $9.95 to $12.95, depending on size. Homemade bread, tossed salad (the sweet and sour dressing is a house specialty), vegetable and starch accompany.

Shrimp cocktail, stuffed mushrooms, fruit salad and clam chowder are the appetizers. Favored desserts include blueberry pie and English trifle.

Full breakfasts are served to the public for $5.25. The wine selection was limited when we visited, but the inn has a full liquor license.

Breakfast, 7 to 11; dinner, 5 to 9; Sunday brunch.

Black Horse Tavern, Route 302, Bridgton. (207) 647-5300.

New in 1988 and a big hit in the Bridgton area was this restaurant in a barn behind a gray house whose front porch looks as if it were straight out of Louisiana. The two structures are joined by a large bar. Most of the dining is in the rear portion, where all kinds of horsey artifacts hang from the walls and stalls have been converted into booths.

The Louisiana farmhouse look is appropriate for the cuisine of native Maine chef Greg Hagerman, who acquired a Cajun flair while cooking in Texas and Louisiana.

The chicken and smoked sausage gumbo, $2.65 a cup and $3.95 a bowl, is a must starter for first-timers at lunch or dinner. Barbecued pork ribs, chicken fingers and macho nachos are other appetizers ($3.65 to $4.95).

Steaks, prime rib, pan-blackened sirloin or swordfish, chicken Creole and scallop pie are among the dinner entrees, priced from $8.95 for fish and chips to $17.95 for beef and reef (prime rib and scallops). Deli sandwiches and light entrees are available for lunch.

Open daily from 11 to 10, weekends to 11, Sunday from 12:30.

Diversions

The area has many attributes, but they tend to be quiet and personal. As the Westways brochure states: "Whether you prefer browsing through local antique shops, visiting the country fairs, watching the sun rise over the misty lake as you fish from your canoe at dawn or spending a quiet evening around the fieldstone fireplace, you are on your own." Some ideas:

The villages. General stores and the odd antiques or crafts shop are about the only merchandising in places like Waterford, North Waterford, Center Lovell and Lovell. But do not underestimate the villages' charms. As humorist Artemus Ward wrote of Waterford: "The village from which I write to you is small. It does not contain over forty houses, all told; but they are milk white, with the greenest of blinds, and for the most part are shaded with beautiful elms and willows. To the right of us is a mountain — to the left a lake. The village nestles between. Of course it does. I never read a novel in my life in which the villages didn't nestle. It is a kind of way they have." Waterford hasn't changed much since, nor have its surrounding towns. For action, you have to go north to Bethel, east to Bridgton or southwest to Fryeberg and North Conway.

The lakes. Kezar, quiet and somewhat inaccessible, lies beneath the mighty White Mountain range, its waters reflecting the changing seasons and spectacular sunsets. The lake is relatively undeveloped and private, with access only from the marina at the Narrows, the beach at the end of Pleasant Point Road and a point in North Lovell. The rest of the time you can rarely even see it (much to our dismay, for we got lost trying). Keoka Lake, at Waterford, has a small, pleasant and secluded beach just east of the village and a crowded village beach just south. Hidden lakes and ponds abound.

Antiques. The Bridgton area, in particular, is a center for antiquers, with a brochure describing 23 antiques shops at last count. The new **Oxford Common Antique Center** on Route 26 south of Oxford is a collection of eighteen dealers and shops, among them **Common Scents** with wonderful potpourris and everything frilly, **Classic Country** with gifts and decorative accessories, a country store, and a lunch room and food shop where you can get things like Shaker herbs and pickled fiddleheads.Cynthia Hamilton's antiques in the **1836 Brick Schoolhouse** in Lovell and the **Kayserhof Alpine Village** with a country store and Christmas shop in North Waterford are shopping destinations. At **Craftworks,** ensconced in a refurbished church in Bridgton, we browsed through the baskets, rugs, candles, Maine wines and foods, and some interesting clothing.

Extra-Special

Hard to find but worth the trip is the **Jones Gallery of Glass & Ceramics** off Route 107 on Douglas Hill in Sebago Center. Here are more than 3,000 works of art, everything from Chinese porcelain and Egyptian glass to Wedgwood teapots and Sandwich lamps displayed in brilliant profusion (admission $2.50). The Gallery Shop has original glass and ceramics, plus books, slides and gifts. Open daily, May to mid-November.

Bonnema Pottery on Main Street in Bethel is a studio and showroom where Garret and Melody Bonnema craft and display their pottery in a barn beside their house. Seldom have we seen such appealing colors; according to the Bonnemas, their glazing is influenced by the colors in the mountains and valleys surrounding Bethel. Tankards, tiles, candelabras, casseroles, teapots and much more are their wares. We fell for some small and inexpensive rectangular vases they call "extrusions," just right for a few wildflowers, and bought several for gifts and for ourselves. Open daily.

Inn Street Mall meets Market Square in downtown Newburyport.

Newburyport, Mass.
A Museum of Living History

Native-son novelist John P. Marquand said Newburyport "is not a museum piece although it sometimes looks it." Well it could be.

Like a phoenix rising from the ashes of doldrums and decay, the smallest city in Massachusetts is stirring again. Once one of the nation's most prosperous seaports, Newburyport slept through the Industrial Revolution and fell upon hard times in the 20th century. Residents balked, however, when the downtown waterfront was to be razed in the name of urban renewal. The prized Federal-style downtown, rebuilt in brick after an 1811 fire, was saved. Grand old houses were restored and 19th-century buildings become shops, artisans' studios, restaurants and inns. Brick sidewalks, gas lanterns, benches and landscaping enlivened the streetscape.

Newburyport offers a panorama "of what early America was really like," according to an Historical Society of Old Newbury brochure. Three-quarters of the city is listed on the National Register. The three miles of High Street are flanked by more buildings from the 17th, 18th and early 19th centuries on their original locations than any street in America. Between the elegant residential thoroughfare and the waterfront is an unexpectedly vibrant downtown.

The city is unique in that it never had either a milltown or a Victorian overlay, notes innkeeper Judith Crumb of the Windsor House. "What we have is an intact, homogeneous, late Federal brick downtown, the only one in the country. People come here just to study the architecture."

They come as well to shop in the restored brick buildings, the Inn Street pedestrian mall, the Ice House Marketplace and the Tannery.

Visitors come also for a sense of space near the sea, which is rare along the urban coast. The Parker River National Wildlife Refuge, a seven-mile-long stretch of marshes and dunes on Plum Island east of town, is a haven for ornithologists, beachgoers and solitude seekers. Garden and nature enthusiasts enjoy the flora and fauna of the impressive new Maudslay State Park.

Away from the mainstream, Newburyport has been bypassed by tourists bound for its better-known neighbors. It lacks the obvious history of Portsmouth and Salem, the endearing quaintness of Rockport, the cachet of Marblehead. Yet it combines all those attributes in a low-key way that qualifies it as a special place.

"This is not a tourist center," innkeeper Crumb cautions. "There's no razzle-dazzle. It's a place people come to be in — not to do."

Inn Spots

Morrill Place, 200 High St., Newburyport 01950. (508) 462-2808.

This handsome, square three-story Federalist mansion once was owned by the junior law partner of Daniel Webster (who was a frequent visitor) and later by the town's mayor. It was acquired in 1979 by Rose Ann Hunter, an ex-Ohioan and her young daughter who three years earlier had opened Newburyport's first B&B.

Thanks to its upgrading and redecoration as Newburyport's first decorator showhouse in 1985, it is now a showplace with eleven guest rooms, some of them spacious and with private baths, and with an uncommon number of public rooms. Although the decorators took with them everything afterward but the paint, wallpaper and $22,000 worth of curtains (which Rose Ann bought), she is enthusiastic about the possibilities, making improvements as time and budget permit.

A long, hanging staircase with six-inch risers leads to the second floor. Bedrooms abound with interesting touches, from a painted pink and green rug on one floor that is so realistic we tried to kick down its turned-up corner to the quilted wreaths and animals on the doors, the ivy painted on a radiator, tin pigs holding candles and a cozy window seat in the front upstairs hall. The dining room mantel has been painted to look like marble, and the front doorway is framed with Sandwich glass. In the Daniel Webster Room, his lithograph above the fireplace looks over the big pineapple four-poster bed. Four third-floor rooms share one bath. One has dark exposed beams, the result of the ceiling having been raised a foot because a former occupant was very tall.

The main-floor library, done up in cheerful reds with enormous bookcases, has the inn's only working fireplace and an aquarium bearing Oscar the fish. A pleasant, brick-floored summer porch looks onto a rear patio. Red Sandwich glass decorates the door into the glass-enclosed winter porch on the second floor, a sunny spot in which to relax and watch TV or movies on the VCR. With wicker furniture and dhurrie rugs, it's also the home of two sociable ring-neck doves. Professional musicians occasionally play the grand piano in the music room.

A continental breakfast of muffins and donuts is served at a long table surrounded by Queen Anne chairs in the dining room.

Rose Ann keeps a whirlwind pace as founder of Country Inns of America, a brokerage service for inns and prospective buyers. She leads seminars and lectures around the country, and the innkeeping sometimes takes a back seat to her other endeavors. She also hosts mystery weekends and wedding parties.

Doubles, $60 to $75.

Windsor House, 38 Federal St., Newburyport 01950. (508) 462-3778.

Built in 1786, this was a ship's chandlery downstairs along the street and a residence facing a pleasant little side courtyard. Today it's an authentic and cozy B&B with six guest rooms, three with private baths.

Daniel Webster was a frequent visitor to the Federalist mansion that's now Morrill Place.

The focus is the sunken kitchen, both because of its size (the chandlery's original shipping room — note the large outside doors and the fourteen-foot ceiling) and because that's where guests gather around the big common table for innkeeper Judith Crumb's English breakfasts. A typical repast the day we visited was smoked turkey and ham, scrambled eggs with herbs and tomatoes from the garden, baked beans and and wholewheat toast. Her partner, Jim Lawbaugh, is known for his Sunday festival breakfasts featuring pancakes, homemade maple syrup sauce and sausage.

Off the kitchen is a guest room in the original ship's chandlery, with a brick wall behind the bed and a private entrance from the street. Also on the main floor are an appealing parlor full of books, pictures and even coronation cups and plates from Great Britain (Mrs. Crumb's parents were British) and a keeping room used for receptions and occasionally English tea.

Upstairs on two floors are high-ceilinged bedrooms, ranging from a front corner bridal suite with a full bath to a nanny's room with inside wooden shutters. Everything is at a four-year-old's height in the nursery room. Rust red woodwork and tons of books along one wall add character to the library guest room on the third floor. Furnishings are appropriate to the Colonial, Georgian and Federalist periods — some of them reflecting Judith's heritage, including a portrait of Queen Elizabeth over the parlor mantel.

Doubles, $85 to $115.

The Essex Street Inn, 7 Essex St., Newburyport 01950. (508) 465-3148.

This converted, century-old boarding house has seventeen guest rooms and suites on three floors linked by two parallel stairways and two more at right angles, but nary a common room and no sign of an innkeeper. You register at a front desk hidden behind the stairways, go to your room and might as well be in an anonymous hotel or motel.

The prevailing color scheme is brown and beige, from carpets to patterned wallpaper. Some rooms are small, with double beds and showers, and we felt sorry for anyone

229

Garrison Inn is Newburyport's largest.　　**Courtyard entrance to Windsor House.**

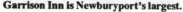

trying to sleep late on the main floor as early risers were departing. Rooms on the third floor have skylights, and one has a spool bed and two rockers. All rooms have phones, television and air-conditioning.

Our one-room "suite" had a working fireplace, a loveseat (the only place to sit and read — no chairs) under a Victorian floor lamp, a queensize four-poster bed, an in-room vanity and two ficus and palm trees that had enjoyed better days. In the enormous bathroom were a jacuzzi bath, a separate shower, a bidet and another sink with chrome and glass fixtures. But the front desk missed our wakeup call, an advance order for continental breakfast in the room would have been $3 each, and we felt all the warmth of a Holiday Inn.

Doubles, $70 to $85; suites, $114.

Garrison Inn, 11 Brown Square, Newburyport 01950. (508) 465-0910.

Renovated into an inn in 1972, this four-story brick structure built in 1809 looks like it belongs in Newburyport's Federalist downtown. Although billing itself as an historic inn, it's really a small hotel with contemporary rooms, a registration desk and an elevator.

Eighteen rooms and six two-level suites with spiral or Colonial staircases have private baths with heat lamps but no extras like shampoos and the like, which you might expect for the price. They are furnished in motel style with reproduction antique furniture, one or two double beds, a desk and a single upholstered wing chair.

The main-floor parlor with a fireplace was occupied by a reception on the day we visited. There are two main-floor dining rooms, one rather formal with Chippendale chairs and another a little more informal, also with reproduction furniture, as well as the downstairs Pub serving a light all-day menu.

Doubles, $65 to $120.

Portside Restaurant and Inn, 421 Bridge Road, Salisbury 01952. (508) 465-1234.

Although best known as a large seafood restaurant with splendid views from its large terrace and dining rooms of the Newburyport waterfront across the Merrimack River, this is also a nicely restored motel with nineteen rooms and four two-bedroom suites, some with kitchenettes.

Each with two queensize beds, the rooms are larger than normal motel rooms and offer full baths, both attributes that are missing in many Newburyport accommodations. Some face the river and others go off the parking lot.

A buffet breakfast is available in the dining room in summer; other times, it's served in the coffee shop. The dinner menu in the vast dining room is priced from $9.75 for a fried clam plate to $16.95 for a twenty-ounce sirloin steak. Lobster pie is $13.50.

Doubles, $70.

Dining Spots

Joseph's Winter Street Cafe, 22 Winter St., Newburyport. (508) 462-1188.

You remember Joseph? He used to have Joseph's Rye on the Rocks, an institution up the coast in Rye, N.H., and also Joseph's Riversmere in Portsmouth. Well, they went the way of so many restaurants. Joseph Pignato tried his hand at teaching and turned up again in 1987 in Newburyport, where he already had been a force behind the founding of the town's two best-known restaurants, 10 Center Street and Scandia, and its highly regarded Alden Merrell Cheesecake Co.

An ebullient man who is typically attired in white and who "*is* his restaurant," according to his manager, he opened this New York-style bistro in 1987 in a good-looking gray shingled building that was part of a train station. Illuminated outside by white lights on trees and inside by candles, it is intimate and romantic at night, with a low dark-beamed ceiling, a pianist playing and gleaming silver dishes and knickknacks reflecting pink lights on the bar. Plans were for the original outdoor patio to be enclosed with a lucite roof for a dine-under-the-stars atmosphere.

The northern Italian and continental cuisine is pleasantly priced from $9.95 for chicken livers madeira to $17.50 for grilled rack of lamb. Service is knowledgeable and flawlessly paced.

Our meal began with a shared appetizer of oysters San Remo ($6.50) and one of the better salads we'd had in a long time, a mix of greens, red cabbage and shredded mozzarella cheese dressed with a dijon vinaigrette. We concurred with one patron's assessment that the rack of lamb was one of the best he'd had, and also liked the skewer of lamb a la Grecque, served with sauteed small red cafe potatoes and a $19 bottle of peppery and flavorful Rutherford Ranch cabernet sauvignon. A creme brulee smothered with fresh raspberries and creme fraiche was a worthy ending for a memorable experience.

Scampi, grilled prawns, scallops provencale, pasta with seafood, mixed grill, filet mignon and Sicilian sausages with roasted peppers are other favorites.

Joseph's also offers an acclaimed jazz brunch on Sundays, at which you might order anything from grilled Lucanico sausage to berries and clotted cream to chicken livers with sour cream and caviar, priced up to $11.95.

Dinner nightly except Monday, 5 to midnight; Sunday, 4 to 8. Sunday brunch to 4.

Scandia, 25 State St., Newburyport. (508) 462-6271.

The reason for the name escapes us, but there's no denying the romance of this dark, intimate storefront restaurant with candles lit even at noontime. The ambiance is Edwardian, chandeliers set an elegant theme, and lucky (?) couples at two tables on either side of the recessed entry get to see and be seen in the front windows.

The dinner menu is continental and rather limited. Six appetizers ($5.95 to $6.25) include seafood sausage, veal pate and baked oysters brie. The ten entrees range from $13.95 for chicken prosciutto to $17.95 for steak Diane; rack of lamb with mustard mint sauce or chutney is $34.95 for two. Shrimp and scallop curry, stuffed yellowtail sole and salmon en croute are seafood standbys. Meals include a salad with a choice of five dressings, including fennel-herb and maple-curry.

Many of the same items (as well as salads, sandwiches and entrees like Moroccan chicken) are available at lunch at prices from $5.95 to $8.95, but we think the candlelit and formal atmosphere is more appealing at an evening meal.

Lunch, Monday-Saturday 11:30 to 3; dinner, Monday-Thursday 5 to 10, Friday and Saturday 6 to 10; Sunday, brunch noon to 4, dinner 5 to 10.

Ten Center St., 10 Center St., Newburyport. (508) 462-6652.

Built in 1790 as the home and shop of a baker, this restaurant was much expanded in 1987 following a kitchen fire. The original tavern and a Colonial dining room upstairs remain, but the building was tripled in size with a reception area, two more upstairs dining rooms and an outdoor deck.

Seating upstairs varies from formal and elegant in the brick-walled Colonial room to light and airy in the contemporary, skylit addition. Dinner in the downstairs pub is dark and intimate and obviously very popular.

Chef Stephen Farrell's eight-page dinner menu is extensive and continental. Two pages are devoted to appetizers, soups and salads, ranging from chilled gazpacho for $2.50 to fettuccine alfredo or smoked salmon for $7.95. More than two dozen entrees are listed under seafood, veal, pasta, poultry and beef at prices from $11.95 for sherried chicken livers to $22.50 for lobster Newbury. Sole with bananas, Brazilian shrimp, Irish veal with smoked salmon, and veal and oysters are some out-of-the ordinary dishes. A house favorite is chicken breasts garnished with prosciutto, mushrooms, artichoke hearts and parmesan cheese.

Entrees are $4.95 to $10.95 at lunch, and $8.95 to $12.95 at Sunday brunch. The pub menu served nightly from 5:30 to 10:30 in the convivial bar is a bargain, with a dozen choices like baked cod with crabmeat, lemon chicken with caper sauce and fricadelles of veal from $4.95 to $10.95.

Lunch, Monday-Saturday 11:30 to 3; dinner, 5:30 to 10:30; Sunday, brunch 10:30 to 3, dinner 4:30 to 10.

Glenn's Galley, 388 Merrimac St., Newburyport. (508) 465-3811.

This is the kind of restaurant we are always looking for and don't often find — by the water, casual but with creative cooking flair. Unfortunately, chef-owner Glenn Mayers had it up for sale in hopes of finding a less seasonal operation.

Hidden behind a marina beside a scenic bend in the river at the west end of town, it's hard to find, but knowing locals consider it the most exciting restaurant around. The atmosphere is casual both inside the pine-walled structure with its pretty light fixtures and outside on a screened porch beside the water.

Glenn cooked in Boston, the Southwest and California before opening his own place. He serves up the likes of Texas or Cajun mixed grill and Maine lobster basted with ginger and garlic from his wood-fired grill in the $10 to $13 range. The nightly specials demand attention: when we visited, blackened bluefin tuna steak with ginger and pineapple salsa, broiled Norwegian salmon with sweet roasted red pepper puree, and grilled swordfish with andouille sausage and crabmeat cream. The pasta was raviolis with lobster and wild mushrooms, basil and garlic.

Entrees are garnished with herbs and flowers, and come with garden salad and vegetable or starch of the day. Wines are interesting (Connecticut, Massachusetts and

Colonial dining room is reflected in mirror at Ten Center St.

Vermont wineries are represented, along with Texas, Washington and California), offered at down-to-earth prices.

"Burn Your Britches" chili, spicy marinated shrimp, chili pesto oysters, nachos and mexi-skins are among the fiery appetizers. Cool off, perhaps, with a mocha hazelnut torte or chocolate mousse cake for dessert.

Just hope, with us, that Glenn's Galley (or at least his cooking) will continue to spark up the area for a long time.

Lunch, noon to 2; dinner, 5:30 to 10 or 11; open April-September.

The Grog Shop, 13 Middle St., Newburyport. (508) 465-8008.

Always crowded, this ramble of rooms with a lively pub downstairs and the quieter Grog Too upstairs is immensely popular with the locals for lunch, dinner and even Sunday breakfast.

The fold-out menu is cutesy and extensive, from "rude food" (chili) and veggie boboli pizza to Thai chicken and Long Island duckling. A Mexican fiesta platter is $8.25, and dinner entrees are good values from $6.95 for chicken or beef sate to $12.95 for grilled scampi.

Among the nine salads during the election campaign of 1988 were Dukakis Greek and Bush spinach. Sandwiches in the $3 and $4 range appeal, and the King of Clubs sandwich ($4.95) can be split for two. No wonder the Grog, whose predecessors date back to the Civil War, is still packing in the crowds.

Lunch and dinner daily, 11:30 to 1 a.m.; Sunday breakfast, 8 to 11.

One Threadneedle Alley, 1 Threadneedle Alley, Newburyport. (508) 465-6601.

The folks from Scandia opened this casual, new eatery almost across the street from their formal restaurant. The main-floor bar is apt to be crowded and noisy, but upstairs is a small dining room with a few window tables overlooking State Street and a trendy,

233

all-day menu of things like California burger ($5.75), sweet potato french fries ($1.95) and New England egg rolls ($5.95).

Entrees served after 5 p.m. range from $7.95 for vegetable stir-fry to $14.95 for chargrilled prime rib. Barbecue items, chicken teriyaki and the day's catch are among the possibilities. With the special blend of coffee touched with chocolate mint, try the strawberry amaretto cake or lemon mousse pie.

Open daily, 11:30 to midnight.

Middle Street Foods, 25 Middle St., Newburyport. (508) 465-8333.

Here is a specialty-foods store, take-out deli and cafe in which patrons take their meals to tiny round tables, seat themselves on folding chairs, and lunch on some of the best food in town amidst a backdrop of classical music, shelves of oils, vinegars and mustards, and hustle and bustle.

The soups and pastries are to die for, we were informed, and the thick and hearty lentil soup and a toffee bar lived up to advance billing. The choice of three salads ($5.25) made an ample and interesting lunch; we wished our burrito with homemade salsa had not been served lukewarm.

Sandwiches are made with breads like onion-dill or anadama; there are small whole wheat pizzas, torta rustica, spring rolls and turkey pot pies. Pick out a seltzer from the cooler, have a chocolate-raspberry tart for dessert, and enjoy.

Open daily from 7 to 7, weekends from 8 to 6.

The Mall, 140 High St., Newburyport. (508) 465-5506.

Long a local hangout, this was rechristened a Yankee grill by new owners in 1988. It's named for the mall, an historic parkland across the street, and is pronounced mal (rhymes with pal, as in England) by the locals.

Potato skins and nachos, omelets and salads, sandwiches and pizzas are the all-day fare. The Yankee grill marinade of apple, soy, lemon and herbs enhances the sirloin tips, chicken and shrimp, or combinations thereof, priced from $7.98 to $12.98 (all the prices end inexplicably in "8"). Some entrees are pecan blackened, and the grilled duckling comes with an orange green peppercorn sauce. The house salad is an extra 98 cents.

Ice cream drinks and liqueured coffees (all $3.88) are featured on a short dessert list.

Open daily, 11:30 to midnight.

Captain's Quarters, Brown's Wharf, 54 Merrimac St., Newburyport. (508) 462-3397.

A new dining room overlooks the Merrimack River, and two large outdoor decks take advantage of the view. Although some think the scenery is better from the Portside across the river (after all, there you get to see Newburyport), this is a favorite with those who want to eat lobster beside the water.

The menu is standard, from broiled scrod ($8.25) to baked lobster pie ($12.95). There's lots of fried seafood, prime rib and sirloin can be blackened, and a clambake with lobster, clams and the trimmings is $18.95.

The cooking begins at 6 a.m. with breakfast and continues all day.

Open daily, 6 a.m. to 9 p.m. (Monday to 3).

Michael's Harborside, Tournament Wharf, Newburyport. (508) 462-7785.

Beside the Route 1 bridge, this is another large establishment favored by those who like their fish beside the water. Baked stuffed haddock ($10.50) is owner Michael Roy's favorite, but you also can get charbroiled swordfish, baked stuffed shrimp and surf and turf for $8.95 to $12.95.

234

Cushing House is one of landmark structures along architecturally rich High Street.

Here there are fried seafood and chicken plates, (the fisherman's combination is $12.95), and sandwiches are available. Strawberry shortcake is the dessert specialty.

Lunch, 11:30 to 3:30; dinner, 5 to 10; hours vary in winter.

Diversions

Historic buildings, nature preserves and shopping are the triple attractions for visitors.

The downtown area is remarkable for its elegant brick Federalist architecture, some choice old homes and the beautiful Unitarian Church, whose photogenic spire is grandly illuminated at night. Wander around the main and side streets to savor the surprises at almost every turn. This is a good walking city, especially along the Inn Street pedestrian mall, nicely landscaped and with a modernistic playground for youngsters, the riverfront boardwalk and Market Square.

Custom House Maritime Museum, 25 Water St. The Classic Revival custom house built in 1835 provides a good introduction to Newburyport, particularly its enlightening fifteen-minute video presentation. Exhibits relate to the Coast Guard, which was founded here, as well as maritime history, shipbuilding and foreign trade. The John P. Marquand Library contains many of the novelist's treasures. Open Monday-Saturday 10 to 4:30 and Sunday 1 to 4, mid-March through December; Monday-Friday 10 to 4, rest of year. Adults, $1.50.

High Street, a three-mile-long residential thoroughfare where the rich once lived (and many still do), is the site of three attractions. The **Bartlett Mall** contains a fountain known as the Frog Pond, the old Hill Burying Ground, the Old Jail built of Rockport granite, and a brick courthouse designed by Charles Bulfinch.

The **Cushing House** (1808), a stark white, three-story Federalist mansion at 98 High St., is operated as a house museum by the Historical Society of Old Newbury. The 21 rooms have priceless paintings, furniture and accessories, the library has valuable manuscripts and the gardens contain century-old plants. Open May-October, Tuesday-Saturday 10 to 4, Sunday 2 to 5; other times by appointment. Adults, $2.

The **Coffin House,** across the city line in Newbury at 14-16 High St. (Route 1A), is vastly different, dating back to 1654 though later expanded. The structural details and furnishings reflect generations of Coffin family residents. Owned and operated by the

Society for the Preservation of New England Antiquities, it's open from June through mid-October on Tuesday, Thursday, Saturday and Sunday from noon to 5. Adults, $2.50.

Parker River National Wildlife Refuge, Plum Island. The southern two-thirds of Plum Island just off Newburyport facing the Atlantic is a choice wildlife refuge. It's so choice, in fact, that you're advised to arrive by 9 or 10 on a summer weekend if you hope to get one of the 150 parking places; otherwise, you don't get in. The ride along the seven-mile road, which starts paved and turns to dirt, is pleasant enough, looking at the colorful dunes and the flocks of Canada geese. But you should park and take the trails over the dunes to the beach or, better, the boardwalks of the Hellcat Swamp wildlife trail and observation tower (Parking Lot 4). One of the few natural barrier beach-dune-saltmarsh complexes left on the Northeast coast, the 4,662 acres harbor more than 300 species of birds along the Atlantic flyway. Beachcombing and swimming (by the rugged — there's a strong undertow) as well as beach plum and cranberry picking are popular pastimes. As you leave this remarkable haven, you may be surprised to see the "So Long, See Ya' Later" farewell on the back of the "Welcome to Plum Island" sign. Open daily, dawn to dusk; $5 per vehicle.

Shopping. The brick sidewalks, the old mews and careful landscaping enhance a shopping experience that is more prominent here than in most cities its size. At the **Tannery,** 12 Federal St., is one of our favorite bookshops, the **Jabberwocky.** Next to it is the **Jabberwocky Cafe,** where you can get light breakfasts, lunches, coffee and desserts. **Homespun Gatherings** is a crafts co-op where you can find handicrafts, antiques and country things, and Henry's Hippo has cute children's clothing and toys. We saw some interesting Australian clothing at **Endeavour Trading Company** and some heavenly desserts at **Nutcracker Cookery.**

Something Sweet, at 21 Market Square, sells homemade saltwater taffy and fruit slices, as well as truffles, caramel corn and fudge. **Sueffles** at 14 Market Square is a kitchen shop and takeout. Try the broccoli pecan salad or "our unbeatable chicken tarragon" served in a pita pocket. Or pick up a picnic basket to take to the beach. The shops at Merrimac Landing are worth a peek. **Aurora** has interesting women's clothing and **Mahri,** jewelry and gifts. Along the Inn Street Mall, stop at the **Rose Medallion** for gifts and cards or at **Churchills** to look at the art and unusual jewelry. **State Street Candle & Mug** has room after room of coffee beans, candles, mugs and gifts, and smells heavenly. **Gabriel** at 90 Pleasant St. sells men's and women's brand-name clothing, including Evan Picone, at 20 to 30 percent off. And, of course, there's a **Benetton** — isn't there always?

Extra-Special

Maudslay State Park, Curzon's Mill Road. (508) 465-7223. Rarely is a state park so special, but this is a new one like no other. Established in 1985, the 485-acre park with two miles of frontage along the Merrimack River was formerly the Mosely estate, named for the family's ancestral home in England. It has lovely 19th-century ornamental gardens, pastoral meadows, pine forests and one of the largest natural stands of mountain laurel in eastern Massachusetts (the sight of the last inspired several poems by John Greenleaf Whittier). Don't expect to drive through and see much of the park; like so much of Newburyport, you have to get out, walk and immerse yourself in it to enjoy it. A state brochure points out park features and three walks of twenty to ninety minutes. When we visited, a children's theater was in residence and autumn hayrides were offered to pick pumpkins and gourds. Hiking, jogging, horseback riding, biking, walking and picnicking are particularly good here. Open daily, 8 to 7.

Motif No. 1 is a must-see attraction for visitors to Rockport.

Rockport, Mass.
Bargains by the Sea

They certainly don't need more crowds, these habituees of Bearskin Neck, Pigeon Cove and Marmion Way. Nor do those who cater to them.

But bargain-conscious travelers can seldom do better than in Rockport, the seaside Cape Ann resort town where the costs of food and lodging consistently remain five years behind the times.

Last we knew, lobster dinners were going for $7.95 at Ellen's Harborside. Rooms in the finest inns and motels cost $60 to $90, about one-third less than they'd command in equivalent locations elsewhere.

Why such bargains? Because Rockport was developed earlier, when costs were lower, than many such coastal resorts. "We were bed and breakfast long before the craze started," notes Leighton Saville, co-innkeeper at Seacrest Manor. Adds William Balzarini, owner of the Old Farm Inn: "The inns here keep their prices down because they don't have new mortgages with high rates." Rockport's century-old ban on the sale of liquor has influenced prices, if only in lowering restaurant tabs when patrons BYOB.

The bargains help swell Rockport's year-round population of 7,000 to 35,000 in summer. Most, it seems, are on the streets near Dock Square and Bearskin Neck. Parking is usually a problem (arrive early or expect to park on distant side streets and walk).

Visitors are drawn by the rocky coast more typical of Maine, the atmosphere of an old fishing village crammed with shops, the quaintness of a "dry" town in which Sunday evening band concerts are the major entertainment, and the lively arts colony inspired by a harbor listed by Walt Disney Productions as one of the nation's most scenic. In fact, Motif No. 1, a fishing shack on the wharf, is outranked as an artist's image only by the Mona Lisa. When it collapsed in the Blizzard of 1978, villagers quickly rebuilt it — such is the place of art (and tourism) in Rockport. The village planned a gala 150th birthday celebration (marking its severance from adjacent Gloucester) for 1990.

All around Rockport are the varied assets of the rest of Cape Ann. They range from the English look of quiet Annisquam, which is New England at its quaintest, to the working fishing flavor of busy Gloucester.

The allure of Rockport is so strong that its devotees return time and again. Crowded it may be, but it's hard to beat the prices.

Inn Spots

Eden Pines Inn, Eden Road, Rockport 01966. (508) 546-2505.

You can't get much closer to the ocean than on the rear patio that hovers over the rocks — or, for that matter, in five of the upstairs guest rooms — at this delightfully secluded inn by the sea.

The setting in what was formerly a summer home could not be more appealing. The lodge-like front parlor with fieldstone fireplace, the California-style side breakfast porch with white furniture and picture windows, the rear porch full of lounge chairs with brick patio below, even a couple of bathroom windows take full advantage of the water view across to Thatchers Island and its twin lighthouses. Although the shore here is rocky, the inn is within walking distance of two beaches.

The six upstairs guest rooms, all with private baths, are unusually spacious. Most have two double beds (Room 6 has striking white seersucker and lace curtains enclosing a canopied bed) and private balconies over the water. We'd choose Room 4, all beige and blue in decorator fabrics with thick carpeting, a comfortable sitting area and an enormous bathroom done in Italian marble with a bathtub, a separate shower and a large window onto the ocean next to the marble vanity.

Innkeeper Inge Sullivan, a blonde dynamo who is partial to marble and pastel fabrics, has redecorated all the rooms in California colors and style.

She and her husband serve a continental breakfast that includes Scandinavian pastries, fruit salad and muffins, as well as mid-afternoon tea and setups for drinks. We know of few more picturesque places for the last than the lounge chairs on the rear patio smack beside the ocean.

The Sullivans also rent a four-bedroom house down the street, $150 a night for two and $200 for four, plus a three-bedroom apartment on Bearskin Neck, $525 a week.

Doubles, $84 to $95; two-night minimum. Open May-November.

Seacrest Manor, 131 Marmion Way, Rockport 01966. (508) 546-2211.

If Eden Pines has the ocean setting and decorator's flair, Seacrest has the lawns and gardens and a breakfast to remember. It also has a sweeping view of the ocean beyond the trees from its second-story deck above the living room.

Leighton T. Saville and Dwight B. MacCormack Jr. have been running their inn since 1972, so personally that many of the repeat guests have left gifts — their own watercolors of the inn, crocheted pillows and countless knickknacks, including a collection of rabbits "which just keep multiplying, as rabbits are prone to do," according to Leighton.

The main-floor library displays many British magazines ("our English guests tell us it feels like home"). The elegant living room where afternoon tea is served has a masculine feel with leather chairs, dark colors and fine paintings, as well as exquisite stained glass and tiny bottles in the bow windows.

The formal dining room is decked out in fancy red linen, Wedgwood china and crystal glasses at five tables for a breakfast that Town & Country magazine called one of the 50 best in America. It begins with fresh fruit cup and fresh orange juice, continues with spiced Irish oatmeal and bacon and eggs, and ends with a specialty like blueberry or apple pancakes, french toast or corn fritters.

Guests have the run of the two-acre property, which includes a remarkable, century-old red oak shading the entire front yard, prolific gardens, a couple of statues and a rope hammock strung between trees in a rear corner. The flower beds supply the small bouquets scattered through the inn.

Six of the eight guest rooms have private baths. Rooms are comfortable if plain; each

Ocean lies just behind Eden Pines Inn.

has kingsize or twin beds, color television, clock radio, a couple of chairs and a desk. The inn touch comes with mints on the bedside table with nightly turndown service, fine soaps and shampoos, overnight shoe shines, and a complimentary Boston Globe at the door in the morning.

Seacrest Manor is a special place that measures up to its motto, "decidedly small, intentionally quiet."

Doubles, $68 to $90. Closed mid-December to mid-February.

Addison Choate Inn, 49 Broadway, Rockport 01966. (508) 546-7543.

An in-town location, a prized antiques collection, a rear swimming pool and some of the best-furnished rooms around draw guests to this attractive, flower-bedecked house built in 1851 and boasting Rockport's first bathtub — in the kitchen, no less.

That bathtub has been replaced, of course, but all seven guest rooms and a two-room suite have large and modern hand-tiled bathrooms with pewter faucets. Each is furnished with rare antiques; the lamps in the blue room with a stunning canopied pine bed are intriguing. The third-floor suite has Laura Ashley fabrics and a stained-glass skylight in the bathroom.

The inn's public rooms include an eclectic parlor with a big leather pig and museum-quality ship's models, a small rear library with TV and rosy mauve benches, and a small dining room with a quilt on one wall.

German-born innkeeper Margot Sweet serves a continental breakfast of fruits and fresh-baked muffins at intimate tables for two on the narrow side porch or in the dining room.

The rear Stable House contains two housekeeping suites with loft bedrooms. The greenhouse suite with a baby grand piano, a spiral staircase and skylights in the bathroom and bedroom has particular flair. Beyond is the small, tree-shaded pool area, so secluded in heart-of-Rockport terms "that you think you're up in the mountains," says Margot.

Doubles, $72 to $79; suites, $100 to $105. No smoking. Closed in winter.

The Inn on Cove Hill, 37 Mount Pleasant St., Rockport 01966. (508) 546-2701.

Close to the heart of town and with a fine view of Motif No. 1 and the harbor from its rear third-floor deck is this Federal-style mansion built in 1791. It's surrounded by a white picket fence and lovingly tended gardens.

Innkeepers Marjorie and John Pratt have completed a lengthy restoration and redecoration of the former guest house. Nine of the eleven bedrooms have private baths; two on the third floor share. Each is nicely decorated in Laura Ashley fabrics and wallpapers, and each has a small black and white television set. Most rooms sport handmade quilts and afghans and crocheted coverlets as well as oriental-style rugs.

The Pratts like to point out the structure's architectural features — such as the spiral staircase with thirteen steps in the entry hall — and the antique furnishings in the small common room. On the coffee table is a book called "Taster's Tattles and Titillations," written by guests who share their local dining experiences. It makes for lively reading.

A continental breakfast with muffins is served on English bone china at outdoor tables topped by yellow and white umbrellas in the side garden or on trays in the bedrooms in cool weather.

Recipes for eight of the Pratts' popular muffins (oatmeal, orange buttermilk and pumpkin, among them) have been printed for guests. A note is appended to the end: "If you find that your muffins are failing, we have conspired to leave out one essential ingredient from each of the recipes; that is umbrella tables in the summer and breakfast in bed in the winter. For access to both, come see us."

Doubles, $44 to $80. Closed late October through March.

Sally Webster Inn, 34 Mount Pleasant St., Rockport 01966. (508) 546-9251.

A good-looking gray house with red shutters and a lovely fan door, this 1832 structure has six guest rooms, each named for one of its former occupants and each with private bath.

The front parlor is known as "Sally's Share," because that is the part of the house that Sally Webster inherited from her father, who built it. It is graced with Sally's Bible, as well as a rather grim-faced portrait of her. Sally's great-great-great-granddaughter has stayed in the inn and gave innkeeper Janet Webster (no relation) more family artifacts.

Double canopy, pencil-post four-poster and Jenny Lind beds are in the guest rooms. Each is attractively furnished to the period and outfitted with colorful ice buckets and a tote bag with which to take your wine to local restaurants.

Janet serves continental breakfast with muffins and biscuits at tables charmingly set with mismatched china and silver in the dining room.

Doubles, $60 to $68. Open April-November plus February and March weekends.

Yankee Clipper Inn, Route 127, Box 2399, Rockport 01966. (508) 546-3407.

One of Rockport's larger and older inns, the Yankee Clipper has been run since 1946 by Fred and Lydia Wemyss and lately by their daughter and son-in-law, Barbara and Bob Ellis.

It began with nine rooms in the main inn, a Georgian mansion situated amid beautifully landscaped lawns on a bit of a point jutting into the ocean. More were added in the 1840 Bulfinch-designed neo-classic mansion across the road, and more contemporary rooms are in the Quarterdeck built in 1960 beside the water. The last has a third-floor penthouse suite with ruffled pillows on two double beds, a sofabed, and two velvet chairs facing floor-to-ceiling windows onto the ocean.

In the inn, there's a grandly furnished living room on the main floor. Downstairs is a new function room, in which chairs are lined up in front of a huge VCR, with a bunch of films at the ready.

Century-old red oak shades front of Seacrest Manor.

The L-shaped dining porch takes advantage of the ocean view. With blue linens and white wrought-iron chairs, it's for non-smokers only; the inner dining room is for smokers.

The food ranges from down-home Yankee to continental. Filet of scrod is topped with sea scallops, Vermont cheddar cheese and galliano cream sauce, scallops are served au gratin in a puff-pastry sea shell, and the steak is grilled with green peppercorn sauce. Veal saltimbocca, chicken saute Creole, tournedos of beef with grand marnier and rich tomato garlic sauces, and lamb chops with mint-onion marmalade are other choices, priced from $9.95 to $18.50. The chocolate grand marnier cake is a favored dessert.

Guests like to check the blackboard on the dining porch for announcements and Fred Wemyss's latest limericks, which he composes as the mood or situation strikes.

The heated saltwater pool is unusually attractive and hidden from the public eye on the nicely landscaped, terraced grounds.

Doubles, $138 to $186, MAP; Bulfinch House, $87 to $96, B&B. Open mid-May to late October.

Seaward Inn, Marmion Way, Rockport 01966. (508) 546-3471.

Across the street from the ocean in a residential area on attractive grounds full of gardens, lawn chairs, boulders and stone fences is this complex of inn, cottages and guest house, totaling 38 rooms with private baths.

Some guests prefer the oceanfront Breakers, a shingled house with a common room and nine homey guest rooms, each with two chairs and a telephone. Others like the accommodations in single or multi-unit cottages.

The main inn has ten rooms as well as a large front common room with flagstone floor, rattan furniture and windows onto the ocean. The beamed dining room is divided into several sections; one wall is strung with clothes pins that have held guests' napkins with their names over the last ten years. Dinner, served nightly to guests, offers a choice of two entrees — roast beef and seafood newburg the night we visited.

White stucco Captain's House hugs waterfront.

"Gracious informality is the way of life at Seaward," according to longtime inn-keepers Roger and Anne Cameron. Their information sheet asks men to wear jackets at dinner "and you ladies look lovely in dresses or pantsuits." At bedtime, the sheet advises, "yes, we too like our glass of milk. Come to the kitchen and let your wants be known."

Doubles, $120 to $156, MAP. Open mid-May to mid-October.

The Captain's House, Marmion Way, Rockport 01966. (508) 546-3825.

A fabulous location right at water's edge commends this white stucco mansion, billed as "a comfortable and casual guest house" by owners Carole and George Dangerfield. Although they've owned it for 21 years, both the exterior and interior have been upgraded lately.

There's a wraparound porch, part of it open to the ocean and the rest enclosed for a library and TV. Inside are a huge parlor with beamed ceiling and fireplace, and a handsome dining room that catches a glimpse of the ocean.

Upstairs are five guest rooms with private baths. Two rooms are particularly large, and those in front have the best views. Each is done in turn-of-the-century wallpaper, have hand-creweled embroidery on the valances, and reproduction Williamsburg furnishings.

Sour cream blueberry coffee cake, muffins and fruit breads are served for continental breakfast in the dining room or on the porches, where guests "feel closer to the water," Carole says. They really feel close to the water in the lounge chairs spread along the rocky shore.

Doubles, $70 to $80. Open April-November

Old Farm Inn, 291 Granite St. (Pigeon Cove), Rockport. (508) 546-3237.

For years, this was tops on everyone's list of favorite eating spots on Cape Ann. The restaurant, run with tender loving care since 1964 by the Balzarini family, was closed in 1986 and Susan and Bill Balzarini have concentrated since on their B&B operation.

The inn is housed in a red structure with white trim built in 1799 and once part of a dairy farm (the Balzarini grandchildren's ponies still graze in the meadow). One of the original dining rooms has been converted to a parlor (the others are closed off); here, in something that resembles grandma's sitting room, sherry and cookies are available in the afternoon. The sprightly garden room with its windows looking out onto birch trees and its 80-year-old cast-iron stove is where guests take breakfast every morning. The fare includes fresh fruit and juice, cereals (and sometimes oatmeal in winter), yogurt, muffins and coffee cake.

Upstairs are three guest rooms with fireplaces, each with private bath and television, wide-plank floors and furnished with antiques. The barn out back has four guest rooms, all with private bath and TV and small refrigerators. They're recently upgraded, comfortable with country decor and rather motel-like.

Doubles, $70 to $78. Closed January-March.

Dining Spots

Hungry Wolf Restaurant, 43 South St., Rockport. (508) 283-8194.

The best restaurant in town in the summer of 1988 was a newcomer, relocated from its old haunt in Gloucester's Rocky Neck. Locals had high hopes for owners Charlie and Laura Wolf to succeed year-round in a spot where others had failed.

Off the tourist path, the Hungry Wolf looks a bit like a country bistro, thanks to Laura's decorating talents: pink, white and deep blue linens, gathered lace curtains, the works of a Rocky Neck artist on the walls, and votive candles and bouquets of fresh flowers on each table. A picture of a wolf in a dinner jacket, with knife and fork in hand, adorns both the entrance and the menu and sets a whimsical theme.

Charlie specializes in fresh fish, vegetables and produce that he shops for each morning. The deceptively simple menu lists a dozen entrees from $9.95 for pork chops or chicken teriyaki to $13.95 for four presentations of sirloin steak (plain, teriyaki, dijon or with garlic butter). Grilled Norwegian salmon with dilled hollandaise sauce might be a special. Start with scallops wrapped in bacon, Italian fish soup or ratatouille au gratin. Homemade croutons dress the complimentary caesar and garden salads. Sourdough bread, rice or potatoes, and fresh vegetables accompany.

Laura makes the desserts, including amaretto bread pudding, peanut-butter fudge brownie pie, apple crisp and pecan pie.

Dinner, Monday-Saturday 5 to 9:30.

The Galley, Bearskin Neck, Rockport. (508) 546-3721.

For more than 25 years, Mike Parillo has been running this no-nonsense restaurant his way, with little in the way of decor beyond some stained glass, hanging plants and a sensational harbor view outside.

The simple menu is augmented by many blackboard specials. "I've had hundreds of dishes," Mike explains, saying he never could have lasted 25 years "without making it interesting, if only for me to maintain enthusiasm for what I do."

When we visited, the appetizers were asparagus spears vinaigrette and clish chowder (you guessed it, for clams and fish), both $2.75. Atlantic chowder — "all good things from the Atlantic," from haddock to lobster — is served in three-size portions ($2.10 to $4.25). Entrees included fresh tuna saute, lobster stew, an avocado, lobster and crabmeat salad plate, baked shrimp Michel and chicken marsala, all in the $10 to $12 range. Listed among "delicious, delicious decisions" for dessert were cheesecake with brandied fruits, lime cream pie and a fresh peach pie with real whipped cream.

The Galley sells its Atlantic chowder and pecan pies for takeout.

Lunch 11 to 5, dinner 5 to 7:30; closed Tuesday. Cash only.

My Place, 72 Bearskin Neck, Rockport. (508) 546-9667.

When Cristull and Robert Sheath decided to open a restaurant in 1982 in an old black and yellow tea house at the very end of Bearskin Neck, they didn't know what to call it, Christull said, "so we called it My Place."

Now taken over by their chef, Charles Kreis, My Place seems to be missing Christull's feminine touch and attention to detail.

You can't argue with the ambiance, blessed with an unbelievable location on the rocks at water's edge and decidedly romantic with an un-Rockport-like rose and aqua color scheme and, at night, flaming torches and pink and blue spotlights on the rocks. As flute music plays while the sun sets, the setting is magical for diners on the two flower-lined outdoor decks and, indeed, for people across Sandy Bay who admire the sight as well.

You can argue with the food, at least at our latest lunch. The menu was pedestrian and expensive (a peanut butter sandwich for $4, "with jelly" for $4.50). Our BLT ($4.50) was a travesty, a tiny sandwich made with wooden winter tomatoes (in August, mind you) at the side of a large white plate devoid of anything but a slice of watermelon. The chef's salad ($7.50) was a mass of slivers of ham, roast beef, chicken and cheese heaped on a bed of iceberg lettuce, with a side of dressing and again a slice of watermelon.

Chef Chaz, who arrived from the market as we were leaving, apologized and said our experience was an aberration. He promised better things at dinner, when entrees are priced from $10.50 for baked scrod in lemon butter to $18 for steak au poivre.

The setting remains one of the best for a restaurant anywhere.

Lunch, noon to 3; dinner, 5 to 9:30; closed Wednesday. Open mid-May-October.

The Greenery, 15 Dock Square, Rockport. (508) 546-9593.

The name bespeaks the theme of this casual place, but nothing prepares one for the view of Motif No. 1 across the harbor from the butcherblock tables at the rear of the L-shaped dining room.

Seafood and salads ($5.25 to $10.95) are featured, as is a salad bar and an ice cream and pastry bar out front. Otherwise the fare runs from what the owners call gourmet sandwiches to dinner entrees like seafood casserole, seafood linguini, chicken Milano and crab salad quiche ($7.50 to $13.95).

For sandwiches, how about the Sproutwich — muenster and cheddar cheeses, mushrooms and sunflower seeds, crammed with sprouts and served with choice of dressing ($3.95). You could order a lobster or crab roll, or a charbroiled hamburger.

Apple pie with streusel topping and cheesecake with fresh strawberries are popular desserts ($2.95 to $3.45). The chocolate chambord and amaretto cheesecakes are available to go.

Open daily, 10 to 9 weekdays, 9 to 10 weekends, May-October.

Ellen's Harborside, 1 T-Wharf, Rockport. (508) 546-2512.

Wholesome food, reasonably priced, is the attraction at this plain, local institution with a front counter and tables and a rear dining room overlooking the water. Crowds start lining up for supper at 4:30 for what other restaurateurs attribute to "total value." When was the last time you saw a dinner menu in which almost everything is in the single digits and drink set-ups are free?

The breakfast special could be eggs Benedict for $3.95. You can get a clam roll for $4.95 along with more mundane fare for lunch, and dinners run from $5.25 for fried squid to $11.95 for lazy lobster, prime rib or Delmonico steak. Most desserts like cranberry-raspberry and orange-pineapple cream pies and pineapple-tapioca pudding are $1.25; the most expensive item when we visited was Ellen's carrot cake with cream cheese frosting ($1.75).

Open daily from 5:30 a.m., early spring through late fall.

Sea Level Cafe, Bearskin Neck, Rockport. (508) 546-2180.

Ensconced on two levels of a stone building with the servers scurrying on the steep

Dining on deck at water's edge is the appeal of My Place.

and narrow stairs between, this new cafe really is at sea level — at least, the lower floor is. Here, the chairs at half a dozen tables and a counter facing the window look onto the water and the setting is nicely nautical, from white chairs and blue and white oilcloths to stone floors and a tray of mustards and relishes beneath a tiny umbrella on each table.

We liked the clam chowder, very creamy and accented with a dash of paprika, and the baked stuffed clams ($2.95) are highly acclaimed. Lunch might be quiche of the day, bacon burger or Italian sandwich (all $3.25) or lobster salad ($7.50). Dinner entrees go from $6.75 for a hot roast beef sandwich with mushroom gravy to $11.95 for boiled lobster. The dishwasher's sister bakes the fabulous pies (among them key lime, pecan and peach pie with granola topping). The chef's mother does the fudge brownies, strawberry shortcake and chocolate mousse pie.

Lunch, 11 to 4; dinner, 5 to 9:30 or 10; weekends only in spring and fall. Closed in winter.

Cove Court Gourmet, Bearskin Neck, Rockport. (508) 546-9249.

Picnics, along with a map of where to take them, are the forte of this new delicatessen cum shop cum restaurant in the heart of Bearskin Neck.

Baked goods and bagels are the breakfast fare. Lunchtime brings pita sandwiches ($2.95), fancy salads ($5.95 to $8.95), French country pate with brie, pesto pasta with chicken or shrimp, and several quiches with salad ($5.95). The dinner menu offers orange-teriyaki chicken, seafood linguini, baked scallops, baked stuffed shrimp and sirloin steak, priced from $9.95 to $12.95, as well as light fare like a summer salad plate and cold pasta plate.

There's a small dining room in the rear with not much of a view, and a shop selling T-shirts and specialty foods up front.

Open daily, 8:30 a.m. to 9:30 p.m. Closed in winter.

Helmut's Strudel, 49 Bearskin Neck, Rockport. (508) 546-2824.

This is not a restaurant as such (although you may share a small rear deck with a seagull or two on a few weathered captain's chairs, put your coffee on a rail and savor the view of the harbor). But this small bakery makes a good stop for heavenly strudels (apple, cherry, cheese, almond and apricot, 90 cents a slice), blueberry croissants (95 cents), coffee, tea and "the best hot chocolate in town." The strudel is real Austrian style with 81 layers of puff pastry. Helmut's is a good break from Bearskin Neck's prevailing seafood and ice cream.

Diversions

The Seashore. Rockport is aptly named — it has the rocky look of the Maine coast, in contrast with the sand dunes associated with the rest of the Massachusetts shore. Country lanes lined with wild flowers interspersed between interesting homes hug the rockbound coast and crisscross the headlands in the area south of town known as Land's End. We like the California look of Cape Hedge Beach from the heights at the end of South Street, the twin lighthouses on Thatchers Island as viewed from Marmion Way, and the glimpses of yachts from the verdant, narrow streets along the water in quaint Annisquam (stop for a lobster roll on the deck right over the water at the Lobster Cove).

Swimming is fine at Front and Back beaches in the center of town, the expansive Good Harbor Beach near the Gloucester line, the relatively unknown Cape Hedge and Pebble beaches at Land's End, and the Lanesville beach north of town. Parking can be a problem, but we've always lucked out.

Bearskin Neck. The rocky peninsula that juts into the harbor was the original fishing and commercial center of the town. Today, most of the weatherbeaten shacks have been converted into shops and eateries of every description. Glimpses of Sandy Bay and the Inner Harbor pop up like a changing slide show between buildings and through shop doors and windows. The rocky point at the end of the neck provides a panoramic view, or you can rest on a couple of benches off T-Wharf and admire Motif No. 1 — the Rockport Rotary Club sign beckons, "This little park is just for you, come sit a while and enjoy the view."

Shopping. Most of Bearskin Neck's enterprises cater more to tourists than residents. Main Street and the Dock Square area generally have better stores. **Serendipity** sells arts and crafts, including pottery and baskets. **Sun Basket** features North American Indian art. Suave clothes are sold at **The Motif.** At the **Square Circle** we marveled at incredible porcelain depictions of antipasto platters, fruit salad and the like, done by a woman from Virginia. **Zini** for wild jewelry and **Zanzibar** for "jewelry and surprises" are worth a stop. **La Mariposa** has Mexican things. We admired the cotton handblocked prints at **Segrets Sun Prints** — a great place to mix and match the wonderful colors. Still more exquisite crafts are found at the **London Venturers Company. Sand Castles** has contemporary clothing and accessories, and **Kids & Company** everything for children. You can watch saltwater taffy being made at **Tuck's Candies.** Proceeds from the well-stocked **Toad Hall Bookstore** further environmental causes.

The Art Galleries. For many, art is Rockport's compelling attraction. More than 200 artists make the town their home, and 37 galleries are listed in the Rockport Fine Arts Gallery Guide. **The Rockport Art Association,** with exhibitions and demonstrations in its large headquarters at 12 Main St., is a leader in its field. John Manship, a past president of the art association and son of Paul Manship, Rockport's famed sculptor whose Prometheus stands in New York's Rockefeller Center, has a gallery at Main and School streets. You could wander for hours through places like Paul Strisik's slick gallery next to the art association or Geraci Galleries in a 1725 complex of buildings at 6 South St.

Band Concerts. The summer Sunday evening concerts presented at 7:30 by the Rockport Legion Band at the outdoor bandstand near the water at Back Beach have been a Cape Ann tradition since 1932. Some of the original members are still active today, providing stirring concert marches, overtures and selections from Broadway musicals under the stars. Other than these, the best entertainment in town may well be, as a couple of guests at Eden Pines put it, "sitting on Dock Square and watching the world go by."

Museums. The Sandy Bay Historical Society and Museum, 40 King St., has early furnishings and exhibits on shipping, fishing and the local granite industry in the 1832 Sewall-Scripture House built of granite (open 2 to 5 daily in summer, weekends in September, free). The **James Babson Cooperage Shop** (1658) on Route 127 just across the Gloucester line, a small one-story brick structure with early tools and furniture, may be the oldest building on Cape Ann (Tuesday-Sunday 2 to 5, free). The **Old Castle** (1678) at Granite and Curtis streets, Pigeon Cove, was scheduled to reopen in 1989 after refurbishing to show early architecture, period furniture and clothing, artifacts and handicrafts, most of local origin (summer weekends, 2 to 4, free). Also at Pigeon Cove at 52 Pigeon Hill St. is the **Paper House,** built nearly 50 years ago of 215 thicknesses of specially treated newspapers; chairs, desks, tables, lamps and other furnishings also are made of paper (daily in summer, 10 to 5, 50 cents).

Extra-Special

Like the rest of Rockport, its museums are low-key. But you have only to go next door to Gloucester to see two of New England's stellar showplaces.

Beauport, 75 Eastern Point Blvd., (508) 283-0800. Interior designer Henry David Sleeper started building his summer home in 1907 to house his collection of decorative arts and furnishings. Most of the 40 rooms are small, but each is decorated in a different style or period with a priceless collection of objects. Sleeper designed several rooms to house specific treasures: the round, two-story Tower Library was built to acccommodate a set of carved wooden draperies from a hearse; the Octagon Room was built to match an eight-sided table. One of the breakfast tables in the Golden Step Room is right against a window that overlooks Gloucester Harbor; many visitors wish the place served lunch or tea. Guided tours Monday-Friday 10 to 4, mid-May to mid-October; also weekends 1 to 4 from mid-September to mid-October; adults, $4.

Hammond Castle Museum, Hesperus Avenue, (508) 283-2080. Cross the drawbridge and stop for lunch or tea and castle-baked pastries at the Roof Top Cafe in this replica of a medieval castle, built in the late 1920s by John Hays Hammond Jr. to house his collection of Roman, medieval and Renaissance art and objects. Concerts are given on the organ with 8,600 pipes rising eight stories above the cathedral-like Great Hall. Marbled columns and lush plantings watered by its own rain system are featured in the Courtyard. Guided tours, daily 10 to 4, May-October; Thursday-Saturday 10 to 4 and Sunday 1 to 4, November-April; adults $3.50.

Renovated 1846 octagonal rotunda is a focal point of Williams College Museum of Art.

Williamstown, Mass.

Arts Town of the East

Blessed with an uncommonly scenic setting and the riches that prestigious Williams College attracts and returns, this small college town in the northern Berkshires has become an arts center of national significance.

Newsweek called the annual Williamstown Theatre Festival "the best of all American summer theaters." Connoisseur magazine said its three leading museums make it "an unlikely but powerful little art capital." U.S. News and World Report reported that educators consider Williams College tops among academic institutions in the country.

Williams, its associates and benefactors have inspired these superlatives. But they have geography and nature to thank for what some call "the Village Beautiful." Set in a verdant bowl, Williamstown is at the foot of Mount Greylock, the highest peak in Massachusetts, and surrounded by Vermont's Green and New York's Taconic mountains.

Not only do these provide great outdoor activities (golf, hiking and skiing in particular). They also help Williamstown retain a charmed rural flavor that seems far more village-like than its population of 5,000 might suggest.

Williamstown is a sophisticated town of great appeal, one that unfolds as you delve. The youthful dynamic of 2,000 college students is not readily apparent in the broader community. Besides natural and cultural attractions, there are good restaurants and selective shops but distressingly few inns.

This is one place that has long been special. If you simply drive around town, you'll miss the real Williamstown. Here you must stop and explore.

Inn Spots

The Orchards, 222 Adams Road (Route 2), Williamstown 01267. (413) 458-9611 or (800) 225-1517.

Opened to the tune of many millions of dollars in 1985, the Orchards was designed to fill a conspicuous gap in terms of inn accommodations. It succeeds "along the lines of an English country hotel" (its words). But it's not the Berkshires' "most gracious country inn" nor "the finest inn in the Northeast," as its publicity hoopla claims (indeed, its strange-looking, salmon-colored stucco facade could be mistaken for a condominium project). Rather, it's a spacious, spanking-new hotel-motor inn with telephones in bathrooms as well as bedrooms, in-room refrigerators and television controls at bedside.

The 49-room, three-story structure meanders around a small, open courtyard containing a little free-form, rock-bordered pool surrounded by an outdoor dining area, lawns and flowers.

The interior layout separates restaurant and shop from guest rooms; winding corridors expand into a drawing room with a high ceiling. Polished antique furniture of the Queen Anne period fills the living room, where complimentary scones and English tea are served on fine china in the afternoon and, perhaps, dessert and coffee or liqueurs after dinner. Coffee and breakfast pastries are served there (gratis) before the dining room opens in the morning.

The guest rooms are large, comfortable and colorful in the Orchards' pink and green theme (the site was long an orchard, but you'd never know it today from the shopping center across the street and the housing tracts behind on this, the most built-up side of Williamstown). Each room is different within the prevailing theme: marble bathroom with terrycloth robes and Lord & Mayfair bath oils and soaps, separate dressing area, and small refrigerator. Some have working fireplaces, four-poster beds and bay windows. Cookies are served when the beds are turned down at night; the pillows are filled with feathers and down.

The inn has a sauna and jacuzzi, environmental chamber, four function rooms, an antiques shop, a cocktail lounge with fireplace and a beautiful dining room (see below).

Doubles, $135 to $180.

River Bend Farm, 643 Simonds Road (Route 7 North), Williamstown 01267. (413) 458-5504 or 458-3121.

This inviting Georgian Colonial was built in 1770 by Col. Benjamin Simonds, one of Williamstown's thirteen founders, and staying here is an experience in 18th-century authenticity.

Preservationists David and Judy Loomis acquired the house in 1977, spent years restoring it with great care and attention to detail, and slowly started sharing its treasures with B&B guests.

Guests enter the rear keeping room, where black kettles hang from the huge hearth, one of five fireplaces off the central chimney. The room is full of hooked rugs, antiques, dried flowers and grapevine wreaths. Here's where the Loomises serve what they call a healthy continental breakfast of fresh fruit, homemade granola, honey from their own beehives, muffins and breads.

All the lighting here and in the adjacent parlor comes from small bulbs in tin chandeliers and period lighting fixtures. The Loomises keep a stash of local menus on a table in the parlor.

The house has five bedrooms sharing two baths, one upstairs with a tub and the other downstairs in the old pantry and containing a marvelous corner shower with tiles that

Dave fashioned from roof slate. Four rooms are upstairs off a hall with a giant spinning wheel. We liked the front corner room with crocheted four-poster bed and plenty of room for two wing chairs in a sitting area. A double bed nearly fills a cozy room in the rear. A downstairs bedroom in a former parlor is lovely, decorated in blues and whites with oriental rugs.

Dave says the B&B proceeds help finance the on-going restoration of this old home and tavern, which is listed on the National Register of Historic Places. Spending a night or two here is to immerse oneself in history.

Doubles, $50.

Field Farm Guest House, 554 Sloan Road, Williamstown 01267. (413) 458-3135.

When the 1948 American Modern-style home of arts patron Lawrence H. Boedel became available following the death of his widow in 1984, the Trustees of Reservations didn't quite know what to do with it. David and Judy Loomis of River Bend Farm proposed running it as a B&B and, true to their word, they ended up doing just that.

Staying in one of the five guest rooms in this rural hilltop home surrounded by 254 acres of conservation land is intriguing, given the home's history. The word "home" is used advisedly, for that's exactly what it is — looking much as the Bloedels left it, with the exceptiion of the fabulous collection of paintings they donated to the Williams College Museum of Art and the Whitney Museum of Art in New York City.

Guests have the run of a spacious living room (here, as elsewhere in the large house, most of the furniture was made by Mr. Bloedel, a 1923 Williams graduate and onetime college librarian), dining room, galley kitchen and grounds, which are striking for their sculptures, views and trails. The property is one of seventy owned by the Trustees, a state land-conservation group that is the largest landowner in Massachusetts.

All five bedrooms retain their original private baths and vary greatly in size. The main-floor Studio Room, which the original owner used as a studio, is enormous with a double bed, two twins, a black walnut floor and a separate entrance.

Upstairs in this house that might be described as a mixture of art nouveau and Danish modern are four more guest rooms. The North Room has tiles of butterflies flanking the fireplace (the tiles on all the fireplaces are interesting), its own balcony, a dressing table with mirrored surface and a walk-in closet with sliding drawers. The master bedroom has a built-in corner dressing unit, a fireplace with tiles of trees and birds, and an enormous private deck. The other rooms are considerably smaller, but the East Room's bathroom is large enough to contain both a shower stall and a tub.

The architecturally interesting house, built of Western cedar and fronted by a mass of yellow creeping hydrangeas, was designed by architect Edward Goodell. It has 5,000 square feet of space, including the quarters of innkeepers Emo and Roselette DeWitt, who took over after the Loomises got the place running.

They serve a continental breakfast of fruit, granola, breads like banana and zucchini, and muffins.

Outside are a tennis court, picnic tables, woodlands, pastures, a pond, and trails for wildlife-watching or cross-country skiing. But don't be misled by the name. Field Farm is not your usual farm, but rather the home lived in by a wealthy and interesting man.

Doubles, $75.

Le Jardin, 777 Cold Spring Road (Route 7), Williamstown 01267. (413) 458-8032.

A wooded hillside lush with pachysandra, a pond, a waterfall from the passing brook and, of course, gardens welcome guests to this French-style restaurant and country inn converted from a 19th-century mansion two miles south of town.

River Bend Farm occupies Georgian Colonial built in 1770 by a founder of Williamstown.

A narrow stairway beside the entrance to the main dining room leads from the entry foyer through a rustic hallway to the seven guest rooms, all with full baths and four with fireplaces. Most choice is the front corner room with a four-poster bed ensconced in a niche, stenciling, hooked rugs and TV, and a tub with a jacuzzi in the large bathroom. Particularly popular in summer is a small new room in the rear with queensize bed and a private balcony facing the woods. The other rooms in country style are somewhat more plain.

The only public sitting area is in the front bar, which has a television set. Continental breakfast is served in the formal dining room (see below), where friendly German chef-innkeeper Walter Hayn has achieved a good reputation.

Doubles, $75 to $85. Closed mid-November through winter.

The Williams Inn, Junction of Routes 7 and 2, Williamstown 01267. (413) 458-9371.

After the old Williams Inn was taken over by Williams College, the Treadway built a replacement (supposedly "on-the-green at Williams College," though not by our definition). We wish we could be more enthusiastic, but this is a Colonial-modern hotel/motel rather than an inn. A pianist was playing in the almost-empty cocktail lounge and a gaggle of giggling girls was being shepherded through the lobby for a swimming-birthday party the Friday afternoon we stopped in.

The 102 air-conditioned rooms on three floors have full baths, color TV, oversize beds and early American furnishings. Facilities include a spacious and comfortable lobby, indoor pool, a whirlpool and sauna, elevators, lounge and restaurant serving three meals a day.

The large and formal dining room with big brass chandeliers and high-back, leather-seat chairs is in shades of raspberry, green and beige. The dinner menu (entrees $12.95 to $18.95) includes such continental choices as pork chop Normandy, roast duck bigarade and veal Oscar, plus, for starters, pickled herring and — would you believe? — egg salad on lettuce and tomato with creamy cocktail sauce, ham julienne and toast.

The inn's gift shop is particularly good, featuring quilted bags, baskets, beveled glass ornaments, porcelain Christmas tree angels, appliqued denim jumpers, animal sculptures and such.

Doubles, $90 to $105.

251

The Orchards is designed in the style of an English country hotel.

Dining Spots

The Orchards, 222 Adams Road, Williamstown. (413) 458-9611.

Upholstered reproduction Queen Anne chairs, rose and green carpeting, forest green walls and well-spaced tables set with soft rose linen, ribbed glassware, flowered German china, silver baskets for the rolls and antique teapots — what could be more elegant than the L-shaped, two-part dining room at the Orchards? We enjoyed a Saturday lunch, settled in comfy high-backed rose velveteen chairs in an airy, two-story greenhouse-like area at one end, looking onto the courtyard. It was the next best thing to dining outside under striped umbrellas (it was too cool that day).

The inn's linen bill must be outrageous, based on the layers cautiously arranged by the teenaged busboy (attired in formal maroon jacket and topsiders) as he changed the cloths. Each table bears intricate covered dishes for sugar and saccharin, pepper grinder and crystal salt shaker.

Poppyseed rolls were served as we sipped the Macon white house wine, a not particularly generous glass for $3.50. Sandwiches, salads and sandwiches are priced from $4.85 for a "grilled sirloin burger" to $7.25 for crabmeat and avocado salad. Swordfish soup with vegetables was an interesting starter, as was the excellent chilled apple curry soup. The chicken salad with papaya slices, apples and pecans was a winner, and a beef bourguignonne special was fine. Not so wonderful was the strawberry almond cake ($2.75) that tasted like a jelly roll; next time we'll try the peanut butter cheesecake or the homemade sorbet.

The dinner menu changes nightly and is respected by area chefs because of its reach. Entrees ($16.75 to $18.25) could be broiled swordfish with anchovy beurre blanc, poached salmon with saffron hollandaise, chicken basquaise, grilled quails with wild mushrooms, veal medallions with morels, calves liver au poivre and sauteed beef tenderloin New Mexico.

Start with sauteed snails on capellini or shrimp diable ($4.50 to $7.75). End with a good-looking apple tart with crumb crust or chocolate roulades from the pastry cart. The extensive wine list is fairly priced, from $12.50 for vouvray to $150 for a 1982 Chateau Mouton Rothschild Pauillac.

Lunch daily, noon to 2; dinner, 6 to 8:30 or 9.

The Mill on the Floss, Route 7, New Ashford. (413) 458-9123.
Genial Maurice Champagne, originally from Montreal, is the chef-owner at this established and well-regarded restaurant. He loves to socialize, so one reason he designed the open, blue and white tiled kitchen was so that patrons could come up and talk with him as he cooked. The dark brown wood building, pleasantly landscaped, was once a mill. Inside it is cozy, with beamed ceilings, paneled walls, a hutch filled with Quimper pottery, white linens and many hanging copper pots. Before dinner, complimentary Swiss cheese and crackers, chicken liver pate, radishes and olives are served.

The menu is classical French. Among starters ($3.50 to $8.50) are duck pate with plum wine, prosciutto and melon, and soups like cold cucumber or black bean. Entrees range from $17 for chicken amandine to $25 for rack of lamb. Sweetbreads in black butter, veal kidneys with mustard sauce, calves liver with bacon and sliced tenderloin with bordelaise sauce are some, and the fish of the day could be halibut meuniere or swordfish.

For dessert (changing daily), you might find a nut torte or a chocolate roll cake filled with grand marnier souffle, or try cafe diablo for two. Wines are quite reasonable.

Since 1986, M. Champagne has taken an additional role as executive chef of **Drummond's,** the more formal of two restaurants at the Country Inn at Jiminy Peak ski resort in nearby Hancock. He and his family make their presence known at both restaurants.

Dinner nightly from 5 (from 4 in July and August). Closed mid-November through April.

Chef Maurice Champagne in his kitchen.

Le Country Restaurant, 101 North St. (Route 7), Williamstown. (413) 458-4000.
A warm, country atmosphere and the personalities of chef-owner Raymond Canales, his wife Beverly and son Gregory pervade this long-established restaurant in the continental tradition. "We're sort of rustic," Beverly acknowledged as she showed the main dining room done up in beige and brown, with beamed ceiling, a mix of shaded lamps and candles on the tables, and a Franklin stove to ward off the chill in winter. The nicest of the three dining rooms with high ceiling and sunken area with a fireplace is used for special occasions.

A striking antique piece from Brittany is decked out with wines, glasses and grapes; it's the sister to one behind the bar. "We want people to enjoy wines, so we don't have much of a markup," Beverly explained when we found some extraordinary bargains (carafes for $9.50, vouvray for $11, chardonnays from $13 to $20 and nothing over $25).

The extensive menu is supplemented by nightly specials, prime rib and veal curry the night we were there. Entrees from $12 for fettuccine carbonara to $19.25 for broiled lamb chops include chicken prepared four ways, veal three, and such standards as duckling bigarade, coquilles St. Jacques and tournedos bordelaise. Southern pecan pie and baba au rhum are featured desserts.

Many of the appetizers and desserts are available at lunch, along with sandwiches, salad plates and entrees from $6.95 to $10.95 for items like chicken fricassee on toast, Spanish omelet and shrimp curry.

Lunch, Tuesday-Friday 11:30 to 1:30; dinner, Tuesday-Sunday 5 to 9.

Le Jardin, 777 Cold Spring Road, Williamstown. (413) 458-8032.

The two partitioned dining rooms are country French and quite elegant, with velvet striped seats, white linens and dark napkins placed sideways, hanging lamps with pierced tin panels, white draperies and plants in every window.

German chef Walter Hayn shares billing for the longest tenure in town with Raymond Canales of Le Country (twenty years). His menu is classic French, from the French onion soup for $3.50 to the herring in sour cream and escargots bourguignonne ($8). Dinner entrees are priced from $12 for chicken Henry IV to $19 for filet mignon bearnaise. They run the gamut from Long Island duckling to pepper steak flambe, all nicely prepared with fine cream sauces. The wine list struck us as strange, though it offered Beaujolais Villages Jadot for $15 and Sutter Home cabernet for a bargain $12.

Desserts tend to be rich — chocolate truffle mousse cake, double fudge chocolate layer cake, hazelnut torte, kahlua cheesecake and pecan pie.

Dinner nightly, 5 to 10; Sunday brunch, 10:30 to 1:30. Closed mid-November into winter.

The Cafe at the College Bookstore, 76 Spring St., Williamstown. (413) 458-4808.

Tucked amid the books and stacks of the College Bookstore, this small cafe was to be remodeled and expanded shortly after our latest visit. Talented chef Scott Avery, a CIA grad who says he has been apprenticing since he was 12, was enthused about plans to open for dinner as well as light breakfast and lunch.

Espresso, cappuccino, twelve kinds of tea and homemade muffins and bagels are the fare for breakfast. Sunday brunch brings champagne fruits with raspberry mayonnaise, omelet with fishberry jam (caviar), and waffles with orange spice butter.

Blackboard specials on our visit were beef duglere soup ($3.50), smoked turkey sandwich ($5.50) and a winter salad of greens, citrus fruits, pecans and cucumber with raspberry dressing ($4). In summer you might find a pesto torta — layers of brioche, pesto, red pepper, ratatouille and two cheeses for $6.50, or seafood ceviche with tomato and cucumber in gold tequila vinaigrette served with blue corn chips, $7.50.

Scott's soups might be gingered carrot and leek, asparagus and lobster bisque, or firehouse clam chowder. "I have 1,500 cakes in my repertoire," says he. One of his tortes is called the "Williams torte" because the lemon cake and blueberry filling represent the college's yellow and purple colors; another is a chocolate layer cake with chambord mousse filling. His frozen cointreau mousse is enveloped in a meringue swan with a sauce of three berries.

The cafe is particularly popular in summer, when tables are set up on the sidewalk outside. Plans were to expand the kitchen and to have a mesquite grill and perhaps a wine bar.

Open at 9; lunch from 11:30.

The 1896 House, Routes 2 and 7 south of Williamstown, (413) 458-8123.

An expansive red dairy-barn structure with a pleasant new outdoor patio in front, this has been a restaurant known for beef dishes since its start in the 1920s. After a brief

Le Jardin offers country French dining and lodging.

fling with regional nouvelle cuisine and a bankruptcy that forced its closing, it was reopened by new owners in the summer of 1988 with its traditional beef and seafood fare (newly advertised as New England cuisine) that was getting good reports.

The menu has a children's section and lists mini-meals for the smaller appetite ($6.95 for lasagna to $8.50 for broiled sea scallops). Regular dinners start at $9.95 for stuffed breast of capon and top off at $14.95 for "hefty open-hearth sirloin" and prime rib. The rest of the fare is predictable, except perhaps for such combination dinners as broiled scrod with prime rib, capon with steak teriyaki or capon with coquilles St. Jacques.

The dining room has an upscale barn interior of red carpeting, blue chairs with beige leather seats, white and beige tablecloths with blue napkins, candles in hurricane lamps, and brass lamps under antique paintings on the dark pine walls. There's entertainment and dancing weekends in the large cocktail lounge, and lunch is served on the patio.

Dinner nightly, 5:30 to 9:30.

The River House, 123 Water St., Williamstown. (413) 458-4820.

Popular with the college crowd, the River House offers a large, varied menu of "New England country fare in an authentic 1870s setting," an original building with beamed ceilings, bare floors and candles in hurricane lamps, a large bar and newer additions where tables are covered by blue mats.

Soups, appetizers, salads, sandwiches, entrees, desserts, wines and bar selections are listed on the straightforward, six-page typewritten menu. The choices are numerous; suffice to say that you can order almost anything you desire, from escargots in mushroom caps to deep-fried onions to an open-face reuben to Indian pudding with ice cream — nothing too trendy or changeable here. Entrees are $9.50 (spaghetti, roast turkey) to $16.95 (lazy lobster, prime rib). The homemade brownie is covered with the extraordinary fudge sauce of Mother Myrick's in Manchester, Vt. All ten wines are $11.50 or less (pina coladas and Bass ale are more popular here).

Dinner, 5 to 10; late-night fare, 10 to midnight; Sundays and holidays, 1 to 9; closed Monday.

Hobson's Choice, 159 Water St., Williamstown. (413) 458-9101.

This cozy little place is a favorite of the locals. Old tools hang on its wood walls, paper mats are on bare tables with Tiffany-type lamps above and mismatched chairs around, and there are a few stools at the bar in back of the room. Around the front door are wonderful panes of stained glass with flowers and birds therein.

The large menus offer something for everyone. At lunch a crock of onion soup, tempura onion rings, buffalo wings, sandwiches and burgers are in the $3.25 to $4.25 range. Fish and chips are served the British way, with vinegar. The same appetizers, sandwiches and burgers are listed for dinner, with ten or so entrees priced from $8.95 for chicken piccata to $12.95 for seafood fettuccine. Cajun catfish is $10.95.

Mud pie, carrot cake, chocolate mousse and cheesecake are some of the desserts. The wine list is limited but cheap, and a bottle of West County sparkling farm cider is $8.

Open 11:30 to 9 weekdays; to 10 Friday and Saturday.

The Grapevine, 100 Water St., Williamstown. (413) 458-2104.

John England, son of the owner of the Potter's Wheel craft shop nearby, runs this new gourmet takeout, where you can get sandwiches, salads and soups at bargain prices. A veggie sandwich with roasted garlic and goat cheese is $3.75, curried chicken is $3.95 and the most expensive item is a French pate sandwich with cornichons, $4.50.

John also has a takeout dinner menu, one item a night plus vegetable and starch, priced from $7.95 to $11.95. Chicken cordon bleu with sweet potato and pear casserole ($9.95) was tempting the day we visited.

Open Monday-Saturday.

Diversions

Williamstown's scenic beauty is apparent on all sides, but less known is the composite of its art and history collections. You get a hint of both on arrival simply by traversing Main Street from the green at Route 7. The hilly street with broad lawns leading to wide-apart historic homes, imposing college buildings and churches is more scenic and tranquil than the main street of any college town we know.

Art and history are best appreciated when viewed close up, away from the crowded settings of the great museums. As Connoisseur magazine reported, this intimacy is "the great gift" of Williamstown.

Extra-Special

Sterling and Francine Clark Art Institute, 225 South St., (413) 458-9545.

The most widely known of the town's museums chanced upon its Williamstown location through an old family connection with Williams and the fact that eccentric collector Sterling Clark, heir to the Singer sewing machine fortune, wanted his treasures housed far from a potential site of nuclear attack. Clark's neoclassical white marble temple opened in 1955 (he and his wife are buried under its front steps) and was expanded in 1973 by a red granite addition housing more galleries and one of the nation's outstanding art research libraries. The Clark's major strength lies in its holdings of French 19th-century paintings, English silver, prints and drawings (the Clark was the single largest source for the Renoir exhibition at Boston's Museum of Fine Arts in 1985-86). Shown mostly in small galleries the size of the rooms in which they once hung, the highly personalized collection of Monets, Turners and Winslow Homers quietly vie for attention with sculptures, porcelain and three centuries worth of silver (Clark liked good food and the silverware to go with it). All this is amid an austere yet intimate setting of potted plants and vases of dried flowers, furniture and benches for relaxation. Amazingly, it's free, Tuesday-Sunday 10 to 5.

Neoclassical white marble temple houses Sterling and Francine Clark Art Institute.

Massachusetts Museum of Contemporary Art. By 1991, if funding and renovations proceed on schedule, the $72 million Massachusetts Museum of Contemporary Art will be open in the old eighteen-building Sprague industrial complex in neighboring North Adams. Inspired by the former director of the Williams College Museum of Art (Thomas Krens, now director of New York's Guggenheim), the new museum is expected to house the largest collection of contemporary art and sculpture anywhere. It surely will cement the Williamstown area's ranking as a major center of art.

Williams College Museum of Art, Main Street. A $4.5 million extension to its original octagonal building in Lawrence Hall makes this museum, itself a work of art with "ironic" columns that are decorative rather than functional, a sleeper in art circles. The eight sides of the 1846 neoclassical rotunda are repeated in soaring newer galleries with skylights, some of their walls hung with spectacular wall art. The museum houses fourteen galleries and a staggering 10,000 works, from 3,000-year-old Assyrian stone reliefs to the last self-portrait by Andy Warhol. In an effort to complement the Clark's strengths in the 19th century, this museum stresses contemporary, 17th and 18th century American art and rare Asian art. It features traveling and special exhibitions rivaling those of many a metropolitan museum; Wallworks by Sol LeWitt brightened the three-story entrance atrium when we visited. Open free Monday-Saturday 10 to 5, Sunday 1 to 5.

Nearby is the **Hopkins Observatory,** the oldest extant observatory in the United States (1836) and used as a planetarium and museum with weekly shows all year long.

Chapin Library, Stetson Hall, Williams College. Nowhere else are the founding documents of the country — original printings of the Declaration of Independence, the Articles of Confederation, the Bill of Rights and drafts of the Constitution — displayed together in a simple glass case on the second floor of a college hall. This remarkable library contains more than 30,000 rare books, first editions and manuscripts — you might ask to see James Madison's copy of Thomas Paine's "Common Sense." One floor below is the Williamsiana Collection of town and gown, while the lowest level of Stetson contains the archives of band leader Paul Whiteman, with 3,500 original scores and a complete library of music of the 1920s. Open Monday-Friday, 9 to noon and 1 to 5. Free.

Williamstown Theatre Festival, Adams Memorial Theater, Williams College. Founded in 1955 (the year of the Clark Art Institute opening), the professional summer festival presents "some of the most ambitious theatre the U.S. has to offer," in the words of the Christian Science Monitor. Such luminaries as Christopher Reeve, Dick Cavett, Edward Herrmann and Marsha Mason return summer after summer to the festival they call home for productions of everything from Chekhov and Ibsen to Tennessee Williams and Broadway tryouts, all the while mingling with the townspeople. The festival uses the theater's main stage, but also includes the smaller Other Stage, emphasizing newer works in the 99-seat Extension added in 1982 to the same building. Leads from the main stage often join the festival's Caberet, which presents late-night revues at area restaurants. Festival performances Tuesday-Saturday, late June through August.

Williams College. Besides the aforementioned highlights, the campus as a whole is worth exploring. Its 50 buildings, predominantly in red brick and gray granite, range through almost every period of American architecture. The lawns and plantings and sense of nature all around contribute to a pleasant walking tour.

Nature. The prime spot — as well as the area's dominant feature — is the **Mount Greylock State Reservation,** a series of seven peaks with a 3,491-foot summit that is the highest in Massachusetts. You can drive, hike or bike to the summit for a spectacular five-state view. Other memorable views are obtained by driving the Taconic Trail through Petersburg Pass and the Mohawk Trail above North Adams. The 2,000-acre **Hopkins Memorial Forest** northwest of the campus is an experimental forest operated by the Williams College Center for Environmental Studies, with nature and cross-country trails, plus the Barn Museum showing old photographs, farm machinery, implements and tools, and the Buxton Gardens, a farm garden designed to have certain flowers in bloom at all times. Williams College also recently reacquired **Mount Hope Park,** a former estate with extensive gardens and grounds.

Recreation. Golf is the seasonal pastime at the Taconic Golf Club, on the south edge of town and ranked as one of the tops in New England, and at Waubeeka Springs Golf Links in the valley at South Williamstown. In summer, you can swim in the 74-degree waters of Sand Springs Pool and Spa, founded in 1813 and the oldest springs resort still in operation in the country. In winter, there's skiing nearby at Jiminy Peak and Brodie Mountain ski resorts.

Shopping. The college-community stores are generally along Spring Street, running south off Main Street opposite the main campus and between campus appendages such as museum, science center and sports complex. The **House of Walsh** is an institution for traditional clothing. Try the **Clarksburg Bread Co.** for chunky cheddar cheese bread or a nutmeg hermit. **Bette's Life and Times** is good for breakfast, served all day, and **Goodie's Cafe** serves Tex-Mex. **The Cow Bell** has nice gifts and needlepoint. The **Library** shows dhurrie rugs, English country pine furniture, linens, china and more.

Water Street, an historic development that blossomed later, has distinctive shops including the **Cottage** and **Mole Hole** gift shops, outdoors equipment at the **Mountain Goat** and high-tech stuff at the **Green River Trading Co.** We always stop at the **Potter's Wheel,** an outstanding shop with stoneware, porcelain, glass, prints, woods, fibres and jewelry by top craftsmen, and once came out with a nifty little acrylic sheep to hang in the dining room window.

At the new **Williamstown Market Place** south of town on Cold Spring Road, you'll find **Wings Unlimited,** calling itself "nature's general store," with bird feeders, decoys and the like. **Little Bo Peep's** has cute clothes for children, the **Cold Spring Eatery** sells ice cream and snacks, and the **Shops at the Green Barn** include a well-stocked Christmas shop, and arts of American Indians.

Chesterwood was summer home and studio of sculptor Daniel Chester French.

Lenox, Mass.
The Good (and Cultured) Life

The gentle beauty of the Berkshires has attracted generations of artists, authors and musicians — as well as their patrons who appreciate the good life. At the center of the Berkshires in both location and spirit is Lenox, a small village whose cultural influence far exceeds its size.

In the 19th century, Lenox was home for Nathaniel Hawthorne, Edith Wharton, Henry Ward Beecher and Fannie Kemble. Herman Melville, Henry Adams, Oliver Wendell Holmes, Henry Wadsworth Longfellow, William Cullen Bryant and Daniel Chester French lived and worked nearby.

Such was the allure of this tranquil mountain and lake country that many prominent Americans built palatial homes here. Lenox became "the inland Newport" for such families as Westinghouse, Carnegie, Procter, Morgan and Vanderbilt (indeed, some of America's 400 summered in Newport and spent the early autumn in the Berkshires).

The artists and the affluent helped make Lenox in the 20th century a center for the arts. Tanglewood, across from Hawthorne's home, is the summer home of the Boston Symphony Orchestra. Edith Wharton's Mount is the stage for Shakespeare & Company. Nearby are the Lenox Arts Center, the Berkshire Theater Festival, Jacob's Pillow Dance Festival and South Mountain Concerts.

The Lenox area's cultural attractions are well known. Less so are some of its hidden treats: the picturesque Stockbridge Bowl (a lake), the Walker sculpture garden, the Pleasant Valley wildlife sanctuary, the Church on the Hill, and the mansions along Kemble and Cliffwood streets.

Attractions of a more specialized nature are offered at the Kripalu Center for Yoga

259

and Health and, starting about September 1989, at Canyon Ranch in the Berkshires, newly ensconced on the Bellefontaine estate.

Staying in some of Lenox's inns is like being a house guest in a mansion. Besides lodging in style, visitors may dine at some of New England's fanciest restaurants and enjoy $44 orchestra seats in the Shed at Tanglewood. The budget-conscious can find more reasonable places in which to stay and eat, and, while picnicking on the Tanglewood lawn, can hear the BSO almost as well as those in the Shed.

Except perhaps for the prices, we don't know anyone who doesn't enjoy the copious charms of Lenox.

Inn Spots

Most Lenox inns require a minimum stay of three nights on summer weekends, and weekend prices usually extend from Thursday through Sunday. Rates quoted here are for weekends in peak season. They are lower for weekdays, and vary by the season. Two-night minimums on weekends are often the rule year-round.

Apple Tree Inn, 224 West St., Lenox 01240. (413) 637-1477.

Imagine sitting by the pool, iced drink in hand, and listening to the music from Tanglewood waft up the hill. If you stay at the Apple Tree Inn, you don't even need to buy a lawn ticket.

We first met this inn, situated across from the main Tanglewood gate, a couple of incarnations ago, when it was Alice's at Avaloch (the original name of the estate) and Alice Brock of Alice's Restaurant fame was the chef. After that, it was the Portofino before it was taken over in 1983 by New Yorkers Greg and Aurora Smith, who spent much energy and money to turn the 100-year-old main house into a proper inn.

High on a hill amidst 22 acres covered with apple trees, the setting could not be more fortuitous. Greg, a keen gardener, has planted 12,000 bulbs and more than 450 varieties of roses, in an effort to give the inn a fourth season — spring. The aforementioned pool, installed by the Smiths in 1985, is contoured to fit into the hillside beyond a restored barn that is now the Smiths' home.

The inn includes a separate structure with twenty motel-like rooms, which the Smiths have upgraded.

Of more interest is the refurbishing done in the main house. Everywhere there is evidence of Greg's construction abilities and Aurora's decorating flair. Since the rooms had never been available to the public before, the Smiths had plenty to do, including replacing ceilings and putting in new bathrooms.

The spacious sitting area is surrounded by walls with arches cut into them, outlined by Tiffany-type fixtures. It has velvet sofas and chairs for lounging in front of the fireplace, and a grand piano often played by visiting musicians.

Several Raggedy Ann and Andy dolls peek through the staircase up to the second floor. They were made by Aurora, who also painted in wondrous colors the old shoe lasts that you'll find in each room.

All eleven bedrooms and two suites on the second and third floors, many with working fireplaces, are picture-pretty. They have quilts and comforters, ruffled pillows and dust ruffles done by Aurora, a sculptor, who says she always has to have handwork to do while she is sitting down. Rooms vary in size; some have twin beds, some have window seats, some on the second floor have skylights. Room 2 is the prize, with a high four-poster bed you have to use a step stool to get into. French doors covered with lace curtains open onto a private porch where you can sit and look at the waters of Stockbridge Bowl shimmering below, if you are not inside enjoying the fireplace.

Blantyre is a Tudor-style replica of a castle in Scotland.

Guests are served continental breakfast (usually muffins, sometimes croissants) and have use of the clay tennis court. Lunch, cocktails and dinner also are available (see Dining Spots).

Doubles, $115 to $210; suites, $245 to $260.

Blantyre, Route 20 and East St., Lenox 01240. (413) 637-3556 or 298-3806 (November-April).

This rambling, Tudor-style brick manor was built in 1902 as a summer retreat for a millionaire in the turpentine business. A replica of the Hall of Blantyre in Scotland, it used to be called Blantyre Castle, and was a memorable place for dining in the baronial style. Today, "castle" has been dropped from the name, but the feeling remains in lodging as well as in dining.

In 1981, the structure was carefully restored even to the inside of the huge closets by Jane Fitzpatrick, whose Red Lion Inn in adjacent Stockbridge has welcomed guests in the old New England tradition for so many years. The result is worthy of a castle: a majestic foyer with staircase of black oak, public rooms with high beamed ceilings, rich and intricate carved paneling, crystal chandeliers and fireplaces with hand-carved mantels, and eight elegant suites and guest rooms, five with fireplaces.

The ultra-deluxe Paterson Suite has a fireplaced living room with a crystal chandelier, a large bedroom with kingsize bed and two full bathrooms. Victorian-style sofas and chairs make comfortable sitting areas at the foot of the ornate queensize four-poster beds in the Laurel and Cromwell suites. Even the smallest Bouquet and Ribbon rooms are fit for would-be barons and baronesses, if only for a night or two.

A typical bathroom has terrycloth robes and piles of towels, a scale, a wooden valet, heated towel racks, embroidered curtains, and at least ten soaps and toiletries.

Twelve rooms in more contemporary style, several of them split-level loft suites, are available in the carriage house. All have decks or balconies and wet bars. Two cottages offer two-bedroom suites with kitchenettes.

Four tennis courts (whites required), a swimming pool and competition croquet courts are available on 85 acres of woods and lawns.

Fruit, wine and cheese await guests on arrival. Cocktails and after-dinner coffee and cordials are served in the main foyer and the crystal-chandeliered music room. A complimentary continental breakfast is served in the breakfast room or on the terrace.

"Proper evening dress" is required in the house after 6 p.m., Blantyre advises. Service is pampering and professional, both for house guests and for the public at dinner (see Dining Spots).

Doubles with continental breakfast, $190 to $260; suites, $235 to $450. Open May-October.

Cliffwood Inn, 25 Cliffwood St., Lenox 01240. (413) 637-3330.

A magnificent classic Colonial built in Stanford White style about 1890 by the then-ambassador to France, this is almost a stage set for the furnishings of innkeepers Joy and Scottie Farrelly, acquired during their periods of residence in Paris, Brussels, Italy and Montreal when he was with Ralston Purina Co.

The three-story mansion has ten working fireplaces, one of them in the bathroom off a third-floor guest room.

A large foyer gives access to all three main-floor public rooms, each of which has French doors opening to the full-length back porch overlooking a swimming pool. At one end of the house is a living room with twelve-foot-high mirrors and a white marble fireplace. The music room in the center leads to the formal dining room, which has a black marble fireplace.

Upstairs are seven air-conditioned guest rooms, all with private baths and six with working fireplaces. Each is named for one of the Farrellys' ancestors (a scrapbook describing the particular one is at the foot of each bed, and it turns out they were an illustrious lot). The new Walker-Linton Suite, with a sitting room fashioned from a former bedroom, has a step-up four-poster bed. A Victorian loveseat faces the fireplace in the Helen Walker Room, pretty in pink, white and rose. A gaily painted lunch pail is a decorative accent in one room, and Joy is doing folk art for the others. You'll be intrigued by many of her ingenious decorating touches.

In the early evening, the Farrellys put out wine and hors d'oeuvres, perhaps salmon mousse, marinated olives and hot artichoke dip. Joy planned eventually to offer "dinners in a party atmosphere" in the off-season.

For what they call a "copious continental breakfast," the Farrellys serve a renowned compote of baked apples with nuts and creme fraiche, homemade yogurt, granola, muffins and cornbread. It's taken in the paneled dining room with tapestried, high-back chairs or on the back porch.

Doubles, $125 to $200.

Whistler's Inn, 5 Greenwood St., Lenox 01240. (413) 637-0975.

Located across from the landmark Church on the Hill, this fine French-English Tudor mansion built in 1820 by Whistler's nephew was acquired in 1978 by Richard and Joan Mears from a member of his family. It has been upgraded gradually into a gracious inn with museum-like public rooms and twelve guest rooms of varying size, all with private baths. The Mearses, who write novels and do photography (some of their output is

Cliffwood Inn is classic Colonial built about 1890 by the ambassador to France.

Tudor facade of Whistler's Inn.   French salon at Whistler's Inn.

evident throughout the inn), were restoring a studio into a gift shop and art gallery at our last visit.

Edith Wharton used the French salon with the grand piano, two fringed green velvet sofas and oriental carpets as the setting for a scene in "Ethan Frome." Beyond is a gracious porch above an Italian sunken garden and seven acres of land, where great effort was going into rejuvenation of the gardens. A fireplace, comfortable chairs for reading and a round table bearing decanters of fine port and sherry await guests in a library full of chintz and cushions.

Blueberry muffins, pastries and boiled eggs are served for breakfast in the formal dining room or on the sun porch and terrace.

Upstairs, guest rooms range in size from large to a tiny single with a small square bathtub. The bathrooms have been modernized and the colorful tiles in most are striking. One room has red velvet bedspreads, another Mrs. Whistler's original Chippendale armoire, and a third has antique paper on walls and ceiling. Original art works and the innkeepers' framed photographs decorate walls throughout the inn. Rooms are furnished with "as many antiques as possible," Joan Mears says.

Doubles, $70 to $180. Closed mid-March to mid-May.

Walker House, 24 Walker St., Lenox 01240. (413) 637-1271.

It's clear that ex-Californians Peggy and Richard Houdek, who opened this B&B nine years ago in the heart of Lenox, like music. A pecan Kimball grand piano in the living room is used for recitals and singalongs, a pump organ is in the front hall and the guest rooms are named for composers, with appropriate memorabilia of the person and the period in each. Dick Houdek was a music critic and Peggy in administration at the San Francisco Opera, which is where they met.

It's clear also that the Houdeks like flowers, which are in profusion everywhere, inside and out, and cats (they have six live ones and uncounted inanimate replicas in the form of pictures, pillows and the like). We loved the poster in the dining room picturing three earnest-looking cats with the message, "we don't want you to smoke."

The result is an engaging clutter that shows the public rooms are clearly meant to be used. Ditto for the screened side porch and the wide rear veranda looking onto a landscaped yard and three acres of woods in back.

All eight guest rooms in the house, built in 1804 as the Walker Rockwell House, have private baths and five have working fireplaces. Some have clawfoot tubs, most have hooked rugs and comforters, and several have canopied beds with high oak headboards. The Verdi room with its wild green and white wallpaper, white iron bedsteads and wicker furniture is in airy contrast to the dark colors and period wallpapers in most of the rooms. The Puccini room downstairs has rose walls, brass bedstead, modern bathroom, fireplace and its own little porch.

Guests keep a running commentary on their local dining experiences in an informative guest book.

Continental breakfast of fresh fruit or baked apples, muffins and croissants is served in the dining room, where a stuffed tiger, lion and lamb are seated at one table. The welcoming aroma of spices fills the room day and night. More than 100 mugs with all kinds of logos on them are hung on a wall. If you're late for breakfast, Peggy advises guests, your coffee may be served in a mug from Cleveland or Fargo, N.D.

Doubles, $90 to $130.

The Gables Inn, 103 Walker St., Lenox 01240. (413) 637-3416.

Edith Wharton made this her home at the turn of the century while she was building her permanent edifice, the Mount. Her upstairs room is one of the most attractive at this restaurant-turned-inn, with the four-poster bed canopied in a pink and white print, a beautiful patterned rug and a deep plum sofa by the fireplace. Ask innkeeper Frank Newton to show you the famous eight-sided library where the author wrote some of her short stories.

The other twelve guest rooms, all with private baths, are full of verve and Victorian warmth as well. It's little wonder that the Jockey Club Suite is most in demand. It has a brass bed in a niche, an ample sitting area with two sofas facing a big-screen TV, and a private entrance from the back-yard pool area.

We like the Show Business Room, full of signed photos of old stars and a library of showbiz volumes, with which to curl up on the chintz loveseat in front of the fireplace. The Presidents' Room is aptly named, with lots of memorabilia and memoirs. You need a stool to climb into the high bed with a notable eight-foot-high walnut headboard in Room 9. The Shakespeare Room has a carved bas relief of the playwright in the bedstead.

Frank, a former banker and sometime pianist, and his wife Ann first operated the Gables as a restaurant before converting their banquet hall into lodging and making it "a special inn."

The breakfast room is spectacular with one long table in the center and, along the sides, six round tables for two skirted in pink, green and white. Sour-cream cake and banana bread are the usual fare.

In the back yard, the Newtons have put in a tennis court and an enclosed, solar-heated swimming pool with a jacuzzi.

"We like to be hosts and to enjoy our guests," says Frank. That they do very well.

Doubles, $80 to $135; suite, $175.

Brook Farm Inn, 15 Hawthorne St., Lenox 01240. (413) 637-3013.

This would be just another charming inn, were it not for the innkeepers' bent for literature and music. "There is poetry here," says the stylish cover of their brochure, and indeed there is.

You'll find it in each of the twelve guest rooms as well as in the front parlor, where Bob and Betty Jacob keep their 750 volumes of poetry and 70 tapes of spoken poetry.

They also have a well-stocked CD library, a piano and games. Bob has taped all of the PBS series, "Voices and Visions," for guests to watch on the VCR.

Every morning, he types out a poem of the day to display on the lectern. He does a poetry reading on Saturdays at tea time, and says guests "go bananas" over his wife's scones. Both acclaimed and would-be poets gather here. Many an aspiring writer has been inspired to try his hand at poetry, and many a poem has been added to the Jacobs' collection. They host writers' events and were thinking of a Brook Farm series of readings at Arrowhead, Herman Melville's house in Pittsfield. All might be expected from an inn that takes its name from the mid-19th-century Brook Farm literary commune in West Roxbury, Mass.

Brook Farm Inn.

The setting attracted the Leonard Bernstein family, which took over the inn for his 70th birthday extravaganza in 1988 at Tanglewood. All guest rooms have private baths, handsome furnishings and, of course, good reading lights on the headboards. Some have fireplaces, colorful stained-glass windows and skylights.

There is more than intellectual nourishment at Brook Farm. The Jacobs are gregarious hosts, and Bob pours a dynamite sherry from his own blend of three. A hearty breakfast could include apple fritters, pancakes, french toast made with thick Italian bread, bacon and eggs, and occasionaly blintzes. Guests also enjoy a heated pool and lovely gardens in back.

Doubles, $85 to $135.

Underledge, 76 Cliffwood St., Lenox 01240. (413) 637-0236.

A large white house with corner turret and solarium atop a hill some distance out Cliffwood Street, known to Lenox residents as *the* street but one often missed by tourists, this estate built in 1900 by two sisters was converted into an inn in 1982 by Marcie Lanoue and her son Tom, a carpenter.

All nine air-conditioned guest rooms and suites have private baths and are of substantial enough size to warrant their description as "parlor bedrooms." Five bedrooms have fireplaces, and all have sofas and loveseats that make for unusually comfortable relaxing. Marcie did the stenciling that enhances a couple of third-floor rooms, one an enormous bathroom converted from a former bedroom. A second-floor beauty has a kingsize bed, fireplace and a private balcony. We're partial to the large room off the stairway landing to the second floor, which has a fireplace framed in oak, two loveseats, a kingsize brass bedstead and a pleasant porch. One summery room on the main floor with a kingsize bed, chintz sofa, fireplace and a large walk-in shower is converted to a breakfast room in winter.

The entry foyer is richly paneled in stained oak. Contemporary off-white sofas surround the fireplace just off the lobby. In the living room are television, stereo, a grand piano and games. Continental breakfast, including muffins made by Tom's wife Cheryl, is served in the solarium in season.

Doubles, $120 to $130.

Gateways Inn and Restaurant, 71 Walker St., Lenox 01240. (413) 637-2532.

The landmark white, dark-shuttered mansion, built in 1912 by Harley Procter of Procter & Gamble and said to resemble a cake of Ivory soap, has long been a fixture in Lenox. Renowned chef-innkeeper Gerhard Schmid sold it in 1988 to Queens caterer Vito Perulli, who is maintaining its reputation and with innkeeper Brenda Mayberry redecorated the lobby to make it more welcoming.

Architect Stanford White inspired the two leaded windows by the main side entrance and the sweeping central staircase, which upon descending makes you feel as if you're floating into a ballroom. The eight guest rooms with private baths on the second floor are richly furnished in Colonial style with antiques and oriental rugs.

A front corner suite lined with books and containing a couch and two fireplaces was home for Arthur Fiedler during his Boston Pops concerts at Tanglewood. A semi-suite has a pillar in the middle with the bed at an angle, while a third room has heavy furniture carved in Austria. The west corner room harbors an eight-piece bird's-eye maple and black walnut Victorian bedroom set.

A full breakfast with a choice of the menu is served in one of the formal dining rooms (see below).

Doubles, $145 to $165; Fiedler Suite, $295.

Garden Gables, 141 Main St., Lenox 01240. (413) 637-0193.

The woman who had run this triple-gabled house as an inn since 1951 retired in 1988 and sold to Mario and Lynn Mekinda, an energetic couple from Toronto. Mario, an engineer who says he loves to tinker and fix things, has done wonders in adding private baths so that each of the eleven guest rooms now has one. The rooms are rather small, but cozy and clean, and are being gradually redecorated by Lynn.

The former gift shop has been transformed into a charming dining room, with views of the spacious five-acre grounds. A continental breakfast of orange juice, cantaloupe, muffins and croissants is served here. The new owners have totally redone the parlor, which has a TV and VCR, and the library, with two rust velvet sofas before the fireplace, decorated with horse brasses.

At our visit, Mario was preparing a new bedroom in back on the main floor with a kingsize bed, porch and large bathroom with jacuzzi.

A 72-foot-long swimming pool is an attraction in summer.

Doubles, $90 to $130.

Dining Spots

Wheatleigh, West Hawthorne Road, Lenox. (413) 637-0610.

"Wheatleigh is singular and stands alone," claims the introduction to the Berkshires' most lavish inn brochure. And so it does, according to knowing food afficionados hereabouts. They say the dining experience is perfect, if pretentious and pricey. The rest of us who cannot — or choose not to — partake must take their word for it.

The aim of innkeepers Susan and Linfield Simon is to have the best restaurant in the Northeast, one that's the match "of any three-star restaurant in New York." They took a giant step with the acquisition in 1985 of chef Bill Holbert, who had been at Parker's at the historic Parker House in Boston, training ground for many a nouvelle chef.

The Minneapolis-born chef is Irish-Dutch, his wife is German and his three young daughters bear French names. But his cuisine is regional nouvelle, with the emphasis on local and fresh — from morels to asparagus, shad roe to baby quails.

Dinner is prix-fixe at $58, and a special tasting menu is $80. Surcharges pop up frequently ($5 for sevruga caviar with wild rice blinis, $7 for seasonal salad, $8 for an assortment of cheeses with walnut bread). We hear that even coffee is an additional $5, and drinks a staggering $9.50.

The changing menu is inventive, to say the least. Aforementioned quails might turn up as an appetizer in a terrine of duck foie gras and quail with champagne grapes, as a soup in a quail consomme with quail eggs and truffles, or as an entree in quail poached with madeira stock and stuffed with veal sweetbread mousse on a nest of Anna potatoes.

Wheatleigh's kitchen is said to be labor-intensive, which is understandable when you see appetizers of duck confit and foie gras in a savoy cabbage pocket with two truffle sauces, or ravioli stuffed with escargots and artichokes in a light herbed bouillon.

Entrees could be black bass braised with champagne and leeks, grilled tuna with a Szechuan glaze and enoki mushrooms, loin of veal with wild mushrooms and a hive of pasta, filet mignon with black truffle sauce, roast squab on caramelized onions and venison loin with huckleberries.

Desserts are out of this world, perhaps a gateaux marjolaine, framboise-scented chevre layered with raspberries in a delicate pastry, a quartet of petite caramel desserts or a tart of clementines, pears and strawberries. Can't decide? Try the grand assortment. In this heady realm, what's $10 more?

The Simons have doubled the size of their wine list, with a number available in half-bottles. "At the high end," says Linwood, "our wines become very reasonable. If you're of a mind to drink Chateau Lafite, this is the place to do it."

The main dining room has been refurbished with Chippendale armchairs imported from England. All the tables are round, dressed in white linens and adorned with individual vases of exotic flowers. Three tile murals, each weighing 500 pounds, were found in England and put up on the walls; they acquire a luminescent quality in the candlelight.

Upstairs are seventeen guest rooms, which vary from spartan to opulent. To us, they have a lonesome feeling. Wheatleigh is a place that seems to inspire fierce loyalty or dislike. Rates range from $165 to $425.

Dinner, Tuesday-Sunday 6 to 9 or 9:30. Reservations required.

Church Street Cafe, 69 Church St., Lenox. (413) 637-2745.

This is the casual, creative kind of restaurant of which we never tire, the one we keep returning to for a quick but interesting meal whenever we're in Lenox. We're not alone, for it's generally No. 1 on the list of everyone's favorite eating establishments in town.

Owners Linda Forman and Clayton Hendrick have furnished their two small dining rooms and outdoor deck simply but tastefully. On one visit we admired all the amusing paintings of zebras on the walls, part of the changing art exhibits and all for sale. We also like the bar stools painted like black and white cows, udders hanging below, as well as the ficus trees lit with tiny white lights, the white pottery with colorful pink and blue flowers, the flute music playing in the background, and the reasonably priced wines.

Once Ethel Kennedy's chef, Clayton also worked in a Creole restaurant in Washington and that background shows. Blackened redfish might be a dinner special; Louisiana Creole gumbo was an entree when we were there. Lately, the fare has taken a Southwest turn, as in red chili pasta with peppers, corn, cilantro, scallions and toasted pumpkin seeds.

The menu lists six appetizers and about a dozen entrees at dinner. Start with charcoal-grilled garlic sausage with croutons and cornichons or black bean nachos with two salsas ($4.95 to $5.50). Chesapeake Bay crab cakes, charcoal-grilled Jamaican "jerk" chicken, eggplant rolatini, marinated pork medallions and Louisiana shrimp saute are among entrees, $11.95 to $16.95.

Lenox inns are known for sumptuous dining facilities, like this breakfast room at The Gables.

Our latest lunch included a super black bean tostada and the Church Street salad, a colorful array of goat cheese, chick peas, sprouts, eggs and red pepper, with a zippy dijon vinaigrette dressing on the side and whole wheat sunflower seed rolls, so good that we accepted seconds. Prices are $5.50 to $7.50.

Among desserts, we recommend the chilled cranberry souffle topped with whipped cream, the apple walnut crisp and the chocolate macadamia nut torte.

Lunch, Monday-Saturday 11:30 to 2:30; dinner nightly, 5:30 to 9; Sunday brunch in summer and fall.

Gateways Inn and Restaurant, 71 Walker St., Lenox. (413) 637-2532.

Noted chef Gerhard Schmid turned over the reins to his sous chef of four years, Jeffrey Niedeck, a Culinary Institute grad, when he sold the inn in 1988. Jeff kept the menu the same and the restaurant's coterie of regulars didn't miss a beat.

One of the formal dining rooms is the small and intimate Rockwell Room, named for the late artist Norman Rockwell, who dined there regularly. The Orleton Room, elaborately refurbished, has a sofa and chairs in the center, surrounded by five tables for dining. It leads to the new Procter Room in back. Fresh flowers grace the tables, set with white linens and fanned pink napkins.

The menu, which rarely changes but is supplemented by fresh seafood and game in season, is a blend of classic American and French. All entrees are a fixed price of $27, including salad and rolls. House specialties are shrimp Andreas (stuffed with crabmeat and mushrooms), rack of lamb, medallions of beef tenderloin, and Norwegian salmon topped with shrimp and lobster meat and finished in a dill-champagne sauce, garnished with hollandaise and toasted almonds. Veal sweetbreads, Dover sole meuniere and duckling with mandarin sauce are other favorites.

Appetizers ($6 to $8.75) include herring with sour cream, escargots, and warm duck salad with raspberry vinaigrette. There are always fresh fruit and vegetarian plates and a pasta of the day (all $18.50).

Among desserts ($4 to $4.50) are Viennese apple strudel, sabayon torte and praline pecan ice cream truffle.

The wine list contains an interesting mix of Massachusetts, California, New York, Pacific Northwest, French, German and Italian wines in that order. Most are priced in the teens and twenties.

An earlybird special including appetizer and dessert is available Monday-Thursday from 5:30 to 7 for $17.50. If the waiter neglects to tell you, ask.

Dinner nightly, 5:30 to 9 or 9:30; closed Sunday in winter.

Blantyre, Route 20 and East St., Lenox 01240. (413) 637-3556.

General manager Roderick Anderson planned to open the Blantyre dining experience to the public "in limited numbers" in 1989.

He envisioned serving lunch (appetizers, $8 to $12; entrees, $16 to $24) to perhaps twenty people on the outdoor terrace, and offering dinners for about forty patrons in the formal dining room or a couple of smaller private rooms.

Investing heavily in the kitchen, Blantyre put in a barbecue for grilling purposes and offered an alternative menu for the health-conscious. Chef Stephen Taub cooks in the Provence style, with a light hand on the sauces.

Five-course prix-fixe dinners are $65. A typical dinner starts with a choice of cucumber vichyssoise with shellfish butter, veloute of avocado, or seafood minestrone perfumed with lemon balm. Next comes perhaps a confit of duck salad with Belgian endive and pears, ravioli of wild mushrooms with white truffles or a duo of oysters in spinach pillows with caviar butter sauce.

A sorbet precedes the main course, perhaps steamed sea bass over red spinach with two caviars, Maine lobster with Thai herbs and tomato, medallion of veal with madeira and chanterelles, or grilled filet of beef with foie gras and zinfandel butter sauce.

Desserts could be Viennese chocolate walnut torte with chocolate ganache, cognac parfait with raspberry coulis and pistachio anglaise, terrine of two chocolates, or a berry compote with praline ice cream. Most guests take coffee and armagnac in the Music Room, where a harpist and pianist play on weekends.

Blantyre prepares some fairly exotic "fantasy picnics" ($30 to $60) for guests headed to Tanglewood.

Lunch, July and August; dinner nightly in season.

Apple Tree Inn, 224 West St., Lenox. (413) 637-1477.

The round dining room still has the spectacular panoramic view and carousel ceiling with ribs of bulb lights that it had when it was Alice's at Avaloch — Alice's upscale restaurant after she moved from Housatonic to the inn across from Tanglewood. It is all pink and white, with Austrian-type curtains.

In cooler months, meals are served in the McIntosh Tavern, a cheery haunt in winter, with red and white checked curtains, red tablecloths, paneled walls, booths and a big fireplace.

Of the five pasta dishes offered at dinner, linguini al Gustav ($17) sounds wonderful: jumbo shrimp in a sauce of tomato, basil, garlic, olive oil and wine. Other entrees ($14.50 to $18) include three presentations each of veal and chicken, as well as broiled salmon, blackened fish of the day with Cajun remoulade sauce and roast Long Island duckling.

Sauteed langoustinos, smoked trout and pate of the day are among appetizers ($6 to $7.50). There are sometimes as many as fourteen desserts ("you'd think you were in a Viennese pastry shop," says owner Greg Smith), with fresh fruit tarts, profiteroles and chocolate mousse cake always popular. Pastry chef Lisa Thomas prepares things like

Kentucky bourbon pound cake with buttered bourbon sauce, chocolate cherry truffle torte and frozen white chocolate frangelico mousse. People often come back after Tanglewood concerts for dessert and coffee.

The wine list is an interesting mix of bottles the Smiths enjoy, balanced between French, Italian and Californian. Drinks are served in summer on the outdoor terrace.

Lunch daily during Tanglewood season, noon to 2; dinner nightly, 5:30 to 9:30. No smoking in dining room.

Cafe Lucia, 90 Church St., Lenox. (413) 637-2640.

Jim and Dianne Lucie have transformed the former Ganesh, which was an art gallery cum cafe, into an expanded cafe with art as a sideline. "We're a restaurant that shows and sells art," explains Jim, who opened up the kitchen so patrons can glimpse the goings-on.

Jim's Italian cuisine is much favored by locals, who praise his pasta creations, baked polenta with homemade sausage and Italian codfish stew. The osso buco con risotto is so good that it draws New Yorkers back annually, and Jim reports he almost had a riot on his hands when he took the shrimp alla Medici off the menu (it was promptly restored, even though he had offered it on specials). Entrees are priced from $12.95 to $16.95 and include house salad.

Among desserts are cold chocolate souffle cake with almonds and amaretto, frangelico and hazelnut cheesecake, gorgonzola and fresh pears, and a sauteed apple, cinnamon and sour cream pie.

Those desserts, a fine port or brandy and cappuccino can be taken on the flower-bedecked patio on warm summer evenings.

Dinner nightly from 5; winter, Tuesday-Saturday from 5:30.

The Village Inn, 16 Church St., Lenox. (413) 637-0020.

Afternoon tea and well-regarded dinners are served in this inn, which has had aspirations to be a focal point in Lenox since it was built in 1771 and carries its age well. The inn was nicely restored lately by Clifford Rudisill and Ray Wilson, who added 25 bathrooms and now offer 29 guest rooms.

Villeroy & Boch china, pistol-handled knives and fresh flowers enhance the white-clothed tables in the Harvest Room. Dinner entrees run from $12.95 for pecan breaded chicken to $16.95 for shrimp tarragon or roasted breast of pheasant served with braised red cabbage and Kentucky bourbon sauce. Chef John Clapper offered a novel pasta — tenderloin tips and jumbo shrimp in creamy herbed bordelaise sauce — on the winter menu. Venison pate and smoked breast of duckling with ginger root and grand marnier glaze were appealing starters ($4.75 to $6.95), and we liked the sound of the mushroom and cheddar "potage."

English tea is served every afternoon from 2:30 to 4:30. Complete tea is $8.25, with variations priced downward (sandwiches and scones, $6.50).

Dinner nightly except Monday, 5:30 to 9:30. No smoking.

Brushwood Cafe, Route 7, Lenox. (413) 637-2711.

Part of the Brushwood Farm complex, this is the 1750 house once occupied by Paolo's Auberge, and when Paolo Eugster left, his chef stayed on.

One-time owner Harold Godwin, New York Post publisher and grandson of poet William Cullen Bryant, had an art studio in what is now the rear dining room. Some of his watercolors are framed into the woodwork surrounding the bar in the waiting room.

Dinner is served in small, elegantly appointed Victorian dining rooms with lace cloths over burgundy and high-back chairs.

Chef Pam Greene's changing menu lists up to sixteen entrees from $11.50 for pasta primavera to $19.50 for marinated lamb chops. Filet of sole with scallop mousse, pork tenderloin with apples, saltimbocca, chicken with goat cheese and stuffed quail with orange sauce are some of the possibilities.

Start with ginger-carrot or oriental chicken noodle soup ($3). Duck galantine with cumberland sauce and escargots in puff pastry are favored appetizers ($4.50 to $6.50).

A tavern menu offers entrees from $8.50 for shepherd's pie to $15.50 for sirloin steak and shrimp. For starters, sausage and onions in puff pastry and fishermen's mussels are $4 and $5.

Dinner nightly except Tuesday from 6.

Wyndhurst, Cranwell Resort Hotel and Conference Center, Route 20, Lenox. (413) 637-1364.

Blessed with the acquisition of two French chefs from Blantyre in 1988, the lovely dining room at this imposing resort fashioned from the Jesuits' old Cranwell preparatory school was highly regarded when we visited in the winter of 1989.

Window table at Wyndhurst.

Cranwell must be seen to be believed — it's a tapestry of marble, 60,000 pounds worth. Marble is everywhere: in the bathrooms, on the floors, along the bar. The resort has 65 guest rooms, the twelve most choice being those in the mansion — spacious and decorated in surprisingly modern style, renting for $259 to $359 a night.

While the conference-center theme is obvious (a group of businessmen was lining up on the main staircase to pose for a photographer when we were there), the **Music Room Lounge,** the **Cranwell Pub,** the **Sun Room** for light fare, the majestic **Grand Ballroom** and the **Rose Terrace** in summer attract transients.

With its lace table cloths, pink silk upholstered chairs, pale green carpet and lovely moldings, the baronial yet intimate Wyndhurst is surely Lenox's most glamorous dining room. The dinner menu is priced from $18 for grilled chicken with a truffle sauce on a bed of leeks to $26 for rack of lamb bouquetiere. Broiled monkfish with a red bell pepper sauce, veal forestiere, sauteed salmon steak, and venison with a puree of apple and celery root are among the choices.

Among appetizers ($8.75 to $13.95), try quail on an endive nest, smoked duck around a savory slaw or ginger shrimp beurre blanc. Desserts might include a poached pear with strawberry demi-glaze, apple puff pastry with caramel sauce and vanilla ice cream, hazelnut torte or lemon mousse pie.

A Sunday buffet brunch is $14.95, and lunch on the terrace is deservedly popular in summer. The wine list, which looks like a scrapbook, includes a page of interesting beers.

Lunch, Tuesday-Saturday; dinner, Tuesday-Sunday 5 to 10; Sunday brunch.

Dakota, Route 7, Lenox. (413) 499-7900.

Rebuilt and expanded following a fire in 1988, this immensely popular steakhouse is part of the Sirloin Saloon group from Vermont. It looks like a ski chalet with rustic, hunting-lodge decor — a far cry from its onetime heritage as a Howard Johnson's.

Patrons wait for up to two hours on busy weekends to get a table in the restaurant, which seats 250 in a variety of rooms. The focal area contains two enormous salad bars (with a spectacular selection, say the local innkeepers), an open grill, a lobster tank, a display case containing slabs of beef, and a table where huge loaves of Buffalo bread are displayed (and cost $10 to take home).

Western grain-fed beef is featured, priced from $11.95 for top sirloin or teriyaki sirloin to $15.95 for prime rib. Mesquite-grilled chicken, swordfish and shrimp are offered separately or in a variety of combinations from $9.95 to $13.95. The day's specials when we were there included Norwegian salmon with lime coriander butter, wood-grilled yellowtail tuna or rainbow trout, and baked scrod. Light entrees, including bread and salad bar, go for $7.95 to $9.95 — little wonder the place is packed.

The all-American wine list has similar values, and New York cheesecake and mud pie are the obligatory desserts.

Dinner nightly, 5 to 10 or 11.

Laura's Scottish Tea Room and Bakery, Lenox House Country Shops, Route 7, Lenox. (413) 637-1060.

This small tea room is a good place for breakfast or lunch. It's the kind of spot where Heinz salad cream is put on the tables, and racks of muffins, scones, cookies, sausage rolls and meat pies beckon enticingly.

The beef and barley soup hit the spot on a winter day, and the beef bridie ($2.95) was garnished with a carrot and raisin salad, the kind that mother used to make. The broccoli and cheddar quiche was delicious, but a paltry portion for $4.95. Chicken and pork pies are $4.95, and various open croissant sandwiches, $4.25.

A full breakfast is served until 2 p.m. and, of course, tea in the afternoon. This goes well with Laura's homebaked Scottish shortbread, which is also available by mail order. Two little sample squares come with your bill.

Open daily for breakfast, lunch, tea and light dinners.

Diversions

Tanglewood, West Street, Lenox. The name is synonymous with music and Lenox. The summer home of the Boston Symphony Orchestra since 1936, the 210-acre estate above the waters of Stockbridge Bowl in the distance is an idyllic spot for concerts and socializing at picnics. The 6,000 reserved seats in the open-air shed sell for $12 to $44; up to 10,000 fans can be accommodated at $8 each on the lawn (bring your own chairs, blankets, picnics and wine, or pick up something from the cafeteria). Concerts are at 9 p.m. Friday, 8:30 p.m. Saturday and 2:30 p.m. Sunday, last weekend of June through August.

Shakespeare & Company, Plunkett Street, Lenox. Edith Wharton's former estate above Laurel Lake, the Mount, is the magnificent outdoor setting for three Shakespeare plays presented in repertory Tuesday through Sunday evenings in summer. The neo-Georgian home of the novelist is open for tours ($3.50) Tuesday-Friday 11 to 5, weekends 9:30 to 5 in summer, Friday-Sunday in fall.

Lenox Arts Center, Citizens Hall, Interlaken. An improvisational music-theater group presents three new productions each summer, Wednesday-Sunday at 9 p.m. Some of its plays and playwrights have gone on to Broadway.

Pleasant Valley Wildlife Sanctuary, West Road off Route 7 north, Lenox. The Massachusetts Audubon Society maintains a 740-acre nature preserve high up Lenox Mountain next to Yokum Brook. A museum of live and stuffed animals and nearly eight miles of nature trails through forests, meadows and marshes are a pleasant refuge for a few hours. Open daily except Monday year-round.

Shopping. Lenox offers some of the most exclusive shops in the Berkshires. Along Main Street, we like **Christopher & Company** for its pottery, especially MacKenzie-Childs from Aurora, N.Y. in lovely colors, and hand-painted animals from Herend, a Hungarian firm. Gifts, cookbooks and the delicious local chocolates, Boomer's Oogies, are sold here. As a women's specialty store for more than three decades, **Elise Farrar** at 361 Pittsfield Road is a classic of its genre. Along Church Street, **Mary Stuart Collections** has wonderful needlework, potpourris and fragrances, children's clothes fit for royalty, and heavenly lingerie. Neat casual clothes are at **Glad Rags,** and fine contemporary crafts at the **Hoadley Gallery.** Ormsby's is an interesting gift, games and accessories shop. **Tanglewool** sells English cashmeres and other handknits, Italian bags, Arche shoes from France, creative jewelry, and imported yarns and knitting patterns; everything here has a flair. Behind the Church Street Cafe, **Weaver's Fancy** displays handsome weavings, from placemats to pillows to coats.

On Walker Street you'll find **Talbot's** for classic clothes and **Evviva!** for contemporary. At the **Curtis House Shops** on the ground floor of the old Curtis Hotel, which has been converted to apartments, are **The Hand of Man,** an interesting crafts gallery, and **Celtic Origins** with Irish and Scottish imports.

Just north of town, the **Different Drummer** (at the Lenox House Country Shops) has all kinds of kitchen ware, contemporary crafts, cards and even a bath shop. There are also good factory outlets in this complex.

Nearby, **Brushwood Farms** is a collection of shops that is fun to browse through. We enjoy the **Brushwood General Store,** crammed full of gifts and goodies, and **White Horse Hill,** a treasure chest of goods from England, Scotland and Wales, from postcards of Penzance to gorgeous mohair sweaters. **The Stables** is a small luncheon spot here where you can get delicious ham sandwiches, made with the country-glazed ham sold in the deli out front. Pea soup, homemade bread pudding and smoked turkey sandwich with raspberry-mayo dressing are in the $1.50 to $4.50 range.

Extra-Special

Chesterwood, Route 183, Stockbridge.

Lenox's next-door neighbor, Stockbridge, has so many attractions — from the Norman Rockwell Museum to the Berkshire Garden Center (even the Red Lion, the epitome of New England inns) — that it should not be missed. Our favorite is Chesterwood, the secluded estate of sculptor Daniel Chester French, who is famed for the Seated Lincoln in Washington. Visitors start at a gallery in the old cow barn, see the 30-foot-high studio in which the sculptor worked and tour the grand Colonial Revival home in which he spent six months a year until he died there in 1931. The period garden, nature trail and museum shop appeal as well. Open May-October, daily 10 to 5. Adults $4.

Chatham, Mass.
Serenity Beside the Sea

Of all Cape Cod's towns, we are fondest of Chatham, a sophisticated, sedate and serene enclave of affluence beside the sea. This is the elbow of the Cape, where the hubbub of much of the south shore yields to treed tranquility before the land veers north to face the open Atlantic and form the dunes of the National Seashore.

Known locally as "The First Stop of the East Wind," Chatham is one of the Cape's oldest towns (settled in 1656) and one of its most residential. Hidden in the trees and along the meandering waterfront are large homes and estates.

Explore a bit and you may see the gorgeous hydrangea walk leading up to a Shore Road mansion. Across from a windmill in a field of yellow wildflowers sparkling against a backdrop of blue ocean, it's the essence of Cape Cod. Or you may follow Mooncusser's Lane and find that the road ends abruptly at the water. Admire the view from the drawbridge on Bridge Street as well as the classic views of the Chatham Light.

Because it's so residential, Chatham has escaped the overt commercialism and tourism of much of the Cape. This is not a place catering to transients; some inns and motels encourage long stays, and many of the accommodations are in cottages or rented houses.

The summer social scene revolves around parties and private clubs. But almost everyone turns out for the Friday evening band concerts in Kate Gould Park.

Although Main Street, which winds through the center of town, seems filled with pedestrians and shoppers, chances are they're residents or regulars. Perhaps its air of stability and tradition is what makes Chatham so special.

Inn Spots

Chatham Bars Inn, Shore Road, Chatham 02633. (508) 945-0096.

This complex of an imposing inn and charming oceanfront houses existed virtually as a private club from its days as a hunting lodge built in 1914 to its acquisition by

South Lounge at Chatham Bars Inn.

Boston real-estate developer Bill Langelier in 1987. Following costly renovations to the 150 guest rooms and public areas, the inn was opened year-round, advertised bargain off-season packages and announced to the world, "we're here — come enjoy."

One of the last great oceanfront resorts, this is unusually appealing, lavish and with-it. It's perched on 80 acres of bluff with half a mile of shoreline overlooking Pleasant Bay and the barrier beach separating it from the Atlantic. Rooms run the gamut from 50 of the traditional type in the main inn to sumptuous suites in 27 cottages, many of them really houses containing two to eight guest rooms and common living rooms with fireplaces. We enjoyed watching the surf pummeling the now-famous breach in the barrier beach from the balcony off the

Pleasant Bay is backdrop for dining room at Wequasset Inn.

plush sitting room of our cottage suite, which was suavely decorated in shades of mauve and rose.

The resort contains an enormous dining room, the casual Beach House Grill, a convivial lounge, a nine-hole golf course, five tennis courts, a pool and a beach.

Chef Roland Czekelius of Boston's Park Plaza Hotel joined the Chatham Bars in 1988 as executive chef. The prix-fixe dinner menu ($32) featured such updated continental specialties as shrimp scampi dijon, grilled duck breast bigarade, chicken francaise and veal Oscar. The Sunday evening buffet ($32) remained a fixture, but the Beach House Grill went back to hot dogs and hamburgers after a brief and wonderful stint with exciting regional cuisine.

Although the new management takes pride in providing luxury rooms, good food and service, the resort is distinguished by its mix of accommodations. You can mingle and make merry in the main inn, or get away from it all in a house by the sea.

Doubles, $230 to $290, MAP; cottages for two, $245 to $425.

Wequassett Inn, Pleasant Bay, Chatham 02633. (508) 432-5400 or (800) 225-7125.

Blessed with a fine location above its private beach and peninsula separating Round Cove from Pleasant Bay, this inn reflects its Indian name for "crescent on the water." The new blends quite nicely with the old in a resort compound with structures dating back 200 years. Eighteen Cape Cod-style cottages, motel buildings and condo-type facilities totaling 103 rooms are distributed across 22 rolling, beautifully landscaped acres amid huge old pines.

Large guest rooms and suites are traditionally furnished with cheery colors, patterned fabrics, pine furniture, quilted bedspreads, duck-print wall hangings and needlepoint rugs. We like best the waterview suites, with windows onto the bay and decks for outdoor lounging. Others are partial to the tennis villas, many with cathedral ceilings and private balconies overlooking the woods or courts. Rooms have cable TV, refrigerators, phones, air-conditioning and, a nice touch, small flashlights — "we go through $7,000 worth a year," says managing partner Clive C.L. Chu. It is touches like these in which Clive excels. The inn earned membership in the prestigious Preferred Hotels association of luxury resorts shortly after his arrival in 1986; Wequasset is the only New England inn so honored.

At the disposal of guests are five tennis courts with a resident pro, sailboats and canoes, a special offshore sailing school program, a large swimming pool and a half-mile-long beach. A boat shuttles guests to Nauset Beach.

Guests may take their meals in the historic "square top" Eben Ryder House, which is acclaimed for fine dining (see below).

Doubles, $150 to $210, EP; suites, $300. Open mid-May to mid-October.

The Captain's House Inn of Chatham, 371 Old Harbor Road (Route 28), Chatham 02633. (508) 945-0127.

Captain Hiram Harding's 1839 home was taken over in 1983 by Philadelphians David and Cathy Eakin, who spruced it up for their first innkeeping venture, added the personal touches that make it so inviting, went on to expand and now are proud that theirs is one of two AAA four-diamond small inns in New England. To a consultant's comment during our latest visit that "this is the standard for all other inns on the Cape," Dave replied simply that "we try to be the best that we can be for what we do." Which is to provide an elegant and comfortable place for a quiet getaway.

Set on shaded lawns screened by high hedges in a sedate residential section north of the village and a pleasant ten-minute walk from the water, the Captain's House is refined and tranquil. The entrance hall and living room retain the original pumpkin pine floors and are furnished with antiques, oriental rugs and period wallpapers.

The ten guest rooms with private baths in the main Greek Revival house have a variety of furnishings, including four-poster beds wih pineapple finials, lacy white fishnet canopies, white eyelet-edged curtains, colorful sheets and comforters, thick towels, braided rugs and soft velvet wing chairs for reading. Two have working fireplaces, and Whytemor & Keach toiletries are provided in the bathrooms.

The most coveted room is in the Captain's Cottage, which was renovated into a sumptuous suite with dark wood paneling, a fine oriental rug on the wide-plank floor, working fireplace, sofa and four-poster bed. Three deluxe rooms were fashioned in 1987 from a rear carriage house.

Cathy Eakin's touch is evident in the kitchen as well as in the gardens. She serves afternoon tea with homemade cookies and scones, which you may top with whipped cream and jam; there are different goodies every day. The Eakins also offer a continental breakfast buffet on the sunny dining porch, set with blue and white mats and big blue napkins. Included are English muffins and delicious homemade nut breads, blueberry muffins and preserves. While we enjoyed an early-morning stroll along the shore road, Dave drove into town to pick up copies of the Boston Globe for people to read with breakfast. He also takes guests out fishing or for a luncheon cruise on his 35-foot sloop.

Doubles, $95 to $140. Closed December to mid-February.

The Queen Anne Inn, 70 Queen Anne Road, Chatham 02633. (508) 945-0394.

Among small inns, Chatham's most posh is the house built by a sea captain in the 1840s as a wedding gift for his daughter. Austrians Guenther and Nicole Weinkopf reclaimed it from near ruin in 1978. Their renovated structure has 30 guest rooms, all with modern baths (some with whirlpools) and telephones, and seven with fireplaces. There is a rather austere, antiques-filled sitting room, plus a downstairs lounge with big-screen television, a spa room with a large jacuzzi and an acclaimed restaurant (see Dining Spots).

All the guest rooms and suites are furnished with antiques, including many kingsize

Captain's House Inn of Chatham occupies residential site north of village.

pencil-post beds (some canopied) and bentwood rockers. The prized rear rooms have private balconies overlooking the rear gardens and Oyster Pond. We were intrigued by the striking map etched in the window panes of the northeast corner room on the main floor.

Guests may swim in the pond or walk ten minutes to the beach. They also may play tennis on three clay courts hidden away in a park-like setting. Guenther, a licensed skipper, offers guests day cruises to Nantucket as well as picnic and sightseeing excursions to the Monomoy Islands. The inn's Tuesday night clambakes in the gardens are popular.

Complimentary continental breakfasts with homemade muffins are served in the dining room or on the porch beside the garden.

Doubles, $96 to $196.

The Bradford Inn and Motel, 26 Cross St., Chatham 02633. (508) 945-1030.

An exceptionally attractive inn evolving from a motel, this venerable establishment is well situated in a residential section just off Chatham's Main Street. For years we had admired its cheery exterior with yellow awnings, as well as the well-kept gardens with flowers of every hue; the interior, we found, is just as nice.

Innkeepers William and Audrey Gray live in the 1860 Captain Elijah Smith House, which also serves as the office and common facility. There is a parlor-lounge, and the Garden Room at the rear is where a full complimentary breakfast (guests choose from a large menu) is served. The apricot pancakes are so good that they draw the public as well. In season, many prefer to linger over coffee on the yellow and white lawn furniture on the garden patio beside the small pool, savoring the extravagant roses and watching the birds feed.

Five large rooms are in the Bradford House in front, which we found cozy with a fire on a fall evening, while four are in the Carriage House near the pool. The most deluxe are four with king and queensize canopy beds, fireplaces and thick carpeting in the newly built Jonathan Gray House. Eleven more are in the L-shaped motel building in back. Five have kitchens and some are suites. All are individually decorated and have private baths, cable television, refrigerators, telephones and air-conditioning.

Ever expanding and refining, the Grays recently added the Lion's Den game room and lounge, opened a two-bedroom cottage as the Captain's Hideway, and were restoring the Mulberry House at 44 Cross St. into an elegant B&B with two luxurious bedrooms and a fireplaced common room, to open in 1989. They now offer drinks and

277

snacks through room service. They also provide the most elaborate mimeographed information sheet we've seen on guest services and area offerings.

Doubles, $90 to $150.

Cyrus Kent House, 63 Cross St., Chatham 02633. (508) 945-9104.

An ex-insurance executive from Hartford is one of Chatham's busiest innkeepers. Richard T. Morris restored an 1877 sea captain's home into this comfortable B&B in 1985, went into partnership and opened the Ship's Inn in 1988, and was preparing to restore and reopen an expanded Cranberry Inn in 1989.

Antiques, original art and fresh flowers from the inn's gardens decorate the Cyrus Kent's eight guest rooms, all with private baths, clock radios and telephones. Some have fireplaces and decks. Eyelet curtains and upholstered wing chairs are special features.

The newest and largest room upstairs in the rear carriage house has a living room with high ceiling and Austrian curtains around the rounded window that is its focal point. The main floor of the carriage house is Horatio Hall, the inn's own art and antiques gallery featuring some of the primitives of inn manager Mary Flagg.

A continental breakfast of fresh fruit and homemade muffins is set up in the center hall, for guests to take to the spacious living room or dining room with their marble fireplaces, the country kitchen or the front porch.

Doubles, $92. Closed Christmas to Easter.

The Ship's Inn at Chatham, 364 Old Harbor Road, Chatham 02633. (508) 945-5859.

If this enlongated, 1839 whaling captain's house bears a resemblance to the Cyrus Kent, it's because Richard Morris is its co-owner and chief restorationist in partnership with innkeeper Peggy DeHan. Located across the street from the Captain's House Inn of Chatham, it is remarkable for its narrow width and extreme depth. "The house is one room wide so you get windows on both sides," notes Peggy.

That provides considerable light, as do the interesting window treatments and decorative touches that are becoming a Morris-DeHan trademark. The theme is set in the living room with its beige sofas: oriental rugs grace white pine floors, striped paper brightens the walls and balloon curtains festoon the windows.

Six guest rooms with private baths and phones are available in one section in front of the living room, up steep ship's stairs from the dining room or in the rear section. Two have fireplaces.

Climb those ship's stairs if you can to see a room with a great window seat full of peach-colored pillows, antique twin beds with carved wreaths on them, a large pine armoire and a stenciled bathroom bearing peach towels. Once here, you may have difficulty leaving — one lanky fellow had to back down the stairs.

A continental breakfast of fruit and muffins is served at a big pine table in the fireplaced dining room or on the side porch where chairs are outfitted in purple fabric.

Doubles, $85. Closed Christmas to Easter.

The Cranberry Inn at Chatham, 359 Main St., Chatham 02633. (508) 945-9232.

Once named the Traveler's Home and later the Monomoy House, this red-frame inn dates from the 1830s and has charmed or suffered accordingly. That is, until 1988, when it was acquired by Richard Morris and Peggy DeHan, who planned a total renovation and addition to be ready in 1989.

The fourteen original guest rooms were to be doubled in size, thanks to an addition on the east end, and all were to have new private baths, telephones and television. Some were to be suites of two or three rooms. Peggy planned light but elegant decor, with her

Comfortable home of former town physician is now the Old Harbor Inn.

striking window treatments, colorful linens and Shaker-style furniture, including pencil-post beds.

On the main floor where the previous owners ran a simple but thriving restaurant, the new owners planned to offer a full breakfast to house guests and were contemplating ultimately reopening the restaurant for dinner. Meanwhile, they were fixing up a rear patio for breakfast and drinks, redecorating the large Colonial-style living room, and expanding the front porch — "the best spot in town to watch the Fourth of July parade," according to Richard.

Doubles, $98. Closed Christmas to Easter.

The Old Harbor Inn, 22 Old Harbor Road, Chatham 02633. (508) 945-4434.

For a change of pace, consider this newer home built for the physician who "delivered half the babies in Chatham," according to owner-renovator Rich Derby. Built in a very different style than the Cape Cod norm, it's smashingly decorated and luxuriously comfortable in a contemporary kind of way.

The stage is set in the living room, all pink and green with lots of chintz, botanical prints on the walls, a rug patterned with flowers and a piano in the corner. To the side is a breakfast porch furnished in white wicker leading onto an attractive deck.

Upstairs are four guest rooms, all with private baths, strikingly appointed and bearing the different names the town was called before it became Chatham. One is all red and white, from the white eyelet comforter to the red towels and a porthole in the bathroom. Another is in blue and white with a wicker loveseat. A third in black and floral-print fabrics has a huge bathroom with a rug that matches the border trim. Still another is all pink and white, with wicker chairs, dhurrie rugs, balloon curtains and a wicker bedstead.

Two more guest rooms have private entrances in a wing off the first floor. They are equally light, bright and airy in shades of pink, green and gray, and contain the thick rugs, candy and Boggs cranberry liqueurs featured in the rest of the house.

A continental breakfast of fruits, cereals, and homemade breads and muffins is served in the morning. On weekends, a more substantial breakfast (maybe eggs and sausages) is available.

Rich and Pat Derby, who opened the inn in 1986, sold it lock, stock and barrel two years later to Sharon and Tom Ferguson, Virginia transplants originally from Connecticut, who planned to operate it as is.

Doubles, $95 to $105.

Chatham Town House Inn and Lodge, 11 Library Lane, Chatham 02633. (508) 945-2180.

This Victorian inn complex, just off Main Street, has grown and grown as Svea and Russell Peterson raised three children on the site and continually sought bigger quarters (they finally built a house at the rear, giving up the last of the family rooms to guests).

The expanding complex, full of eccentricities, is a hodgepodge of rooms new and old, of varying sizes and homey decor. If the whole does not hold together as well as its individual parts, that's because, like a family house, it's still evolving (we even had trouble finding the entrance, after several aborted dead-ends). Sixteen rooms are in the main house built in the 1820s and in a wing opened in 1977. An adjacent lodge has seven rooms, including a two-bedroom cottage, and another building has a two-bedroom cottage with living room and kitchen (like the family home it once was) and a large guest room fashioned from a garage.

All have private baths, air-conditioning, color television, room phones and small, prominently placed refrigerators. Attractive quilts, painted furniture, hooked rugs, bath amenities and queensize beds (some canopy) are the norm.

In their nautical dining room, Svea, who managed a hotel in Stockholm, Sweden, and Russell display a rare set of show plates and champagne glasses from the liner S.S. United States. The one-of-a-kind set of china is the backdrop for a breakfast of eggs, homefries, bacon or sausage served in the cheerful dining room. It is complimentary; the Scandinavian specialties (Norwegian smoked salmon with eggs, wine marinated smoked pepper mackerel filet or, on Sundays, Svea's Finnish oven-baked pancakes with fresh fruit melange) are $5 extra for houseguests, $7 for the public.

Doubles, $98 to $155. Closed January to mid-February.

Chatham Wayside Inn, 512 Main St., Chatham 02633. (508) 945-1800.

When we first vacationed in Chatham nearly three decades ago, the Wayside seemed the quintessential New England inn — located in the heart of town and containing a lively tavern that was perfect for an after-dinner drink. Today, with the proliferation of inns everywhere, it no longer seems that way, although new owner Guenther Weinkopf of the Queen Anne Inn has set about to change the situation.

Renovations are under way in the elongated structure dating from the 18th century to produce 25 guest rooms. The finished ones we saw were outfitted with four-poster beds with crocheted canopies, a single wing chair, TVs tucked away in hutches, telephones and full baths.

There's an outdoor swimming pool, and plans were to renovate a couple of cottages.

Off the main lobby are two restaurants. The popular **Sam Bellamy's Tavern,** which looks properly tavern-like, features an all-day menu from nachos to kabobs, nicely priced in the $5 to $9 range. The long, slate-floored dining room with beamed ceiling has been rechristened **Harbor Seafood,** the theme borrowed from Boston's popular Legal Seafoods restaurants, according to manager Tony Raine. Fresh fish — baked, broiled or blackened — is priced from $12 to $15, including salad and choice of red-skin potatoes or mild spiced rice. The British-born manager keeps up a busy summer schedule of entertainment Wednesday through Saturday in the tavern, with comedy nights Tuesdays in the dining room. Off-season he was planning celebrations of Guy Fawkes Day and Boxing Day.

Doubles, $85 to $105, EP; cottages, $120 to $150.

Creative dining is offered on porch at Christian's.

Dining Spots

Christian's, 443 Main St., Chatham. (508) 945-3362.

For a fine meal, a raw bar, cocktails on an upper deck, or nightly entertainment and a pub menu in the classic English bar, Christian's is a favorite choice among locals.

With the help of his brother and his parents, chef Christian Schultz offers a creative dinner menu in the airy, casual porch or the more formal dining room with white linens, beamed ceilings, oriental rugs and latticed dividers.

With drinks comes a complimentary chicken liver pate served with melba toast. Appetizers range from $6 for Portuguese egg rolls to $10 for a plate of imported and domestic caviars with fried wontons and ginger sour cream, which we ordered and enjoyed but felt did not include enough caviar to be worth the tab. On another occasion we liked the crab beurrecks wrapped in phyllo dough and a special called "cockles and such," which happened to be four Monterey oysters in a choron sauce.

Entrees run from $15.95 for fish of the day to $24 for veal medallions sauteed with lobster, shrimp and scallops. Roast duck with a fresh fruit sauce (once raspberry, the next time pear and pink peppercorns) is the house specialty, and filet mignon might be prepared three ways — bearnaise, au poivre or stuffed with brie. On various visits, we've enjoyed fresh halibut sauced with asparagus hollandaise, a superb veal and shrimp saute, the duck with kiwi and raspberries, and calves liver in a cabernet sauce. These came with interesting vegetables — once green and yellow squash, carrots and rice, another time green beans, cauliflower and turnip puree — plus crusty French bread and a simple salad of hearts of palm with a zesty herb and cheese dressing. The portions are so large that few have room for dessert, though we once splurged for a grand marnier torte topped by a chocolate shell filled with grand marnier.

After dinner, adjourn to **Upstairs at Christian's** for cordials and special coffees. A laid-back, luxurious space, it has a handsome curved oak bar, African mahogany paneling, shelves filled with books, and an interesting mix of eaves and niches with leather sofas and loveseats. When we stopped in, a banjo player, "proud to be a preppy from North Chatham," sang rousing ditties while one of a collection of old movies was shown in "The Critic's Corner."

Dinner nightly, 6 to 10; closed Thanksgiving-March.

The Impudent Oyster, 15 Chatham Bars Ave., Chatham. (508) 945-3545.

With a name like that and an innovative menu, how could this place miss? Run by Michele and Peter Barnard and always jammed and noisy to the point (for us) of turn-off, patrons crowd together at small glass-covered tables under a cathedral ceiling, plants in straw baskets balanced overhead on the beams.

The international menu, based on local seafoods, is an intriguing blend of regional, Chinese, Mexican, Indian, Greek and Italian cuisines, among others. For dinner, we couldn't resist starting with the drunken mussels ($4.95), shelled and served chilled in an intense marinade of tamari, fresh ginger, Szechuan peppercorns and sake, with a side portion of snow peas and red peppers. The Mexican chicken chili and lime soup, one of the best we've tasted, was spicy and full of interesting flavors. Also delicious were the spinach and mushroom salads with either creamy mustard or anchovy dressings.

Among entrees ($14 to $21), it was difficult to choose from such imaginative offerings as celestial oysters (poached in champagne, topped with hollandaise and served on pasta), shrimp Sardinia, grilled bass Mediterranee, scallops San Cristobal with avocado and cilantro, and Barbados bluefish. A spicy pinot grigio for $12.50 went well with such assertive fare. A plate of several ice creams made with fresh fruit was a cooling finale.

The menu changes frequently, and is supplemented by nightly specials. It's the kind of cuisine of which we never tire, although we would prefer to have it in a more peaceful setting. We also could do without being told by the hostess that "Mary Lou will be cocktailing you this evening."

Lunch, 11:30 to 3; dinner, 5:30 to 10.

The Queen Anne Inn, 70 Queen Anne Road, Chatham. (508) 945-0394.

For a restaurant with distinguished cuisine, the Earl of Chatham at the Queen Anne Inn is in a rather undistinguished room. There are twelve tables with uncomfortable bentwood chairs, pink linens, stenciling, dark oak wainscoting and oriental rugs.

The hand-written menu offered by a team of three chefs imported from Austria and Switzerland changes frequently. The pricetag is dear (make that staggering): a cream of butternut squash soup served with diced sweetbreads for $6 is par for the course. Appetizers run from $6.50 for a tomato salad with goat cheese to $12.50 for sauteed quail with a salad of french beans and enoki mushrooms or homemade ravioli with confit of duck, served with sauteed foie gras and black currant sauce.

Main courses begin at $25 for sauteed haddock (that's right, haddock) with a red butter sauce or sauteed monkfish, sole and scallops with lobster cream sauce and fettuccine. Prices top off at $28.50 for a veal chop filled with lobster and spinach. Loin of lamb might come with a garlic-thyme sauce and medallions of venison with creme de cassis.

Innkeeper Guenther Weinkopf is proud of the desserts, which he compares favorably with those of any pastry shop in Europe. We've heard great things about the sachertorte, and the fresh fruit mousses and homemade sorbets are said to be out of this world.

The limited wine list, compiled by the head waiter, starts at $19 and contains some not-often-seen American vintages.

Dinner nightly except Tuesday, 6:30 to 9, late spring through December.

Wequasset Inn, Pleasant Bay, Chatham. (508) 432-5400.

Among area restaurants, we know of no more majestic water view amid more elegant surroundings than from the restored 18th-century sea captain's mansion that houses the

Queen Anne Inn is known for its dining room as well as its lodging.

Wequasset Inn's dining room. Light lunches and cocktails are served on the large outdoor terrace covered by a yellow and white canopy, with pink geraniums framing a view of the sea. Floor-to-ceiling windows on three sides is all the decor you need in the main dining room with sturdy wood chairs and candles in hurricane lamps.

Chef Frank McMullen, a Culinary Institute grad who accompanied managing partner Clive Chu from Pier 66 in Fort Lauderdale, is partial to fresh seafood and continental cuisine. For starters, we liked his escargots with pinenuts in puff pastry ($6.50), a coarse country pate with champagne mustard sauce ($5.50) and a green salad topped with grilled chicken and wild mushrooms. Among entrees ($15.50 to $22.50), standouts were beef tenderloin with wild mushrooms, grilled cornish game hen, and gulf shrimp over tri-colored pasta. Key lime pie and a strawberry tart were refreshing desserts.

Salads, sandwiches and light entrees are offered at lunch on the patio, or at the **Outer Bar** beside the pool.

Lunch daily, 11:30 to 2; dinner, 6 to 10; open mid-May to mid-October.

Oyster's Garden Cafe, 483 Main St., Chatham.

An outdoor oasis of greenery at the rear of a complex of shops called the Swinging Basket, this is a fine spot for lunch or a snack on a sunny day. It's filled with the Cape's trademark blue hydrangeas and colorful flowers. Sit on a kitchen chair at an umbrella-covered table and order Wellfleet oysters ($5.95 for half a dozen), a pate plate, salad nicoise, clam chowder or a fruit and cheese plate ($9.75 with a half carafe of wine). The turkey, avocado, tomato and brie sandwich is $4.75. Wash it down with an Amstel light or Old Chicago seltzer water. Desserts include fruit tarts, fruit compotes and chocolate decadent torte.

Open daily 11 to 9 (unless it is raining), mid-June through September.

The Chatham Squire Restaurant, 483 Main St., Chatham. (508) 945-0945.

Once little more than a bar and still a hangout for summering collegians, the Squire has soared lately with its food, to the point where on our latest visit everyone was mentioning it as one of the best in town. The atmosphere is perky, the decor old Cape Cod, with murals of local scenes and the bar decked out with old license plates and sailing flags. Regulars love to sit near the windows and watch the passing parade on Main Street as they slurp a wonderful fish chowder or peel their own shrimp.

At lunch, burgers are served with those great Cape Cod potato chips. Three bucks buys dessert — cappuccino mousse, highland berry pie and french custard are a few.

Dinner entrees are from $12 for chicken Tudor to $17 for tenderloin of beef with madeira sauce, and pastas $4.50 to $12, depending on whether they are ordered as appetizers or entrees. Fettuccine with shiitake mushrooms, snow peas, prosciutto and garlic butter sounds first-rate. Bouillabaisse is $16 and includes fennel and saffron. A bottle of Beringer sauvignon blanc for $15 would be a good accompaniment. On Thursdays an acclaimed paella is on the docket, and Wednesday is classic curry night.

Lunch daily, 11:30 to 4:30; dinner nightly, 4:30 to 9:30 or 10.

Pate's, Route 28, Chatham. (508) 945-9777.

This substantial steakhouse that's a panorama of red decor with pinkish lights is not the kind of place we look for when vacationing on the Cape. But it's filled nightly with locals seeking good steaks and seafood, and has been for 31 years.

The Pate family retired lately, turning over the reins to Bob Gardner, who's maintaining their tradition. The list of appetizers offers the old standbys, from vichyssoise to French onion soup, from clams casino to oysters Rockefeller. Entrees run from $11.50 for fried haddock to $18.95 for lamb chops. Filet mignon, baked stuffed shrimp and prime rib are relative bargains in the $15 to $16 range, and if you can't decide, settle for surf and turf ($14.95). Tossed or caesar salad and potatoes come with; desserts like brownie a la mode and chocolate parfait are $3.75 extra.

Dinner nightly from 5:30; closed Monday in off-season and mid-October to spring.

Soup to Nuts Cafe, 155 Crowell Road (at Chronicle Court), Chatham (508) 945-0565.

Quiches are specialties at this small cafe-deli. You can get one for breakfast with toast for $3.25. Homemade cinnamon toast is 85 cents. At lunch, a crabmeat pocket and a reuben are in the $4.50 range. Spinach salad comes with chopped egg, bacon, cheese and mandarin oranges for $3.95. Beer and wine are available. Open from 7 a.m.

Diversions

From Chatham's choice location at the elbow of Cape Cod, all the attractions of the Cape are at your beck and call. People who appreciate Chatham tend to head north to Orleans or into Wellfleet and the Truros, if they leave Chatham at all.

Beaches. Chatham has more beach area and shoreline than any other Cape Cod town, but much of it is privately owned or not easily accessible. Those with boats like the seclusion of the offshore sandbar at the southern tip of the Cape Cod National Seashore, a barrier beach that sheltered Chatham from the open Atlantic until it was breached in an infamous 1987 winter storm. (Roads to the shore between Main Street and Chatham Light have since been closed to the public to deter sightseers and beach erosion.) Swimming is available by permit at such town beaches as Harding Beach on Nantucket Sound or the sheltered "Children's Beach" at Oyster Pond. Those who want surf and open ocean head for Orleans and the Coast Guard and Nauset state beaches.

Monomoy National Wildlife Refuge. Accessible by a short boat trip from Morris

Island, this wilderness island stretching south into the Atlantic is a haven for birds — 309 species, at latest count. It's a major stopping point for migratory waterfowl along what ornithologists call the Atlantic Flyway.

Chatham Fish Pier. The fish pier down the slope off Shore Road is popular with sightseers who want to see the real thing. Boats make their run to the fishing grounds ten to one hundred miles into the Atlantic and return with their catch to the pier starting in the early afternoon, depending on tides. Visitors may watch from an observation balcony.

Museums. The Old Atwood House (1752) on Stage Harbor Road, owned and maintained by the Chatham Historical Society, is one of the town's oldest houses. Among its offerings are seashells, Sandwich Glass and the nationally known murals of Alice Stallknecht Wight, "Portrait of a New England Town." Changing exhibits illustrate Chatham life through photos, paintings and artifacts. The museum is open Monday, Wednesday and Friday from 1 to 5 in summer; adults, $3. Also open summer afternoons is the 23-year-old **Railroad Museum,** the former town depot now filled with more than 8,000 models, relics and photos, plus a 1910 caboose. Other historic sites are the **Mayo House** on Main Street, the 1820 home of the Chatham Conservation Foundation and furnished with period furnishings; the old **Chatham Grist Mill,** and the **Chatham Light.**

Shopping. Some of Cape Cod's finest shops are located along tree-lined Main Street; just stroll along and poke inside any number that appeal. We've always liked the **Tale of the Cod** at 450 Main, a collection of rooms filled with interesting gifts and furniture. Almost across the street is the **Swinging Basket** complex of boutiques; a highlight is the **Afterhouse Gallery** with its collection of antique prints and maps. **Mark, Fore & Strike** has classic apparel. We never can resist a stop at **Chatham Cookware** at 524 Main, a fine kitchen store and food shop. Check the linens from France and the colorful pottery from Fitz and Floyd; we especially like the tureens. Take your pasta salad a la Grecque or coffee and a chocolate shortbread to the small outside deck. On our last visit, we admired the handpainted clothing at **Frillz** on Main Street, especially the shirts decorated with irises. For wild beachplum or wild blackberry preserves, go to the **Chatham Jam and Jelly Shop** at 10 Vineyard Ave. at the corner of Route 28.

West of town on Route 28 is a special shopping area of interest to gourmets: The newly expanded **Fancy's Farm Market,** the **Pampered Palate** with specialty foods and great deli items to go, and **Chatham Fish and Lobster's** extensive selection — all the makings for a picnic or a party at one stop.

Extra-Special

Town Band Concerts.
It's hard to imagine in sophisticated Chatham, but upwards of 6,000 people turn out for the Friday evening band concerts, a town tradition every July and August, in Kate Gould Park. The 40 instrumentalists, most of them townspeople who rehearse weekly during winter, are joined by the multitudes for rowsing singalongs. The natural amphitheater is good both for listening and for watching the children (and often their elders) dance to the music.

Nantucket, Mass.
Island of History and Romance

Stepping onto Steamboat Wharf after a two-and-a-half-hour ferry ride twenty miles into the Atlantic is a bit like stepping onto another land in another time.

"This is the island that time forgot," announces one of Nantucket's visitor guides. "Steeped in tradition, romance, legend and history, she is a refuge from modernity."

Flanked by brick sidewalks, towering shade trees and gas lamps, the cobblestone streets lead you past more fine old sea captains' homes still standing from Nantucket's days as the nation's leading whaling port than most people see in a lifetime. The more than 400 structures from the late 1700s and early 1800s that make up the historic district represent the greatest concentration in America, evoking the town's description as "an architectural jewel."

So much for the island that time forgot. The island's romance draws thousands of well-heeled visitors to a sophisticated side of Nantucket that is uniquely chic and contemporary. More distant than other islands from the mainland and yet readily accessible to the affluent, Nantucket is all the more exclusive.

That's the way island businessman-benefactor Walter Beinecke Jr. planned it when he created the Nantucket Historical Trust in 1957 and later co-founded the Nantucket Conservation Trust. His efforts led to the preservation of 6,100 acres of open space — one-fifth of the island's land total. Through his historic and real-estate interests, the village has been transformed into what New England Monthly magazine termed "a perfect oasis — neat, tidy and relentlessly quaint — for upscale vacationers."

It's a bit precious and pricey for some tastes, this town in which whaling fortunes were amassed and which now is predicated on tourism for the elite. (Once you get away from Nantucket village and Siasconset, the folks on the south beaches and the west side of the island let their hair down). The week our family roughed it, so to speak, in a cottage near the beach at Surfside was far different from the fall weekends a decade later when we returned, as so many couples do, for getaways in Nantucket village, 'Sconset or Wauwinet.

Nantucket is perfect for an escape — away from the mainland and into a dream combining Yankee history and the Preppy Handbook. You don't have to wear Nantucket pink trousers or dine at Le Chantecleer, although many do. Simply explore the village's treasures, participate in its activities, or relax and watch a select world go by.

Inn Spots

The inn and B&B phenomenon started later on Nantucket and is changing faster than in most areas. The town's traditional boarding and guest houses are being upgraded, and more and more are staying open longer each year. As elsewhere in this book, rates here are quoted for peak season, which generally runs from June through September and the Christmas Stroll. Off-season rates are lower.

The Wauwinet, Wauwinet Road, Box 2580, Nantucket 02554. (508) 228-0145 or (800) 426-8718.

Grandly restored in 1988, this understated "country inn by the sea" is the most elegant on Nantucket and among the most deluxe in New England. Newton (Mass.) developers Stephen and Jill Karp, longtime Nantucket summer home owners, spared no expense in turning the weathered old Wauwinet Hotel into the ultimate in taste and comfort.

Wicker-furnished back porch looks onto harbor at The Wauwinet.

The Wauwinet holds a fond place in the memories of the island's gentry, which helps explain the success of its restaurant and the number of sightseers who oohed and aahed over the intricacies of its transformation in its first season. Certainly the location is unmatched — a private, parkland/residential area on a spit of land with the Atlantic surf beyond the dunes across the road in front, the waters at the head of Nantucket Harbor lapping at the lawns in back.

Twenty-eight rooms are available in the inn and twelve more in five cottages across the road. Our "superior" room — as opposed to deluxe or suite — was not large but was nicely located on a third-floor corner facing the harbor so that we were able to watch spectacular sunsets every night. Fresh and pretty, it had a queensize bed with a striped dust ruffle and lace-trimmed pillows, wicker and upholstered armchairs, and a painted armoire topped with a wooden swan and two hat boxes (one of the inn's decorating signatures). The modern bathroom contained a multitude of thick white towels and a basket of Crabtree & Evelyn amenities. During turndown service, the towels were replenished, mints placed by the bed and the radio turned on.

All the rooms we saw had different, striking stenciled borders (some turning up in the most ingenious places), interesting artworks and sculptures, ceiling fans, and such fillips as clouds painted on the ceiling. The deluxe rooms had bigger sitting areas, but many did not seem to be as well located as ours.

The main floor harbors a lovely living room and library done in floral chintz, a back veranda full of wicker that you sink into, a couple of guest rooms, the restaurant and a small, classy lounge. Outside, chairs are lined up strategically on the back lawn, a croquet game is set up, drinks and snacks are availble at a small beachside grill, and a resident pro gives lessons on two tennis courts tucked away in the woods. You can swim from a dock or a not particularly inspiring beach along the harbor, or walk a couple of minutes from the hotel through the dunes to the most gorgeous, endless and unoccupied strand we've seen on the Atlantic coast. Sailboats and sailboards are available.

Friendly service is provided by a staff of 110, an unusually high ratio for the maximum of 80 guests, according to general manager Russell Cleveland, who came to the

Wauwinet from the top executive posts at the Williamsburg Inn in Virginia and Salishan Lodge in Oregon. A van is available to transport guests back and forth to town for shopping or to catch the ferryboat.

Three meals a day are available in the spacious Topper's (see Dining Spots) and an adjacent patio facing the harbor. A complimentary continental breakfast of fresh orange or grapefruit juice, melons with berries, breads and breakfast pastries is served either in Topper's or in your room. Heartier eaters may order from a menu that includes eggs Benedict, Portuguese frittata, tri-pepper western omelets and sourdough pancakes ($6.50 to $8). They come garnished with enough sliced fruit that we needn't have ordered the mixed fresh fruit plate ($7.50) to start. That plate must have included twelve or more kinds of fruit, and was enough for an army.

Doubles, $250 to $450, B&B; suites, $450 to $675. Add $52 per person MAP. Open April 20 through October.

Jared Coffin House, 29 Broad St., Nantucket 02554. (508) 228-2405.

One of New England's grand old inns, the famed Jared Coffin House is rather fancy and handsomely furnished with museum-quality pieces. It's also active and busy — like a train station 24 hours a day, some islanders say.

The public rooms, restaurant, tap room with entertainment and outdoor patio are busy, that is, for this is a center for Nantucket life and a must visit for tourists, if only for a drink or to sample one of the restaurant's brunches or buffets.

The restoration of the island's earliest three-story house was accomplished by Walter Beinecke Jr. and the Nantucket Historical Trust, which acquired it in 1961 for $10,000, renovated and furnished it, and finally sold it in 1975 to innkeepers Phil and Peg Read for more than $750,000 — an example of the gentrification of Nantucket.

The 60 guest rooms are scattered in six buildings, two of which are connected to the main 1845 Jared Coffin House. Three are in houses 30 feet on either side of the main complex. All have private baths and most have television.

Some guests prefer the seven twin and double rooms upstairs in Jared's former home, each furnished with period antiques, artworks and island-woven fabrics. Others covet one of the three large rooms with queensize canopy beds and sitting areas in the 1700s Swain House attached to the main building or, across the street, one of the eighteen queensize canopy rooms in the 1821 Henry Coffin House and the Greek Revival Harrison Gray House.

The public areas are a sight to behold, the living room and library furnished in priceless Chippendale and Sheraton antiques.

Jared's, the inn's large main dining room, features classic American cuisine and changing seasonal menus. Dinner entrees are $19.95 to $30.95 for items like Nantucket bluefish with sauce nicoise, orange spiced duck or melange of lamb (breaded rack of lamb with marinated leg and sausage with an anise glaze). Less formal dinners in the beamed, pine-paneled **Tap Room** downstairs are $12.95 to $15.95. Lunch on the patio might be the "Pride of New England," a choice of broiled jumbo frankfurter or deep-fried codfish cake with baked beans, brown bread and cole slaw.

Doubles, $110 to $175, EP.

Cliff Lodge, 9 Cliff Road, Nantucket 02554. (508) 228-9480.

The eleven rooms and one apartment in this sea captain's home dating to 1771 are more comfortable and have more flair than many in town. And there are all kinds of neat places to sit, inside and out.

Innkeeper Mary Coughlin Patton keeps a trained eye and a firm hand on the upkeep as well as the guests' comfort. She puts out a breakfast buffet in one of the sitting rooms, or guests can adjourn to the patio or take trays to their rooms. Fresh fruit, cereal, sour-cream coffeecake, special breads to toast, and muffins like oatmeal-pecan are typical fare. In the afternoons, she offers hot or iced tea, plus popcorn, cheese and crackers.

Rooms are notable for spatter-painted floors, Laura Ashley wallpapers, frilly bedding, fresh flowers and antiques. All have private baths, telephones and remote-control TV sets neatly built into the walls or concealed in armoires, and some have kingsize beds and fireplaces. Room 6 has a view of the ocean.

The five sitting rooms on three floors, a rooftop walk with view of the harbor, reading porches and the brick patio beside a secluded garden provide plenty of gathering spots for guests.

Doubles, $90 to $140.

Centerboard, Center and Chestnut Streets, Box 2697, Nantucket 02554. (508) 228-9696.

Possibly the most elegant — and certainly the most romantic — of Nantucket's small inns is this winner of a restoration at the edge of the historic district. It's owned by Long Island artist and interior designer Marcia Wasserman, who calls it the fulfillment of a fantasy. She bought the guest house in 1985 and finally reopened it in 1987 after renovations took seven times longer and cost three times more than originally planned.

There's a big window seat in the living room, outfitted with a TV and stereo, and the floors have a pickled finish. Adjacent is a casually formal dining room, with cane chairs around a handful of tables, where "the largest continental breakfast you could imagine is served," says resident manager Reggie Reid. A big bowl of fruit (from kiwi to blueberries), granola and cereals, four or five kinds of muffins and Portuguese breads are the fare. Wine and cheese are served afternoons in season.

A two-room suite on the first floor was inspired by a masculine sitting room in an English manor house. It has a fishnet canopy bed with down comforters, a green marble bathroom with an oversize black marble shower and jacuzzi tub, a TV in the armoire and a fireplace.

Upstairs, "the theme is romantic — one of Victorian elegance and charm," says Mrs. Reid. All with queens or two double beds, private baths, telephones, TVs and refrigerators stocked with soft drinks, the four guest rooms here are bright, airy and decorated in soft pastels. They have ceiling fans, iron and brass bedsteads, lacy pillows, bathrooms with baskets of Gilcrest & Soames toiletries, and even a couple of murals painted by a Martha's Vineyard artist. A studio apartment in the basement has built-in double beds and a teeny kitchen.

Doubles, $125; studio, $150; suite, $195.

76 Main Street, 76 Main St., Nantucket 02554. (508) 228-2533.

A costly restoration in 1984 upgraded the old White Eagle Inn into an elegant B&B in an 1883 sea captain's home. It's the only one on central Main Street, a residential section of stately 19th-century mansions.

Innkeeper Shirley Peters, who arrived in Nantucket by way of Wellesley, Japan and England, and her late husband restored the original cherry, oak and walnut floors that had been covered by rugs and papered the walls hidden behind layers of paint. They added private baths for the twelve guest rooms, each furnished with queensize beds, upholstered chairs and antiques.

The large front corner room on the main floor with four-poster bed and Victorian furnishings is a showplace renting for $130 a night. Besides the other guest rooms on the second and third floors (plus an extra bathroom with shower for use of departing

Front room at 76 Main Street has wing chairs and canopied four-poster bed.

guests returning from the beach after they have checked out) are six family units with TV and refrigerator in a motel-style annex.

Off a grand entry hall are a formal Victorian parlor for reading and the kitchen with dining area, where a continental breakfast of fruits, cereals, and homemade muffins and breads is served. Outside are a sheltered courtyard and shady patio with a peach tree in the middle.

Doubles, $110 to $130.

Eighteen Gardner Street, 18 Gardner St., Nantucket 02554. (508) 228-1155.

Large, impressive public rooms appeal in this 1835 home, acquired and remodeled in 1988 by Mary and John Keenan, former innkeepers on Martha's Vineyard. Besides a formal parlor where sherry is offered, there's a formal dining room with Queen Anne chairs around a Sheraton cherry table. Cereals and homemade breads and muffins are served here for continental breakfast. Guests read magazines and relax on an informal side porch with a BYO bar, TV and deck chairs.

Upstairs are ten guest rooms, all with private baths and some with fireplaces, which the Keenans hoped to get in working order. They were adding queensize beds, upgrading the wallpaper and importing furnishings from their former inn. A two-bedroom apartment with a kitchen on the third floor is good for families.

Doubles, $90 to $130.

Ten Lyon Street Inn, 10 Lyon St., Nantucket 02554. (508) 228-5040.

This is located away from the mainstream in what the Chamber of Commerce refers to as "a transitional neighborhood" (which, in Nantucket terms, is relative). Housed in an 1850 barn and livery stable, it's also a refreshing departure from Nantucket's relentlessly dark and similar Colonial inns.

The layout is interesting, the rooms bright and airy, and some of the bathrooms have to be seen to be believed. One enormous bathroom has converted gas fixtures with the original etched-glass shades. Barry Foster, innkeeper with his wife Ann Marie, is an electrical contractor, which explains some of the unusual lighting and plumbing touches. They call a room on the third floor "the tree house room," because they frequently have to prune a tree limb when it starts growing through the window.

Altogether, the inn has seven spacious bedrooms, all with private baths, country antiques, and handsome quilts and rugs on wide-board floors. Most have queensize beds. There are a sitting area in the upstairs hall and a main-floor common room with a breakfast area.

Ann Marie makes muffins to accompany cold cereals and fresh fruit cups for continental breakfast. She also provides dishes of nuts and dried fruit in the living room for snacks.

Doubles, $90 to $135. Closed mid-December to mid-April.

Anchor Inn, 66 Centre St., Nantucket 02554. (508) 228-0072.

Built by a whaling ship captain, this B&B in the heart of the historic district was the home in the 1950s of the Gilbreths of "Cheaper by the Dozen" fame, who wrote of their experience in the book "Innside Nantucket." Today it's run very personally by Charles and Ann Balas, active Nantucket promoters.

The interior retains its original random-width floorboards and antique paneling. Eleven guest rooms, named after whaling ships, have private baths, queen or twin beds, and period furnishings. There are the usual Nantucket parlor with a rust-colored corduroy sofa and wing chairs, and a side porch with checked cafe curtains. Here is where Charles's homemade muffins are served for continental breakfast to the accompaniment of classical music.

There's a pleasant patio with lounge furniture in the side pocket-garden.

Doubles, $85 to $115.

Fair Gardens, 27 Fair St., Nantucket 02554. (508) 228-4258.

The gardens here are lovely and rather spacious for Nantucket, and include a renowned Shakespearean herb garden. A rear deck and patio take full advantage of the view, as do three rooms in the Garden House facing the gardens.

The main Colonial house has eight rooms with private baths, some with canopy beds and fireplaces. One with a four-poster bed and rag rugs opens off the dining room.

Muffins, coffee and juice are served in the garden, the bedrooms or a sunny breakfast room.

The inn was purchased in 1986 by Lee and Stuart Gaw, who started with the **Great Harbor Inn** at 31 India St. a year earlier. Although not near the water, the Great Harbor does offer nine guest rooms with modern baths, TVs and canopy or four-poster beds, an attractive living room in gray and rose, and a colorful rear patio. Rates and continental breakfasts are the same as at Fair Gardens.

In 1988, the Gaws acquired the **Brass Lantern Inn** at 11 North Water St., and were upgrading ten rooms and adding baths in the main house there. Eight contemporary rooms in a wing built in 1983 were as comfy as ever. Muffins, coffee and juice are served in the rooms. One of us had to go out for breakfast after consuming the tiny muffin he was served here a few years ago. Doubles at the Brass Lantern are $70 to $95 in the main house, $120 to $140 in the wing.

Doubles at Fair Gardens, $95 to $130.

Carlisle House, 26 North Water St., Nantucket 02554. (508) 228-0720.

The fifteen guest rooms in this 1765 house range from a large corner front with fireplace, queensize canopy bed with eyelet cover and rose spread to a small single with pencil-post bed and shower. A third-floor room with strawtop canopy bed and wicker furniture has an inviting, summery air. Nine have private baths, and each has an antique bed with iron or brass headboard or canopied four-poster.

Nowadays in Nantucket, "people want more than a rooming house — they want a place to gather," says owner Peter Conway, who since has opened the deluxe Harbor Light Inn in Marblehead. He has provided an attractive common room with a fireplace, a sun porch with wicker furniture where breakfast is set up buffet style in summer, a Victorian lounge looking onto the garden, and a pleasant back yard.

In the winter, breakfast is served at a huge trestle table by the original kitchen fireplace with its beehive oven and cauldron. Breakfasts include fresh fruits, homemade fruit breads and Portuguese bread. On Sunday afternoons, Peter might offer guests some wine or a bit of brandy.

Doubles, $65 to $120.

Dining Spots

21 Federal, 21 Federal St., Nantucket. (508) 228-2121.

New in 1985 and a smash success ever since, this restaurant now is making waves on the mainland since founding chef Robert Kinkead opened another Twenty-One Federal in Washington, D.C. His chef de cuisine, Ris Lacoste, was part of the "swat team" that invaded Washington Square at 1736 L Street N.W., according to partner Chick Walsh. But Chick and chef Carl Keller are continuing their style of American grill cuisine in Nantucket and doing very well, thank you.

One of Nantucket's larger restaurants, 21 Federal is on two floors of a sand-colored house with white trim, designated by a brass plaque and elegantly decorated in Williamsburg style. There are six dining rooms, some with their white-linened tables rather too close together for privacy.

Our latest lunch in a small room next to the convivial bar produced a smashing pasta ($15) — spaghettini with two sauces, one thyme-saffron and one smoked tomato, topped with crabmeat-stuffed shrimp — and a grilled shrimp salad with Greek olives, feta cheese, pinenuts and spinach ($14). Three varieties of breads came with, and a tropical fruit sorbet was a refreshing ending.

Even more memorable was a summer lunch in the courtyard, served on large wicker trays. The pheasant and wild rice soup of the day and a linguini salad with shrimp and pinenuts were out of this world.

At dinner, entrees are $23 to $27 for the likes of sauteed breast of pheasant with fresh fruit relish, grilled tenderloin of veal with risotto and oyster mushrooms, and a trio of grilled lobster tail, ravioli and lobster cake, supplemented by such specials as grilled salmon with lobster tomato cream sauce and crab fritters. Start with grilled oysters with pancetta, seared raw tuna with nori rolls and smoked salmon, or zarzuela, a Southwest seafood stew. Finish with a palette of chocolate, creme brulee tart with fresh fruit, or one of the great homemade ice creams and sorbets.

This is Nantucket dining at its best, not as pretentious (though just as pricey) as some and more exciting than many. Catering to the local trade, the restaurant also is one of the few that stays open most of the year.

Lunch daily, 11:30 to 2:30; dinner, 6 to 10. Closed March and Sundays in off-season.

Le Languedoc, 24 Broad St., Nantucket. (508) 228-2552.

Although the Grennan family have twenty guest rooms in four buildings, their attractive white building with blue shutters across from the Jared Coffin House complex is noted most for its dining.

Downstairs is a cafe with checkered cloths. Upstairs are four small dining rooms with

One of six dining rooms decorated in Williamsburg style at 21 Federal.

peach walls and white trim, windows covered with peach draperies and valances, and prints and posters framed in chrome. Windsor chairs are at nicely spaced tables bearing hurricane lamps with thick candles and vases, each containing one lovely salmon rose.

Among appetizers ($7 to $15), smoked Nantucket pheasant with cranberry relish was very good and very colorful with red cabbage and slices of apples and oranges on a bed of lettuce. Good warm French bread compensated a bit for the lack of salad ($5 extra).

Of the entrees ($24 to $28), one of us sampled noisettes of lamb with artichokes in a rosemary sauce. The other had sauteed sweetbreads and lobster in puff pastry, in a sauce that included shiitake mushrooms, cognac and shallots. Nicely presented on piping hot oval white plates, they were accompanied by snow peas, broccoli, pureed turnips, yellow peppers, sweet potato and peach slices. Other interesting choices were wok-seared halibut with papaya and lime, roast duckling with Jamaican caramelized lemon sauce and veal chinoise with garlic and ginger.

For dessert, we passed up strawberry pie and pears poached in a reduction of port to share a dense chocolate hazelnut torte spiked with grand marnier. The wine list seemed a bit strange and pricey.

You can dine light but well in the cafe, where some of the upstairs appetizers and salads are available and there are always fish and pasta specials. Lunch is available on a canopied sidewalk terrace.

Le Languedoc is owned by the Grennan brothers, Neal, who is chef, and Alan. Michael Shannon, a friend who runs the Club Car, sometimes cooks here on nights his restaurant is closed.

Lunch in season, daily except Monday and Tuesday 11:30 to 2:30; dinner nightly except Monday 6 to 10.

The Second Story, 1 South Beach St., Nantucket. (508) 228-3471.
The second floor of a building across from the harbor is done up in pink walls and

linen, pink and green floral overcloths, and green napkins. Mismatched chairs with cane seats are at tables topped by mums in bud vases and enormous hurricane lamps enclosing candles. An alcove area beside the window onto the harbor is awash with comfy pillows. At night, the place is illuminated entirely by candles, and the setting could not be more glamorous.

The fare served up by chef-proprietors Patricia Tyler and David Toole is a mix of Mexican-Spanish, French, Cajun and lately Thai.

Their hand-written dinner menu changes monthly and is sufficiently obscure as to require explanation by the servers. Appetizers ($6 to $14) might be Bo Bun or littlenecks Sesimbra, oysters and soft-shell crayfish Bayou Teche or spicy Thai sesame shrimps with lemon-paprika sauce. We sampled the hot country pate, a huge slab of goose, duck, chicken and sausage, piping hot and bathed in a creamy green peppercorn sauce. Good monkey bread was hot as could be. The Parducci chardonnay was chilled in a large silver ice bucket, and salt was in a crystal dish.

Entrees are priced from $23 for grilled sweetbreads with truffles and mushroom sauce to $30 for lobster and avocado enchilada with goat cheese, jalapeno and cumin sauce, and spicy red pepper salsa. The scallops au gratin (with avocado, tomato, garlic and cream) was a portion so ample that we needed neither salad (an extra $3) nor appetizer. The Thai shrimp with black bean and coriander sauce was super spicy and left the mouth smoldering long into the night.

For dessert, the amaretto souffle turned out neither hot nor cold, but more like a mousse with only a hint of amaretto. Better choices might have been coeur a la creme with raspberry sauce or pears in puff pastry with caramel sauce.

Dinner nightly, seatings at 7 and 9:15. Open April to mid-December.

Straight Wharf Restaurant, Straight Wharf, Nantucket. (508) 228-4499.

Marian Morash of television and cookbook fame was the original force behind this summery restaurant on the waterfront. She wrote the encyclopedic Victory Garden Cookbook in 1982 with inspiration from her husband Russell, a television producer and weekend gardener, plus Jim Crockett and Julia Child, and finally left the restaurant in 1987 to finish a second cookbook.

Seafood is featured in this popular spot that is the height of chic and priced to match. The complex includes a fish market, a gourmet shop called **Provisions** and a contemporary restaurant, consisting of a large room with soaring, shingled walls topped by billowing banners made by owner Elaine Gifford, a canopied and rib-lit harborfront deck, and a popular bar where appetizers, light entrees and desserts are served.

The menu changes weekly. Appetizers ($5 to $10) could be lobster and fish cakes with tomato-basil beurre blanc, tuna sashimi and fish soup with rouille. Entrees ($23 to $28) run the gamut from poached salmon and scallops with champagne ginger sauce and grilled swordfish with ancho chili butter to roast rack of Australian lamb with ratatouille. We enjoyed a complimentary bluefish pate that came with drinks, some first-rate lobster crepes and a grilled salmon with tarragon mustard sauce, and the peach Bavarian laden with raspberry sauce. We were not impressed with the vaunted vegetables, which turned out to be plainly cooked broccoli and carrots.

Regulars rave about the bar menu, where you can sample some of the Straight Wharf specialties like spicy shrimp with sesame spinach salad, swordfish kabobs with barley salad, and pork chops with black bean salad and cornbread at wallet-pleasing prices ($10 to $12). Or stop in for espresso and one of the delectable desserts.

Dinner nightly except Monday, 6:45 to 10; bar menu, 7 to 10:30. Closed Mondays and October through mid-June.

Second-floor dining room is handsome in shades of peach at Le Languedoc.

The Club Car, 1 Main St., Nantucket. (508) 228-1101.

The red train car at the side of this luxurious establishment brightened by petunias in flower boxes outside the windows is a sedate lounge that's open from noon daily and enlivened by a piano bar nightly. Beyond, the elegant dining room has cane-backed chairs with rose colored velvet cushions at crisp, white-linened tables. Large artworks and a shelf of copper pans add color.

This is where chef Michael Shannon serves up the island's priciest food (entrees $24 to $33.50) to a loyal clientele that includes competing chefs on their nights off.

The formerly French menu lately has been Americanized in translation, but many items remain the same. Appetizers start at a staggering $7 for squid in the style of Bangkok and rise rapidly through duck foie gras with raspberry vinegar ($21.50) to Beluga caviar with Solichnaya vodka ($45). Seasonal salad is an extra $6.50.

The preparation of most of the nine entrees, from Irish salmon and grey sole to Indian curry, veal sweetbreads and rack of Vermont lamb, varies daily. The wine list and desserts are worthy of the rest of the menu.

Dinner nightly, 6 to 10; weekends only in off-season. Closed mid-December to Memorial Day.

Boarding House, 12 Federal St., Nantucket. (508) 228-9622.

The Boarding House provided our most memorable meal when we first visited Nantucket in 1972. It had just opened in the downstairs of a former boarding house on India Street and was the culinary hit of the summer. The restaurant since has moved to larger quarters around the corner at Federal and India streets, but the food continues to be highly regarded.

A sidewalk courtyard and the cathedral-ceilinged Victorian lounge with small marble tables are popular for lunch, perhaps an excellent carrot and dill soup followed by a spicy pizza with andouille sausage ($7) or the day's pasta special, in our case beet linguini with scallops and a rich lobster sauce ($8.50).

Dinner might be more serene downstairs in the sunken room that has an Italian feel, curved arches and along the far wall a striking if strange mural of asparagus stalks and small crabs on a sandy beach. The limited menu might begin with carpaccio of beef sambal with garlic crisps, sauteed shrimp in oriental marinade, smoked salmon with tarragon-lemon creme fraiche or Javanese barbecued chicken ($8 to $10). Entrees ($24 to $27) could be grilled swordfish with macadamia nut butter, steamed salmon with tomato pistou or grilled loin lamb chops with rosemary garlic sauce. Among desserts are a bourbon-flavored bread pudding and a frozen brandy mousse with crushed praline.

Lunch daily, noon to 2:30; dinner, 6:30 to 10.

Topper's at the Wauwinet, Wauwinet Road, Nantucket. (508) 228-0145.

Named for their dog, whose portrait is in one of the dining rooms, Topper's succeeded beyond its owners' dreams in its initial season in 1988, thanks to heavy local patronage and/or curiosity. Plans were in the works for expansion, particularly of the kitchen designed to serve 100 dinners and frequently called upon to put out half again that many. Chef Keith Mahoney, who was imported from Stuart, Fla., was staying year-round to oversee the expansion, as well as development of a spa menu.

Most outside diners come for a stroll through the refurbished inn, a drink on the outdoor terrace and a look at the Wauwinet's famous sunsets.

Dining is leisurely in two elegantly appointed, side-by-side rooms with large windows. Upholstered chairs in blue and white are comfortable, tables are well-spaced (or screened from their neighbors), and masses of flowers are all around.

The menu is printed daily but changes only modestly, and prices range from $8.50 to $10.50 for appetizers, $24 to $27 for entrees. Among the former, we were impressed with lobster and crab cakes with smoked corn and a wonderful mustard sauce, grilled shrimp with buffalo mozzarella and grilled pizza, and grilled quail on a toasted brioche. We were less impressed with the chilled oysters with pickled ginger mignonette and hot (as in incendiary) blackened swordfish with crayfish and grilled cornbread. The caesar salad is so good that some regulars order it with every meal.

Good main courses are things like grilled rack and leg of lamb with a tomato-eggplant timbale and sauteed veal with wild mushrooms and risotto, both accompanied by baby vegetables (tiny pattypan squash and carrots about a big as a fingernail) and a wedge of potatoes. Seafood dishes like grilled salmon with spicy black beans and striped bass with a hot vegetable relish proved the chef likes to leave a fiery after-taste. That can be cooled with dessert, perhaps a refreshing pineapple-papaya sorbet or pecan-praline ice cream, although the selection is heavy on rich pastries like linzer torte, creme brulee and fruit tarts with cheese filling.

The water comes with a lemon slice, the bread is crusty, salt and pepper are served only on request, and the wine list is choice but pricey, starting at $16 with most in the $30s and up.

Lunch daily, noon to 2; dinner nightly, 6 to 9:30.

American Seasons, 80 Centre St., Nantucket. (508) 228-7111.

A simple square room with Southwestern decor, eclectic American food and moderate prices made this newcomer Nantucket's restaurant hit of 1988. Brothers Stuart and Everett G. Reid III made a conscious decision "not to charge Nantucket's awful prices" at their out-of-the-way site, which requires a bit of an effort to reach. Islanders at heart, they opened their own restaurant after a year at the Summer House in Siasconset and various stints in Boston, New York and Newport.

The two Culinary Institute of America graduates do all the cooking. They turn out such treats as pan-fried Louisiana catfish with hot and sweet pepper tartar sauce, grilled Pacific salmon with artichoke pancakes and crayfish-coriander butter, grilled South

Boats are docked at waterfront area near Nantucket's Commercial Wharf.

Carolina quail with dirty rice, grilled Idaho trout with jalapeno-peach chutney and grilled bluefin tuna with an Arizona cactus relish. You get the idea, but you'll be shocked (pleasantly) by the tab ($12 to $22 for entrees). Start with raviolis of smoked duck and crayfish or a grilled artichoke and fried oyster salad. End with a bourbon banana-cream pie, strawberry shortcake with blood oranges, fresh blueberry and peach crisp or honey-cinnamon pecan pie with maple ice cream. With one of the reasonably priced bottles from the all-American wine list, you'll get out for what would be considered normal mainland prices.

Fifty-two patrons can be seated in the dining room, simple yet pretty with Southwestern red and deep green wood trim, paint-spattered floors and white-linened tables topped with hurricane lamps and pots of cactus. Twenty-five more can be accommodated on the outdoor patio.

Dinner nightly except Wednesday, 6 to 10. Closed in winter.

The Morning Glory Cafe, Old South Wharf, Nantucket. (508) 228-2212.

Although not in the luxury category, this is listed as a perennial favorite by most Nantucketers, who gather on the wharf patio at breakfast to wake up with strong coffee and Morning Glory muffins as they trade gossip from the night before.

An impressive variety of breakfast, lunch and dinner fare is put out by owner Liz Gracia from an open kitchen inside the small cafe, which has stunning trompe l'oeil paintings on the walls and a handful of tables. At lunch, interesting salads, sandwiches and pizzas are in the $6 to $8 range. Dinnertime brings a handful of appetizers, four or five pastas and entrees, priced from $8.50 for fettucelle with fresh basil-tomato meat sauce to $15.95 for sauteed veal cutlet with spinach and capers. Save room for one of the delectable desserts.

Breakfast, daily 7 to 11:30; lunch, noon to 3:30; dinner, 6 to 9:30. BYOB. Open Memorial Day to mid-September.

North Wharf Fish House, 12 Cambridge St., Nantucket. (508) 228-5213.

Seafood and pastas with a northern Italian touch are offered at this intimate, casual place where we encountered one of our more enjoyable meals in Nantucket.

After refusing to be jammed together in a lineup of deuces, the two of us lucked into our own table for four. A huge salad served family style, sea scallops fra diavolo, a hot and spicy pasta special, a complimentary basket of after-dinner fruit and an interesting wine list made dinner a relative bargain.

Entrees are priced from $15.95 to $19.95 for the likes of shrimp scampi, calamari provencale, Cajun pasta, mixed-shellfish pasta and steak marsala.

Dinner nightly, 6 to 10:30 or 11. Closed January-April.

The Tavern Restaurant, Harbor Square at Straight Wharf, Nantucket. (508) 228-1266.

Thoroughly casual and popular with tourists is this place owned by the folks from the Brotherhood of Thieves restaurant. It has a canopied patio and a two-level interior where some window tables offer a view of the waterfront buildings.

The dinner entrees are limited ($11.95 for chicken of the day to $17.95 for grilled swordfish and prime rib). This is hardly the kind of food to make a gourmand swoon, but for a basic burger, fish and chips or an oversize sandwich, it's a good spot for lunch or a light meal.

Open daily in season from 11:30 to midnight.

Diversions

Nantucket's attractions run the gamut from beaches to history to architecture to art and antiques. Except for the beaches, almost everything the visitor needs or wants to do is right in Nantucket village, and easily reached on foot or by bicycle. A number of pamphlets detail interesting walking tours.

Fourteen buildings and exhibits of special interest are maintained by the **Nantucket Historical Association,** which offers a combination pass to eleven for $6.50. Among them:

The Whaling Museum, the largest complex and one most visitors pass just after they leave the ferry, is considered the nation's best after the New Bedford Whaling Museum. Originally a candle factory, it contains an original beam press still poised to render whale spermaceti into candles and oil. Rooms are devoted to scrimshaw, whaling equipment and objects brought home by seamen from the South Seas. A whale jaw with teeth, the skeleton of a 43-foot whale and whalecraft shops — a sail loft, cooperage, shipsmith and such — are among the attractions.

The Peter Foulger Museum next door recreates the town's early days, particularly the folk life of its population, from Indians to Quakers. Exhibits range from Nantucket silver and lightship baskets to artifacts from the Great Fire of 1846 and relics of the China Trade.

Fair Street Museum and Quaker Meeting House. Nantucket's art museum records the lives of early citizens in portraits. An upstairs gallery houses more recent works and special exhibitions. The adjoining Meeting House was built in 1838.

Farther from the center of town are the **Oldest House** (1686), the **Old Mill** (1746) and the **Old Gaol** (1805). Numerous other structures are under Historical Association auspices, but if you simply walk any of the streets fanning out from the center you'll stumble on your own finds. Don't miss central Main Street, particularly the three Georgian mansions known as "The Three Bricks."

Walking Tours. The best of several is that led by Roger Young, former town selectman and an energetic semi-retiree, who goes "where the buses don't," through hidden alleys and byways, all the while spinning tales of Nantucket lore. Well worthwhile, the two-hour tours leave daily at 9:30 or 1:30 (the first to make a reservation sets the time); adults, $6.

Art Galleries and Antiques Shops. Besides beaches and good food, it's said that

Cobblestoned Main Street is decorated for Nantucket's annual Christmas Stroll.

visitors are attracted to Nantucket by all the galleries and antiques shops. They certainly have a wide choice: one brochure is devoted to antiquing on Nantucket, and one of summer's big events is the annual antiques show in early August. Such Nantucket scenes as cobblestoned streets, deserted moors and rose-covered cottages in 'Sconset appeal to artists, whose works hang in galleries all along the wharves. Erica Wilson's needlepoint shop is a local attraction.

Shopping. Nantucket is a shopper's paradise and, were it not for the cobblestoned streets and salt air, you could as easily picture yourself in Lexington or New Canaan. Specialty stores with names like **Very Terry** (for terrycloth) and **Nobby Clothes** compete with the more traditional like **Murray's Toggery** and **Mitchell's Book Corner,** all across the several square blocks of "downtown" Nantucket. One of the best gourmet food and takeout shops anywhere is **Que Sera, Sarah** with the makings for great picnics at rather stiff prices. We love the **Lion's Paw,** an exceptional gift shop full of cheerful pottery; check out the animal's tea party. Two outlets of **Nantucket Mills** offer "lower than mainland prices" for sweaters and sportswear.

Extra-Special

Nantucket Lightship Baskets.

The lightships that protected boats from the treacherous shoal waters off the south and east ends of the island in the mid-18th century spawned a cottage industry indigenous to Nantucket. The crews of the South Shoal Lightship turned to basket-weaving to while away their hours on duty. Their duty ended, the seamen continued to make baskets ashore — first primitive and heavy-duty types for carrying laundry or groceries, later more beautiful handbags appealing to visitors. The latter were inspired by the Sayle family, who continue the tradition at their shop on Washington Street Extension. Today, Nantucket's famed baskets come in all shapes and sizes (including 14-karat gold miniatures) and seem to be ubiquitous in the shops and on tanned arms. The handbags have ivory carvings on top and carry hefty price tags. The Four Winds Craft Guild on Straight Wharf claims to have the largest collection.

Edgartown, Mass.
Fall for the Vineyard

One of the best things about visiting an island is the ferry ride over from the mainland. The ringing of ships' bells, the whistle as you depart, the hustle and bustle of getting cars on and off — it all adds to the anticipation of what is to come.

Even though the trip to Martha's Vineyard from Wood's Hole takes less than an hour, that's time enough to listen to the buoys clanking, and to watch one shore fade in the distance and another grow closer.

It's time enough also for a transition — to leave mainland cares behind, before arriving at Vineyard Haven or Oak Bluffs and stepping into a different milieu.

The Vineyard is nothing if not varied. Oak Bluffs is a Methodist campground and Victorian beach resort, its many-splendored gingerbread cottages a rainbow of hues. At the other end of the island are the Indian-owned restaurants and shops atop windswept Gay Head, its cliffs a mosaic of colors and the East's mini-version of the Big Sur. In the interior of West Tisbury and Chilmark, the landscape is such that you might not even think you were on an island.

Then there's Edgartown, as up-to-date as a resort town can be while still reflecting a heritage back to 1642. It's a prosperous seaport village, which boomed during the whaling days of the 19th century and became a yachting center in the 20th century.

Long a retreat for the rich and famous as well as the rich and not-so-famous, Edgartown is best appreciated in the off-season. The crowds are gone, but the charms remain as autumn lingers at least through Thanksgiving. The beaches are deserted except for strollers. The waters are left for the fishermen and a few hardy sailors and wind-surfers. Cottages and condos are battened down for the winter.

Autumn is the season that islanders and knowing visitors look forward to, particularly in Edgartown, a year-round haven for retirees and escapees from the mainland. Many inns and restaurants remain open most of the year, but prices are reduced. You can be near the ocean in a moderate clime, and immerse yourself in a delightful community.

"Fall for Martha's Vineyard," the magazine ads entice in trying to boost autumn trade. It's hard to imagine how anyone wouldn't.

Waterfront view of Egartown, including the Seafood Shanty restaurant.

Inn Spots

Rates at Edgartown inns vary seasonally, and seasons vary from inn to inn. "In-season" is generally from sometime in June to sometime in September or October, "off-season" is usually from November to March or April, and "interim season" is the period in between. Rates quoted here, as elsewhere, are for peak season.

Charlotte Inn, South Summer Street, Edgartown 02539. (508) 627-4751.

You register at a front desk so old and ornate that it is pictured in the centerfold of the Architectural Digest inn book. At one side of the main floor are a two-room art gallery and a gift shop that are destinations in themselves. Behind is a small, deluxe restaurant in which you dine romantically in an indoor-outdoor garden reminiscent of New Orleans or Europe. You relax beforehand on the side porch running the depth of the Summer House, rejoicing in the fountains and flowers and a scent resembling eucalyptus; the ice for your drinks comes in a green leather bucket. And later you retire to one of 25 guest rooms that are so lavishly and tastefully furnished as to defy expectation.

The Charlotte Inn compound, which Gery and Paula Conover have developed from a private home he acquired in 1971, is nothing short of a masterpiece. Such an aura of elegance could make the inn seem aloof. But it turns out that the boyish-looking man talking to the painters is Gery (for Gerret, pronounced Gary), who might be mistaken for his 25-year-old son, and the youngish blonde helping out as a waitress at breakfast identifies herself as Paula. This is, after all, a very personal place, a reflection of Gery's

Coach House Suite at Charlotte Inn.

desire to have an art gallery (he runs a restoration business as well) and of Paula's flair with flowers, decorating and stitchery (she made many of the pillows and comforters that enhance each guest room).

Rooms are in the main two-story 1860 house, a rear carriage house that Gery built (without blueprints!) in 1980, the 1705 Garden House (so called because of its lovely English garden in back) across the street, the 1840 Summer House next door, and the new Coach House Suite.

The much-photographed deluxe suite upstairs in the Carriage House has an English hunting feel to it: a queensize bed with brass bedstead, a mahogany sleigh bed redecorated as a sofa, a working marble fireplace, a beamed cathedral ceiling, thick beige carpeting, walls covered in hunter green or red and green stripes, a TV and stereo hidden away in a chest, and a treasury of bric-a-brac from a gentleman's riding boots to one of the earliest cameras perched on a tripod in the corner. Even more to our liking is the Coach House Suite, opened in 1987, bigger and less masculine, outfitted like a well-planned house. The bed is covered with lace, there's a tiny balcony with wicker chairs, and the living room, with its easy chairs and hassocks, is exquisite. The walk-in dressing room/closet is a fantasy of hats, fans and hat boxes. Downstairs is what manager Carol Reed routinely calls the garage; it would be a museum anywhere else. Here — amid so many museum-quality treasures — it goes relatively unnoticed by all but the Coach House occupants, who have their own museum for the duration upstairs. The suites rent for $325, and Gery says they're booked almost every night.

After seeing these and a sampling of other opulent rooms, we wondered about ours (the last available and at the other end of the price scale). No. 18 in the Summer House had a private entrance off the wicker-filled side porch (we happened to be its only users on a couple of mild October days and nights). Although relatively small, it was luxuriously comfortable, with a four-poster bed in front of shelves of books, two wingback chairs and many antiques.

The compound is a landscaper's dream, full of exotic greenery, vivid flowers, trickling fountains and trellised arbors. Gery laid the spacious courtyard in front of the Coach House Suite brick by brick, and tends to the flowers with old watering cans from one of his many and diverse collections.

Continental breakfast is served in the conservatory dining room and terrace that houses the inn's restaurant, L'Etoile (see Dining Spots). Classical music and a trickling fountain are the backdrop for fresh orange juice, tea or coffee and breads (perhaps raisin or cranberry) and muffins (walnut-sour cream, cheese, cranberry and apple) served with raspberry preserves and marmalade. More substantial breakfasts are available at extra cost, a choice of raspberry waffles or a sour cream and asparagus omelet, preceded by broiled grapefruit at our visit.

Dinners at L'Etoile, whose space is leased by chef-owner Michael Brisson, are considered the priciest and most elegant on the island. After dinner, you can wander around the art gallery, watch television or play games in the small fireplaced common room of the Garden House, or simply relax on the wicker rockers on the porch of the Summer House, taking in the sights of the illuminated Charlotte Inn compound and the sounds of the fountains and the church bells on the hour. What a way to end a day!

Doubles, $115 to $265.

The Victorian Inn, South Water Street (Box 947), Edgartown 02539. (508) 627-4784.

Located across from the famous Pagoda Tree in an area of ship's captain's homes, the Victorian with masses of impatiens in front of its striking exterior is an anomaly. It's as Victorian as can be (well deserving of its listing in the National Register) and also as luxurious as can be, from its elegantly furnished rooms to the gourmet breakfasts served in the English garden out back.

New innkeepers Lewis and Arlene Kiesler are embellishing the fourteen lovely guest rooms, all with private baths (only one with tub) and inviting sitting areas, on the second and third floors. Pink, rose and green are the prevailing colors, and some of the sheets and shower curtains have patterns of roses. One room has two green velvet chairs in a bay window and a cedar chest topped with cushions at the foot of the bed. Another has a kingsize bed with ruffled canopy, damask sofa, rose wallpaper and rose easy chair. Tiny balconies offering glimpses of the harbor are attractions for two rooms on the third floor. A deluxe room at the rear has a porch with deck chairs and loungers overlooking the English garden and the carriage house of the abutting Charlotte Inn.

Decanters of sherry and bowls of apples are put out in the Victorian parlor.

Arlene does the cooking at breakfast, which also is available to the public for $7.75. Fresh fruits and juices, homemade muffins and granola precede such main courses as fruit-filled crepes, brandied french toast, quiche or eggs with cheese in pastry. Breakfast is taken in a dining room with delicate pink wallpaper, polished floors and hanging

English garden behind Victorian Inn backs up to Charlotte Inn property.

plants or, in summer, outside at white tables shaded by blue umbrellas on a delightful brick patio amid the greenery and flowers of the English garden.

Doubles, $87 to $177.

Point Way Inn, Main Street at Pease's Point Way, Box 128, Edgartown 02539. (508) 627-8633.

Remodeled from a 150-year-old whaling captain's house, this fifteen-room inn offers a variety of fine accommodations and personality galore. The personality emanates from owners Ben and Linda Smith, who landed in Edgartown Harbor in 1979 after a 4,000-mile sailing cruise and spent that winter turning the house into an inn reflecting family interests through and through.

You'll enjoy the pictures of their 38-foot ketch, the Point Way (on which they used to offer cruises off Florida or the Caribbean islands in winter), as well as the memorabilia of the Edgartown Mallet Club, a croquet group that Ben formed to play on the inn's lawn, all the yachting and golfing trophies, the photos of the Yale Whiffenpoofs of which Ben was a member, and the paintings by his mother, who was of the Boston School of Impressionists.

Each of the guest rooms, grouped off various stairways in separate sections of the house, has a private bath and ten have fireplaces. Canopy and four-poster beds, colorful quilts, wing chairs, wicker or tweedy sofas, a couple of tiny porches and a large deck — it's a delightful mishmash that's comfortable as can be. Each room also has nice touches like decanters of sherry, stamped envelopes, pin cushions and taffy.

The cozy public rooms have oriental rugs, a fireplace, games, a spectacular jigsaw puzzle and an honor bar. An assortment of sailing trophies hold fresh flowers. Flags that Ben used on his boats are under the glass-covered tables in the breakfast room, in which fresh orange juice, popovers, coffee cakes, muffins and breads are served buffet style.

Tea or lemonade and cookies (oatmeal just like our mothers used to make on our last visit) plus clams — if guests have been successful on clamming expeditions — are an afternoon highlight in the ivy-covered outdoor gazebo, which is part of the mallet club. Guests as well as members may play croquet if they wish.

Doubles, $110 to $185 (for a two-room suite with deck, private entrance and fireplace).

The Shiverick Inn, Pent Lane at Pease's Point Way, Box 640, Edgartown 02539. (508) 627-3797.

Built in 1840 for the town physician, this mansion was restored in 1984 by Philadelphia descendants of the Shiverick line and opened as the Dr. Shiverick House, a fancy if somewhat austere-feeling inn. New owners from Washington acquired the inn in 1987, closed it for ten months for top-to-bottom renovations, and reopened with an antiques-filled masterpiece that some find a tad intimidating.

The theme, as described in the inn's brochure, is a "grandly romantic sequence of visual pleasures and physical comforts purposely designed to enchant the senses and enrich the spirit." Inside the oak double-door entry is a high-ceilinged entrance hall with the original mahogany staircase and a remarkable showpiece spool cabinet.

Ahead is a formal parlor/dining room, notable for gorgeous rugs over random-width floorboards restored from a barn in Vermont. A crystal chandelier hangs over the dining table, and porcelain figures line the mantel. Balloon draperies frame the parlor's windows onto a spacious garden room, which has a long sofa along one wall, wrought-iron furniture with ivy-patterned seats, and a long tiled counter (painted with ivy) for breakfast or cocktail service. Beyond is a delightful patio and garden colorful with pink and white flowers, which are also on view from an upstairs porch.

Upstairs is the library, a sunny room in which the mementos of innkeepers Claire and Juan del Real may be of more interest than the books. Juan, a lawyer for 22 years, was general counsel for the U.S. Department of Health from 1981 to 1985 and his wife was press secretary for Sen. Strom Thurmond. Autographed photographs, White House Christmas cards and the like tell how esteemed they were by the Reagan administration and top Washington political circles.

Well-connected Republicans ought to feel at home in any of the ten guest rooms and suites on the first and second floors. Each has a full bath and all but one a working fireplace. They are sumptuously furnished with four-poster or canopy beds, a variety of art objects and antiques, oriental rugs, and rich wallpapers and fabrics.

A continental-plus breakfast of fresh fruit, cereal, yogurt, granola, muffins and breads is served in the morning.

Doubles, $135 to $185; suites, $215 to $325.

The Daggett House, 59 North Water St., Edgartown 02539. (508) 627-4600.

For a waterfront location, this bed-and-breakfast inn with 24 rooms in two houses and a cottage is unsurpassed in Edgartown. The long, narrow rear lawn with flowers, benches and umbrellaed tables slopes down to the water and a private pier next to the Chappaquiddick Ferry landing.

Guest rooms, all with private baths, are in the main 1750 Daggett House with its historic tavern downstairs, the newer (early 1800s) and larger Captain Warren House across Water Street, and the Garden Cottage, which has three double rooms. New innkeeper Sue Cooper-Street, an effervescent ex-Marylander who took over in 1988, was upgrading the rooms, which are generally quite spacious and furnished with antiques. Oversize canopy and four-poster beds, artworks and decorative fireplace screens painted by her artist husband, Tom Street, and custom-made coverlets and draperies were in the works.

304

Trees shade front of Shiverick Inn.   **Trellis frames entry to Point Way Inn.**

After its location, the next best thing is the historic downstairs tavern room, which dates from the 1600s and above which the house was later built. The island's first tavern, it still looks the way an early tavern should look, with its unusual beehive fireplace chimney, dark beams, old tools and bare wood communal tables for six, where conviviality is the norm. Continental breakfast — with wonderful toast made from a recipe of the late Lucille Chirgwin, who with her husband Fred owned the inn for 40 years — is complimentary. Full breakfasts are extra, a fine eggs Benedict going for $6. Breakfast is available to the public as well, and the ambiance is such that people gladly wait for a table over coffee served on the rear terrace.

Hidden near the fireplace in the tavern room is a secret staircase that provides steep, low-ceilinged access to an upstairs guest room with kingsize bed, gold wallpaper and a view of the harbor.

Off the entrance to the main inn is a small living room with sofas, wing chairs and a television set. Among the fourteen rooms in the Warren House are several efficiencies and suites good for families. Although upgrading the facilities, innkeeper Sue planned to continue the tradition of homey warmth with such innovations as optional breakfast in bed, complementary hors d'oeuvres during cocktail hour on the rear terrace on Saturdays, and potential dinner service for houseguests.

Doubles, $100 to $140. Main house open all year; Captain Warren House and Garden Cottage open early April to late October.

The Chadwick Inn, Winter Street at Pease's Point Way, Box 1035, Edgartown 02539. (508) 627-4435.

Pure white with black shutters, on a nicely landscaped corner lot, this Greek Revival-style house built in 1840 has been an inn since 1979. It has been upgraded by Peter and Jurate Antioco, Connecticut transplants who opened an antiques shop around the corner, were smitten by the Vineyard and bought the inn in 1988.

Federal furnishings, marine paintings and a collection of majolica from their Summer

305

Landing shop now enhance the public rooms. Among them is an elegant front parlor where comfort is the theme — "I have a passion for foot stools, where you can stretch out your legs and rest," says Jurate, who was abrim with decorating ideas for a second parlor she was transforming into a library. She already had created a delightful sun porch full of wicker and plants, with supplemental light from two hand-painted Italian chandeliers in the form of flowers.

An enormous antique English sideboard fills one end of the cheery dining room; Jurate laughs as she recalls Peter struggling to wheel it down the street from the shop late one night. Here, at four glass-topped tables, guests partake of full breakfasts cooked by Peter. Fresh berries from the locally well-known Thimble Farms, raspberry crepes, light and airy waffles made with yeast, and fresh-ground coffee from Kenya are typical fare.

The main house has six guest rooms, all with private baths, king and queensize beds, high ceilings, wide-plank floors, period furnishings, area rugs and the decorative flair that marks the public rooms.

A suite and eight more bedrooms are housed in a two-story garden wing, which goes off the main house in an L-shape. The exterior is architecturally in keeping with the original, but the interior is modern, although Jurate planned to put in some antique metal bedsteads.

A pleasant, shaded veranda beside a flower garden faces the ample grounds. One room in the original house also has its own veranda. Decanters of sherry are put out in the afternoon.

Doubles, $85 to $155; suites, $185 to $225.

The Governor Bradford Inn, 128 Main St., Edgartown 02539. (508) 627-9510.

Young innkeepers Robin and Stephen Prentiss oversee a mid-19th century house that has been converted into an appealing inn of comfort and style. All sixteen rooms on three floors have private baths, kingsize brass or four-poster beds, and ceiling fans, most have color TV, and some have Queen Anne wing chairs.

Sherry is provided guests in the formal front parlor full of Victorian antiques. Afternoon tea with "whatever we feel like baking," says Robin, is served in the television room, decorated in colorful gold and navy and oriental rugs. The garden room has white wicker chairs with green corduroy seats and a refrigerator with ice and setups.

Cereals and muffins are served in the breakfast room, which has bentwood chairs at round tables dressed in pink linen and a willoware collection on display in the Sheraton china cabinet.

Doubles, $85 to $175.

Dining Spots

Warriners, Post Office Square, Edgartown. (508) 627-4488.

Tops on everyone's list of favorite restaurants in Edgartown, this is actually "two concepts under one roof," as owner Sam Warriner advertises it. Changing prix-fixe menus, fine wines and an elegant, home-like setting amid fine china and antiques combine for luxurious dining in the **Library.** The new, adjacent **Sam's** is billed as casual elegance (with the emphasis more on elegance, since this was, after all, part of the original Warriners), but the menu is informal, the prices moderate and the ambiance spirited.

The decor consists of "all the favorite things we've seen and pulled together," Sam Warriner says. He obtained the striking Dudson china (with everything matching, even vases and salt and pepper shakers) from the late Reject Shop in London and the heavy print mats for the English reproduction mahogany tables from another trip to England.

Table in the Library at Warriners.   **Conservatory dining room at L'Etoile.**

It's little wonder that the dark-paneled main dining room with Queen Anne chairs, bow windows and brick fireplace with oriental fan in front is now officially called the Library. Small brass lamps with pleated shades and vases of alstroemeria grace the well-spaced tables, and china and books glow in a back-lit corner cabinet.

The prix-fixe $34 dinner might begin, as ours did, with a pate of duck accompanied by a beach plum chutney, fettuccine with crawfish, bacon and pinenut pesto, or grilled quail with honey poppyseed mustard. These were followed by a carved loaf of fresh bread and a house salad of endive, lettuce and cucumber with a strawberry vinaigrette.

Entrees range from medallions of salmon with watercress and lillet to tournedos Diane. We liked the peppered duck steak mousseline with zinfandel sauce and the roulade of lamb brunoise with prosciutto, nicely presented with an array of brussels sprouts, cherry tomatoes and small red potatoes, and — an appropriate touch — garnished with a bunch of small wild grapes. The dessert tray included a tasty kiwi cake, a grand passion genoise with liqueur, butter cream and kiwi, chocolate pate with creme celeste, a dish of four kinds of chocolate truffles and Sam's favorite raspberry mousse with chocolate sauce.

Accompanying all this was a good Clos du Bois pinot noir for $18, chosen from a magnificent wine list containing more than its share of bargains among pricier offerings up to $650. The house wines are $8.50 a bottle and available by the glass, as are several other select wines.

On our latest visit, we thoroughly enjoyed Sam's, where you can pick and taste from an inspired menu. We shared a seafood terrine ($6) before digging into a generous dish of fettuccine with shrimp in basil, garlic and tomato butter sauce and an equally hefty plate of curried chicken India (both $10.25). A frozen blueberry mousse with the consistency of ice cream was a refreshing dessert ($4.50). With portions and prices like these, it's no wonder that Sam's quickly became everyone's favorite dining spot, but the waits can be lengthy since no reservations are taken.

Dinner nightly in season, 6 to 9 in Library by reservation, to 10 in Sam's; open Thursday-Sunday in winter.

307

L'Etoile, South Summer Street, Edgartown. (508) 627-5187.

Ensconced at the rear of the Charlotte Inn, this bow-windowed conservatory-dining room is charming. It's handsomely furnished with white linen, white bentwood and cane chairs, brick walls, skylights, paintings, lush ferns and a blooming hibiscus tree.

But somehow the uncomfortable chairs and the stark brick and stone floors seem more inviting for the inn's breakfast or the acclaimed Sunday brunch than for a leisurely, four-course dinner that often amounts to $150 to $200 a couple.

Chef-owner Michael Brisson and his wife, Joan Parzanese, overcome what could be a chilly environment with exquisite food and artistic presentation. The 28-year-old chef, who cooked for four years at the acclaimed L'Espalier in Boston, takes special pride in his treatment of game, lamb and native seafood. He also is partial to the understated place settings of white, gold-edged Villeroy & Boch china, the Reed & Barton silverplate and fluted crystal wine glasses at white-linened tables seating 45 inside. Another twenty or so can be served on a patio beside a trickling fountain outside.

The $45 prix-fixe menu starts with a choice of five appetizers: perhaps basil ravioli with pinenut and chive cream sauce and tomato concasse or a confit of game birds, rabbit and baby vegetables with tomatillo chutney and honey mustard. Or you can sample a soup of island shellfish, a salad of marinated goat cheese, or sauteed fresh foie gras with leeks and cognac-soaked golden raisins.

A homemade sorbet or a salad precedes the main course, which could be a saute of lobster and scallops with ancho chilis and corn, lobster bourbon and cilantro sauce, roasted pheasant with warm figs and a cognac and thyme sauce, rack of lamb with a salad of couscous, mint, tomato and rosemary, or grilled filet mignon with oyster and chive butter and a roasted tomato stuffed with spinach and cheese. Extravagant dishes, these, and some items carry surcharges.

Desserts could be chocolate marquis, lemon-lime tart with strawberry coulis, creme courvoisier with peach coulis, or caramelized macadamia ice cream with Bailey's creme anglaise.

The wine list starts with many champagnes, since for most this is special-occasion dining. But it offers a variety of good French and California choices priced from $15 to $110.

Dinner nightly in summer, 6:30 to 9:30; weekends rest of year; Sunday brunch, 10:30 to 1.

Shiretown Inn, North Water Street, Edgartown. (508) 627-3353.

In season, the large indoor-outdoor dining room and covered terrace at the rear of the Shiretown Inn is one of the more popular spots in Edgartown. Pink linen and pink and green wallpaper provide a soft backdrop for the garden setting, and many diners like to have drinks in the garden or the Pub adjacent to the dining room.

Well-spaced tables, soft candlelight and quiet music provide a glamorous backdrop for the widely acclaimed fare of chef Jack Hakes, one of the island's veterans. Seafood is the specialty, particularly among appetizers (shrimp and raspberry compote with haricots verts, baked littlenecks and garlic, $4.50 to $7.50), and the inn boasts the best clam chowder on the island ($3). Typical entrees ($17 to $22, except $35 for a two-pound lobster stuffed with crabmeat) are yellowtail tuna, sauteed shrimp romana, seafood brochette, rack of lamb dijon, veal Martiniquaise and tournedos sauteed with crabmeat and brandy, served with avocado pate and bearnaise sauce.

Three kinds of breads in a basket and salads with caesar dressing and pinenuts preceded our entrees of four jumbo shrimp in a rich garlic sauce, accompanied by baby vegetables that were past their prime, and an enormous helping of baked Norwegian salmon in puff pastry.

Fancy ice creams are the dessert specialty, among them the Shiretown wonder: ice cream with hot fudge sauce, creme de menthe and shredded coconut. We decided instead on a slice of tangy key lime pie, smothered with whipped cream, from the pastry cart. Dinner nightly except Wednesday, 6 to 9 or 10, spring to mid-fall.

Savoir Fare, Post Office Square, Edgartown. (508) 627-9864.
What began as basically a gourmet takeout shop has expanded into a small but full-fledged restaurant known for the best lunches in town. In 1988, owners Scott and Charlotte Caskey added dinners as well. Chef Scott, who used to cook in Vail, works in an open kitchen at one end of the small restaurant, which is a picture of pristine white from its glass-covered linened tables to the lights on a ficus tree. There's a counter with four chairs, but most of the action is outside at tables on a deck.

For lunch, you order inside from a blackboard menu and the staff brings your choices to the table. We savored a caesar salad ($6) topped with grilled chicken, which everyone seemed to be having that day, and a combination plate ($6.50) of curried chicken and pesto-pasta salads, accompanied by good French bread and a glass of Spanish wine. At night, food comes from a changing menu of nouvelle cuisine. Typical summer fare might begin with appetizers ($5.75 to $6.25) like Vineyard bay scallops ceviche, antipasto of sliced prosciutto and fresh figs, and goat cheese tart with sun-dried tomatoes and roasted garlic. Lobster in brioche and smoked-duck salad are offered as light dinners. Cioppino heads the list of main courses ($14.50 to $19.50), which could be grilled tuna steak with mango chile salsa, fettuccine with bacon, feta cheese and pinenuts, and sauteed tournedos of beef with wild mushroom ragout.

Chocolate mousse cake with pecan crust, baked apples in pastry and hot fudge pudding are among the interesting desserts.

Lunch, Monday-Saturday 11 to 3; dinner, Tuesday-Saturday 6 to 10; slightly shorter hours in off-season. Closed Christmas to March.

Andrea's, Upper Main Street, Edgartown. (508) 627-5850.
This northern Italian restaurant is one of those places that locals either love or dislike. On our last visit we heard an equal mix of both, with nothing in between. The setting is a large white house, built in 1890, with a wide front porch, a side garden patio, and a downstairs bar-lounge and wine cellar.

The airy dining rooms have bare wood floors and large windows framed by lacy white curtains. Deep green tablecloths contrast with the white walls. The fare is about what you'd expect: hot and cold appetizers of melon and prosciutto, clams casino and mozzarella in carozza, a dozen pastas, four salads, and the usual array of veal, seafood, chicken and beef dishes from $14.95 to $26.95. The veal Andrea is sauteed in white wine and baked on a bed of fresh spinach and herbs before being topped with cheese. Dinner nightly except Sunday, 6 to 11.

Martha's, 71 Main St., Edgartown. (508) 627-8316.
What could be more New Yorkish than Martha's, the arty, unbelievably colorful and crowded downstairs restaurant and the upstairs nightspot with a glassed-in waterfall behind the bar, tiny theater lights that flash on and off, and a small front porch where patrons vie in warm weather for the few tables overlooking the Main Street goings-on? It seems an unlikely spot for the busloads of elderly tourists who jam it every October lunchtime we're in town, but it turns out, they're the ones who will.

'Tis a pity the food and service no longer measure up to the setting. The menu is appealing and the food good, we understand, if you can get it. Quiches, omelets and salads in the $6 to $9 range are featured at lunch. Dinners are more international and pricy, with entrees from $14 for vegetable stir-fry with Japanese tofu and a couple of pasta dishes to $50 for rack of lamb bouquetiere for two.

A sushi bar, a raw bar, cafe menu, brunch, afternoon snacks — you name it, Martha's offers it. The locals, who must know something the tourists don't, no longer will buy.

Open daily from 11 to 10:30.

David Ryans, 11 North Water St., Edgartown. (508) 627-3030.

Named for the two sons of owner Dennis Maxwell, who also owns restaurants in New Hampshire, this is a lively bar and cafe favored by the young set on the main floor. Upstairs, an effort is being made toward serious dining in a contemporary room that is a mix of tables left bare or covered with glass, some with mats and some with cloths. One deuce has a view of the harbor across the rooftops, while most look onto the street.

The extensive dinner menu embraces everything from swordfish Creole to chicken caribe, veal Oscar and steak madagascar. The price range is from $16.25 for vegetable stir-fry to $24.95 for mixed grill over pasta. Pricey salads, sandwiches (a croissant turkey club is $7.50) and burgers are featured at lunch. Cafe fare is available at night.

Open daily from 11:30.

The Square-Rigger Restaurant, Upper Main Street at West Tisbury Road, Edgartown. (508) 627-9968.

The folks who run the immensely popular Home Port seafood restaurant in Menemsha acquired this 1800 house and turned it into a restaurant of deceptively large size, specializing in grilled American foods. The theme is nautical at tables set with woven blue mats and surrounded by captain's chairs.

From an open hearth come a variety of charbroiled entrees, from bluefish and swordfish to sirloin steaks and lamb chops. There are also prime rib, roast duck and bouillabaisse for those who prefer. At first glance the prices seem steep ($16.50 for chicken breast to $28 for swordfish), but they include appetizer — anything from house pate to shrimp cocktail — salad, beverage and dessert (from parfaits and sorbets to chocolate truffles). No wonder it's a favorite with families.

Dinner nightly from 5:30.

The Seafood Shanty, 31 Dock St., Edgartown. (508) 627-8622.

This contemporary, three-level spot is anything but a shanty. Edgartown's best harbor view for dining is from the upstairs deck with a raw bar above a glass-enclosed porch with water on three sides. Unusual plastic chairs with blue mesh frames, bare tables with blue and white mats and bare wood walls add up to an attractive nautical setting.

You pay for the location. Our lunch for two came to $30 for a cup of clam chowder and a spinach salad, plus a pasta salad loaded with seafood; the sunny Indian summer setting was such, we admit, that we lingered over a second beer.

Dinner entrees are fairly traditional, from $14.95 for broiled scrod or bluefish to $17.95 for a fried seafood platter; rolls and salad or cole slaw, baked potato or french fries accompany. After all this, who needs the desserts, which are standard anyway?

But you might want to adjourn upstairs to the Shanty Cabaret, where ten singers (mostly from Yale) perform show tunes and such from 8:30 to midnight in summer.

Lunch daily, 11:45 to 3; dinner, 5 to 10:30. Open May-October.

The Wharf, Dock Street, Edgartown. (508) 627-9966.

With an enclosed deck, a dining room with a soaring ceiling and windows toward the harbor, and a usually crowded pub, this is popular for casual and light meals.

A seafood salad and fried oysters vie with the raw bar as attractions at lunch. Seafood Wellington, pan-blackened yellowfin tuna or bluefish, bouillabaisse, linguini alfredo

310

with duckling, sauteed veal steak and filet mignon are among the dinner entrees ($10.95 to $18.95). Surf and turf mixed grill ($16.95) combines barbecued beef rib, marinated chicken breast and half a swordfish steak. In case you're interested, this is the only place in town to get Beluga caviar, $35 as an appetizer.

Open daily from 11:30 to 11.

Mad Martha's, North Water Street, Edgartown.

One of a group of ice-cream parlors around the island, this offers an incredible variety of flavors (we loved the Bailey's Irish cream overflowing from its crackly cone, $1.75) and concoctions, from walkaway waffle sundae to oreo cookie nookie. The most outrageous is the pig's delight ($14.95): a dozen scoops of ice cream topped with banana-split trimmings; "order by saying 'oink,'" says the sign at the door. Some do.

Extra-Special

Chicama Vineyards, West Tisbury. (508) 693-0309.

The wild grapes that gave Martha's Vineyard its name are now being cultivated by ex-Californians George and Catherine Matheisen and winemaker son Tim, who makes "the kinds of wines we like to drink," Catherine says. They specialize in dry viniferas, among them a robust red zinfandel, a new Summer Island red that's meant to be drunk young, and the first Martha's Vineyard-appellation merlot. Much of the winemaking operation is outside and rather primitive, as you might expect after negotiating Stoney Hill Road, a long mile of bumps and dirt that we'd rename Stoney Hole. Several hundred people make the trek on a busy summer day and relish the shop's choice of wine or herbal vinegars, dressings and jams, all neatly displayed in gift baskets and glass cases lit from behind so the herbs show through. In fall, the Christmas shop offers festive foods, wreaths and hot mulled wine. Open daily 11 to 5, Sunday 1 to 5.

Vinegars on display at Chicama Vineyards.

Diversions

Edgartown is an eminently walkable town and everything (except some of the beaches) is within walking distance. That's fortunate for in summer the place tends to be wall-to-walk people, bicycles and cars. The shops, restaurants and inns are compressed into a maze of narrow streets leading from or paralleling the harbor. Interspersed with them and along quaint side streets are large white whaling captain's homes, neatly separated from the brick sidewalks by picket fences and colorful gardens. Here you see and sense the history of a seaport village preserved from the 19th century.

Walk around. Don't miss the churches: The Old Whaling Church, the tall-columned Greek Revival structure that doubles as the Performing Arts Center; the little St.

Andrew's Episcopal Church with wonderful stained-glass windows, a cheery interior and a carillon that tolls quite a concert across town in the late afternoon; the imposing First Federated Church with old box pews and a steeple visible far at sea. Other highlights are the towering Pagoda Tree brought from China as a seedling in a flower pot early in the 19th century and now spreading over South Water Street to shade the Victorian Inn and the Old Sculpin Art Gallery showing works of various artists

The Dukes County Historical Society, at School and Cooke streets, is a block-size museum complex worth a visit. The twelve rooms of the 1765 Thomas Cooke House are filled with early island memorabilia. You're apt to see historians at work in the Gale Huntington Library of History, through which you pass to get to the Francis Foster Museum, which has a small maritime and island collection. Outside is a boat shed containing a whaleboat, fire engine and old wagon, plus the original Fresnel lens from the old Gay Head Lighthouse, mounted in a replica of the lighthouse lantern and watch room, and still lighted at night. Open mid-June to mid-September, Tuesday-Saturday 10 to 4:30; adults $2, children 50 cents. Rest of year, Thursday and Friday 1 to 4, Saturday 10 to 4, free.

Chappaquiddick Island. Reached by a 25-cent and five-minute ride on the On Time ferry from Edgartown, it has a public beach facing the Edgartown Harbor at Chappy Point, plus the Cape Pogue Wildlife Refuge and Wasque Reservation beaches. These are remote and secluded, three miles from the ferry — best reached by car as bicyclists may find it difficult negotiating some of the sandy roads (but parking is limited). On the way you'll pass the forested Mytoi Trustees Preservation and the Chappaquiddick General Store and gasoline station, surrounded by abandoned cars and the only commercial enterprise of size on Chappaquiddick.

Shopping. Main Street and adjacent streets are crammed with interesting stores. **The Fligors'** (billed as the Vineyard's most delightful store for 30 years) is an intriguing maze of rooms and levels that make it almost a department store; suave gifts, dolls, resort clothing, toys, Christmas shop, a fantastic basement sale room — you name it, Carol and Richard Fligor probably have it. **Tashtego** is a one-of-a-kind shop with lovely china and furniture from antique through contemporary. We liked the speckled Stippleware from California. **Henley's** has unique and sophisticated clothing as well as many kaleidoscopes and the fascinating life-like sculptures and cityscapes of Michael Garman; billed by owner John Henley as "like a 3-D Norman Rockwell," they sell for up to $1,850 but most are considerably less. Pick up your foul-weather gear at **Sundog;** the **Snake River Trading Company** offers "clothes for your comfortable life style." **Country Life** has exquisite decorative accessories from hand-painted linens to Italian pottery. The **Unicorn Tales Bookshop** also offers funny cards and island memorabilia. We enjoy popping into the **Vermont Shop,** the idea for which was thought up in the winter of 1980 by Robin Burke, who has a ski house there, when there was very little snow. It has expanded to the point that 40 percent of the merchandise mix comes from elsewhere, but you'll find Woody Jackson cows, Vermont pottery and foods like common crackers and cheeses; we liked the ceramic steamers and came out with an interesting pair of titanium earrings. There are branches of such well-known shops as **Crabtree & Evelyn** and **Carroll Reed. Nevin Square** is a conglomeration of nice shops behind the Colonial Inn; the leather handbags, belts and custom-made sandals at **Harness & Reed** are good-looking, as are the grapevine baskets. **Embellishments, Optional Art** for fine jewelry and **The Great Atlantic** for clothes are others we liked.

If you get bushed from all this shopping and walking, rest awhile on the benches atop the Memorial Wharf pavilion, a salubrious vantage point for contemplating the harbor.

Newport waterfront is on view from dining deck at Clarke Cooke House.

Newport, R.I.
A Many-Splendored Place

For the visitor, there are perhaps five Newports.

One is the harborfront, the busy commercial and entertainment area along the wharves and Thames Street. This is the heart of Newport, the place from which the Tall Ships and America's Cup winners sailed, the place to which the tourists gravitate.

Another Newport is a world apart. It's up on fabled Bellevue Avenue among the mansions from the Gilded Age. Here the Astors, Vanderbilts, Morgans and others of America's 400 built their summer "cottages," palatial showplaces designed by the nation's leading architects. Here near the Casino at the turn of the century was a society summer resort unrivaled for glitter and opulence.

A third Newport is its quaint Point and Historic Hill sections, which date back to the 17th and 18th centuries when Newport was an early maritime center. Here are more Colonial houses than in any place in the country, and some of the oldest public and religious edifices as well.

A fourth Newport is the windswept, open land around Ocean Drive, where the surf crashes against the rocky shore amid latter-day mansions and contemporary showplaces. This is the New England version of California's Pebble Beach and Seventeen-Mile Drive.

And then there's the rest of Newport, a bustling, Navy-dominated city that sprawls south along Aquidneck Island, away from the ocean and the other Newports.

Join these diverse Newports as history and geography have and you get New England's international resort, a wondrous mix of water and wealth, of architecture and history, of romance and entertainment.

You can concentrate on one Newport and have more than enough to see and do, or try to savor a bit of them all. But likely as not, you won't get your fill (unless you tire

313

of fighting the crowds of a summer's weekend). Newport will merely whet your appetite, its powerful allure beckoning you back.

Inn Spots

The Inn at Castle Hill, Ocean Drive, Newport 02840. (401) 849-3800.

Gnarled trees on a hillside, reminding us of the olive groves in Portugal, make the approach to the Inn at Castle Hill a bit mysterious as well as picturesque. When you reach the brown shingled inn at the crest of the hill, the view of Narragansett Bay and the Atlantic is breathtaking.

Calling itself a "country inn by the sea," Castle Hill seems rather more sophisticated than that, with its fine restaurant and elegant Victorian air. Well-aged oriental rugs and well-cared-for wood paneling and carving abound. The fireplace of inlaid wood in the sitting room, where a fire is usually lit, is a sight to behold.

Seven of the ten rooms in the inn have private baths; the smaller three rooms that were in the servants' wing share two. Most are huge, and smashingly decorated with splashy coordinated prints in her inimitable style by Ione Williams of the Inn at Sawmill Farm in Vermont.

In one room, the peach covering of a loveseat and chair, beside a bay window that appears to be perched right over the ocean, is matched in the peach chair in front of the dressing table in the large bathroom. Other bedrooms have chestnut or pine paneling, chaise longues, Victorian furniture and plush carpets, and most have wonderful views. On the third floor is a suite with sitting room; another room is all green and white and wicker, and even the clawfoot bathtub is wallpapered. The Nun's Room in the former servants' quarters, transformed from a large closet, has enough room to accommodate a twin bed and a sink "for the person who can't afford our rates," says innkeeper Paul McEnroe.

He collects and displays the paintings of Helena Sturdevant, a Newport artist early in the century.

In the lovely little breakfast room, named after Alexander Agassiz, the naturalist who was first owner of the house, continental breakfast is served to inn guests all year, buffet style from April to October. The inn's bar is a stunner and its restaurant widely acclaimed (see Dining Spots).

In summer, six motel-like units are available in the Harbor House, just in front of the inn. Eighteen cottages (typical New England tacky beach cottages, says the innkeeper, but they're rented a year in advance) right on the water are available by the week.

The property upon which the inn resides was put up for sale in 1988, but the $20 million asking price drew no immediate takers.

Doubles with private bath, $85 to $175, depending on season; shared bath, $50 to $80; suite, $120 to $225. Harbor House, $110. Beach cottages, $625 or $675 weekly.

The Victorian Ladies, 63 Memorial Blvd., Newport 02840. (401) 849-9960.

All is light and airy in these two Victorian beauties, one behind the other and separated by a lovely brick courtyard with a gazebo, birdbath, wicker furniture and tempered-glass tables, surrounded by colorful flower boxes. Innkeepers Helene and Donald O'Neill gutted and renovated the houses, opening one of Newport's most inviting B&Bs in 1987.

The nine guest rooms, all with private baths, are decorated in a Victorian theme with a light touch. One of the nicest has a queensize bed and sitting area; it is fresh and feminine with dhurrie rugs and rose carpeting, puffy curtains, down comforters, eyelet ruffles, thick pink and blue towels, potpourri and vials of dried flowers on the doors.

Guest room at Inn at Castle Hill has windows onto Narragansett Bay.

Although Helene had never decorated before, she did a gorgeous job throughout. The small pink and blue parlor has a crystal chandelier and crystal sconces on the mantel; the fireplace was ablaze the chilly October morning we were there. Balloon curtains grace the parlor and the adjacent dining room, where an enormous English oak hutch displays plates and country knickknacks.

Don, a contractor, built the gazebo and the courtyard, and his green thumb shows in a profusion of flowers. He was adding an outdoor redwood hot tub for 1989.

Helene serves up a marvelous breakfast, from all kinds of muffins to french toast grand marnier, eggs Benedict, or an egg and spinach casserole. "She loves to cook and keeps expanding her repertoire," says Don. "I'm the dishwasher."

The personable young innkeepers share the limelight with Wylie, a loveable and loving golden retriever who has gained nine pounds since the O'Neills opened as a result of guests sneaking him tidbits at breakfast.

Doubles, $120. Closed in January.

Admiral Fitzroy Inn, 398 Thames St., Newport 02840. (401) 847-4459.

The newest of Jane and Bruce Berriman's three Admiral inns in Newport, this is also the most luxurious — a far cry from its former status as the St. Mary's Church convent. A plain, square box on the outside, it's very appealing inside, especially the striking and incredible hand-painted decorative touches everywhere. Done by a young artist, they vary from borders to murals and entire walls, and are worthy of a gallery.

An elevator serves the eighteen rooms and suites upstairs, most of them quite spacious and artfully furnished with antique queensize or twin beds, upholstered or wicker loveseats and chairs, thick carpeting, and plump, lace-edged pillows and white duvet comforters. All have modern baths, telephones, air-conditioning, and small TVs and refrigerators, some of them hidden in brightly painted cabinets. Check out Room 10's large mural of an apricot tree in a clay pot, so realistic it even has bugs and a butterfly.

Two rooms on the fourth floor have decks offering a terrific view of the harbor.

A full breakfast is served at white tables in the main-floor dining room, its walls highlighted by hand-painted garlands of flowers. Cheese and parsley omelets and blueberry or banana pancakes are typical fare. Tea and crackers and cheese are set out in the afternoon. If you'd like to make a cup of tea or coffee in your room, you'll find an electric kettle and the fixings.

The inn is named for the admiral who developed a barometer that allows the average person to forecast the weather. Several examples are on display and for sale in the impressive Chinese-red entry hall.

Doubles, $100 to $110.

Cliffside Inn, 2 Seaview Ave., Newport 02840. (401) 847-1811.

Ex-Californian Kay Russell made this inn a block from the ocean what it is: a lovely old formal Victorian house with a high Victorian flair. When we visited in October 1988, she was looking to retire after eight successful but tiring years as a doting innkeeper; we were assured the inn would continue in good hands.

Built in 1880 by the governor of Maryland as a summer villa, the inn has ten guest rooms with private baths. The four on the second floor are the nicest with high ceilings and tall windows, an armoire here and an in-room sink there. All are elaborately furnished with period antiques. Miss Beatrice's Room is the largest; she was a well-known artist who summered in the house and guests still admire the flowers she painted on the door panels. Her room has an antique, Lincoln-style queen bed and a huge bathroom converted from a former bedroom — the toilet looks like a throne behind lacy eyelet curtains.

A small sitting room on the third floor offers a TV set, and there's a library-landing with books and games. Guests like to congregate in the large fireplaced parlor, cheerfully decorated in tones of green and peachy-orange, or on wicker furniture on the wide front veranda, which yields glimpses of the ocean down the street.

A continental breakfast with homemade rolls is served at two big tables in the parlor.

In each room is an informative, opinionated (though accentuaing the positive) guide to Newport restaurants, handwritten by a member of the inn's staff. Guests share their experiences in an ongoing book called "Past, Present and Future."

Doubles, $65 to $85. Closed November-April.

Ivy Lodge, 12 Clay St., Newport 02840. (401) 849-6865.

Headlined "Description of a Beautiful Place," an article in a local newspaper of 1886 called this "one of the prettiest cottages in Newport." Today, it's one of the town's most inviting B&Bs, thanks to some spectacular architectural touches, comfortable furnishings and the T.L.C. of energetic young innkeepers Ed and Mary Moy.

The most striking feature is the three-story entry hall, 33 feet high and paneled in carved oak. There's "no plaster in any part of the hall," as the newspaper article put it. Upstairs rooms go off galleries, supported by fluted and carved columns, around the hall.

A small reception parlor, inviting in pink, wicker and chintz, is enhanced by a fireplace and floral prints. Beyond is a large green living room, elegant and comfortable.

The twenty-one-foot-long table in the dining room is set for fourteen, with room to spare. Here, the Moys serve fruit salad or banana casserole, fresh breads and muffins, hard-boiled eggs or quiche for breakfast. Smoked salmon and bloody marys might be offered on weekends. Ed, a knowledgeable chef, does all the cooking at his huge professional kitchen in back, and will prepare dinners for guests on special occasions with advance notice.

Mary's elaborate stenciling graces the eight guest rooms, six of which have private (and stenciled) baths. "I went on a stenciling frenzy," she concedes; "Eddie says he

316

Striking entry hall at Ivy Lodge.

expects to wake up some morning and find his forehead painted!" Each of the rooms is outfitted in vibrant colors. Laura Ashley fabrics, eyelet trims, lace-edged towels, brass or wicker headboards, and the odd skylight are features.

Two efficiency suites are available in an annex to the lodge and in a carriage house.

This is a residential area of substantial homes with spacious grounds, so there's a tranquility that's rare among Newport inns. A wraparound veranda is great for lounging, and some spirited croquet games are played on the side lawn. The Moys offer beach chairs and bicycles for guests to use.

In the afternoon, candles are lit on the fireplace mantels and hot cider, cookies and popcorn are put out to welcome guests.

Doubles, $85 to $95; suites, $135.

Admiral Benbow Inn, 93 Pelham St., Newport 02840. (401) 846-4256.

Located on Newport's Historic Hill on the first street in the country to be lit by gas lamps, this gray clapboard house built in 1855 by a retired sea captain has both an historic and a nautical air. The first of Jane and Bruce Berriman's Admiral inns, it is overseen by manager Maggie Wiggins and her mother, innkeeper Joan Fleming.

The fifteen guest rooms on three floors have canopy and four-poster beds, antique bureaus, cozy armchairs and Victorian settees, tall windows with print curtains and private bathrooms with showers. Some of the upper rooms have harbor views, and Room 12 has a deck overlooking much of Newport.

Continental breakfast (homemade breads and muffins) is served downstairs in a walkout basement with old stone walls, wide-board floors and a wood stove. Here, deck chairs and a sofa are grouped around a TV set, and tea is available on winter afternoons.

The inn has a distinctly maritime flavor (it's named for the inn in *Treasure Island*). Quite a collection of antique English barometers is on display (and for sale) in the front hall and downstairs common room.

Doubles, $75 to $100.

The Inntowne, 6 Mary St., Newport 02840. (401) 846-9200.

This inn built in 1980 after a fire destroyed the original structure is aptly named. It couldn't be more in town, just off Thames Street, its side rooms facing on the busy main street and those on the third and fourth floors catching a glimpse of the harbor.

Run by Betty and Paul McEnroe of the Inn at Castle Hill, this also reflects the decor of their friend Ione Williams of Vermont's Inn at Sawmill Farm. All 26 rooms are different, but oh-so-decorated in colorful and contemporary matching fabrics (right down to the shower curtains and wastebaskets), thick carpeting, canopy beds, upholstered wing chairs and wicker furniture.

A fourth-floor corner suite has a pencil-post bed, a sofabed and two upholstered chairs. A twin room is flanked by a narrow patio, which has two wrought-iron chairs against a brick wall. Terrycloth robes are provided in the only room with a hall bath.

The inn's Restoration House a couple of doors away at 20 Mary St. offers a basement apartment with kitchen, sitting room and bedroom. Upstairs are six more rooms and suites, several with kitchenettes and small balconies, individually decorated in white on gray, blue on white, white on taupe — you get the picture.

A continental breakfast of croissants, muffins and fresh orange juice is served in a small dining room amid oriental rugs and antiques. Tea and cookies are put out there every afternoon (you can buy your teacup if you like).

The small front sitting room, with sofas and chairs in colorful chintz, has shelves of books and magazines for reading. Off the inn's fourth floor is a large plant-filled sundeck, popular on sunny days.

Doubles, $95 to $150 (suites and apartments, $125 to $170).

Wayside, Bellevue Avenue, Newport 02840. (401) 847-0302.

There's no street number, no advertising nor brochure, and the sign on the gate is so discreet that many miss it. In the midst of the mansions along fabled Bellevue Avenue and looking very much at home is Wayside, the beige brick Georgian summer cottage built by Elisha Dyer of New York, almost across from the Elms and just down the street from the Astors and Vanderbilts.

After a period as a dormitory for Salve Regina College, it was converted into an inn in 1976 by Al and Dorothy Post. Here you can partake of Newport's gilded past, staying in a gigantic room amid Victorian furnishings at prices that are out of the past as well.

Enter Wayside through heavy doors under the portico into the foyer, its fifteen-foot-high ceiling, oak parquet floor and paneled walls setting the stage for things to come. Coffee and pastries are served here on a wicker table at breakfast. To the right is the Library, a bedroom with a tall carved fireplace crowned with an ornamental Florentine mantel. The room is so vast that the front has a queensize bed and armoire, the center section is a comfortable seating area available for meetings and television-watching, and built-in bookshelves are on all sides.

A beautiful, quarter-cut oak staircase leads to seven more guest rooms off a wide hall on the second floor, each with private bath and each seemingly bigger and more impressive than the last. Crystal knobs on the doors, inside and out, are among the extravagant touches. Twelve-foot-high ceilings dwarf the canopy beds in the rooms, which have colorful wallpaper, shiny wood floors and pleasant sitting areas, usually with wicker furniture (Dot, says her husband, is a wicker nut). The largest room, Number 5, has two double beds, a wicker table, and a grouping of two upholstered chairs and a rocker. The bathroom for Number 6 is almost as large as the bedroom.

The third floor has three more guest rooms, each with in-room wash basins but sharing two baths. One bedroom, fashioned from a storage area, has a sitting room and, up a few stairs, a "crow's nest penthouse" containing a brass bed.

All rooms have small black and white TVs for those who "want to watch the news," Al says. Children are welcome at this inn, and cribs are available.

A swimming pool behind the inn beckons on summer days.

Doubles, $75 to $85.

Villa Liberte, 22 Liberty St., Newport 02840. (401) 846-7444.

This small hotel has one of the most striking exteriors we've seen, its square, green and terra cotta facade punctuated by an enormous arched window. Other windows are covered by intricate iron grills and softened with flower boxes. Formerly a German restaurant and before that a bordello, it was thoroughly renovated in 1987 into twelve units that include four suites. The place takes its name from its Mediterranean-looking exterior and from its address.

Innkeeper Anne Mosco proudly shows off the rooms, each of which has an archway into a dramatic black and white tiled area where a sink stands; the adjacent bathroom

Wayside looks very much at home among mansions of Bellevue Avenue.

is similarly tiled. Each room is done in peach and seafoam green colors and has a small TV; suites have refrigerators. Most rooms as well as the wide halls, with columns painted a terra cotta color, contain prints of Ansel Adams photographs.

A continental breakfast of juice, croissants and muffins is served buffet style. Guests may take it to the spacious outdoor deck off the second floor, or to one of two small sitting areas in the halls on the second and third floors.

Next door is a house renovated into three units for families and groups.

Doubles, $95 to $140.

Hydrangea House, 16 Bellevue Ave., Newport 02840. (401) 846-4435.

Two antiques dealers opened this B&B in 1988 in former office space above a Bellevue Avenue storefront. So you expect it to be decorated to the hilt. The furnishings come from Jennifer's Junque, owned by Dennis Blair, partner in the B&B venture with innkeeper Grant Edmondson.

A walk-up stairway between two stores leads to a wide hall with stippled gold walls painted with a pastry brush to look like marble. To one side is a small room with an antique reception desk. To the rear is a large deck with a more residential, verdant feeling than you'd guess from the front.

Five guest rooms with small private baths are decorated with splashy draperies and wallpapers that match; the fabrics may be repeated on the bed headboards or, in one case, a valance over the shower. A sixth room, in the works downstairs when we visited, was to have a private entrance, deck and jacuzzi.

Grant serves pastries for continental breakfast at a tiny sitting area in the hall or outside on the deck, where afternoon tea is offered in season. Or guests can take breakfast in a European-type coffee shop downstairs.

Doubles, $115 to $125. No smoking.

The Pilgrim House, 123 Spring St., Newport 02840. (401) 846-0040.

A large rooftop deck off the third floor with a panoramic view of the harbor is the main attraction at this Victorian B&B, opened in 1987 by Bruce and Pam Bayuk in a former boarding house. The front faces a busy street, but once you're ensconced on high at tables and chairs on the rooftop deck, the busy Newport scene in front seems far away.

Lots of books and magazines are at the ready in the pleasant, fireplaced living room. Three of the eleven air-conditioned guest rooms are on the main floor. All but two have private baths, most of them small, in what obviously used to be closets.

Continental breakfast is served at tiny round tables in the third-floor hallway leading to the deck or, on nice mornings, at tables on the deck. Fresh fruit or spiced pears and apples, homemade muffins, and blueberry or banana bread are the fare. A refrigerator here is available for guests' use.

Doubles, $85 to $95. No smoking.

Dining Spots

The Black Pearl, Bannister's Wharf, Newport. (401) 846-5264.

Our favorite all-around restaurant in Newport — and that of many others, judging from the crowds day and night — is the informal tavern, the fancy Commodore's Room and the deck with umbrella-topped tables that comprise the Black Pearl.

Up to 1,500 meals a day are served in summer, the more remarkable considering it has what the manager calls "the world's smallest kitchen." Waitresses vie with patrons for space in the narrow hall that runs the length of the building; white-hatted chefs and busboys run across the wharf, even in winter, to fetch fresh produce and fish — sometimes champagne — from the refrigerators in an outbuilding.

It's all quite colorful, congenial in spirit and creative in cuisine.

You can sit outside under the Cinzano umbrellas and watch half the world go by while sipping a zesty bloody mary or sampling Newport's best clam chowder (creamy, chock full of clams and amply herbed, served with a huge soda cracker) for $1.75 a cup, $3 a bowl. You also can get a Pearlburger with mint salad in pita bread and good fries for $4.75 and a variety of other sandwiches, salads and desserts.

Inside is the hectic and noisy tavern, offering the outdoor fare as well as heartier items that can serve as lunch or dinner. In winter, we thoroughly enjoyed our lunches of eggs Copenhagen (smoked salmon instead of ham) and the famed Pearlburger. Among desserts, we remember a delectable brandy cream cake, a dish of golden grand marnier ice cream and an apple-raisin bread pudding. Last time we were there, we watched as a woman at the next table tried to finish (but couldn't) a huge slice of blueberry pound cake with lemon icing, just out of the oven and "awesome," according to the waitress. Espresso as strong as it should be or a cup of cappuccino Black Pearl ($3), with courvoisier and kahlua, set you up for the rest of a winter's day.

Candlelight dinners are lovely in the Commodore's Room with its beamed sloped ceilings, the lights of the waterfront twinkling through small paned windows.

Chefs Marjorie and Daniel Knerr use light sauces and stress vegetables and side dishes. Entrees run from $13 for chicken sauteed with lemon butter to $21 for steak au poivre. Shrimp, scallops and lobster in a light sauce Americaine, soft-shell crabs meuniere, duckling sauteed with brandied raisin sauce, noisettes of veal with a watercress cream sauce, and loin of lamb with thyme and truffle sauce are possibilities. Appetizers ($4.50 to $5.75) include oysters, escargots and tuna with red pepper sauce.

Tavern and outdoor cafe open daily from 11; dinner in Commodore Room from 6. Closed in January or February.

La Petite Auberge, 19 Charles St., Newport. (401) 849-6669.

Chef Roger Putier opened Newport's first classic French restaurant with classic French service in 1975 in the historic Stephen Decatur house, and has been thriving

Classic French cooking of La Petite Auberge emanates from historic Stephen Decatur house.

ever since. Smack against the sidewalk, the severity of the dark green exterior is warmed by roses climbing fences and trellises beside a small outdoor courtyard.

The inside seems indeed petite, many people never getting beyond the two intimate and elegant main-floor dining rooms, one with five tables and the other with four. But up some of the steepest stairs we've climbed are three more dining rooms. Out back is a little-known tavern where regulars linger over brandy and chat with Roger.

Chef Putier's hand-written French menu is so extensive and his specials so numerous that the choice is difficult. His sauces are heavenly — from the escargots with cepes ($6.25), a house specialty (the heavily garlicked sauce demanding to be soaked up by the hot and crusty French bread), to entrees of veal with morels and cream sauce and two tender pink lamb chops, also with cepes and an intense brown sauce.

Soups and appetizers ($4.50 to $7.95) include a fine Marseilles-style fish soup and a mousse of chicken livers with truffles. Entrees are priced from $16 for frog's legs provencale to $23 for lobster Americaine, and include classic poultry and meat dishes. Vegetables on our visit were green beans and creamy sliced potatoes topped with cheese. Desserts are classic as well. We enjoyed strawberries Romanoff, but regretted that the cafe filtre listed on the menu was really espresso.

Dinner, Monday-Saturday 6 to 10; Sunday, 5 to 9.

The Clarke Cooke House, Bannister's Wharf, Newport. (401) 849-2900.

A 1790-vintage Colonial house offers an informal menu downstairs in the bistro-like Candy Store Cafe and formal dining upstairs on several levels, including a breezy, canopied upper deck with a great view of the waterfront. In these rarefied heights, the staff's demeanor is more haughty and the prices more lofty than need be, but as the clipping from "W" out front attested, the Clarke Cooke is one of those places with style, as defined by W.

Entrees are in the $21.50 to $24.50 range for things like roast rack of lamb persillade with minted tarragon glaze and onion marmalade, fricassee of sweetbreads steamed with morels and lobster and madeira sauce, and grilled sea scallops on chive pasta with a champagne and chanterelle vinaigrette. For starters ($7.25 to $12.50), try fried oysters on a warm spinach and bacon salad, a salad of Farmland quail with sesame dressing and oriental mushrooms, or terrine of duck, pheasant and rabbit with caramelized chestnuts and cranberry chutney.

Owned by the owner of Locke-Ober of Boston, Clarke Cooke features Locke-Ober's Indian pudding a la mode for dessert, along with chocolate grand marnier mousse and warm apple crepes flambe.

Lunch in the casual **Candy Store Cafe** is fun, when you sit at tiny marble-topped tables on bentwood chairs and eat things like clam chowder ($2.75), stir-fried chicken with snow peas and ginger on angel-hair pasta ($7.95) or a Candy Store burger topped with roquefort and bacon ($6.50). A $10.95 brunch includes a mimosa or bloody mary.

Dinner, nightly 6 to 10 or 10:30, weekends only in winter; cafe, 11:30 to 11 in season.

Le Bistro, Bowen's Wharf, Newport. (401) 849-7778.

Its large windows on the airy second and third floors looking toward the water, Le Bistro is a bit fancier than a run-of-the-mill bistro. The second-floor dining rooms have an air of elegance, the menu is regional American and a new bar menu is served all day on the third floor. Chef-owners John and Mary Philcox continue their tradition of a fine wine list and a series of prix-fixe dinners with cuisine from different regions of France.

Dinner entrees run the gamut from bouillabaisse ($14.95) to steamed lobster beurre blanc ($28.50). In between are grilled duck salmis with wild mushrooms, sea scallops sauteed with endive and cream, and veal steak with leeks and mushrooms. Desserts, baked daily on the premises, include green grapes in puff pastry with whipped cream, Ivory Coast chocolate rum cake, walnut cake and Creole bread pudding.

For lunch from a menu on which everything sounds (and later looks) good, we enjoyed a fine salade nicoise ($7.25) and a classic bouillabaisse ($10.95). The hot sausage with hot potato salad is a wonderful dish on a cold day.

Lunch daily, 11:30 to 2; dinner, 6 to 11; Sunday brunch, 11:30 to 2.

The Inn at Castle Hill, Ocean Drive, Newport. (401) 849-3800.

The most sumptuous bar in Newport is tucked away in the front corner of this fine inn, its tall windows taking in the grand views of bay and sunset as you sip a drink and snack on crackers with a zippy spread.

Beyond is a three-sided dining porch with rounded walls that juts out toward the water, all very inviting with white tables and chairs and flowered seats. Also available are a plus a fancy small room where breakfast is served in winter, and a large formal dining room, richly paneled but for one wall of deep blue and rose wallpaper.

The continental menu with a touch of nouvelle is highly regarded. Dinners could begin with sweetbreads in pastry, raw Cajun tenderloin or lamb noisettes provencale.

Entrees ($18 to $25) include halibut paupiette, veal with chanterelles, Dover sole, and sliced duck with raspberry and peppercorn sauce. We can vouch for a fine filet of sole stuffed with scallop mousse and an excellent tournedos au poivre from meals past.

Salads, sandwiches and entrees in the $7 to $11.50 range are served at lunch. Jazz is played on the lawn during Sunday brunch.

Lunch, Tuesday-Saturday noon to 2:30; dinner, Monday-Saturday 6 to 9; Sunday brunch, noon to 4. Restaurant closed November to mid-April. Jackets required at dinner.

Recorder's Restaurant, 673 Thames St., Newport. (401) 846-5830.

This French restaurant run by an Irish family is a gem. Patrick O'Byrne, a chef who was second in command at Boston's Ritz-Carlton, acquired the quarters formerly occupied by a restaurant bearing the name of Volker Frick, a well-known Newport restaurateur. Patrick shored up the building's infrastructure, enhanced the two small dining rooms with white linens and fresh flowers, and voila, Frick's was rechristened Recorder's.

The food is classic French, but the prices are down-home and the service is endearing. Patrick's wife Gloria is hostess and waitress, their son Fitz is chief pot-washer, and thirteen-year-old son Tony is busboy and waiter — "one of the best waiters in the state, according to our customers," his father reports proudly. Indeed, his mother thinks he puts her to shame in explaining the menu; "he's a great seller of desserts," she says.

The twelve entrees ($15 to $19) come with good French bread, fresh vegetable, and potato or rice. Among the possibilities are Norwegian salmon in parchment, Gulf shrimp with a cognac and dill sauce, scallops sauteed with maitre-d'hotel butter, veal scaloppine with cognac and green peppercorn cream sauce, two versions of lamb steak and a French lamb stew. Noticeably missing on the 1988 menu were any beef dishes other than a beef consomme.

Pate bigarade, two versions of escargots, sauteed mushrooms and roasted red peppers comprise the list of appetizers ($4.50 to $6.50). Among the desserts that young Tony says he likes best to sell are a caramelized apple cake with apple rum sauce, a Swiss chocolate walnut cake with strawberry sauce, meringues shaped like swans and filled with chocolate mousse, and "the best creme caramel anywhere."

The restaurant's hours are limited by the sons' schooling. "It's a total family operation and there's just the four of us," Patrick explains. "So when the boys are in school, we have to close."

Recorder's has a beer and wine license.

Dinner, Tuesday-Sunday 6 to 10 in summer; Friday and Saturday in spring and fall. Closed November-April.

Scales & Shells, 527 Thames St., Newport. (401) 846-3474.

Plain and exotic seafood is simply but assertively prepared in what owner Andy Ackerman bills as Newport's only "only fish" restaurant.

A retired sea captain, Andy cooks up a storm in the open kitchen near the entry. The well-spaced tables are covered with black and white checkered cloths, the floors are bare and, but for a few models of fish on the walls, the decor is stark.

The food is foremost. A blackboard menu offers an enormous range of seafood, from mussels marinara ($9.75) to lobster fra diavolo ($32.95 for two). There are mesquite-grilled bluefish, tuna and lobster ($9.95 to $14.95), but no non-seafood items at all..

You can pick and choose from a raw bar near the front entrance, appetizers like a grilled clam pizza ($5.95), and desserts like Italian gelatos and tarts.

A blackboard wine list offers a limited selection of Italian and California wines from $8.95 to $26. The $100 bottle of Dom Perignon that heads the list seems out of place.

Dinner, Monday-Saturday 5 to 9 or 10, Sunday 4 to 9; extended hours in summer.

Muriel's, corner of Spring and Touro streets, Newport. (401) (401) 849-7780.

One of a number of good little funky restaurants in town, this gets the most accolades in the Cliffside Inn's rundown on local eateries — five stars and a rave review: "The only thing that outdoes Muriel's unique menu which has the freshest ingredients and colorful display with a flair is her hospitality and beautifully designed restaurant."

Life-like mannequins make visitors do a double-take at the entrance, and the "water closet" turns out to be unisex. The tables, covered with glass over lace over green, are rather close together. Lace curtains with little houses on them cover the windows, the floors are bare, and ceiling fans and globe lamps hang from the ceiling. When we lunched there, background music could not muffle the sounds of two squawking babies in separate parts of the room.

Muriel Barclay-deTolley, something of a Newport institution, makes the soups, but leaves most of the rest of the cooking chores to her chef, Billy Rose. Her son, Paul, who is co-owner and host, touts the award-winning seafood chowder, rated first in the 1987 great chowder cook-off at the Newport Yachting Center and a recent prize winner in Seattle. It's distinctive and laced with dill, but we wished it were not quite so thick.

The luncheon crepe ($4.50) — spinach, mushrooms, cheese and tomatoes — was a classic of its kind, and the side salad of greens with slivers of cheddar cheese dressed with creamy dill was extraordinary. A hefty bowl of spinach salad ($4.75) was topped by apple slices, a new one to us, and lots of crisp bacon.

Crepes and salads also are available at dinner, when you can get appetizers like escargots, pate and baked brie for $3.95 to $5.95. Entrees are priced from $6.50 for vegetable stir-fry, lasagna and fettuccine to $13.95 for filet mignon with bearnaise sauce. Desserts range from $2.95 for raisin bread pudding with butter rum sauce or carrot cake with orange glaze to $3.50 for bananas Foster.

The dinner menu notes that "the first serving of French bread is on us; additional servings — .50/person." Now that's funky.

Breakfast, Monday-Saturday 8 to 11:30; lunch, 11:30 to 2; dinner from 5. BYOB.

Puerini's, 24 Memorial Blvd. West, Newport. (401) 847-5506.

Since Dan Puerini opened his tiny, cafe-like Italian restaurant in 1986, it's been a favorite of locals and visitors alike. Patrons squeeze together at perhaps twenty tables in two narrow, side-by-side dining rooms with tile floors, lacy curtains and not much else in the way of decor. The tables are covered with strips of paper, the lighting is bright, prices are gentle, and the food is true.

The menu seldom changes (it doesn't need to), and among antipastos ($2.25 to $6.95) you can always find spinach pie, pepperoni and cheese calzone, and hot cherry peppers stuffed with prosciutto and provolone. The spinach salad with a creamy pesto dressing ($6.95) includes gorgonzola cheese and walnuts and is out of this world.

All the pasta is made fresh daily. It comes in sixteen versions, from spaghetti with meatballs ($6.75) to five presentations with chicken ($9.95 to $12.95). The linguini with pesto and pinenuts was voted the best in the state. Shrimp scampi and fish of the day (perhaps sole stuffed with lobster, pinenuts, brie and sun-dried tomatoes) are other entrees, and there are many choices for vegetarians.

Desserts include tartuffo, gelato, rice pie with custard and raisins and apple strudel. Although there's no liquor, mineral water, espresso and cappuccino are available.

Dinner nightly, 4 to 10 or 11. BYOB. No smoking. No credit cards.

Sardella's, 30 Memorial Blvd. West, Newport. (401) 849-6312.

A couple of doors away from Puerini's, Sardella's is a world apart in terms of atmosphere. Formerly known as Barclay's, the restaurant changed names and cuisines in 1987. Fine, European-style Italian dining is advertised, and translates into two serene dining rooms, one with red woven tablecloths and the other all in white, against a backdrop of European paintings on exhibit and for sale.

A heady aroma of garlic greets patrons as they enter, and turns up in mussels, chicken and other dishes. Escarole and bean soup, two versions of mussels, fried mozzarella with tomato sauce, snail salad and caesar salad are popular starters ($2.75 to $4.75). Eight pastas are offered, plus fifteen entrees from $10.50 for baked fish with a marinara sauce to $15.50 for grilled sirloin with garlic butter. Veal is offered five ways, and there are many daily specials as well. The wine list is all Italian, priced from $12.50 to $37.50.

In the rear of the large establishment is a pub with TV and pool tables, an outdoor patio and a regulation bocce court.

Dinner nightly, 5 to 10 or 10:30; lunch in summer.

Amsterdam's Bar & Rotisserie, 509 Thames St., Newport. (401) 847-0550.

The once-trendy Southern Cross, an Australian restaurant, gave way in 1988 to Newport's newest trend-setter, Amsterdam's Rotisserie, a branch of two New York City restaurants that opened in a small storefront here in 1987. Its move was prompted by the desire for more space and a full liquor license.

A casual place with red and white woven cloths and black chairs, it still specializes in roasted chicken. We bought one to take home and found it delectable. With fresh green herb sauce, three-green salad and super fried potatoes, a half chicken is $7.95. At dinner, start with soup of the day, maybe tomato-basil or potato-leek, or buffalo mozzarella with fresh basil, tomatoes and extra virgin olive oil. Smoked trout ($5.50) is garnished with freshwater caviar sauce, cucumber and watercress. Entrees are simple, with roast and pasta of the day changing daily, shell steak, grilled shrimp and grand salad with roasted meats comprising most of them. Prices go up to $14.95 for the shrimp.

At lunch, look for a chicken sandwich with green herb mayonnaise and sun-dried tomatoes ($4.25) or sliced sirloin sandwich with fries ($5.95). The small wine list has reasonable prices. Desserts change every day, but there's always key lime pie.

Lunch daily, noon to 5 (weekends only in winter); dinner nightly, 5 to 11; Sunday brunch, noon to 4:30.

Pronto, 464 Thames St., Newport. (401) 847-5251.

When Amsterdam's Rotisserie moved to larger quarters in 1988, one of its chefs, Nora Forbes, stayed behind to cook in the open kitchen at the rear of this small bistro. Black chairs, wild flowered cloths, bare floors, and pressed tin walls and ceiling set a colorful backdrop for a limited menu of Italian specialties.

Mix-and-match pastas with the sauce of your choice (the one with olives, prosciutto, anchovies, garlic and olive oil sounds terrific) are featured, $5.95 to $8.75. That's about it, except for a few appetizers like wild mushroom crostini, antipasto, and mozzarella salad, chicken and steak of the day ($7.95 and $10.50 respectively), and a couple of fish specials — broiled swordfish with aioli and broiled bonita with a spicy ginger and sesame mayonnaise the night we were there.

Three desserts are offered nightly: chocolate mousse, cheesecake and a changing seasonal fruit like poached pears. A handful of Italian and California wines are offered from $11 to $24.50.

Dinner nightly, 5 to 10 or 11. No reservations, no credit cards.

The Mooring, Sayer's Wharf, Newport. (401) 846-2260.

For outdoor dining right by the water, you can't beat this casual place with tables under blue umbrellas on a lower brick patio and under a green and blue canopy on an upper deck.

The building used to belong to the New York Yacht Club. Inside all is blue and nautical with votive candles flickering on light linens and a large fireplace ablaze in winter.

This is a place for grazing: perhaps a bowl of prize-winning clam chowder and steamed mussels or cold shellfish medley, or a frozen marguerita and cheesecake with strawberries. The fairly extensive menu is served all day (sandwiches from $5.25, entrees $14.25 to $23.95). The steak and seafood fare is serviceable, if hardly exciting, but the setting is rewarding.

Open daily, 11:30 to 10 or 11. Closed in January.

325

Shore Dinner Hall, Waites Wharf, Newport. (401) 848-5058.

Something Newport has needed for a long time, this casual, inexpensive family seafood place opened in 1987. The cavernous room has huge doors that open onto the water, seating is at picnic tables, and you can BYOB.

A lobster boil with corn chowder, mussels and potatoes is $12.99. Fish and chips, steamed mussels and steamers, lobster salad roll, clam cakes and hot dogs are listed.

The Shore Dinner Hall is part of the new, multi-million-dollar **Newport Harbour Market,** site of Harbour Market Provisions, a liquor store and the **S.S. Newport,** a moored ship that has been restored for fine dining. Although it served ambitious dinners in the summer of 1988, it closed unexpectedly in the fall for restoration and a change of management. The owners said it would reopen for meals in the summer of 1989.

Shore Dinner Hall, open April-October, daily from 11 to 10 or 11.

Newport Star Clipper, 19 America's Cup Ave., Newport. (401) 849-6933 or (800) 432-4343.

What do you get for the town that has everything? Why, a dinner train, of course.

Folks from Waterloo, Iowa, started their second dinner-train venture in Newport in the fall of 1988, and the hospitality trade here was agog. We happened to be in town during its opening, and tourist officials and innkeepers alike were full of praise after the maiden excursion for invited guests the night before.

The two-hour train ride takes diners to Portsmouth and back as they eat a four-course dinner in two luxury dining cars of old. Although it was dark outside that inaugural evening, the train's spotlights illuminated passing scenery. Everyone lauded the corn-fed Iowa prime rib of beef, extra-thick and juicily tender. Other choices were broiled swordfish and roasted cornish game hen.

The tab is a staggering $49.50 per person, for lunch, dinner or Sunday brunch, gratuities and drinks extra. But Newporters anticipated that the excitement of it all would make it fly or, rather, ride.

Departures daily except Monday at noon and 7 p.m. from the Newport Depot near the Gateway Transportation and Visitors Center. Payment and menu selections required at time of ticket order.

The Everyday Gourmet at the Perry Mill Market, 337 Thames St., is a good place to pick up a sandwich (some named after famous women). Priced from $3.50 to $4.50, they include the Lady Di — hot turkey, brie and broccoli. There's always a big pot of soup cooking here, maybe french onion or clam chowder, and delectable desserts like bourbon-glazed orange cake and peanut-butter chip brownies.

The Wharf Deli on Bowen's Wharf also has good sandwiches and you can build your own. Smoked fish plates with lemon, capers and horseradish sound good; wash one down with a pint of Guinness stout.

Cappuccino's, 92 William St., is a nifty little breakfast and lunch cafe with a takeout and gourmet shop in the uptown Bellevue Avenue area. The salads are great, and the broccoli quiche was one of the best we've tasted.

Diversions

The Mansions. Nowhere else can you see such a concentration of palatial mansions, and nine are open to the public under individual or the collective auspices of the Preservation Society of Newport County. If you can see only one, make it Cornelius Vanderbilt's opulent 72-room **The Breakers,** although romantic **Rosecliff** of "The Great Gatsby" fame and the museum-like **Elms** would be other choices. If you've seen them all, as we have, you may like best the Victorian **Kingscote,** which looks lived-in and eminently livable. **Hammersmith Farm,** the childhood summer home of Jacqueline Kennedy Onassis and the Kennedy summer White House in the early 1960s, has more of a country feeling, a salubrious setting overlooking Narragansett Bay and lovely grounds and gardens. Schedules and prices vary, but all are open daily at least from May through October; some are open weekends in winter.

Historic Sites. Newport has more than 400 structures dating from the Colonial era. **Touro Synagogue** (1768), the oldest place of Jewish worship in the country, offers fascinating though limited guided tours. **Trinity Church** (1726) at the head of Queen Anne Square has the only remaining central pulpit and the second oldest organ in the country. The **Quaker Meeting House** (1699) is the oldest public building in Newport. **St. Mary's Church** (1848), where Jacqueline Bouvier was married to John F. Kennedy, is the oldest Catholic parish in Rhode Island. The **Redwood Library** (1748) is the nation's oldest library building in continuous service. The **Old Colony House** (1739) is the nation's third oldest capitol building and is still used for public ceremonies. The **Hunter House** (1748) is rated one of the ten finest Colonial homes in America, while the **Wanton-Lyman-Hazard House** (1690) is the oldest house still on its original site.

Water Sites. Ocean Drive winds along Newport's spectacular rocky shoreline, between Bailey's Beach where the 400 swam (and still do) and Brenton Point State Park, past clapboard estates and contemporary homes. The Cliff Walk is a must for a more intimate look at the crashing surf and the backs of the mansions. Narragansett Bay is visible along the nine-mile trip run by the Old Colony & Newport Railway to Portsmouth. The ocean surf rolls in at Easton's Beach.

Sports sites. Yachting reigns across the Newport waterfront; the America's Cup Gallery, the new **Museum of Yachting** at Fort Adams State Park, and the wharves off Thames Street and America's Cup Avenue appeal to sailing interests. In the landmark Newport Casino is the **International Tennis Hall of Fame,** housing the world's largest collection of tennis memorabilia and the Davis Cup Theater, where old tennis films are shown; outside are thirteen grass courts for tournaments and public use.

Shopping. Innumerable and oft-changing shops line Thames Street, the Brick Market Place, Bannister's and Bowen's Wharves, Christie's Landing, the Perry Mill Market and, uptown, fashionable Bellevue Avenue. If the past is an indication, there will be more when you're there. Some of our favorites are the **Spectrum,** representing American artisans and craftsmen; **Cabbages & Kings** for gifts and accessories that appeal to those who still live in Newport's "cottages," **Sampaguita** for gifts and incredible jewelry (we liked a necklace with pink flamingos dangling from it), and **Frillz** for women's clothes painted with flowers by artists in Boston.

Extra-Special

Green Animals, Cory Lane off Route 114, Portsmouth.

It's worth the drive north of town to see the incredible topiary gardens that live up to their name, Green Animals. Run by the Preservation Society of Newport County, it has 85 trees and shrubs sculpted into shapes of a camel, giraffe, lion and elephant at the corners of the original garden, plus a donkey, ostrich, bear, horse and rider, dogs and more. The animals are formed of California privet, while the geometric figures and ornamental designs are of golden and American boxwoods. The delightful site sloping toward Narragansett Bay also has espaliered fruit trees, dahlia and vegetable gardens, and a gift shop. Open May-September, daily 10 to 5; weekends in October. Adults, $4.

Old Lighthouse Museum is landmark at Stonington.

Watch Hill and Stonington
Vestiges of the 19th Century

They face each other across Little Narragansett Bay from different states, these two venerable towns so different from one another.

Watch Hill spreads out across a point at the southwesternmost tip of Rhode Island, a moneyed seaside resort of the old school and something of a mini-version of Newport. "Still echoing with the elegance of past years" (according to the brochure of the Inn at Watch Hill), the resort has enjoyed better days, although the large brown shingled "cottages" remain respectable, the shops fashionable and the atmosphere clubby. It is here that sheltered Long Island Sound gives way to Block Island Sound and the Atlantic, opening up the surf beaches for which Rhode Island's South County is known.

Stonington, on the other hand, is a peninsula cut off by travel and time from the rest of southeastern Connecticut. Quietly billing itself as "a place apart," it's an historic fishing village and an arts colony. The old houses hug the streets and each other, and the Portuguese fishing fleet adds an earthy flavor to an increasingly tony community.

328

Better than anywhere else along the Connecticut shore, the Borough of Stonington lets you sense times gone by.

These two choice vestiges of the 19th century are linked — in terms of geography — by the small Rhode Island city of Westerly, through which you drive from one to the other, unless you go by boat.

In recent times, Watch Hill and Stonington have been upstaged by Newport and Mystic, and thus bypassed by many of the trappings of tourism, particularly in terms of overnight accommodations. Neither town wants — nor can handle — crowds. Each in its own way clings to its past.

Inn Spots

Shelter Harbor Inn, Route 1, Westerly, R.I. 02891. (401) 322-8883.

The area's best choice for both lodging and dining is this expanded farmhouse dating to the early 1800s, set back from the highway and off by itself not far from the edge of Quonochontaug Pond.

The original three-story main house contains a fine restaurant (see Dining Spots), a sun porch with a bar, a small library with the original fireplace and ten guest rooms, plus a new rooftop deck with a hot tub and a water view that you must see to believe. Suffice to say that it's a scene straight out of California. The barn next door has been renovated with ten more guest rooms, plus a large central living room on the upper level opening onto a spacious redwood deck. Newest accommodations are in the front Coach House, which has four deluxe rooms with fireplaces, upholstered chairs and telephones.

All rooms have private baths, many have king or queensize beds, and about half have color TV. As innkeepers Jim and Debbye Dey continue to upgrade and expand with a contemporary flair, their most select rooms may be those recently renovated or added upstairs in the main house. Three on the second floor have wonderful terraces with a view of Block Island Sound in the distance. One particularly nice room with brick fireplace, brass screen, rose carpet and terrace is a steal for $92 a night.

Out front are two paddle tennis courts. In summer, Jim runs guests across the pond in a motor boat for a day at what he calls the finest beach along the Rhode Island shore.

A full breakfast, sometimes banana or ginger-blueberry pancakes, is served guests. Doubles, $78 to $92.

Weekapaug Inn, Weekapaug, R.I. 02891. (401) 322-0301.

Destroyed by the hurricane of 1938, the Weekapaug Inn reopened without missing a beat in the summer of 1939, so 1989 was cause for celebration. This grand seaside resort of the old school — venerable, refined and ever-so-Yankee — planned a 50th anniversary observance that would trigger the memories of many of the bluebloods whose photographs grace the walls of the club-like lobby. After all, an inn dating to 1889 and run like a private club by four generations of one family has a tradition to uphold.

Weekapaug is family, social, unpretentious and fun. The guests tend to be repeat and long-term. Many of the friendly young staff came here earlier with their families. Owners Bob and Sydney Buffum, whose winters are spent running the Manasota Beach Club in Englewood, Fla., get to know most of their guests — a trait being continued by their son Jim, the new innkeeper.

The rambling, weathered-gray, three-story hotel doesn't look quite as you'd expect, perhaps because its reincarnation is a product of the late 1930s. But there are few waterfront inn sites to rival it on the East Coast: on its own peninsula, with a saltwater pond in back, the ocean to the distant front and starboard, and lawns, a yachting basin, tennis courts and a mile and a half of private beach in between.

Shelter Harbor Inn is acclaimed for both food and lodging.

The 65 guest rooms, all with twin beds (some placed together to form kingsize) and old-fashioned baths, are simple but immaculate. A few small rooms have been joined to make larger rooms. One guest's room is painted just the way she likes it; after all, she stays the whole season. She and her neighbors occupy the nicest wing, which the staff calls "The Gold Coast."

The common areas are larger and more distinctive than in similar resorts. On the ground floor, a summery dining room has floor-to-ceiling windows onto the wildflowers outside. Above it on the second floor are the front desk and lobby full of games and books. Off it is the large and comfy Sea Room, a living room also used for games, bingo and movies. In front is a wonderful card room — all windows on three sides. Then there's the paneled and beamed Pond Room in which guests pour their own drinks from bottles they have stashed in their cubbyholes and warm their tootsies by the fire.

A full breakfast is served, and lunch is a nicely presented buffet. Dinner attracts the public as well (see below).

Rates, $135 per person, full AP; children, $80. Open mid-June to Labor Day.

Randall's Ordinary, Route 2, Box 243, North Stonington, Conn. 06359. (203) 599-4540.

A dirt road lined with stone walls leads to this remote ordinary (British definition: a tavern or eating house serving regular meals). It's anything but ordinary, from its hearth-cooked meals (see Dining Spots) to its overnight accommodations in a rural farmhouse dating to 1685 or in a restored barn that seems rather contemporary.

First the accommodations. Anyone cherishing the past would enjoy the three rooms upstairs in the main house with queensize beds and handloomed coverlets, working fireplaces, air-conditioning and private baths with whirlpool tubs. They are spacious and, except for modern comforts, look much as they would have in the 18th century.

Nine newer-feeling rooms and suites are located at the rear in a restored 1819 barn, which was dismantled and moved from Richmondville, N.Y. It's attached to a milking shed and a silo, which has been converted into the home of innkeepers Bill and Cindy Clark and their family. Designed in what might be called a rustic contemporary style, rooms retain original beams, barn siding and bare floors. They have queensize canopy (and occasionally trundle) beds, private baths with whirlpool tubs and heat lamps, and some have TVs and phones. Three are loft suites with sitting areas in the lofts; in one, a circular staircase leads up to a platform with a built-in sofa nestled under a skylight. The decor is spartan, if authentic, but the place certainly is interesting. A would-be common room, still in progress when we last visited, has enough room for contra dances.

Guests are served continental breakfast of fresh fruit and muffins in the main house. Hearth breakfasts are available on weekends for $8; they include Indian ground cakes, scrambled eggs, bacon and coffee.

Doubles, $80 to $125.

330

The Inn at Watch Hill, Bay Street, Watch Hill, R.I. 02891. (401) 596-0665.

Something of a misnomer, this strip of motel-type units above the shops along Bay Street was totally renovated in 1982 from what was once a ramshackle rooming house with 32 rooms.

You enter from a hilltop parking lot at the rear, register at a tiny shingled house that serves as an office, and descend to one of sixteen spacious rooms, each with contemporary furnishings and sliding doors opening onto small balconies above the street, with the municipal parking lot and harbor beyond.

Rooms have bare wood floors, white brick walls and queensize beds. They're plain but pleasant, all with full baths and color TV, and certainly located in the midst of Watch Hill activity. Most have a sink, microwave and refrigerator, and prices vary accordingly.

Doubles, $131 to $155, EP. Open May-October.

Watch Hill Inn, 50 Bay St., Watch Hill, R.I. 02891. (401) 348-8912 or (800) 356-9314.

This large, unassuming white wood structure with waterfront terrace and dining room was renovated in 1987 by new owners who changed the name from the Narragansett to the Watch Hill Inn and became the only resort in town to stay open year-round.

Four guest rooms were eliminated to make space for private baths for all sixteen rooms on the second and third floors. Two rooms are junior suites, with a sofabed that accommodates an extra guest, and four efficiency suites were in the works when we visited, as was a weekend spa program.

Formerly advertised as rustic and quaint, rooms are now billed as "charming." Although only a few in front have water views, all are carpeted and have double or twin beds with frilly spreads and pillows, lacy curtains, telephones, fans, and tubs or showers. They look a lot more comfortable than they used to.

That said, we wish we could be more positive about this inn, but it's really more of a hotel-motel — complete with a makeshift front office/porch that outdoes many a motel. There are no welcoming common rooms; instead there may be lots of coming and going from the 200-seat Positano Room, a banquet facility, and the **Deck Bar & Grill.**

A casual Italian menu is featured in this mirrored, two-level facility that might be more at home in Atlantic City. The outdoor deck is where the action is on a summer day, and the views of the sunset here are spectacular.

A continental breakfast is served beside a potbelly stove on an enclosed porch.

About all the activity: the inn's brochure says it's not surprising. "With celebrity Dana Valery Catalano as owner you never know who might drop in." Oh.

Doubles, $100 weekdays to $130 weekends; suites, $115 to $145.

Antiques & Accommodations, 32 Main St., North Stonington, Conn. 06359. (203) 535-1736.

An attractive yellow house built in 1861 with the gingerbread trim of its era was turned into a Victorian B&B in 1988 by Ann and Thomas Gray. The name is appropriate, for the Grays are antiques dealers who sell many of the furnishings in their showplace home in the center of the quaint hamlet of North Stonington.

"Fond memories of traveling in England inspired us to furnish our home in the Georgian manner with formal antique furniture and accessories," says Ann.

Most coveted is a downstairs bedroom with a working fireplace and a stereo system. Upstairs are another guest room and a two-bedroom suite. All have canopied four-poster beds and private baths.

The Grays, who are into cooking, almost enrolled in the Johnson & Wales culinary program but decided to open a B&B instead. They serve a full English breakfast by candlelight in the elegant dining room or on the flower-bedecked porch. It always includes fresh fruit in an antique crystal bowl, plus Tom's acclaimed crepes or omelets.

Doubles, $95 to $125. No smoking.

Dining Spots

The Harborview, Water Street at Cannon Square, Stonington, Conn. (203) 535-2720.

The hurricane candles in the large dining room are lit even at noon at this dark and romantic establishment from which you can glimpse Stonington harbor through small-paned windows. The darkness of wood paneling and the blue-clothed tables is brightened by pink napkins and fresh flowers.

Classic French food has been the specialty of this acclaimed restaurant, which was about to change owners when we last visited. Among fifteen dinner appetizers ($4.50 to $6.95), we especially have enjoyed the crevettes remoulade, a dinner plate full of five huge shrimp on a bed of tender lettuce covered with a piquant sauce, and a sensational billi-bi soup, creamy, mussel-filled and redolent with herbs.

Favorites among entrees ($13.95 to $18.95) have been a Marseillaise bouillabaisse, sauteed shrimps chinoise with pea pods and ginger butter, Jamaican shrimps sauteed with dark rum, kiwi fruit and lime, and veal prepared three ways. We liked the veal sweetbreads in a vol-au-vent pastry and the veal scallops in a calvados cream sauce, a portion large enough for two, served with apple, julienned vegetables and tiny new potatoes, still in their jackets and swimming in butter.

Many dinner items are available at lunch (entrees $6.50 to $8.95). The rustic bar, lately expanded and with a warming potbelly stove, offers daily specials and reasonably priced entrees (how about roast duckling muscadet with grapes, walnuts and pearl onions for $9.95)? We like the lavish Sunday brunch buffet ($10.95), which has unusually interesting hot dishes and enough food to keep one full for a couple of days.

Lunch, 11:30 to 3; dinner 5 to 10; Sunday brunch, 11 to 3. Closed Tuesday in winter.

Shelter Harbor Inn, Route 1, Westerly, R.I. (401) 322-8883.

The highly regarded dining room at the Shelter Harbor Inn was expanded in 1985 by a large addition with dining on two levels. The original dining room with stone fireplace has bare floors, country curtains and bentwood chairs at white-linened tables topped with hurricane lamps and, at our fall visit, colorful mums in carafes. Beyond is the new two-level dining room, which has rough wood beams and posts, brick walls, comfortable chairs with curved backs and white linens, and overlooks a flagstone terrace with white furniture.

The food is worthy of the setting. At Sunday brunch, we liked two of the day's specials, baked oysters and lamb shanks with rice pilaf, both $6.95. Although the former was smallish and the latter too large, we managed by sharing the two as well as feasting on the "surprise salad" of greens, radicchio, orange slices, cantaloupe, kiwi and strawberries with a creamy poppyseed dressing. Two glasses each of champagne came with. How they can do it for the price ($5.95 to $7.95, depending on choice of entree), we don't know. But it's always good.

At dinner, be sure to try the Rhode Island johnny cakes with maple butter ($1.25) and, among appetizers ($3.95 to $5.95), the honey-mustard scallops with peppered bacon or the smoked bluefish with strawberry horseradish. Entrees run from $11.95 for hazelnut chicken with orange-thyme cream to $15.95 for double lamb chops with mint pesto and grilled pork tenderloin with brandied prune sauce. Highly rated are the seafood pot pie chock full of shrimp, scallops and lobster, and roast duckling with the inn's tart beach plum sauce. You can even get finnan haddie poached in milk with bacon.

Hearthside cooking is featured in 1685 farmhouse called Randall's Ordinary.

Desserts in the $2 to $3 range include genoise, chocolate raspberry cake, lemon custard tart, blueberry crisp and Rhode Island Indian pudding. The interesting wine list offers bargains like Dry Creek zinfandel for $13.50 and Firestone chardonnay for $17.

Lunch daily, 11:30 to 2:30; dinner, 5 to 10; Sunday, brunch 11 to 3, dinner 4 to 9.

Randall's Ordinary, Route 2, North Stonington, Conn. (203) 599-4540.

In 1987, culinary entrepreneurs Bill and Cindy Clark transformed a hobby of cooking dinners for friends and private parties over an open hearth in their former home in South Salem, N.Y., into a unique Colonial restaurant and inn in their native Connecticut. Such was the response that the restaurant operation just kept growing (hearthside cooking lessons were offered and a Colonial cocktail hour was in the making when we visited).

Cooking with antique iron pots and utensils in reflector ovens and an immense open hearth in the old keeping room, the Clarks serve food from the 18th century in an authentic setting — three atmospheric but spartan dining rooms in a farmhouse dating to 1685. Patrons gather at 7 o'clock in a small taproom where they pick up a drink, popcorn, crackers and cheese before they tour the house and watch cooks in Colonial garb preparing their dinners on the open hearth.

Dinner is prix-fixe at $25 with a choice of three entrees, perhaps roast turkey with wild rice stuffing, roast rib-eye beef or Nantucket scallops with scallions and butter. The meal includes soup (often carrot or clam chowder), whole wheat walnut or spider corn bread, squash pudding, a conserve of red cabbage and apples, and desserts like Vermont gingerbread, pumpkin pie or Indian pudding.

With similar food but less fanfare, lunch is a la carte. Entrees are $4.50 to $7.50 for the likes of hearth-grilled swordfish, breast of duck and roast capon sandwich.

Don't worry about that hearthside heat in the summer. The structure is air-conditioned.

Lunch daily, noon to 2; dinner nightly at 7.

Weekapaug Inn, Weekapaug, R.I. (401) 322-0301.

Meals in this venerable inn of the old school are available to the public by reservation. Be advised, however, that the dining room has a clubby air (most of the guests are old-timers), you must bring your own bottle for cocktails in the Pond Room, and jackets and ties are required at night.

The six-course menu ($27 to the public, including tax and tip) changes daily. Following a chilled juice, there's a choice of two appetizers, perhaps steamed mussels and smoked salmon pate. Then come lobster bisque, chilled melon or jellied madrilene and a salad with choice of dressings. The six main-course offerings could be grilled pigeon breasts, sauteed rainbow trout with almonds, grilled tuna with grapefruit beurre blanc, sauteed sea scallops with garlic and tomatoes, sauteed calves liver, and grilled sirloin with hazelnut butter. Buttered carrots, rice with walnuts and corn on the cob might accompany.

For dessert, how about hazelnut dacquoise, white chocolate mousse, banana rum cake, fresh berries or ice cream and cookies? No one leaves the table hungry here.

Dinner nightly, 6:30 to 8. BYOB. No credit cards.

Noah's, 113 Water St., Stonington, Conn. (203) 535-3925.

The price certainly is right at Noah's, a hip, casual and immensely popular operation that has expanded into a second dining room with a service bar at the rear.

When did you last find soup for $1.30 or homemade clam chowder for $1.45, broiled flounder with salad and vegetable for $8.25 and desserts like German chocolate pie or tartuffe di chocolate (this is a good place for chocolate freaks) for $2? Those are dinner prices; an omelet for breakfast is $1.75 and a fruit and cheese plate for lunch, $3.95.

With a bowl of clam chowder and half a BLT plus a bacon-gouda quiche and a side salad, two of us had a fine lunch for less than $10.

The blackboard specials are as appealing as the regular menu: blackfish stew at lunch, regional and ethnic specialties nightly. Such luncheon salads as Greek country or sliced breast of chicken in the $4 range are masterpieces. The most you can pay is $12.95 for a large filet mignon. Save room for the chocolate yogurt cake, bourbon bread pudding or what one customer volunteered was the best dessert he'd ever had: fresh strawberries with Italian cream made from cream cheese, eggs and kirsch.

Owners Dorothy and John Papp have decorated their two-section storefront restaurant colorfully with pastel linen tablecloths and fresh flowers beneath a pressed-tin ceiling. They have a full liquor license, with all but two French wines priced in the teens.

Breakfast, 7 to 11; lunch, 11:15 to 2:30; dinner, 6 to 9 or 9:30. Closed Monday.

The Skipper's Dock, 66 Water St., Stonington, Conn. (203) 535-2000.

Part of the Harborview restaurant operation, this casual place on the fishing pier has two interior dining rooms and a smashing outdoor deck, right over the water.

On a sunny November day we sat underneath the canopy beside the water and reveled in a lunch of Portuguese fishermen's stew and a tasty linguini with shrimps and clams, studded with black olives, red pimentos, artichokes and capers (both $5.95). The bloody mary was huge, the loaf of hot bread so good we asked for seconds, and the main portions ample enough that we couldn't face dessert.

At night, you might start with fish house chowder, a plate of pickled herring or a bowl of Stonington steamers ($2.25 to $6.95). Besides blackboard fish specials, you can continue with a kettle of that great Portuguese fishermen's stew, scallop pie, stuffed shrimps or linguini with clams and shrimp ($12.95 to $14.95). Lobster is served steamed, baked or as the star of a clambake. Choices for non-seafood eaters are filet mignon with rum butter, rack of Block Island grilled boar ribs and barbecued chicken caribe. Ice cream puff with mocha ice cream and pina colada cheesecake are among the desserts. Wines are reasonably priced by the glass or liter.

Lunch, daily 11:30 to 4; dinner from 4. Closed in off-season.

Owners Jerry and Ruth Mears at Abbott's Lobster in the Rough.

1 South Broad Cafe, Route 1, Stonington, Conn. (203) 535-0418.

The owner of this successful little cafe in a shopping plaza, Tricia Shipman, planned to move it lock, stock and name in mid-1989 to larger quarters in what formerly was the Village Pub at 201 North Main St. near the viaduct in Stonington borough.

Everything is done from scratch, even the tortilla chips for the nachos, which, Tricia claims, are the best in the state. A blackboard lists the day's dishes, which change frequently and are international in nature (even the egg rolls and wontons are homemade). Cheddar and vegetable chowder, grilled mussels, stuffed mushrooms, tostadas, nachos and super nachos, shrimp and tortellini salad, deli sandwiches and international burgers are typical fare.

Dinner entrees are priced from $8.95 for fettuccine alfredo to $14.95 for scampi. Beggar's bouillabaisse and mixed grill (perhaps fish, chicken and sausage) are among the possibilities.

The nicely priced wines are mainly Californian, and many are available by the glass. Lunch, Monday-Saturday 11:30 to 3; dinner nightly, 5 to 10 or 10:30.

Extra-Special

Abbott's Lobster in the Rough, 117 Pearl St., Noank, Conn. (203) 536-7719.

If it's lobster you're after, make the short trek west through Mystic to the quaint shore town of Noank, where the busiest place day and night is Abbott's. Here, seated at brightly colored picnic tables placed on mashed-up clamshells, you watch the passing parade of marine traffic in and out of Mystic Harbor as you feast on the freshest of seafood. You order at a counter inside and take a number; bring your own drinks and maybe some cheese to tide you over while you wait. The lobster (about $9) comes with a bag of potato chips, cole slaw, melted butter and the obligatory bib. Also available are steamers, mussels, clam chowder, shrimp, lobster or crab rolls and hot dogs for the kids. We think this is the neatest lobster pound south of Maine.

Open daily, noon to 9, May-Labor Day; Friday-Sunday noon to 7, through Columbus Day.

Diversions

Watch Hill and Stonington are small, choice and relatively private places off the beaten path. The crowds head east to Rhode Island's South County beaches, particularly the vast Misquamicut State Beach where the surf thunders in, or west to Mystic, where Mystic Seaport and the Mystic Marinelife Aquarium combine to make the area Connecticut's busiest tourist destination.

Stonington Borough. We cannot imagine anyone not falling for the historic charms of this once-thriving seaport, founded in 1649 and not all that changed since the 19th century. The last commercial fishing fleet in Connecticut is manned by the resident Portuguese, who stage a colorful Blessing of the Fleet ceremony every mid-July. To savor fully the flavor, walk the two narrow streets through the borough. They and their cross streets are lined with historic homes, many of them marked by the Stonington Historical Society and some once occupied by the likes of John Updike, Eve Merriam, Peter Benchley and L. Patrick Gray. The house where artist James McNeill Whistler painted Whistler's Mother later was home for Stephen Vincent Benet. Edgar Allen Poe and Capt. Nathaniel Brown, who discovered Antarctica, also lived here. Much local memorabilia is on display in the fine **Old Lighthouse Museum,** full of whaling and fishing gear, articles from the Orient trade and an exquisite dollhouse, at the end of Water street (open Tuesday-Sunday 11 to 4:30, May-October; adults $1).

Watch Hill. This staid, storied resort community protects its privacy (parking is limited and prices are high), but things get busy on summer weekends. Stop for a tart, thirst-quenching lemonade at the old-fashioned **Olympia Tea Room** (serving three meals a day since 1916). Youngsters line up at the entrance to the Watch Hill Beach for 25-cent rides on the **Flying Horse Carousel,** established in 1879 and thought to be the oldest merry-go-round in the country.

Napatree Point. If you find a place to park, hike out to Napatree Point conservation area, extending half a mile beyond the Watch Hill parking lot. The walk to the ruins of a Spanish-American War fort at the far end opposite Stonington can take an hour or a day, depending on beachcombing and bird-watching interests.

Shopping. Along Water Street in Stonington are several special shops. At the **Hungry Palette,** silkscreened and handprinted fabrics can be purchased by the yard or already made up into long skirts, wrap skirts, sundresses and colorful accessories like Bermuda bags. **Quimper Faience** deals exclusively in handpainted French earthenware. **Water Street Antiques** sells interesting antiques, gifts and mahogany furniture. **Deja Vu** offers decorative accessories and garden statuary. In Watch Hill, **William Coppola Inc.,** **Lily's, R.W. Richins** and **Ninigret Men's Shop** specialize in clothing and resort wear; **Beauty and the Beach** has accessories, gifts and quilts; **Finitney & Co.,** elegant gifts and linens, and **McMonogram,** personalized bags, aprons, sweaters and such. Unique American crafts are featured at **Puffins,** where we liked the aluminium sandcast pieces by Arthur Court and pottery birdhouses from Tennessee.

Between expeditions, you might stop in Stonington at **Stonington Vineyards,** Taugwonk Road, where Nick and Happy Smith run a fledgling winery. Among their premium vinifera wines are a fine chardonnay and an estate-bottled pinot noir ($10.99 and $12.99 respectively). The less expensive Seaport white and blush wines reflect the winery's proximity to the historic Stonington and Mystic Seaport areas, Happy Smith reports. In North Stonington, **Crosswoods Vineyards** at 75 Chester Maine Road has a state-of-the-art winery (tours by appointment) and a small retail shop offering prize-winning chardonnays and merlots. If you're like us, you'll likely leave with a $15 bottle — or a case — of Hugh and Susan Connell's masterful chardonnay.

Prudence Crandall House in Canterbury is among historic structures in Northeast Corner.

Northeast Connecticut
The Quiet, Gilded Corner

Few people realize that Connecticut's oft-overlooked "Quiet Corner" once was a fashionable summer resort of the Lenox-Newport ilk.

Starting in the late 1870s, it was known as "Newport without the water." During its gilded days, wealthy New Yorkers and Bostonians summered in Pomfret and Woodstock on vast country estates with dreamlike names like Gwyn Careg, Courtlands and Glen Elsinore.

John Addison Porter, a Hartford newspaper editor and Pomfret resident, wrote in 1896 that his town was "one of the natural garden spots of the state — the ideal peaceful New England landscape. It bears on its face the unmistakable signs of being the abode of people of culture. No town of its size in Connecticut represents more wealth, but this is used unostentatiously and is in perfectly good taste."

The Depression and post-war priorities took their toll on the wealth, as did the move to the South of the textile mills upon which the local economy had been based. "The quiet corner was the neglected corner," said innkeeper Terry Kinsman. "When the mills closed, people here gave up."

Herb and Terry Kinsman moved back East from California in 1982 to open the area's first B&B. "Everybody thought we were crazy," says Terry. "But now there are thirteen or fourteen B&Bs and two inns."

Adds restaurateur Jimmie Booth, who moved from New York to her husband's family farm and launched the renowned Golden Lamb Buttery: "Everything's changing out here. We're not the quiet corner any more. The developers are building in all the woods around."

Developers indeed are at work, but the change everyone talks about locally is relative. Northeast Connecticut remains the state's poorest and least-developed area. "The Street" in Pomfret carries much of the grace of a century ago. A low-key sophistication is lent by Pomfret, Rectory and Marianapolis preparatory schools, the cultural offerings at the conference and training center of Data General Corp. on the campus of the defunct Annhurst College, and the headquarters of firms like Crabtree & Evelyn, the area's largest employer.

The visitor has a rare opportunity to share in the good life here. You can stay in restored inns that once were the homes of the rich and famous. You can have bed and breakfast with the aristocracy in houses filled with family treasures. Your host may be an artist, a furniture maker, an arts promoter, a pediatrician, a professor or a carpenter. In no other area have we found the innkeepers and their faciliities as a group so understated and so fascinating.

You'll feel as if you're a character in a Currier & Ives etching in this area of rambling stone walls, rolling hills and fertile farmlands, languishing mill towns and tranquil villages. But get yourself going. The Quiet Corner may not be quiet forever.

Inn Spots

The Inn at Gwyn Careg, Route 44, Box 96, Pomfret 06230. (203) 928-7768.

One of the potentially great small inns of the East opened quietly in June 1988 on the exotic estate upon which the Marquis and Marquessa de Talleyrand had entertained guests from across the world in the 1940s and 1950s. An air of mystery prevails in its thirteen-going-on-seventeen guest rooms and suites, a restaurant with an acclaimed chef, a Japanese teahouse on stilts over a four-acre pond, and thirty acres of formal gardens, rare ornamental trees and eleven-foot-high stone walls and archways.

The estate, named for "pure stone" in Welsh, was featured as one "of unusual beauty and originality" in a four-page spread in 1933 in House Beautiful magazine. The vision for the emerging inn is that of George R. Flonnes, a carpenter by trade from Hartford. He paid $65,000 in 1980 for the abandoned property, which was in disrepair after being misused as a private school for difficult boys. After four years of fixing up the grounds, he moved inside and, leveraging its rising real-estate values, mortgaged his way to completion of the building in 1989.

The impressive, white brick mansion totals 25 rooms, of which six suites on the second floor are the most luxurious. Some have working fireplaces. All have large private baths and are handsomely decorated with period antiques in colors matching their names: Delphinium, Primrose, Morning Glory and such. Our quarters in the Suite William were ample (although we only used the small sitting room for its former function as a dressing room and the steam radiators knocked off and on through the night). The Marquis Suite is the most extravagant, all in white except for two green wing chairs, and with an elaborate carved chest at the foot of the lace-canopied four-poster bed.

Upstairs in what were the servants' quarters, George has fashioned six more rooms, four rented as two-bedroom suites with adjoining baths. The Crow's Nest intrigues with its wood-slat ceilings and walls and an incredible window seat upon which you can loll on tons of pillows and get a bird's-eye view of the lavish Spanish and Italian gardens.

A seventh room is available on the first floor. A teahouse perched over the pond was scheduled to be ready with four more guest rooms by the summer of 1989. More accommodations are planned in the artist's studio and the carriage house.

The main floor includes a spacious entry hall, a small restaurant (see Dining Spots), a tea room that looks like a board room, a vast fireplaced living room in need of more furniture, and an enclosed terrace used for the many weddings the inn attracts.

Where the Talleyrands and their predecessors had dozens of servants, George and his mother, who is sometimes in residence, had a chef, a housekeeper and five waitresses

Owner George Flonnes at garden wall in front of restored Inn at Gwyn Careg.

on call when we visited in winter 1989. Operating on a shoestring made for some lapses (the continental breakfast in which we had to ask for every item was a case in point). But with the promise of a seasoned innkeeper and the ongoing realization of the estate's grandeur, something great could emerge. "Gwyn Careg is still just a shadow of its former self," George said. "It will take another few years, but there's no limit to its potential."

Doubles, $65 to $100; suites, $85 to $130.

The Inn at Woodstock Hill, Plaine Hill Road, Woodstock 06267. (203) 928-0528.

The 1816 Christopher Wren-style home of Henry Bowen, whoseshocking-pink summer cottage is a landmark up the road, was willed in 1981 to the University of Connecticut, which had no use for it. Enter Ruth Jensen who, after a career on Wall Street, became the resident manager for a changing group of investors who restored the house with great taste and opened in 1987 with more ambition than the locale could immediately afford.

The atmosphere of an English manor house pervades the inn's common rooms, restaurant (see Dining Spots) and nineteen guest rooms and suites. The small dining rooms, main living room and morning/TV room in particular are a kaleidoscope of chintz fabrics, fine paintings, plush orientals and tiled fireplaces.

More Waverly floral chintz accents the prevailing peach, pink and blue color scheme in the guest rooms. All are sleek and comfortable with reproduction antiques and wicker furniture, chairs and loveseats, thick carpeting and modern baths, some with double marble sinks. Quiet rooms with rear views look across the valley. One room has a beamed cathedral ceiling and a large cedar closet off one room on the third floor has been made into a bathroom.

An outside entrance leads to a cozy lounge, where colorful wine labels under glass top the bar. A spacious, L-shaped dining room overlooks a rear deck, which Ruth Jensen planned to enclose in glass for use as "a wicker winter garden."

Her assistant and childhood friend from Denmark, Kirsten Miller, bakes the

Former Bowen home and carriage house are now the Inn at Woodstock Hill.

restaurant's desserts. She's up at dawn to prepare coffee cake, brioches, muffins and sticky buns for continental breakfast.

Doubles, $75 to $140.

Selah Farm, Routes 44 & 169, Box 43, RR 1, Pomfret 06259. (203) 928-7051.

This imposing, gray-shingled mansion on a hilltop commands a view of the pond at the Rectory School across the street. One of the great country estates, it was built in 1928 by a stock broker from Providence and acquired in 1964 by Newell Hale, who owned textile mills in Putnam. It really is a gentleman's farm, says his wife Betty, with 27 acres, horses, walking paths and formal gardens.

Upstairs off a hall running the length of the house are four guest rooms. One double room with bath connects to a twin bedroom, making a suite for families on their way to Pomfret or Rectory schools. Even the closet is wallpapered in a third room that is cheery in blues and greens. The fourth guest room uses an adjacent hall bath that has been refurbished in blue and white. It has a new shower and a whirlpool tub but keeps the original sinks. Across the hall in Newell's office is a bed that is pressed into service on busy parents' weekends. An upstairs sitting room with TV is cozy in pinks and blues.

The main floor appeals with an enormous living room harboring two rust-colored velvet sofas, walls of books and a grand piano and an enclosed sun porch spectacularly decked out in blues and deep peach, with windows onto a terrace and pool (Newell designed the fabrics both for the sofas in the living room and on the sun porch). On the other side of the large entry hall is a formal dining room where guests may eat breakfast, although most prefer to join the Hales as they make preparations in the sunny, oversize kitchen.

Newell, who learned to cook many years ago in the Coast Guard and makes meals in his extra basement kitchen for a local soup kitchen, prepares the main course after Betty serves a fruit plate. His specialty is strata with homemade sausages, but he's also partial to oatmeal and omelets, and has been known to offer guests bloody marys for breakfast.

Betty, who serves guests welcoming drinks upon arrival, is full of talk about the arts and culture. She's an arts coordinator who brings visiting entertainers to the Data General cultural center and sets up theatrical productions for area school children.

Doubles, $75.

Cobbscroft, Routes 44 & 169, Box 104, Pomfret 06258. (203) 928-5560.

This rambling white house almost up against the road is home to Janet and Tom

340

McCobb as well as a gallery for the works of watercolorist Tom, who has a studio in the rear barn, and those of artist-friends.

Guests are received in a library with a gorgeous needlepoint rug and deep shelves full of books and a TV. Beyond is a large gallery/living room hung with a variety of art, all for sale and all very enticing. Off the library are a double and single guest room joined by a bathroom, rented as a family suite. Upstairs are three more guest rooms with baths. One with twin beds has lacy white spreads and curtains, a sofa and knickknacks including little dolls. A front corner room has charming stenciling done by Janet, a four-poster bed, chaise longue and oriental rug. Its bathroom has gold-plated fixtures and an oval, clawfoot tub like none we've ever seen; Janet says it's called a birthday tub and can hold all her four granddaughters at once. Over the living room is what the McCobbs call the bridal suite, a wondrous affair with windows on three sides, a working fireplace, a loveseat, dressing table and a bed covered in frilly white linens.

Breakfast is served at a long table in the dining room, full of lovely country touches like a collection of lambs. The table is flanked by Queen Anne chairs and topped by two wooden chickens and eggs as a centerpiece. In her extra B&B kitchen (away from the family quarters), Janet prepares hot apple crisp or melon in season, croissants, scrambled eggs, quiche or strata. In the afternoon, she serves tea with cinnamon toast or fruit bread and offers a drink, and offers brandy in the living room after dinner.

Doubles, $60; suite, $75.

Grosvenor Place, Route 97, Pomfret 06258. (203) 928-4633.

When Garfield W. Danenhower III completed his Army service as a physician in Thailand in 1973, he and his wife Sylvia, Southerners both, bought this lovely beige Colonial 1720 house sight unseen. It was built by her great-grandmother ten times removed and had been in the family ever since, so the Danenhowers knew something of what they were getting.

Their B&B guests since 1984 know they are in for great comfort and Southern hospitality. A focal point of this elegant home is the spacious dining room filled with silver, portraits, chairs with needlepoint seats and oriental rugs. The living room is done with flair in reds and off-whites and a collection of family pictures. Indian shutters in the windows protect a study full of books, a piano and a jigsaw puzzle in progress.

Watercolor of Cobbscroft adorns cover of its brochure.

341

A large guest room with private bath and fireplace occupies a front corner of the first floor. It has a half-canopy bed with crewel draperies, a sofa, plants and a deep-hued oriental rug atop a wide-plank floor. Up some very steep stairs is another large guest room with a four-poster bed that belonged to Sylvia's grandmother in Boston. This room is unusually warm in peach tones with a taupe rug and period antiques. An adjacent single room ("good for bringing a child to school," says Sylvia) is between it and the modern bathroom.

Sylvia offers her guests tea or sherry upon arrival. She and her pediatrician-husband Woody (for Woodruff, his middle name) serve a breakfast of homemade muffins and rolls, supplemented on weekends by french toast from a recipe they acquired in Malaysia. They grind their own coffee beans and set out exotic teas.

Doubles, $60.

Ebenezer Stoddard House, Routes 171 and Perrin Road, West Woodstock 06267. (203) 974-2552.

Romance is the theme and couples the clientele at this early 19th-century house with working fireplaces in each guest room and an upstairs ballroom. Lynda Hennigan, a hairdresser who operates "The Front Parlour" at the side of the house, has decorated her B&B with exceptional verve. The small parlor is all in shades of blue, from a blue sofa with a pattern of irises to lace curtains with blue swags. Blue tiles flank the fireplace.

Across the hall is another fireplaced parlor, a quiet retreat for two where a valentine theme prevailed in February (Lynda changes her decor with the season, and had eleven Christmas trees — including one in each guest room — at Yuletide).

The breakfast room retains its original pine floors and offers three tables for two, all set differently. Here Lynda and her husband Don, a school teacher, serve a dish of fresh fruits followed by blueberry or cranberry mousse, quiche, harvest cake or bread pudding with maple syrup tapped from a tree on the property.

The Hennigans light the fireplaces in their three guest rooms while their occupants are at dinner. Upon their return guests find a tray of candies, cookies and cordials. Each room has its own bathroom, fancy wallpaper and floral arrangements. Extra touches like a christening gown, a collection of evening purses, antique gloves and knickknacks abound. Two 1700 fireside chairs face the fireplace in a suite, which has stenciled wide-board floors and a queensize canopy bed.

Guests are greeted with tea and perhaps a piece of pie, which they can enjoy on a screened porch or a new rear patio beside a little fountain. Lynda sells a few nifty items handcrafted by friends in her beauty shop.

Doubles, $75; suite, $95.

Wintergreen, Routes 44 and 169, RFD 87AA, Pomfret 06258. (203) 928-5741.

A substantial gray Victorian house at the end of a long driveway turns out to have been built for the head gardener of the old Clark estate. It's now a B&B, and innkeeper Doris Geary points out other structures still on the vast property, which affords a view across the valley.

Doris and her husband Stan, business manager at the Rectory School, offer four guest rooms (two with private baths) and the potential for two more rooms on the third floor. Most coveted is the front corner room, which has striking blue painted Italian furniture, including an incredible bedstead with an oval mirror in the headboard. The furnishings, nicely set off against peach walls, can be admired from a mushroom velvet loveseat. Plush beige carpeting enhances a rear room with a sofa, twin beds and a porch in the making for taking in the valley view. A third room has a wood stove in the fireplace,

Southern-style hospitality is dispensed in 1720 Colonial house known as Grosvenor Place.

while a fourth has a queensize bed with a quilted headboard and stuffed dolls amid the pillows.

On the main floor is a colorful entry hall with bright green walls, window seats and turn-of-the-century spool banisters framing the stairway. Guests enjoy a formal, fireplaced parlor and a dining room with another fireplace and a long polished table.

The Gearys serve a full breakfast of fresh fruit and a main dish like pancakes or french toast stuffed with cream cheese and nuts. "We ask our guests the night before what they'd like and cater to their wishes," says Doris, reflecting a theme that prevails at most of the area's B&Bs. She provides tea or a drink upon arrival, and planned to offer dinners when her professional kitchen was finished.

Doubles, $55 to $65.

Friendship Valley, Route 169, Brooklyn 06234. (203) 774-0746.

Prudence Crandall, the Canterbury educator who was hounded out of town for teaching blacks in her academy in the 1830s, named this 18th-century, Georgian-style country house when it was occupied by one of her benefactors. The name fits, for Leslie and Dick Wendel — she a marketing consultant and he an economics professor at the University of Connecticut — run a very friendly B&B with their three effusive springer spaniels.

Dick comes from a family of painters and their works are all around the common rooms and the two guest suites in this gorgeous house, which is listed on the National Register. Some of the most striking were done by one of their sons, an artist in New York. Welcoming drinks are served in the front parlor or the library, richly decorated in the style of Provence with a marble fireplace and prized possessions from the Wendels' extensive travels in France.

A rear suite on the main floor has an inviting parlor trimmed in Colonial red (it doubles as Leslie's writing office). The bedroom off a side hall has twin beds joined as a king, antique blue and white coverlets, and a lovely oriental rug. Another guest room upstairs has twin beds, dhurrie rugs and one of the home's eight working fireplaces. A sitting room reserved for occupants of this room has a queensize sofabed; the Wendels were

343

thinking of adding a TV and VCR. Crabtree & Evelyn toiletries are in the bathrooms, as they are in most B&Bs in this area where the company is headquartered.

The Wendels join their guests for continental breakfast in a dining room full of antiques, silver and oriental rugs. Fresh orange juice, croissants and apricot muffins are typical fare. Beyond is a flagstone-floored sun porch furnished in wicker, overlooking a garden and a pool.

Doubles, $70.

The Felshaw Tavern, Five Mile River Road, Putnam Heights 06260. (203) 928-3467.

"Welcome to Yesterday," proclaims the brochure for this inviting B&B in a pre-Revolutionary tavern dating to 1742. Terry and Herb Kinsman, he a homesick Yankee, moved into the house from California, restored it to the hilt and opened it in 1982 as the area's first B&B.

Herb, a woodworker of note, did most of the restoration himself. The results are evident everywhere, but nowhere more so than in the keeping room/library, where the remarkable ceilings are made of stained pine, and in the adjacent living room full of orientals. He also put together the grandfather clock and the lowboy of black walnut in the formal dining room.

Upstairs past colorful birds in stained glass on the landing are two large guest rooms, each with fireplace and bath. One with a queensize Mississippi rice-carved four-poster is full of fine French furniture, including a Louis XIV chest and a Napoleonic chair. The other has a queensize four-poster, an Empire sofa, a 1790 bowfront dresser and a remarkable Connecticut highboy that Herb built of cherry. Guests can watch TV in an upstairs sitting room paneled in wood.

In a sunny, cathedral-ceilinged breakfast room that Herb built from scratch, the Kinsmans serve a full meal of scrambled eggs with sausage and bran or corn muffins. They offer tea or sherry in the afternoon. Guests may lounge on the European-looking little terrace or in a four-season garden with a fountain out back.

Doubles, $70.

Dining Spots

The Golden Lamb Buttery, Hillandale Farm, Bush Hill Road, Brooklyn. (203) 774-4423.

For more years than we care to remember, Golden Lamb Buttery has been our favorite restaurant. We love it for summer lunches, when the surrounding fields and hills look like a Constable painting. We love it for summer evenings, when we have cocktails on a hay wagon driven by a tractor through the fields and listen to Susan Smith's pure voice as she sings and plays guitar. We love the picnic suppers and plays put on in the barn on occasional Thursday nights. And we love fall lunches and dinners ensconced beside the glowing fireplace. We know we would love the Elizabethan dinners served in December, but we haven't been able to get to one as yet. And everyone loves Jimmie and Bob Booth, the remarkable owners of the farm on which the restaurant stands — she the wonderful chef and he the affable host.

You can tell as you enter through the barn, where a 1953 Jaguar convertible is displayed among such eclectic items as a totem pole and a telephone booth, that you are in for an unusual treat. Step out on the back deck and gaze over the picturesque scene as waitresses in long pink gingham show the blackboard menu ($45 prix fixe) and take your order. After you are seated following the hayride, the table is yours for the evening.

Appetizers consist mostly of soups, and Jimmie makes some knockouts. Using herbs

Pond is on view from Golden Lamb Buttery.   **Dining room at Inn at Gwyn Careg.**

from her garden — especially lovage, her favorite — she might concoct country cottage, minestrone mother earth, cabbage soup made with duck stock or, in summer, a cold soup like raspberry puree or cucumber.

There is usually a choice of four entrees, always duck and often salmon, chateaubriand and lamb. These are accompanied by six to eight vegetables, served family style and to us almost the best part of the meal. Marinated mushrooms are always among them, and depending on the season and what's in the garden, you might find celery braised with fennel, carrots with orange rind and raisins, tomatoes with basil and lime juice or a casserole of zucchini and summer squash with mornay sauce. Jimmie cooks without preservatives or salt, and believes strongly in fresh and healthful food. Desserts, prepared by a neighbor, might be chocolate roll made with Belgian chocolate, lemon or grand marnier mousse, or butter cake with fresh berries.

At lunch, entrees in the $8 to $13 range could include pasta parmesan, seafood crepes, red salmon quiche, Hillandale hash and Londonderry pork stew.

This unfoldment takes place in dining rooms in the barn or the attached building with a loft that was once a studio used by writers. The old wood of the walls and raftered ceilings glows with the patina of age, as do the polished wood tables in the flickering candlelight. Colored glass bottles shine in the windows, and the whole place is filled with barny things like decoys, deacons' benches, pillows, bowls of apples and rag rugs. Add classical music on tape or Susan Smith's folksongs and a bottle of wine from Bob's well-chosen wine list, and you will find yourself part of a midsummer night's dream.

Lunch, Tuesday-Saturday noon to 3; dinner, Friday and Saturday, one seating from 7. Closed January-May. No credit cards. Dinner reservations required far in advance.

The Harvest at Bald Hill, Route 169 and 171, South Woodstock. (203) 974-2240.
Two chefs who had turned around the Brown University Faculty Club in Providence teamed up in 1988 to buy this cozy barn of a restaurant that museum curator Wylie Cumbie had put on the gastronomic map a decade earlier. Peter Cooper and Carol Twardowski take turns in the kitchen and out front, and change their menu seasonally to reflect the restaurant's name.

The screened porch is the favored place for summer dining, although Peter was thinking of enclosing it to double the size of the 50-seat restaurant. The decor is comforting: peach linens in summer, dark green in winter; Dudson English china, flickering oil candles, comfortable cane arm chairs, and dark wood walls and ceiling.

At lunch, three of us enjoyed good French bread, a shared appetizer of gyoza (tasty Japanese dumplings), sauteed scrod with winter vegetables ($8.50) and two excellent — and abundant — salads, oriental seafood and tuna nicoise, $6.75 and $7.25 respectively. These were so filling we couldn't begin to think of desserts such as truffle cake, linzer torte, baked bread custard with a calvados sauce and a classic marjolaine.

The dinner menu appeals as well. Entrees run from $11.95 for pasta with spinach, cheese and spiced sausage to $22.95 for veal with lobster. Other tempters are stuffed shrimp with sherry, poached salmon with a peppercorn hollandaise, roast duckling with raspberry sauce, sirloin steak bearnaise and "gentlemen's grill" of filet and lamb chop. Shellfish bisque, gravlax, gyoza, country pate and basil fettuccine are among the starters. The fairly extensive wine list is nicely priced, and our only quibble was over a $3.50 charge for a cup of cappuccino. Splurge instead on a specialty liqueured coffee.

Lunch, Tuesday-Friday 11:30 to 2; dinner, Tuesday-Saturday 5:30 to 9 or 10; Sunday, brunch 11 to 2:30, light dinner 5 to 8.

The Inn at Woodstock Hill, Plaine Hill Road, Woodstock. (203) 928-0528.

This new restaurant acquired its third chef in its first year with the arrival in December 1988 of Matthew D'Errico, a Culinary Institute grad who cooked at the Summer House on Nantucket and earlier had his own restaurant in the Hamptons on Long Island.

His menu changes nightly, offering the winter evening we were there a choice of five entrees ($12.95 to $18.25): honey glazed roast duckling, shrimp scampi, tournedos with green peppercorn sauce, sauteed scallops and grilled chicken with casino butter. Seafood ragout or cream of watercress soup might precede. Kirsten Miller's desserts follow, perhaps trifle, Dutch hazelnut cake, white amaretto mousse or chocolate-almond torte laced with grand marnier. A good wine list is fairly priced.

In winter, tables are set in the inn's small dining room and library, cozy and colorful with Queen Anne chairs, Villeroy & Boch china and pink napkins stashed in big wine glasses. The site changes the rest of the year to the spacious restaurant in the carriage house, which has banquettes draped in chintz, blue arm chairs and crystal chandeliers, and an outdoor deck. The locals consider this special-occasion dining.

Dinner nightly except Monday, 5:30 to 9; Sunday, brunch 11 to 3, dinner 4 to 8.

The Inn at Gwyn Careg, Route 44, Pomfret. (203) 928-7768.

In an attempt to launch "a world-class restaurant," owner George Flonnes hired one of Connecticut's best chefs — Raymond Terrill, who had helped put Ivoryton's Copper Beech Inn on the map. Now Ray is cooking for a small dining room lit almost entirely by candles and with conversation muted by classical music. The room is elegant with parquet floors, Victorian parlor chairs upholstered in green velvet, pink cloths and built-in shelves full of china.

The limited menu is classic Terrill, from lobster ravioli as an appetizer to an entree of veal stuffed with spinach, mushrooms, tomatoes, cheese and artichoke hearts — whew! Among appetizers ($4.50 to $8.50) are vegetable strudel with a mild curry sauce, baked stuffed mushroom caps duxelle, artichoke hearts a la Grecque and roasted clams corsini. Entrees run from $15.50 for chicken piccata to $22 for poached salmon and tenderloin of beef roquefort with port wine sauce.

We enjoyed sauteed pork medallions finished with calvados, cream and sliced apples, accompanied by a melange of winter vegetables and tiny potatoes. We were disap-

Dark red barn is home of the Harvest at Bald Hill.

pointed with the "grilled noisettes of lamb with fresh goat cheese raviolis and orange basil sauce." The noisettes were pounded like minute steaks, tasted like veal, lacked the goat cheese raviolis, bore no trace of basil and came with the same sauce and accompaniments as the pork. We also were surprised that a kitchen of this caliber tossed its green salad with a dressing not of its own making but one that bore the unmistakable taste of Newman's Own.

The bread was chewy and good, and the strawberry brulee with grand marnier was a worthy ending even with a burnt topping. Service was friendly and professional. A $17.50 Belvedere merlot proved a good choice from an interesting wine list. We only wished that more of our food had matched the surroundings, and that the small pre-dinner drinks in the living room hadn't cost $4.50 each.

Dinner, Wednesday-Saturday 5:30 to 9; Sunday, brunch 11 to 2, dinner 5 to 7.

Vernon Stiles Inn Restaurant, Route 193, Thompson Hill. (203) 923-9571.

Built in 1814, this venerable stagecoach tavern is what a New England restaurant should look like: a homey old place with a fire blazing in the pub, three dining rooms and a great picture of the inn made with what looks to be pieces of tiles. The place was named for one of its more colorful landlords, who claimed "more stage passengers dined there every day than at any other house in New England."

A winter tradition that is always sold out is the weekly Stew and Story sessions on Wednesday evenings. Cocktails and a supper of stew (perhaps lamb or beef) precede a fireside story told by local actors or professors in the reading room. The event attracts 40 people a week, and manager David Landry regrets having to turn many more away.

Chef-owner Joseph Silbermann oversees a continental menu that is well regarded locally. Dinner entrees start at $9 for two pastas and $10.50 for four chicken dishes and top off at $17.25 for the larger sizes of broiled steak or filet mignon. Five versions of veal are $14.50. Other choices include seafood saute, broiled scallops, roast duckling and beef Diane.

Luncheon is a mixed bag from omelets ($4) to filet mignon ($13.95).

Lunch daily, 11:30 to 2:30; dinner, 5 to 9 or 9:30. Closed Tuesday.

The Paddock, Route 101, Dayville. (203) 774-1313.

Popular with local residents seeking good food and casual surroundings is this nondescript place beside the railroad track in downtown Dayville. One door at the front entry leads to the bar and the other to a small dining room with formica tables set with red paper mats and flanked by captain's chairs.

The dinner hour starts here at 4:30. Crackers and bread sticks with a zippy cheese spread come with drinks, so you could skip the few appetizers — soup du jour, chowder on Fridays only, fruit juices and shrimp cocktail. Dig instead into down-home main courses like ham steak with pineapple, broiled pork chops, tenderloin tips en casserole, broiled or fried scallops, and shrimp scampi. Prices go from $5.95 for fish and chips with cole slaw (Thursday and Friday only) to $14.95 for surf and turf. Prime filet, sirloin, prime rib and lobster casserole are in the $12 to $14 range.

Salads are $1.50 extra and big enough to share. Desserts include puddings, cheesecake, carrot cake and home-baked pies, among them pineapple cream pie.

Lunch, Tuesday-Friday 11:30 to 2; dinner, Tuesday-Saturday 4:30 to 9.

Diversions

Roseland Cottage, Route 169, Woodstock. Roses and the Fourth of July were the twin passions of Woodstock native Henry C. Bowen, a New York merchant and publisher who planted roses outside his summer house, upholstered much of its furniture in pink and named it Roseland Cottage. To his wild pink Gothic Revival mansion trimmed in gingerbread for his famous Independence Day celebrations came the day's luminaries, among them Ulysses S. Grant, Benjamin Harrison, Rutherford B. Hayes and William McKinley. The house, its furnishings and pink parterre garden remain much as they were in the 19th century. In the rear barn is the oldest extant bowling alley in a private residence; balls of varying sizes line the chute. Open Wednesday-Sunday noon to 5 in summer, Friday-Sunday through October. Adults $2.50.

The Prudence Crandall House, Routes 14 and 169, Canterbury. The site of New England's first black female academy has a fascinating history to reveal. Asked to educate their children, Prudence Crandall ran afoul of townspeople when she admitted a black girl in 1833. They withdrew their children, so she ran a boarding school for "young ladies and misses of color" until she was hounded out of town. Now a museum, the house is interesting for its architecture and exhibits on 19th-century Canterbury, blacks and Miss Crandall. Open Wednesday-Sunday 10 to 4:30, mid-January to mid-December. Adults, $1.25.

Hamlet Hill Winery, Route 44, Pomfret. One of New England's better farm wineries is displayed to excellent advantage in a contemporary setting. Start by viewing a twelve-minute video in a circular room whose walls are covered with labels. An informative self-guided tour along a wraparound observation deck leads past winery points of interest; the visitor gets to walk through an oversize wine cask. Frenchman Henri Maubert oversees the production of some bottlings of chardonnay, dry riesling and seyval brut, and champagnes were released in 1989. Prices in the retail shop vary from $4.95 for Woodstock white proprietor's reserve (we took home a bottle for dinner that night and it was fine) to $13.50 for charter oak red. Open daily, 10 to 5 or 6.

Hill Towns and Mill Villages. A booklet of this name, prepared by the Association of Northeastern Connecticut Historical Societies, helps in touring rural Woodstock, Pomfret, Brooklyn and Canterbury as well as the nearby mill towns of Thompson, Putnam, Killingly and Plainfield. We particularly enjoy "The Street" lined with academic buildings, churches and gracious homes in Pomfret, the Woodstock Hill green with a three-state view behind Woodstock Academy, and the Thompson Hill common.

Other little treasures are the spireless **Old Trinity Church** in Brooklyn, the oldest Episcopal church now standing in the oldest diocese in the country (open some summer afternoons but used only on All Saints Day), and the brick one-room **Quassett School** in Woodstock. The Brooklyn and Woodstock fairs are among the nation's oldest.

Mashamoquet Brook State Park offers the Brayton Grist Mill (a one-man mill operation), swimming and an adventurous trail to the Wolf Den, where local Revolutionary War hero Israel Putnam killed the last she-wolf in northeastern Connecticut. One can almost visualize him stalking that beast in the cave.

For seasonal local color, visit Mervin Whipple's annual **Christmas Wonderland** of 24,000 lights, mechanized scenes, outdoor displays and a chapel — surely the biggest extravaganza of its kind. Much of it is gaudy but much is tasteful, including animated figures that once were in window displays in New York department stores. Signs point the way for the 40,000 visitors who come from miles around to see the nightly spectacle each December along Pineville Road in the Ballouville section of Killingly.

Shopping. For many, shopping begins and ends at **Scranton's Shops** in South Woodstock, a ramble of rooms in an 1878 blacksmith shop, full of country wares from more than 90 local artisans. The array is mind-boggling, and we defy anyone to get out without a purchase. Behind Scranton's is **Fox Hunt Farms,** a gourmet shop purveying the wonderful Woodstock Hill Preserves and doling out sandwiches and salads. We lunched on a good sandwich of country pate on French bread and a warm croissant filled with chicken and red peppers. Nearby are changing shops beside the 1760 Samuel McLellan House, including **Country Kettle.**

The folks at Scranton's recommend that serious shoppers visit **Cornucopia Crafts** for baskets, **Brunarhans** for wood furnishings, the **Woodstock Orchards Apple Barn** and the **Christmas Barn,** all scattered about Woodstock. At the **Irish Crystal Co.** you may find exquisite Tyrone crystal of the same quality as Waterford, says proprietor Celine Swanberg, at much lower prices. From perfume decanters to wine glasses to lamps, it all shimmers in the Woodstock showroom. We liked the primitives and local crafts at **Meadow Rock Farm,** an antiques and gift shop run by Georganna Dickson in a small barn behind her imposing country home in Pomfret. **Heirloom Antiques** in Brooklyn is considered one of the area's better shops. Nearly 100 dealers show at **Pomfret Antique World.** It's a jungle inside **Logee's Greenhouses,** a must stop for gardeners and plant lovers in Killingly. Begonias, orchids amd geraniums are specialties, but you can find just about anything else that grows.

Extra-Special

Caprilands Herb Farm, Silver Street, Coventry. (203) 742-7244.

Herbalist Adelma Grenier Simmons, an indomitable octogenarian with a twinkle in her eye, presides over 31 theme gardens, herbal lectures and luncheons, an array of shops and her book-writing endeavors at historic Caprilands, a don't-miss attraction in Coventry. Most people book far in advance for the daily luncheons, which start about 11 o'clock with herbal tea and canapes in the greenhouse. Following a noon lecture on herbal and seasonal topics by Mrs. Simmons, visitors move to her 18th-century farmhouse for lunch. It includes canapes and a punch that's quite punchy, bread, soup, salad and a main course of perhaps shrimp and mushroom casserole, accompanied by a couple of vegetable dishes. Dessert and more tea are served afterward in the greenhouse. Then browse through the Bouquet and Basket Shop, the Bookstore, the Herb Shop and the main gift shop as well as the gardens. Grounds and shops are open daily 9 to 6. Herbal luncheon programs April-Dec. 24, $15.

Essex and Old Lyme, Conn.
River Towns, Arts and Charm

Nearing the sea after lazing 400 miles through four states, the Connecticut River wends and weaves between forested hillsides and sandy shores. Finally it pauses, almost delta-like, in the sheltered coves and harbors of Essex and Old Lyme before emptying into Long Island Sound.

A sand bar blocked the kind of development that has urbanized other rivers where they meet the ocean. Indeed, the Connecticut is the nation's biggest without a major city at its mouth.

It is in this tranquil setting that historic Essex was settled in 1635, its harbor a haven for shipbuilding in the past and for yachting today. From Essex the first American warship, the Oliver Cromwell, was launched in time for the Revolution. From Essex, leading yachtsmen sail the Atlantic today.

Touted by the New Yorker magazine as "a mint-condition 18th century town," Essex relives its past in the River Museum on Steamboat Dock, in the boatworks and yacht clubs along its harbor, in the lively Tap Room at the Griswold Inn, in the lovely old homes along Main Street and River Road.

Across the river from Essex is Old Lyme, which has less of a river feel but exudes a charm of its own. In a pastoral setting that is now part of an historic district, artists gathered at the turn of the century in the mansion of Florence Griswold, daughter of a boat captain. The American Impressionist movement was the result, and the arts are celebrated and flourish here to this day.

Just inland from old Essex along the Falls River are Centerbrook and Ivoryton. They and Old Lyme provide a setting in which fine inns and restaurants thrive. Up river are Deep River, Chester, Hadlyme and East Haddam, unspoiled towns steeped in history.

You still have to drive the long way around to get from one side of the river to the other, unless you take the tiny ferry that has been plying between Chester and Hadlyme for 200 years. The Valley Railroad's steam train and riverboat link the towns as in the past, offering visitors scenic ways to see both river and shore.

Inn Spots

Old Lyme Inn, Lyme Street, Box 787 B, Old Lyme 06371. (203) 434-2600.

With eight sumptuous guest suites, an addition opened in 1985 has transformed what was basically an acclaimed restaurant into a full-service inn of distinction.

The north wing has been so tastefully added that the casual passerby in Old Lyme's carefully preserved historic district wouldn't know it was new. On two floors, the rooms are individually decorated in a plush Victorian theme — canopy and four-poster queensize beds with Marblehead mints perched atop their oversize pillows, comfortable sofas or chairs grouped around marble topped-tables, and large, gleaming white bathrooms outfitted with Dickinson's Witch Hazel (made in Essex) and herbal shampoos. The new rooms are so attractive they make the five smaller rooms in the original 1850s farmhouse seem almost dowdy in comparison.

Innkeeper Diana Field Atwood has furnished guest rooms and public areas alike with Empire and Victorian pieces acquired at auctions, tag sales and antiques shows. Many of the inn's notable collection of paintings represent the Old Lyme School of artists who were based at the Florence Griswold House across the street.

Guests have use of Sassafras's Library (named for the inn's aged cat), which has a

New addition expands lodging capacity at Old Lyme Inn.

marble-topped fireplace and television. The Victorian bar dispenses drinks, shellfish from a raw bar, light snacks, special coffees and dessert pastries.

Homemade croissants and granola are served for continental breakfast in the Rose Room. Lunch and dinner are available in three formal dining rooms (see Dining Spots).

Doubles, $95 to $125.

Copper Beech Inn, 46 Main St., Ivoryton 06442. (203) 767-0330.

Long rated highly as a restaurant (see Dining Spots), the Copper Beech has catered to the luxury market in lodging since it opened nine guest rooms in 1986 in a restored carriage house behind a mansion shaded by the oldest copper beech tree in Connecticut.

Eldon and Sally Senner from Washington, D.C., he a banker and she an interior decorator, purchased the inn in 1988 and enhanced it with their extensive collection of fine antiques, marine paintings and oriental porcelains. They also restored the dining experience to levels it had not matched since the restaurant's glory days in the 1970s under founders Jo and Robert McKenzie.

The nine new guest rooms are furnished in "country chic," with comfortable sitting areas and TV sets. Each has a jacuzzi bathtub and French doors that open onto an outdoor deck overlooking landscaped gardens. Second-floor rooms have cathedral ceilings.

Rooms in the main inn are attractive as well. Nicely decorated in rich shades of blue, the master suite has a striking floor-to-ceiling fabric canopy enveloping a kingsize bed, a loveseat in front of the fireplace, a chaise longue across the room and a large table for two in the front dormer window.

Another room is bright and cheery with wicker furniture and brass bed. All the rooms have good-looking furnishings and antiques as befits a mansion once occupied by an ivory merchant.

There's a small sitting area upstairs in the spacious hall. In season, one of the more pleasant places to relax is the large greenhouse behind the inn, nicely outfitted with colorful garden furniture and an abundance of plants. It's popular for cocktails and after-dinner drinks. The Senners are restoring the gardens around the inn, have planted 4,000 bulbs, and plan terraces of annuals and perennials.

Guests are served continental-plus breakfast in the Copper Beech Room, a handsome dining room with a view of the great tree, blue oriental carpets on the floor and tables spaced well apart.

Doubles, $105 to $145.

Bee and Thistle Inn, 100 Lyme St., Old Lyme 06371. (203) 434-1667.

Stately trees, gardens all around and a flower-bedecked entrance welcome visitors to this cheery yellow and white frame inn, set on five acres bordering the Lieutenant River in the historic district of Old Lyme. Built in 1756 with subsequent additions and remodeling, the structure is a delightful ramble of parlors and porches, dining rooms and guest rooms.

It is this scene that attracted Bob and Penny Nelson in 1982. Wishing to leave the corporate life in northern New Jersey, they were looking to buy a traditional New England inn. A broker told them of one they weren't familiar with along the Connecticut shore. "It was only two hours from home so we said we'd go look," Bob Nelson recalls. "We walked in the front door, saw the center entrance hall and graceful staircase and said, 'This is it.'"

With sofas to sink into and fireplaces ablaze, the parlors on either side are inviting. On sunny days, the enclosed porches beyond are great for lingering over breakfast or lunch. The Nelsons have refurbished most of the inn's public spaces and guest rooms, and upgraded the restaurant as well (see below).

Nine of the eleven guest rooms upstairs have private baths and all have fresh flowers and what Bob calls "country old" furnishings. Four-poster, fishnet canopy and spool beds are covered with quilts or afghans. Some rooms have wing chairs and ruffled curtains, and one even has a washstand full of flowers. Nooks are full of games and old books are all around.

A winter feature of this inn, voted the most romantic in Connecticut, is afternoon tea. Served Monday, Wednesday and Thursday from 3:30 to 5 for $5.95, it's generally booked solid. Fresh scones, four tea sandwiches and a dessert accompany the beverages.

Full breakfasts are available in the sunny dining porches, a great place to start the day. Breakfast in bed can be ordered the night before. The Bee and Thistle popover filled with scrambled eggs, bacon and cheese ($4.50) draws the public as well as overnighters.

Doubles, $78 to $105, EP.

Riverwind, 209 Main St., Deep River 06417. (203) 526-2014.

Innkeeper Barbara Barlow found a dilapidated 1850 house in 1983 and spent a year restoring it into a B&B, doing most of the work herself. Her contractor didn't blanch when she told him in 1987 she wanted to build an addition 150 years older than her existing inn. The result is a skillful blend of old and new, from eight guest rooms with private baths to an equal number of common rooms affording space for mingling or privacy. This is a cozy inn crammed full of antiques and folk art, with a noteworthy collection of pigs in all guises, all over the house.

Barbara, who grew up in Smithfield, Va., and whose dad is a hog farmer there, serves up slices of the red, salty Smithfield ham for breakfast every morning to her guests. The hams hang from the ceiling in her kitchen, where cupboards are made of wood from a gristmill in upstate New York and the counter is a 200-year-old piece of hemlock. Guests eat breakfast by candlelight at a table for twelve in the new dining room and at a smaller table in the adjacent room. Coffee cake, real southern biscuits in the shape of pigs, egg dishes (perhaps sliced hard-boiled eggs with artichoke hearts and mushrooms in a cheese sauce), fresh fruit in summer and hot curried fruit in winter, and her homemade jams and preserves are the fare.

Dining porch at Bee and Thistle Inn. **Living room at Riverwind.**

There'a s twelve-foot stone cooking fireplace in the "new" 18th-century keeping room. We're always attracted to the original fireplaced parlor loaded with antiques and neat touches. Quilts, wooden animals, hooked and woven rugs, a set of blocks shaped like houses spelling "welcome," a wonderful lighting fixture of wooden animals holding candles and a piano topped with all kinds of sheet music make for an exceptionally welcoming room. A decanter of sherry is always out for guests. An antique checkerboard is among games in the trophy room, and there's a library with a fireplace in the upstairs study. In summer, the long narrow porch in front is set with white wicker furniture and looks as if it were made for Scarlett O'Hara.

Up steep stairs, lined with old preserve jars filled with dried flowers, are the older guest rooms. The Smithfield Room, all red, white and blue, has bluebirds stenciled around the walls and a high rope maple bed with a chamber pot underneath. A stenciled floor and her grandmother's carved oak hall tree and carved oak headboard give Zelda's Suite a decidedly Gatsby flavor. Flowers on the bedroom wallpaper, hearts on the bathroom wallpaper and a heart-filled stained-glass window are featured in the Hearts and Flowers Room. The ultimate is the Champage and Roses Room with a private balcony, a bathroom with a Japanese steeping tub, a bottle of champagne awaiting on a table between two wing chairs, and a fishnet canopy bed too frilly for words.

Is it any wonder that Barbara bills Riverwind as a place for romance? To add to the romantic atmosphere, she was recently married to Bob Bucknall, now her co-innkeeper, and has become a justice of the peace so that she can perform weddings. Her newly acquired classic Bentley limousine parked out front simply intensifies the aura.

Doubles, $75 to $135.

Griswold Inn, Main Street, Essex 06426. (203) 767-1812.

The Griswold Inn has an historic appeal matched by few inns in this country. There's the requisite tap room containing a steamboat-Gothic bar, potbelly stove and antique popcorn machine — Lucius Beebe called it "probably the most handsome barroom in America." Unpretentious meals and an unexcelled Hunt Breakfast are served in four dining rooms that are treasuries of Americana. And the floors in some of the guest rooms list to port or starboard, as you might expect of an inn dating to 1776 when it was built as Connecticut's first three-story structure.

Commandeered by the British during the War of 1812, the inn was found to be long on charm but short on facilities. Today, most of the 23 guest rooms in the main inn, the annex and a house have private baths, but are unabashedly simple and old-fashioned. One upstairs front room facing the street has a beamed ceiling and sloping floor, twin beds, marble-topped table and a small bath with shower. Two new suites erected over the Steamboat Room during a massive kitchen renovation in 1989 are a cut above.

A continental breakfast buffet of juice, coffee and Danish pastry is put out in the dark paneled, book-shelved Library.

The "Gris," as it's known to locals and visitors from near and far, serves hundreds of meals a day (see Dining Spots), and the Sunday Hunt breakfast is an institution. Before and after dinner, the Tap Room is a happy hubbub of banjo players, a singalong pianist and sea chantey singers, depending on the night. You can snack from the raw bar, sample popcorn from the old red machine, hoist a few brews and readily imagine you've been transported 200 years into the past.

Doubles, $75; three suites, $90 to $165.

Dining Spots

Fine Bouche, Main Street, Centerbrook. (203) 767-1277.

For consistency and creativity, Fine Bouche stands at the head of the list in an area known for fine restaurants. It's also a relatively good value, having reluctantly raised its fixed-price menu to $36 after holding at $32.50 for three years ("some people were saying we were too cheap — that there must be something wrong," chef-owner Steven Wilkinson acknowledged candidly).

Trained in London and San Francisco before opening his small French restaurant and patisserie in 1979, Steve since has been acclaimed among the top chefs in Connecticut. But he remains unassuming and personable, chatting with patrons on a first-name basis and running special wine-tasting and culinary events.

As you enter through the patisserie, stop for a look at some of the delectable desserts you might order. As you await your table in a small reception parlor, scan the interesting memorabilia from the owner's career — empty bottles of rare wine, special menus from London and such — discreetly on display in two lighted glass cases.

Beyond are two small interior dining rooms seating a total of 45, one with pictures of grapes and vines on cream-colored walls and the other darker with pretty green and flowered wallpaper and old French prints. A pristine, cafe-style wraparound porch is particularly inviting with white, not-quite-sheer full-length curtains, arched lattice-work over the windows, peach-colored walls and rattan chairs, their seats covered by a dark green chintz dotted with exotic lilies.

The $36 prix-fixe menu might start with a choice of smoked salmon with celery root remoulade, galantine of pheasant and duck, poached oysters wrapped in spinach, and snails with an anchovy-walnut sauce. The soup or fish course could be a choice of a delectable mussel soup with fennel and saffron, pheasant soup, coquilles St. Jacques or grilled salmon with fresh oyster mushrooms.

After a green salad comes the piece de resistance. How about medallions of veal with onion compote, sauteed duck breast with sour cherries and brandy, tournedos of beef with two sauces, rack of lamb with roasted garlic and anise, or breast of pheasant with madeira and truffle sauce?

Desserts are superlative, particularly the almond-hazelnut dacquoise and the mar-

Chef-owner Steven Wilkinson in front of Fine Bouche.

jolaine, a heavenly combination of almond praline, hazelnut meringue, creme fraiche and bitter Belgian chocolate. Those with more resistance than we can order a fresh fruit sorbet.

The a la carte menu offers a few additional choices. Entrees are $17 for coquilles St. Jacques to $25 for rack of lamb.

Although we've been happy dining here on numerous occasions, we'll never forget one dinner of warm duck pate in puff pastry, grilled oysters with fresh herb sauce, sweetbreads, filet of veal with mushrooms, madeira and tarragon, and a rich genoise for dessert.

The superb wine list, winner of Wine Spectator's Grand Award, is especially strong on French but with an interesting selection of other European imports as well as Californias, quite reasonably priced.

Behind the restaurant, a country inn with twelve deluxe guest rooms was under construction for a planned opening in 1989.

Dinner, Tuesday-Saturday 6 to 9. Patisserie, 10 to 5.

Daniel's Table, Ivoryton Inn, 115 Main St., Ivoryton. (203) 767-8914.

After apprenticing at the Old Lyme Inn and Restaurant du Village in Chester, Daniel McManamy opened a restaurant of his own in leased quarters in the Ivoryton Inn in 1988. Almost immediately, word traveled among the culinary cognoscenti that Dan knew how to make his eleven tables sing.

The place is serene and simple: an L-shaped room with lace curtains, bare floors, recessed ceiling lights, and stenciling and a few sconces on the plain walls. The white-linened tables are canvases for the chef's artistry.

Among appetizers ($3 to $7.50), we tried the rabbit pate — two enormous slabs garnished with orange nasturtiums and cornichons, and enlivened by a zesty mustard in a leaf of radicchio — and a superb crab ravioli with sweet red pepper sauce.

Hot, crusty rolls and a composed salad of tiny lettuces (oakleaf, frise, nasturtiums, etc.) precede the entrees, priced from $17.50 to $19. We liked the salmon on a basil beurre blanc and roast pork loin in a grand marnier sauce with orange and cranberry. Saffron rice with pernod and perfect little haricots verts accompanied. Other choices

could be filet of sole with grapefruit and caviar, filet of beef madeira with morels, leg of lamb with anything-but-mundane garlic mashed potatoes, and breast of pheasant with an apple-onion compote.

A luscious frozen hazelnut souffle with frangelico and kahlua sauces and a peach crisp with white chocolate and bourbon sauce were among the desserts. Chocolate pate with raspberry sauce, passion fruit creme brulee and apple galette with cinnamon ice cream are other possibilities.

The wine list, small but excellent, contains good values.

Dinner, Tuesday-Thursday 5 to 9:30, Friday-Sunday 5:30 to 9:30.

Daniel McManamy outside his restaurant.

Bee and Thistle Inn, 100 Lyme St., Old Lyme. (203) 434-1667.

Head chef Francis Brooke-Smith, who trained at the Ritz in London, delights in innovative touches and stylish presentations at this highly regarded dining room. Among them are edible flowers for garnishes and fresh herbs grown hydroponically year-round.

Dining on the enclosed side porches overlooking the lawns is a treat. Ladderback chairs are at tables with blue and rose cloths or mats. Baskets hang from the ceiling and windows open to let in the breeze. Thriving African violets, other plants and knick-knacks are all around.

Luncheon choices in the $6.95 to $9.95 range include quiche, omelet, oriental pasta salad, smoked seafood plate, Maryland crab cakes and petite filet mignon.

Candlelight dinners are served on the porches or in a small rear dining room, where a guitar-playing couple sings love songs on Friday nights and a harpist plays in a corner on Saturdays.

Dinner entrees range widely from $16.95 for medallions of Shaker pork or chicken sauteed with garlic, cream and walnuts, served with fettuccine, to $25.95 for rack of lamb with a mint pesto in pastry. Country quail, pheasant and venison were on the latest winter menu.

Start with the house-dried gravlax with green peppercorns and herbs, a duck and hazelnut pate or cold poached shrimp with remoulade sauce among appetizers ($6.95 to $8.95). Finish with banana mousse terrine, brandied pear trifle or chocolate mousse torte. Bob Nelson, who studied wines at the Cornell University Hotel School, put together the wine list with an eye for reasonable prices.

Lunch, daily except Tuesday 11:30 to 2; dinner nightly except Tuesday 6 to 10; Sunday brunch, 11 to 2.

Old Lyme Inn, Lyme Street, Old Lyme. (203) 434-2600.

Thrice given the top three-star rating by the New York Times and its desserts featured in successive 1985 issues of Bon Appetit magazine, the Old Lyme Inn has been a mecca for traveling gourmets since Diana Field Atwood took it over in 1976.

The food is inventive and the setting is formal in three large dining rooms, all regally furbished in gold and blue. Tables in the long, high-ceilinged main dining room are angled in perfect formation, a vase with one perfect rose atop each. Beyond are two more dining rooms, one with an intimate windowed alcove containing a table for four.

Chef Chris Hawver, who trained in Paris and Zurich, oversees an ambitious menu. Dinner appetizers ($7 to $9.50) run the gamut from pecan poultry pate and Irish smoked salmon to shrimp roulade and venison pate garnished with pickled okra. Seasonal "interludes" might be truffled brie and field salad with goat cheese.

Entrees ($17.50 to $26) include grilled swordfish with macadamia nut butter, Norwegian salmon in a potato crust with a ragout of mushrooms, roast Connecticut pheasant with apples and endive, loin of venison with a chestnut puree, sweetbreads with manzanilla olives, and lamb medallions with mint, coriander and fava beans.

The inn's raspberry cheesecake Japonaise was pictured on the cover of Bon Appetit. Other desserts are homemade sorbets and ice creams and fancy confections like cranberry linzer torte, lemon shortcake tart and chocolate almond rice torte.

The wine list is choice and pricey. Cafe Diana with chambord and chocolate liqueur is a worthy finale.

The lunch menu includes interesting salads (venison with a wild mushroom couscous and a currant-brandy vinaigrette, or pheasant and duck ringed by a whole grain salad with a port wine and toasted pecan vinaigrette), a grilled chicken and cheese sandwich, omelets, cashew bourbon chicken, calves liver and grilled salmon ($6.50 to $12). We loved the curried cream of yellow squash soup and a special of Niantic scallops.

A light bar menu in the evening offers things like parsnip soup, vegetarian platter, sea scallops with Thai herbs and coq au vin. The six entrees are priced in the $12 to $15 range.

For the month of December, the inn puts on a Dicken's Feast with wild boar, wild Scottish hare, baron of beef, Christmas goose and the like.

Lunch, Tuesday-Saturday noon to 2; dinner, Tuesday-Saturday 6 to 9; Sunday, lunch noon to 4, dinner 4 to 9.

Copper Beech Inn, Main Street, Ivoryton. (203) 767-0330.
The level of dining at the Copper Beech dropped somewhat following the departure of founding innkeepers Jo and Robert McKenzie. It was raised again in 1988 by new innkeepers Sally and Eldon Senner and their chef, 25-year-old chef Armand Mazzulli, who reduced the scope of the large menu, taking away some of the heavier dishes, while maintaining the high-for-the-area prices (dinner entrees, $22.50 to $25.25).

The main Georgian Room is elegant indeed, with three chandeliers, wall sconces, subdued floral wallpaper and crisp white napkins standing tall in the water glasses. The dark Comstock Room with beamed ceiling looks a bit like the old billiards parlor that it was, lately enhanced by the paintings collected by the Senners. Nearby is a pretty little garden dining porch, its four tables for two spaced well apart amid the plants. In each dining room, tables are centered by one perfect red rose. Windows in the blue Copper Beech Room afford views of the great tree outside.

The menu is printed in French with English translations. The ten hors d'oeuvres start at $7.95 for country pate and top off at $27.50 for fresh foie gras with a fruit compote. Scotch smoked salmon, clams topped with crabmeat, and timbale of sweetbreads and chicken are other possibilities.

Among the dozen entrees, some of the more inspired are bouillabaisse, grilled tuna with a sauce of sun-dried tomatoes, pheasant under glass, tournedos with roasted chestnuts and brandy-cream sauce, sauteed pork loin with potato and leek cakes, and beef Wellington with a truffle sauce.

Desserts in the $4 to $5 range include chocolate crepes, sacher torte, white chocolate mousse with strawberries in a pastry tulip and English trifle. Finish with one of the fancy liqueured coffees or fine brandies for an occasion to remember.

Dinner, Tuesday-Saturday 6 to 9, Sunday 1 to 9.

Griswold Inn, Main Street, Essex 06426. (203) 767-1812.

The famed "Gris" was serving an abbreviated menu every day in the winter of 1989 while its old kitchen was closed and a new one was built. You'd expect no less from an institution that since its founding in 1776 has served "precisely 3.1416 times the number of meals which had been cumulatively prepared in all the steamships of the Cunard Line, the dirigibles Graf Zeppelin and Hindenburg, and the Orient Express," as a statement to customers noted.

"Our aim is to create New England's finest kitchen," said innkeepr Bill Winterer. "The old one lasted 213 years and we expect the same performance from the new one."

A meal at the Gris, whether prepared in old kitchen or new, is an experience in Americana. There's much to see in a variety of dining rooms: the important collection of Antonio Jacobsen marine oils in the dark paneled Library, the Currier and Ives steamboat prints in the Covered Bridge Room (actually fashioned from a New Hampshire covered bridge), the riverboat memorabilia in the Steamboat Room, the musket-filled Gun Room with 55 pieces dating to the 15th century. All together, they rank as one of the outstanding marine art collections in America.

The atmosphere is the match for the food, which is country New England, fresh and abundant. "We have no pretenses," says the informative Innkeeper's Log. "Our menu is printed in English. We call fish fish and beef beef." The menu is a mixed-bag of seafood, fish and game, priced at night from $13.95 for fried oysters or fried catfish to $19.95 for medallions of venison. Steak and kidney pie, Irish lamb pie, English mixed grill, seafood gumbo, grilled shrimp oregano, carpetbagger steak and barbecued ribs are among the offerings.

The inn's patented 1776 sausages are served in a mixed grill with sauerkraut and German potato salad for $13.95 at dinner. They're in even more demand for lunch, when they come in four versions for $6.95. You also can get shirred eggs or Welsh rarebit, salade nicoise or a bucket of steamers or mussels, $4.75 to $9.50.

The Sunday hunt breakfast is an enormous buffet of dishes ranging from kippered herring and creamed chipped beef to eggs and grits. The adventuresome get their fill of specialties like braised goose, roast partridge, braised rabbit and grilled moose served in the Colonial tradition during December at the inn's annual Christmas feast.

Lunch daily, noon to 2:30; "lite bite," 2:30 to 4; dinner, 5:30 to 9 or 10; Sunday, Hunt Breakfast 11 to 2:30, dinner 4 to 9.

8 Westbrook Restaurant, 8 Westbrook Road, Centerbrook. (203) 767-7085.

This promising eatery opened in January 1989 in a restored house with a rear view of a mill pond. Its two small dining rooms on two floors are connected by a narrow stairway that has patrons wondering how the staff manages to negotiate.

The airy upstairs room, across the hallway from the kitchen, is pristine with pink and white linens, sturdy blond wood chairs with pink seats, and brass lamps and interesting art for sale on the teal-colored walls. Votive candles are in crystal holders, and there's a lovely fireplace. The downstairs room with its mulberry walls appears warm and cozy.

Chef-owner George Tilghman, who formerly ran the eclectic Finest Kind restaurant on Mount Desert Island in Maine, and his wife Polly change their menus seasonally. Their first featured cream of celery soup with walnuts, crab cakes with lemon butter, Thai shrimp, duck with green peppercorn sauce, calves liver with currants and pinenuts, and filet stuffed with smoked oysters, $12.95 to $17.95.

Among appetizers ($4.25 to $6.95) were mozzarella crostini with a caper sauce, vegetable torte with two sauces, and artichokes and snails in phyllo. One of the salads was endive with watercress and beets, and among the three pasta dishes was crab ravioli ($7.25).

Historic Griswold Inn in Essex, as viewed from Griswold Square shops.

Homemade desserts include a chocolate angel cake with white chocolate frosting, the Queen Mother's chocolate cake with chocolate mousse, orange-walnut crepe and homemade ginger ice cream.

The Sunday brunch menu brings fare like omelets with sour cream and caviar, eggs sardou and welsh rarebit, $4.95 to $6.95. A liquor license was pending.

Dinner, Monday-Saturday 6 to 9 or 10; Sunday brunch, 11 to 2.

Elephant Walk, Old Lyme Shopping Center, Halls Road, Old Lyme. (203) 434-1900.

A Caribbean-style decor in pink and green, with rattan furnishings and safari prints and masks of exotic animals on the walls, commends this new eatery at the rear corner of a small shopping plaza. Glass etched with elephants separates the bar from the dining room. Soaring windows on the main floor and a mezzanine used for overflow look out across the Lieutenant River marshes, and the setting is quite stunning.

The dinner menu is rather ambitious, ranging from chicken tarragon and tuna steak nicoise to scallops mornay, veal hunter and brace of quail stuffed with a mushroom duxelle and topped with a sauce of shiitake mushrooms, port and rosemary. Entrees are priced from $10.50 to $19.95. The lengthy list of appetizers includes a smoked seafood collage ($10.95), domestic and beluga caviar, items from a raw bar, baked brie with fruit and a dish called lumache, snails with pesto and capers on a bed of arugula ($6.50).

The same appetizers are available at lunch, when sandwiches like the "elephant burger (actually beef)" and a variety of entrees from $6.25 for stir-fried chicken to $9.95 for petite tenderloin steak served on a souffle are offered. Desserts might include a raspberry or hazelnut torte, or Bailey's Irish Cream mousse.

Lunch daily, 11:30 to 2:30; dinner, 5 to 9 or 10. Closed Sunday in winter.

The Black Seal, Main Street, Essex. (203) 767-0233

The legendary Tumbledown's Cafe gave way in 1988 to the Black Seal, a casual and appealingly nautical place run by Joe O'Neal and Mauricio Salgar. All the stuff to look at along the walls of the front tavern and in the rear dining room could distract one from the food, of which there's something for everyone day and night.

Basically the same fare is offered at lunch and dinner, though lunch brings more sandwiches and dinner more entrees. Graze on chili nachos, fire-pot chili, stuffed potato skins, Cajun shrimp, Rhode Island clam chowder, California burger, and cobb and hunters salad anytime.

At night, entrees run from $9.95 for stir-fry vegetables to $14.95 for steak au poivre. "Seals Delight" is mussels, clams, scallops, shrimp and calamari in red clam sauce over pasta ($13.95). Sunday is roast night (beef, ham, turkey and such), offered in addition to the regular menu. Wednesday is for pasta ($7.95), while Thursday there are Mexican specials and Friday brings prime rib for $9.95.

Desserts ($3.50) include white satin torte and Mississippi mud cake. The house Napa Ridge chardonnay and cabernet sauvignon are $2.50 a glass.

Lunch, daily 11:30 to 3:30, weekends to 4; dinner, 5 to 10 or 11; Sunday, brunch 11 to 2:30, dinner 5 to 10.

Oliver's Taverne, Plains Road (Route 153), Essex. (203) 767-2633.

This establishment named for Essex's first ship, the Oliver Cromwell, is a casual spot in a breathtakingly high space in the former Hitchcock furniture store. The decor is mostly wood with a massive stone fireplace and a three-story window with large hanging panels of stained glass to catch the light. Upstairs is a long oak and mahogany bar from Cicero, Ill., at which Al Capone once drank, and a suave lounge area with modern sofas and chairs and a fascinating collection of baskets on the wall.

Huge sandwiches served with french fries, burgers, salads and a few entrees like quiche or scallops baked in a cheese sauce are in the $4.75 to $5.50 range at lunch. Snacky things like nachos, potato skins, fried calamari and such are also offered at night, when entrees go up to $14.95 for steak and lobster tail. "Steak lovers," slice-your-own sirloin, is $24.95 for two. The barbecued pork ribs are praised by those in the know, and we lamb lovers wonder how they can do loin of New Zealand lamb for $11.95. Bailey's Irish Cream mousse cake and chocolate chip cookie pie are popular desserts.

With a children's menu, the place is popular with families as well as singles.

Lunch daily, 11:30 to 5; dinner, 5 to 10:30; Sunday brunch, 11:30 to 4.

Diversions

The Essex Waterfront. As a living and working yachting and shipbuilding town, the Essex waterfront is a center of activity (on our last visit, half the merchants in town were in New York at the boat show).

Connecticut River Museum, Steamboat Dock, 767-8269. Restored in 1975 from an 1878 steamboat warehouse, this is a living memorial to the Connecticut River Valley in an area from which the first American warship was launched. The main floor has changing exhibits. Upstairs, where windows on three sides afford sweeping views of the river, the permanent shipbuilding exhibit shows a fullsize replica of David Bushnell's first submarine, the strange-looking American Turtle, plus a new model of a Dutch explorer ship that sailed up the river in 1614, given by the William Winterer family of the Griswold Inn. Old-timer Albert F. Dock, one of the Connecticut River Foundation founders and benefactors, often is around to share an insight or two. The museum is open Tuesday-Sunday from 10 to 5, April-December, and weekends in the winter; adults $1.50.

The foundation property also includes a small waterfront park with benches and the 1813 Hayden Chandlery, now the Thomas A. Stevens maritime research library. Just to the south off Novelty Lane are the historic Dauntless Club, the Essex Corinthian Yacht Club and the Essex Yacht Club. The venerable structures here and elsewhere in town are detailed in a walking map, available at the River Museum.

Uptown Essex. Besides the waterfront area, Methodist Hill at the other end of Main Street has a cluster of historic structures. Facing tiny Champlin Square is the imposing white **Pratt House** (circa 1648), restored and operated by the Essex Historical Society

Florence Griswold Museum was once the retreat of the Old Lyme artists.

to show Essex as it was in yesteryear (open June-September, Friday-Sunday 1 to 4, $1.50). The period gardens contain herbs and flowers of the 18th century. The society also operates the adjacent **Hill's Academy Museum** (1833), an early boarding school that now displays historical collections of old Essex (Wednesday-Friday 10 to 3, $1).

Old Lyme. The long main street of one of Connecticut's prettiest towns is lined with gracious old homes, including one we think is particularly handsome called Lyme Regis, the English summer resort after which the town was named. Lyme Street, once the home of governors and chief justices, is a National Historic District.

The **Florence Griswold Museum,** 96 Lyme St., is the pillared 1817 landmark in which the daughter of a boat captain ran a finishing school for girls and later an artists' retreat, with most of the rooms converted into bedrooms and studios in the barns by the river. Now run as a museum by the Lyme Historical Society, it has unique painted panels in every room, but especially prized is the dining room with panels on all sides given over to the work of the Old Lyme artists, who included Childe Hassam. Across the mantel the artists painted a caricature of themselves for posterity. The arts colony thrived for twenty years and its works are exhibited in the second-floor galleries. Open daily except Monday 10 to 5 and Sunday 1 to 5, June-October, and Wednesday-Sunday 1 to 5, November-May. Adults, $1.

The **Lyme Art Association** gallery, next door to the Florence Griswold Museum, was founded in 1921 and exhibits three major shows each season (afternoons, late May to mid-September). Nearby is the handsome **Lyme Academy of Fine Arts,** with changing exhibits and workshops (weekdays 9 to 4:30). The works of Lyme's American Impressionists also are hung in the Town Hall, and the public library often has exhibits. Art and antiques are featured in the town's few shops, among them the Cooley Gallery.

Deep River, just above Essex and reached most rewardingly via the River Road, is a sleepy river town best known for its ancient muster of fife and drum corps. Portrayed lately by the New York Times as on the verge of chic between Essex and Chester, its downtown has a couple of good shops — **Celebrations,** which has a purple door, for neat cards and paper goods, as well as jewelry, children's clothes and toys and wonderful papier mache cats, and, next door, **Pasta Unlimited.** Here pasta of all shapes and flavors (we liked the tomato basil and the black peppercorn) is made in the front window and goodies like broccoli-almond salad with fusili pasta, "not your Mom's" macaroni and cheese, and key lime mousse are available for takeout. Try one of the sandwiches in pita ($2.75) for a picnic.

Shopping. Most first-timers are impressed by the quality of shopping in Essex, much of it nautically oriented. One concentration is at Essex Square: **E.J. Danos & Co.,** an intriguing place advertising sports art and antiques, has decoys, ducks and carved animals of all shapes and sizes. **Seaflowers** is a whimsical garden shop with a mechanical cat lying in a basket in the window, great hanging wall baskets and exotic dried flower arrangements. The **Clipper Ship Bookstore** specializes in nautical volumes. For fashions, visit **The Talbots, Silkworm, Camps** and the **Nantucket Mills** shop. At Griswold Square, the **Hide in the Woods** shop has fine leather goods and wood things, and the **Cheese Shop & Deli** is a good place to pick up soup and a sandwich. We also like **Connecticut River Tapestries** here, with decoys and nautical art. The soaring and colorful **Boat House** at Dauntless Boat Yard is very contemporary, very nautical and full of interesting gifts; **All Decked Out** offers sportswear for the yachtsman. **The Queen's Museum,** a gift shop at Champlin Square, is one of those places where you covet almost everything. There are enormous stuffed fabric tulips, intriguing California necklaces bearing fish or watermelons, Bartlett prints, tote bags and purses, dolls and lamps.

The Yellow Daffodil on Main Street, Centerbrook, is as trendy and contemporary as can be, its relocated showroom filled with sophisticated cards, paper goods, glassware, toys, furnishings and exotic jewelry. Also in the new Spencer's Corner shops is **Plaza Sweet,** an ice cream parlor with choice candies like cafe au lait truffles, cappuccino and espresso, light entrees for lunch and assorted gifts. The homemade waffle cones might envelop caramel peanut, wild berry crunch or chocolate cherry truffle ice cream. In the same complex is **Seaflour Foods,** a gourmet takeout. Sandwiches (Stacey's includes roast turkey, sprouts, bacon, avocado and Swiss cheese on dill-onion bread) are $3.50 to $4.95. Luncheon and picnic entrees feature soups like carrot-ginger, English pies, spinach and ham turnovers, stradas and goulash.

LuEllen at 24C Main St., Centerbrook, is a choice catering and specialty-foods center where you can pick up wonderful soups, pizzas, salads and entrees for lunch or take an entire meal home for dinner. We especially enjoyed a winter soup of sausage and sweet potato and some pizza with goat cheese, and stoutly resisted a piece of coffee heath bar cheesecake.

Extra-Special

The Valley Railroad, Exit 3 off Route 9, Essex. (203) 767-0103.

Its whistle tooting and smokestack spewing, the marvelous old steam train runs from the old depot in the Centerbrook section of Essex through woods and meadows to the Connecticut River landing at Deep River. There it connects with a riverboat for an hour's cruise past Gillette Castle to the Goodspeed Opera House and back. The two-hour trip into the past is rewarding for young and old alike. Trips run daily in summer, mainly weekends in spring and fall and at Christmas. The Saturday evening Dixieland or country music cruises, three hours of jam-packed nostalgia, are a fun-filled Connecticut summer tradition. Adults, $9.95 train and riverboat; $6.95, train only.

Stanley-Whitman House dating to 1660 houses Farmington Museum.

Farmington Valley, Conn.

The Best of Both Worlds

A long mountain range separates the Hartford area from its outlying western suburbs. Talcott Mountain — the "mountain," as it's called locally — shields the Farmington River valley from the Capital City and creates a place apart.

It is a special place of bucolic landscapes, meandering streams, venerable structures and lingering history. It's the place where their founders established no fewer than five private preparatory schools, where an industrialist's daughter gave her home as a prized museum, and where many executives of corporate Hartford today make their homes and provide living space for their families.

The "valley," as it's called locally, expands or contracts, depending on who is doing the defining. It always includes historic Farmington, home of the exclusive Miss Porter's School and some of the area's finest estates as well as office parks and corporate headquarters. Here you find a country club occupying one of the prime four corners in the center of town.

It includes Avon, a forested expanse of newer houses that command the region's highest prices. It includes Simsbury, a schizophrenic suburb that has lost more of its obvious 17th-century heritage than Farmington but has retained more sense of community than Avon. It includes Canton, where suburban sprawl starts yielding to rural wilderness. For these purposes, the valley does not include Granby, Burlington, Harwinton or, for that matter, our hometown of West Hartford, which is the largest town in the regional tourism district but does not consider itself part of the valley at all.

The valley is a place more for seeing and doing than for contemplation. Hot-air ballooning, hang-gliding, horseback riding and river tubing are the sports of note after tennis and golf. There are museums to explore, countless shops (from boutiques to art galleries), interesting restaurants, rural byways and lately, a handful of inns that qualify the valley as an inn spot as well as a special place.

Although this is suburbia, don't expect to see tract houses or commercial strips. Most of the houses are tucked away on large lots off winding roads in the woods. The shops, except along the main Route 44, are in old houses and new clusters.

Stray from the mainstream, which is easy to do in the valley. You won't believe that a "suburb" is just around the corner, or that Hartford is just beyond the looming mountain. Partake of suburban and rural pleasures, but know that the diverse offerings of Connecticut's largest city are only a dozen miles away.

"We have the best of both worlds," says Suzanne Besser, director of the Farmington Valley/West Hartford Visitors Bureau. She has much to promote and increasingly receptive takers.

Inn Spots

Simsbury 1820 House, 731 Hopmeadow St., Simsbury 06070. (203) 658-7658.

Listed on the National Register of Historic Places, this country manor on a gentle rise above Simsbury's main street has been restored by some of Hartford's movers and shakers, among them a corporate leader, a decorator and a restaurateur. The result is an inn and a restaurant of distinction.

A veranda full of wicker and baskets of hanging flowers greets guests at the entrance of the imposing gray building, reopened as an inn in 1986. The entry is notable for deep purple walls, leather chairs and a crystal chandelier. The public rooms retain the remarkable wainscoting, carved molding and leaded-glass windows of the original structure; all the gilt-framed oil paintings are reproductions. The living room, sun room and dining room are furnished as you might expect of a country gentleman's estate.

Reproduction and English antiques grace the 23 guest rooms and suites on the inn's three floors. King and queensize four-poster beds, wing chairs, chintz curtains, and shades of mauves and blues predominate. Most of the private baths have windows and have been tucked ingeniously into the nooks and crannies with which the house fascinates (one bathroom goes around a corner and is almost bigger than its bedroom). Most rooms have comfortable sitting areas for reading but not for watching television — the TVs are entrenched in front of the beds.

Across the side lawn designed by Frederick Law Olmsted, the Carriage House offers eleven more rooms and suites, some of them on two or three levels and decorated in dark and masculine tones, a couple with an equine theme. Particularly interesting is the "executive suite" with its own garden terrace, a sitting room like a men's club and, up a couple of stairs, a room with a kingsize four-poster bed and an armoire. Beyond is a bathroom with a jacuzzi tub big enough for two, a separate shower, and his and her sinks. "European romance in Southern New England," one guest said of her stay here.

A continental breakfast of fruits, juices, granola, cereal, homemade muffins and breads is taken in the inn's sun room. Dinner is served nightly in three serene, candlelit rooms downstairs (see Dining Spots).

Doubles, $85 to $125; suite, $135.

The Simsbury Inn, 397 Hopmeadow St., Box 287, Simsbury 06089. (203) 651-5700.

New in 1988 and stylish as can be, this is really a sleek, gracious hotel, with concierge service for all 100 rooms and a front-desk staff dressed in morning coats. A fireplace warms the soaring lobby with its parquet floors that lead to a gift shop and the Nutmeg Cafe coffee shop. Upstairs is Twigs, a lounge with a semi-circular bar flanked by stools carved like saddles with horse hooves for feet. Guests pass a wine cellar along the hallway to Evergreens, the inn's main restaurant (see dining spots). An indoor pool opens to the outside in summer and adjoins an exercise room with whirlpool and sauna.

Up the elevators are curving hallways leading to the light and pleasant guest rooms

Historic country manor has been converted into Simsbury 1820 House.

on three floors. Pineapples top the headboards of the beds, each covered with custom-designed pastel spreads that are the inn's signature. Lace curtains or draperies, antique clocks, remote-control TVs, closets with removable coat hangers and two double beds or one kingsize are standard. Bathrooms have superior lighting, solid brass fixtures, mini-refrigerators, built-in hair dryers and a basket of the inn's own amenities, including a sewing kit. Beds are turned down nightly and fresh towels are added to the ample supply on hand.

The living room of each suite is attractive in Colonial Williamsburg style with a chintz sofa, an oriental rug over deep blue carpeting, a round table circled by four Queen Anne chairs and a TV with VCR hidden in an armoire. Another TV and a kingsize four-poster on a raised platform are in the adjoining bedroom. Extra touches like electric shoe polishers set the inn apart.

Breakfast is available in the coffee shop or dining room.

Doubles, $120, EP; suites, $175 to $350.

The Barney House, 11 Mountain Spring Road, Farmington 06032. (203) 677-9735.
You can live as the Farmington gentry do in this stately 1832 mansion, situated amid formal gardens on a winding street of secluded estates. It was donated by the family of the head of the Hartford Electric Light Co. to the University of Connecticut Foundation, which turned it into a low-key educational conference center and a B&B of character.

Business magazines and conference accoutrements are evident in the main-floor rooms, among them two dining rooms, a great hall lit by crystal chandeliers, a fireplaced library, and spacious porches framed with wisteria and awash with wicker. They give way on the second and third floors to seven unusually spacious rooms with private baths. Only the fact that six have twin beds hints at the conference-center use. The double bed in the third floor's Yale Room "is for the honeymooners," our guide pointed out. The smallest room in the house with lots of angles and ells, it's big enough to accommodate a twin bed as well.

Each room is distinguished by high ceilings, tall windows fronted by free-standing plants, well-worn oriental rugs and period furniture. Each has a small TV set and a phone. The rear Farmington Room is especially appealing, with huge closets, an

B&B guests are welcome at Barney House, suburban mansion turned into conference center.

enormous bath with separate shower and tub, and a pink chaise longue for enjoying the many books. Through the window you can watch the sun set over a pond.

Guests enjoy the grounds, particularly the open side lawn, the formal gardens with a Victorian greenhouse whose lettuce and herbs later turn up in the dining room, and the long, deep swimming pool. They also enjoy a continental breakfast of juice, cereal and a basket of fresh fruits, muffins and breads in the roomy second-floor hall where a sunny window seat is awash in pillows. A small refrigerator in the third-floor hall contains sodas and tonic water, and a hot pot is at the ready for tea or coffee.

If they're lucky, overnight guests may happen onto a conference and enjoy a fine luncheon buffet for $12 or a dinner of highly regarded new American cuisine (prices vary, depending on the fare). Two chefs prepare meals for the conferences, and overnight guests are welcome to eat by prior arrangement. A typical dinner might be assorted hors d'oeuvres, grilled lobster with saffron mayonnaise and tropical fruit, a salad of greenhouse lettuce, grilled rack of lamb with brandied mushroom sauce and stir-fried vegetables, and a tuscan rum cake with ice cream.

Doubles, $85.

The Farmington Inn, 827 Farmington Ave., Farmington 06032. (203) 677-2861.

Totally gutted and refurbished in 1988, the old Farmington Motor Inn was transformed into an inn of taste and exceptional value. We barely recognize the place where we stayed during a house-hunting trip nearly two decades earlier.

More than most refurbished motels, this seems like an inn, from its lovely reception area with a fireplace, a couple of comfortable seating groupings and a basket of shiny red apples, to the jaunty second-floor dining area. A continental-plus breakfasts of fruit, cereals, muffins and pastries is served here.

Seventy-two rooms and "junior suites" go off interior hallways. Each has a recessed door beneath an overhead spotlight and bears a brass nameplate — "like entering your own home or apartment," as gregarious young manager Glenn Faria puts it. Rooms have king or two double beds and are decorated in country or traditional style. The country involves light pine furniture and overstuffed club chairs. The traditional means dark cherry furniture, teal carpeting and mauve Queen Anne wing chairs. Framed small pieces of handmade quilts adorn the walls. Bathrooms have lucite fixtures, separate vanities, and baskets of Lord & Mayfair toiletries.

The TVs are hidden in armoires in the junior suites, far from the bed and at an awkward angle from the sofas in the oversize rooms. With swagged draperies and substantial furnishings in teal and pink decor, the suites for $105 represent unusual value.

Doubles, $80 to $105.

Avon Old Farms Hotel, Routes 10 and 44, Box 961, Avon 06001. (203) 677-1651 or (800) 228-1651.

What started long ago as an ordinary motel has grown like Topsy up and around a hill through two major additions and many levels into first an inn and now a hotel. The original motel with exterior doorways remains opposite the main entrance and the large, homey lobby where coffee is put out all day near the fireplace. Above the lobby, a long second floor curves around to become the main floor, and eventually the visitor enters the grand new wing, a soaring spectacle of three marble floors with an open lobby, curving staircases and an elevator.

The 164 rooms have kingsize or two double beds or a queensize bed with pullout sofa. They are distinguished by handsome watercolors of Farmington Valley scenes — more than 400 originals in all — and the current month of the Travelers Insurance Cos. calendars of Currier & Ives etchings framed on the walls.

Rooms increase in size and price as they wind up the hill. Those in the new Georgian-style wing adopt a luxury-hotel style with kingsize pencil-post beds, stenciled borders matching the fabrics, remote TVs and bathroom scales. Many have woodland views. The mini-suites have sofas and three Queen Anne chairs.

Seasons Cafe, which includes a semi-circular back room with windows looking out onto the trees, is colorful in pink, green and white with balloon curtains festooning the view and green beams on the ceiling. It

Soaring lobby at Avon Old Farms Hotel.

serves three meals daily, tending toward simple fare like baked scrod, grilled shrimp and petite filet mignon (dinner prices, $7.95 to $9.25).

There are an exercise room and sauna, and the twenty acres of grounds include a stream and a pool.

Doubles, $85 to $150, EP.

Hartford Marriott Hotel/Farmington, 15 Farm Springs Road, Farmington 06032. (203) 678-1000.

A deluxe suburban hotel, this low-slung structure opened near the end of a forested office park in 1982 and did so well that a three-story wing in 1987 added 42 more rooms, 34 of them on a concierge level. The 381 rooms are spacious and individually decorated. Many have small balconies.

The setting is pleasant, hidden in the trees off Interstate 84 with roundabout roads upon which to walk or jog, outdoor tennis courts, and indoor and outdoor swimming pools and a jacuzzi. The hotel has all the urban amenities of a staffed health club, a video game room and a lively lounge frequented by suburban singles.

The casual **Village Green** restaurant serves an ample luncheon buffet for $7.50 as well as a varied menu for lunch and dinner (entrees from $9.15 for tortellini Italiano to $15.50 for shrimp tempura or sirloin steak).

The main dining room is **Champignon,** unexpectedly small and intimate on two levels centered by a lighted aquarium full of exotic fish. Dressed in pink, it's quiet and romantic for dinner — perhaps cioppino over pasta, broiled shrimp platter, Cajun swordfish, veal with peaches or prime rib. Straightforward seafood is the theme, at prices from $13.75 to $23.95. Lunches are in the $6.95 to $9.95 range.

Doubles, $126 to $135, EP; weekends, $99.

Dining Spots

Apricots, 1591 Farmington Ave., Farmington. (203) 673-5405.

Outside on the jaunty terrace beside the Farmington River. Inside on the enclosed porch, its windows taking full advantage of the view, its white walls painted whimsically with branches of apricots. Beyond in a more formal dining room of brick and oak. Or downstairs in a cozy pub with exposed pipes painted with more apricots. These are the varied settings offered by one of the Hartford area's more appealing restaurants.

The food is usually equal to the setting, thanks to the inspiration of Ann Howard, the Farmington resident known for her cooking lessons and later the Ann Howard Cookery, from which she and her staff cater some of the best parties in town. In 1982 she reopened an abandoned French restaurant in an old trolley barn sandwiched between Route 4 and the river, calling it Apricots, "a juicy pub."

We know folks who eat dinner at least once a week in the cozy, convivial pub, but we prefer the upstairs porch with its view, even though the glass on the windowside tables sets our teeth on edge. For lunch, we've enjoyed the spinach and strawberry as well as the cobb salads, pizza a la Mexicaine, the specialty chicken pot pie, fettuccine with crab and mushrooms, grilled lime chicken and wonderful mussels ($3.50 to $9.95).

At night, when at least the inner dining room (without the glass-topped tables) turns serene, entrees range from $13.50 for pasta of the day to $28 for roast rack of lamb with a mustard hollandaise. Roast quail with a cranberry beurre blanc, poached sea scallops in a champagne watercress cream, and sauteed veal with sweetbreads are seasonal favorites. Start with lobster and brie in phyllo or a multi-layer terrine of scallops. Finish with apricot gelato, frozen nougat glace or one of the heavenly cakes — marquise au chocolate, charlotte russe, New York cheesecake with strawberry puree and lemon roulade, all $4.50 — for an experience to remember.

The wine list has been upgraded lately with a wide selection of wines priced from $12 to $155.

The friendly staff, some of whom have been at Apricots for years, treats customers like old friends, many of whom are.

Lunch, Monday-Saturday 11:30 to 2:30; dinner nightly, 5 to 10.

Simsbury 1820 House, 751 Hopmeadow St., Simsbury. (203) 658-7658.

The dark and intimate lower floor of the Simsbury House provides a refined setting for some of the valley's better meals. Brick archways, deep green walls and carpeting, reproduction Chippendale chairs, hunting prints and deep green-rimmed china service plates on white linens are the backdrop for three cozy dining rooms and a small bar. A single rose graces each table.

Trademark items like steamed fillet of sole salad with spinach and fresh vegetables popped up on the menu after Hartford restaurateur John Chapin signed on as a management consultant in 1988. Other luncheon favorites are eaglewood salad with

Porch dining room overlooks Farmington River at Apricots.

smoked Canadian bacon and turkey, braised lamb stew, Maryland lump crab cakes with Creole sauce and an omelet of asparagus, lobster and brie ($5.95 to $14.95).

At dinner, we liked the grilled bluepoint oysters served chilled with a splash of pernod and a rather diminutive trio of smoked fish with lime-horseradish sauce ($7.75 and $8.25 respectively). The eight entrees ($17 to $22) include poached halibut with a basil-orange hollandaise garnished with chopped pistachio nuts, braised Norwegian salmon with leeks and tomatoes, veal with wild mushrooms and tomatoes in madeira sauce, and sauteed tournedos of beef with roasted garlic and balsamic vinegar. We can vouch for the roast duckling sauced with black currants and white port wine and the sliced loin of lamb with two sauces, one of basil and curry and the other a rosemary brown sauce garnished with wild mushrooms and Holland peppers. Good, crusty French bread comes with; salads are extra.

Among desserts are chocolate terrine on a raspberry puree, peach torte, and chef Tim Smith's favorite, French chocolate cake with vanilla sauce. The Simsbury House coffee — with chocolate liqueur, grand marnier, whipped cream and orange zest — is said to be lethal.

Lunch, Monday-Saturday 11:30 to 2; dinner nightly, 5:30 to 9 or 10; Sunday brunch, 11:30 to 2.

Hop Brook, 77 West St. (Route 167), Simsbury. (203) 651-0267.

Go here for the ambiance — a restored 300-year-old mill beside Hop Brook waterfall, with dining on a multitude of levels, some of them with windows right beside the falls.

Go here also for the food, a contemporary melange without pretense. Three pasta dishes, grilled chicken and more seafood have lightened up the new menu. Among dinner specialties ($10.95 to $17.95) are buttermilk fried chicken with a maple syrup and pecan glaze, turkey pot pie, roast duckling with a maple syrup and cranberry glaze, two versions of veal, calves liver laced with applejack, and rack of lamb with cheddar crust. Prime rib with popover, filet mignon and steaks come in assorted sizes and prices from $15.95 to $24.95.

Appetizers are a mixed bag, from Cajun shrimp in a spiced beer sauce to country pate with homemade chutney and Maryland crab cakes with homemade ketchup. Ditto for desserts, from apple crisp and chocolate bread pudding to rum pecan pie. There's a light tavern menu as well. The all-American wine list has unusual reach and pleasant prices, especially the house Sonoma wines with Hop Brook labels.

The grister's platter of chicken tarragon salad, tuna salad, fresh fruit, vegetables and smoked cheese ($5.95) makes a good lunch. Almost every entree, from banana nut pancakes to smoked salmon omelet, appeals on the $10.95 champagne brunch menu.

With interesting place settings (circular service mats with the restaurant's striking logo and sprays of flowers in white china dogs atop dark green stained-wood tables centered with copper inlays) and those great views from so many different levels, the whole place is a winner.

Lunch, Monday-Friday 11:30 to 2:30, Saturday noon to 3; dinner, Monday-Saturday, 5 to 10 or 11; Sunday, brunch 10:30 to 2:30, dinner 4 to 9.

The Chart House, Routes 10 & 185, Simsbury. (203) 658-0059.

The Chart House chain sure knows how to pick its locations — this one the 1780 Pettibone Tavern, which has offered respite to the traveler for two centuries. The mustard-colored inn has tables in a ramble of properly historic rooms as well as two pretty sun porches, summery all year long in green and white wicker. Even the enormous upstairs lounge is comforting with leather sofas, Hitchcock chairs, oriental rugs and wood artifacts all around.

Ask one of the waiters in Hawaiian shirts to tell you about the ghost of the house, who can be seen in a portrait in the front foyer (ours was a believer after she'd heard him call his name). She's been known to drop dishes, make glassware move and the like. But she only operates at quiet times, which are rare when the Chart House is open, such is its popularity.

The menus and the table tops bear the chain's trademark sea charts. Entrees, served with unlimited salad and fresh breads, are priced from $13.45 for Santa Fe or teriyaki chicken to $19.95 for baked stuffed shrimp or shrimp teriyaki. Top sirloin, New York steak, filet mignon with bearnaise and prime rib are featured, and mahi-mahi, broiled swordfish and baked stuffed scrod could be specials. Vegetables (even wild rice and baked potato) are extra. The smoked fish and cheese plate ($5.75) is a good appetizer and mud pie is the dessert of choice.

Dinner, Monday-Saturday 5:30 to 10 or 11, Sunday 4 to 9.

Avon Old Farms Inn, Routes 44 & 10, Avon. (203) 677-2818.

Established in 1757, this is one of the twenty oldest inns in the United States, although now it's strictly a restaurant (a hotel of similar name but separate ownership is across the street).

Seven dining rooms sprawl through a series of additions and are usually filled. Book early and then walk the length of the building to the Forge Room. A splendid tavern atmosphere is this, with rough dark stone walls, flagstone floors, cozy booths made from old horse stalls, and lots of equestrian accessories hanging from dark beams. Bright red tablecloths and red leather chairs add color to the room, which is one of the most atmospheric around.

The Sunday brunch for $10.95, including two glasses of champagne, has been voted best in the state for ten years by Connecticut magazine. Set up in the main dining room, the spread is ladled out by twenty servers at two long banquet tables, then taken to one of the six other rooms, which have enough nooks and crannies to offer privacy. Up to 700 people may be served at three seatings.

American food in a quintessential Yankee setting is featured at lunch and dinner, when service is personal and each dining room functions almost as its own restaurant. The

Simsbury Inn offers stylish accommodations plus gracious dining in Evergreens.

extensive dinner menu (entrees $16.95 to $21.95) goes from liver pate and herring in sour cream through baked onion soup, a salad of mozzarella and sun-dried tomatoes, to seafood Rockefeller and chateaubriand. Veal sentino, a house specialty, combines tender medallions with layers of Danish cheese, asparagus and mushrooms. Other entrees include chicken with peaches and grapes, broiled salmon bearnaise, roast duckling bigarade and tournedos with two sauces. It's festive dining, and the English trifle is a masterpiece among desserts.

Lunch, Tuesday-Saturday noon to 2:30; dinner, 5:30 to 9:30 or 10; Sunday, brunch 11:30 to 3:30, dinner 5:30 to 8:30.

Evergreens, Simsbury Inn, 397 Hopmeadow St., Simsbury. (203) 651-5700.

The gracious main dining room at this new inn has wood pillars, brass sconces, lace draperies and a mural of 18th-century Simsbury. Tables are set with English bone china, crystal and sterling silver.

The fare served at the inn's opening party outdid any we've seen or savored in years of attendance at such events. Critics have written since that it's uneven and marred by slow service, although we noted neither at a private function a year later.

Dinners begin with the plunking of a lemon slice in each water glass and end with the presentation of warm, scented towels. Following a complimetnary plate of hummus with pita bread, you might order a lobster turnover, escargots in phyllo, eggplant gateaux or black peppercorn pasta prepared tableside with smoked goose and chanterelles ($5.95 to $8.25).

Entrees generally run from $17.50 for roast free-range chicken with sausage cornbread stuffing to $23.95 for veal chop on a tomato fondue. More costly are lobster for $25.95 and rack of lamb, $42.95 for two. Poached halibut, salmon with a scallop mousseline, roast rib of beef with a Vermont cheddar popover, medallions of venison, beef Wellington and pheasant with a pumpkin frangelico sauce are seasonal choices.

Most of the house-made desserts ($3.50) are triumphs, among them key lime pie, white chocolate mousse and pumpkin cheesecake. Wines come from a cellar visible off the entry hall.

Besides an a la carte menu, an interesting luncheon buffet is served for $11.95.

Lunch, Monday-Friday 11:30 to 2:30; dinner, Monday-Saturday 5:30 to 9:30; Sunday brunch, 11 to 3.

Cafe Chanticleer, Riverdale Farms, Route 10, Avon. (203) 677-6026.

A standing sheep, attired in black vest and white gloves, holds the blackboard specials at this restaurant in the middle of the shops of Riverdale Farms, where one of us has enjoyed many a good lunch and shopping spree with "the girls." Lately it has expanded and serves dinners.

Advertising itself as "a touch of Normandy," Chantecleer sports a French country look. The original dining room (now with a small bar and serving a blackboard pub menu at night) has tile floors, bare tables, ladderback chairs and lace curtains. Adjacent is a popular outdoor dining porch. The newer dining room has similar tables and chairs amid spotlit paintings, carpeting and a rounded wood ceiling.

The lunch menu is basic — a handful of burgers, sandwiches, croissants and salads in the $3.75 to $6.25 range — because the list of specials is extensive. The chantiburger with bacon, cheese, onions and green pepper is terrific. We're fond of the croissant filled with spinach souffle and the spinach and mandarin orange salad with almonds and a sweet and sour dressing. Soups here are outstanding and could include seafood bisque or curried chicken.

Country pate served with fresh fruit and a mini baguette or baked brie topped with almonds make good starters at dinner. Try the raspberry chicken salad ($6.50) and make it a meal. Or go on to entrees like black cherry cognac glazed chicken, grilled shrimp in an orange-ginger glaze, scallops dijonnaise and baked sole stuffed with shrimp and broccoli. Prices go from $8.95 for pasta of the day to $17.95 for New York sirloin with cracked pepper in a burgundy sauce.

The acclaimed desserts include chocolate truffle cake, hot apple spice cake with whipped cream, raspberry charlotte russe and chocolate triple torte. The cafe has a small but adequate and reasonable wine list. One of the good aperitifs is champagne kir, made with homemade raspberry sauce.

Lunch, Monday-Saturday 11:30 to 3; dinner, Tuesday-Saturday 5 to 9.

Lily's, 160 Albany Turnpike (Route 44), Canton. (203) 693-8558.

Named in memory of co-owner Barbara McCarthy's mother, Lily's is a tiny bistro in a little white house where the front porch is painted pink and the picture window is outlined in white lights. Barbara and her husband Robert, the extraordinary chef, put the place together in 1988 with a shoestring budget and a lot of sweat.

Ten or so tables are topped with paper mats and votive candles in etched glasses. Bentwood chairs, bare floors ("we stripped four layers to get to the hardwood," says Barbara) and funky old cans and packages — remember Duz? — are the decor. In the corner are shelves with old linens and a mannequin with ribbons for hair. Classical music plays in the background, and the atmosphere is friendly and unpretentious.

You might think the food here would be casual as well, but at night it takes on a continental flair. Bob, who has had thirteen years of experience in country clubs, restaurants and as a caterer, cooks impeccably fresh food in a down-home manner (roast loin of pork with pan gravy and mashed potatoes is one popular dish) but with elegant touches. Along with a thick and hearty lentil soup, we sampled escargots in mushroom caps ($5.95) in an ethereal sauce, so good we asked for more bread with which to soak it up. Clams casino ($5.95) and baked brie en croute ($6.95 for two) might also be on the menu.

The blackboard usually lists six entrees, priced from $12.95 to $15.95. Before them comes a salad of mixed greens topped by shredded carrots with choice of vinaigrette, honey-mustard or a creamy french with herb dressing. Our party of three was delighted with a perfectly cooked salmon filet with dill-lemon butter sauce, sea scallops sauteed with mushrooms and garlic butter, and linguini with clams, scallops and shrimp. All portions were generous, fresh as could be, and served with good rice pilaf and a side dish of summer squash in a zesty tomato sauce.

The McCarthys seem to love bananas. You might find banana sherbet (sensational), banana chocolate mousse or grilled banana bread for dessert. Chocolate pecan torte, lemon cheesecake and warm gingerbread are others.

At lunch Lily's serves hot sandwiches like sauteed breast of chicken with bacon and cheddar on a bun, cold ones like egg salad made with caramelized onions, and salads, in the $3.25 to $5.25 range. At breakfast on weekends, you'll find that grilled banana bread (the recipe from Barbara's mother), and her aunt Sonia's sour cream coffee cake, as well as buttermilk biscuits, omelets, corned beef hash and homefries.

Breakfast, Saturday 8 to 11:30, Sunday 8 to 2; lunch, Tuesday-Saturday 11:30 to 3; dinner, Tuesday-Saturday, 5:30 to 9. BYOB. No credit cards.

One-Way Fare, 4 Railroad St., Simsbury. (203) 658-4477.

One of the valley's restaurants with staying power is this eclectic, noisy place in which on one side of you, a portly white-haired man in tennis shorts quaffs a gin and tonic and eats fish chowder while on the other side, four "ladies who lunch" figure out their check to the nth degree after enjoying a large pot of crabmeat fondue.

Ensconced since 1975 in Simsbury's old railway station with all the appropriate decor, this is not for quiet, leisurely dining. We found the bar that runs the length of the main room jammed even at mid-afternoon on a Monday. The Underground Railway lounge downstairs with original brick and stone walls is lively with entertainment at night.

The all-day menu is presented on a small ticket-like paper at the table without prices and scrawled on blackboards around the room with prices. You may get a strained neck trying to decide among things like tomato-rice soup with an overstuffed sandwich, chili, cheese fondue ($8.95 for four), mushroom quiche, station salad (ceviche for $6.50) and steak and stout, at $7.95 the most expensive item we could see last time we were there. The waiter said specials change all day and go up to $12.95 for tenderloin at night.

The casual formula with limited but changing specials obviously works, because the place is usually jammed. The New York Times Sunday brunch is a local tradition.

Open daily from 11:30 a.m. to 11:30 p.m. or later; Sunday brunch, 11:30 to 2:45.

Diversions

Stanley-Whitman House, 37 High St., Farmington. 677-9222. The most painstakingly accurate restoration said to have ever been undertaken in a New England house preceded the 1988 reopening of this 1660 structure that houses the Farmington Museum, one of the best examples of a 17th-century frame overhang house in New England. With rare diamond-paned windows, it is furnished with early American pieces, many the gifts of local residents. It offers a fascinating glimpse into the life and conditions enjoyed — or endured — by the early colonists. Open May-October, Wednesday-Sunday noon to 4; Sundays in early spring and late fall, noon to 4; closed January-February. Adults, $3.

Massacoh Plantation, 800 Hopmeadow St., Simsbury. Three centuries of Simsbury history dating to Indian days are recreated in this little complex of buildings most interesting for its lofty reproduction of a 1670 meeting house, nicely hedged and screened from a nondescript shopping plaza. The adjacent 1771 Elisha Phelps House shows the furnishings of an early tavern and canal hotel. The low-key complex also has a 1740 school house, a pastor's cottage, sheds full of Victorian carriages and, surprise, the Arlene McDaniel gallery of contemporary art and sculpture. Open May-October, daily 1 to 4 (guided tours at 1 and 2:30); Phelps House also open November-April, weekdays 1 to 4. Adults, $3.

Farmington Valley Arts Center, Avon Park North, Route 44, Avon. A park-like setting of century-old buildings contains a complex of studios for twenty artists, who open at their whim but often can be seen at work on weekends. The Fisher Gallery Shop is open all year, Wednesday-Saturday 11 to 4. Its annual Christmas show and sale is a great place to pick up holiday gifts. Free.

The Farmington Polo Grounds, Town Farm Road off Route 4, is the scene each May of the nationally recognized Children's Services horse show and country fair. On selected weekends in summer and fall it draws huge crowds for the the Farmington Antiques Weekend and crafts expositions.

Heublein Tower, Talcott Notch State Park, Route 185, Simsbury. The landmark tower built as a summer home by the Gilbert Heublein family (of Heublein liquor fame) atop Talcott Mountain is open to the public as an observation tower and small museum. The four-state view from the top is especially smashing during fall foliage, but worth the 1.2-mile climb from the parking lot at any time. Along the ridge you may see members of the Connecticut Hang Gliding Association soaring from the cliffside trail that's considered one of the best gliding spots anywhere. Open free, April 15 to Labor Day, Thursday-Sunday 10 to 5; Labor Day-November, daily.

Hot-Air Ballooning. For reasons best known to those involved, the same mountain and valley that are so good for hang-gliding are also favorable for balloonists. No fewer than six outfits now float over the area, presenting a colorful spectacle at dawn and sometimes at dusk. The hour's ride is quite an event, which must explain the price ($175 to $200 per person). Boland Balloon Rides and KAT Balloons Inc. both leave from the "balloon farm" off Meadow Road, Farmington. Matt Fenechal of Airventures leaves from Simsbury Farms or Weatogue. Reservations are required long in advance.

The **Farmington River** is popular with canoeists and bird-watchers. Hikers can walk along sections of its banks in Farmington, Avon and Simsbury. Water-skiers may be seen jumping in the Collinsville section of Canton. The latest sport is tubing. Young and old alike enjoy riding double-inflatable tubes down the river from Satan's Kingdom State Park in New Hartford to Canton. North American Canoe Tours rents tubes at Satan's Kingdom from Memorial Day to Labor Day for $7.50 a ride.

Hiking and **bird-watching** also are attractions of McLean Game Refuge in Simsbury and the scenic Metropolitan District Commission reservoirs astride Talcott Mountain in West Hartford.

Shopping. This sophisticated suburban area provides a variety of shopping opportunities, from the upscale stores (Lord & Taylor, Brooks Brothers, Abercrombie's and such) at **Westfarms Mall** on the Farmington-West Hartford border to free-standing shops throughout the valley.

Farmington center offers **Tweeds & Tees** and **Eleanor Rose** for women's classic clothing and the **Ann Howard Cookery** for sensational breads and maybe a corned beef and swiss croissant to take out for a picnic along the river. Farther out Route 4 in ever-increasing numbers are shops like **Design Forum, Lexington Gardens** and the **Natural Gourmet,** an extensive grocery store that sells hummus sandwiches, broccoli quiche, lentil salad and the like.

Worth a trip in itself — if you like things Scandinavian — is the **Tre Kronor Gift Shop** at 248 Main St., always full of choice Scandinavian crystal, stainless steel, colorful painted horses and trivets, cards and much more. Upstairs is a little coffee shop

Fine Colonial Revival country house is home of prized Hill-Stead Museum.

where you can get open-face sandwiches on Swedish rye. Priced from $1.95 to $2.95, they include smoked salmon and sliced eggs with sardines. Next door at **Scandinavian Foods,** Carl Dahlberg cooks things that smell great and purveys all the foods that Scandinavians from across the state seek out, especially at Christmas time.

An historic atmosphere pervades the site and shops of **Old Avon Village** along Route 44. Browsers like the setting and such unusual stores as the **Player Piano Emporium, Little Silver Shop,** the **Tinker's Drum** for handmade gifts, the **Candle Shop, Blumen Laden** for floral arrangements, **Herbs & Whey** for natural foods, **Le Chapeaux, Kids & Company** and **Roxie Taylor** vintage clothing.

Nearby is Avon's newer **Riverdale Farms,** which advertises "today's shopping amid yesterday's charms." A 19th-century dairy farm provides the base for such trendy shops as **Oxford Baggs Outfitters, Jillian Thomas** women's apparel, **C.J.'s Paper Place** and the **Yellow Daffodil,** a wondrous ramble of rooms full of gifts for all occasions.

The best shops in Simsbury are gathered at **Simsburytown Shops,** which has the **Salt Box** for fashions, **La Grande Pantrie, Book & Candle** and **Bathtique.**

Extra-Special

Hill-Stead Museum, 35 Mountain Road, Farmington. (203) 677-9064.

This cultural treasure is important on three fronts: art, architecture and furnishings. The 29-room white clapboard house with rambling wings and a Mount Vernon facade is considered one of the finest Colonial Revival country houses in America. Willed as a museum by its last occupant, architect Theodate Pope Riddle, it's a pleasantly personal masterpiece of a mansion that remains as she left it. Hung on its walls is the matchless collection of one of the earliest American collectors of Impressionist paintings before they became fashionable — what Henry James in 1907 called "wondrous examples of Manet, of Degas, of Claude Monet, of Whistler." The furnishings include remarkable mementoes of an early 20th-century family, from Corinthian pottery and Chinese porcelain to a first edition of Samuel Johnson's *Dictionary* and a handwritten letter from Franklin D. Roosevelt. As you are guided on an hour-long tour, it is "as if the owners, having to be away for the afternoon, nevertheless invited you to stop for a time to delight in their house and collection," as director Katherine Warwick writes in the new guide to this priceless place. Open Wednesday-Friday 2 to 5, Saturday and Sunday 1 to 5; closed mid-January to mid-February. Adults, $5.

Lake Waramaug provides backdrop for wines at Hopkins Vineyard.

Litchfield-Lake Waramaug
Connecticut's Colonial Country

Nestled in the hills of Northwest Connecticut, picturesque Lake Waramaug boasts an alpine setting that appeals enough to a couple of Austrian innkeepers to call it home. Nearby is Litchfield, the quintessential Colonial Connecticut town preserved not as a restoration in the tradition of Williamsburg, with which it has been compared, but as a living museum community.

The lake and the town, though ten miles apart, are linked by a mystique of timeless isolation.

Hills rise sharply above the boomerang-shaped Lake Waramaug. Its sylvan shoreline is flanked by a state park, fine summer homes, and four country inns. With little commercialism, it's enveloped in a country feeling, away from it all.

Litchfield, a small county seat whose importance long has transcended its borders, is perched atop the crest of a ridge. Its beautiful North and South streets are lined with gracious homes and history (George Washington slept here, Harriet Beecher Stowe was born here, Ethan Allen lived here, the nation's first law school and its first academy for girls were founded here). The village is so preserved and prized that only in the last few years has it attracted inns and the kind of shops that affluence breeds.

Between the hills and lakes are fine natural and low-key attractions — Connecticut's largest nature sanctuary, a world-famous garden center, two farm wineries, state parks and forests. Connecticut's entire Northwest Corner has much to commend it, but there's no more choice a slice than Litchfield and Lake Waramaug.

376

Inn Spots

The Boulders Inn, Route 45, New Preston 06777. (203) 868-0541.

Its setting just across the road from Lake Waramaug, its handsome and comfortable sitting room and its fine kitchen make this an unusually appealing inn. Built as a private home in 1895, it has been a small inn since about 1950. Kees and Ulla Adema of Fairfield, he a ship's broker from Holland and she born in Germany, took over the inn in 1988 as a retirement venture. "We were thinking of a three-room B&B," recalls Ulla. "Instead, we bought an inn with a restaurant and now we seem to be running a restaurant with an inn."

The food operation (see Dining Spots) keeps them busy, but the Ademas are making gradual improvements to the inn's five guest rooms and the eight contemporary rooms in outlying duplex chalets. They also were adding a rear carriage house in 1989, with three more guest rooms and their own family quarters. After its completion in the summer, they planned to create a sixth guest room in the inn in the space they vacated.

The inn rooms come with plush carpeting, comfortable sofas or chairs, and king or queensize beds, a couple of them covered with handsome quilts. Three rooms that face the lake have large, cushioned window seats that take in the view, and the South West corner room has its own balcony. The rear corner suite has a kingsize bed and separate sitting room. All have private baths, as do the eight rooms in duplex chalets scattered along the hillside behind the inn. The chalets are in great demand because they're like private country houses, some with refrigerators and second bedrooms. Each has a deck with a glimpse of the water through the woods. Five with sofas and chairs grouped around free-standing fireplaces are especially popular with the New Yorkers who comprise the bulk of the Boulders clientele.

Back in the inn, a basement game room offers pingpong and skittles, a small den has a color TV and the dark-paneled living room, with picture windows overlooking the lake (binoculars are provided), is a lovely mix of antiques and groupings of sofas and wing chairs in reds, blues and chintz. In one corner are book shelves and a stereo with many records. A Russian samovar has been used to dispense tea in winter months, and guests also enjoy cocktails here.

In summer, swimming, sailing and canoeing are favorite pastimes. If you feel lazy, just sit in the beach house's wicker swing and watch the changing moods of the lake.

Full breakfast for inn guests is served by the windows in the six-sided Lake Dining Room. A help-yourself cold buffet is set up with fresh fruit and juices, prunes, melon in season, cereals and coffee cake. Eggs any style, omelets, french toast and pecan, apple or blueberry pancakes with bacon, sausage or ham can be ordered and are accompanied by English muffins or homemade whole wheat toast.

Doubles, $95, B&B; $160, MAP.

Toll Gate Hill, Route 202, Litchfield 06759. (203) 567-4545.

The rural 1745 landmark home near the Torrington town line in which Captain William Bull once took in travelers on the Hartford-Albany stage route was handsomely restored and reopened as a small inn and restaurant in 1983. Inviting it is, situated back from the road in a stand of trees, its red frame exterior dimly illuminated at night and appearing to the traveler much as it must have more than two centuries ago.

Such has been the demand for rooms that innkeeper Fritz Zivic opened four more guest rooms in the adjacent "school house" and started construction of a new building with ten more guest rooms and a lobby/reception area in 1989.

Overnight guests at the inn — listed on the National Register of Historic Places — are in for a treat. When we last were there, the most choice rooms were those in the school house, splashily decorated with comfort in mind (plus direct-dial telephones and cable TV for business travelers). Fritz's wife Ann, a Superior Court judge, did the decorating, leaning to coordinated Hinson fabrics, canopy queensize beds, and upholstered chairs and loveseats. A couple of suites have fireplaces, and the bathrooms are outfitted with 4711 and Pavlova colognes.

The nicest rooms in the main inn are the three larger ones on the second floor, each with a working fireplace. But all have modern bathrooms, air-conditioning, comfortable sitting areas with upholstered chairs or loveseats, sprightly Laura Ashley-style decor and color-coordinated fabrics.

A small parlor for house guests is located on the second-floor landing next to the ballroom. Continental breakfasts of juice and muffins baked by chef Michael Louchen's wife are served in the rooms or in summer on the outdoor patio.

Doubles, $90 to $100; suites, $130. Closed most of March.

Hopkins Inn, Hopkins Road, New Preston 06777. (203) 868-7295.

This landmark yellow inn astride a hill above Lake Waramaug is known far and wide for its cuisine (see Dining Spots), and we often recommend it when asked where to take visitors for lunch in the country. Its reputation was built by Swiss-born innkeepers and has been continued since the late 1970s by Austrian Franz Schober and his wife Beth.

Built in 1847 as a summer guest house, the Federal structure with several additions was converted from a boarding house into an inn in 1945, and the guest rooms have been considerably enhanced by the Schobers. Warmed only by small heating units (thus used only from April through mid-November), the nine guest rooms on the second and third floors have been sparingly but comfortably furnished with brass or wood bedsteads, thick carpeting, floral wallpapers, chests of drawers and the odd rocker. Seven of the nine rooms have private baths.

Guests share a couple of small main-floor parlors with restaurant patrons, and may use the inn's private beach on the lake. There's no better vantage point for lake-watching than the expansive outdoor dining terrace, shaded by a giant horse chestnut tree and distinguished by striking copper and wrought-iron chandeliers and lanterns. Breakfast is available for house guests.

Doubles, $42 to $50, EP.

The Inn on Lake Waramaug, North Shore Road, New Preston 06777. (203) 868-0563 or (800) 525-3466.

From private home to village inn to boarding house for summer guests, this has grown since the 19th century into a year-round destination resort with an indoor pool, sauna, whirlpool, game room, meals in two dining rooms or at lakeside, a beach and twenty-three guest rooms, five in the main inn and the rest in redecorated guest houses below.

This is the place for people who like activity. Barbara and Kevin Kirshner, new innkeepers for the Baron Group owners, keep things busy with traditions like lake

Inn on Lake Waramaug has evolved from original building into year-round resort.

Landmark 19th-century hilltop structure above Lake Waramaug houses Hopkins Inn.

excursions on the inn's 50-passenger Showboat in summer and horse-drawn sleigh rides in winter. Monthly special events include an old-fashioned ice harvest, maple sugaring festival, a frog jump, Scottish dancing day, Huck Finn raft race, Halloween masked ball and olympic events for turkeys (real ones, that is).

Yellow webbed lawn chairs are lined up in rows around the grounds, the better for watching all the fun.

All guest rooms have cable television and air-conditioning; eight in the guest houses have fireplaces, and many have canopy beds, maple furniture and upholstered chairs. The top of the line are the eight master bedrooms with fireplaces and water views.

Three meals a day are served in peak season in the inn's dining rooms, on the terrace or beside the lake, where hot dogs and hamburgers are barbecued at lunchtime. The Honeycomb Gift Shop was being converted into a cocktail lounge with a wood stove in 1989.

Doubles, $148 to $198, MAP.

The Birches Inn, West Shore Road, New Preston 06777. (203) 868-0229.

The dining room and a secluded waterfront location are the attractions at this rustic inn run in Alpine style since 1977 by Austrians Heinz and Christa Holl.

Of the ten guest rooms, all with private baths, the most choice are the three in the lakefront cottage across the shore road, each sharing part of an extended back porch directly over the water. They're used seasonally, and one that is good for families has four beds in a loft. One of the two guest rooms upstairs in the inn has two double beds, an assortment of chairs and a large front window onto the lake. The other five rooms are in a guest house behind the inn.

Guests have use of the private beach and boat dock; canoes and bicycles are available for rent. They also join restaurant patrons in the cozy bar, pleasantly situated with an excellent lake view.

Christina Holl is the dinner chef; her wiener schnitzel and apple strudel are renowned. Other specialties on the continental menu include Hungarian goulash soup, chicken

Kiev, sauerbraten and pork Styrian style, among more traditional entrees like chateaubriand and grilled salmon with dill sauce, priced from $11.95 to $16.95. Apple strudel, sachertorte and strawberries Romanoff are among the desserts.

Lodging rates include a full breakfast and four-course dinner. Dinner is served nightly except Tuesday; also Sunday brunch.

Doubles, $140 to $150, MAP. Closed most of March.

Litchfield Inn, Route 202, Litchfield 06759. (203) 567-4503.

Set back from the road west of the village on a vast expanse of lawn in need of more landscaping, the Litchfield Inn is a fairly new (1982) white Colonial-style inn with modern accoutrements, 31 guest rooms and a couple of suites, two restaurants, a banquet facility and plans for 70 more rooms, a function hall and a swimming pool/health club.

Furnished with early American reproduction pieces, rooms with a single double bed or two double beds have private baths, color TV and air-conditioning, and some have wet bars. Rooms that appeared sparsely appointed were being redecorated when we were there.

The formal main-floor sitting room is elegantly furnished, if a bit austere. More cozy is the Tack Room with a fireplace and comfortable armchairs. There's weekend entertainment in the **Tapping Reeve Room** bar and lounge.

Breakfast is available in the narrow, skylit Greenery. A lunch buffet for $7.50 is served in the **Joseph Harris Room,** properly decked out in hand-hewn beams, wide-plank floors, ladderback chairs and nicely spaced tables. Myriad plants, copper pots, baskets and such hang from the ceiling. An extensive dinner menu lists twenty entrees from $11.95 for pasta primavera or Boston scrod to $19.95 for three honeyed lamb chops with ginger and rosemary. Other possibilities are pepper-broiled swordfish, Jamaican pork tenderloin, veal Creole and filet mignon. Key lime mousse is a favorite dessert.

Lunch daily, 11:30 to 2:30; dinner, 5:30 to 9 or 10.

Doubles, $80.

Dining Spots

Toll Gate Hill, Route 202, Litchfield. (203) 567-4545.

Innkeeper Fritz Zivic, who founded the late Black Dog Tavern steakhouse chain in the Hartford area in the 1960s, features a changing menu of what he calls "light, unencumbered food" in two small, charming old dining rooms on the inn's main floor and upstairs in a ballroom complete with a fiddler's loft for piano or live entertainment.

His chef the last few years, Torrington native Michael Louchen, won the Connecticut Restaurant Association's seafood competition in 1988 with a ragout of Stonington clams and sauteed Long Island Sound bluefish served with grilled polenta and cucumber spaghetti. Local fans consider his meals the best in Litchfield County.

Michael features what he calls "updated New England fare" on a lengthy menu supplemented by nightly specials. The winter dinner menu listed a dozen entrees from $17 for grilled honey-glazed chicken with cranberry catsup to $24 for grilled rack of lamb with dried apricot and ginger demi-glace. We've heard rhapsodic comments about the shellfish pie, and the duck breast with maple-vinegar sauce and the pan-seared tuna with sun-dried tomatoes sound good. So do specials of roast pheasant stuffed with pheasant mousse and veal sauteed with bacon, pinenuts and porcini mushrooms.

For appetizers ($6 to $8.75), look for seafood terrine with roasted red pepper coulis, beef carpaccio on watercress or smoked salmon tartare. Desserts, prepared by a master baker from Europe who teaches at the Culinary Institute of America, are to groan over.

Priced from $4 to $5, they include bread pudding with dark rum sauce, chocolate zabaglione torte, bing cherry cheese tart and chocolate pate with grand marnier creme anglaise.

The wine list is choice and quite reasonably priced, the soups are creative and our

Corner table at Toll Gate Hill.

summer dinners a few years ago of shrimp in beer batter and sauteed sea scallops with sweet butter and braised leeks were outstanding.

The original tavern room with its dark wood, wide-plank floors and well-spaced tables covered with peach linen, Villeroy & Boch china, heavy silver and tiny lamps is attractive. Some prefer the more formal dining room with oriental rug and arched corner cupboard, while still others go for the piano music on weekends in the upstairs ballroom under a vaulted ceiling and brass chandeliers. All the dining rooms have working fireplaces.

Brunch items are offered on weekends in addition to the daily luncheon menu, which lists many of the dinner appetizers, sandwiches and entrees like sauteed fish cakes, seafood puff pastry and mixed grill ($6.95 to $10.95).

Lunch daily, noon to 3; dinner, 5:30 to 9:30 or 10:30. Closed Tuesdays November to July, and most of March.

The Boulders Inn, Route 45, New Preston. (203) 868-0541.

Boulders are a good part of the decor at this inn, jutting out from the walls of the intimate inner dining room as well as in part of the smashing six-sided addition, where, through large windows, almost every diner has a view of Lake Waramaug. Three levels of a spacious deck/terrace are the setting for lunch and cocktails in season.

Chandeliers with pierced lampshades made by innkeeper Ulla Adema hang from the ceiling. Other light is provided by hurricane lamps on the white-linened tables.

Chef Martin Carlson, who's been cooking at the Boulders for eight years, has added game dishes to the menu — pheasant in sauerkraut, rabbit with mushrooms and artichoke hearts, and venison with lingonberries the February night we were there. The limited menu is priced from $11.50 for angel-hair pasta with broccoli, red peppers and pesto to $19.75 for broiled lamb chops with tarragon butter. The menu is supplemented by up to ten specials, perhaps salmon with seafood mousse and cucumbers, cioppino or Indian spiced monkfish.

Appetizers ($4 to $6.50) could be dill-cured salmon, smoked breast of duck with sweet and sour mustard, Belgian endive with walnuts and blue cheese, goat cheese on radicchio, squid vinaigrette or potted pork. For dessert, try chocolate cake with fresh raspberries, grand marnier tart, pecan pie or a Huguenot tart of apples and nuts layered with whipped cream.

We remember from a previous dinner the tasty chicken paprikasch and the kashmir lamb in a sauce of tomatoes, ground almonds, yogurt and curry spices.

381

An extensive luncheon menu includes five or six hot dishes, among them veal curry and steak Diane, delicious salads (one is curried chicken with fresh mango) and interesting sandwiches like mozzarella pesto and open-face shrimp. Prices are in the $5.75 to $9.50 range.

Sunday brunch ($11.95) starts with a choice of appetizers like pears in port, California salad and a fresh pineapple sherbet boat. Entrees include blueberry blintz, lamb kidneys madeira, and sour cream and caviar omelet. Champagne is $2 a glass.

The wine list is reasonably priced from $10 to $38. We heartily applaud the fact that no smoking is allowed in the coveted Lake Dining Room.

Lunch in summer and foliage season, noon to 2; dinner nightly except Monday, 6 to 8:30 or 9 in summer, Wednesday-Saturday in winter; Sunday brunch.

Hopkins Inn, Hopkins Road, New Preston. (203) 368-7295.

On a warm summer day or evening, few dining spots are more inviting than the large outdoor terrace under the giant horse chestnut tree at the entrance to the Hopkins Inn. With the waters of Lake Waramaug shimmering below and a bottle of wine from the Hopkins Vineyard next door, you could imagine yourself in the Alps. No wonder Austrian chef-owner Franz Schober feels right at home.

Dining inside this 1847 Federal structure is a delight as well. Two dining rooms stretch around the lakeview side of the inn; the overflow goes to a paneled Colonial-style taproom up a few stairs. One dining room is Victorian, while the other is rustic with barnsiding and ships' figureheads on the walls.

The blackboard menu changes daily, but always includes the Austrian and Swiss dishes of the chef's heritage. Prices are surprisingly reasonable. You might start with pate maison ($2.75), baby trout or escargots ($4.75). Dinner entrees are $13.25 to $17.25 for dishes like wiener schnitzel and sweetbreads that we remember fondly from years past. In spring, you can get shad roe; Beth Schrober says her husband's roast pheasant with red cabbage and spaetzle is especially popular in fall. How about trout meuniere or backhendl with lingonberries, both in the $14 range? Vegetables are special, especially unusual things like braised romaine lettuce.

Regulars cherish the grand marnier souffle glace and strawberries Romanoff, the priciest desserts at $3.25 and $3.50 respectively. Pear Helene, creme caramel and chocolate mousse are others. The wine list has twenty cabernet sauvignons from $14 to $80 as well as four Swiss and two Austrian whites and an incredible list of bordeaux and burgundies. Finish with a flourish: Irish or Jamaican coffee for $3.25.

Lunchtime brings many of the same specialties at even lower prices. Entrees run from $6.75 for lamb curry to $9.50 for sirloin steak. It's not surprising the place is so popular.

Lunch, Tuesday-Saturday noon to 2; dinner, 6 to 9 or 10, Sunday 12:30 to 8:30; closed Monday. No lunch in April, November and December. Closed January-March.

Le Bon Coin, Route 202, Woodville. (203) 868-7763.

The small white dormered house along the road from Litchfield to New Preston is home for classic French cuisine, lovingly tendered by chef-owner William Janega, who moved from Le Parisien in Stamford in 1983 with his wife and sons to take over this off-again, on-again country establishment. He describes his cooking as "classic French, flavorful but light."

The dark, cozy barroom has copies of French Impressionist paintings on the walls and Hitchcock chairs at half a dozen small tables. On the other side of the foyer is a dining room, barely larger but brighter in country French style. Colorful La Fleur china tops the double sets of heavy white linen cloths at each table, and the rooms are most welcoming.

Dinner with flowers at Mary Dugan's.   **Dining room at the Boulders Inn.**

The oversize menu is handwritten in French with simple translations. Dinners might begin with pate of pork and duck, a pastry shell of seafood, smoked tuna or Maryland crabmeat cocktail ($5.25 to $9.50). The onion soup and shrimp-lobster bisque are classics.

The dozen entrees run from $16.50 for calves liver with raisins to $23 for filet mignon with foie gras and truffles. Dover sole, frog's legs provencale, pepper steak, duckling with black currants and sweetbreads du jour are among the offerings. Desserts include a plate of ice creams and sorbets, floating island, poached pear with raspberry sauce, chocolate rice souffle and creme caramel.

Chef Janega is proud of his wine list — mostly French — and of his new front entry, decorated with wine casks, spigots and crate labels plus some handsome stained-glass windows.

Lunch, Monday and Thursday-Saturday noon to 2; dinner, 6 to 9 or 10, Sunday 5 to 9. Closed Tuesday.

Mary Dugan's, On the Green, Litchfield. (203) 567-3161.

A well-regarded restaurant that closed in 1988 in New Milford, Mary Dugan's popped up again in early 1989 on the green in Litchfield. Judging from the crowds we saw during a weekday lunch, owner Steve Cardonsky has another winner in his new location.

A long narrow room is flanked by black booths and a row of blond-wood-edged black formica tables down the center. One wall is brick; the other has a charming mural of cows and barns. Paper mats top the tables, the chairs are windsor, the place is jolly and noisy (everyone seems to know everyone else) and the atmosphere at breakfast and lunch is most casual. At night, when white linens are used, the lights are lowered and a gorgeous arrangement of flowers is spotlit, it's a bit more formal.

For lunch we enjoyed a cup of split-pea soup, so thick a spoon could stand up in it, and a generous spinach salad with a yogurt-dill dressing. We felt the polenta with roasted red peppers, mushrooms and cheese could have used more cheese. Other possibilities on the menu that changes daily were clam chowder, burgers, a philly steak sandwich we heard was the best thing offered, a cold meatloaf sandwich and a tuna melt. Prices are in the $2.50 to $5.95 range.

The dinner menu also changes nightly, with appetizers (seafood sausage, pizza fritta, breaded deep-fried mushrooms) from $2.25 to $4.50. Main courses run from $5.50 for a hamburger with fries to $16.50 for T-bone steak with new potatoes. Granny's meatloaf, sesame-seed catfish, southern fried chicken and rack of lamb are other choices. Mary Dugan's is nothing if not eclectic.

Lemon yogurt cake, derby pie, rice pudding and apple crisp are some of the desserts. A liquor license was pending.

For breakfast, try Irish oatmeal with warm milk and bananas ($3.45) or a three-egg western omelet with homefries and toast ($4.50). Big eaters and spenders might like Sam's dream breakfast, eight ounces of freshly squeezed orange juice, three eggs, toast, homefries, steak, sausage and pancakes, $13.95. That should set anyone up for the day (or week).

Who is Mary Dugan? Read your paper placemat and you'll find out. There's a touch of whimsy here: the staff served on New Year's Day in their pajamas and on Friday the 13th they break mirrors and walk under ladders. Our service was of the "so, what would you guys like to drink?" variety.

Open Monday-Friday, 6:30 a.m. to 10 p.m.; Saturday, 7:30 to 10; Sunday, breakfast 7:30 to 3, lunch 11:30 to 8, a couple of dinner specials after 5.

The Inn on Lake Waramaug, North Shore Road, New Preston. (203) 868-0563.

Dining here is in a large, pleasant room with Hitchcock chairs, swagged draperies and pink over burgundy linens and an adjacent, more airy room in deep burgundy. There's also an outdoor deck, and barbecue lunches are served by the lake in summer.

New innkeeper Barbara Kirshner, a former food professional in New York, describes the cuisine as "inventive American." Old favorites are made sophisticated, as in grilled breast of chicken on a sauce of roasted peppers and garlic flavored with brandy, sauteed shrimp and scallops in a roasted pepper and raspberry vinegar butter sauce, and grilled tournedos with gorgonzola butter. Entrees are $15 to $21. Appetizers ($5.95 to $6.95) could be escargots served in red wine and herb butter sauce or homemade pasta tossed with smoked chicken, crimini mushrooms and parmesan cheese. Among desserts are rice pudding, apple crisp, pies and brownies.

The inn barbecues hot dogs and hamburgers for lunch at lakeside in the summer, and the new innkeepers were looking to open the Lake House for steamed clams and other casual fare. A Sunday buffet brunch for $12.95 is popular.

Lunch in season; dinner, Monday-Saturday 6 to 9; Sunday, brunch 11:30 to 2:30, dinner, 4 to 7 or 8.

La Tienda Cafe, Sports Village, Route 202, Litchfield. (203) 567-8778.

A green neon cactus beckons in the window of this two-room Mexican cafe with a bar in the rear. Glass tops the cloths of wide, bright stripes and a cactus in a small pot is on each table. Colorful prints and rugs adorn the walls.

Crispy homemade tortilla chips and a fairly hot salsa are served. We found a lunch of Mexican pizza ($5.50) was almost more than one could handle: a flour tortilla topped with ground beef, cheese, lettuce, tomato, chilies, guacamole and sour cream. One half had hot peppers, the other mild. An order of burritos ($5.75), one stuffed with cheese and scallions and one with chicken, was also delicious and hearty.

Both dinner and lunch menus have "north of the border" dishes, but who would come here for strip steak? Black bean soup, flautas, Arizona-style nachos (topped with ground beef) and quesadilla are some of the appetizers ($2.50 to $4.75) and there's even a

Dining table with a view at the Inn at Lake Waramaug.

Mexican egg roll. Dinners include rice and refried beans, and are $7.50 for folded tacos to $10.50 for chimichanga. Everything may be ordered mild, medium or hot. Lime pie is the most requested desert, but flan and sopaipilla are popular as well. Fajitas (chicken or flank steak) had been added to the dinner menu for $9.95 the last time we were there. Create your own at the table and top with a choice of ten items like guacamole, green chilies, refried beans and Mexican rice.

Carafes of margaritas, pina coladas and daiquiris are $9.50. Many beers are available, including Lone Star of Texas.

Lunch, Monday-Saturday 11:30 to 2:30; dinner, 4:30 to 9 or 10, Sunday 3 to 9.

Wickets, Litchfield Commons, Route 202, Litchfield. (203) 567-8744.

Named for the American version of cricket, which was first played on these shores at the Tapping Reeve Law School in Litchfield, this is a large, contemporary establishment in the Litchfield Commons shopping complex. Prints and cricket paraphernalia adorn the cheerful pink walls. Tables downstairs and in the solarium are left bare with pink inlays; those in the airy upstairs dining room are set with white linens for dinner. The outdoor terrace is favored in season.

The menu when we last visited was in transition, a new chef just having been acquired from the venerable Village restaurant in town. Veal was her specialty, in six presentations. The rest of the dinner fare was fairly standard, from chicken divan ($14) to filet mignon "with champignons." Dinners come with soup and salad. Desserts run to apple pie and different cakes.

A buffet lunch was served the day we visited, but management was expecting a regular lunch menu soon.

Lunch, Tuesday-Saturday 11:30 to 2:30; dinner, 5 to 8:30, 9 or 10; Sunday brunch, noon to 4.

Strudel Cafe, The Uncommon Strudel, Litchfield Commons, Route 202, Litchfield. (203) 567-4327.

Seductive aromas emanate from this bakery turned cafe turned mail-order food business. Known for its gourmet desserts, the cafe also offers lunch items at six tables. The namesake, spinach and feta or chicken and broccoli strudels, are in the $6.50 range. Other possibilities ($6 to $8) are shrimp and crab in puff pastry, torta rustica, sesame noodles, herbed chicken salad, salad nicoise and oversize sandwiches. Not inexpensive, these, but ever so good.

Try one of the desserts — creamy cheesecake with a nut crust, Swiss chocolate torte, Brazilian meringue cookies, Queen Mother's torte ($2.75 to $3.25) — and you'll become addicted. You can always get more to take home. Stosh's ice cream is served here — how about a turtle cone, of chocolate chips, nuts and caramel?

Open daily except Tuesday 10 to 5:30; lunch, noon to 4; tea til 5; Sunday brunch, 11 to 2.

Litchfield Food Company, On the Green, Litchfield. (203) 567-3113.

Lately doubled in size, this specialty foods shop and catering service par excellence has added tables for partaking of its goodies on the premises. Smoked ham and turkey with cranberry-orange mayonnaise in a hard roll and the three-salad combination plate are lunches of choice, in the $3.50 to $5 range. Changing soups, delectable salads and exotic meats are available.

Box lunches range from $12 to $38, the latter for eastern nova salmon and capers, artichoke hearts, chicken breast stuffed with spinach and parmesan, fruit, dessert and more.

Retired New York advertising executive Dale Puckett and his wife Irma have lined their walls with framed testimonials from the rich and famous. They make as interesting reading as the shelves of foods do browsing.

Open daily, 9:30 to 5:15.

Diversions

Lakes and Parks. Lake Waramaug State Park at the west end of the lake is a wonderfully scenic site, its picnic tables scattered under the trees right beside the water. The lake's Indian name means "good fishing place;" it's also good for swimming and boating, and blessedly uncrowded. On the north and east sides of the lake are the forested Above All and Mount Bushnell state parks. Not far from Lake Waramaug on the road to Litchfield (Route 202) is **Mount Tom State Park.** It has a 60-acre spring-fed pond for swimming and again picnic tables are poised at shore's edge. A mile-long trail rises to a tower atop Mount Tom.

White Memorial Foundation and Conservation Center, Route 202. Just west of Litchfield are 4,000 acres of nature sanctuary bordering Bantam Lake. Thirty-five miles of woodland and marsh trails are popular with hikers, horseback riders and cross-country skiers. This is a great place for observing wildlife, birds and plants in a variety of habitats. The Conservation Center in a 19th-century mansion has a natural history museum with good collections of Indian artifacts, butterflies, live and stuffed animals, and an excellent nature library and gift shop. Grounds open free year-round; museum, $1.

White Flower Farm, Route 63, Morris. This institution south of Litchfield is a don't-miss spot for anyone with a green thumb. In fact, people come from across the country to see the place made famous by its catalog, wittily written by the owner under the pen name of Amos Pettingill. Eight acres of exotic display gardens are at peak bloom in late spring; twenty acres of growing fields reach their height in late summer. Greenhouses with indoor plants, including spectacular giant tuberous begonias, are pretty all the time. Shop and grounds open daily, mid-April through October.

Litchfield Historic Sites. The Litchfield Historic District is clustered along the long, wide green and out North and South streets (Route 53). The seasonal information center on the green has maps for walking tours, which are the best way to experience Litchfield.

Note the bank and the jail with a common wall at North and West streets. Along North Street are Sheldon's Tavern, where George Washington slept, plus the birthplace of Harriet Beecher Stowe and the Pierce Academy, the first academy for girls. South Street is a broad, half-mile-long avenue where two U.S. senators, six Congressmen, three governors and five chief justices have lived. Here too is the **Tapping Reeve House and Law School** (1773), the first law school in the country. The house with its handsome furnishings and the tiny school with handwritten ledgers of students long gone are open Thursday-Monday noon to 4, mid-May to mid-October, $1. The newly renovated **Litchfield Historical Society Museum** at South and East streets has four galleries of early American paintings, decorative arts, furniture and local history exhibits. Open Tuesday-Saturday 10 to 4, April-November.

Litchfield Congregational Church.

Wineries. Two of New England's premier wineries occupy hiltop sites overlooking the beauty of Litchfield and Lake Waramaug. **Haight Vineyard,** Connecticut's first farm winery just east of Litchfield, occupies a new, English Tudor-style building with a large tasting room and gift shop across Chestnut Hill Road from its original barn. Guided winery tours on the hour and a fifteen-minute vineyard walk are among the attractions. You can pick up a bottle of award-winning Covertside white or chardonnay plus a pink T-shirt ("Never bite the foot that stomps your grapes"), wine accessories and such. Open Monday-Saturday 10 to 5, Sunday from noon.

Hopkins Vineyard, Hopkins Road, New Preston. A hillside location with a good view of Lake Waramaug marks this family operation run by Bill and Judy Hopkins, dairy farmers turned winemakers. The rustic red barn provides a quick, self-guided tour from an upstairs vantage point and the fine Hayloft Gallery showing works of local artists. The gift shop sells wine-related items like baskets, grapevine wreaths and stemware, even handmade linen towels. The winery's cat may be snoozing near the wood stove, upon which a pot of mulled wine simmers on chilly days. On nice days, you can sip a superior seyval blanc or Lakeside white ($5.99 to $7.50) in a small picnic area overlooking the lake. Open daily 11 to 5, May-December; weekends rest of year.

Shopping. Good shops have sprung up lately in the center of Litchfield and its western environs. Enter the ever-so-suave **Mason Gift Shop,** just off the common, to smell the Arkansas potpourri called Scent of Spring and to check out some delightful gifts. **The Litchfield Exchange,** where practically everything is handmade, including lovely clothes for children, the **Cobble Court Book Shop** and the **Kitchenworks** are worth visiting in the courtyard around the corner. On the green is **Workshop Inc.,** a boutique with updated women's apparel and accessories; downstairs is a gallery of home furnishings, from wicker furniture to pillows and dhurries to two-tone china and unusual placemats. **Fox & Lane,** which smells divine, offers clothing, accessories, gifts, kitchenware, paper goods and more. **Weekenders** features casual clothing for men and women of weekend leisure. **House in the Country** has a great collection of home accessories, while neighbor **R. Derwin** stocks men's clothing and country furniture in two shops.

Litchfield Commons, a cluster of shops in an attractive grouping around a brick walk, is worth a stop as you traverse Route 202 west of town. **Mother Goose** is an outstanding toy shop, **Puddlejumpers** has clothes for children, and **Tweeds & Tees** recently moved into expanded quarters here.

New Preston, a mountain hamlet just down the hillside from Lake Waramaug, is experiencing a flurry of shop openings. We never can leave **J. Seitz & Co.** without making a purchase. In a converted garage overlooking a waterfall, Joanna Seitz shows clothing, antiques and accessories from around the world, with a decided emphasis on the American Southwest. The coats made of old Pendleton Indian blankets for $425 are unique, as is the handpainted furniture. Also expanded is **Brittania Books,** a used-book store that started New Preston's revival and is now in new quarters on Church Street beside the waterfall. Other shops worth browsing are **Timothy Mawson Bookseller,** specializing in gardening, landscape architecture and English country life; the **Cottage Garden,** with all kinds of decorative things for the garden, herbs and tea supplies; the **Village Barn** for decoys and paintings; **Jonathan Peters** for fine linens and lacy things, and **R. Cogswell Collection** for antiques and quilts. Two more boutiques and a take-out gourmet shop were in the works for the spring of 1989 in what Joanna Seitz said was coming to be called "the Rodeo Drive of Connecticut" in terms of quality merchandise.

Just south of Route 202 in tiny **Washington Depot, Jackeroos,** advertising "sturdy country gear," features Australian outback wear. We liked its Dessert Design batik summer wear and the waxed cotton "travel coats" in bright colors, $219. At the **Tulip Tree Collection** you'll find Canadian antiques, porcelain, terra cotta, painted boxes and baskets and the like. **Kiddippity,** with its colorful rainbow striped awning in front, sells fashions and toys for children. **Le Mystere** is a lingerie store with European imports. **Nimble Fingers** has wonderful yarns and handmade sweaters. **Hickory Stick Bookshop,** which also has a large room full of stationary and gifts, is super for browsing.

Extra-Special

The Pantry, Washington Depot. (203) 868-0258.

One of our favorite places for lunch and shopping is this upscale gourmet shop lovingly run by Michael and Nancy Ackerman. A counter displays and a blackboard lists the day's offerings from an extensive repertoire, and you can get anything to take out as well. The fare is innovative, with especially good soups, salads and desserts. Our latest winter visit brought forth oriental vegetable soup amd watercress puree; tortellini with walnut pesto and endive salad, smoked salmon assiette, vegetable risotto with stuffed butternut squash and gingered carrot salad ($5.95 to $6.95) sounded appealing, and we wished we could have tried the parsnip cake. Summer favorites are poached salmon, curried chicken salad and seafood salad with raspberry vinaigrette. Tables, decorated with lilies in flat bowls, are set amidst high-tech shelves on which are just about every exotic chutney, mustard, vinegar, extra virgin olive oil and the like that you could imagine, as well as kitchenware and tableware, baskets and pottery. Open Tuesday-Saturday 10 to 5:30, lunch from 11 to 3:30, tea from 3:30 to 5.

Index

391

Also by Wood Pond Press

Getaways for Gourmets in the Northeast. The first book by Nancy Webster and Richard Woodworth appeals to the gourmet in all of us. It guides you to the best dining, lodging, specialty food shops and culinary attractions in 22 areas from the Brandywine Valley to Montreal, Cape May to Burlington, the Finger Lakes to Monadnock, the Hudson Valley to Nantucket. Published in 1984; fully revised and expanded in 1988. 474 pages to read and savor. $12.95.

Weekending in New England. The best-selling travel guide by Betsy Wittemann and Nancy Webster details everything you need to know about 18 of New England's most interesting vacation spots: nearly 1,000 things to do, sights to see and places to stay, eat and shop year-round. First published in 1980; fully updated and revised in 1988. 290 pages of facts and fun. $10.95.

Water Escapes in the Northeast. The latest book by Betsy Wittemann and Nancy Webster relates the best lodging, dining, attractions and activities in 36 great waterside vacation spots from Chesapeake Bay to Cape Breton Island, from the Thousand Islands to Martha's Vineyard. Everything you need to know for a day trip, a weekend or a week near the water is told the way you want to know it. Published in 1987. 420 pages to discover and enjoy. $12.95.

The Best of Daytripping & Dining. Another book by Betsy Wittemann and Nancy Webser, this is a companion to their original Southern New England and all-New England editions. It pairs 25 featured daytrips with 25 choice restaurants, among 200 other suggestions of sites to visit and places to eat, in Southern New England and nearby New York. Published in 1985. 186 pages of fresh ideas. $7.95.

The Originals in Their Fields

These books may be ordered from your local bookstore or direct from the publisher, pre-paid, plus $1.50 handling for each book. Connecticut residents add sales tax.

Wood Pond Press
365 Ridgewood Road
West Hartford, Conn. 06107
(203) 521-0389